Land Economics

Land Economics

RICHARD T. ELY

AND GEORGE S. WEHRWEIN

MADISON, 1964

THE UNIVERSITY OF WISCONSIN PRESS

Published by
THE UNIVERSITY OF WISCONSIN PRESS
430 Sterling Court, Madison 6, Wisconsin

Second printing 1941

Printed in the United States of America

Library of Congress Catalog Card Number 64-15100

FOREWORD

In the history of land economics, the Ely-Wehrwein volume is probably the single most influential book. Originating as a textbook for teaching the basic principles of land economics at the University of Wisconsin, it has with the years become a classic in the mainstream of Wisconsin tradition.

It is generally agreed that formal coursework in land economics originated at the University of Wisconsin, one of the first offerings being the course in land tenure given in 1915 by Richard T. Ely and Henry C. Taylor. In the following years, Ely, Taylor, and Benjamin H. Hibbard regularly conducted this graduate seminar, which was later called "land problems." George S. Wehrwein had worked with these men as a student before taking his Ph.D. degree in 1922. When he was appointed professor in 1927, he joined Hibbard in conducting this course. After Hibbard's retirement, Wehrwein and Leonard A. Salter, Jr., taught the course jointly until Wehrwein's sudden death in 1945.

The introductory course in land economics from which this book derived most directly was first offered in 1926 by Hibbard, who was assisted at times during the next four years by Bushrod W. Allin and Roland R. Renne. Wehrwein assumed responsibility for this course in 1931 and continued to teach it and to write this book during the next decade. As described in the Preface following, earlier drafts were mimeographed and tested in the classroom before revision for the edition published by Macmillan in 1940.

During the same period, Wehrwein was extensively involved in other courses. He began a graduate seminar in land income in 1929, and an undergraduate course in urban land economics in 1932, offering both courses until his death. For several years, he participated in a pioneer interdepartmental offering in rural regional planning, and he was instrumental in sponsoring courses in wildlife management given by Aldo Leopold. These wide interests are evident throughout this book.

Wehrwein's active teaching covered the period of burgeoning

interest in land economics. More than 700 students were enrolled in the introductory land economics course during Wehrwein's tenure. Another 700 — mostly graduate students — attended his other courses. It is hardly an exaggeration to say that Wehrwein taught a whole generation of the graduate students who were later identified with land economics work in universities and government. This is the book from which these students were taught, and they in turn have passed its ideas on to following generations.

A reader can hardly fail to notice the intimate relationship between the classroom and the research of the period. Wehrwein and his students were deeply involved in a variety of research activities, and footnotes include many references to pioneering (then current) studies of rural zoning, forest crop taxation, land use planning, conservation, water use, recreation, and public land management. In this edition, the original footnotes have been retained, not only to preserve the flavor of an unusually wide-ranging inquiry but also because some of the citations are not otherwise available. However, the 16-page bibliography, described originally as a sampling of "various sources of American literature dealing with land economics," has been omitted in this reprinting.

The history of land economics shows it to be a field strongly oriented to current social problems. The land economics problems of the United States about 1940 with which this book deals are not the problems that concern later generations of resource economists. In some cases — as, for example, the problems associated with prospects for a declining population — applicability to today's problems is barely imaginable. But others of the resource problems, which dated in the United States by standards of the 1960's, are actually not far removed from current problems of underdeveloped areas.

This reprint is offered in the belief that *Land Economics* is one of the classics that teachers and researchers will want for its historic (and, in some cases, sentimental) value. But it is also a useful book — a simple, brief, and clear presentation of basic ideas for beginning students and laymen.

C. W. LOOMER

Madison, Wisconsin
November, 1963

PREFACE

"The starting point as well as the end point of our science is Man," says Roscher in opening his treatment of Economics. The starting point of Land Economics is the relation of population to land. Land Economics deals with the utilization of land by man, but more specifically with the relations of man to man arising out of the relations of man to natural resources. Land utilization takes place within three frameworks: the physical, the institutional, and the economic.

The use of land must first conform to natural laws, especially in this modern age when man himself has become a geographical factor with science, machinery, and earth-born energy at his command. The more important physical factors conditioning land use are presented in the second chapter.

Secondly, land utilization is also influenced by customs, traditions, laws, and institutions. Arthur Young once said, in essence: Give a man a barren piece of soil in private ownership and he will convert it into a garden; but give him nine years' lease of a garden and he will convert it into a desert. While this statement cannot be accepted without reservations, it serves to illustrate the effect of stability of tenure afforded by private property on the manner in which land is used. Although Chapter IV provides the specific introduction to this subject, the institutional conditioning of land use will be discussed throughout the treatment of all land resources.

In the third place, the operator in a commercial society is guided by costs and income in his decisions concerning land use. He will proportion the factors of production in such a way as to get the largest net profit. When land is cheap and labor and capital are expensive, land may be used so lavishly that later generations may discover that the natural resources have been wasted. The economic principles of land use, land income, and value are set forth in Chapter V, but are also applied to various types of land in the succeeding chapters.

Since the unique characteristic of land which differentiates it most from other capital goods is space and spatial relationships, Land Economics may be defined as *the science which deals with the utilization of the earth's surface, or space, as conditioned by property and other institutions and which includes the use of natural forces and productive powers above or below that space over which the owner has property rights.*

The first five chapters serve to present these frameworks and the remainder of the book treats their application to the various types of land and natural resources. It is important that the land economist be equipped with a general knowledge of all types of land and understand their interrelationship before concentrating on a specific kind of land or on a given region. Since land problems are regional in character, the material presented here will have to be supplemented by local subject matter.

The illustrations have been selected to make the principles of land use clear and more graphic, but they should be considered only as illustrations. Others might have been selected from a multitude of sources. The many splendid activities of state and federal governments have been cited in the same way, with no intention of slighting any. Their functions, operations, and accomplishments are adequately described in easily available public documents. Maps, pictures, and diagrams are essential in presenting land economics, yet have been kept to a minimum in this book because so much excellent illustrative material is being published by the various departments of the federal government, the state colleges, experiment stations, universities, and planning boards. Citations in footnotes and in the bibliography have been made to such publications. It was decided to include a few portraits of persons who have been prominent in land economics, in the conservation of natural resources, or in the formulation of American land policies. These are selected from a collection of over one hundred portraits begun in 1922 by Dr. W. E. Grimes and the junior author, G. S. Wehrwein, and continued by the latter after 1924, in co-operation with the Diemer Photographic Laboratory, Madison, Wisconsin.

The content and arrangement of the subject matter of the *Land Economics* are the outgrowth of twenty years' experience in presentation and teaching. In 1922 three volumes were published in a mimeographed edition under the general title, *Outlines of Land Economics;* Volume I, *Characteristics and Classification of Land,* Volume II, *Costs and Income in Land Utilization,* and Volume III, *Land Policies,* by Richard T. Ely, assisted by Mary L. Shine and George S. Wehrwein. In 1928 and again in 1931 the subject matter was revised and rearranged and published in a single volume,—*Land Economics,* by Richard T. Ely and George S. Wehrwein.

In the preparation of this volume we wish to acknowledge the encouragement and help of many colleagues, friends, and students who have been associated with us since the course in Land Economics was started in the University of Wisconsin in 1919–20. In the past few years Warren Bailey, Scott Keyes, Charles Loomer, Louis Upchurch, Joseph Kenas, and Pearl Rosenthal have assisted with individual chapters and the mechanics of publication. Miss Rosenthal also prepared the Index. We are particularly indebted to John A. Baker for his assistance on the entire book, and especially for his helpful criticisms. Finally, we are obligated to Miss Dorothy McGuire for her efficient help with the preparation of the manuscript.

R. T. Ely
George S. Wehrwein

March, 1940

CONTENTS

I

LAND AND POPULATION

The Malthusian Law of Population. Although Thomas Robert Malthus was not the first to observe the pressure of population on subsistence, his statement of the principle as he saw it in 1798 centered men's thoughts on the relation of man's increase to the material world as never before. One effect of his theory was to demolish the prevailing theories of the natural desirability of an increase in population. Malthus used the now familiar illustrations of a geometric ratio for the increase in population and an arithmetic ratio for the increase in subsistence to indicate the tendency toward wide divergence of the two within a relatively short time. Starting as 1 to 1, in two centuries the ratio of population to food supply would be as 256 to 9, and "in two thousand years the difference would be almost incalculable." [1] He based his estimates on conditions in the United States, where the population had doubled every 25 years, a rate of growth which he termed the "natural increase" of people. The remarkable increase in American population had also been observed by Franklin. Not more than 80,000 Englishmen had migrated to America, but by natural increase their numbers had exceeded 1,000,000 by the end of the eighteenth century, and, by doubling every 25 years, in another century the number of Englishmen in America would exceed the number in England itself.[2]

Malthus was, in fact, very conservative in his estimates of man's reproductive powers. Under ideal conditions an average woman could give birth to five or six children between her 17th and 27th years. If four of these children lived to be 27 years of age and reproduced at the same rate, population would double every 27 years even if no one lived beyond that age. If no one lived beyond

[1] *An Essay on the Principle of Population* (1st ed., London, 1798), p. 26.

[2] "Observations concerning the Increase of Mankind and the Peopling of Countries" (1751), *Complete Works of Benjamin Franklin,* ed. John Bigelow (New York, 1887), II, p. 232.

35 years of age but had six surviving children, population would triple in 35 years.[1]

Malthus believed that the prolific nature of mankind would be ultimately checked by a shortage of food supply, which would arise because of the limited supply of land. "Even though subsistence can be increased and be greater than any assignable quantity; still the power of population being in every period so much superior, the increase of the human species can only be kept down to the level of the means of subsistence by the constant operation of the strong law of necessity acting as a check upon the greater power." [2] In other words, there is a fixed ceiling above which the numbers of animals and human beings cannot rise. Animals are often reduced in numbers by actual starvation and this is also the fate of mankind at times, but usually the lack of sustenance operates in a more indirect manner. Malnutrition of infants, invalids, and the aged, and wars among primitive peoples for food are attributable to the pressure of population on the food supply.

In many cases, however, population is far below the limit of subsistence. This is due to the "positive checks" as enumerated by Malthus. Death, accidents, "severe labor and exposure to the seasons, extreme poverty, excesses of all kinds, the whole train of common-diseases and epidemics, war and plagues," he listed in this category. Some of these, however, may also be attributed to lack of sustenance.[3] The epidemics and devastating religious wars of the Middle Ages often reduced populations to such low figures that there was fear of underpopulation instead of anxiety concerning overpopulation.

Malthus also observed that human beings were not reproducing at their full power because many deliberately chose not to have offspring. Although impelled by the same powerful instinct of reproduction as animals, man, being endowed with reason, asks himself whether he will not increase his hardships and lower his rank in life if he marries early and raises a large family. All

[1] Warren S. Thompson, "Human Populations," Chap. III of *A Handbook of Social Psychology* (Clark University Press, 1935), p. 53.

[2] *An Essay on the Principle of Population* (2d. ed., London, 1803), p. 8.

[3] See E. F. Penrose, *Population Theories and Their Application with Special Reference to Japan* (Food Research Institute, Stanford University, 1934), pp. 12–13, 17–18.

practices which prevented people from being born Malthus classed as "preventive checks."[1] He recognized the postponement of marriage as a preventive check, but (in his first edition) held that this or any other tampering with the sex instinct would result in vice and misery. The human race was therefore caught on the horns of a dilemma. The use of "preventive checks" meant vice and misery, but to let population increase to the starvation limit and thus encounter the "positive checks" was no happier solution.

His insistence on unhappiness as the destiny of mankind evoked many sharp criticisms. In his later editions, Malthus made significant changes in his statement of the law of population, softening some of his expressions. For instance, he now said postponement of marriage "too frequently produces vice," and he admitted of a third check, "moral restraint"—a preventive check "which is not followed by irregular gratification." He defended this check, saying "the virtue of chastity is not, as some have supposed, a forced product of artificial society; it has the most real and solid foundation in nature and in reason; being apparently the only virtuous means of avoiding vice and misery which result so often from the principle of population."[2]

Penrose has pointed out that it is impossible to understand Malthus without considering his social theory.[3] Central in his thinking were property, the family, and the "narrow principle of self-interest" as the factors to which "we are indebted for all the noblest exertions of the human genius, for everything that distinguishes the civilized from the savage state." He held that man was indolent by nature and was stimulated into activity by his desire for marriage and, after marriage, by the necessity for supporting a family. The preventive check of postponing marriage therefore acted in a dual capacity: it provided the stimulus to work and saving so necessary to human advancement before marriage and also kept down the excess of births. After marriage there was to be no birth control. "I should always particularly reprobate any artificial and unnatural modes of checking population, both on account of their immorality and their tendency to remove the necessary stimulus to industry. If it were possible for each mar-

[1] First ed., *op. cit.*, p. 27.
[2] Second ed., *op. cit.*, pp. 483–84, 493.
[3] Penrose, *op. cit.*, pp. 21–35.

ried couple to limit by a wish the number of their children, there is certainly reason to fear that the indolence of the human race would be greatly increased. . . ." [1]

Considering Malthus' theological background, it is interesting that he emphasized the relationship of "stimulus to activity" to marriage throughout all his editions, and that he used it as an argument against birth control instead of ethical or religious scruples. He based his arguments against Utopias on the same grounds. In fact, the chief purpose of the first *Essay* seems to have been to discredit Utopias, while his later editions were aimed at the Poor Laws. Both removed the need for worrying about supporting a family, and encouraged early marriages and procreation. With the preventive check thus removed, he feared that so many children would be born that the positive checks would eventually have to reduce population. William Godwin tried to meet this argument by claiming that the sex passion might one day be extinguished, but Malthus claimed "that the passion between the sexes was necessary and will remain nearly in its present state." [2]

In spite of changes in the later editions of the *Essay,* the stern implications of the principle of population remained. After all, postponement of marriage and moral restraint are feeble compared to the sex instinct, and Malthus probably realized this. One of the most significant features of the Malthusian law was its insistence upon the *constant operation* of the pressure of population upon subsistence at all times and all places.

"It is probable that the food of Great Britain is divided in as great plenty to the inhabitants, at the present period, as it was two thousand, three thousand, or four thousand years ago. And there is reason to believe that the poor and thinly inhabited tracts of the Scotch Highlands are as much distressed by an overcharged population, as the rich and populous province of Flanders." [3] In other words, if population pressure could be measured by some kind of gauge, it would indicate the same pressure everywhere, no matter whether a nation is rich or poor. Since the pressure point is always productive of misery, Malthus concluded that in the

[1] Malthus, *An Essay on the Principle of Population* (6th ed., London, 1826), p. 574.

[2] Second ed., *op. cit.,* pp. 483–84, 493.

[3] Malthus, 1st ed., *op. cit.,* pp. 137–39.

natural development of a people, "there would not be a single period, when the mass of the people could be said to be free from distress, either directly or indirectly, for want of food." [1]

Population and the Economic Supply of Land. When Malthus set a limit to the possible increase of the supply of agricultural commodities by stating that subsistence could only increase in arithmetic ratio, he implied the *secular law of diminishing returns.* As stated by Marshall this law reads: "Whatever may be the future development of the arts of agriculture, a continued increase in the applications of labor and capital to land must ultimately result in a diminution in the extra produce which can be obtained from a given extra amount of capital and labor." [2] Unlike the *static law of diminishing returns* (to be discussed later), which has as its premises a given place, time, and technique of production, the secular law predicts definitely that future generations will be rewarded by steadily decreasing returns per unit of labor and capital costs.[3] In some respects this is merely restating the law of population by granting an increasability of sustenance but one not sufficient to keep pace with the growth of numbers.

One of the reasons for pessimism in regard to the future land supply is to be found in the classical statement of rent. James Anderson in 1777 noted the fact that land was of unequal fertility, i.e., that it existed in gradations. Later writers, West and Ricardo, claimed that in the "progress of society" the most productive land or that most conveniently situated with respect to a market would be cultivated first and, as new land was needed to support the inevitable increase in population, progressively poorer grades would have to be used. This order of land use itself was a basis for the belief in the secular law of diminishing

[1] *Ibid.*, pp. 138–39.

[2] Alfred Marshall, *Principles of Economics* (8th ed., London, Macmillan, 1920), p. 153.

[3] It is important to keep the *secular* and *static* laws separate and distinct. There is considerable confusion on this point. See F. Lester Patton, *Diminishing Returns in Agriculture* (Columbia University Press, 1926), Chap. VII, "The Problem of Secular Diminishing Returns in Agricultural Development"; Theodore W. Schultz, "Diminishing Returns in View of Progress in Agricultural Production," *Journal of Farm Economics,* October, 1932, pp. 640–49; John W. Boldyreff, "The Law of Diminishing Fertility of the Soil, from the Point of View of Some of the Russian Economists of Today," *Journal of Farm Economics,* July, 1931, pp. 470–85; and George M. Peterson, *Diminishing Returns and Planned Economy* (New York, Ronald Press, 1937), Chap. 6, "Diminishing Returns and Population."

returns. Henry C. Carey, the American economist, claimed that the "order of land use" was exactly the reverse, and he therefore is classed among the "optimists."[1]

It may seem strange that the early economists should have had so little faith in the increasibility of production per acre through new discoveries and techniques.[2] At the time of Arthur Young, a contemporary of Adam Smith, soil, which for a thousand years of mediaeval history had produced only 10 to 12 bushels of wheat per acre, was yielding 20 to 24 bushels. John Stuart Mill's life span was almost identical with that of Justus von Liebig, whose discoveries made possible yields of 30 to 32 bushels of wheat, yet Mill accepted the secular law of diminishing returns and the Malthusian principle and built, not only a theory of rent, but a theory of distribution of wealth upon them. His reasoning may be stated as follows: Since the secular law of diminishing returns prevents subsistence from increasing as fast as population, the constant pressure of people on resources makes the landowner the favored member of society. As population increases, subsistence becomes more costly, rents increase, land values rise, and all except the landowner obtain a progressively smaller share in the distribution of wealth. Quoting John Stuart Mill, "The economical progress of a society constituted of landlords, capitalists, and laborers tends to the progressive enrichment of the landlord class; while the cost of the labourer's subsistence tends on the whole to increase, and profits to fall. Agricultural improvements are a counteracting force to the two last effects; but the first, though a case is conceivable in which it would be temporarily checked, is ultimately in a high degree promoted by those improvements; and the increase of population tends to transfer all the benefits derived from agricultural improvement to the landlords alone."[3]

[1] L. H. Haney, *History of Economic Thought* (3d ed., New York, Macmillan, 1936), pp. 315–29.

[2] Perhaps it is unfair to criticize the classical economists when as late as 1898 Sir William Crookes predicted that even if all the wheat growing countries of the world added to their area "to the utmost capacity" the additional acres and yield would be "just enough to supply the increase in population among bread eaters till the year 1931." Crookes, *The Wheat Problem* (London, John Murray, 1899), p. 15.

[3] *Principles of Political Economy,* ed. Sir W. J. Ashley (New York, Longmans, 1926), Book IV, Chap. III, § 5, pp. 723–24. The later classical economists used "standard of life" rather than "subsistence."

It is sometimes said that the Malthusian law was merely a statement of what will happen *if* the trend of population takes a given turn. Thus, if population increases very fast, a shortage of subsistence will arise; if it increases at a moderate rate, improvements in agriculture will more than keep pace with the growth in numbers; and if population declines or remains stationary, there may even be "pressure of food supply on population." However, the classical statement of secular diminishing returns and of rent had no "ifs" in it; the "progress of society" was regarded as predestined and involved an increase in numbers, a scarcity of land, and a rise in rent and land values, with the enrichment of the landowning classes at the expense of the other classes of society.

Even with its later modifications, the Malthusian theory had a mechanistic tone about it which was an effective argument against Godwin's idealistic philosophy of human perfectibility, but it also left the human race with little hope of happiness under any conceivable arrangement of society. For this reason reformers like Karl Marx and Henry George refused to accept the Malthusian law. The law also inferred that the causes of vice and distress are due to impersonal forces, and thus absolved the ruling classes of all responsibility for the poverty of the poor. Henry George accordingly devoted several chapters in his *Progress and Poverty* to showing that poverty may be due to the "injustice of society not the niggardliness of nature," but he failed to overthrow the law itself.[1]

Corollaries of the Malthusian Law. That "population invariably increases where the means of subsistence increase" is a natural corollary of the Malthusian law. In his *Political Economy* Malthus speaks of "that quality peculiar to the necessaries of life, when properly distributed, of creating their own demand, or of raising up a number of demanders in proportion to the quantity of necessaries produced." [2] He considers all agricultural improvements and the discovery of new lands as mere breathing spells. "No agrarian regulations in their utmost extent could remove the pressure of it even for a century." In other words, if the ceiling is

[1] See Frank A. Fetter, "Price Economics vs. Welfare Economics," *American Economic Review,* September, 1920, pp. 467–87.

[2] *Principles of Political Economy* (London, William Pickering, 1836), Chap. III, Sec. 1, p. 140.

raised it will take only a short time for population to fill the new space and to restore the former pressure.

He also stated the results of opposite conditions, concluding that in a period of distress the difficulty of rearing a family is so great that population comes to a standstill. It would be logical also to conclude that those classes in society with the largest means would have the most numerous families and those in poverty the smallest, which unfortunately is rarely the case.

In his later editions Malthus was more optimistic about the possibility of adjusting population to land. "It would appear to be setting the tortoise to catch the hare. Finding, therefore, that from the laws of nature we could not proportion the food to the population, our next attempt should naturally be to proportion the population to the food. If we can persuade the hare to go to sleep, the tortoise may have some chance of overtaking her." [1]

Population Growth since Malthus. The Malthusian law must be considered in the light of the time and place in which it was formulated. The various editions of the *Essay* were published during the early stages of the agricultural and industrial revolutions and during the Napoleonic Wars, when food was a vital factor for insular England. Probably from 70 to 80 per cent of the total population was engaged in mere food and fiber production, and neither the railway nor the steamship had been perfected for the bringing of food from overseas. The next half century, however, witnessed a complete reversal of these conditions. Mechanization and modern agricultural methods reduced the man-power needed to feed the nations. Industry absorbed the people released from food production and stimulated urbanization and industrialization. The "bee hives" of Europe began to import food from the now accessible new continents—America, Africa, and Australia. Famines became a thing of the past in mechanized nations, and modern science helped to reduce the "positive checks" to population.

The first effect of this revolution was a demonstration of Malthus' contention that subsistence "raises its own demanders." In 1700 the population of the world was about 500,000,000; it increased to above 600,000,000 or 700,000,000 by the time of Malthus, reached 1,500,000,000 by 1900, and was reported to be

[1] Quoted in Harold Wright, *Population* (New York, Harcourt, 1923), p. 37.

2,000,000,000 in 1930. The world's population has trebled since 1800, and that of Europe has doubled. The greatest increase has been in Japan and among the white races, not only in Europe but in the Americas, Australia, New Zealand, and Africa. The popu-

TABLE 1

POPULATION INCREASE AND IMMIGRATION, UNITED STATES, 1800–1940[1]
(000 omitted)

YEAR	U. S. POPULATION	INCREASE	PERCENTAGE INCREASE	IMMIGRATION BY DECADES		
				Total	Immigrants from Canada	Immigrants from Mexico
1800	5,308	1,379	35.1	—	—	—
1810	7,240	1,931	36.4	—	—	—
1820	9,638	2,399	33.1	—	—	—
1830	12,866	3,228	33.5	143.4	—	—
1840	17,069	4,203	32.7	599.1	—	—
1850	23,192	6,122	35.9	1,713.3	41.7	3.2
1860	31,443	8,251	35.6	2,598.2	59.3	3.1
1870	39,818	8,375	26.6	2,314.8	153.9	2.2
1880	50,156	10,337	26.0	2,812.2	383.6	5.1
1890	62,948	12,792	25.5	5,246.6 *	393.3 *	1.9 *
1900	75,995	13,047	20.7	3,687.6 *	3.3 *	1.0 *
1910	91,972	15,978	21.0	8,795.4	179.2	49.6
1920	105,711	13,738	14.9	5,735.8	742.2	219.0
1930	122,775	17,064	16.1	4,107.2	924.5	459.3
1940	131,669	8,894	7.2	—	—	—

* Immigrants from Canada, Newfoundland, and Mexico not reported 1886–94 inclusive.

lations of China and India are increasing very slowly if at all, and the black race is not increasing in Africa.[2]

In spite of this increase in the numbers of people, the new world of mechanization, energy, and science created conditions under which the tortoise outstripped the hare; food production kept ahead of population in the western world. This was cer-

[1] From *Statistical Abstract of the United States* (Department of the Interior, 1935), and releases of the 1940 census.

[2] W. Russell Tyler, "Increase in Contemporary Peoples," *North American Review*, Vol. CCXVIII, pp. 619–20.

tainly true of the United States, Canada, and other new countries. Here the cry was rather for more population to people the wilderness. Europe got the benefit of the abundant food and raw materials supplied by these virgin lands, doubled her population, and increased her standard of living. Malthus became a "forgotten man."

In the United States, population increased about 33 per cent every ten years from 1800 to 1860 (Table 1). This was largely due to natural increase, since immigration did not assume important proportions until 1840. After 1880 immigration became more noteworthy, and was especially significant in the increase of almost 16,000,000 people in the first ten years of the present century. In this decade population seemed to outstrip the land supply. The increase in food prices and in farm land values gave notice that the period of rapid expansion of the farm area was drawing to a close. Forests and minerals once considered "inexhaustible" were discovered to be limited. The nation became "conservation conscious" under the magnetic leadership of President Theodore Roosevelt, and in the conservation movement such men as Gifford Pinchot, James J. Hill, and Andrew Carnegie took a prominent part. The World War, with its extraordinary demand for food and fiber, redoubled the pressure, and nations began to take stock of their resources and of trends in population. The Malthusian devil, chained for more than half a century, was unloosed again.[1] Within a few years after the World War eight books on population appeared, most of them rather pessimistic in tone, as expressed by such titles as "Mankind at the Cross-roads" and "Standing Room Only?" [2]

Canada had a very conservative rate of increase before 1900, but in the first decade of the present century population increased by one-third and in the next two decades by about one-fifth per decade. Part of this increase was due to heavy immigration. During these thirty years over 5,000,000 people moved into Canada, a substantial proportion of whom went from the United States. On the other hand, almost 3,500,000 people left Canada during this period, leaving a net gain through immigration of about

[1] John M. Keynes, *Economic Consequences of the Peace* (New York, Harcourt, 1920), Chap. II.

[2] Edward M. East, *Mankind at the Cross-roads* (New York, Scribners, 1923). E. A. Ross, *Standing Room Only?*, (New York, Century, 1927).

1,500,000 people. Natural increase offset the 3,500,000 loss.

Since 1920 a new man-land ratio has established itself in the United States. On the one hand the economic supply of land has increased enormously, for reasons to be discussed later, while the rate of population growth has steadily been going down. In the revival of Malthusianism in the "conservation era" we were unaware of the fact that instead of pre-Civil War increases of 33 to 36 per cent per decade, the rate was steadily declining and was only 7 per cent between 1930 and 1940. Around 1925 the population of the United States was increasing by 1,800,000 a year, but in 1934–35 the increase was only 800,000 per annum. The decrease in the birth rate began as early as 1800 when New England became industrialized, and during the past century the decline spread westward and southward with the advance of urbanization.[1]

If the present trends in birth and death rates continue in the United States, and if no change in immigration occurs, a maximum population of about 135,000,000 by 1950 can be expected. After that, population will become stationary, or may even decline, according to O. E. Baker's predictions. Others place the time at which the peak will be reached at a somewhat later date, with a higher maximum population, but all authorities are agreed that a stationary, if not a declining, population is inevitable.[2]

However, the United States is not the only nation with a low or declining rate of increase. The western nations are all approaching a stationary population. In France the balance of deaths and births has been in favor of deaths for some of the years during the past decade. England was expected to reach her maximum of population in 1936. Even for Japan a limit of eighty to one hundred million has been predicted.[3]

It is not easy for nations used to a psychology of "bigger and better" population to adjust themselves to the prospect of a sta-

[1] O. E. Baker, *The Outlook for Rural Youth,* (U. S. Dept. of Agriculture, Extension Service Circular 223, September, 1935).

[2] However, the trend in the birth rate in the United States was upward in 1937 and 1938. The Scandinavian and Baltic countries, England and Wales, northern Ireland, Australia, New Zealand, and the Union of South Africa also have had increases in birth rates in recent years, although no official efforts were made to stimulate births as has been the case in Germany and Italy. Nevertheless, the gains are not yet enough to keep most of these countries from an ultimate decrease in population. See *Statistical Bulletin* of the Metropolitan Life Insurance Co., Vol. 20, February, 1939, pp. 3–5.

[3] Penrose, *op. cit.,* p. 104.

tionary or decreasing population. Instead of more mouths to feed, farmers are now faced with declining markets; in fact, all engaged in extractive industries will feel the lessened demand for lumber, iron, steel, bricks, and fuel. Much of the subject matter of Land Economics as applied to the United States deals with the readjustment of land uses to the new situation.

In passing it may be well to point out some corollaries to the phenomena of a declining birth rate. More and more people will be found in the older age groups and fewer in the younger and middle ages when strength of mind and body are normally at the maximum. The support of the aged necessarily falls on the second group, an increasing share falling on public agencies. Recent legislation and old age "movements" are indications of this fact. The change in age structure will also influence demands for food and housing, which in turn affect land uses. Aging people become more conservative in business, political, and social life. A rise in the death rate is inevitable, and as more people move out of the reproductive years a still greater decrease in the birth rate will follow. This illustrates Dublin's statement, "If population can increase in a geometric ratio, it can also decrease in the same ratio." [1] Some writers fear the effects of a declining population, others are more optimistic about the outlook.[2]

The Decline in the Death Rate and the Birth Rate. Population increase is the resultant of two variables, the birth rate and the death rate, the rate of natural increase being the excess of births over deaths. All three are usually expressed in terms of "per 1,000 living persons." Considerable confusion arises if attention is centered on only one of the two factors. For instance, in 1930 the birth rate of India was 32.9 and of New Zealand only 18.8. Taken by itself the birth rate would thus indicate almost twice as high a rate of population increase in India as in New Zealand. However, the death rate in the former was 26.8 and in the latter only 8.6. Judged by these figures, people were dying almost three times as fast in India as in New Zealand; the natural increase

[1] Louis I. Dublin, "The Statistician and the Population Problem," *Papers and Proceedings of the American Statistical Association,* March, 1925; P. K. Whelpton, "Increase and Distribution of Elders in Our Population," *ibid.,* March, 1932, pp. 92–101.

[2] Compare P. K. Whelpton, "The Future Growth of Population of the United States," in *Problems of Population,* ed. G. H. L. F. Pitt-Rivers (London, Allen and Unwin, 1932), pp. 83–85, with O. E. Baker's opinions; also Penrose, *op. cit.,* p. 119.

was greater in New Zealand than in India in that particular year.[1]

The beneficial effects of modern science have really helped to increase population by giving man greater control over the positive checks upon population. Modern medicine and sanitary engineering banished many of the epidemics that had decimated medieval Europe. Infant mortality, especially, has decreased and the average expectancy of life has been lengthened. The "large" family, in the sense of bringing a large number of children to maturity, is a product of the modern age.[2]

"Death control" has been the most potent factor in increasing the population of the world. However, science cannot reduce this rate much more, because it is decreed that man must finally "return unto the ground from which he was taken." Besides, the regulation of population should not come through an increase in deaths. Human happiness is not enhanced by increases in infant mortality, disease, famine, starvation, or war. People have to die but they do not have to be born.

If western civilization created conditions favorable to an enormous increase in numbers, it also created within itself the mechanism for keeping down population. In spite of the greater well-being, better homes, more efficient medical care, and more abundant food, the birth rate has fallen. In 1850 the birth rate in Germany was 36.1 per thousand, but in 1928–32 it was only 17. England's birth rate dropped from 33.4 to 16.1 in the same period. France had a birth rate of 31.4 in 1810 but today it is only 17.7. She has not reduced mortality as much as other European nations and her stationary population is to be attributed as much to a relatively high death rate as to the much discussed decline in her birth rate. Even Italy has had a steady decrease in the birth rate, from 36.9 in 1870 to 25.5 in 1928–32. The same holds true for all western nations, for the United States, and—contrary to popular belief—for Japan as well.[3]

In spite of the weak preventive checks suggested by Malthus, the size of the family and the population of nations in earlier ages were results of blind biological forces based upon the satisfactions of the sex instinct. With modern contraceptive methods, the size

[1] Warren S. Thompson, *Population Problems* (2d ed., New York, McGraw-Hill, 1935), pp. 123 and 175, Tables of Crude Death and Birth Rates, 1808–1932.

[2] Penrose, *op. cit.*, pp. 117–18.

[3] *Ibid.*, pp. 102–8.

of the family is based on choices determined by the social and economic factors surrounding the parents, and there is no particular relation between the sex instinct and procreation. Modern people decide whether to remain childless, how many children they intend to rear, and when they want them. Limitation of families is, however, not a modern phenomenon. Infanticide and abortion were, and still are, practiced among primitive peoples. Methods of contraception were not unknown even among the ancients. However, Christianity, with its emphasis on the sacredness of human life, considered even contraception the taking of human life—a view which is held by some groups today.

The reason why "demanders" have not been "raised up" in response to the increased means of subsistence lies in the reactions of individuals to moral, economic, religious, social, and occupational factors, many of them contradictory. It has been found that the same economic forces are at work determining the size of families within religious groups opposed to birth control.[1] Some of these factors are closely associated with land utilization and the social psychology of those on the land.

Size of Families in Rural and Urban Areas. The country is traditionally the better place to bring up children, and rural families are large in comparison with city families. This can be seen by comparing the number of children below five years of age per 1,000 women of 15 to 44 years of age. This ratio is placed upon a unit representing the reproductive element of the population and is therefore more reliable than births per 1,000 of *total* population, which includes men and women, the children and the aged. In fact, population statisticians claim that birth and death rates expressed in terms of total population are very misleading and give us a too optimistic rate of natural increase at the present time.

Cities in general do not have a birth rate high enough to maintain their numbers whereas the rural non-farm people, living mostly in villages, in 1930 had 471 children per 1,000 women in the reproductive years, or more than were necessary to keep population stationary. But the real surplus is on the farms, especially in certain rural areas. The most outstanding example seems to be eastern Kentucky, with 915 children per 1,000 women, yet this

[1] Samuel A. Stouffer, "Trends in Fertility of Catholics and Non-Catholics," *American Journal of Sociology,* September, 1935, pp. 143–66.

ratio is somewhat lower than prevailed in the United States as a whole when Malthus used America as his example of "normal" population growth. About 370 children per 1,000 women 15 to 45 years of age were necessary to maintain a stationary population in 1930.[1]

The reasons for large families on farms are essentially economic, although some weight must be given to the fact that the knowledge of contraception is not yet as widespread in rural districts as in cities, and that religious scruples against birth control are stronger in the country. The family farm is conducive to large families. The wife and children contribute to the income of the enterprise; the children can help even at an early age. The patriarchal tradition has also made the family an old age insurance institution for the parents. The more primitive and self-sufficing farms have larger families than the "commercial" farms. The Corn Belt, New England, and the Pacific states have the smallest rural families, whereas in the South and in the Inter-mountain states the number of children per family is above the average.

However, a prolific rural population is not necessarily inherent in agriculture. Much depends upon the social and economic institutions. The system of dividing the farm equally among the heirs of French farmers would eventually have made the farms too small, so the "two-child family" was evolved to lessen excessive fragmentation of the land.[2] Before the Russian revolution the land was distributed periodically among the peasants on some of the *mirs* in proportion to the number of sons in the families. Families would speculate whether the expected baby would be a boy and hoped it would arrive before the redistribution of land took place. Fecundity was at a premium, and in this part of Russia the increase in population was twice as great as in sections where the *mir* system did not prevail.[3]

In cities, except among those in unskilled occupations, the birth rate is lower than in the rural areas. The individual and not the family is the economic unit. The ambitious youth who is

[1] See J. C. Folsom and O. E. Baker, "A Graphic Summary of Farm Labor and Population" (U. S. Dept. of Agriculture, Miscellaneous Publication 265, 1937), Figs. 48, 51–54.

[2] Francis Walker, *Land and Its Rent* (Boston, Little Brown, 1883), pp. 213–14.

[3] E. A. Ross, "The Soil Hunger of Russia," *Century Magazine*, Vol. XCV, p. 877. The *mir* was a form of village community in which land was held in common, but for purposes of cultivation was distributed periodically by households or individuals.

preparing himself for a profession cannot support a wife and family during his years of training. As in the days of Malthus, he postpones marriage. Women are no longer dependent on marriage as a "meal ticket" and often continue in their occupations after marriage; in fact, their earnings sometimes help support the husband while he is still in school. Childbearing interferes with the ambitions of both, and they choose to remain childless until they are ready for a family. The number of couples who prefer to have no children at all, however, seems to be small. Social and economic prestige, the desire for luxuries and for mobility, and perhaps pure selfishness also tend to keep families childless or smail.[1] Urban people as a rule move often and want to travel. The farmer, on the other hand, is tied to the land by his occupation and has less desire to move. Even a vacation is difficult to arrange. All these factors constitute the urban "luxury check" on population, or high standard of life, defined as "the number and character of wants which a man considers more important than marriage and family." [2]

In cities children are not economic assets as they are on farms. As a rule the urban father's work is not near the home nor is it of such a nature that the children can be of help. However, in more patriarchal families the parents have been known to put the children to work as early as possible and appropriate their wages, even to the point of actual exploitation. The school attendance and child labor laws have interfered with this system and it is claimed that one of the major reasons for family limitation among the proletariat of England and France was the passage of laws regulating the work of children.[3] Modern children are dependent on the parents for at least eighteen to twenty years. Since the parents do not expect the children to support them in their old age, they try to accumulate life insurance and investments for this period of their life. Under such conditions the number of children that can be reared with a given income and a given standard of living is distinctly limited. Most parents prefer to keep the size of the family below this "economic maximum" in order

[1] Anon., "Must I Have a Child?" *Forum*, January, 1933, pp. 52–54.

[2] Richard T. Ely, *Outlines of Economics* (6th ed., New York, Macmillan, 1937), pp. 434–35. See also Mark Jefferson, "Looking Back at Malthus," *Geographical Review*, April, 1925, pp. 187–89.

[3] East, *op. cit.*, p. 266.

to enjoy a fine home, a car, travel, and the other luxuries and necessities of modern life.

The social theory of Malthus that man is "indolent" and needs the prick of necessity to make him work does not apply to the wealthier classes. Here the "striving spirit" for wealth, power, and prestige is so great that it becomes the very reason for small or childless families. On the other hand, in the other income groups supporting the family may or may not be a driving force.

The number of children seems to be in inverse proportion to the ability of the parents to rear them. Professional and wealthy classes choose small families because of the "luxury checks"; at the other end of the scale are those who take a fatalistic attitude toward reproduction and let the Lord or society do the worrying about the future of their children. The relation of the poor laws to the size of families, which troubled Malthus, appears to find its counterpart in the relief problems of today. But even in the intermediate groups the same relationship holds to a considerable extent. It seems to hold a direct relationship to occupations. Every student of population has noted the difference in the size of the families of business and professional men and those of laborers. Skilled workers have smaller families than the unskilled laborers, who in turn have almost as many children born per 100 wives as farm owners. Farm laborers averaged 9 per cent more children born than the renters and these had 12 per cent more than the owners of farms.[1] It is interesting, however, that in recent years there is a tendency in Sweden and Germany for the richer people to have larger families than those of more modest means, a fact also observed in Brazil and rural China.

Finally, the city with all its material advantages has been designed for adults and for their occupations and pleasures, not for children. Housing, traffic congestion, noise, and the dangers of the street have added to the cost and inconvenience of raising children. There is no reason, however, why a city could not be so planned, and the houses, streets, and other features so adjusted as to make the urban home and the city as good as, if not better than the farm as an environment in which to rear children.

Those who are living in countries with a declining rate of

[1] Data compiled from the Census of 1910 by the Milbank Memorial Fund. See Folsom and Baker, *op. cit.*, Fig. 54.

population should not overlook the fact that *more than half of the world still lives under the Malthusian law.* The pressure of people against subsistence is ever present, and whenever conditions are improved, population merely increases to fill the vacuum. With the increase in subsistence in India and Egypt, population rose at once. China, Porto Rico, Java, and tropical nations in general are still other examples. Whether this great proportion of mankind can liberate itself from the vicious circle of poverty and progeny remains to be seen. Probably the question is pertinent whether the population policies of some nations will permit them to liberate themselves from this cycle. In Russia, population doubled in the last sixty-five years, and the average increase of 3,000,000 per year will cause another doubling within the next forty years. "In fact the Bolshevik leaders are attempting to whip up the population rate even more, to add 'new hundreds of millions.' "[1] The population policy of Germany is to "arrest the declining curve of population and turn it upward."[2] Italy is pursuing the same course.

Unequal Population Density of Nations and Regions. Nations with a low man-land ratio, a large "number of units of resources" per capita, and a high standard of living cannot live by themselves alone. They are threatened by the nations with large populations. Just as "highs" and "lows" of barometric pressures are the causes of cyclones, so uneven population pressure may be the direct or indirect cause of war. In ancient times starvation forced people to migrate and clash with their neighbors. In modern times the conflict appears in more subtle guise and involves control over mineral and power resources as much as control over food and markets. Even without war an underpopulated nation may be subject to "peaceful penetration" by immigration unless foreigners are barred. Growing nationalism, however, has closed the door to immigration from overpopulated nations. Besides, it is debatable whether emigration has ever offered permanent relief to overcrowded countries. If the emigration results in easier living conditions there may result a tendency to "be fruitful and multiply" and fill the gaps in the population.

[1] Bruce Hopper, "Population Factors in Soviet Siberia," in Isaiah Bowman. *Limits of Land Settlement* (New York, Council of Foreign Relations, 1937), p. 91.

[2] Franz Heske, *German Forestry* (New Haven, Yale University Press, 1938), p. 247.

Population pressure assumes different forms and produces different effects in agricultural as compared with industrial nations. China, India, and the countries of eastern Europe are examples of agricultural nations with dense populations. The poverty of these nations is said to result more from "over-population than from any other one cause, if not more than from all other causes combined." Being largely agricultural, the dense population operates small farms, and the great bulk of the food produced must necessarily be consumed by the farmer's family and his livestock. These peoples have been reduced to a cheap vegetable diet and have very little surplus above subsistence to exchange for comforts or luxuries. The farmers of the United States have from 5 to 20 times the surplus of the farmers of these countries to spend for the amenities of life. Their lack of livestock also contributes to the lack of fertility and low yields. A low standard of life precludes proper education. "A vicious circle becomes established. Because population is dense it is poor. Because it is poor it cannot afford education. Because it is uneducated it makes poor use of its resources. Not only that but the lack of education leads to unwise and unnecessary multiplication of numbers; and the chain begins all over again." [1]

The need of agricultural nations is for more space, hence the pressure to add territory taken from a neighbor or to find colonial possessions. The former alternative is of little avail in Europe, where any territory that may be annexed is already densely populated.

Industrial nations have no internal limit to their population in the strict Malthusian sense. They obtain food in exchange for their manufactured products, and the limit to their population is set by their ability to buy food and raw materials with the goods they have fabricated. They draw upon the whole world for their sustenance, keeping "their stomachs away from home, drawing sustenance from afar through umbilical commercial cords." However, a population larger than a food and raw material base is safe only as long as sources of raw material are available and as long as markets exist for their finished products. Hence the scramble for colonies, "mandates," "spheres of influence," and the

[1] E. Dana Durand, "Agriculture in Eastern Europe," *Quarterly Journal of Economics,* February, 1922.

rivalry for markets. England could not help but "view with alarm" the expanding foreign trade of Germany and the development of the German merchant marine before the Great War. But as under-developed countries begin to become industrialized, they cease to furnish raw materials for the older industrial nations, and also deprive them of their markets.

Nations depending upon stored and non-replaceable resources sooner or later find themselves faced by increasing costs as these

MAN-LAND RATIO IN THE UNITED STATES AND CANADA

REGION	POPULATION PER SQUARE MILE	RELATIVE MAN-LAND RATIO
UNITED STATES		
1 NORTH EASTERN	192	100.0
2 CORN BELT	92	47.9
3 LAKE	53	27.6
4 SOUTH	50	26.0
5 PACIFIC	26	13.5
6 100TH MERIDIAN	20	10.4
7 MOUNTAIN	4	2 1
ALASKA	0.1	0.05
CANADA		
8 MARITIME PROVINCES	20	10 0
9 ONTARIO	9	4.7
10 QUEBEC	6	3.1
11 SASKATCHEWAN	4	2.1
12 MANITOBA	3	1.6
13 ALBERTA	3	1.6
14 BRITISH COLUMBIA	2	1.0
YUKON	0.02	0.01
N.W. TERRITORIES	0.008	0.004

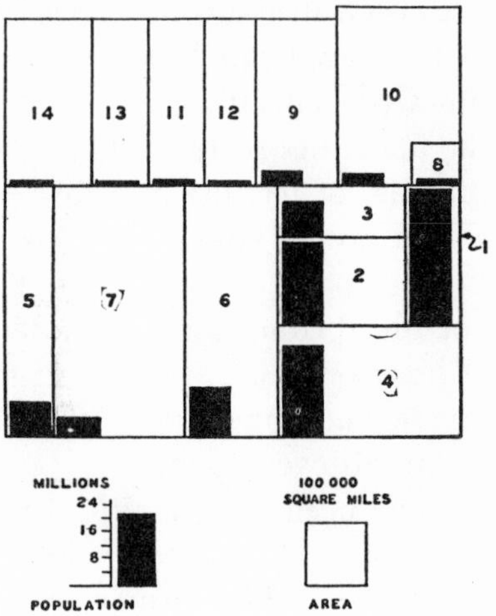

MILLIONS 24 16 8 POPULATION

100 000 SQUARE MILES AREA

Fig. 1. Relation of Population to Land, by "Economic Regions" as Shown in Figure 3

resources approach exhaustion. In 1865 W. Stanley Jevons, in his book *The Coal Question,* called the attention of the British people to the fact that their population rests on coal. With it they are able to command the food and raw material resources of the rest of the world. But coal does not bring an "annual and ceaseless income," and "once turned into light and heat and motive power, is gone forever into space." As the supplies of coal become less and the costs of mining become greater, the ability to exchange it for other raw materials on favorable terms is decreased. Such a nation can maintain her trade only by superior skill or greater energy, or it must be satisfied with a lower standard of life, unless its population is gradually adjusted to the diminishing resources. Finally, a sort of stationary state may be expected.[1]

Even within a given country the uneven distribution of population as related to resources creates problems of man-land adjustments. Figure 1 shows the ratio of people to land in the United States and Canada. This diagram has been so constructed as to make the area of the northeastern region and the size of the oblong representing its population almost equal, and so the man-land ratio for this region can be expressed as 100.[2] This part of the United States has a population density of 192 per square mile, or about the same as France. The Corn Belt has less than half the density of the Northeast, even though it includes Chicago, St. Louis, and other large cities. The Lake states and the South have a little more than one-fourth of the number of people per square mile found in the Northeast; the Pacific states have one-eighth, and the Mountain states have only one-fiftieth as many.

The low population density of Canada is indicated by the fact that the Maritime provinces have a man-land ratio almost identical with that of the 100th Meridian states and all other regions have a drastically lower density. This has given an erroneous impression, however, because the parts of Canada actually inhabited have a population density comparable to the adjacent region of the United States, but the average is brought to a low figure by the enormous thinly settled areas stretching northward from the "line." Nevertheless, the "large open" white spaces of Figure 1 help to explain the insistent desire for more people in parts of the United States and in practically all of Canada.[3]

In contrast with the low population density of Canada and parts of the United States are the man-land ratios of Europe and some nations of Asia. Table 2, nevertheless, shows that Rhode Island is almost as densely populated as the Netherlands; Massachusetts and New Jersey are more thickly peopled than Japan, Italy, or Germany; Sweden has fewer people per square mile than Iowa. Comparisons such as these are very misleading as measures of "population pressure," however. In some cases a small urbanized state is compared with an entire nation or an industrial country is placed in contrast with an agricultural nation or state.

[1] See the full discussion of this problem in Wright, *op. cit.*, Chap. V.

[2] See Chap. II for a discussion of these regions.

[3] W. A. Mackintosh, "Canada as an Area for Settlement," in Bowman, *Limits of Land Settlement, op. cit.*

Neither do these figures reveal the true man-land relationship. A given population on poor land may be as "congested" economically as a city slum. The only alternative is for the surplus population to migrate to other regions or to cities, a normal movement of population from rural areas and as old as civilization. The

TABLE 2

POPULATION PER SQUARE MILE OF SELECTED COUNTRIES AND STATES WITH YEAR OF ENUMERATION [1]

Country/State	Pop.	Year	Country/State	Pop.	Year
Belgium	707	1937	Czechoslovakia	272	1930
England and Wales	685	1931	New York	281	1940
Netherlands	674	1936	Switzerland	255	1930
Rhode Island	674	1940	Pennsylvania	220	1940
New Jersey	553	1940	France	197	1934
Massachusetts	546	1940	Maryland	184	1940
Japan	375	1935	Scotland	164	1931
Germany	363	1933	Illinois	141	1940
Italy	355	1936	Iowa	45	1940
Connecticut	350	1940	Sweden	40	1936

West with all its "wide open spaces" has probably all the population it can support under present conditions, and between 1920 and 1930 the South sent 1,400,000 more people into the rest of the nation than migrated to this region. This exodus was so marked that notwithstanding the fact that its natural growth is about four times that of the nation it had a slightly smaller proportion of the total population in 1930 than in 1920. The depression reversed the trend to some extent, which did not help the situation.[2] The high birth rate among French Canadians has forced them to migrate to the north and west, to the cities and the United States. It is estimated that over 2,000,000 people of French-Canadian origin live in the "States."[3]

Population Policies vs. Land Policies. The suggestion of Malthus to "proportion population to food" intimates the possibility of a national policy of limiting population to the amount of available natural resources instead of letting blind biological forces

[1] From the *Statesman's Yearbook, 1938; Statistical Abstract of the United States* (Department of Commerce, 1937), Table 5.

[2] Carl C. Taylor, "Constructive Measures for Dealing with the South's Population Problems," *Rural Sociology*, September, 1938.

[3] André Siegfried, *Canada* (London, Jonathan Cape, 1937), pp. 78–80.

determine numbers. This raises many difficulties. In the first place it calls for a determination of the proper "man-land ratio." What is the optimum population? Is it a population enjoying a high standard of living? Other elements of the same policy might include the ideas of a high quality population, healthy in mind and body, and its proper distribution within the nation to avoid both congestion in cities and the isolation of sparse settlements.

Even if an optimum population were agreed upon there would still be the problem of framing a policy and setting up the mechanism to put the policy into action. With the size of the family decided by likes and antipathies, by choices involving a "good time," by economic welfare and social prestige as compared with children, population is now left to choices just as blind and planless as if abandoned to biological instincts. What social controls can be used to coerce people to marry and to impel parents to increase or decrease the size of their families? Public opinion is probably more ready to accept regulations necessary to secure health and prevent the propagation of the unfit than to regulate numbers.[1]

However, population policies of the present age seem to be aimed at increasing rather than decreasing the visits of the stork. Some authorities are afraid that America is moving too rapidly in the direction of a stationary population. It is suggested that more people be settled on farms and in villages so as to give them the environment conducive to large families and thereby reverse the fall in the national birth rate.[2] Germany is making her land tenure policies serve the same purpose. Some nations try to stimulate the growth of numbers by the exhortations of dictators, taxes on bachelors, rewards for large families, or by granting special privileges to parents. Paradoxically it is often the very country that complains of the need for more room, more resources, or more colonies that is following this form of population policy.

[1] Warren S. Thompson, "Population Policy and Child Welfare," *Children's Home Record*, March, 1934; and *Factors Conditioning a Population Policy for the United States*, Publication of the American Sociological Society, August, 1935.

[2] O. E. Baker, "Rural-urban Migration and the National Welfare," *Annals of the Association of American Geographers*, June, 1933, pp. 59–126.

II

LAND AS NATURE

Man is interested in land either for direct use as a consumption good, such as a home site or for recreation, or as a factor of production, a means of making a living. He uses it as an instrument for the creation of economic goods or services, either for the satisfaction of his own wants or to exchange with others for goods and services they have to offer. Thus man selects from the entire physical universe only that part or those resources which can serve in the production of economic goods or satisfy human wants. This serves to distinguish the *economic* supply from the *physical* supply of land.

The economic supply of land is a constantly shifting one. Resources once thought to be useless or a laboratory curiosity are made important by some invention or discovery, as, for instance, the use of helium in dirigibles. In other cases land or resources may pass out of their spheres of usefulness. The discovery of coal tar dyes made indigo growing uneconomical and thousands of acres of land had to be shifted to another use or passed out of production entirely.

Land as defined by the economist is more than mere surface. Mention "land" and the picture that comes to mind is the space on which crops are raised, land used for building sites, or perhaps forests. The very terms in which land is measured tend to focus our attention on the two-dimensional concept of land. It is difficult to conceive of water, minerals, air, light, heat, the forces of gravitation and cohesion as "land." As a matter of fact, the "economics" of the utilization of "natural resources" would come closer to expressing the nature of land economics than any other term and would be preferable were it not for the accepted use of the word "land" in economics to cover the physical universe outside of man himself.

Even though the physical facts concerning nature and natural resources belong to the realm of geography and other physical sciences, the economist must take them into consideration; in fact, they are the framework within which the economics of land operates. Land policies must be based upon the operation of nature's laws as well as upon the economic drives of man. Too often the "conquest of nature" benefiting immediate generations has resulted in the "conquest of man" by those natural forces operating into eternity.

The Effect of Physical Conditions on Man Himself. In looking upon land as a factor of production, the emphasis is placed upon the power of the earth to produce economic goods and services. However, the earth is the inert and man the active factor in the partnership. The natural resources were just as abundant when the Indians owned America, yet the land supported only a few million people; under modern techniques, a population of 250,000,000 could be maintained upon the same area without undue pressure of population on the food supply. The production of goods depends upon the intelligence, inventiveness, culture, and stage of civilization of a people. Why these differences exist is beyond the scope of this book, but a word should be said about the influence of physical conditions on the productive powers of man as a "factor of production."

Climatic conditions have a direct influence on man himself as a "factor of production." The geographer, Ellsworth Huntington, has made a careful study of the effects of climate on the energies of man. According to Huntington the most favorable temperature for creative work lies between the mental optimum of 38° and the physical optimum of 60° or 65°, but there should be changes in temperature from day to day and season to season for the best results. The best work seems to be done with a relative humidity of 75 per cent in the spring and fall but at a higher point in winter and lower in summer. The region of cyclonic storms fulfils these conditions. Huntington's regions of optimum climate or "energy regions" correspond very closely with the areas having the highest civilizations.[1]

Not all geographers place the same emphasis on the influence of climate that Huntington does. However, be it much or little, the fact that the productive capacity of man is so conditioned must be considered in explaining the utilization of land. Certain re-

[1] Ellsworth Huntington, *Civilization and Climate* (3d ed., New Haven, Yale University Press, 1924), especially Chap. VII; also Huntington and Williams, *Business Geography* (New York, John Wiley and Sons, 1922); and Huntington and Cushing, *Principles of Human Geography* (New York, John Wiley & Sons, 1922).

gions are low in human productive energy. The monotonous cold of the northern regions, which seems to reduce the mental and physical energy of people, must be taken into consideration when Siberia, Alaska, and northern Canada are considered as sources of future food supply or the homes of future pioneers.

More important than the Arctic regions from this standpoint is the broad belt bordering the Equator. Great difference of opinion exists among scientists as to the effect of climate on the energies of man, whether it be on natives inured to the climate or on temperate zone peoples bent on exploiting the Tropics. However, not only the heat, the humidity, and the monotony of climatic conditions, but also disease, difficulties of agriculture, isolation, and lack of transportation facilities must be overcome. Australia, by maintaining a "White Australia" policy under which all colored races are excluded, insists that it is feasible for the white race to conquer the tropical portions of her domain.[1]

There are other regions whose utilization is limited by the fact that white men have difficulty in overcoming physical disadvantages. In Rhodesia the tsetse fly, malaria, and "nervous strain" are severe handicaps. The latter seems to be the effect of altitude and of sunshine. The actinic rays of the sun are more concentrated and have a definitely harmful effect. The problem increases in northern Rhodesia and Nyasaland where the altitudes are higher and the sun's rays more intense.[2]

Some writers carry the influence of physical factors beyond the mere influence of climate, etc., on productive powers. They claim that man's life is "determined" by his physical environment, and even see differences in the institutions, actions, and opinions of men as the result of living on different soil types. Others swing to the opposite direction; while not denying the relation of man to his physical universe, they place the emphasis on man as the determining factor of his own social and economic life. These philosophies cannot be ignored by the land economist, because proposed land policies are often based upon such premises.[3]

[1] H. Wilkinson, *The World's Population Problem and a White Australia* (London, P. S. King, 1930).

[2] *Pioneer Settlement,* Cooperative Studies by Twenty-six Authors (New York, American Geographical Society, 1932), pp. 212–13.

[3] Charles E. Kellogg, "Soil and the People," *Annals of the Association of American Geographers,* September, 1937, pp. 142–48.

Preston E. James, *An Outline of Geography* (Boston, Ginn, 1935), pp. 8–10.

Man's Modification of Nature. Primitive man was dominated by nature. He had to depend on the spontaneous production of the earth and on hunting and fishing for his source of food. Population was limited by a food supply gleaned from an untilled soil. Even after tillage was introduced, the simple hand tools and implements drawn by man or animals kept agriculture in a primitive stage for thousands of years, and man's power to subdue the earth was limited to a mere scratching of the surface. His simple weapons were too weak to have much effect on the wild life in woods and waters.

This condition was changed suddenly with the Industrial Revolution. Minerals were mined to make machines which in turn mined more metals and energy-producing minerals. Machines, at first propelled by horse power, conquered the prairies, but the truck, tractor, and combine pushed the frontier of wheat production far into the arid regions of the United States and Canada. The early sawmill depending on water power gave place to the steam driven saw, and in less than a century 500,000,000 acres of forests were removed by the ax and fire in the United States and another 500,000,000 acres in Canada. The steam shovel, dredge, and other earth-moving machinery have given man powerful tools with which to gouge the earth's surface. Gun powder and high-power repeating guns have made man superior to wild life, even the largest and fiercest, and entire species have disappeared.

A prophetic book by George P. Marsh called *Man and Nature, Physical Geography as Modified by Human Action,*[1] in which he treats of the reaction of man on nature, appeared in 1864, long before the more powerful earth-carving machines and the more modern forms of energy were invented and discovered. He pointed out that man has become a geographical factor along with wind, water, and climate, changing the character of his environment and sometimes with more destructive speed than nature itself. In removing forests and cultivating the land the balance of nature is disturbed and the soil is subjected to the action of wind and water, causing erosion and silting of streams, and adding to the violence of floods. Man transfers, modifies, and extirpates

[1] New York, Scribners, 1864.

vegetable and animal life only to find that he has loosed unforeseen forces.

In some cases, our knowledge of the forces of nature has been inadequate to forecast the devastating results of man's attempt to utilize the earth as a factor of production in a machine civilization, although often science was and is able to give the answer. But this does not necessarily stop the disastrous practices. Even if scientists know that "deserts are on the march," nothing will be done until the public becomes conscious of the problem and until the private owner of land can be induced to adjust his utilization so as to conserve the resources. Land Economics therefore has to concern itself not only with the "private" economic factors in land utilization but even more with the "political economy" of the conservation, restoration, and augmentation of natural resources.

PHYSICAL FACTORS CONDITIONING LAND USE

The relation of man to physical factors rests primarily upon his dependence on plant and animal life. Only in exceptional cases does man live far from land capable of supporting vegetation. Until trade, commerce, and manufacturing made agglomerations of population possible, the distribution of conditions favorable to plant life practically determined the distribution of people.

Temperature and Sunshine. Every plant has its own temperature requirements consisting of total heat, the distribution of heat throughout the season, and the length of the growing season, that is, the number of days between the last killing frost in the spring and the first killing frost in the fall. The climatic boundaries for the intensive production of corn (maize), for instance, are a "mean summer temperature of 70° to 80°, an average daily minimum summer temperature exceeding 58°, a frostless season of more than 140 days," and a rainfall of 25 to 50 inches of which at least 7 inches should occur in July and August. Corn is grown beyond these boundaries but practically no corn is grown where the summer temperature averages less than 66° or where the night temperature falls below 55°.[1]

[1] A. J. Henry et al, "Weather and Agriculture," *Yearbook of the United States Department of Agriculture,* 1924, p. 503. For illustrations see O. E. Baker, *A Graphic Summary of Physical Features and Land Utilization in the United States* (U. S. Dept. of Agriculture, Miscellaneous Publication 260, 1937), Figs. 2–10.

Temperature sets up zones of vegetation along latitudinal lines—tropical, then subtropical, temperate, and finally the frozen zones with treeless tundra. These zones, however, do not follow lines of latitude exactly and in some cases not even closely. The lines of summer temperature swing upward in western Canada so much that wheat can be grown as far north as 62° north latitude. Northern Norway extends beyond 70°, but the influence of the Gulf Stream is such that the average January temperature is the same as New England and the Corn Belt and the average July temperature permits wheat production, though not in commercial quantities. The Pacific currents also ameliorate the climate of southern Alaska.

Even within climatic regions local variations affect the length of the growing season and the temperatures. Some parts of the West, of the Lake states, and of Maine have only ninety days of growing weather, thus limiting the number and kind of crops. The presence of bodies of water makes certain small areas suitable for fruits, as in Door County, Wisconsin, with its cherries, the peach district of Michigan, and the grape area of western New York.

Altitude has the same effect as latitude. As a general rule, temperature decreases about 3° for every 1,000 feet. Even in the Tropics the traveler can go in a short time from sugar cane and tropical vegetation through various climatic zones to perpetual snow. Mountains rising from dry plains are often forest covered on the upper elevations and cultivated on the lower slopes. However, an inversion of temperatures may occur where air drainage occurs; the valleys are often more subject to cold and frosts than the hillsides. This fact is of considerable importance in selecting land for fruit growing. Treacherous "frost pockets" often make the difference between success and failure on otherwise identical soils.

Sunshine is necessary for the physical development of plants. It accelerates photosynthesis, promotes transpiration, and raises the temperature of plants. For this reason a longer growing day can make up for the lower temperatures of the higher latitudes. Extended hours of sunshine also reduce the frost hazard and promote the rapid development and early maturity of crops.

Although the total possible hours of sunshine for the entire year are approximately the same for all parts of the globe, the farther north or south one goes from the equator, the greater progressively become the hours of sunshine during the growing season. In the southern part of the United States the longest day has 14 hours of possible sunshine, in the northern part 16 hours. The 19 to 20 hours of sunshine per day in June in the Peace River country and Matanuska Valley permit agriculture in these far northern areas.

The possible number of hours of sunshine may be lowered by fog, rain, and cloudiness. At such times the effectiveness of sunlight is much reduced and diffused. In the Pacific Northwest and the Great Lakes region the sun shines less than half of the daylight hours, increasing from there to Arizona where the percentage of possible annual sunshine is over 85. Another factor related to plant growth is the intensity of solar radiation, which also increases from the Northeast to the West and Southwest in the United States. Thus it happens that the same regions with a dry climate and high temperatures also have the most intense sunlight and a large percentage of the total possible hours of sunshine.

Rainfall and Evaporation. Equal in importance with temperature in the utilization of land for agriculture and forestry is humidity. The amount of water needed by plants during their growth is astounding. It is said that it takes two tons of water to grow the wheat necessary to produce a loaf of bread. A fully stocked beech stand consumes 1,560 to 2,140 tons of water per acre or 1.15 acre-feet per year.[1]

Vegetation not only uses water to carry the food materials but uses it in plant growth. Cellulose is half water. Forests under certain conditions act as desiccators, as was observed when the Landes district of France and the Pontine marshes of Italy were reforested. On the other hand, even ordinary rainfall brings more moisture than is supposed. An inch of rainfall deposits more than 100 tons of water on an acre of ground.

From the standpoint of plant growth, not only is the total amount of precipitation important, but also its nature—whether gentle or torrential, whether or not it is distributed properly

[1] Raphael Zon, "Forests and Water in the Light of Scientific Investigation," in *Final Report of the National Waterways Commission* (1912), Senate Document 469, 62d Congress, 2d Session, p. 29.

throughout the year and comes at the critical time for crops. The eastern parts of North America receive rainfall from the Atlantic Ocean, principally from the tropical air-masses moving northward over the continent. The maximum rainfall of over 60 inches in Florida and in the southern Appalachians gradually shades off to 10 inches or less on the Great Plains. The northeastern states have a very even distribution of precipitation; so, also, have the southeastern states. The autumn is drier than other seasons in the Cotton Belt, which is favorable to the harvesting of the cotton. The heavy summer rainfall of the Corn Belt is exactly right for the production of a "bumper crop." [1] On the Great Plains the maximum rainfall occurs during the growing season, which tends to offset the low total rainfall and high evaporation of this region. The mountains "catch" the westerlies from the Pacific, which results in extremely high rainfall on the coast (80 to 120 inches in Washington), but decreasing toward the south. The heaviest rainfall takes place in winter, the summers being practically rainless.

After precipitation reaches the earth, the water follows three courses before it finally falls again as rain. Some of it, called the "fly-off," evaporates directly; part of it enters the soil to become ground water or returns to the surface via the plants or capillary action; and the remainder flows over the surface to the oceans as "run-off." This has been called the "hydrologic cycle" and is illustrated in Figure 2.

Evaporation carries away water from all exposed surfaces into the air, even in winter, but is especially active in the hot, dry regions where humidity is low and winds are brisk. These conditions cause a rapid loss of the already meager rainfall on the Great Plains, less in the cooler northern regions than in the high plains of the South. However, the cold, dry, heavy polar masses moving southward also absorb moisture, become heated, and are eventually transformed into tropical air masses. It is estimated that the polar currents absorb six million cubic feet of water per second in a three-day passage from North Dakota to Florida.

[1] "In Ohio alone, in a period of 60 years, an average increase of 1/4 inch in rain in July, at the critical rainfall period, caused an average increase in the yield of corn of 6,000,000 bushels, while a 1/2 inch increase in rain made an average increase in the yield of over 15,000,000 bushels." J. Warren Smith, "Speaking of the Weather," *Yearbook, U. S. Dept. of Agriculture,* 1920, p. 200.

Thus, not only the visible rivers but the titanic invisible air currents transport water from the land to the seas, and tropical air masses moving into the interior of the continent bring ocean-evaporated moisture back. The available moisture and surface run-off are roughly the difference between evaporation by the former and the precipitation due to the latter, if these two air

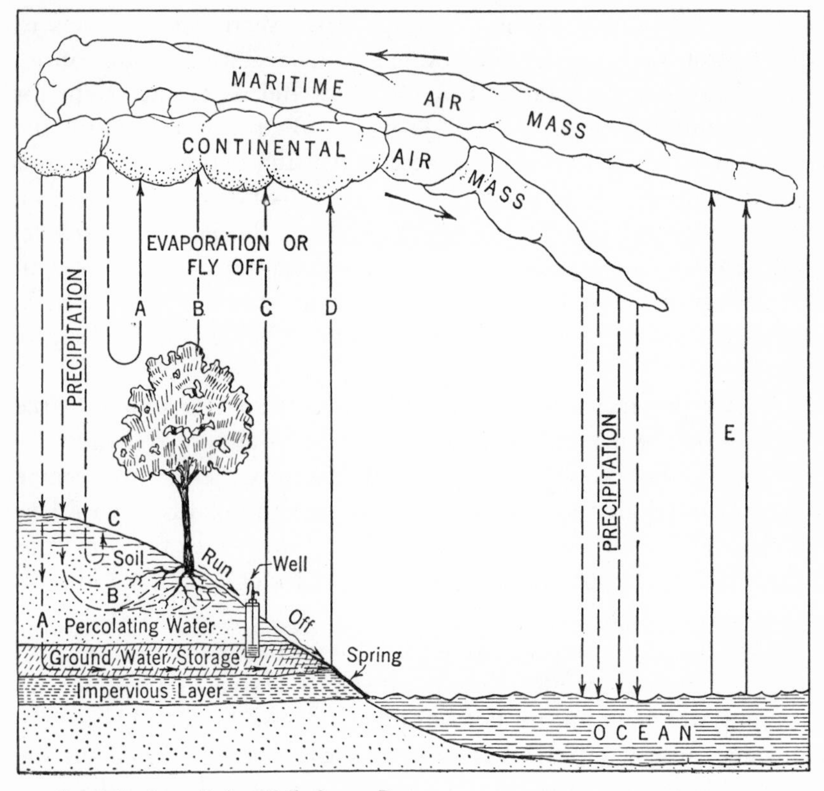

Precipitation—Rain, Hail, Snow, Dew

Evaporation

A. From air.
B. Transpired and evaporated.
C. From land surface.
D. From lakes, streams, marshes, etc.
E. From ocean.

Percolating Water

A. Through soil to underground water storage—leaches soil.
B. Enters roots of plants and trees.
C. Returns directly to surface and is evaporated.

Fig. 2. The Hydrologic Cycle [1]

[1] From Diagram, p. 90, *Soil Conservation*, Oct., 1937.

masses were the only ones concerned.[1] Evaporation in the United States ranges from 20 inches per year in the moist northeastern and northwestern parts and near the Great Lakes to 80 inches in the Imperial Valley of California.[2]

Three broad classifications of land can be made on the basis of rainfall—arid, semi-arid, and humid. In general, arid lands are those with less than 10 inches of precipitation, generally unsuited to crops without irrigation, except where soil and temperature are especially conducive to conserving moisture. Grazing is possible on the better watered lands of this class, but even so, it may take 75 acres or more to maintain a head of stock. About one-fourth of the earth's surface receives less than 10 inches of rainfall.[3]

TABLE 3

PERCENTAGE OF THE CONTINENTS WITH VARYING AMOUNTS OF RAINFALL[4]

	UNDER 20 INCHES	20–40 INCHES	OVER 40 INCHES
Australia	66%	22%	12%
Africa	54	18	28
Asia	67	18	15
North America	52	30	18
Europe	47	49	4
South America	16	8	76

Semi-arid lands are those with 10 to 20 inches of precipitation. These are used primarily for grazing, and for crops only in the moister, cooler areas. Regions with less than 15 inches of rainfall are doubtful for crop production. Half of the earth's surface has less than 20 inches of rainfall; fully two-thirds of Asia and Australia

[1] C. Warren Thornthwaite, "The Hydrologic Cycle Re-examined," *Soil Conservation,* October, 1937, pp. 85–91. See also Benjamin Holzman, *Sources of Moisture for Precipitation for the United States* (U. S. Dept. of Agriculture, Technical Bulletin 589).

[2] *National Resources Board Report,* December 1, 1934 (Washington, Government Printing Office, 1934), p. 299. (This work is hereafter referred to as the N. R. B. Report.) Evaporation is measured in inches as it vaporizes from a free water surface. Less water is lost from a soil surface or where water has penetrated the earth.

[3] This is an over-simplification of a complex subject. See the classifications of Köppen used in James, *An Outline of Geography, op. cit.,* and other works; and Thornthwaite, *Geographical Review,* Vol. XXI, 1931, and Vol. XXIII, 1933.

[4] From Griffith Taylor, "Frontiers of Settlement in Australia," *Geographical Review,* January, 1926.

and about half of Europe, Africa, and North America face problems of aridity. The longest battle front of the "pioneer fringes" is on the frontiers of deficient moisture. However, Europe leads in the proportion of its area with a rainfall of 20 to 40 inches, and Africa and South America in the area with more than 40 inches of moisture. It is in these continents that agriculture is made difficult and even impossible by an excess of moisture. Certain parts of the Tropics have such an extreme rainfall and such a steady tropic warmth that they are covered with huge trees, interlacing vines, ferns, and other growths which defy clearing. Parts of the Pacific Coast of the United States and Canada have rainfall ranging from 75 to 125 inches, and it is suspected from stream flow observations that 250 inches fall on certain mountain slopes. Snow depths of 50 feet are found at higher elevations.[1] An excess of moisture also produces swamp and overflow lands which are useless for agriculture until reclaimed.

Topography. Nearly one-fifth of the land area of the United States is unfit for crop production on account of unfavorable topography, irrespective of climatic and soil limitations. It is difficult to carry on farming operations on steep slopes, especially with machinery. Mechanization has tended to shift agriculture from hilly and sloping land to the level soils where large-scale farm machinery and tractors can be used. Besides, steep slopes are especially subject to erosion. In older countries terraces have been built to hold the soil, as for instance on the banks of the Rhine for the wine lands and in the rice fields of the Philippines. However, the tree crops and forests or heavy grasses are in many cases the best and only uses for steep hillsides.

Mountainous regions, because of the differences of altitude, slope, elevation, and exposure, have almost an infinite diversity of climate, and this necessitates the adjustment of crops to each climatic district. It is said of Colorado that it has as great a variety of climates as one would pass through in going from Virginia to Greenland. Variations in altitude alone account for fourteen differences in factors affecting plant and animal life, including differences in air pressure and in the intensity of ultra-violet rays.[2]

[1] *N. R. B. Report*, pp. 296–97.

[2] Wilfred W. Robbins, *Native Vegetation and Climate of Colorado in Their Relation to Agriculture* (Colorado Agricultural Experiment Station, Bulletin 224, 1917), pp. 28–30.

Mountains, however, are often rich in mineral deposits and water power; great mining and manufacturing centers may arise in extremely rough country. Valleys and mountains also determine lines of transportation, canals, railways, and highways; in general elevations add to the cost of transportation, because vehicles and goods must be *lifted* to considerable heights as well as propelled over the surface horizontally. Agriculture is often concentrated in coves and valleys and, because of inaccessibility, tends to be self-sufficient rather than commercial.

Because of their magnificent scenery many mountain regions have become noted as recreational areas. Switzerland, Germany, Norway, Canada, Colorado, and the Pacific Coast are obvious examples, but even lower ranges such as the Appalachians, the Ozarks, and the Green Mountains of Vermont have their appeal for the nature-lover and tourist.

Soils. Soil consists of parent material derived from rocks acted upon by chemical and physical forces with the assistance of the action of fungi, bacteria, plants, and animals. Climate has a profound effect on the soil, not only by the weathering process and by its influence on percolating water, leaching, and chemical reactions, but also by determining the vegetation under which soil develops. Climatic conditions have produced three general types of natural vegetation: forests, grasses, and desert. The soils developed under a grass cover are quite different from those developed under a forest cover; soils and plants evolve together. So close is the association of soils with climate that boundaries of climatic regions roughly correspond with those of the great zonal groups, although discrepancies occur as, for instance, on the margins of the prairie soils. In the humid eastern part of the United States these zones have an east to west trend similar to the trend of rainfall lines and isotherms; in the western prairie and semiarid section the soil zones run north and south and correspond to the direction of lines of rainfall and native vegetation—tall grass, short grass, and desert plants. Kellogg sums up the interaction of these factors as follows: "In the natural landscape all factors are interdependent. There is a relationship between soil and vegetation, between soil and climate, between climate and vegetation, between soil and parent rock, between soil and slope, and even between climate and slope, but all these factors cooperate in the production of an actual soil. The soil is the final synthetic expression of all these factors working together, and by which the nature of landscapes can be characterized, better, more directly and completely, than by any other factor or combination of factors."[1] The relationship of climate, native vegetation and soils to agriculture and land utilization is shown in Table 4.

Within each of the general soil classes there are a great many sub-classes. For instance, differences in relief will develop radically diverse soil types on the same parent material and in the same climate, producing corresponding differences in fertility. The difference between a good soil and a poor one is often very subtle. In the Connecticut Valley land is worth $300 an acre if the water table is just right for growing Sumatra tobacco; lacking this one quality it is worth less than $3.00 as hay or grain land.[2]

WATER AND LAND

The present configuration of the landscape—of mountains, hills, valleys, plains, and deltas—is largely the result of the action of water on the earth, especially in humid areas. In arid regions wind and other agencies may be more important. Rainfall helps to make the soil and transport it over the earth's surface. It penetrates this soil, serves plants, and works as underground water. It flows over the surface and forms creeks, lakes, and mighty river systems which are useful to man as paths of commerce, for water power, irrigation, and recreation. Both underground and surface water serve man for domestic, industrial, and urban purposes. There is hardly a form of land use that is not related to water directly or indirectly. The hydrologic cycle will assist in understanding these relationships.

Ground Water. As already stated, some of the precipitation disappears sooner or later as "fly-off," including the transpired water. Percolating water, not absorbed by vegetation, moves downward until it reaches rock, hardpan, or some other more or less impervious material. Here it forms an underground lake, the upper level of which is called the "water table." Underground water flows to lower places in response to gravity, just as surface

[1] Kellogg, "Soil and the People," *op. cit.*, p. 142. See also his *Development and Significance of the Great Soil Groups of the United States.*

[2] O. E. Baker, "The Middle Atlantic Trucking Region," *Economic Geography*, January, 1929, p. 44.

TABLE 4

GENERAL CHARACTER AND RELATIONSHIPS OF THE PRINCIPAL ZONAL GROUPS OF SOILS, U. S.[1]

CLIMATE	NATIVE VEGETATION	ZONAL GROUP OF SOILS	NATURAL FERTILITY FOR CROPS	PREDOMINANTLY* IN	CHIEF FORMS OF AGRICULTURE
Cool-moist.	Coniferous forest	Podzol	Low	Northern New England and Lake States	Small subsistence farms, wide variety of crops. Also recreation and lumbering.
Cool-moist, temperate.	Deciduous forest	Gray-brown Podzolic	Medium	East and Eastern Corn Belt	Small farms, general farming, wide variety of crops, including corn and wheat.
Moist. Warm to temperate.	Largely Coniferous forest	Yellow	Low	South	Small or medium sized farms, wide variety of subsistence crops; little livestock. Tobacco, cotton, peanuts. Local fruit and truck.
Do.	Largely Deciduous forest	Red	Medium	South	Small farms, some livestock. Wide choice of subsistence crops —considerable cotton and tobacco.
Temperate, moist.	Tall grass prairie	Prairie	High	Western Corn Belt, Eastern 100th Meridian	Medium sized or small farms—general farming—considerable livestock.
Temperate to cool-subhumid.	Tall grass prairie	Chernozem	Very high	100th Meridian	Rather large farms with wheat dominant, cereals, few subsistence crops.
Temperate to cool-arid.	Mixed tall and short grass	Chestnut	High	Western 100th Meridian Eastern Mountain States	Large farms—wheat dominant.
Do.	Short grass	Brown	High	Mountain	Very large farms—wheat with some ranching—irrigation.
Do.	Short grass to desert	Sierozem and desert	Medium	Do.	Ranching. (High fertility if irrigated.)

* Most of the Pacific and Mountain states are classified as "Mountains and Mountain Valleys (Undifferentiated)."

[1] Adapted from Table 1 of Charles E. Kellogg, *Development and Significance of the Great Soil Groups of the United States* (U. S. Dept. of Agriculture, Miscellaneous Publication 229, April, 1936), pp. 33–34, Figs. 4 and 5.

water does, and finally either emerges as springs above ground or quietly seeps into lakes, streams, or the ocean. It is not generally realized how much of the water in streams comes from ground water. It is rarely less than 40 or 50 per cent and may be nearly 100 per cent in the glacial deposits of the Lake states.[1] It is this seepage which produces "spring fed" lakes and keeps rivers going during long periods of rainless weather.

Underground water, when tapped by wells, becomes available for human use. About half of the people of the United States use water from wells to supply their domestic demands, in addition to the industrial and agricultural demands upon the same source. With the increase of population the water table has been lowered appreciably in many parts of the country, a situation which becomes more acute when droughts reduce the rainfall.

Percolating water is of significance in agriculture because it dissolves vital elements of the soil. Whenever the water moves upward, these elements are carried to the surface and deposited there as the water evaporates. This is of particular significance in arid lands. When the water moves downward, on the other hand, it carries away or "leaches" these elements into the rivers and lakes. In the Tropics and other regions of heavy rainfall the movements of water through the soil are often so rapid that the soil is depleted of its fertility. The mineral content of water also determines its "hardness" or "softness," which is important in the domestic and industrial uses of water.

Run-off and Erosion. Water which does not evaporate or penetrate the soil forms the "run-off"; gathering in creeks, lakes, and streams, it finally reaches the oceans. Where the force of water is sufficient and conditions are favorable, soil is loosened and carried away in suspension or by dragging over the surface. Other soil elements are dissolved by the surface water. This process of *erosion* is the antithesis of soil building. It is estimated that for the usual type of rock in our range of climate it takes 4,000 to 6,000 years, and perhaps longer, to produce a foot of soil. Soil erosion experiments in Missouri indicate that cultivated soil without any protective covering can lose a foot of soil in less

[1] H. S. Person, *et al., Little Waters* (Soil Conservation Service, *et al.,* 1935), p. 10.

than 50 years.[1] Erosion is as much a process of nature as is soil building, but it has been accelerated under the utilization of the earth by man. Under natural conditions an equilibrium was established between soil building and soil eroding forces, with the balance in favor of the accumulation of soil over a large part of the earth's surface. Forests and heavy grasses do much to check the flow of water over the earth's surface and, in general, assist the absorption of the water by the soil. To that extent, run-off, erosion, and floods are prevented. Man has disturbed this equilibrium by removing vegetation, loosening soil by cultivation, and in some cases increasing the run-off by making the surface more impervious. Erosion has become one of the most serious land utilization problems and will be discussed again in connection with agricultural land, forests, and water resources.

Run-off and Stream Flow. The volume and character of stream flow depends upon the nature of the rainfall and run-off. Given a steep slope, a heavy beating rain, an impervious, frozen, or saturated soil, most of the water will be removed as run-off. Such conditions cause serious floods. The Dayton flood of March, 1913, which caused damages of over $190,000,000 and the loss of about 400 lives, was the result of 8–10 inches of downpour within five days, falling on ground which had been saturated by the rainfall of previous months. In California, the seasonal character of the rainfall and steep slopes of the mountains contribute to sending three-fourths of the precipitation to the oceans within forty-five days after it falls, but on the level Great Plains the run-off is often as low as 3 per cent of the rainfall. For the country as a whole between 20 and 30 per cent of the rainfall reaches the seas.[2]

The reason that all original run-off does not reach the oceans is that much of it is returned to the "fly-off" en route, especially where it lingers in lakes, marshes, swamps, and reservoirs and wherever a large surface is exposed to the action of wind and sun. These bodies of water are collecting and retarding agencies and serve to regulate the volume of the streams. This helps to prevent floods and is very desirable for water power. Niagara, with four

[1] F. L. Dudley and M. F. Miller, *Erosion and Surface Run-off under Different Soil Conditions* (Missouri Agric. Exp. Station, Research Bulletin 63, 1923), p. 31.

[2] *N. R. B. Report,* p. 301. See also the maps.

of the Great Lakes as a storage basin, is ideal in this respect, and the lakes of the Laurentian Shield of Canada serve in the same capacity. Stream flow is also retarded by obstructions such as stones, logs, beaver dams, bends, and meanders.

With the settlement of the country many of the natural conditions which had retarded run-off and reduced the velocity of streams have been disturbed. Forests and grass have been removed; hard surfaced roads, railroads, and buildings now shed water instead of assisting its absorption. In some cities buildings and paved streets cover practically the entire area, and their efficient drainage systems send almost the entire run-off into the rivers. Bridges, piers, factories, and other man-made features have encroached on streams, thereby reducing their cross sections. Lakes and other bodies of water have been filled in or drained. Drainage of farm lands has hastened the removal of water and added to the run-off.[1]

Running water not only erodes material on the land surface but also cuts the channels of rivers, the two actions being responsible for differences in the character of valleys, gorges, and other features of the landscape. The power of water to erode and transport material depends on its velocity. When the velocity of water is doubled, its transporting power is not doubled, but increased sixty-four times; and so is its power to batter down its banks and the earthworks intended to hold it in control. The velocity of a stream increases when its bed slopes more steeply or when it is forced into a narrower channel. Since the increase in velocity multiplies the power to carry sediment, even a small decrease will cause a deposition to take place. When a stream leaves a narrow channel to take a broader one, or when the degree of slope is reduced, the river lays down its silt, causing formation of sand bars. Secondary channels are cut through the accumulated material and even the level of the river bed itself tends to rise. These are important considerations in flood control measures and in keeping rivers navigable.

Silting of Lakes and Reservoirs. Deposition also takes place whenever a swifter stream discharges into a gentle river. Lake

[1] If thoroughly dried out, drained areas act like a sponge or an empty reservoir by absorbing water until the earth is saturated before discharging it into streams. In fact, one of the dangers of desiccated peat marshes is from fires which often destroy the entire fertile layer of earth before they are extinguished.

Pepin on the Mississippi is a result of the damming of this river by the sediment dropped by the more rapid Chippewa. This also happens where a river discharges into a lake. It has been said that "rivers are the mortal enemies of lakes," and this also applies to swamps, marshes, artificial lakes, reservoirs, and dams. The coarser material is dropped first. The finer material is transported further and tends to settle to the bottom where it is carried by underflows to the remainder of the dam or lake bed. Thus the top of the water may be clear, yet deposition is going forward in the deeper waters. The significance of this in connection with irrigation, water power, recreation, and municipal water storage will be discussed in appropriate chapters. However, it is apparent that unless land utilization on the streams supplying the reservoirs is designed to control erosion, the "death" of dams, lakes, and other water storage is only a matter of time. This means that use of the irrigated land dependent on this water is also doomed. It is estimated that some of the dams on the federal irrigation projects will be filled in seventy-five years and, unless the dam is raised, the land will revert to desert. A series of structures to catch the eroded material will be helpful until they are also filled.

The popular proposal to get rid of silt by opening gates in dams is of little avail. Systematic venting by properly arranged gates might draw off the finer material but would do little to remove the heavier sediment deposited where the stream enters the reservoir. After the dam is completely filled, opening a gate merely causes a narrow channel to be cut in the accumulated silt from the gate to the inlet. Hydraulic dredging and mechanical removal cost from five to fifty times as much as the original storage.[1]

Deltas. The final place of deposition is at the mouth of the river where deltas are formed, provided the sediment is not carried away by currents. The Mississippi now flows through a delta which began at Cairo. The bed of the lower Mississippi is all alluvium; borings show a mean depth of alluvial deposits of 131 feet from the mouth of the Ohio to New Orleans, and logs have been found 100 to 300 feet below the present land surface. The process of "robbing Peter to pay Paul" is still going on; every year a

[1] Henry M. Eakin, *Silting of Reservoirs* (U. S. Dept. of Agriculture, Technical Bulletin 524, July, 1936), pp. 2–7, 125, 126.

billion cubic yards of earth are taken from the vast drainage basin of the Mississippi and dumped into the Gulf of Mexico.[1] Deltas are usually flat fertile plains conducive to intensive agriculture and dense populations. The deltas of the Ganges, Yangtze, Nile, Po, Rhine, and our own Mississippi are examples.

Flood Plains. Whenever a river is in flood and natural conditions permit, the water leaves the channel and spreads over the

TABLE 5

PERCENTAGE OF THE ECONOMIC REGIONS OF THE UNITED STATES IN LAND OF VARIOUS GRADES [2]

REGION *	PERCENTAGE OF LAND AREA IN EACH GRADE				
	Grade 1	2	3	4	5
Northeastern	.71%	16.94%	25.61%	30.67%	26.06%
South	1.53	10.40	28.20	32.08	27.79
Corn Belt	35.89	24.52	23.21	11.05	5.33
Lake	13.73	28.66	17.13	15.03	25.45
100th Meridian	4.46	18.06	30.00	23.41	24.07
Mountain	0.00	.07	3.06	11.06	85.81
Pacific	.23	1.51	5.11	12.53	79.81
All U. S.	5.3	11.1	18.1	19.1	46.4

* See Fig. 3 for grouping of the states which constitute these regions.

adjacent flat country. As it does so, its velocity is decreased and the silt is deposited. The "fertilizing mud" of the Nile has maintained the productiveness of the valley since the beginning of agriculture in Egypt. Before levees were built the Mississippi also roamed over its flood plain, depositing silt and building up the soil. The heavier sediment is deposited first, producing natural levees near the stream. In the Mississippi Valley these levees slope 3 to 4 feet per mile away from the river, whereas the slope to the Gulf is only 8 inches per mile. Swamps and secondary river systems paralleling the main stream are the result. Man covets the rich soils of the flood plains, and, by levees and drainage, millions of acres of land have been reclaimed, the more spectacular among them being the Zuyder Zee in Holland, the Pontine Marshes of

[1] Arthur DeWitt Frank, *The Development of the Federal Program of Flood Control on the Mississippi River* (Columbia University Press, 1930), p. 103.

[2] Calculated from Table 7, "Preliminary Inventory of Land Productivity Classes of the United States," *N. R. B. Report,* p. 127.

Italy, and the flood plain of the Mississippi. However, those who live behind dikes and levees do so at the constant peril of floods.

Rivers also have the unhappy facility of changing their courses, making bends and oxbows, and then cutting them off. The Mississippi formed secondary channels which once took the water out of the main stream and later returned it, or, in Louisiana, sent the water directly to the sea. This makes navigation difficult and interferes with the use of the land for farms, industries, and cities.

Gradations in the Quality of Land. When the land of the United States is classified into five classes on the basis of physical productivity the area of excellent land or "Grade I" land is surprisingly small.[1] Only 5.3 per cent of the total land area of the United States is classed as "Grade I" land, whereas 46.4 per cent is placed in the fifth grade, described as "essentially incapable of tillage." The distribution of the first-grade land among the states is even more extraordinary. Iowa has about one-fourth of all the "Grade I" land, and three-fourths of this class is located in Iowa, Illinois, Minnesota, Missouri, Nebraska, and Indiana, essentially the Corn Belt states. Seventeen states have no first-grade land and six have no soil of either grades one or two. The distribution of these soils by regions is shown in Table 5.

Below the agricultural margin, forestry and grazing may still be profitable land uses. Forests can endure conditions which crops cannot; grasses can grow in arid regions where grains and even forests cannot exist. It is estimated that there are about 262,000,000 acres of *absolute* forest land in the United States and about 468,000,000 acres of land suitable only for grazing, with approximately 66,000,000 acres that could be used for either. The extreme physical limit of crop production is placed at 973,000,000 acres. In 1935 the United States had about 514,000,000 acres of crop land, about 53 per cent of the potential arable acreage.[2]

Forest land also has gradations ranging from soils highly efficient for the growing of trees to soils submarginal for tree production. The same is true of grazing. The carrying capacity of

[1] *N. R. B. Report,* pp. 126–27. These figures are preliminary and subject to revision. They have been mapped in O. E. Baker, "A Graphic Summary of Physical Features and Land Utilization in the United States," *op. cit.*, pp. 12–14.

[2] L. C. Gray, *et al.*, "The Utilization of Our Lands for Crops, Pasture, and Forests," *Yearbook of the U. S. Dept. of Agriculture,* 1923, p. 431.

pasture and range land varies from 2 acres per cow in the Corn Belt to 75 acres in Nevada and other parts of the West.

Gradations in land have more than passing interest to the economist. In the first place, these grades are practically permanent and are only locally subject to change by man. Something can be done by drainage, irrigation, fertilization, or other amelioration, but only with the expenditure of labor and capital. The physical characteristics become translated into economic characteristics. Each grade and class of land becomes associated with specific types of agriculture, with certain sizes of farms and patterns of rural occupation. Rich soils mean greater income per man and per farm, higher land values, and a substantial tax base which can support schools, roads, and other community institutions. Marginal areas lack these advantages.[1] The Corn Belt is an illustration of the economic consequences of a "Grade I" soil. It covers only 8 per cent of the total area of the United States yet in 1920 it had 13 per cent of the farms, 25 per cent of the value of all crops, and 35 per cent of the value of all farm real estate of the entire nation. The value per acre of its crops was 60 per cent greater than that found in any other agricultural area.[2]

In the second place, differences in grades of land became the basis for the classical doctrine of rent. In 1777, a year after the appearance of Adam Smith's *Wealth of Nations,* James Anderson published a pamphlet which explained rent on the "differential" principle. Ricardo used this concept and combined it with Malthus' "law of population" and the law of diminishing returns (noted by Edward West in 1815) in his statement of the theory of rent and distribution of wealth in 1817.

Regions. In any country as large and diverse as the United States the variation in physical conditions produces differences in the economic interests of the people, different cultural patterns, and differences in outlook upon life. However, within given areas natural factors tend to be uniform enough to produce a uniformity of occupations, interests, and cultural patterns so that a "region" can be distinguished. This is recognized in everyday life when

[1] Ellsworth Huntington, "The Handicap of Poor Land," *Economic Geography,* July, 1926, and "The Quantitative Phases of Human Geography," *Scientific Monthly,* October, 1927.

[2] O. E. Baker, "The Agricultural Regions of North America, Part IV, The Corn Belt," *Economic Geography,* October, 1927, p. 447.

people refer to the Cotton Belt, the South, the Corn Belt, or New England. The question of regions and regionalism has become very popular, especially with those who think in terms of planning. It recognizes that the differences in natural conditions and people are such that no one ironclad system of local government, for instance, can be forced upon the nation or even within some states. It also recognizes that regions requiring similar treatment rarely coincide with state and county boundaries; nevertheless, these units of government must provide the machinery for the utilization of a particular resource. As an example, the seven states in which the Colorado River lies tried to use the device of a "state compact" before the river could be utilized for irrigation, power, and water supply.[1]

Regions may be set up from many points of view. Geographers describe the earth in terms of broad zones, and O. E. Baker has delineated the agricultural regions of North America, which in some respects are subdivisions of the broader geographic regions (Figure 3). Another type of region is based upon the hinterland of the chief cities or upon their metropolitan influence. Such regions are primarily economic in character. Drainage basins have been made the basis of another set of regions, and from the standpoint of federal administration a multitude of regions or districts have been created.[2] The National Resources Committee suggests another arrangement, based upon planning problems for natural resources, that corresponds closely to O. E. Baker's "agricultural" regions.[3] Naturally, large general regions are divisible into many sub-regions, and much fine work has been done to determine "type of farming" areas in various states and by the federal Department of Agriculture.[4]

The United States Census has divided the country into three "sections"—North, South, and West—and subdivided these into a total of nine divisions, and statistical data are available by sec-

[1] National Resources Committee, *Regional Factors in National Planning and Development,* December, 1935, Chap. VI, "The Interstate Compact."

[2] Howard Odum, *Southern Regions of the United States* (Chapel Hill, University of North Carolina Press, 1936). The T.V.A. is an example of the *region* based on a drainage basin.

[3] *Regional Factors in National Planning and Development, op. cit.,* p. 166.

[4] See Fifteenth Census of the United States, Census of Agriculture: *Types of Farming in the United States;* also studies of types of farming made by the state colleges.

tions, divisions, states, counties, and "minor civil divisions." The groupings of states of the census are useful for many purposes but they rarely coincide with geographic or agricultural regions. For this reason a new grouping has been made as shown in Figure 3 and used in Table 5. These "economic regions" will be referred to throughout this book.

The Pacific and Mountain states are the same as the census divisions. British Columbia on the Canadian side has the characteristics of both regions, just as eastern Washington, Oregon, and California share the attributes of the Inter-mountain area.

The 100th Meridian states or Great Plains are set aside because of their position as the transition states between humid agriculture and the areas with low rainfall, including the famous "Dust Bowl." Alberta, Saskatchewan, and Manitoba share the characteristics of the Plains region of the United States.

The Great Lakes states, usually attached to the Corn Belt, have unique land use problems and deserve separate treatment. A part of Ontario corresponds to the Lake states, but the Laurentian Shield is a region with its own characteristics. It dips into the Great Lakes States and swings to the northwest and northeast in such a manner as to cover more than two million square miles, which is more than half of the surface of Canada. It is characterized by sparse forests, a barren rocky terrain with a great abundance of lakes, rivers, and potential water power. Agricultural soils are lacking except in the valleys and other scattered areas. Minerals and forest products are of importance, however. This area was a barrier to westward expansion. Population was deflected by the shield to the south until, at the end of the nineteenth century, one-third of the Canadian-born population lived in the United States. "These were days of depopulation when the Scriptures, according to a Canadian Finance Minister, were said to 'begin with Exodus and end with Lamentations.' "[1] The barrier was finally bridged by railroads built at enormous expense.

New England and the Middle Atlantic states, plus West Virginia, Maryland, and Delaware, are placed in the Northeastern region in which industry and commerce overshadow agriculture. Over 31 per cent of the people of the United States live in these

[1] W. A. Mackintosh, "The Laurentian Plateau in Canadian Economic Development," *Economic Geography*, October, 1926, pp. 537–49 at 541.

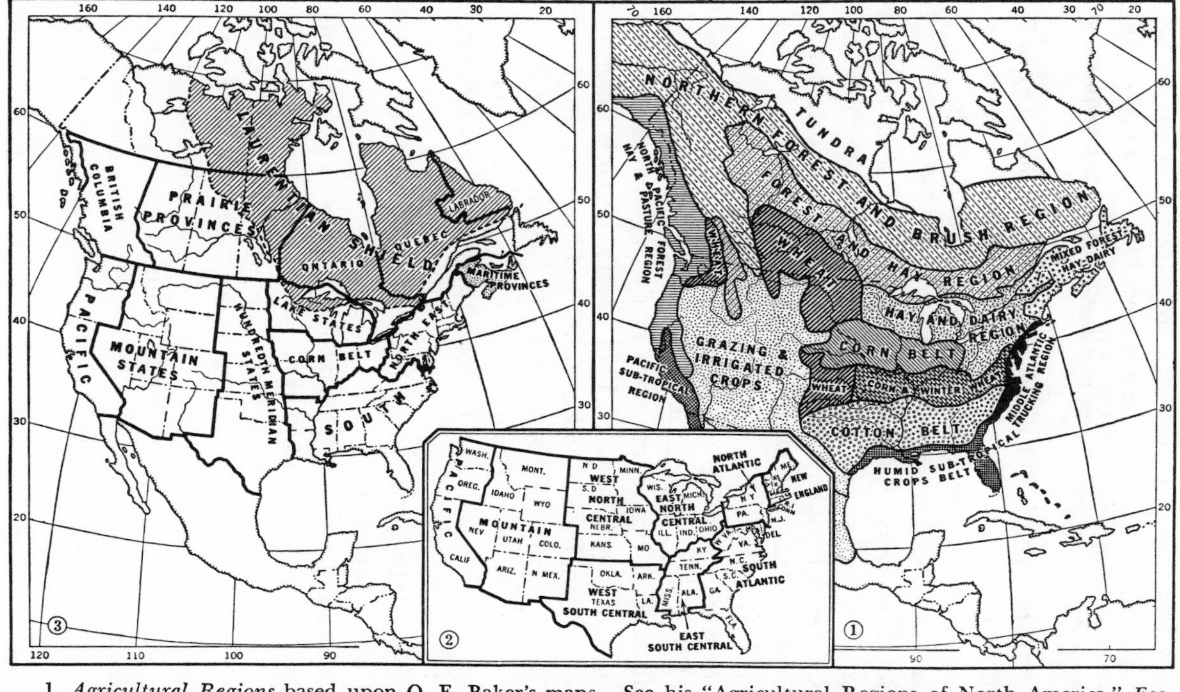

1. *Agricultural Regions* based upon O. E. Baker's maps. See his "Agricultural Regions of North America," *Economic Geography*, Oct., 1926, and U. S. Dept. of Agriculture Miscellaneous Publication 260, *op. cit.*
2. *Geographic Divisions* as used by the United States Census.
3. *Economic Regions* as used throughout the book, based in part on Maps 1 and 2 above.

FIG. 3. REGIONS OF UNITED STATES AND CANADA

twelve states, and almost 80 per cent were classed as urban in 1930. Corresponding areas in Canada are eastern Ontario, Quebec, and the Maritime provinces, which have 70 per cent of the population of the Dominion.

The Corn Belt consists of five states, none of which lie wholly in the belt, as is shown on the agricultural regions map; and parts of Minnesota, South Dakota, and Nebraska properly belong in this region.

The South includes all the states lying in the Cotton Belt, the Gulf subtropical region, and border states between the cotton and corn belts. Texas has so much cotton that much of it rightly belongs with the South, but because of its importance as a Plains state, it has been placed with the 100th Meridian states.

Mere expediency in the use of census material by states and provinces has prompted the groupings suggested above. The "regions" fall short of expressing much of the regional character of the United States and Canada. They ignore the Gulf Coast, the Ozark-Appalachian, the Columbia Basin, and Northeastern Forest regions. They make no allowance for the diversity of the Pacific states, British Columbia, Ontario, Texas, or the Lake states, to mention only a few examples. Quebec is distinctive enough to be a region by itself. However, as facts call for other groupings, other regions will be suggested to bring out an adequate treatment of a particular resource.

Classification of Land or Natural Resources. Early economic literature often treated land as if it were homogeneous, having identical characteristics and an income of a peculiar nature called "rent." However, as soon as land users were confronted with the practical problems of conserving our soils, growing forests, irrigating land, and taxing resources, it became clear that each type of land had its own attributes. There is no one principle of income, utilization, conservation, valuation, or taxation which can apply to all of them.

For purposes of separate treatment certain broad classes of land or resources are easily distinguished. The following classification will be used in this work: [1]

[1] These broad classes are used in Charles R. Van Hise and Loomis Havemeyer, *The Conservation of Our Natural Resources* (rev. ed., New York, Macmillan, 1930) and in the *N. R. B. Report.*

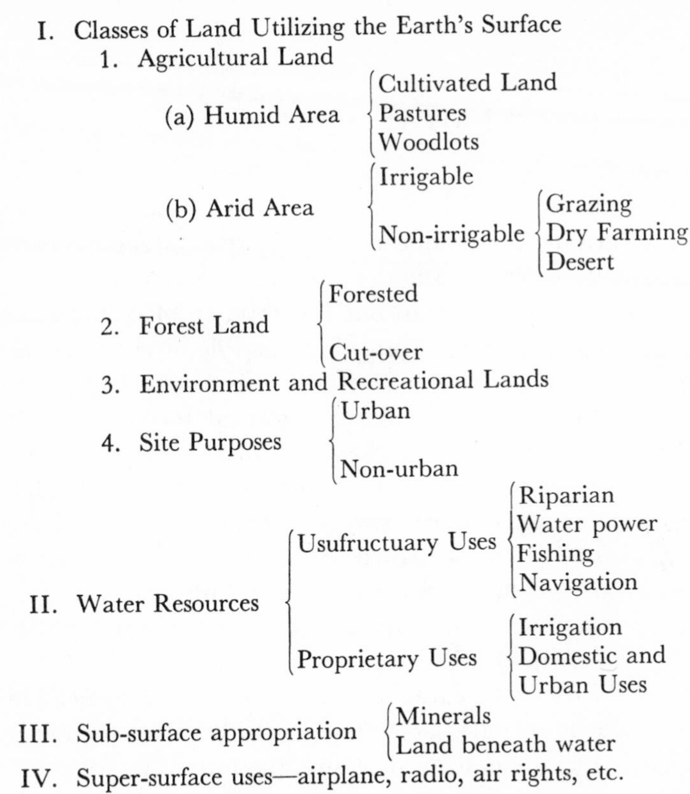

I. Classes of Land Utilizing the Earth's Surface
   1. Agricultural Land
      (a) Humid Area — Cultivated Land; Pastures; Woodlots
      (b) Arid Area — Irrigable; Non-irrigable — Grazing; Dry Farming; Desert
   2. Forest Land — Forested; Cut-over
   3. Environment and Recreational Lands
   4. Site Purposes — Urban; Non-urban
II. Water Resources
   Usufructuary Uses — Riparian; Water power; Fishing; Navigation
   Proprietary Uses — Irrigation; Domestic and Urban Uses
III. Sub-surface appropriation — Minerals; Land beneath water
IV. Super-surface uses—airplane, radio, air rights, etc.

Although land falls into rather distinct classes, these classes cannot be separated in a treatment of resources or in the framing of land policies. Forest, recreational, ranch, and arable lands compete for the earth's surface. Coal, gas, and petroleum are rivals of wood as fuel and power; iron, steel, stone, brick, and cement are substitutes for wood. On the other hand, the uses of resources may be complementary. Forests can be used for recreation and, if carefully supervised, for grazing. Inasmuch as forests have a pronounced effect on stream flow and erosion, large areas of land may have to be dedicated to forest use primarily for the purpose of keeping streams navigable, keeping reservoirs from silting, for flood control, and for the protection of farm land. Production of forest products may be incidental or even negative in "protection forests." [1]

[1] Frank A. Waugh, "Reconciliation of Land Uses," *Journal of Land and Public Utility Economics,* February, 1936, pp. 87–89.

III

LAND AS SPACE

Whereas agricultural, forest, and mineral lands are useful because they yield physical products, urban land is valuable merely because it furnishes space, standing room, or extension. It is paid for because people want to build a store, an office building, a bank, or to park their cars. Instead of tangible products, urban land yields intangible services. However, this fundamental attribute is common to all land, whether agricultural, forest, or urban; in fact, Marshall says it is the one characteristic that marks off land "from the material things which we regard as products of land." [1] Commons puts it even more strongly when he says, "Land is valuable primarily because it furnishes only *room* and *situation*. This is practically all that is furnished in agriculture and notoriously all that is furnished in other industries. These are its only original and indestructible powers." [2]

Indestructibility of Physical Space. Taking land in general, extension is no doubt the most indestructible characteristic of land. A forest may be destroyed by fire, the humus converted to ashes, yet the acres of surface remain as before. Farm land may be devastated by erosion and reduced to bare rock, yet the area has not shrunk. Even a mine will occupy the same space relationships when excavated as when newly opened. While space and extension are of the greatest economic significance in cities and suburban areas, they are not without importance in other resources. Plants and trees need room for both roots and leaves and only a limited number can be supported on an acre. As was pointed out earlier, overcrowded agricultural nations are looking for more room, more space, because of this attribute of the agricultural use of land.

The Law of Diminishing Returns. Land in itself is not productive. It yields wheat, forest products, or office space only when labor and capital are applied to it. While land yields greater re-

[1] *Principles of Economics* (2d ed., London, Macmillan, 1891), pp. 197–98.
[2] John R. Commons, *Distribution of Wealth* (New York, Macmillan, 1893), p. 137.

turns with the application of more labor and capital, and while we say that the yield is greater under *intensive* than *extensive* utilization, there comes a point where the "static law of diminishing returns" sets in and the yield is no longer in proportion to the input.

If successive small units of labor and capital are applied to a *fixed area of land* under a given technique of production, an increase in output per unit of input will take place until a maximum or optimum is reached. After that a decrease in output per unit of input takes place, and finally even the total product will be reduced. This law sets a limit to agricultural production on a given area at a given time. If additional "doses" of input always produced equal units of output, the products or services from a fixed area of land would be an infinite quantity. There would be no need to extend cultivation to poorer soils; in fact, the area necessary to supply the world with food could be shrunk to a small proportion of the best land now in use. The realization that this law sets a limit, even though an elastic one, to agricultural production prompted John Stuart Mill to say that it "was the most important proposition in political economy." He, with many preceding economists, considered its operation peculiar to land; however, the law applies not only to farm land but to all other resources and all other factors of production. It should be noted, furthermore, that it is based upon physical phenomena and is therefore independent of capitalism, socialism, or any other economic system.

It is also important that the static nature of this law be noted. It holds for a given space, at a given time and with a given technique of land utilization. Its behavior will change when a new fertilizer is introduced, a superior method for drilling oil is invented, or steel construction is substituted for masonry.

The operation of the law has repeatedly been observed practically or experimentally, the "doses" usually consisting of a single item of labor and capital instead of a complete composite unit of input. For instance, Table 6 shows the varying yields of wheat on a series of equal-sized plots with varying quantities of irrigation water. Diminishing returns are indicated by the decrease from 7.56 bushels per inch on Plot 1 to less than one bushel per inch on Plot 8, on which 50 inches had been applied. However, the soil contained almost 14 inches of natural soil moisture in addition to artificial irrigation water; but even in terms of the total supply there was a consistent decrease. Other illustrations of diminishing returns are related to depth of plowing, amount of seed planted, fertilization, and the number of cultivations.[1]

TABLE 6

YIELDS OF WHEAT WITH DIFFERENT QUANTITIES OF IRRIGATION WATER[2]

(Water in acre-inches)

Plot No.	Inches of Irrigation Water	Rainfall and Soil Water	Total Water	Yield of Wheat per Acre	Increment Bushels	Yield per Inch of Irrigation Water	Yield per Inch of Total Water
1	5.00	13.74	18.74	37.81	...	7.56	2.02
2	7.50	"	21.24	41.54	3.73	6.39	1.96
3	10.00	"	23.74	43.54	1.99	4.35	1.83
4	15.00	"	28.74	45.71	2.17	3.05	1.59
5	25.00	"	38.74	46.46	.75	1.86	1.10
6	30.00	"	43.74	47.51	1.05	1.58	1.08
7	35.00	"	48.74	48.55	1.04	1.39	.99
8	50.00	"	63.74	49.38	.77	.99	.77

Table 7 is a hypothetical table designed to show the operations of the law and the proportioning of the factors of production to be discussed later. The first column merely numbers the units of inputs of composite "doses" of labor and capital. The second column shows the product (which may be called pounds for convenience) which the land yields as successive units of input are expended on the fixed area of land. The third column shows the "increment" or the product due to the particular unit of input. For instance, the second unit adds 15 pounds; this does not mean that the second unit is more productive than the first (since all are of the same size), but that the second in co-operation with the first *adds* 15 pounds to the total. Thus the "increment" assignable to the fifth input is 45 pounds. It will be observed that the increments increase up to the fifth unit, then consistently decrease,

[1] W. J. Spillman and E. Lang, *The Law of Diminishing Returns* (New York, World Book Co., 1924); Patton, *Diminishing Returns in Agriculture, op. cit.*

[2] Based on Tables 2 and 3, John A. Widtsoe and L. A. Merrill, *The Yields of Crops with Different Quantities of Irrigation Water* (Utah Agricultural Experiment Station, Bulletin 117), pp. 76, 77.

and finally become negative, and the total product decreases. The "increments" due to additional inputs of irrigation water (Table 6) also decline but are more erratic than in the hypothetical table, partly because the inputs increase irregularly. Plot 2 receives 2½ inches more water than Plot 1, but Plot 5 was given 10 inches more than Plot 4. The final column of Table 7 shows the average

TABLE 7

INCREASING AND DECREASING RETURNS

I "Inputs" Units of Expenditure of Labor and Capital	II Output or Product	III Increases Due to a Given Unit of Input or "Increment"	IV Average per Unit of Labor and Capital
1	5	5	5
2	20	15	10
3	45	25	15
4	80	35	20
5	125	45	25
6	162	37	27
7	196	34	28
8	224	28	28
9	243	19	27
10	260	17	26
11	275	15	25
12	288	13	24
13	299	11	23
14	308	9	22
15	315	7	21
16	320	5	20
17	323	3	19
18	324	1	18
19	323	−1	17
20	320	−3	16
21	315	−5	15
22	286	−29	13
23	253	−33	11
24	216	−37	9
25	175	−41	7

production *per unit of input;* these increase up to the seventh and eighth units and then decrease.

Just where do diminishing returns take place? If one could disregard scarcity and costs completely, the operator might add inputs of labor and capital until the product actually decreases.

Measured in terms of the fixed factor (land), there is no decrease until the nineteenth unit of input has been expended. But in terms of the variable factor two points can be located either (1) where the increment no longer increases (Input 5), or (2) where the output per unit of input declines, namely the seventh or eighth "dose." Practically, these points are mere guides to the operator, whose combination of the factors will be determined by the relative prices of land, labor, and capital on the one hand and of the products or services of the land on the other. This will be discussed in a later chapter; at this point it is merely necessary to point out that the same *space* can be made to yield from 5 to 324 "pounds," depending on the inputs of labor and capital the operator places on this space.[1]

Expansibility of Economic Space. "The area of the earth's surface is fixed; the geometric relations in which any particular part of it stands to other parts are fixed. Man has no control over them; they are wholly unaffected by demand; they have no cost of production; there is no supply price at which they can be produced." This is Marshall's statement in regard to the supply of space and man's power over this supply.[2] That the physical area of the earth's surface is fixed no one can deny, but the *economic* supply of space is not the physical supply. Area for economic purposes is always area for a specific use and when so considered is not a fixed expanse, at least not until this particular use has absorbed the entire earth's surface.

The most valuable spatial use of all is urban land. The space actually occupied by all the cities and villages of the United States covers only 10,000,000 acres out of the 1,903,000,000 acres of total land area. This is less than half of the area in farmsteads. It has

[1] The hypothetical table shows increasing, maximum, and decreasing returns, whereas actual illustrations and practical experience show only decreasing returns. One reason is that even experiments are not, or cannot be set up in such a way as to show the increasing return phase. In the irrigation experiment the wheat on the first plot had almost 19 inches of water instead of the input of 5 inches. This is like starting with Input 7 in Table 7. To be comparable with the hypothetical table the experiment should be conducted on water-free soil and an input of say 2½ inches of water placed on Plot 1, 5 inches on Plot 2, etc., thus providing for five additional plots previous to the first one as now set up. In actual land utilization the operator knows by experience about what combination to make between land and the inputs of the other factors under expected prices, and neither increasing nor decreasing returns are readily observable.

[2] Alfred Marshall, *Principles of Economics, op. cit.,* 8th ed., pp. 144–45.

been calculated that if the entire population of the globe were placed in a super-city with a density of population equal to that of Paris "this monstrous honeycomb would extend outward in a circle for not more than 75 miles." [1] Land for site purposes therefore occupies only an infinitesimal part of the space available for this purpose.

Cities can always expand by absorbing new land taken out of farm or forest use and, where values are high enough, land is often "manufactured." The areas of Milwaukee and Chicago were enlarged by filling in Lake Michigan. From the standpoint of the total land area of America the space so created was insignificant, but from the standpoint of economic values it was of great consequence. At one time it was proposed to extend Manhattan Island into the Upper Bay so as to create six additional square miles for New York City. It was estimated that the value of the land so produced would have been equal to the value of all the farm land, excluding buildings, of the Middle Atlantic states, as urban and rural land values stood in 1920–24.[2] This "estimate," however, neglected entirely the depressing effect of adding six square miles to the total land supply of New York City. During the land boom in Florida, land was made at the rate of five acres a month and sold before the dredges were started. In Seattle, hills were literally washed away to make space for buildings. Treasure Island, the site of the San Francisco World's Fair (1939) is a 400-acre tract created by dredges, one of the largest islands ever built by man.

It might be argued that in such cases man has not really created space: he has merely taken space from Lake Michigan, New York Bay, or the Atlantic in order to add it to dry land. The total area of the earth has not been changed. This simply means that physical space *per se* has little significance. No one would spend money to produce extension in Nevada where area is plentiful. What is significant is that *economic space* can be created where it is needed.

Another way of creating economic space is by increasing the height of buildings. The skyscraper is a mechanism designed to

[1] "The Problem of the Tall Building as a French Architect Views It," *Western Architect*, September, 1925, p. 96.

[2] *Literary Digest*, December 10, 1921, p. 18.

furnish usable space. It is possible to create almost 1,800,000 square feet of net rentable space with office room for approximately 20,000 tenants on a city lot 200 by 405 feet.

However, the creation of economic space is also limited by the law of diminishing returns. "Net rentable space" is the test of the efficiency of an office building. Table 8 shows the net rentable space available in a series of buildings ranging from 8 to 75 stories and placed on the same sized lot. In theory every

TABLE 8

DECREASING RENTABLE SPACE WITH INCREASE IN HEIGHT OF OFFICE BUILDINGS[1]

Building No.	Stories	Net Rentable Area	Total Increment in Rentable Space	Average Net Rentable Area per Floor	Average Increment per Floor *
		Square feet	*Square feet*	*Square feet*	*Square feet*
1	8	513,420	....	64,178	...
2	15	803,102	289,682	53,540	41,383
3	22	983,806	180,704	44,718	25,815
4	30	1,165,862	182,056	38,862	22,757
5	37	1,313,346	147,484	35,495	21,069
6	50	1,491,259	177,913	29,825	13,686
7	63	1,653,342	162,083	26,243	12,468
8	75	1,791,914	138,572	23,892	11,548

* Total increment in rentable space divided by the number of floors between "stories."

one of the 75 floors should have the same gross area as the ground floor; there should be no diminution in the available floor space as the height of the building increases, and consequently no "diminishing returns." However, rentable space *decreases* with the height of the building because more and more space has to be given over to elevators, stairs, and service facilities. Moreover, in the case of the building used as an illustration in Table 8, the zoning laws required a "set back" and the gross floor space afforded by the 200–by–405 lot above the first eight floors was reduced to 137 by 166 feet in the remaining tower floors. So, in this instance, both physical and legal factors were responsible for diminishing returns. Although the building height is increased

[1] Based on Table 8, W. C. Clark and J. L. Kingston, *The Skyscraper* (New York, American Institute of Steel Construction, 1930), p. 42.

from 8 to 75 stories, or over nine times, the net rentable space is increased only three times. The decrease is even more marked if measured in terms of the "increment," best shown in the last column where the increment is expressed in terms of floors.

Ground area is no more an indication of the limitation of creating economic space than a given area is an indication of its capacity to produce farm products. In both cases the yield in services or products depends on the number of inputs of labor and capital placed upon the land under the operation of diminishing returns. The same lot can provide office space ranging from 100,000 to 2,000,000 square feet, depending upon the height and efficiency of the building. In fact, buildings twice as high as any existing structure are entirely feasible from the engineering standpoint. The maximum *economic* height, however, seems to have been reached. It is determined by the balance of increasing costs as against the income derived from rental of diminishing space as the building mounts in height.[1]

Increasing Economic Space by Transportation. The area of land for a specific purpose is therefore not "unaffected by demand"; in fact it is highly sensitive to demand. The area of urban land can be increased at will either by horizontal or vertical expansion. Even an island city like New York expands to neighboring mainlands or other islands and rises into the air. Whether one or the other method is used depends upon the economy of horizontal as compared to vertical transportation. While the original space might have little or no cost of production, economic space is not costless. Although ferries, bridges, and tunnels give access to land across the waters surrounding New York, barriers in the form of time and cost in getting to and from work, inconvenience and congestion still remain. Besides, the ferries, tunnels, bridges, trains, and busses are all man-made and have to be paid for. Every improvement in horizontal transportation tends to overcome these public and private costs, and the most effective argument for decentralization of industry and population is that it will make these costs unnecessary or at least reduce them. The increasing cost of providing space as the height of the building is increased acts as an elastic barrier in the vertical creation of space.

[1] See Chap. V.

Physical Immobility of Land. Another element in the spatial aspects of land lies in the fact that the relation of one part of the earth's surface is definitely and unalterably fixed to every other part. This is axiomatic yet of great importance in the economics of land use. Stated in another way, land is physically *immobile.* Immobility prevents the moving of land from where it is plentiful to where it is scarce. Heavy taxes can be placed on real estate, yet the owner cannot move land to another state to escape taxes, which is one of the arguments used in favor of land taxation. Movable capital goods can be transported to escape taxes or to take advantage of price differences. If horses become scarce in the East they can be driven or transported from the West where they are cheap; not so the ranch on which they were raised.[1] The attribute of immobility is also found in the more permanent capital goods, skyscrapers, factories, bridges, and dams. Of course, they can be taken down brick by brick or piece by piece and rebuilt on a new location, but only at enormous expense. This practice seems to be largely confined to the moving of old castles from Europe to America by millionaires.

The immobility of land and buildings produces unusual gains or extraordinary losses for the landowner. Unexpected gains arise if the city moves in his direction, a new street or bridge is opened, or new transportation lines make his particular piece of land more valuable for business or homes. On the other hand, the encroachment of business, "blighted districts," or the moving in of undesirable races or nationalities often decreases values.

Space and Possession. "The use of a certain area of the earth's surface is a primary condition of anything that man can do; it gives him room for his own actions, with the enjoyment of the heat and the light, the air and the rain which nature assigns to that space," is a further observation of Marshall.[2] In other words, the ownership of area or space entitles the possessor to all the forces of nature connected with that space or, as Bye defines *land,*

[1] Immobility of land does not necessarily imply immobility of soil. With modern machinery it is physically possible to move hills. The topsoil can be stripped from fertile farm land without much engineering difficulty. Whether this is permitted or not is a legal matter. French gardeners are allowed to take with them a certain portion of the topsoil when they move, and in parts of China the ownership of the soil is separate from the land space. The one is physically mobile, the other immobile.

[2] *Ibid.*

as "all natural resources and productive power over which *possession* of the earth's surface gives control." [1] "Possession," however, involves the concept of property in land. Whether the products or services of a given space on the earth's surface are permitted to go to private owners or to the public depends upon the institutions set up by society.

Favorable winds, excellent climate, or a beautiful view cannot be enjoyed without purchasing or renting the land with which these are associated, unless the land is owned publicly. Very often the ownership of a small area of land carries with it forces of nature or rights to amenities far out of proportion to the space involved. The owner of a small piece of land surface may control an important water power site or, in a ranching country, the owner of a spring or water hole may monopolize grazing on all the land depending on this watering place.

Since the ownership of a particular space excludes every other person from using or enjoying it, and since no two pieces of land are alike, it is often held that the owner has a monopoly. However, if by monopoly is meant that the owner or owners in collusion have *exclusive* control over the supply and through supply fix the price of either the land itself or the products of the land, the resources that can comply with this definition are extremely limited. The agricultural land of the United States is in over six and one-half million separate tracts, individually owned. Farmers have had so little success in getting concerted action to control the supply of farm products and "fix prices" that the Agricultural Adjustment Administration was created to help them to adjust crops to demand. The ownership of most mines is widely diffused and in some cases competition is so intense that all efforts at conservation have been dismal failures. The same is true of timberland ownership even though there was fear of monopolization some time ago.

The ownership of superior grades of land, as, for instance, the best home site in a neighborhood, the "100 per cent location" in a business area, or the best soil in a given region, is merely differential advantage of location or fertility and not complete monopoly.[2] Land exists, nearby, only a little less advantageously sit-

[1] Raymond T. Bye, *Principles of Economics* (New York, Knopf, 1924), p. 103.
[2] *Exclusive* control can rarely, if ever, be achieved. "Pure competition" is de-

uated or a little less desirable than the best. However, a few cases of ownership of certain natural resources approach monopoly control.

Economists in classifying monopolies use the term "natural monopoly" to designate cases where a physical limitation in supply gives monopolistic control to the owners. It is significant, however, that the public is sensitive to such situations and is quick to control and regulate such lands, or to convert them into public ownership. Wharves are either publicly owned or publicly controlled. Water power is closely guarded in the public interest, and, in the West, irrigation water is regulated or declared to be the property of the public or the state. The classic example of a natural monopoly was anthracite coal. This coal is concentrated on 500 square miles in five Pennsylvania counties. By 1901, 96 per cent of the deposits were owned by railways, and the other owners could be kept in line by the railways over which the coal had to be shipped. As long as a strong demand for this superior fuel existed, the owners could control production and price. However, competition from gas, oil, and other coal has cut the output from 89,000,000 net tons in 1911–15 to 70,000,000 in 1930, and in recent years "bootlegging" from these deposits has still further dethroned the former "monopolists." The diamond industry was once considered a complete monopoly, yet enough small operators appeared throughout the world to threaten price control.[1]

It is also true that large blocks of urban and farm lands have from time to time come into the ownership of individuals or groups who were in a position to withhold the land from sale until they got their price. Henry George acquired his philosophy

---

fined as that in which *no one* has any *degree of control*. Complete control of price is impossible so long as there are a large number of buyers and sellers and all producers are not producing identical goods and selling them in identical markets. The first condition makes for more competition; the second introduces monopoly elements. Of special significance is the lack of an "identical market" in the retail commercial section of a city. Space relationships are such that all stores cannot have the same relationship to the stream of traffic of shoppers. A small area becomes the favored "100 per cent location"; all others have inferior positions. This Chamberlain calls a "spatial monopoly," i.e., "that control over supply which is the seller's by virtue of his location."—Edward Chamberlin, *The Theory of Monopolistic Competition* (Cambridge, Harvard University Press, 1933), pp. 7–9, 62–63.

[1] "Why Diamonds Remain Costly," *Current Opinion*, April, 1925, p. 472.

of the taxation of land in the atmosphere of land frauds and wild speculation in urban and agricultural lands of California where both Mexican and American land policies had favored concentration of ownership and the bona fide settler found great difficulty in acquiring land.[1]

The Measurement of Land. Land is bought and sold on a spatial basis. Even mining claims are based upon possession of part of the earth's surface. Because land is sold in terms of surface measurements, a simple and accurate method of measuring, designating and recording area is important. In order to secure legality of title, land ownership is the subject of many regulations, including that of registering ownership with a description of the land so owned, in some public office.[2]

In the older parts of the United States and Canada land is usually described and registered by "metes and bounds." In this case, natural objects such as trees, streams, and rocks are used to designate the points connecting the surveyor's lines. However, soon after the federal government acquired the public domain the so-called "rectangular system" of land surveying was incorporated into the earliest land laws (1784–85).[3]

In the public land survey system surveying is begun from a base line. For example, in 1855 such a base line was started from the Missouri River on the 40th parallel of latitude, which became the boundary between Kansas and Nebraska. It was run due west for 108 miles and here the 6th principal meridian was run due north and south. Every six miles east and west of the principal meridian other lines were run north and south, and, measuring along the principal meridian, east and west lines were run, thereby dividing the land into blocks six miles square called "townships." These were sometimes called "survey" or "government" townships to distinguish them from the civil divisions of counties also known as "towns" or "townships." These units of local govern-

[1] Arthur Nichols Young, *The Single Tax Movement in the United States* (Princeton University Press, 1916), Chaps. II and III.

[2] In most states this official is called the county "registrar of deeds" or some similar title.

[3] Modified forms of the rectangular survey were used in some of the colonies previous to its adoption by the federal government. See Amelia C. Ford, *Colonial Precedents of Our National Land System as It Existed in 1800* (Bulletin of the University of Wisconsin, 352, 1910).

ment are descendants of the old New England and New York "towns" and should not be confused with the popular term meaning village or city.

Figure 4 shows how the public domain was surveyed from the various principal meridians and base lines. Some of the states, such as Ohio and Mississippi, have been surveyed from several base lines, but in general much larger areas are "governed" by a

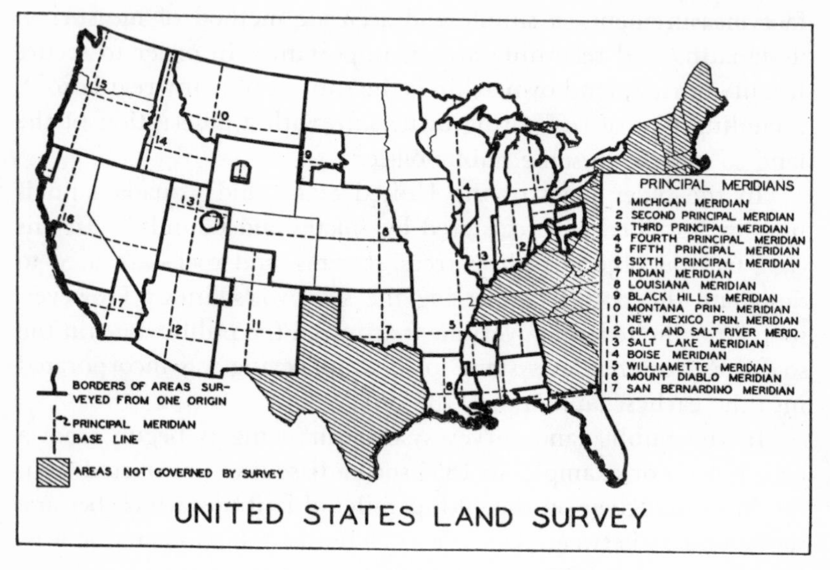

Fig. 4

given base line and principal meridian. Kansas, Nebraska, and most of Colorado and Wyoming were surveyed from the 6th principal meridian.

Townships are designated by two figures. Running north or south from the base line they are called "Township 7 North" or "Township 10 South." Running east and west from the principal meridian they are indicated by "Range 2, West" or "Range 5, East." For example, the first homestead entered and patented under the Homestead Act of 1862 is located in Township 4 North, Range 5, East, of the 6th principal meridian. Thus it is possible to locate a piece of land under the rectangular survey without reference to states, counties, or other units of government.

Since lines running due north from a base line converge as

they approach the Pole, townships are narrower at the northern boundary than at the southern and become smaller and smaller as the Pole is approached. This convergence is noticeable in the shape of states and provinces bounded by lines of longitude, notably Alberta and Saskatchewan. In order to keep the township as near 36 square miles as possible, surveyors have established new base lines known as "correction lines" from which north and south lines again run six miles apart. These correction lines account partly for the noticeable jogs in north and south roads following section lines but may also be due to discrepancies and errors in the original surveying.

Townships are divided into 36 sections a mile square, each containing 640 acres and numbered as shown in Figure 5. The Canadians reverse the American order in designating sections. The section is subdivided into quarter sections, which in turn are divided into forties. A simple system of designating the parts of a section has been devised which can be extended to include parts of forties, with the result that the legal description of a farm can be written in two lines or less. For instance, the first homestead is described as S½ of NW¼; NE¼ of NW¼ and SW¼ of NE¼ of Section 26, Township 4 North, Range 5 East of the 6th Principal Meridian.

Because townships do not contain the full 36 square miles, sections and their subdivisions are also deficient. However, surveyors try to make forties of standard size in the main body of the township and adjust the deficiencies in the forties on the northern and western boundaries. The actual areas of these "fractional forties" or "lots" are entered on the official map as shown in Figure 5. Uneven sized forties also occur because of inaccuracies in surveying or where two areas, surveyed by different men, join.

Wherever lines cross bodies of water one of two methods was followed. In the case of small lakes the surveyor ran his line across them as if they were dry land and the land was sold as if the tract were a full forty, quarter section, etc. (Lake A). Where the lines encountered larger bodies of water they were run merely to the water's edge and then along the high water level of the lake, with every change in the direction of the line duly recorded as part of the survey. The resulting tracts are numbered and recorded as "lots" on the official map, including the area of each lot (Lake B).

Wherever lines touch large bodies of water, large streams, or in some cases the boundary of a state, the tracts are also surveyed and inscribed as "lots."

Bodies of water surveyed in this way are called "meandered" lakes or streams. The difference between "meandered" and "unmeandered" bodies of water is important in some states because

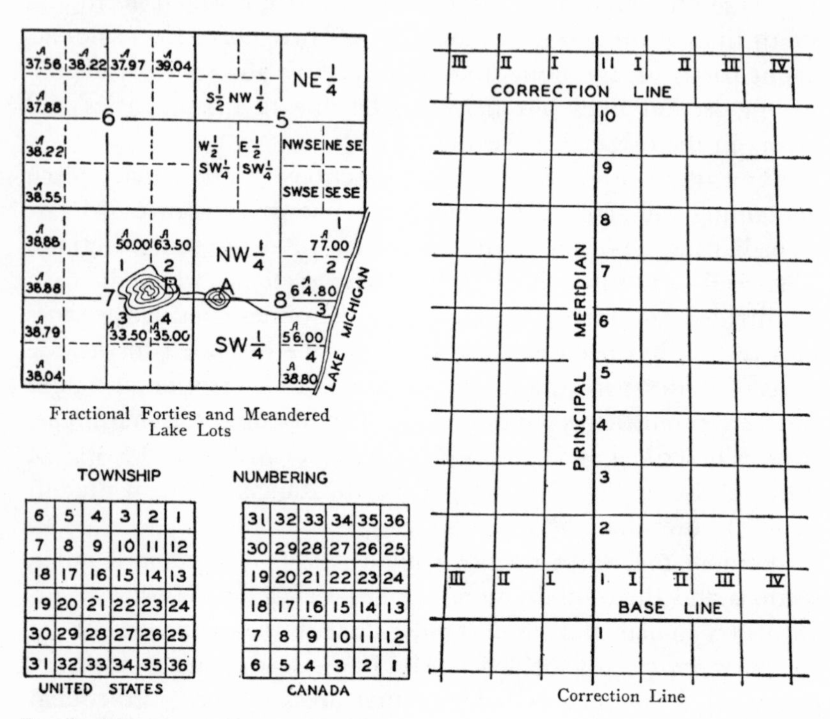

FIG. 5. METHODS OF DESIGNATING TOWNSHIPS, SECTIONS, AND DIVISIONS OF SECTIONS

the former are declared to be legally navigable waters whereas unmeandered bodies are not.

A third method of surveying and recording land descriptions is known as "platting." The surveyor makes a careful map to scale, which is placed on record in city, town, or county offices. The subdivisions of the plat are numbered as lots and blocks similar to "lake lots." This method permits the laying out and easy designation of small and irregular tracts which do not fit into the rectangular system. For purposes of taxation and for recording of deeds and mortgages the land can be described as "Lot 1, Block

3 of X subdivision." This method is especially adapted to the needs of cities, suburban areas, and recreational lands.

Canada has various systems of surveys. Quebec has narrow and deep lots, the result of the seigniorial system of land tenure, whereas Ontario adopted the 1000-acre system with 100-acre farms in 1829. A new system, however, was installed in northern Ontario with townships of 9 square miles. Under the Dominion Land Survey Act of 1908 the 36-section township system of the United States was adopted.[1]

The rectangular system of surveying had a temporary influence on the size of farms. The "quarter section" was the conception of the proper size under the Homestead Act, and this notion became an obstacle to a change in the land laws for the arid regions where a much larger tract was needed for an economic holding.

The six miles square "survey township" has become the accepted area for the civil town wherever this unit of government has been transplanted from New England and New York to the Middle West. Surveyor's lines have become county boundaries. The Plains states are almost complete checkerboards of identically shaped counties. Section lines determine road layout, forcing the traveler to go along the outside of a triangle instead of along the hypotenuse, or roads are laid out over hills or through swamps. Even the street layout of a city like Chicago owes much of its gridiron structure to the checkerboard pattern of the rural highways which preceded it. The rectangular and gridiron system of road and street layout are the despair of planners even more than the "cowpath pattern" of city streets in the older parts of the country.

Economic Location. The geometric relations of the earth of which Marshall speaks are geographical locational factors. The relation of a particular hill to a river or stream is fixed by nature. However, as soon as man desires one spot rather than another for business, recreation, or a home, human choice enters, these spots acquire economic significance, and *situs* is created. Situs has been defined as physical location plus human choice.[2] Economic loca-

[1] Thomas Adams, *Rural Planning and Development* (Ottawa, Commission of Conservation, 1917), Chap. III.

[2] H. B. Dorau and A. G. Hinman, *Urban Land Economics* (New York, Macmillan, 1928), pp. 167–69.

tion or situs is always orientation in relation to some other economic factors. The business man who has a "good location" is near the center of business, near "traffic," or near the amusement district. When he buys or rents a place he pays for this privilege. All this grows out of the spatial relations of land. Only one store, one building, or one farm can occupy the best site; the others must be arranged side by side until the last one lies at the edge of the business district or the outer circle of farm land utilization. Land uses are conditioned by their relations to such centers, and cities themselves are the most important centers of all.

As soon as cities arise they begin to influence the uses of land around them according to a principle which no one else has stated so well as Johann Heinrich von Thünen in his *Isolated State,* written in 1826.[1] In order to segregate the influence of location on the utilization of the soil he conceived of a large city in the center of a fruitful plain of uniform soil and climate. Differences in crops and methods of farming are therefore not attributable to soils, rainfall, temperature, or any other physical factors, but to the purely economic factor of distance from a market. A wilderness lies beyond the cultivated area which separates the Isolated State from the rest of the world. The one large city is the only source of the manufactured products needed by the state; likewise, the surrounding country is the only source of food for the city. Mines and saltworks are near the city and supply the entire population.

Von Thünen was a practical farmer as well as an economist and used the accounts of his estate, Tellow, to work out his conclusions. He asks, "How would I manage my estate were it located at some particular spot in this State? What economic effects would I experience if I moved my farm towards the periphery of this hypothetical State, or nearer to the city?"

He begins with the price of a farm product fixed by supply and demand in the city. The price of wheat, for instance, on a farm five miles from the city, becomes equal to the city price minus the cost of wagon transportation, which is the only mode considered by the author. Based on a price of 1.5 thaler in the

[1] *Der Isolierte Staat,* with introduction by Heinrich Waentig (Jena, Gustav Fischer, 1910).

city, it will be worth less and less as the distance from the farm to the market is increased, as follows:

Place				Price
At city				1.500
5 miles	from	city		1.313
10	"	"	"	1.136
15	"	"	"	.968
20	"	"	"	.805
25	"	"	"	.656
30	"	"	"	.512
35	"	"	"	.374
40	"	"	"	.242
45	"	"	"	.116
50	"	"	"	.000

It is evident that wheat will not be raised beyond 50 miles from the city even if it has no cost of production. But since there are costs of production, wheat growing will cease long before the 50-mile locations are reached. According to von Thünen's calculations, cereal cultivation will cease 31.5 miles from the city. This outer limit is in the form of a circle equidistant from the market.

Other crops, more perishable or more or less bulky than wheat, will have their own limits. Perishable crops which cannot stand transportation for long distances, such as berries, fruit, and whole milk, will be produced in a narrow zone just outside of the city. Their prices will generally be so high in proportion to wheat or grain that the farmer will find the intensive crops more profitable.[1]

It appears curious from the modern standpoint that the second zone should be devoted to forests. But in von Thünen's time forests furnished both fuel and building materials which are very bulky. With only wagon transportation available it was quite natural that the forests should be near to the city. This also implies that the forests were "man made" and deliberately placed in the second zone.

It is an interesting fact that in pre-railway days in the Middle

[1] As will be shown in another chapter, the utilization of the Isolated State is the result of the competition of crops and uses for the land. Distance, perishability, bulk, and difficulties of transport are physical factors which affect prices, costs, and income in such a way as to give certain crops or uses predominance in each zone or concentric circle of the state.

West, wherever wood products had to be transported by wagon onto the nonforested prairies, the difficulty of transportation became a determining factor in the location of settlements and vil-

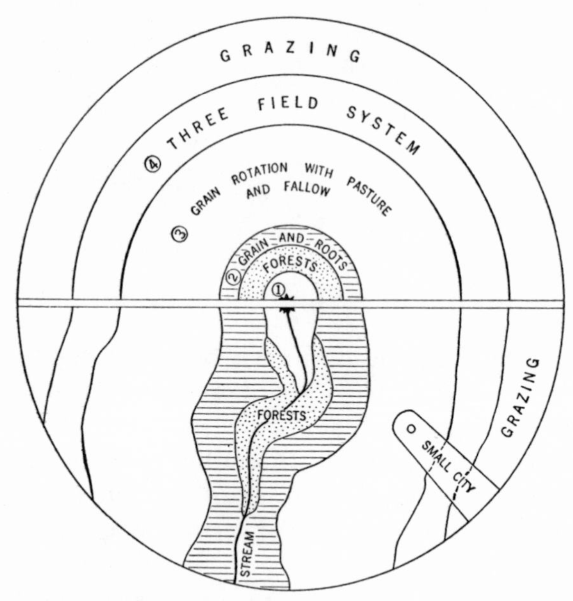

The upper part of the diagram shows the concentric circles of land utilization before the introduction of the influences of water transportation and the smaller city. The crop and farm management system used by Von Thünen is as follows for the numbered circles:

1. *Freie Wirtschaft*—characterized by the fact that no regular order of crops is followed. Crops are planted to suit the climate, soil and market.
2. *Frucht Wechsel Wirtschaft* (Grain rotation culture) in strict sense implies a rotation of grain with leafy plants such as legumes, root crops, etc. A, Von Thünen gives as examples—(1) Potatoes, (2) Barley, (3) Clover to be mowed, (4) Rye, (5) Legumes, (6) Rye. B, Norfolk rotation—(1) Winter grain, (2) Roots, (3) Summer grain, (4) Clover.
3. *Koppel Wirtschaft* (Rotation culture) introduces pasture and fallow. Von Thünen himself used this system with seven parts in the cycle, (1) Rye, (2) Barley, (3) Oats, (4), (5), (6) Pasture, (7) Fallow.
4. *Dreifelder Wirtschaft* (Three field system) was the dominant system from 800 to 1800 in most of Europe. Characterized by permanent pasture and meadows. Von Thünen mentions (1) Rye, (2) Barley, (3) Fallow.

FIG. 6. LAND UTILIZATION AS DETERMINED BY LOCATION, MODIFIED FROM DIAGRAMS IN VON THÜNEN'S *Isolated State, op. cit.*, p. 387

lages. "Railroads did not exist and overland wagon haul for lumber was out of the question; hence local supplies of timber were controlling forces in the settlement of these grasslands, which could not be sold unless several acres of forest land were included.

The relative value of prairie and forest land per acre was about 1 to 7, the former commonly selling for $5.00 and the latter $35 per acre."[1] "The names of some of the early villages, Dry Grove, Blooming Grove (later Bloomington), and Funk's Grove, are significant; for few settlers ventured away from the timber before 1850."[2]

The forest areas of America were all located by nature, hence have no such relation to points of consumption as the forests of the Isolated State. However, in the future, when our forests have to be re-established, their location in relation to population centers will have to be given serious consideration. The great lumber markets are in the East and here the price is set. The price of stumpage in any part of the country is determined by the price in this market minus the cost of transportation and manufacturing costs. The nearer the market the higher the value, almost irrespective of the quality of the timber. "Small second growth white pine in Massachusetts and New Hampshire since 1900 has brought on the average five times as much on the stump as the very large and high-quality Douglas fir in the Pacific Northwest."[3]

In the third zone of the Isolated State an intensive form of agriculture reasserts itself. A "grain rotation culture," consisting of an alternation of grain and leafy plants such as the famous Norfolk rotation of England—winter grain roots, summer grain, and clover—was used in von Thünen's scheme. In the fourth zone the agriculture becomes less intensive. Pasture and fallow are introduced. In the fifth zone, he says, the ancient "three field system" of (1) rye, (2) barley, (3) fallow, will prevail, the identical cropping practice which existed in Europe from 800 to 1800 A.D. This is the last zone for cereal culture; beyond this cattle will be raised and driven to market. However, he concludes that butter could be manufactured at this distance from the city and transported at a profit because of its small bulk and high value. The last zone is devoted to hunting since the valuable pelts can be transported with comparative ease.

After having discussed the simple plan of a single city and

[1] Edith Muriel Poggi, *The Prairie Province of Illinois* (University of Illinois Bulletin, Vol. 31, No. 42, 1934), p. 98.

[2] *Ibid.*, p. 99.

[3] W. B. Greeley, *et al.*, "Timber, Mine or Crop?" *Yearbook of the U. S. Dept. of Agriculture,* 1922, p. 146.

only one mode of transportation, von Thünen introduces a navigable river, as shown in the other half of the diagram. Assuming that the stream cuts the cost of transportation to one-sixth that of wagon transportation, the first zone will be extended along the river in such a manner that the combined land and water costs will be equal to the costs of land transportation for those parts of the state not having the advantage of the river. The other zones will be elongated in a similar fashion.

The influence of another city is also shown in this diagram. The smaller city develops circles of influence of its own, but as long as it is smaller than the central city the price of grain in its sphere of influence is still determined by the price in the larger city. This, says von Thünen, is shown by the relation of prices of grain all over the world to the price in London. Even though the other European countries do not export or import, their price is fixed on a London basis, and when this market is closed the price of grain drops in all Europe.[1]

As will be pointed out more fully later, prices are the determining factor in the scheme of land utilization of the State. Every change in price shifts the circles and changes the zones and von Thünen introduces other interesting diagrams to show how the diameter of the zones changes with increases or decreases in prices. Just as prices of farm products fall as distance from the city increases, so the prices of machinery, fertilizer, clothing, and other goods produced in the city tend to rise. Likewise interest rates, skilled labor, and professional services become progressively more costly, thereby increasing the expense of production and the cost of living for the more distant farmers. Curiously enough, this picture also depicts the historical development of agriculture from hunting and fishing on the periphery of the area to the intensive agriculture in the first zone.

Von Thünen wrote before the revolution of transportation. His crude example of the influence of a river on the cost of transportation and on land utilization has been repeated and magnified repeatedly. Canals were the first improvement over rivers and wagons. After the Erie Canal was finished freight rates from

[1] A good statement of how Liverpool fixes wheat prices is found in F. E. Clark and L. D. H. Weld, *Marketing Agricultural Products in the United States* (New York, Macmillan, 1938), pp. 508–15.

Albany to Buffalo dropped from $88 to $6 per ton. The success of this venture led to feverish activity in canal building in the United States which collapsed with the coming of the railways.

Railways became "empire builders" and the locational advantage of farm land along the seaboard was broken. Grain, sheep, and cattle shifted westward to the frontier, and butter and cheese were replaced by fluid milk. This new mode of transportation opened up new lands and gave them the advantages of the market in the urbanized East. Before the era of railroads each city was dependent upon the local supply for its fruit, truck, and vegetables. Then fast sailboats brought vegetables from the Chesapeake to Philadelphia and Baltimore. Long Island and the eastern shore of Lake Michigan likewise supplied New York and Chicago, respectively, by water. About 1860 the Illinois Central began to bring in fruits and vegetables from southern Illinois. After the Civil War the trucking regions of Tennessee, Mississippi, Arkansas, and Texas were developed.[1]

The automobile, the truck, and modern hard-surfaced roads have opened up new means of accessibility, and the airplane may be the fourth factor in revolutionizing transportation. It is already a factor in passenger traffic and may become a rival of surface traffic in the transportation of certain products.

Permanence of the Spatial Factor. No matter how much transportation is perfected it can never become instantaneous, effortless, or costless. There will always be a cost of overcoming friction, gravitation, and loss of time in moving goods and people. Farmers near a city will always have some advantage over those farther from the market who are raising the same crops and who have identical transportation facilities. The "first zone" still has the advantage over other regions in raising perishables and bulky products. The market afforded by the presence of 13,000,000 people in the urbanized district from Washington to Boston is largely responsible for the persistence of the Middle Atlantic trucking belt.

The distance from which people can commute comfortably is still a matter of time, convenience, and costs, complicated many times by the congestion caused by modern transportation. Traffic within the city has become so congested that very often a

[1] *Yearbook of the U. S. Dept. of Agriculture,* 1900, pp. 437–42.

vehicle spends more time in standing still than in moving. One argument for the skyscraper is that it permits the concentration in one building of all those with whom the tenants are likely to have business contacts, or they are located in other buildings near by. In spite of the telephone and telegraph most business deals are made in person.[1] This emphasizes once more the importance of accessibility and rapid transportation.

Space with Negative Value. Not all space is valuable. Land which has become submarginal for agriculture may no longer furnish food or fiber; it does not even remain private property in many instances. It is mere space, its one "indestructible" attribute, which in this case becomes a public detriment. When the truck, tractor, and automobile made six million horses and mules useless they quietly passed out of existence with no further costs for feed and maintenance. The same factors helped to make millions of acres of farm land submarginal, but the space still exists. Roads have to be built through submarginal land and maintained. The remaining scattered farmers must be supplied with the usual public services, at high costs per capita. If the land is cut-over or forested it has to be protected from fire, and at all events has to be policed and government must be maintained. Idle land is never neutral; it always places a burden on private or public owners. Uninhabited marshes, sand plains, deserts, and mountains therefore have more than negative value, as the Canadians discovered when they had to build railroads across the "Shield." Mackintosh remarks, "In the early development of transportation it would have been much better for Canada had the Laurentian country been completely covered by water, for water unites but land divides and for many decades the remnant of the old continent of Laurentia divided one half of Canada most effectively from the other half." [2]

Zimmermann points out that excessive space, even if not "negative land," is a weak point in the American resource pattern.[3]

[1] "The skyscraper facilitates personal contacts in a way never possible before. From my office on the 28th floor of a building in the Times Square district, I can get to practically every person of importance in the architectural and building field in 15 minutes time."—Harvey Wiley Corbett, "New Stones for Old," *Saturday Evening Post,* March 27, 1926, p. 150.

[2] W. A. Mackintosh, "The Laurentian Plateau in Canadian Economic Development," *op. cit.,* p. 543.

[3] *World Resources and Industries* (New York, Harper's, 1933), pp. 151–54.

Places and resources are so far apart. Our transportation system, of which we are so proud, is really an expense which more compact nations do not have. The automobile, which the European envies, is our invention to overcome space. Much of the energy we get from coal, gasoline, and water power is used to move coal and gasoline, to build railroads, and to construct roads, bridges, and other means of transportation, all of which we must have to move the consumption goods that satisfy our wants.

If space is "a weak point in the resource pattern" of the United States, it is even more critical for Canada. Ninety per cent of the population lives in a thin strip along the northern boundary of the United States within 200 miles of the border and is broken into sections by intervening geographical barriers such as the Rockies, the Laurentian Shield, and the Appalachians. To overcome this obstacle Canada has built 43,000 miles of railways; she is the fourth in the world in total mileage and first in per capita mileage. Canada has invested in this $400 per capita, compared to $143 per person in the United States. Air transportation met with instant favor for the same reasons. In 1937 Canadian planes carried three-fifths of all the air express and freight of the British Empire and a quarter of a million passengers. More freight was carried by air in Canada than in any other country.[1]

[1] "Canada the Siren," *Fortune,* September, 1938; Burt M. McConnell, "The Race for Aerial Trade Routes," *Yale Review,* Winter, 1938, p. 359.

IV

LAND AS PROPERTY

So far the physical framework within which man uses land has been discussed. In addition to the physical factors which condition land utilization there are various group habits in the relations between men which affect their behavior in the use of natural resources. These widespread habits, customs, and arrangements in production, distribution and consumption of goods are economic institutions. Generally adopted customs are frequently crystallized into law. Thus we have another framework within which individuals make choices and perform services in connection with the use of land. Inheritance, government, taxation, credit, competition, and monopoly are examples of such institutions, but the most important institution which affects the use and income of land is property.[1]

Among the simpler customs or folkways that influence land uses is the convention of flowers for funerals, weddings, and other occasions. This "institution" plays a large part in the florist industry and expensive land in cities and in the suburbs is placed under glass for the cultivation of flowers. Silk, cotton, rayon, wool, furs, skins, and rubber are all used for the protection of the body against the elements but which will be worn in modern society will depend not only on the efficiency of the material in keeping out heat, cold, or the rain, but also upon customs, habits, fashions, religion, and the social standing of the wearer. People demand furs even though the wilderness is disappearing which has made the raising of fur-bearing animals a new land use. Animal husbandry on a large scale is unknown in the Orient, where religion forbids the use of animal foods, even though vast areas are available for pasturage. The custom of placing graves in the midst of tilled fields in China takes much needed land out of cultivation. It is estimated that the crop area in eight agricultural

[1] John R. Commons, *Institutional Economics* (New York, Macmillan, 1934), pp. 69–74. "If we endeavor to find a universal principle, common to all behavior known as institutional, we may define an institution as Collective Action in Control of Individual Action" (p. 69).

regions could be increased by 2,552,000 acres, enough to support 400,000 Chinese families, if the land now in graves were cultivated.[1]

Inheritance is another institution which is an important factor in determining land utilization. Under primogeniture the entire estate falls to the oldest son. While this more or less disinherits the other heirs, the land never becomes subdivided and reduced to less than an economic unit. In contrast is the French code requiring equal division of the land among the children. In France this has resulted in small families, but in Quebec, where large families are the rule, the observance of this code has resulted in "ribbon farms" only a few rods wide and a mile or two long.

The Nature of Property. The most important institution touching land is *property,* which will be discussed in this chapter, not so much in its legal manifestations as from the standpoint of its influence on land utilization and land value.

"Property is the exclusive right to control an economic good,"[2] or, as Blackstone stated in more exaggerated language, "that sole and despotic dominion which one man claims and exercises over external things of the world in total exclusion of the right of any other individual in the universe."[3] Property in its more tangible forms implies (1) an owner, (2) the property object, (3) the state to protect the owner in his rights over the property object. The third is the most important. As long as the individual maintained possession of an object by sheer force on his part there was no "property," but when the state guaranteed and enforced his rights property emerged. Before the formation of the modern state, family, clan, or tribal governments served as the third party to enforce property rights.

Property is an attribute of human beings. Chattels cannot own property, although there is an oft repeated story of a tree in Athens, Georgia, that is said to own the land on which it grows. As long as people are willing to respect the wishes of the man who deeded the land to the tree and not place any taxes on it all will be well, but there is no legal foundation for this

[1] John Lossing Buck, *Land Utilization in China* (The University of Chicago Press, 1937), pp. 178–79.

[2] Richard T. Ely, *Property and Contract,* Vol. I (New York, Macmillan, 1914), p. 101.

[3] *Commentaries on the Laws of England,* Book II, Chap. I.

ownership.[1] A 600-acre forest deeded to God in Pennsylvania reverted to the state for non-payment of taxes.[2]

Property also implies human relationships. It has been observed that a Robinson Crusoe could not be a proprietor because there was no one to exclude. Men are brought into all types of relationships with one another because of their relationship to property, as, for instance, landlord and tenant. These relationships do not extend to all external nature but only to economic goods. "Free goods" and objects not appropriable are not property. Land beneath the ocean beyond a certain point has no owner. On the other hand, all land within the jurisdiction of a state or nation always has an owner. If it is not owned privately it automatically becomes public property.

Property is not a material thing but consists of *rights* which extend over the property object, or rather over the activities which involve the use of things. As legal writers have said, it is a "bundle of rights." Prominent among these are the right to use as one pleases, the right to sell the property, to bequeath it to one's heirs within established but varying limits, or to give it to another.

Many examples of the "bundle of rights" of property can be cited. A tenant rents a house or a farm. In doing so he splits the bundle of rights between himself and the landlord. For a period of time the latter surrenders some of his rights to the land, especially that of using it. For this privilege the tenant pays rent. In the same way a neighbor may buy the right to use a part of a lot for a driveway without buying the lot itself.

Property rights change from time to time, depending on laws and institutions of society. Women, children, and slaves were once property. The property object is not always a tangible thing. The owner of land bordering on a stream has the right to use the water but does not own the substance itself under the riparian doctrine of water rights. Even more intangible are franchises, patents, copyrights, the good will of corporations, or the right to a certain radio wave length "on the air."

Kinds of Property. Most of the property objects in capitalistic countries belong to individuals, corporations, or partnerships and are therefore *private* property. Land and other objects owned

[1] Richard T. Ely, *Property and Contract, op. cit.,* p. 96.
[2] *American Forests,* February, 1931, p. 112.

by an organized government are *public* property. Political subdivisions of a state also have the right to own property but only as this right is granted to them by the state. Where organized governments do not exist there is a less formal, but nevertheless recognized, ownership by tribes or clans. The hunting grounds of the American Indians were tribal property. Sometimes, however, the land was divided into separate areas and allotted to individual hunters whose exclusive right to the game in this territory was respected by the tribe. In essence this was private property, whereas the holding of the land by the tribe is often called "common" property.

Not all types of property have fully developed rights, nor does the bundle consist of as many sticks in one case as in another. In free goods, in a legal sense, individuals have no rights at all; in full private property they have many. Between the two extremes is a group of objects which have uncertain status, called *qualified* property. In many states, dogs are not strictly private property unless the owner complies with certain regulations.[1] Fish and game are generally considered the property of the state "in trust for the public," which means that the state may control wild life but does not own it. The state cannot make a business of selling wild animals except when the game is confiscated as part of punishing violations. Game and fish become private property when shot or captured in accordance with the laws of a particular state, but many states prohibit the sale of game after it has been shot or captured. Neither state nor private individuals have exclusive rights to wild life in America. Special acts of the legislature have been necessary to give fur farmers full rights to certain wild animals which they are raising under regulations. In many foreign countries, however, game is private and not qualified property while it is on an individual's land, but the "owner" loses control over it whenever the animals leave his premises.

In New England the commons are interesting features of the towns. Most of them are today owned by the town and therefore public property. However, in the early days they were *common property* owned as an undivided unit by a restricted number of

[1] Note the following South Carolina statute (Code of 1922, Article I, 349. Section 7. Dog Tax): "No dog which is not returned for taxation as required by this Section, shall be held to be property in any of the courts of this state."

private landowners who obtained right in the common lands by virtue of their private ownership in nearby city lots or other land. Usually these rights were grazing rights, but the use was decided by the vote of the common owners. Under this system the proprietors did not own a tangible property object, but merely had rights which were transferable, and subject to lease and taxation.[1] This type of property is more of historical than of practical interest although it exists in European *Allemande*. In England and Wales about 2,000,000 acres of land are still in "commons" of a somewhat different type. Their origin is obscure but goes back to feudal times when certain tracts were open to common pasturage and other uses. Other land became private property but these commons remained without absolute ownership. Legally adjoining owners have rights to graze cattle and sheep, dig turf, cut bracken or heather on the commons; in practice, however, they are used by people in general for walking, riding, and enjoyment of nature. Some of them are found in the environs of London.[2]

PROPERTY IN LAND

Property in land is measured, bought, and sold on a spatial basis in surface measurements. Under English law, however, the ownership of the surface carries with it rights to soil within this space down to the center of the earth and indefinitely upward. This concept has been modified considerably. Ownership of the surface of the earth may be entirely different from the ownership of the minerals below the surface. Even different strata may be in separate ownership. In China the landlord may own the space while the tenant owns the soil-body representing the man-made fertility.[3]

[1] Herbert B. Adams, "The Germanic Origin of New England Towns," and "Village Communities of Cape Ann and Salem," *Johns Hopkins University Studies in Historical and Political Science* (1883), I, 34–38. In 1881 there was still a common field in the town of Sandwich of Cape Cod, restricted in ownership to the heirs of twenty-four original proprietors. Adams says, "Every spring for many years has appeared a public notice calling the proprietors of the Town Neck at some store in the village, to choose a moderator and a clerk, and to regulate the letting of cow rights for the ensuing year. . . . I met in Provincetown a man who said he was taxed for one-sixth of a cow right in Sandwich, which he had inherited from his grandfather." p. 35.

[2] Shaw-Lefevre, G. J., *English Commons and Forests* (London, Cassel, 1894).

[3] A. Kaiming Chiu, "The Division of Rent between Landlord and Tenant in China," *Journal of Farm Economics,* October, 1929, pp. 651–53.

A strict interpretation of the old principle that "he who owns the soil owns it up to the sky" would make aviation legally impossible. In the United States and England no written law confirms such claims, and the federal government has the constitutional right to control aviation as part of its power to regulate interstate commerce. The right of the public to the upper air space, above 1,000 feet in congested areas and 500 feet elsewhere, is similar to the rights on a navigable stream.

However, an airplane has to use the lower air spaces as it leaves or approaches a landing field. This leads to a conflict between the use of the air by the plane and its use by tall buildings, towers, smoke stacks, poles, and high-power transmission lines, all of which make "taking off" or landing difficult and dangerous. The landowners' rights are paramount and about the only way to obtain the use of the lower air spaces is to acquire enough land for the airport so that trespass on neighboring air space is unnecessary, or else to zone the height of the surrounding structures as part of a general height limitation ordinance. Another plan is to buy or acquire an easement or *air right* to the air over neighboring land, under which the owners agree to keeping their structures low. This form of air right has been used by skyscraper owners who do not want other high structures to blanket their buildings.

Another form of air right consists in selling all the space above a certain point for building purposes plus just enough of the earth's surface for the pillars which support the building. This legal device has made possible the economic utilization of land that otherwise would be used only for railway tracks. The Daily News Building and Merchandise Mart in Chicago and the Grand Central, Pennsylvania, and Hudson terminals in New York are examples.[1]

The relative permanence of land has made landed property of peculiar significance. The rights of property appear in full force in dealing with objects that exist in perpetuity. The owner has limited life; property, in land, has not. Out of this fact has grown the need for legal arrangements involved in the *inheritance* of land—bequest by will, entail, and primogeniture. Courts

[1] William D. Pence, "Railway Terminal Air Rights Developments and the Movement of Local Land Values," *Journal of Land and Public Utility Economics*, May, 1929, pp. 150–68.

have upheld deed restrictions which bind future users of land and reduce its usefulness. In 1833 a tract of land was bought in what is now the Chicago Loop and when resold the owner reserved a strip 177 feet long and 10 feet wide for a cowpath. Air rights above it are used but the surface of the land is left unoccupied. It has been used to advertise the International Live Stock Show by driving a steer through or milking a cow in the passageway.

Because of the perpetuity of landed property various kinds of ownership have developed based upon time. An individual's right to property may be limited to his own lifetime, until a pertinent event takes place during the lifetime of another, or in other ways. All rights in realty measured by duration in time, in terms of a life or lifetimes, are called *real* property, whereas all rights measured in other terms are called *personal* property.

Immobility is the basis for another legal characteristic of land. The law has divided *commodities* into realty and personalty and *property* into real property and personal property. The distinction between realty and personalty is based upon the idea of immobility. Land, being the most immobile of all commodities, is denominated *realty*. Likewise all things attached to land are called realty. Trees and minerals were always considered a part of land. Buildings and all "the erections on the surface of a permanent and fixed character" are also considered realty and are known as "fixtures"; when land is sold they go with the land no matter who has placed them there. Just what objects are fixtures and what are not depends upon the law in each state. *Personalty* consists of all things not realty.

Because of the complex legal and economic characteristics of land, title and the transfer of titles are of peculiar significance. States have set up officers and mechanisms for the proper recording of deeds, mortgages, leases, and other instruments relating to land. Even in a country as youthful as the United States these records have become so involved that a new and simpler method of registration is desirable.[1]

Property Rights as Related to Land Tenure and Mortgages. If property in land is considered as a bundle of rights, then ten-

[1] Dorr Viele, "The Problem of Land Titles," *Political Science Quarterly*, September, 1929, pp. 421–34. See also the Torrens System.

ancy may be considered as a form of ownership in which the sticks in the bundle are divided between landlord and tenant. The owner who offers its use to others may be considered a middleman who has bought all the future services of the land and sells the annual uses at retail. For a limited time the landowner transfers certain of the rights of ownership, particularly that of using it, to the tenant. The legal aspects of this division of rights and the payment for them (contract rent) have been the result of a long development reaching far back into feudal and Roman law.

Whenever a landlord and a tenant have shared rights in a given tract of land or real estate they are considered to hold a kind of qualified tenure. The bundle of rights which any person holds in property in land and its fixtures is an *estate*. The full owner is considered to hold an *estate in fee simple,* that is, he has permanent possession. If the owner transfers the right of possession to another for a given period of time, this conveyance is said to create a *lesser estate* which is owned by the tenant, who may exercise all the rights of possession, excluding all others from these rights, even the landlord. However, the transfer of rights to a tenant is usually accompanied by a contract stipulating the conditions under which the property may be used and the rights and duties of landlord as well as tenant. Inasmuch as the farm tenant, for instance, has no long-time interest in the land and may be careless about its conservation, or, if he is a clever farmer, may actually exploit the soil, good farm leases should stipulate the farm practices expected of the tenant. On the other hand, many improvements are incorporated with the land or become "fixtures" which remain the property of the owner; hence, a good tenure system such as has been evolved in Great Britain makes provision for safeguarding the rights of the tenant to his contribution to the fertility or to the permanent ameliorations by paying him for unexhausted improvements.

However, the mere fact that land is used or cultivated by a person other than the owner does not always mean legal landlord-tenant relationships. The laborer working for a farmer has no rights in the land as such. If the right of possession is not conveyed by the owner a tenancy or lesser estate is not created. This is one of the most important though less appreciated differences between the sharecropper and tenant. The cropper, though a cultivator of the land, is not a legal tenant but a laborer with no rights in the land and rights to the livestock or crops only to the extent of a servant's lien for wages. Croppers are not confined to the South, and this distinction has been made not only by southern courts but in other states as well.[1]

In determining whether or not specific arrangements do or do not create a lesser estate, the courts have established several principles. The payment of a cash rent has been considered to imply the intention to enter into landlord-tenant relationships. Share rent arrangements may or may not imply the creation of a tenancy. The intention of the parties as reflected in the wording of the agreement is usually considered as governing. If the instrument of the lease speaks of the owner's portion as "rent," the courts usually hold that the intention was to create a tenancy. However, if the owner retains any supervision of the farming operations, courts have considered it a tendency to show that there is no tenancy because the cultivator does not enjoy the full possession of the land. If no tenancy is created there is only a cropper contract. Some states have, by statute, set up the difference between the two; for instance, in Georgia and South Carolina all share rent arrangements are cropper contracts. In these states "standing renters" are considered to have the same status as cash renters, namely, that of tenant and not of cropper, which accounts for the unusual number of tenants of this class in the two states. In most of the southern states, the renting arrangement under which the landowner furnishes all the requisites of production except the labor and receives one-half of the product is denoted by the statutes as a "cropper contract."[2]

Agricultural land is usually leased for comparatively short periods; in fact, some of the states set a definite limit to the length of time farm land may be rented.[3] In cities, long leaseholds are common, many being for 99 years, and leases for 999 years are not unknown.

[1] For instance: *Dixon* v. *Nicolls,* 39 Ill. 372; *Warren* v. *Abbey,* 112 Mass. 355; *Taylor* v. *Bradford,* 39 N. H. 129.

[2] Standing renters are those who give a specified amount of the crop for the use of the land, in place of a share of the product. Croppers are defined by the census as those share tenants to whom the landlord furnishes all the work animals.

[3] The Wisconsin Constitution (Art. I, Sect. 14) limits leases and grants of agricultural lands to 15 years.

Another splitting of the bundle of rights takes place whenever land is mortgaged. Under some state laws the title to the land actually passes to the mortgagee when the mortgage is executed and is restored to the mortgagor when the debt is satisfied. In other states the title does not pass until default by the mortgagor, and in still others the mortgage creates only a lien or encumbrance upon the land and not a transfer of title. In all cases, however, two parties share in the rights to a given piece of property while the mortgage is in force.

Development of Private Property in Land. The rise of property and especially of private property in land is shrouded in obscurity, and many conflicting theories have been advanced to explain its origin. It seems that private property in personal possessions came first: in jewels, weapons, slaves, and women. The hearth and household goods followed. Burying grounds, springs, and wells seem to have become private property very early in history.

Property in land began to have significance when agriculture superseded grazing. Nomadic peoples have no conception of private property in land, although they may recognize ownership in wells made by human labor. Agriculture could make little headway until the group was ready to protect the right of the owner to a given piece of ground so that he could reap where he had sown. For the others to stand by and see the cultivator reap his harvest and not pounce upon it meant considerable self-denial. The self-control necessary to do this was a step toward a higher culture, and the evolution must have been exceedingly gradual because it "required the development of three fundamental requisites of progress, namely foresight to plan for the future, abstinence resulting in the accumulation of food capital to tide over the period of crop production and coöperation or organization for mutual protection to prevent the spoliation of the individual or tribe by those who still preferred the savage state. . . . Undoubtedly the higher qualities of mind and character thus called into play laid the foundations for the further progress of civilization."[1] Yet, in other cases, agriculture developed under a communal rather than under a private property regime.

[1] Herman Haupt Chapman, *Forest Finance* (New Haven, Tuttle, Morehouse and Taylor Co., 1926), p. 4.

FEUDAL LANDED PROPERTY

In contrast to the scattered farms of America, primitive tillers of the soil settled in villages for gregariousness and defense. The agricultural village or "Dorf" is still the universal pattern over most of the world. The New England towns, Mormon villages, and French Canadian settlements are somewhat on the same order. Each village was a miniature "isolated state," surrounded by common pastures and forests which separated it from its neighbors. This common land was in the least intensive ownership, whereas the land around the dwellings in the village was in the most intensive ownership. The arable land and meadows outside of the village were divided into many strips which were redistributed from time to time.[1] Each farmer operated many widely scattered and often distant tracts of land, a decidedly uneconomical method of farming. Everyone was forced into the same pattern of land utilization by this system. If anyone thought of making improvements in his farm practices he was deterred from doing so by the fact that benefit would go to the next owner. Not the soil, but human institutions were at fault that the earth was not more fruitful.

The village remained the unit under the feudal system. In all great nations of the Old World, landed property went through the manorial-feudal era. Partly by conquest and partly through internal development this institution was evolved. Ownership of all land was vested in the sovereign in England, all others holding their rights under him. Under the king were lords of various ranks, who owed obligations and services to the king. The lord in turn had peasants and serfs who paid rents and services to him. The lord of the manor had rights in all the land and had more or less exclusive rights of the chase in the forests. The significant fact is the division of rights to the land among so many individuals from the serf to the sovereign. As the feudal system declined the services performed by tenants or serfs were converted into money rents, or else they paid "lump sums" to ex-

[1] The influence of a religious institution on land tenure is illustrated by the Mennonite colony at Rosengart in Manitoba. Although founded in 1875, it adopted the medieval pattern of the village with a common hay field and pasture where the cattle were grazed in care of the village herdsman. Three sections were divided into sixteen strips and each family was granted a strip in each section. C. A. Dawson, *Group Settlement, Ethnic Communities in Western Canada* (Toronto, Macmillan, 1936), pp. 111–12.

tinguish the services entirely. Gradually *free proprietorship* emerged as the rights of the cultivator became more intense and those of the lords less so. Consolidation of fields, larger farms, individual ownership, and a great increase in production also took place in some countries.

Seigniorial Tenure of Quebec. America was settled while the feudal system was still in practice in Europe, and several attempts were made to introduce it on American soil. The most successful and long-lived example existed in Quebec from 1626 to 1854. This is more than an historical example of modified feudal land tenure; it also illustrates the bundle of rights of property and the manner in which institutions often hamper the proper utilization of land.

Under the seigniorial system, the king of France granted lands to "seigneurs," usually individuals but sometimes religious orders and institutions. In return the seigneur pledged fealty and homage to the king and was required to perform military service for the colony. This was more than a nominal duty because of the incessant wars with the Indians and with the New England colonies. Many of the seigneurs were on military duty for years, to the neglect of their duties at home. These duties consisted of granting lots to settlers or "habitants" and clearing land, duties upon which the king insisted. The seigneur was also obligated to build a mill for the settlers, furnish pasture, build roads, and erect a church. Periodically he was required to take a census of his estate; he acted as governor over his people, administered justice, and enjoyed a certain social prestige. The only other obligation was the payment of a *quint* or one-fifth of the value of the seigniory whenever the property changed hands otherwise than by direct inheritance. Not all seigneurs were members of the aristocracy and some of them were in such straitened circumstances that they failed to carry out their obligations.

The seigneur in turn granted land to settlers who had the right of occupation and use upon the payment of a small annual rent (*cens et rentes*) in money or in kind or both. Whether this payment was a real rental or merely a "symbol of seigniorial dominance" is not established.[1] The habitant could also be called

[1] William B. Munro, *The Seigniorial System in Canada* (Toronto, The Champlain Society, 1908), pp. 85–88.

upon to work for the seigneur to clear land or build roads. This "corvée" seldom exceeded six days per year under the French regime, but was increased considerably on some estates under English rule after 1763. The habitant also was obliged to patronize the mill built by the seigneur. This seeming monopoly was no hardship in the earlier days but became a matter of irritation later on.

The habitant obtained definite rights in the land. He could sell his right to occupy and use to another, but whenever a transfer of title was made, otherwise than by direct inheritance, the seigneur levied a tax equal to one-twelfth of the value of the property, the *lots et rentes.* In the earlier period inheritance was the rule and this tax was of little consequence, but in later years, especially near the cities, transfers were more frequent and the tax became important. In fact, after the English conquest it acted as an unwholesome check on land transfer.

The seigniory could also be sold or divided through inheritance, and whenever this happened the habitants had a new master. After 1763 many French seigneurs preferred to go to France and sold their estates to English merchants and officials who looked upon their properties in a more commercial light than the former owners. The habitants disliked the new seigneurs, "representatives of an alien race and a heretical creed." Besides, later settlers were obtaining land under fee simple without obligations to seigneurs, and the habitants began to consider their lot burdensome and unfair in comparison. The seigniorial system had outlived its usefulness, and in 1854 it was legally abolished. The seigneurs were paid for the loss of their privileges; the annual *cens et rentes* was retained but the habitants could convert it into a lump sum payment and free themselves of all vestiges of feudal tenure.[1] This commutation, however, was not accomplished in a short time; in fact, as late as 1935 a plan was proposed under which the various rural municipalities of Quebec would furnish the money for this purpose, the farmers to reimburse the municipality by installment payments over twenty or more years.[2]

[1] C. Cagne, "The Seigniorial Tenure in Canada," *Proceedings of the Fifth International Conference of Agricultural Economists, 1938* (London, Oxford University Press, 1939), pp. 316–25.

[2] "Quebec's Feudal System to Go," *New York Times Magazine,* October 6, 1935.

The manner of granting seigniories and of subgranting land to habitants had a greater influence on the size and shape of farms and on the utilization of land than the rectangular survey and land laws exercised on farming in the United States and western Canada. The desirable land in Quebec was that fronting on the St. Lawrence, from the standpoint of both accessibility to transportation and fertility. This frontage was limited, however, whereas the land back of the river was practically "unlimited." Grants were made with frontage on the waterway as the basis, but the seigniory ran back for miles into the uplands. The seigneur himself preferred this system because it reduced his share of the cost of roads, which usually paralleled the river. The shape of the seigniories has determined the shape of the present counties of Quebec which, in many cases, are coextensive and bear the same name.

The same factors were also responsible for the oblong-shaped farms of the habitants. They wanted to be near neighbors and have access to the river and the road. Besides, farms which ran back from the river gave all farmers a complete cross section of the available land—the slope near the river for plow land, the uplands for pasture, and the hills farther inland for fuel and timber. When the land passed to the next generation, however, under the law of equal division, every heir wanted frontage on the river and road, with the result that the famous "ribbon farms" were created. Today the houses and barns form almost continuous villages along the main roads of Quebec. Extreme cases of farms 2 miles long and only 300 feet wide are to be found on the Island of Orleans and on the Beaupré coast. To prevent subdivision from going too far the king of France in 1745 issued a decree prohibiting the construction of farm buildings where lots were less than 288 feet wide. Buildings were actually demolished under this decree.[1]

The long narrow farms interfered seriously with the proper management of the farm. The distance to the far end was such that only the land near the buildings was cultivated and the rest remained wild. Rotation of crops and improvements in agriculture were hindered or prevented, and in a short time the area

[1] Cagne, *op. cit.;* Munro, *op. cit.*, pp. 79–85.

became too small to support a family. Thus the paradoxical situation arose of an artificial scarcity of land in a pioneer country with abundant and unused land resources.[1]

LANDED PROPERTY IN THE UNITED STATES: THE PUBLIC DOMAIN

The British Crown was considered the owner of all land in America under the British flag, and when the king granted land to proprietors and companies the rights to the soil were transferred also. The proprietors sold or granted lands to settlers; in some cases they instituted modified forms of feudal tenure on American soil, but never as completely as the French did in Quebec. The proprietors of New York, Pennsylvania, Maryland, and the Carolinas collected quit-rents. In New York the manorial estates and services established by the "patroons" were not extinguished until the "anti-rent wars" of the 1840's. On the other hand, free proprietorship was established very early in New England.

The Revolutionary War not only was a struggle to obtain political freedom but also swept away the quit-rents and other remnants of feudal land laws. Legally, these were abolished by the legislation of the several states a few years after independence was declared. By the Ordinance of 1787 primogeniture and entail were prohibited and full ownership in the soil was guaranteed in the Northwest Territory. Property in land tended to become like almost any other property in the freedom of its transfer and in inheritance.

After the Revolution the federal government became successor to the rights of the Crown and the actual proprietor of the vast Public Domain. Those of the thirteen colonies which had claims to western lands ceded them to the federal government with only minor reservations. It was generally recognized that

[1] The results of uneconomic farm layout can also be observed in the United States. It was observed in New York State that long narrow farms have a similar effect on the use of the land. "Fields too remote to be cultivated economically are kept in hay almost continuously. If the hay from such fields is to be sold, it is usually stacked or drawn to a nearby barn rather than to the main buildings. Fields too distant to be profitably cropped with hay are used for pasture. . . . On many farms, the remote fields are never manured and are continually getting poorer. Frequently such fields, too distant to be farmed economically by their owner, are directly across the road from a neighbor's house."—W. I. Myers, *An Economic Study of Farm Layout* (Cornell Memoir 34, 1920), p. 435.

the Indians also had rights in the soil and these were extinguished by treaties and by conquest, the theory being that the Indian tribes had some of the attributes of nations.

By cessions of the original colonies, by purchases such as the Louisiana and Florida, by conquest, and by treaty, the federal government became the owner of 1,309,591,680 acres of land, exclusive of Alaska and insular possessions. This area is less than the total area which has come under the legal jurisdiction of the United States because some of the land was already in private possession, or was so claimed, and when Texas entered the Union she retained possession of the lands within her present borders and disposed of them under her own land acts. Under the federal constitution, as interpreted by the courts, the United States has the same power over the public domain as it has over other property belonging to the federal government. This includes the right to prevent trespass, to control, sell, grant, or otherwise dispose of this land, the right being vested in Congress "without limitation." [1] The states cannot exercise the right of eminent domain over it nor can these lands be taxed. Change in the status from territory to statehood or changes in boundaries do not affect the complete power of proprietorship of the national government in the public domain. This is highly significant, because there has been a feeling that the public domain lands are owned by the United States merely as a trustee and, with certain exceptions, should be turned over to the states for ownership or converted into private ownership without reservation.[2] Such an interpretation would make federal forests, the regulation of grazing, or any other federal land policy on the public domain impossible.

Having the actual possession of these 1,309,591,680 acres of land, with all the rights that go with possession, the United States could, theoretically at least, have retained full control over the utilization and conservation of this vast area. However, the nation adopted the policy of alienating the public domain to private

[1] Art. IV, Sect. 3 of the Constitution; *U. S.* v. *Gratiot* (14 Peters 526). In *Gibson* v. *Chouteau* (13 Wallace 92) it is stated: "Congress has the absolute right to prescribe the times, the conditions, and the mode of transferring this property or any part of it, and to designate the persons to whom the transfer shall be made."

[2] This view is elaborated in Charles E. Winter, *Four Hundred Million Acres* (Casper, Wyoming, Overland Publishing Co., 1932).

landowners. Not until 1872 was there any indication that the federal government would retain possession of any part of the land except for such purposes as military reservations, forts, post offices, etc., under the delegated powers of the constitution. In that year Yellowstone National Park was set aside, the first of the park reservations, and in 1891 forest land was withheld from alienation, thereby initiating the federal forest policy.

The philosophy behind this policy of alienation was the belief that private property would create a nation of freeholders whose self-interest would give us maximum production, automatically conserve our natural resources, and, with each owner "under his own vine and fig tree," guarantee a certain equality in the distribution of wealth. If inequalities resulted they would be due entirely to the superior skill, thrift, and hard work of the owner. Besides, taxable wealth would be created for the support of local governments and institutions. No distinction was made between agricultural and forest land. "Almost without exception the Secretaries of the Interior and the Commissioners of the General Land Office had the idea that their duty was to get rid of the land. 'What shall we do about timber? Get rid of it.' That was the common attitude," writes Gifford Pinchot.[1] With some reservations this was also our mineral land policy.

Although the early statesmen believed in the "magic of private property," they also saw in the millions of acres of public domain a source of revenue for the struggling new nation. Even Jefferson looked upon the western lands as a "precious resource" which would "liberate us from our domestic debt, and perhaps, too, from our foreign one." So the first plan (1785) was to sell in large tracts—by townships and parts of townships in fact—and at a minimum of $1.00 per acre. In 1796 the size of the tracts was reduced but the price raised to $2.00. This price was retained till 1820, after which it was reduced to $1.25, where it remained, until the law became more or less inoperative in 1891. The land was offered at auction with the hope that more than the minimum figure would be realized. This method brought occasional prices as high as $25 or $30 per acre but as a rule the sales were at or near the minimum. After the auction was over the remaining

[1] "How Conservation Began in the United States," *Agricultural History*, October, 1937, p. 260.

lands might be purchased at the local land offices at $1.25 per acre.

As early as 1790 Congress debated the advisability of grading the land and selling the better tracts at higher figures, but the uniform price system was officially adopted. Under it an automatic classification was taking place; presumably the settler would select the best land first and would bid higher at the auction for A grade than for C grade land. The principles of *laissez faire* and *caveat emptor* (let the buyer beware!) prevailed; if the settler bought submarginal land he alone was to blame! That some selectivity was taking place is indicated by the "refuse lands" left unsold throughout the Middle West. Senator Benton, after some thirty years of agitation, finally got the Graduation Act enacted in 1854 under which the price was progressively reduced from $1.25 to finally 12½ cents an acre if the land had not been sold within thirty years after it had been proclaimed for sale.[1]

The use of the public domain to obtain revenue or in lieu of revenue was incorporated in other land acts. Soldiers were given lands and later negotiable land scrip which could be converted into cash. Land was granted to build roads, canals, and railways, or to furnish funds to drain land. States received generous grants for public improvements and for the support of education, beginning with the donation of Section 16 of every township under the Ordinance of 1787. About 221,000,000 acres were granted to the states, an area larger than Texas and Oklahoma.

The intention of Congress was that the states should likewise sell the land and use the proceeds for the purposes stated in the act; however, some grants were made without specifying a purpose. Most of the states were so anxious to attract settlers and get the land on the tax roll that they sold their land at a low figure; others, however, realized substantial sums. In some cases the federal grants specified a sum below which the land might not be sold. Since much of the land proved submarginal for agriculture it is still state property. It is important to recognize that the states are proprietors and charged with the administration of about 91,000,000 acres, an expanse almost equal to the area of

[1] Benjamin H. Hibbard, *A History of the Public Land Policies* (New York, Macmillan, 1924), pp. 289–305.

Montana. This figure includes also the lands reverted for taxes, forests, parks, game refuges, etc., and about 37,651,000 acres which are leased and bring some revenue to the states.[1]

Texas, which retained its own public domain, followed the example of the federal government in alienating its land. The need for revenue also prompted Texas to sell land as a means for raising money. It granted 3,000,000 acres to a syndicate for the erection of its state capitol. In 1935 it still owned almost 22,000,-000 acres, making Texas the largest landowner among the states.

As a revenue measure the sale of the public lands was unimportant. The federal government had competitors in the states and agencies to whom it had granted land, and much land was offered below $1.25 per acre. If surveying and administrative costs are considered the United States realized very little from its "precious resource."

From the settler's point of view a price on the raw wilderness was undesirable, to say the least. The typical frontiersman or emigrant had very little capital, and whatever money he had went into moving and converting the wild land into a factor of production.

What prevented settlers from moving en masse onto the public domain and taking possession of the land? They were prevented from doing so because a legal title could not be obtained by mere possession. Title could be secured only as the settler acquired the land according to the established procedure—purchase, preemption, homesteading, and the other methods set forth in the various land acts. The squatter had no rights against the holder of a patent from the United States and the latter could dispossess the settler even if improvements had been made on the land. Thus the legal title furnished an effective check against the mere taking possession of the soil or direct acquisition from the Indians.

The patent or title was important to the settler in still other ways. Without legal ownership it was practically impossible to borrow money since the frontiersman had very little of the world's goods to use as collateral. The patent became the basis for all subsequent titles. States were also anxious for private title to be established as soon as possible in order to get the land on the tax

[1] *Certain Aspects of Land Problems and Government Land Policies,* Part VII of the Supplementary Report of the Land Planning Committee to the National Resources Board, 1935, pp. 88–91.

THE UNITED STATES OF AMERICA,

To all to whom these presents shall come, greeting:

CERTIFICATE No. 22616, } **Whereas,** Simon Robe of Grant County Wisconsin

has deposited in the GENERAL LAND OFFICE of the UNITED STATES, a CERTIFICATE of the Register of the Land Office at Mineral Point whereby it appears that FULL PAYMENT has been made by the said Simon Robe. according to the provisions of the Act of Congress of the 24th of April, 1820, entitled "An act making further provision for the sale of the public lands," for the North East quarter of the North West quarter, and the South West quarter of the North West quarter of Section three in Township three North of Range two West, in the District of lands Subject to Sale at Mineral Point, Wisconsin, containing eighty five acres and forty four hundredths of an acre.

according to the OFFICIAL PLAT of the Survey of the said Lands, returned to the GENERAL LAND OFFICE by the Surveyor General, which said Tract has been purchased by the said Simon Robe

Now know ye, That the ***UNITED STATES OF AMERICA,*** in consideration of the premises, and in conformity with the several Acts of Congress in such case made and provided, HAVE GIVEN AND GRANTED, and by these presents DO GIVE AND GRANT, unto the said Simon Robe and to his heirs, the said Tract above described; **TO HAVE AND TO HOLD** the same, together with all the rights, privileges, immunities and appurtenances of whatsoever nature thereunto belonging, unto the said Simon Robe and to his heirs and assigns forever.

In testimony whereof, I, Franklin Pierce PRESIDENT OF THE UNITED STATES OF AMERICA, have caused these letters to be made Patent, and the Seal of the GENERAL LAND OFFICE to be hereunto affixed.

UNITED STATES GENERAL LAND OFFICE

Given under my hand, at the CITY OF WASHINGTON, the first day of October in the year of OUR LORD one thousand eight hundred and fifty six and of the Independence of the United States the Eighty first

BY THE PRESIDENT: Franklin Pierce

By [illegible] Sec'y.

[illegible] Recorder of the General Land Office.

RECORDED, Vol. 45, Page 213,

Courtesy of Norman Nybroten and L. A. Brunckhorst, Sr.

FIG. 7. THE FACSIMILE OF A LAND PATENT

roll; even speculatively owned land was better than the public domain in this respect. In the early days the patent was considered so important that this document had to be signed personally by the president of the United States. However, in Andrew Jackson's time the grants became so numerous that the law was changed to permit a secretary to sign for the president.[1] Figure 7 is a facsimile of a patent granted in 1856 under the Act of 1820, carrying the name of Franklin Pierce.[2]

However, to obtain title first and pay for land before he could make it earn did not fit into the settler's program. In the first place, in the rush of settlement land was sometimes selected ahead of surveys, and in the second place the frontier farmer rarely had the money to pay $1.25 per acre. If he had any savings they were needed to improve the land. Turner estimated the cost of preparing a 320-acre Illinois farm at the edge of the prairie, of which one-half was broken and fenced, at $1,000.[3] When the sale opened at the land office the settler's claim might be sold to an outsider if he was not present, or he might be overbid by some speculator even if he were present. In fact, speculators watched for the opportunity to bid on partly improved farms. Naturally the settlers considered this rank injustice and formed "claim associations" whose business it was to attend the land sales and discourage bidding on descriptions occupied by settlers. The means used to daunt bidders were truly western and usually effective. Sometimes a single individual was appointed to act for the association, bidding the minimum price on all tracts claimed by the members.[4]

The Preemption Act of 1841 incorporated some features the settler desired. Under this act he could select a tract of land ahead of the sale (and sometimes ahead of the survey), start clearing, and when the land was sold he had the exclusive right to purchase 160 acres at $1.25 per acre. At the auction his quarter section was simply not open for competitive sale.

Although pre-emption was a step toward the settler's goal, the

[1] See Report 734, 30th Congress, 1st Session H. R., June 23, 1848, from *Reports of Committees,* 1st Session, 30th Congress.

[2] Note that the grant is without reservations from the United States of America to Simon Robe of the described tract, "together with all rights, privileges, immunities, and appurtances" to him and "to his heirs and assigns forever."

[3] Frederick Jackson Turner, *The Rise of the New West, 1819–1829* (New York, Harper's, 1906), pp. 86–87.

[4] Hibbard, *op. cit.,* pp. 198–209.

price was still a matter of irritation. The settler's ideal was *free* land, and his frontier experiences strengthened his belief that he was entitled to it. He was bearing the cost of developing a farm while facing the dangers of the wilderness, the Indians, and wild beasts. His industry was "creating values," not only on his own farm, but on the lands held by the speculators, the railroads, and even on the remaining public domain and state-owned lands. The farmer was producing business for the cities and freight for the railroads.[1] The least Uncle Sam could do was to grant the raw land free of charge.

As soon as the West was more or less adequately represented in Congress, leaders like Senator Benton championed the frontier view in Congress. The homestead idea had the ardent support of Horace Greeley, but because of partisan and sectional politics it was not enacted into law until after secession of the southern states in 1862.[2]

Under the homestead act a quarter section was granted free (except for nominal fees) to any settler who lived on the land and improved it according to law. At the end of five years, upon bringing proof of compliance, the patent was issued. The settler could shorten this period by "commuting," i.e., by paying the regular $1.25 per acre, or $2.50 under some conditions.

The homestead method of acquiring land not only suited the settler but discouraged speculation and kept prices of privately owned land on a reasonable level. Meanwhile another change in the land laws favored the settler. The earlier acts set a lower limit to the size of the tracts sold by the government; this suited the speculator but not the bona fide settler who was interested only in an economic unit for himself. Both the pre-emption and homestead acts set an *upper* limit which favored the farmer but deterred speculation.

However, homesteading did not do away with speculation and land frauds. The "commutation clause" permitted pseudo-settlers to "homestead" and, after paying the $1.25 per acre, to sell to speculators, ranchmen, lumber companies, and others engaged in

[1] It is estimated that every settler creates $400 per year of new freight traffic in Canada. Bowman, *Limits of Land Settlement, op. cit.*, p. 82.

[2] The first homestead, entered by Daniel Freeman January 1, 1863, was made into "The Homestead National Monument" by an act of Congress, March 19, 1936. See Addison E. Sheldon, *Land Systems and Land Policies in Nebraska* (Nebraska Historical Society, 1936), pp. 74–75, 364.

blocking up large holdings. Unfortunately, the law permitting the regular sales was also kept on the statute books and defeated many of the benefits of the homestead act.[1] Finally, when settlement reached the semiarid West the act itself was no longer suitable. This particular point will be elaborated in Chapter VIII.

About 954,000,000 acres, or one half of the total land area of the United States, has been alienated under the various land acts. The public domain has been "picked over" and Uncle Sam is the owner of roughly 430,000,000 acres, an area equal to all the Mountain states, excluding Utah and Nevada. This figure, however, includes both the original public domain and the land in forests, parks, game refuges, etc. It is important to distinguish the two types of federally owned lands: (1) those under the administration and management of some branch of the government, such as the Forest, National Park, or Indian services—about 210,000,000 acres, and (2) "vacant, unappropriated and unreserved lands," i.e., the original public domain. Exclusive of Alaska the federal government still owns over 220,000,000 acres of public domain, including withdrawals pending further disposition and unperfected titles. However, under the Taylor Grazing Act, 142,000,000 acres of this have been withdrawn for grazing districts.[2]

ALIENATION OF THE CANADIAN PUBLIC DOMAIN

Canadian experience with the alienation of public lands is similar to and yet unlike that of the United States. It differs in that the eastern provinces made no cession of land to the federal or dominion government as did the original colonies of the United States. In fact, a federal domain did not appear until 1869, when the territory west of Ontario and east of the Rockies was acquired by the Dominion from the Hudson's Bay Company. However, federal ownership of land met with provincial resistance almost from the start, and in 1871 a system was inaugurated of granting subsidies in lieu of land to the provinces. The prairie provinces were given their grants as soon as organized. However, the agitation grew for granting the federal land to the provinces,

[1] Paul W. Gates, "The Homestead Law in an Incongruous Land System," *American Historical Review*, July, 1936, pp. 652–81.

[2] *N. R. B. Report, op. cit.*, p. 236. The 142,000,000 acres were approved June 28, 1934.

and in 1930 the unalienated lands were handed over to those provinces in which they were located. Notwithstanding the fact that the provinces now own their public domain, the subsidies have been continued.[1]

From time to time there has been in the United States a similar movement demanding the cession of the public lands to the states, especially in the West. In fact, in 1930 a congressional committee recommended that this be done in such states as would accept the grant.[2] However, the generous donations to states in earlier times and the Taylor Grazing Act and other land laws of the last decade have kept the states satisfied with the present arrangement. Nevertheless, problems are constantly arising whenever one unit of government owns land lying within the jurisdiction of another, one reason being that public lands are "off the tax roll."

The Dominion's method of alienating its roughly 112,000,000 acres of public domain was strikingly similar to that of the federal government of the United States.[3] A policy was adopted to permit homesteading of 160 acres with the right to purchase adjoining land. Fully 90 per cent of the 58,000,000 acres that went to settlers was homesteaded. Canada felt obliged to grant as liberal terms as the United States because on both sides of the line settlers were pushing beyond the 100th meridian and the two countries were in direct competition for farmers. Canada attracted many people from the "States" during this period. As in the United States, public lands were used to reward soldiers, by negotiable scrip to South African War veterans and by direct grants to World War soldiers.

By 1870 the wild enthusiasm for railways in the United States and the princely railway grants had been replaced by cries of monopoly and the demand for regulation. Canada might have profited by this experience, but the demand for transportation, especially as a bond of union between eastern and western Canada,

[1] The Dominion also owned some land in British Columbia and retains a public domain in the Northwest Territories and the Yukon. J. A. Maxwell, "Alienation of the Federal Domain in Canada," *Journal of Land and Public Utility Economics,* November, 1936, pp. 398–409.

[2] Report of the Committee on the Conservation and Administration of the Public Domain, January, 1931.

[3] Canada separated "under rights" from surface rights and disposed of them separately. About 47,000,000 acres of under rights were alienated between 1870 and 1930. Maxwell, *op. cit.,* p. 400.

was so insistent that history repeated itself. Almost a third of the entire Canadian public domain was granted to railways and in a few years the reaction of the people was similar to that in the "States." No further grants were made to railroads after 1894. However, Canadian railroads did much to settle the prairies by their enlightened colonization policies, which in many respects were superior to those followed by the railroads of the United States.

Another point of similarity was the setting aside of two sections of land in each township for the endowment of schools. Unlike the practice in the United States, these sections were not donated to the provinces but were sold by the Dominion, the funds invested, and the income turned over to the provinces. By withholding the sale of the school sections, despite provincial protests, until opportune times, a much higher price was obtained than was the rule in the United States.[1]

INDIAN LANDS AND TITLES

One of the tragic consequences of the contact of the European races with the Indians was the difference in their concepts of property in land. The Indians had little or no concept of private property and were not aware of the rights they were surrendering when they ceded the soil to the "Great White Father" and moved westward. Today most of them are on "reservations" scattered throughout twenty-four states, from New York and North Carolina through Wisconsin and Iowa to the Far West. The total area of Indian reservations is roughly 52,000,000 acres, or an area the size of Kansas. The title to these reservations usually rests in the federal government but the land is used by the Indians in common.[2]

Granting land in full fee simple to Indians has almost universally resulted in failure because of their lack of understanding of property rights, mortgages and leases. The Dominion of

[1] Maxwell, *op. cit.,* pp. 402–5, 407–9.

[2] Whether the title rests with the United States or not depends upon the manner in which the land was acquired by the federal government. Where the Indian tribes have reserved certain lands by treaty, the title never came into the possession of the government, but the reservation is treated as though the fee title were in the United States but held in trust for the tribes. The Pueblo lands are held in fee and not in trust because they are grants to the Indians from the Spanish king or the Mexican Government and were so recognized by the treaty of Guadalupe Hidalgo.

Canada granted to each half breed, born before 1885, a cash scrip of $240 or a land scrip of 240 acres. Almost 3,000,000 acres were alienated to Indians, most of which was promptly sold to speculators.[1]

In 1887 the United States Congress passed the General Allotment Act permitting the granting of land to individual Indians but under a qualified title. The land was held in trust for the Indian for twenty-five years, during which period it could not be sold, mortgaged, or taxed, but it might be leased with the permission of the government. However, if the Indian was "competent" he could be given a full fee simple title and the land became subject to taxation and all limitations as to its sale were removed.[2] The same privilege could be extended to an "incompetent" Indian with the approval of the Secretary of the Interior. This was an opening for the whites to get the land from the Indians, and the 138,000,000 acres of allotted land which they owned in 1887 had shrunk to about 52,000,000 by 1935.

Another result of this system has been that descendants of the original allottee now have rights in unalienated allotted land. As many as 100 heirs have equities in tracts as small as 60 acres, and one Indian may have equities in 20 allotments. These cases again show how the rights to property may be split, and also illustrate a form of "qualified property." The Wheeler-Howard Act of 1934 is an attempt to "unscramble" the situation and restore tribal ownership and tribal social organization and civilization, as well as to enlarge the reservations.[3]

SOCIAL ASPECTS OF PROPERTY

Social Privileges of Land Ownership. Historically, certain social, economic, and even political privileges have been associated with land ownership which stratified human society and gave special values, economic as well as psychic, to land as property. The entire feudal system with its ranking of men was based on land; but even after it had passed away and the Industrial Revolu-

[1] Maxwell, *op. cit.*, p. 404.

[2] The term "competent" Indian refers to an individual who is considered capable of making his living by his own efforts, but the term is subject to interpretation by the Bureau of Indian Affairs. The Indian passes from the status of "incompetent" to "competent" upon his own application and he sometimes prefers the former status because of the privileges attached to it.

[3] *N. R. B. Report, op. cit.*, pp. 227–35.

tion had ushered in a new era, social and political privileges still clung to landownership. Only landowners could be members of Parliament in Ricardo's time in England, and the landowning Junkers of Prussia were and still are a powerful political influence in Germany. English colonists brought these ideas with them to America. The large landed estates of such men as Lord Fairfax, whose lands were surveyed by George Washington, are evidence of this feeling regarding the desirability of land as property. It gave them a prestige that the ownership of stocks, bonds, and capital goods could not give. In both England and Germany those who became rich in industry have bought land in order to get into the privileged class. In most of the American colonies only landowners were allowed to vote, while ownership of a considerable amount of land was demanded for eligibility to public office. Some of the early state constitutions contained similar qualifications for suffrage and office.

However, when liberal land laws made everyone a landowner, there was no particular social prestige to be gained by owning even large estates. In certain sections the landowner still has a higher social standing than the tenant, and at times certain political rights or privileges are reserved for landowners. For instance, Wind Erosion Conservation districts may be set up in Texas if the majority of the "legally qualified property tax paying voters" favor such a measure.[1] Many wealthy people like to own country estates and "play farms" which are largely owned for pleasure and prestige. These are often numerous enough in the vicinity of large cities to form "estate sections" and to dominate the institutions, land utilization, and valuation of the area. Bankers, merchants, and other residents of small cities in agricultural regions like to own farms and to be called "farmers."

Certain foreign farmers also have a hereditary passion for landed property which causes them to cling to the soil even if better economic opportunities exist elsewhere. The high percentage of farm ownership among foreign-born whites in the United States is partly due to the intense desire for land, sharpened by the fact that they could not satisfy their craving in their native land.

Wherever land is sought for social reasons in addition to economic reasons, the resulting price of land is likely to be higher

[1] Chapter 337, 44th Texas Legislature, Regular Session, 1935.

than if it were bought and sold on the economic basis alone. This is one of the reasons for the observation by George Tucker, of the University of Virginia, in 1859: "It may be remarked that land, including lots and houses in town, yield less than the average profits of capital, partly on account of the greater security of the capital, and partly because, being visible to all and appreciable by all, they confer on the proprietor somewhat more of influence in society than personal property."[1] In older countries the extra-economic factors are often more important than the purely economic factors in determining land values. A land policy must be based as much, if not more so, upon these human or social attitudes toward land than upon its physical-economic characteristics. Wherever the property sense of a people is still in a primitive state, land reforms must also proceed along entirely different lines from those in a nation in which the opposite is the case.

Political and Social Control through Landed Property. The possessor of the surface to a certain degree "owns all." Landowners in a self-supporting community practically control local politics, the schools, roads, churches, and community life. They determine the religion, language, and social customs. Closely settled communities remain impervious to outside influences.[2] Nations sometimes resort to colonizing to penetrate such groups. Because of the political significance of landownership, most nations limit the possession of the soil by foreigners and circumscribe the manner in which land may be owned or leased. California and other western states afford an example of the exclusion of Orientals from owning or even leasing land, and other nations on the Pacific have similar laws. Japan also has restrictions on foreign landownership.

Ownership of land extends power over other things closely associated with land. Some mining and lumbering corporations and manufacturing establishments make it a practice to own all the land and houses occupied by their employees in order to have full control over them. Throughout the world there is an aversion to concentration of landownership, whether it be agricultural, forest, mineral, or even urban land. This is another important factor to be taken into consideration in formulating land policies.

[1] *Political Economy for the People* (Philadelphia, C. Sherman, 1859), p. 64.

[2] See Dawson, *op. cit.* An example of such a community in the United States is the Amana Colony of Iowa.

It has been said that the cure for the perils of democracy is more democracy. In the same spirit land policies were designed to prevent the evils associated with concentration of land and landlordship by promoting widespread ownership of land and homes.[1] In fact, Jefferson built his philosophy on the belief that "equality needed the buttress of widespread land ownership. His dream was a nation of free-hold farmers, each with a tract of sufficient size to maintain his independence."[2] No doubts existed in the minds of the framers of our land policies that private ownership promotes the best use of the land and spurs the operator to put forth his best efforts. At its best, though not necessarily, this means the conservation of the soil and a maximum production for the benefit of society as a whole. Arthur Young remarked, after seeing the thrift of the French peasant proprietors, that the magic of property turns sand into gold. "The true savings bank is the soil," said Sismondi, when he observed in owner-operation a potent check to population, since the small French family was the result of the inheritance laws coupled with the inborn thrift of the peasants.[3] However, the experience of the last sixty years with private ownership of natural resources has raised doubts in the "magic of property" as a conserving force, even in agricultural land.

Private ownership of land has also been favored because it has proved to be a stabilizing force in society. This is a weighty argument for home ownership in both city and country. The landless have no stake in the soil and nothing to lose by changes in institutions. Agrarian unrest is always greatest where attachment to the land is least or where it is likely to be broken by the loss of the home or farm through foreclosure.

The Non-Partisan League had its greatest following in the under-developed farm sections of the Northwest, whereas the rich agricultural counties were not so ready to follow the "new deal" of that day. Before the World War an agrarian movement started

[1] "By an overwhelming majority the nation stands by a civilization based on private ownership. M. J. Bonn says in his *American Adventure* that the United States is the only country that has 'Evolved a system of undiluted capitalism. . . . Property is a sacred national institution. Participation in property, not its abolition, is the national aim.' "—R. E. Turpin, "Five Basic Tenets: Will They Prevail," *New York Times Magazine*, July 31, 1938, p. 2.

[2] *Ibid.*

[3] Francis Walker, *Land and Its Rent, op. cit.*, pp. 216–17.

among the tenants of Texas and Oklahoma which was the main support of the Socialist Party in this section. "Renters' Unions" were formed and the tenant issue was injected into a gubernatorial campaign in Texas in which the successful candidate said in his speeches, "A man will fight for a home but not for a boarding house." The stabilizing influence of land ownership is stressed by McBride in his discussion of land reforms in Mexico:

"The proprietor is by nature a conservator of law and order. His interests are all with established institutions. His home and land, his crops and domestic stock are exposed in every outbreak of violence. He not only will seldom start a revolution, but he can be counted on to oppose it. He needs peace for the security of his property. The propertyless individual, on the contrary, recks little of political turmoil or the overturn of established systems. Individually he has nothing to lose. He may even gain by a completely new deal. This attitude is recognized in the industrial classes of our large cities, who have no permanent interests tied up in the plants in which they work." [1] One of the chief stumbling blocks to uniting farmers and laborers into one political party is this difference in attitudes toward property, especially landed property. It is also the chief distinction between eastern and western "liberalism" in the United States.

Validity of Private Property in Land. In feudal times landed property and landlords played the predominant role in society because of their political power and their lion's share in the distribution of wealth. However, the feudal system was one of duties as well as rights, and with the passing of this regime the duties associated with land largely disappeared and rights became intensified under full ownership. With the development of modern thought, inquiring minds questioned the social order. Among other factors the classical doctrine of rent, assigning an ever-increasing share of the income of society to landlords, raised the question of the validity of private property in land. John Stuart Mill denied the right of private land ownership on the basis that land was not produced by man, yet modified his principle insofar as labor had been incorporated into land. Henry George, however, disregarded the latter consideration and made a clear-cut dis-

[1] George McCutchen McBride, *The Land Systems of Mexico* (American Geographical Society, New York, 1923), pp. 3–4.

tinction between land and "wealth" on the "labor test" basis, excluding land from the realm of legitimate private property.[1] Furthermore, the feeling grew that everyone had a "natural right" to the soil. The absolute rights of an individual to the "heritage of all" was attacked by such men as Herbert Spencer. Land nationalization was actively propagandized by Alfred Russel Wallace and others.

During the same period the entire concept of property was also re-examined. Malthus and his contemporaries considered private property necessary for the best interests of society; William Godwin and others attacked it. Since then opponents and adherents have tried to justify private property by some theory of its origin in line with their prepossessions. Proudhon and Marx claimed that property originated in theft and robbery, and Henry George was inclined to agree with them. Others, favorable to private property, looked upon it as ordained by God or as a "natural right" and therefore unassailable. Those legally inclined said it was a creature of law, or of social contract or social compact. Others claim that it is an outgrowth of human nature, that man craves property and needs it for his full development. Adam Smith, John Stuart Mill, and Henry George felt that it had its roots in labor and, being the result of man's effort, society should guarantee to the producer the results of his toil.[2]

None of these theories is sufficient to justify private property. It is justified only on the *social theory of property,* namely that it is established and maintained for social purposes. Under this theory agricultural land is retained as private property because it is believed that the nation enjoys the greatest well-being under private ownership. Whenever social welfare is better served by shifting from private to public land the state has the power to make this change. It also has the power to make the right of the individual to land less absolute.

Modifying the Rights of Property. "Supposing the entire habitable globe to be so enclosed," said Herbert Spencer, "it follows that if the landowners have a valid right to its surface, all

[1] Mill, *Principles of Political Economy, op. cit.,* Book II, Chapter II; Henry George, *Progress and Poverty,* Book VII, Chap. 1; Francis Walker, *op. cit.,* Chap. III, "Recent Attacks upon Landed Property."

[2] See Ely, *Property and Contract,* Vol. II (New York, Macmillan, 1914), Chap. XXII: "Theories of the Origin of Private Property," pp. 531–55.

who are not landowners have no right at all to its surface. . . . Save by the permission of the lords of the soil, they can have no room for the soles of their feet. Nay, should the others think fit to deny them a resting place, these landless men might equitably be expelled from the earth altogether."[1] This is a dramatic over-statement of the rights of property in land. In the first place rights to the soil may be *exclusive,* never *absolute.* The great definitions of property all limit the owner's rights by adding, "providing he must not use it to the injury of others." No man's house is his castle to the extent that he causes injury or discomfort to others. His right to sell, inherit, or bequeath may be restricted or prohibited, as in the case of sale of land to foreigners. The waste of natural resources is being curtailed even though no particular individual is injured thereby.

Sometimes custom reduces the intensiveness of property rights. The right of the public to use footpaths across the fields in Palestine and England or in the forests of Germany is an example of social rights on private land. In many states of the Union the owner has the privilege of letting his stock roam over all the neighboring land and he who does not want grazing on his property is expected to fence his land to keep the roaming animals out. Only after a "stock law" has been passed is the owner of stock required to fence his land to keep the animals enclosed. Stock owners even assume the privilege of burning over forests they do not own to insure better grazing, a practice usually detrimental to forest reproduction.

The power to regulate the use of property is part of the inherent power of government. The major uses of this power are found in the police power, the power of taxation, and eminent domain. All property is bought, sold, and owned subject to the exercise of these powers. Of the several layers of government in the United States, ranging from the town or village to the federal government itself, the power of sovereignty is in the several states, except as these have been delegated, specifically or implied, to the federal government by the United States Constitution.[2] Local

[1] *Social Statics* (New York, Appleton, 1873), p. 132.

[2] The division of powers between the federal and state governments is stated in the 10th Amendment: "The powers not delegated to the United States by the constitution nor prohibited by it to the States, are reserved to the States respectively or to the people." An example of this division is shown in the A. A. A. decision

governments possess only those attributes of sovereignty which have been delegated to them by the state governments.

Unlike the United States, "Canada proceeds upon the theory of a single sovereign power expressing itself through different agencies, some national and others provincial." The police power, i.e., the power "to make laws for the peace, order and good government," is exercised by the Dominion in all matters not exclusively assigned to the legislatures of the provinces.[1]

This division of powers vitally affects land utilization and planning. As matters now stand neither the federal government nor a state is in a position to conserve wild life because of legal obstacles. A national plan of land utilization cannot be carried out without the co-operation of the states, which alone can use the police power and have the power to levy an apportioned property tax. The state in turn may have to depend upon local communities for certain phases of planning, zoning, and land use control.

The Police Power and Zoning. The police power relates to the sovereign power of the government to limit personal liberties and property rights for the public health, morals, and safety. More recently the courts have held that the "same restrictions may be imposed upon the use of property in the promotion of the public welfare, convenience, and general prosperity."[2] Since the federal government has only those powers expressly granted to it, the term "police power" has come to refer to the power of the states to legislate for these purposes.

Some everyday examples of the use of the police power are the municipal ordinances requiring all rooming houses to be equipped

(*U. S.* v. *Butler,* January 6, 1936), in which the Supreme Court declared that Congress had no power to regulate agriculture. Since this power was not specifically granted to the federal government, it is therefore a power reserved to the states or the people by the 10th Amendment. The Soil Conservation Act of February 29, 1936, sets up a plan of grants to the states, to be administered by the states but subject to certain standards enforceable by the Secretary of Agriculture, which meets the test of constitutionality since it is optional with the states. A similar law was declared constitutional (*Commonwealth of Massachusetts* v. *Mellon,* 262 U. S. 447, decided in 1923). See Charles Bunn, "The A. A. A. Decision and the Soil Conservation Act," *Journal of Land and Public Utility Economics,* May, 1936, pp. 199–200.

[1] Herbert Arthur Smith, *Federalism in North America* (Boston, Chipman Law Publishing Co., 1923), pp. 12–13.

[2] *Carter* v. *Harper,* 182 Wis., 148.

with fire escapes, prohibiting slaughter houses within city limits, or forbidding the use of inflammable buildings within certain parts of the city. Billboards have been prohibited at intersections on the grounds of safety, and infected cattle may be killed to prevent the spread of diseases. In all such cases the cost of making the change or losses must be borne by the owner without public compensation, although some states have paid for cattle slaughtered in campaigns to eradicate bovine tuberculosis.

Zoning, however, is the most important form of the police power affecting land utilization. The state grants this power to municipalities, towns, and counties. Under it a city can divide its territory into one or more residential, commercial, and industrial zones or districts. For each zone a list of permitted and prohibited uses is placed in the ordinance. For instance, in a "Class A" residence district only one-family dwellings, churches, schools, libraries, and truck gardening may be allowed, and all other uses prohibited. Usually the regulations also limit the height of the house, the size of the yards, the distance the house must be placed from the street, and the percentage of the lot that may be occupied by buildings. Similar restrictions are placed on structures in other zones. New York City in 1916 introduced regulations as to height, area, and bulk of commercial buildings—all of which have had a marked effect on the architecture of skyscrapers.

The effect of zoning on land utilization is far-reaching. The owner is not permitted to decide the use of his land on an economic basis. He may see an opportunity to use his lot for an apartment, a store, or a filling station, yet the ordinance may restrict him to a one-story dwelling. Although no one has directly robbed him of his property, he has suffered the loss of income. In all such cases there is no public indemnity for losses of income or values. Instead of having "absolute, sacred rights" which "cannot be violated on any pretense," as Herbert Spencer said, the owner of land today is asking where his rights leave off and confiscations begin.[1]

However, there is a limit to the use of the police power. As exercised by the states, the limit is found in the "due process" clause of the 14th Amendment of the federal constitution: "nor shall any state deprive any person of life, liberty or property with-

[1] Charles Warren, "What Is Confiscation?" *Atlantic Monthly,* August, 1927.

out due process of law." The same provision is also found in the 5th Amendment, which refers to the right as it is exercised by the United States under delegated powers. Most state constitutions have similar provisions.

If the owner feels he has been deprived of property he can bring suit and then the court will consider whether the ordinance was really concerned with public morals, health, safety, or public welfare and whether the individual was actually deprived of life, liberty, or property. The owner always has this recourse under the "due process clause," which does not refer to the mechanism of law but to the purpose of the law. Every decision is a balance between the public purposes to be served on the one hand, and the invasion of private rights on the other. The decision will depend to a large extent on the economic philosophy of the court, whether the judges will lean in the direction of protecting the rights of the individual or in the direction of the public rights or welfare.[1]

The ruling of the United States Supreme Court in the Hadacheck case brings out the essential factors involved in a typical zoning case. Said the court: "A municipal ordinance enacted in good faith as a police measure, prohibiting brick making within a designated area, does not take, without due process of law, the property of an owner of a tract within the prohibited district, although such land contains valuable deposits of clay suitable for brick making which cannot profitably be removed and manufactured into brick elsewhere, and is far more valuable for brick making than for any other purposes, and had been acquired by him before it was annexed to the municipality, and had long been used by him as a brick yard." [2]

This decision was one of the most drastic ever rendered because it affected property whose use had been lawfully established before the ordinance was passed. Such uses, called "non-conforming uses," are usually permitted to remain undisturbed, and this is sometimes provided specifically in the state enabling act itself.

[1] Naturally there have been great variations in the decisions of the courts of various states and at various times. This has prompted an eminent jurist to say, "There be three things which are too wonderful for me, yea, four which I know not: The way of an eagle in the air; the way of a serpent on a rock; the way of a ship in the midst of the sea; and the way of the Supreme Court with the Due Process Clause."—Warren, *op. cit.*

[2] *Hadacheck* v. *Los Angeles,* 239 U.S. 394, 60 L. Ed. 348.

Zoning should be applied retroactively as well as for the control of future land uses. If a new non-conforming use affects public health, morals, safety, convenience, and public welfare, so does an established use of the same nature. Bassett holds that "theoretically the police power is broad enough to warrant the ousting of every non-conforming use."[1] The courts would consider the ousting of an expensive apartment built before the ordinance was passed as unreasonable, yet the Hadacheck case and two New Orleans cases ordering a grocery and drug store to cease operation indicate that even permanent structures may be abated as non-conforming uses.[2] Courts, however, are inclined to distinguish between mere *land* uses such as tennis courts, skating rinks, etc., and fairly substantial buildings, and also to allow time for the use to be amortized and gradually discontinued. Several ordinances in Long Island provide for the abatement of billboards and automobile junk yards, but the former were granted five years and the latter three to six years to amortize the investment.[3]

While the general constitutionality of zoning has been firmly established, especially in the Euclid case, the courts have not upheld every ordinance.[4] In the case of apparently unreasonable restrictions or of an arbitrary and discriminatory exercise of the police power, or where the ordinance had no relation to public health, safety, morals, general welfare, or protection of the community, the courts have ruled against particular ordinances.

Eminent Domain. Sometimes it is necessary to convert private into public property, as, for instance, when land is needed for a park, street, or playground. This power to take private property without the consent of the owner, but with compensation, is known as eminent domain. It is an inherent power of the state government and an implied power of the federal government. In regard to its exercise by the federal government, the 5th Amendment provides that "no person shall be . . . deprived of life, liberty or property without due process of law; nor shall private property be taken for public use without just compensation."

[1] Edward M. Bassett, *Zoning* (Russell Sage Foundation, 1936), p. 112.

[2] *La. Dema Realty Co.* v. *Jacoby,* 168 La. 752, 123 S. 314 (1929); *Dema Realty Co.* v. *McDonald,* 168 La. 172, 121 S. 613 (1929).

[3] Bassett, *op. cit.,* pp. 112–16.

[4] *Euclid* v. *Ambler Realty Co.,* 272 U.S. 365, 71 L. Ed. 303; W. L. Pollard, "Outline of the Law of Zoning in the United States," *Annals of the American Academy of Political and Social Science,* May, 1931, pp. 15–33.

States are limited in the same manner by the "due process clause" of the 14th Amendment, as interpreted by the courts. The federal government may exercise eminent domain independently and without the consent of the states involved, but only in the furtherance of those activities allowed by the various delegated powers. For example, since the power to establish post offices is expressly conferred upon the federal government, it can obtain sites for buildings by eminent domain.[1] However, the federal government may not exercise this power outside of its delegated sphere except through state action and state consent. Thus, obtaining land for national forests by eminent domain requires a state statute permitting such federal purchases.[2] Land utilization plans involving public purchase must therefore be made within the framework of the constitution.

Eminent domain may be granted by the state to local units of government, to quasi-public and even to private bodies if public welfare is served thereby. Railroads obtain their rights-of-way in this manner, power companies may flood land, and irrigators lay their ditches over other men's farms under this right.

Eminent domain is limited to purchase of land for *public purposes.* The land may not be condemned and then be used for a private purpose, but what is meant by public purpose is not always clear. The opening of a new street is a public use. "Excess condemnation" consists of obtaining land on each side of the proposed street for replanning and resale to private owners. Harmonious development is secured in this way but the courts have not been uniform in their decisions whether this is permissible under eminent domain. The point in question is whether the purchase of the additional land is for a public purpose. Not only may the land be taken bodily, but *certain rights* may be taken for the public good. "Land and all estates, rights, interests and easements in, or appurtenant thereto, may be taken under the power of eminent domain." [3]

Eminent domain is another invasion of private rights in property. In the use of the police power the owner is deprived

[1] *Kohl et al.* v. *U. S.,* 91 U. S. 367, 23 L. Ed. 449.

[2] This does not affect the establishment of forests on the public domain, however. This land has always been the property of the federal government.

[3] John Lewis, *A Treatise on the Law of Eminent Domain in the United States,* Vol. I (3d ed., Chicago, Callaghan, 1909), p. 618.

of some of the rights; in this case all of the rights in the entire bundle are seized. The title to the property is left undisturbed under the former power, but when eminent domain is exercised the title to the land usually passes to the state or municipality, although this is not always the case. The chief difference, however, is that the owner must be compensated whenever property is taken for a public use, whereas losses in value or income due to the use of the police power must be borne by the owner. In the purchase of land by a public body, eminent domain is usually the last resort; most of the "deals" are made as ordinary sales.

Taxation. The state can also regulate and direct land utilization incidental to its power of taxation. "The power to tax involves the power to destroy," said Chief Justice Marshall, but the same power may also be used to guide and induce private activity.[1] Taxation has been used as a means of social control in New Zealand, where a graduated land tax was designed to break up large estates. Some states have used tax exemption of houses to stimulate building construction; others have exempted wood lots on farms from taxation, provided they are managed and utilized according to a law.

In conclusion, society has at its disposal the means to interpret the rights of property—public and private—and to set its metes and bounds. The state can change the number of rights in the bundle assigned to owners, landlords, tenants, mortgagors, mortgagees in such a way as to secure an equitable system of land tenure, promote the best utilization of land, conserve the natural resources, and insure an equitable distribution of the income from land. It has the power to change private to public property, or vice versa, and to use taxation in order to secure the same ends.

[1] Marshall was quoted as saying, "the power to tax *is* the power to destroy," by Justice Miller in *Citizens Saving and Loan Association* v. *Topeka,* and this version has become the oft quoted axiom. Marshall actually made the statement in the famous *McCulloch* v. *Maryland* case.

V

THE ECONOMICS OF LAND UTILIZATION

Most of the world lives under a regime of private property in land. This means that the owner is generally free to use his land as he pleases, and that his selection of land uses depends on the forces that direct his own preferences and activities. As a rule the operator aims to make the land yield the highest net return to himself. This does not mean, however, that in a capitalistic society the landowner is directed entirely by economic pressure. Institutional factors, customs, and sentiment may be just as powerful as costs and prices in deciding the pattern of land utilization. Nor is the private landowner always permitted to use the land as he wishes. Society uses the police power, taxation, and the right of eminent domain to modify and direct land uses. Zoning ordinances, for instance, may confine all land within a certain area to residential use, even though an individual owner could make more money by using his lot for a filling station.

Another instance of land usage which is more or less uninfluenced by prices and costs is self-sufficing agriculture. If *complete* self-sufficiency prevailed the farmer would select his crops so as to provide himself with an abundance of food, clothing, and shelter. The significant fact about subsistence or self-sufficing farming is that prices have no influence on the choice of crops; the land use pattern is determined by the needs and preferences of the individual. However, except in the most primitive regions, there is always some contact between the farmer and the commercial world, some buying and selling, and therefore a relationship to the "price system." To the extent that agriculture is commercial it is dominated by the action and reaction of prices as they affect the individual operator, which in turn determines the use of the land. As a matter of fact, very little agriculture is either completely self-sufficing or entirely commercial, and therefore the utilization of land is actually the result of both factors.

PROPORTIONALITY: RENT AND VALUE OF LAND

Proportioning the Factors of Production. In the discussion of diminishing returns it was pointed out that the output of land is not a fixed amount of products or services but depends upon the number of inputs of labor and capital which the operator places on a given area. Table 7 indicates that from 5 to 324 units of produce can be raised on one acre, contingent upon the inputs which range from 1 to 18. This is stating the problem in purely physical terms: the number of inputs the operator actually chooses to make depends upon the relative costs of land, labor, and capital on the one hand, and the price, or anticipated price, of the product on the other.

In order to demonstrate the reaction of prices on inputs, yields, and production, it is well to reduce the problem to its essential features; to state it in rather oversimplified terms and base its solution upon given premises. Let us assume that the producer makes those choices which will give him the greatest net return or the smallest loss. For the sake of simplicity it is assumed that the operator raises but one crop and that he is familiar with the schedule of increasing returns from land. Furthermore, since decisions have to be made before the price of the product and the cost of the outlays are known, the operator must base his decisions on anticipated costs and income. This assumption, at least, is realistic!

Let us return to the *Isolated State* and select five spots at various distances from the city from A to E (Table 9 and Figure 8). The price of wheat varies from $1.00 to 30 cents because of the distance to the market, for reasons already discussed in the former chapter. Since the land is assumed to be perfectly uniform physically, the physical reaction of inputs to land is the same everywhere, whether at A or E. The soil is capable of yielding from 3 to 40 bushels per acre, depending upon the number of inputs the operator places on the acre. Column 3 of the table indicates that the law of diminishing returns so operates that the increments per given unit of input increase up to the fourth input and then decrease until the tenth adds only one bushel to the total product. The eleventh probably adds nothing or may even cause a decrease in the total product. So much for the physical aspects of the problem.

Let us assume further that land is free but is "fixed" in area, i.e., labor and capital inputs are the variable factor while land is

TABLE 9

PROPORTIONING THE FACTORS OF PRODUCTION, AND RENT ON A GIVEN AREA OF LAND AT VARYING PRICES FOR THE PRODUCT

INPUTS	TOTAL PRODUCT	INCREMENT	E	D	C	B	A
			Value of the Increment @				
			30¢	40¢	50¢	70¢	$1.00
1	3	3	$ .90	$ 1.20	$ 1.50	$ 2.10	$ 3.00
2	7	4	1.20	1.60	2.00	2.80	4.00
3	12	5	1.50	2.00	2.50	3.50	5.00
4	19	7	2.10	2.80	3.50	4.90	7.00
5	25	6	1.80	2.40	3.00	4.20	6.00
6	30	5	1.50	2.00	2.50	3.50	5.00
7	34	4	1.20	1.60	2.00	2.80	4.00
8	37	3	.90	1.20	1.50	2.10	3.00
9	39	2	.60	.80	1.00	1.40	2.00
10	40	1	.30	.40	.50	.70	1.00
Value of Product.............			5.70	12.00	17.00	25.90	39.00
Cost of Inputs @$2.00 per input..			8.00	12.00	14.00	16.00	18.00
Excess Income over Inputs (Rent).			−2.30	0	3.00	9.90	21.00

held "fixed" at one acre. Labor and capital can be obtained in unrestricted quantities but cost $2.00 per composite input at all points in the State. It is also assumed that these inputs are highly divisible and can be applied in equal small "doses," as is indicated by the $2.00 per unit of cost. Finally, we will also postulate identical efficiency of management for all five tracts so that it cannot be said that differences in income or productivity are "due to the man."

At D, wheat is worth 40 cents per bushel. This price determines the value of each increment due to inputs worth $2.00 per unit. It will be observed that the operator can afford to go beyond the point of the greatest increment down to the sixth input, which brings 5 bushels—just enough to pay for the cost of

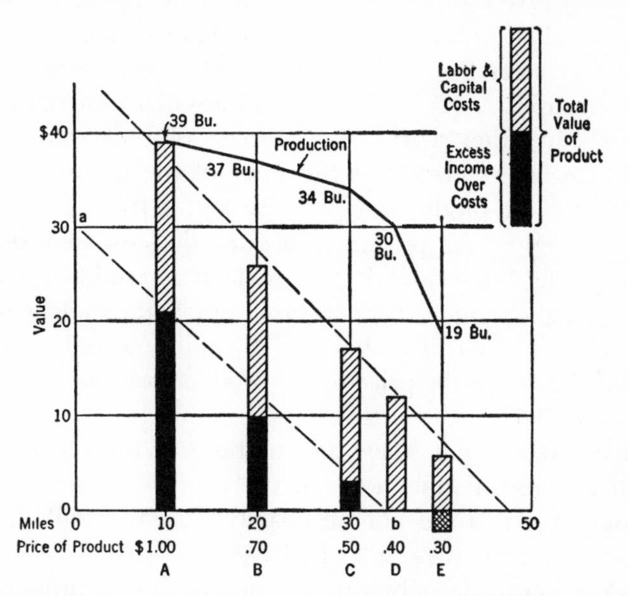

FIG. 8. PROPORTIONING THE FACTORS OF PRODUCTION, AND RENT ON A GIVEN AREA OF LAND WITH VARYING PRICES FOR THE PRODUCT

that particular input. The next input returns only 4 bushels, which is not enough to repay the cost at the price wheat sells for at D. The *total* cost of the six inputs is $12, and the total income is the same (30 bushels at 40 cents each). In other words, the operator just covers his labor-capital costs and no more.

About 30 miles from the city, at C, wheat sells for 50 cents, and a similar calculation indicates that the operator increases the intensity of land use by expending seven units of labor and capital, thus increasing the yield to 34 bushels. In spite of the greater cost of production ($14 per acre), there is a surplus of $3.00 over labor and capital costs. It is evident that wheat growers at B and at all other points still nearer the city can profitably increase their inputs and costs of production over those of C or D, obtain greater yields, and have a still greater surplus above labor-capital costs. Those attempting to grow wheat beyond 35 miles, where wheat sells below 40 cents a bushel, will not even make enough to cover labor-capital costs. In other words, D is the *margin* for wheat production.

The results of the interaction of prices on costs in land utilization, with a given area of land and price of inputs as shown by Table 9 and Figure 8, can be summarized as follows: (1) Physical production varies from 19 to 39 bushels, depending upon the number of inputs. (2) The same land absorbs from 4 to 9 units of input. In other words, the *capacity* of the land to absorb profitably becomes greater as the price of the product increases. (3) The cost of production per acre varies from $8.00 to $18; again, the higher the price, the greater the cost of production. (4) A specific labor-capital ratio to land is established at each point, i.e., a given *intensity of culture* or of land use, depending on prices. (5) The surplus above labor-capital costs becomes progressively greater as the price of the product increases.

As a corollary of these principles it should be noted that yields in agriculture are not solely an attribute of the fertility of the soil but are also, if not more so, the result of costs and prices. Decreases in yields are not necessarily a sign of soil depletion; they may be merely the result of a lower intensity of use prompted by lower prices for farm products or higher costs of inputs. A rise in price stimulates greater intensity of production on every acre of land in use and makes profitable the use of land below the extensive margin, D. It may be that the response to the new price will be such that a heavy increase of products takes place, prices fall, and a new adjustment has to be made.

This example also illustrates the difference between economic and physical space. Space itself is not scarce, but space that can serve as a factor of production is. It makes little difference to the people in the city whether the land beyond the margin is limited to a few thousand square miles or whether it is unlimited; they cannot expect to obtain any products from it as long as the land lies beyond the margin set by the cost of transportation. Economic space is also scarce because nations and states have definite boundaries; so have farms and city lots, and the organization of individual enterprises and the use of land by peoples must function within these space limitations.

Rent. Table 9 and Figure 8 show that certain parts of the State are so situated that the price of wheat is high enough to leave a surplus above the outlays for labor and capital. This residual above the cost of the inputs is the share of the total income assignable to land, differences in management being ignored for the present. This excess or residual is *economic rent,* also called "ground rent" to distinguish it from the rent of buildings or the hire of automobiles and other capital goods. "The rent of land may be defined to be that portion of the value of the whole produce which remains to the owner of the land, after all the outgoings belonging to its cultivation, of whatever kind, have been paid, including the profits of the capital employed, estimated according to the usual and ordinary rate of the profits of agricultural capital at the time being," is the statement of Thomas Robert Malthus. Later he simplifies the definition by saying that it is "the excess of value of the whole produce, or if estimated in money, the excess of the price of the whole produce, above what is necessary to pay the wages of labor and the profits of capital employed in cultivation." [1]

Applying this concept of rent to Table 9 and Figure 8, it will be noted that no such surplus is assignable to land at D, the marginal land, and to try to use land at E results in a loss or "negative rent." At C, where wheat sells for 50 cents a bushel, an economic rent of $3.00 emerges, and a still larger sum results on all lands nearer the city than C.

Rent and Differences in Physical Productivity. In assuming uniform physical conditions for the Isolated State, the influence of location was segregated from other factors. However, other influences besides location determine land uses. In agriculture

[1] Malthus, *Principles of Political Economy, op. cit.,* p. 136. The term rent has not always been used to designate the income assignable to land. The French use it to include the income from any kind of property, and the Germans speak of "ground" rent and "capital" rent, or interest as the term prevails in English usage. Some English and American economists, noting that the "differential," first observed in land, was universal, speak of the "rent element" in wages and profits, and even "consumer rents." Were it not for the fact that economic terminology has insisted on calling the income of the landowner *rent,* for the sake of avoiding confusion the phrase *land income* would be the better term. The concept of rent as stated above was expressed by Malthus in 1815, two years before Ricardo published his *Principles of Political Economy and Taxation.*

and forest culture differences in soil, climate, topography, and other physical factors are such that two tracts respond very differently to the inputs of labor and capital. This likewise introduces differences in intensity of use, production, income, and rent.

To illustrate this Table 10 is presented, in which the price of wheat is assumed to be 50 cents per bushel and the cost of

TABLE 10

DIFFERENCES IN PRODUCTIVENESS AND RENT ON LANDS OF DIFFERENT QUALITY

Inputs	A		B		C	
	Total Product	Increments	Total Product	Increments	Total Product	Increments
1	3	3	3	3	1	1
2	8	5	7	4	4	3
3	14	6	12	5	8	4
4	21	7	19	7	13	5
5	29	8	25	6	20	7
6	38	9	30	5	24	4
7	44	6	34	4	27	2
8	48	4	37	3	29	1
9	51	3	39	2	29	0
10	53	2	40	1		
Value of Total Product @ 50¢ per Bushel	$24.00		$17.00		$12.00	
Cost of Inputs @ $2.00	16.00		14.00		12.00	
Rent	8.00		3.00		0.00	
Cost of Production per Bushel (excluding Rent)	.333		.411		.50	

the inputs $2.00 as in Table 9. In this case prices and costs are held constant, the varying factors being differences in productivity, causing differences in increments per unit of input. Not all the calculations are shown in the table, but by using the same method as was employed in Table 9, A is seen to have the capacity to absorb 8 inputs and produces 48 bushels of wheat. The value of the total product less the cost of the inputs leaves a rent of $8.00. Each of the other grades of land absorbs fewer inputs and produces fewer bushels, and, while B yields a rent of $3.00, C is "no-rent land."

Every acre of land is subject to the influence of both location and productivity, and rent and value are the result or composite of both. Poor land with a good location may find its most profitable use for intensive crops such as fruits, vegetables, and truck. On the other hand, land below the margin at D in Table 9 will become supermarginal if the quality of the land is such that its labor-capital costs are below 25 cents per bushel.

Gradations in land due to differences in fertility or location are not the cause of rent; they merely explain why one tract produces more income than another. To make this clear let us assume a hypothetical zone of definitely limited area around a city with land having uniform physical qualities and with differences in location eliminated completely. Rent would not arise as long as any part of the area was not used. The price of the products could not rise above the expense of production, represented by the labor-capital costs, say, 25 cents per bushel for wheat. However, if the demand continues to increase after the entire area is in use, the scarcity of wheat will cause the price to rise above 25 cents, and rent will arise simultaneously over the entire area. The demand will be met by a more intensive use of the limited zone, since no new land is available under our hypothesis. Rent arises as soon as land becomes *scarce,* whether this is absolute scarcity or whether the scarcity is caused by costs of transportation, or by the fact that the operator has to cultivate land where inputs are rewarded with less productivity than on the better land.[1] The gradations in land quality, such as those of the National Resources Board, become of economic significance when inputs of labor and capital are applied to the various grades and rents and values become established on the basis of productivity. Land as physical nature is not scarce, but A grade land is scarce, only 5.3 per cent of the United States being classed as such. It therefore commands the highest rents and values.

[1] Note that rent is defined as the differential and not as the difference between the total return and the cost of utilization in the following: "Each site tends to be put to the use whereby it will yield the maximum total return over the costs involved in utilizing it. These costs include, among other things, such returns in the form of profits as are necessary to attract business ability. The differential remaining, which is due to the superiority of the profit-making opportunities afforded by one site as compared to another, is rent, and is put into the hands of the landlords by the competition of entrepreneurs for the best opportunities."—Edward Chamberlin, *The Theory of Monopolistic Competition, op. cit.,* p. 203.

Value of Land. Because supermarginal land yields an income, competition sets in for the right to own and use it. In this competition a price is established which tends to hold a direct relationship to economic rent. If buyers and sellers expect future rents to be a series of relatively stable incomes, the present or "lump sum" value of these anticipated incomes is expressed by the "capitalization" formula, $v = \frac{a}{r}$, in which *a* is the annual rent and *r* the current rate of interest. Thus an acre of farm land expected to yield $5.00 rent over a long period of time, capitalized at 5 per cent, would sell for $100. On the other hand, if buyers and sellers expect land incomes to increase in the future, this hope will be reflected in the selling price of the farm and the market price of the same land may reach $150 or $200 per acre. It should be emphasized that the value of land is always a reflection of its *future* productivity as estimated by buyers and sellers. Thus cut-over land, which has no present income-producing use and which everyone recognizes cannot be brought into such use for decades, nevertheless has a price in the market. Vacant urban or farm land yields no economic rent, yet sells at a figure which reflects its *expected* income-yielding qualities. Farm land near cities sells on the basis of anticipated urban uses rather than on capitalized agricultural rents.

For the sake of separating the "anticipated value" from that established by capitalizing present income, the term *productive value* has been applied to that part of the value of a farm obtained by the formula $v = \frac{a}{r}$, and *anticipated value* to that part based upon expectation of an increase in rents. The formula embodying both is $v = \frac{a}{r} + (\text{or} -) \frac{i}{r^2}$, in which *i* is the anticipated annual *increase* in rents. However, sometimes land income is expected to *decrease*, hence both the + and the — in the formula.[1]

The farmer is sometimes willing to pay for qualities of a given farm not included in the money income. A beautiful view, nearness to the church of his choice or to a good school, a desirable neighborhood are subtle factors which enter into land values and

[1] E. H. Wiecking, "Farm Real Estate Values and Farm Income," *Annals of the American Academy of Political and Social Science,* March, 1930, pp. 233–45.

are called *amenity values*. Amenity values may subtract as well as add to the purely economic values as established by rents. The market price of a given farm becomes a composite of productive, anticipated, and amenity values.[1]

Some land is not a factor of production but is a consumption good, such as owner-occupied residential lots and recreational land. Here the value is almost all amenity value. In this case direct competition for the land—or supply and demand—sets the price, although rentable value may also be imputed to this type of land and capitalized.

The above is a streamlined statement of two very complex and even debatable subjects, rent and value. It should be emphasized that the value of land is the result or end-product of a series of price and cost relationships, going from the cost of labor-capital inputs and price of the products of land, through rent, to estimation of the course of *future* rents, then value. The price of land is determined by the price of the products and not the reverse.[2]

Proportionality, Rent and Value with the Factors "Flexible." So far the proportioning of the factors has been based upon the premise that the operator had a fixed area (one acre) upon which he placed varying numbers of inputs of labor and capital. Land was considered to be free, but labor and capital had to be paid for and it was assumed that the operator would keep on adding inputs until the last unit just paid for itself. Under this assumption a certain ratio of labor-capital inputs to land was established and a given rent emerged. However, it is necessary to consider other conditions which are not "always equal," and other circumstances. To do so Table 11 is presented, an elaboration of Table 7 used in connection with the discussion of diminishing returns. New columns have been added, introducing a price of 10 cents per unit of product and $1.00 as the price of each input. The first six columns show the interaction of prices and costs with land free, and the remaining three columns with a rent of $10 per acre.

With land rent-free, the operator may be more interested in get-

[1] The English recognize amenity, prestige, monopoly, and sporting values, as well as agricultural values, in a given tract of farm land. C. Dampier Whetham, "The Land and the Nation," *Economic Journal*, March, 1926.

[2] Note the reasoning in the following quotation from a newspaper: "As population increases the price of land rises steadily inevitably. The result is that the price of farm products also rises."

Table 11

PROPORTIONING THE FACTORS OF PRODUCTION

1 "Inputs" Units of Expenditure of Labor and Capital	2 Output or Product	3 Value of Output or Product at 10¢ a lb.	4 Increases Due to a Given Unit of Input or "Increment"	5 Value of "Increment"	6 Average per Dollar of Labor and Capital	7 Value Units of Expenditure and $10 Rent	8 Average per Dollar of Rent	9 Average per Dollar of All Expenses
1	5	$ .50	5	$ .50	$ .50	$11	$ .05	$ .04
2	20	2.00	15	1.50	1.00	12	.20	.16
3	45	4.50	25	2.50	1.50	13	.45	.34
4	80	8.00	35	3.50	2.00	14	.80	.57
5	125	12.50	45	4.50	2.50	15	1.25	.83
6	162	16.20	37	3.70	2.70	16	1.62	1.01
7	196	19.60	34	3.40	*2.80*	17	1.96	1.14
8	224	22.40	28	2.80	*2.80*	18	2.24	1.24
9	243	24.30	19	1.90	2.70	19	2.43	1.29
10	260	26.00	17	1.70	2.60	20	2.60	1.30
11	275	27.50	15	1.50	2.50	21	2.75	*1.31*
12	288	28.80	13	1.30	2.40	22	2.88	1.30
13	299	29.90	11	1.10	2.30	23	2.99	1.29
14	308	30.80	9	.90	2.20	24	3.08	1.28
15	315	31.50	7	.70	2.10	25	3.15	1.26
16	*320*	32.00	5	.50	2.00	26	3.20	1.23
17	323	32.30	3	.30	1.90	27	3.23	1.19
18	324	32.40	1	.10	1.80	28	*3.24*	1.15
19	323	32.30	−1	−.10	1.70	29	3.23	1.11
20	320	32.00	−3	−.30	1.60	30	3.20	1.06

ting the highest return per dollar of his investment, i.e., in labor and capital, rather than in carrying the inputs until the last unit just pays for itself. For instance, column 6 shows that if he employs 7 or 8 units of input he will receive $2.80 for every dollar invested. If he goes to the thirteenth unit (which just pays for itself), he receives only $2.30 for each dollar invested. However, inasmuch as he has a fixed area of land and no other opportunity to use the extra 5 units of labor and capital, he will be better off to use them than not to use them on this acre. He will be ahead as long as the value of the increments exceeds the cost of the inputs. The subsistence farmer thinking in terms of his own labor and time instead of money costs may even go to the eighteenth input, adding labor as long as it returns anything at all. On the other hand, he may prefer to take his leisure rather than cultivate in the hot sun, especially when the last cultivations add only a few pounds to the total. Likewise, the farmer who can get "outside" work may balance the income from this source against possible returns from extra efforts on his farm.

So far it has also been assumed that the operator was restricted to a given area of land and therefore would find it profitable to intensify his culture. To the extent, however, that land is not restricted in area, the operator will not carry the inputs until the last unit just pays for itself but will aim for the greatest return per dollar of the valued factors. By doing so he achieves not only this purpose but also the highest total production at the lowest cost. For instance, to use 16 inputs on one acre would yield only 320 units of output and return $2.00 for every dollar of labor and capital; placing 8 units on 2 acres would result in a total output of 448 units of product and a return of $2.80 for every dollar expended. Should the operator be restricted to 10 units of input, he would still be better off to put the first 8 units on one acre and the other 2 units on one-fourth of another acre. Any other combination of labor and capital with land would result in less total productivity and a lower return per dollar of investment.

Carrying the inputs until the last unit just pays for itself brings the highest production per acre, but stopping at the point of greatest return per input results in the greatest production in terms of labor and capital, which usually also means *per man*.

It is to the interest of the operator to aim at the greatest production per man rather than per acre. These two points mark the upper and lower limits of profitable combination, the actual point at a given time being determined by the relative flexibility of the factors and their costs.

Proportioning cannot be divorced from the question of the relative fixity or flexibility of the factors of production. In a densely settled agricultural country, where additional land cannot be bought or rented, the operator with abundant labor has no choice but to use his labor lavishly until the last application adds nothing to the total product. At the other extreme is the ranchman in the "free grass" days, with no restrictions on the area he wanted to graze. With a given herd and outfit, more or less inflexible, he spread his operations over a vast domain until the last units of land grazed added nothing to total production.

Sometimes labor may be the most inflexible factor of the three. With the family as the unit, and no outside labor available, the labor force is fixed because the farmer cannot "fire" his family. Hence he selects the enterprises, if not the size of his farm, to fit the man power afforded by himself, his wife, and his children. In the plantation area of the South this adjustment is most easily made; the landlord gauges the size of the tract he rents to a tenant by the labor the family can deliver at the peak loads of chopping and picking the cotton. This practice becomes an inducement to rear large families among the poorest croppers and renters. On the other hand, the mere existence of a large "force" measured in terms of the size of the family is not an adequate measure of the labor power of the family. It is important to know how many members are hunting and fishing and how many are actually working and for how many days and hours.

Temporarily the area of a given farm may be fixed because of inheritance, land laws, or the impossibility of buying or renting more land. That farmers are trying to adjust the size of their farms is shown by the fact that in 1935 almost 700,000 farmers rented land to supplement their "owned" acres.

The pressure for larger farms has become more intense since the tractor and other large-scale farm machinery have made extensive farm enterprises more profitable. However, considerable flexibility exists within the farm. The operator can shift from intensive to extensive crops or even shrink his working acreage by letting some of the fields lie idle. In urban land the size of lots and the division of the land into a multitude of ownerships tend to make the area for a given operator a fixed one.

Capital may be fixed for some operators. Young farmers who have bought land without too much money may find that they have sunk the bulk of their cash in land and left an insufficient amount for tools, machinery, animals, and other equipment. For a time, at least, the ratio of labor-capital inputs to land is too low and the full services of the land are not realized. Every operator makes the best combination possible under the circumstances of price and availability of the factors, resulting in a given intensity of culture, volume of production, and rent, which might well be different if he had the opportunity to make the ideal combination.

Influence of the Size of the Units of Input on Proportionality. In the discussion so far it was presumed that the operator could obtain labor and capital in small, equal doses. It is true that fertilizer can be applied in units of any size from a few pounds to several tons per acre, but the farmer must use a whole tractor, combine, or mower. Office buildings grow by stories; the builder cannot add "a few dollars' worth" of building. For this reason, inflexibility in the size of the units of capital often determines the organization and the size of the enterprise. In cotton farming, the mule and the plow are often the deciding factors. Instead of a given area of land to which the operator adds mule after mule, the situation is just the reverse. Land is the divisible factor, and the work animal becomes the unit to which the area is adjusted. Table 12 shows that the optimum number of crop acres per mule is 20 to 23. An acreage greater or smaller than the optimum results in lower returns measured in the money income per mule or percentage return on the investment.[1]

At the other extreme are the mechanized wheat farms of Montana; they also indicate increasing, optimum, and decreasing returns as more or less land is associated with a given unit of equipment. According to tests made by the Montana Agricultural Experiment Station in 1927, the minimum practical unit of power

[1] A. G. Smith, "A Farm Management Study in Anderson County, South Carolina" (U. S. Dept. of Agriculture, Bulletin 651, 1918), p. 17.

TABLE 12

RELATION OF CROP AREA PER WORK ANIMAL TO FARM EFFICIENCY [1]

Number of Crop Acres per Work Animal	No. of Farms	Percentage Return on Investment	Income per Mule
11 or less	7	2.64%	$238
12–15	13	3.30	267
16–19	33	3.67	324
20–23	26	4.32	422
24–27	23	3.62	396
28 or more	6	2.86	386

for the family farm was a three-plow tractor with its outfit of equipment operating 800 acres of land. This acreage was the optimum; variations in either direction caused reductions in net income. Other sizes of power had their own optimum acreage; the four-plow tractor with 1,100 acres, six-plow with 1,800, and twelve-plow with 3,000 acres gave the best results in low-cost operations.[2]

Influence of the Value of Land on Proportionality. For the sake of establishing the principles of proportionality step by step, the price of land, either as a purchase price or annual rent, has so far been ignored. However, the operator has to consider the value of land at all times. Until the Homestead Act of 1862, even the federal and state governments asked a price for raw land. Competition for the land has driven the price up to the full capitalized value of its income, in fact, many times above this value, through speculation and other factors.

How will land costs affect the operator's decisions in combining the factors? Table 11 can serve to make this clear. In column 7 a rent of $10 is introduced, making the first outlay $11 instead of $1.00. All other inputs are $10 higher than the corresponding input in column 1.

If land is obtainable in any quantity, the object will be to get the highest return for every dollar of *total* investment. Column 9 indicates that this takes place with 11 units of input, 3 inputs

[1] *Ibid.*

[2] E. A. Starch, "Experiments in the Use of Large Scale Machinery under Montana Conditions," *Journal of Farm Economics,* April, 1932, pp. 336, 338, 340.

TABLE 13

SUMMARY OF INVESTMENT COST, GROSS AND NET INCOME, AND RETURN UPON INVESTMENT WITH BUILDINGS OF VARYING HEIGHTS[1]

(Assuming land value at $200 per square foot)

	8-Story Building	15-Story Building	22-Story Building	30-Story Building	37-Story Building	50-Story Building	63-Story Building	75-Story Building
Investment			(in	thousands	of dollars)			
A. Land (81,000 sq. ft. @ $200)	$16,200	$16,200	$16,200	$16,200	$16,200	$16,200	$16,200	$16,200
B. Building	4,769	7,307	9,310	11,775	13,808	16,537	19,390	22,558
C. Carrying Charges:								
1. Interest during construction:								
(a) Land (6% on cost for full period)	810	972	1,134	1,296	1,458	1,620	1,780	1,944
(b) Building (6% on cost for half period)	119	219	326	471	622	826	1,065	1,353
2. Taxes during construction—Land	292	350	408	466	524	584	642	700
3. Insurance during construction	3	5	8	12	21	35	65	95
Total Carrying Charges	$ 1,224	$ 1,546	$ 1,876	$ 2,245	$ 2,625	$ 3,065	$ 3,552	$ 4,092
D. Grand Total Cost	22,193	25,053	27,386	30,220	32,633	35,802	39,142	42,850
Total assignable to Land	17,302	17,522	17,742	17,962	18,182	18,404	18,622	18,844
Total assignable to Building	4,891	7,531	9,644	12,258	14,451	17,398	20,520	24,006
Income								
E. Gross Income	1,819	2,780	3,483	4,181	4,755	5,581	6,302	6,901
F. Expenses:								
1. Operating	311	482	592	723	814	942	1,058	1,213
2. Taxes	479	541	591	653	725	774	846	926
3. Depreciation	95	146	186	235	276	331	388	451
Total Expenses	$ 885	$ 1,169	$ 1,369	$ 1,611	$ 1,795	$ 2,047	$ 2,292	$ 2,590
G. Net Income	934	1,611	2,114	2,570	2,960	3,534	4,010	4,311
Net Return								
H. Net Return on Total Investment	4.22%	6.44%	7.73%	8.50%	9.07%	9.87%	10.25%	10.16%

[1] Based on Table 1, Clark and Kingston, *The Skyscraper, op. cit.*, p. 21.

more than when only labor and capital were considered as valued factors. If he has more than 11 units of labor and capital, the operator will do well to put the excess on another acre or fraction of an acre at the same 11-to-1 ratio. He will depart from this ratio if one or the other factor is "fixed." For instance, if restricted in area the operator will again carry his units of input until the last "dose" just pays for itself, namely the 13th unit of input of Table 11.

In applying this to actual business conditions, the return is expressed in percentage of the total investment. Table 13 and

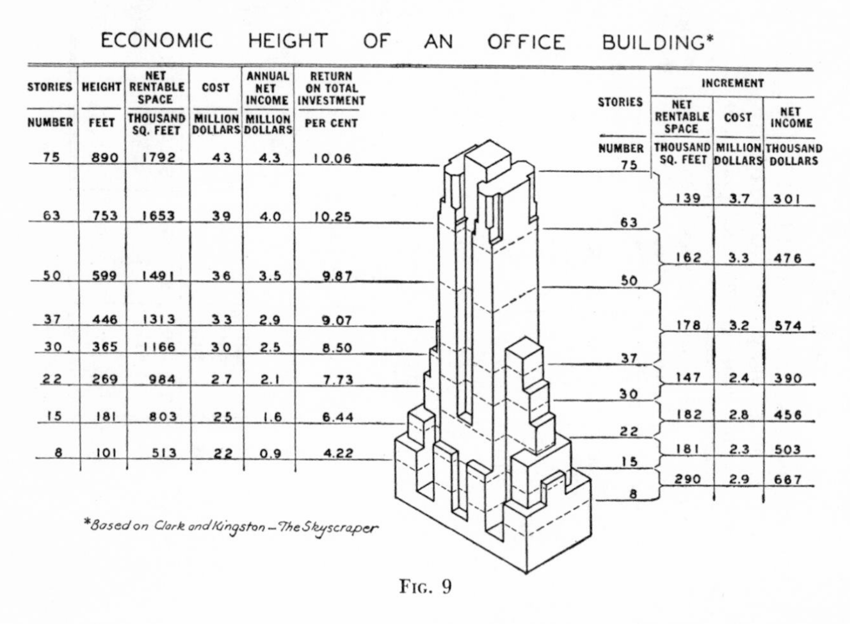

ECONOMIC HEIGHT OF AN OFFICE BUILDING*

STORIES	HEIGHT	NET RENTABLE SPACE	COST	ANNUAL NET INCOME	RETURN ON TOTAL INVESTMENT
NUMBER	FEET	THOUSAND SQ. FEET	MILLION DOLLARS	MILLION DOLLARS	PER CENT
75	890	1792	43	4.3	10.06
63	753	1653	39	4.0	10.25
50	599	1491	36	3.5	9.87
37	446	1313	33	2.9	9.07
30	365	1166	30	2.5	8.50
22	269	984	27	2.1	7.73
15	181	803	25	1.6	6.44
8	101	513	22	0.9	4.22

STORIES	INCREMENT		
	NET RENTABLE SPACE	COST	NET INCOME
NUMBER	THOUSAND SQ. FEET	MILLION DOLLARS	THOUSAND DOLLARS
75			
	139	3.7	301
63			
	162	3.3	476
50			
	178	3.2	574
37			
	147	2.4	390
30			
	182	2.8	456
22			
	181	2.3	503
15			
	290	2.9	667
8			

*Based on Clark and Kingston—The Skyscraper

Fig. 9

Figure 9 show the proportioning of a building to land in the case of a skyscraper. On land valued at about $16,000,000 successive inputs in the form of stories are placed, at costs indicated in the table. The return on the investment for the 8-story building is only 4.22 per cent. It rises to an optimum of 10.25 per cent for the 63-story structure; after this the return declines and a projected income curve indicates that the net income will vanish entirely at a height of 131 stories.[1]

The fact that tall buildings or intensive use of land are associated with high land values gives the impression that high rents and

[1] Clark and Kingston, *op. cit.*, pp. 24–25.

land values force the operator to intensify his land use. Table 11 shows that with a $10 rent the operator finds it profitable to use 3 more units of input than when land is free. Table 13 likewise shows that the services of the land, at a given demand for those services, will not be released unless the proper building is placed upon the site. To this extent the operator is forced to intensify his land use because any other combination of building with land would yield a lower income than the optimum.

Calculations of the economic height of skyscrapers as illustrated in Table 13 indicate that while a 63-story skyscraper on land worth $16,000,000 is the most profitable height, on higher priced land a 75-story building is more profitable. It should be pointed out, however, that this holds true only if the price paid for the land accurately reflects its earning power and is not a speculative value. If a 63-story office building is erected on land valued at $16,000,000, of which $6,000,000 is "inflated," the operator not only has the task of paying for the extra six millions but he has an uneconomic building with which to do it.

Furthermore, these calculations are based on a given level of office rents and do not take into consideration the possible effect of the addition of one and a half million square feet of office space on the rental market of the city. Should the market be depressed appreciably thereby, the 63-story building will prove to be uneconomical for the site.

The tall office building and the illustrations used in Tables 9 and 11 also leave the impression that intensity of use and high capacity of land are always associated with high rents and land values. This is not necessarily true. Sometimes a small application of labor and capital will bring forth production of high value, leaving a large difference between the values of inputs and product to be assigned to land as rent and capitalized into land values. This is strikingly illustrated in urban land uses. Within a given area of very similar land values, an office building, a hotel, a department store, a theater, a filling station, and even a parking lot may exist side by side. Each structure is suited to its particular use, yet the height of the building and capacity of the land are merely incidental to that use and all uses release the services of the land equally well. The office building sells space (and services which make the space usable—heat, light, elevators, etc.), and to get the maximum of space economically a towering structure is necessary. The department store sells merchandise and space is subordinate to that function; the result is a building of moderate height. In this case the capacity of the land is much less than for the skyscraper; it is still less for the filling station and is practically non-existent for the parking lot.

The productivity of land is two-dimensional and consists of *capacity* and *efficiency*.[1] The latter refers to the ratio of output to input and is illustrated by the $2.80 return per $1.00 of input in Table 11. Some land can absorb only a few inputs of labor and capital but each unit returns a large output; the reverse is true for other types of land use. The skyscraper calls for high capacity and a moderate efficiency, or return per unit of labor and capital, whereas the filling station can operate at a low capacity but has extremely high returns for every dollar of input. In fact, it is not usual to think in terms of return to labor-capital inputs at all in this case.

The same differences in capacity and efficiency of land may be found in agriculture. While land about cities is usually cultivated intensively, rye, an "extensively" grown crop, finds a place on the farms of eastern New York, New Jersey, and Pennsylvania because the demand for straw for bedding, packing fruit trees, and pottery, and for the manufacture of straw articles is such that it can compete with more intensive uses and hold its position on high priced land.[2] Another comparison may be made between the cotton section and the Corn Belt. The former has small farms, large families per farm, much hand labor, and, in some sections, intensive use of fertilizer, yet land values are relatively low. Iowa has large farms, small farm families, large-scale machinery operations—all evidences of lower intensity of land use than in the South—yet this state has the highest farm values for the entire country.[3] However, if the residual character of rent is kept in mind, these facts are not difficult to explain.

[1] Henry C. Taylor, *Outlines of Agricultural Economics* (New York, Macmillan, 1931), Chap. XI; John D. Black, *Introduction to Production Economics* (New York, Holt, 1926), Chap. 13. See also Peterson, *Diminishing Returns and Planned Economy, op. cit.*, pp. 59–64.

[2] Vernon C. Finch and O. E. Baker, *Geography of the World's Agriculture* (Washington, U. S. Dept. of Agriculture, 1917), p. 27.

[3] Conrad H. Hammar, "Intensity and Land Rent: An Overlooked Aspect of Economic Theory," *Journal of Farm Economics*, November, 1938, pp. 776–91.

The Factor of Management in Rent. In the presentation thus far management has been held as a uniform, constant factor. However, experience shows that two farmers expending the same inputs may achieve very dissimilar results. Simply more intelligent use of time, materials, and land will secure greater production at lower per unit costs, and shrewd marketing may bring a higher price for the product. In urban buildings the combined efforts of promoter, architect, and building manager may create an exceptionally beautiful and efficient structure at the same cost as an ordinary and uninteresting building. The returns from the former may be such that the capitalized income exceeds the purchase price of the land plus the cost of constructing the building. The difference between the two has been called "improved value." On the other hand, a poorly designed and inefficiently managed building may have negative "improved value."[1]

Table 9 and Figure 8 show the production of the land and the rents with the same degree of efficiency of management, but if a superior manager were in charge of any one of the tracts the surplus above labor-capital costs would be greater. Assume, for example, that the average farmer has an excess of $3.00 over labor-capital costs on C land, but that in the hands of a better farmer this surplus or residuum becomes $6.00. It might appear that the $6.00 would be absorbed by rent and capitalized. Insofar, however, as the better manager can outbid inferior or average operators, all he has to offer for the use of the land is a little above the maximum the latter can pay. An offer of $3.10 will outbid the ordinary farmer, and $2.90 goes to the more skillful manager.[2] It can be said that from the standpoint of the successful renter the $3.10 is a cost and the $2.90 a residuum. From the landlord's point of view, however, the $2.90 may be considered a cost, i.e., the sum necessary to attract the superior farmer, and the residuum will be land income or rent.[3] This assumes that the competition for a given piece of land is between men of different levels of ability; should several tenants of equal and more than average skill bid for the land, less of the surplus will go to

[1] Frederick M. Babcock, *The Valuation of Real Estate* (New York, McGraw-Hill, 1932), pp. 100–108.

[2] For a detailed statement of this principle see H. C. Taylor, *op. cit.*, Chap. XVII, "Rents and Profits."

[3] Chamberlin, *op. cit.*, p. 202.

the operator. There is always a tendency to capitalize the results of good utilization into the value of the land. "Improved value," according to Babcock, is assigned to the land and not to the building nor to the services of the men who were responsible for the superior building. "It is an interesting sidelight that because it is not necessarily more costly to build beautiful buildings and because land value is residual, the beauty of a molding may appear as land value."[1]

Institutional Factors in Rent and Value. The proportioning of the factors, rent, and value are not the result of automatically operating economic forces but are determined by human and institutional elements which form the framework within which the so-called economic forces operate. In proportioning the factors of production, a price was assumed for labor. This price is ascertainable for most urban purposes—in constructing and maintaining stores, hotels, and office buildings. But where the labor consists of the toil of a farm family it is impossible to assign a market value to "family labor," yet the manner of calculating economic rent is such that rent will be high or low in indirect proportion to the price assigned to such labor. It is almost absurd to use the capitalization formula to translate rents into values under such conditions, least of all in regions of more or less self-sufficing farming under owner-operation where the returns from all factors go to the operator.

But wherever land is leased in a commercial agriculture "contract rent," whether paid in cash or on shares, is not a theoretical residual but a definite payment for the use of land, often determined by the relative bargaining power of landlords and tenants. The superior bargaining power of the landlords and the intense competition for land under certain conditions often cause rents to arise which can be paid only by reducing the wages of the renter and his family, which in turn means a lower standard of living for the tenant. Also, races and nationalities satisfied with a low scale of living outbid those trying to maintain a high standard of living, even supplanting the farmer with higher managerial ability. Wherever landlords have the advantage over tenants, "rack" rents tend to become converted into land value.

On the other hand, sometimes the advantage lies with the

[1] *Valuation of Real Estate, op. cit.,* p. 95.

tenant, both on farms and in cities; then landlords are looking for renters instead of tenants crying for a farm, home, or office space. This has been known to happen even in such rapidly growing cities as Chicago. "Medium class houses, 7000 of which were vacant in the West Side alone in 1890, were in such poor demand in the old sections of the city as a result of the exodus to the suburbs and the growing popularity of apartments . . . that middle class as well as poor class residential land remained stationary or declined in this period." [1]

Rents are often influenced by custom and tradition. Richard Jones pointed this out when he criticized Ricardo's theory. He believed that in the majority of cases rents were not the result of economic forces at all. These he called "peasant rents," in contrast to the "farmer rents" of the more capitalistic countries.[2] It is true that in many parts of the world peasant rents prevail, and even in the United States rents are not altogether economic or "farmer" rents.

Among other institutional factors which affect land values are the amenity values mentioned above, social prestige, and the desire for security. Many people invest in land as an "anchor to the windward," feeling that investment in the solid earth is not like ephemeral stocks and bonds. The "subsistence homesteads" movement is based upon the idea of security on the land in times of depression. The fact that land values tend consistently to be above the level of values as justified by rents adds to the difficulty of paying for land and, when the land is paid for, the "inflation" means a low rate of return on the investment.

COMPETITION OF LAND USES

Competition of Land Uses in Non-Urban Areas. Having discussed the nature of rent and land income, we can now use them as tools to assist in explaining the pattern of land utilization. In Figure 8 the rents are shown by the shaded part of the bars, and the line a–b may be called the "rent line" because the distance from this line to the base is the rent for any given tract of land used for wheat culture—about $30 at a and "no rent" at b. This

[1] Homer Hoyt, *One Hundred Years of Land Values in Chicago* (Chicago, University of Chicago Press, 1933), p. 189.

[2] Richard Jones, *Peasant Rents* (London, Macmillan, 1895).

has been exaggerated for the sake of simplicity in this diagram, but in Figure 10 the rent line for wheat is more realistic, the rent being $5.00 adjacent to the city and gradually approaching the no-rent margin at 35 miles from the city, similar to conditions in the Isolated State.

However, other products will be used and demanded by the people of the city, among them corn. Let us assume that the

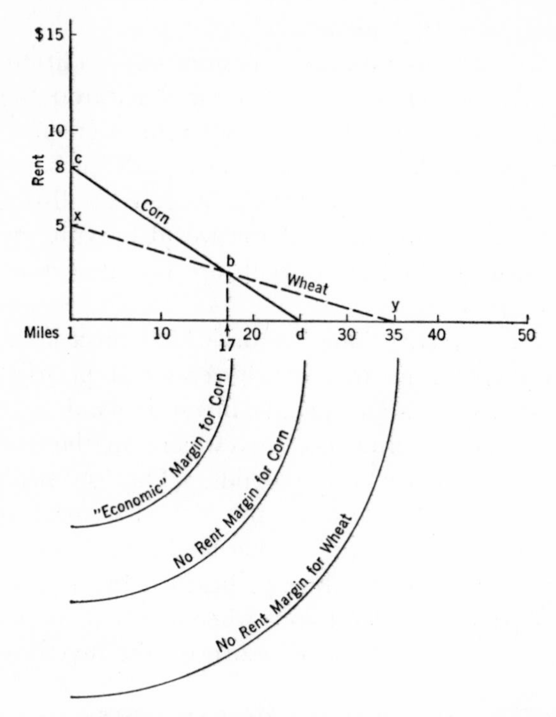

FIG. 10. RENT AND MARGINS FOR WHEAT AND CORN

price of corn and the cost of growing it is such that a rent of $8.00 per acre arises near the city, but that bulk and perishability make the cost of transportation so high that the no-rent margin is 25 miles from the market, as shown by the line c–d. With the two lines superimposed it will be seen that within a radius of 17 miles of the city corn culture produces a higher rent than wheat and will therefore occupy the land. At b, 17 miles from the city, it is a matter of indifference, but beyond this point wheat will yield more rent. b is the *margin of transference*. Thus corn cultivation ceases about 8 miles before the "no-rent corn margin" is reached. Beyond b, wheat, an extensive but more easily and cheaply transported crop, can outbid corn for the use of the land.

Figure 11 introduces a still more intensive but less easily transportable product, milk, and also ranching, a very extensive type of land use whose "products" can transport themselves if necessary. Margins of transference occur at A and C, which, pro-

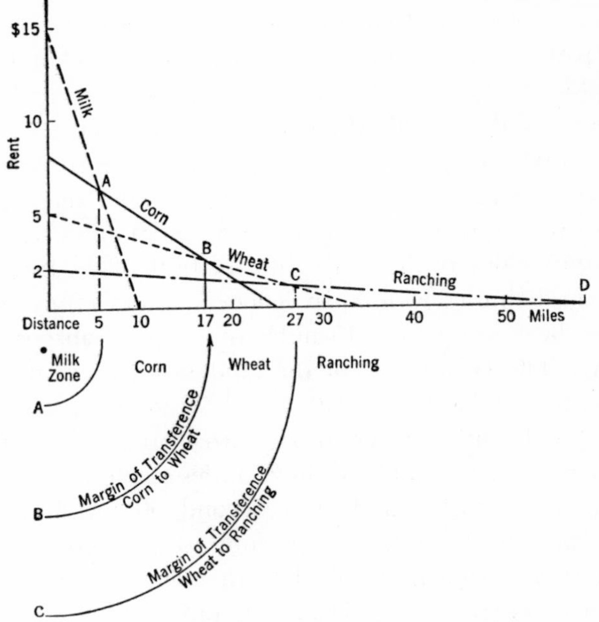

FIG. 11. COMPETITION OF LAND USES: MILK, CORN, WHEAT, AND RANCHING

jected to the base, indicate a "milk zone" of 5 miles radius, a "corn zone" between 5 and 17 miles, wheat in a concentric band 17 to 27 miles from the city, and ranching beyond that. Thus it is the competition of land uses *through rent* that explains the concentric circles of land utilization in the Isolated State. The use which can pay the highest rent at a particular place occupies the land. At the city four land uses compete, but ranching can afford to pay only $2.00 rent per acre, wheat $5.00, corn $8.00, and milk outbids them all with $15.00, therefore becoming the *highest and best use* for this zone. Between A and B corn growing is the highest use, and beyond C, cattle ranching.

Better and cheaper transportation will permit the more distant lands to come into the market. With demand unchanged, prices will come down and the "rent line" tend to flatten out, because the locational advantage of the land near the city becomes less important whereas rent emerges on the more distant lands. If the cost of transportation in time and money were reduced to zero, and the area of land were to remain unlimited, rents would disappear insofar as they are based on locational advantage. The price everywhere would fall to labor-capital costs of production.[1]

The pattern as determined by the competition of land uses and graphically pictured by von Thünen is illustrated by data in all parts of the world where wagon transportation is still in use, but usually the haul is to a railway rather than to a city. In the United States and Canada in the pre-motor age the patronage of railroads was confined to a belt 30 to 50 miles wide (15–25 miles on either side of the road), but the bulk of the freight came from a belt 10 miles wide.[2] In Rhodesia grain crops will ordinarily not bear more than 15 miles of ox-cart transportation to a railway. The occupation of the land may be extended to 25 miles if cotton, tobacco, or butter and cheese are produced, but to only 10 or 15 miles under corn (maize) production. Roughly the zones are: "farm land" within 25 miles of the railway, "ranch land," 25 to 50 miles, and land beyond 50 miles is of little practical value to the settler. The contrast of motor with wagon transportation is shown by the fact that with trucks it pays to carry tobacco as far as 300 miles to the railhead.[3]

An illustration involving physical and locational factors is found in a study of agriculture in the vicinity of Louisville, Kentucky.[4] The soils around the city are not uniform; a strip of land extending along the Ohio is almost wholly used for trucking and here soil is the predominating influence on land use. In spite of this, the power of accessibility to the market is remarkable, as is indicated by Tables 14 and 15. The latter table is set up on a

[1] Charles N. Cooley, *The Theory of Transportation,* Publications of the American Economic Association, May, 1894, Chap. 9.

[2] W. A. Mackintosh, *Prairie Settlement, The Geographical Setting* (Macmillan, Toronto, 1934), p. 55.

[3] Isaiah Bowman, *The Pioneer Fringe* (New York, American Geographical Society, 1931), pp. 216–19. For other illustrations see pp. 255, 285, 313, and 320.

[4] J. H. Arnold and Frank Montgomery, *Influence of a City on Farming,* (U. S. Dept. of Agriculture, Bulletin 678, 1918).

TABLE 14

RELATION OF DISTANCE FROM THE CITY TO SIZE OF FARM, RENTS, VALUE, AND TYPES OF CROPS[1]

Distance from Louisville (Miles)	Size of Farm (Acres)	Rent of Land per Acre	Value of Land per Acre	Percentage of Receipts from		
				Truck and Potatoes	Dairy	Other
8 or less	102	$11.85	$312	68%	10%	22%
9–11	221	5.59	110	35	12	53
12–14	256	5.37	106	34	20	46
15 or more	257	4.66	95	20	27	53
All Farms	211	6.80	158	38	18	44

somewhat different basis and is not strictly comparable with the former. Distance to the farms was measured from the city market place, located at least 2 or 3 miles within the city limits.

The first zone is within 8 miles of the market place. Here truck and potatoes provide 68 per cent of the farm income, whereas in the last zone only 20 per cent comes from this source,

TABLE 15

RELATION OF DISTANCE FROM THE CITY TO FARM ORGANIZATION[2]

Distance from Louisville (Miles)	Average Area of Improved Land (Acres)	Operating Expenses per Acre	Gross Receipts per Acre	Land Earnings per Acre	Value of Fertilizer Used per Acre
9	44	$73	$96	$23	$19.25
12	121	36	45	9	6.50
13	212	15	20	5	5.20
16	420	14	18	4	4.25

even though the soil especially suitable for truck extends more than 20 miles along the river. At 15 miles or more dairying and general farming take the place of the intensive crops.

The greater intensity of land use near the city is shown by the smaller farms, greater operating expenses, and more lavish expenditure for fertilizer. Gross receipts are five times as high

[1] Based on Tables 7 and 9, Arnold and Montgomery, *op. cit.*

[2] Based on Tables 8 and 10, *ibid.*

per acre 9 miles from the city as 16 miles, and "land earnings" almost six times as great.[1] This is reflected in the rents actually paid and in the land values, as shown in Table 14. Probably anticipated urban uses are reflected in the price of $312 per acre within the 8-mile zone.

Competition of Land Uses in Cities. Nowhere is the competition of land uses greater or more noticeable than in cities. At some intersection or in a particular block is the "100 per cent location," the place where more customers congregate than any other, especially women shoppers.[2] Here are the highest land values and rents. All types of merchandising establishments would like to be located at this point, but their rent-paying abilities vary enormously; those that can pay the highest prices for the land or the topmost rents crowd out those that cannot. In this sorting process, stores, offices, and banks are assigned to the place where they "belong" in the order of the choices of the buyers of urban land services. There is a tendency for the uses to form concentric circles around the "100 per cent location," but the pattern is usually disturbed by geographical factors and street layouts.

The merchant or skyscraper operator who is looking for "location" is buying *accessibility,* which Haig defines as "ease of contact, contact with relatively little friction." Even in buying a residence, "a purely consumption proposition one buys accessibility precisely as one buys clothes or food."[3] Accessibility is a substitute for transportation; both have to be paid for, the former in the rent or value of land, the latter in time, inconvenience, and cost of conveyance.

In response to the demands of consumers for the products

[1] "Land earnings," as defined by the authors, "is what is left after paying all operating expenses, which include all current expenses, 6% interest on working capital, and the farmer's estimate of the value of his labor and services as manager, amounting for the average farmer to about $600. Land earnings would be then what the landlord might expect as rent." Arnold and Montgomery, *op. cit.,* p. 12. It will be noted that the term "land earnings" corresponds very closely to "economic rent" as defined in this chapter.

[2] Mark Levy, "One Hundred Per Cent Locations," *Journal of Real Estate Management,* February, 1938, pp. 291–99.

[3] Robert Murray Haig, "Toward an Understanding of the Metropolis; The Assignment of Activities to Areas in Urban Regions," *Quarterly Journal of Economics,* May, 1926, pp. 421–23, at 423.

and services of land, as expressed in price, land uses become arranged in certain patterns. Rent acts as the "sorter" and "arranger" of this pattern. Drug stores occupy strategic corners because people, by their purchases, "vote" to have drug stores on corners rather than furniture stores. The choice of the consumer makes it possible for the drug store to pay more rent, or to outbid the furniture store. In agriculture it is demand—and the physical ability of the earth to fill the demand—plus transportation which determine land uses. Countries which have abolished the price system and economic rent must find some other way to determine the most convenient and efficient way to use the land.

Principle of First Choice. So far our discussion of the land use pattern has largely ignored the reaction of differences in physical conditions and in soils. Figures 10 and 11 assume that the entire area is equally suitable for milk production, wheat, corn culture, and ranching. However, some soils are so peculiarly adapted to certain crops that the areas become akin to natural monopolies. Only certain soils can grow superior Burley tobacco or the choice grapes from which the wines of France are made, but most soils can grow a variety of crops. Whenever crops are competing the one with the most circumscribed area physically will tend to exclude the others. Assume that a certain region, say the South, can grow wheat, cotton, and corn equally well and that at a given time the three crops are being grown in about the same proportions. Wheat is a crop which can be grown over a wide variety of climates and soils. If the price of wheat rises, new lands will readily be brought in on the "dry" and "cold" frontiers; practically every farm operator can and will transfer some of his acres from corn or cotton to wheat as soon as the price is attractive enough. The easily augmented supply will keep the price of wheat from rising very far.

On the other hand, corn cannot be grown as far north or west as wheat. With a rise in price, less land can respond to fill the demand than in the case of wheat and prices will tend to be such that corn will replace wheat to a large extent in this hypothetical region. Cotton, being still more circumscribed than corn, will, if the price rises high enough, exclude both corn and wheat. This *principle of first choice* has been stated thus: "Prices will tend to be such that the one with the more limited total potential area will have the choice of the territory." [1] This principle has application to some extent in cities. In a seaport, land available for wharves may be so scarce and the demand so great that all other buildings—factories, parks, and residences—are excluded from the waterfronts. The "principle of first choice" grows out of the physical scarcity of land for specific uses and helps to explain the rent and value of land due to this cause.

Nevertheless, it must not be concluded that economic competition will of itself direct the land into uses most beneficial from the standpoint of society. We once tried to "let the crops fight it out! Corn vs. oats; potatoes vs. pine; pine vs. popple," on the theory that "whatever finally paid most or best should have the land and the economic right of way," but forests disappeared and were not replenished for reasons to be discussed later.[2] Unregulated and unrestricted competition among urban land uses has given us the "insensate industrial town" and "megalopolis" described by Lewis Mumford.[3] Hence the need for planning, zoning, and social control over land uses.

Comparative Costs and Advantages as Factors in Land Utilization. Industries dependent on natural resources, i.e., the *extractive industries,* are "earth-bound"; they must be carried on at the source of the materials. Given a definite market, they may be so located with reference to this market that they remain unused under given price relationships. The forests of Alaska, Siberia, and the Tropics exist physically but are not economic resources because of their inaccessibility. Coal, iron, and other heavy minerals remain unexploited in many places, awaiting higher prices or cheaper methods of transportation. Gold and diamonds, on the other hand, being of small bulk and high value, are mined in the remotest parts of the world. As long as it is uneconomical to transmit electricity more than three or four hundred miles many water power potentials of the West and on the Laurentian Shield remain scenery.

If, instead of one highly restricted market, such as von

[1] H. C. Taylor, *op. cit.,* pp. 59–60.

[2] P. S. Lovejoy, "Concepts and Contours in Land Utilization," *Journal of Forestry,* April, 1933, p. 383.

[3] Lewis Mumford, *The Culture of Cities,* (New York, Harcourt, 1938), Chaps. III and IV.

Thünen's city, there are many markets or widely dispersed consumers, and if the source of supply is localized, the price to the consumer becomes the cost of extraction *plus* transportation charges. This can be shown by a diagram similar to the concentric circles of the Isolated State, with *isotims* connecting points of equal delivered price (Figures 12 and 13). In this

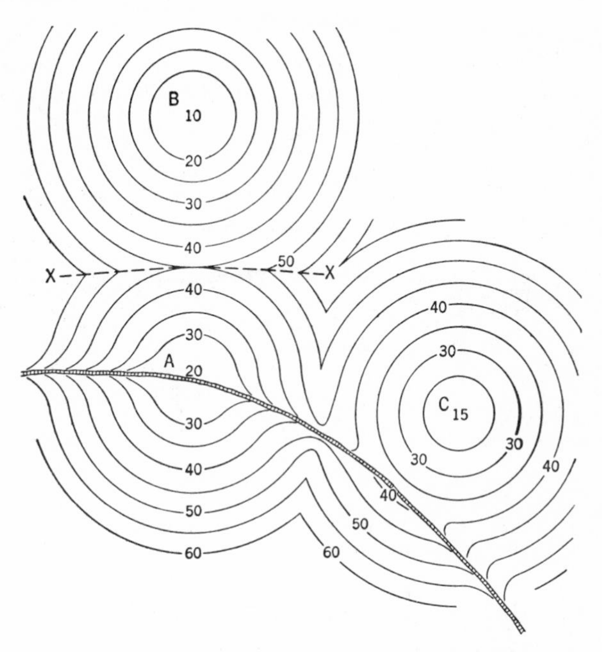

FIG. 12. ISOTIMS OF EXTRACTIVE AND DISTRIBUTIVE ENTERPRISES [1]

case, the center, instead of being the point of consumption with prices decreasing, becomes the point of production with prices increasing as the radius of the circles becomes greater. Figure 13, showing the isotims of the average farm price of potatoes, illustrates this principle. Prices are lowest at the centers of production and become progressively higher with the distance from these centers. Given two points of extraction competing for the same market, the one having the lowest cost of production—costs of transportation being the same—will outsell the high-cost pro-

[1] Based on Edgar M. Hoover, Jr., *Location Theory and the Shoe and Leather Industries* (Cambridge, Harvard University Press, 1937), Figures 3 and 4.

ducer (B and A in Figure 12). On the other hand, given the same cost of production, the one enjoying the more convenient, more efficient, or cheaper form of transportation will penetrate the market area of the other. This principle is of special importance in the distribution of goods to retail outlets from wholesale points.[1]

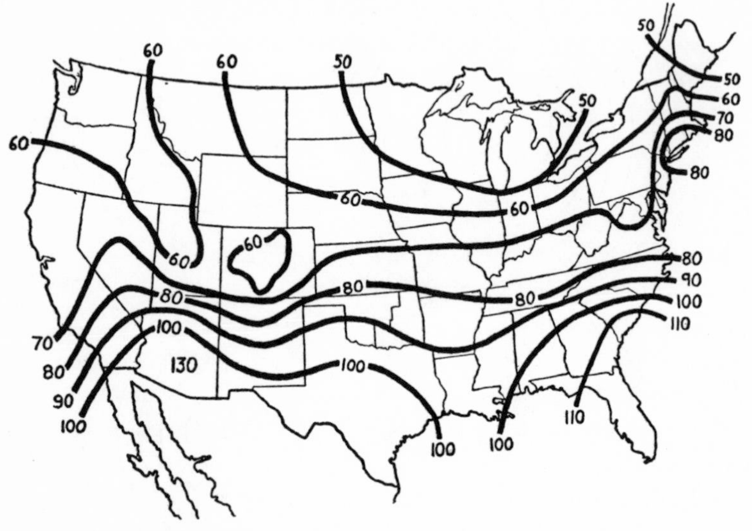

Fig. 13. Isotims (Lines of Equal Price) of Ten-Year Average Farm Price of Potatoes, December 1, 1906–1915 (cents per bushel)[2]

Cost of production also influences utilization through the principle of *comparative advantage*. Comparative costs may be expressed in terms of labor and the yield in physical units. Two regions may be capable of raising the same crops or producing the same minerals but at different labor costs per unit of output. Both regions could be self-sufficing if they wished, but it will be to the mutual benefit of each to produce that crop in which its advantage lies and to buy the others from its neighbors.

For purposes of illustration let us assume that A and B can raise potatoes and corn in the amounts indicated per unit of labor.

[1] Edgar M. Hoover, Jr., *Location Theory and the Shoe and Leather Industries op. cit.*, Chap. II, "The Extractive Industries."

[2] From Holbrook Working, *Factors Determining the Price of Potatoes in St. Paul and Minneapolis* (Minnesota Agricultural Experiment Station, Technical Bulletin 10), p. 6.

	A	B
Corn	30 bushels	35 bushels
Potatoes	60 "	10 "

If each has two units of labor available and both raise corn and potatoes, the total production will be 65 bushels of corn and 70 bushels of potatoes. But if each specializes in the crop in which it has the advantage there will be 120 bushels of potatoes and 70 bushels of corn. The difference will be more apparent if the unit of labor is valued at $30 and the cost of producing the products expressed in money.

	A	B
Corn	$1.00	$ .85
Potatoes	.50	3.00

Three dollars for potatoes in B and a dollar for corn in A are the prices consumers would have to pay if each bought in the "home market." However, if the interchange of products is unimpeded the citizens of both A and B will do better to buy their potatoes from A and their corn from B and let each region specialize in the product in which it has the advantage of lower costs of production.

In reality the problem becomes much more complicated. Instead of two regions, many areas may be involved. Sometimes one area may be superior to another in every product, yet trade will take place in the product in which the second area has the *least disadvantage*. Each area *tends* to produce those commodities for which its ratio of advantage is greatest or its ratio of disadvantage least.[1]

Many factors such as costs of transportation, tariffs, and trade restrictions impede the free flow of goods from nation to nation and even within the United States, which nullifies the principle of comparative advantage. It operates best in a 100 per cent complete exchange and price economy and is inoperative under self-sufficing agriculture or under attempts to produce regionally rather than on a national or international scale.

COSTS OF LAND UTILIZATION

Up to this point the discussion has been concerned with the income which land yields to the operator upon the application

[1] John D. Black, *op. cit.*, Chap. V, "The Principle of Comparative Advantage."

of land and capital, how this rent becomes value, and how rent influences the pattern of land use. Costs of land utilization will now be considered.

Cost of "Producing" "Economic" Land. It is a common assumption that land has no cost of production, that it is a "gift of nature" and therefore unlike capital goods which are produced by labor. However, while land as nature has no cost of production, land is *not* a factor of production or even a consumption good until it has been modified, or "produced." Land is not ready for urban housing until certain public improvements have been made. The home buyer wants a home site, and not just land. Production includes leveling, filling, drainage, sidewalks, curbs, streets, trees, and other improvements. If these facilities are not provided by the subdivider they must be paid for by the individual owner after he has bought the *space* for his home. Even space for standing room is often man-made. Earth dumped into Lake Michigan produced the space which is now Grant Park; certainly it was as much man-made as the bricks which might have been made of the same earth and used in the construction of buildings.

Land in its natural state is not ready to be used even for agriculture except for such extensive uses as grazing or wild hay. To prepare land to function as a factor of production in farming requires the expenditure of labor and the use of capital. The least that needs to be done for farm land is to survey it. Clearing, removing stumps, drainage irrigation, levees to hold back flood waters are examples of "production costs" on agricultural land. The Report of the National Resources Board estimates the cost of getting an acre of cut-over land ready for agricultural production at from $10 per acre in the South, $50 in the Lake states, to $200 an acre in the three Pacific states. The area of irrigable land can be increased by 7,000,000 acres if we are willing to spend $100 an acre for reclamation, and 10,000,000 additional acres can be irrigated at costs up to $200 an acre. At least $30 an acre will have to be expended to bring the best one-third of our drainable lands into production.[1]

Another way to bring farm land into the category of a factor of production is to make it accessible. If land within 25 miles

[1] *Op. cit.*, pp. 128–32.

of a railroad is "farm" land, from 25 to 50 miles "ranch land," and beyond that has no economic use, the expenditure for roads and trucks "manufactures" new land just as successfully as the drainage of a swamp.

To repeat, land as nature is not scarce but land as a factor of production is, and one of the reasons is the cost in money, time, labor, and inconvenience necessary to increase the economic supply of land. No manager of a resettlement project, charged with the duty of creating a farm with enough cleared acres to be a going concern, and equipped with buildings and fences, has any illusions about land as a free gift of nature.

Costs and difficulties of converting raw nature into a factor of production act as a barrier to increasing the economic supply of land. Some of the western cities grew by leaps and bounds, whereas the farming area about them was restricted by the difficulty of clearing the heavy forests. While the demand for farm products exceeded the supply the farmers on the small cleared area had a "monopoly" in furnishing milk, vegetables, and fruit. Land values for a while exceeded the cost of reclaiming the land and after that tended to approximate this cost.

The Time Element in Land Utilization Costs. Not all costs in land utilization are direct expenses which can be observed, such as reclamation, cultivation, excavation, construction of buildings, and maintenance of the land services. Some costs are subtle and indirect and are due to the time which necessarily elapses between the beginning of utilization and the time when the operator can harvest a crop or obtain an income. In agriculture the period between seedtime and harvest is usually only a few months but in orchards, livestock, and other long-time uses it may be years.

Let us refer again to the cost of supplying office space (Table 13). The operator has to consider the fact that as much as two years will elapse before old structures can be razed and a modern 75-story structure can be ready for occupancy. During this interval the land yields no income; besides, taxes and interest must be paid on an investment of over $16,000,000 in the land. An almost equally large sum accumulates as interest charge on building outlays and insurance during construction. Over $4,000,000 of *waiting costs* or carrying charges are amassed in the two years.

No wonder every effort is made to speed up construction to avoid the loss of income and the waiting costs which are associated with changing from one land use to another.

TABLE 16

COSTS ASSIGNABLE TO LAND UP TO TIME OF CONSTRUCTION, SUNNYSIDE GARDENS, L. I., 1924–28 [1]

Land	$ 859,581
Interest on Capital @ 6%	102,493
Taxes	43,302
Interest on Taxes	4,991
Public Improvements (Sewers, curbs, sidewalks, etc.)	376,145
Interest on Public Improvements	7,485
	$1,393,997

Costs of the same nature are encountered when bare land is prepared for housing. The Sunnyside Housing Corporation bought its land for about $860,000 and spent over $376,000 on public improvements such as sewers, water, sidewalks, etc. These were the visible costs; the "invisible" costs consisted of interest on all outlays from the time they were made until construction was started, calculated separately for each parcel of land. Table 16 shows that this amounted to almost $115,000. Similar waiting costs, which are not included in Table 16, had to be paid from the time construction began until the building was actually sold.[2] All in all, the investment assignable to land as such had practically doubled over the price paid for the bare land, yet the costs incurred by the City Housing Corporation were considered very reasonable. The land was bought before the rise in real estate values took place in this area, and careful planning of public improvements, economies in building, rapid construction, and quick sale of the properties kept waiting costs low.[3] All of these costs must be considered whenever the operator wishes to test the economic feasibility of his project or to establish a rental or sale price for his building.

[1] Rosalind Tough, "Production Costs, Building Costs and Total Costs at Sunnyside Gardens, L. I.," *Journal of Land and Public Utility Economics,* February, 1932, Table VI, p. 51.

[2] *Ibid.*

[3] *Ibid.,* p. 54. See also articles in the same journal for May, 1932, April, 1926, and August, 1928.

Even though the pioneer is primarily concerned with visible reclamation costs, he also has indirect costs. In a cut-over region the average settler will do well if he clears from 3 to 5 acres per year. At this rate it takes 20 to 25 years to clear an 80-acre farm; meanwhile he pays taxes, interest, and other carrying charges on the uncleared acres. Waiting costs are of particular importance in irrigation and drainage enterprises.

The time factor is even more important in the production of tree and forest products. If the forest owner starts with bare land he has visible outlays in the cost of the land, planting expenses, and protection costs.[1] Then comes a waiting period of 25 to 30 years if he produces pulpwood, and a much longer interval if saw timber is to be grown. During these unremunerative years, until he cuts the trees, the owner pays 25 to 30 annual taxes and interest on all moneys invested. His invisible costs soon exceed the direct costs. "Ten cent stumpage obtained from the public lands in 1880 and carried at 6% simple interest on first cost and current outlays for taxes and protection becomes 80 cent stumpage in 1916 and $3.20 stumpage in 1940." [2]

Reforestation is popularly considered a phase of forest conservation. However, the above example shows why private individuals hesitate to "conserve" forest resources. The costs accumulate very rapidly, even with simple interest. It is generally conceded, though debated, that in cases involving long waiting costs with no income until the end of the period, compound instead of simple interest is justified since the operator has the alternative opportunity of placing his money in a savings institution and reinvesting the annual interest.[3]

The private owner also hesitates to practice forestry because of the risks involved—fire, insects, wind damage, and other dangers—and especially because of the uncertainty of future prices. Every investor gambles on a distant and uncertain price to balance his accumulating investment in long-time land uses such as timber, rubber, coffee, or oranges. In more primitive com-

[1] Not all reforestation requires planting on bare land. Partly grown forests with considerable natural restocking are available in many sections. See Chap. IX.

[2] W. B. Greeley, *Some Public and Economic Aspects of the Lumber Industry* (U.S. Dept. of Agriculture, Office of the Secretary, Report 114, 1917), p. 17.

[3] This also holds whenever bare land is held for a higher use. See Rosalind Tough, *op. cit.,* pp. 46–47.

munities the absence of law and order and the lack of stable institutions are also deterring factors. Zimmermann points out the significant fact that half of the twenty commodities which have been the subject of price control are perennials and tree crops.[1]

As another illustration of the importance of the time factor in conservation, let us assume a full grown forest ready for cutting. Here growth and decay tend to balance each other, and no further physical increment can be expected. Suppose the owner decides to hold it for future generations as an act of conservation. Immediately he is confronted by the usual invisible costs, intensified in this case by the fact that the initial investment is large and taxes usually are in proportion to the investment. Similar costs arise whenever "conservation involves a reduction of the rate of disappearance or consumption and a corresponding increase in the unused surplus at the end of a given period." [2]

Ripening Costs. In a growing community land uses are not static. Near cities agricultural land moves into suburban uses. Within the city stores and apartments supplant residences. In such cases land may be said to "ripen" into the higher use. Ripening costs arise because the land is suspended between the old and new uses, yet the owner can derive an income only from the present but "lower" use. Near cities, for instance, farm land remains in agricultural use until it is subdivided, but in the interim the land is assessed on a suburban valuation. It may also be subject to special assessments for sewerage and other utilities, yet not derive any benefits from these facilities. All these costs are being paid out of the current income from the land as a farm. However, the owner will retrieve all costs whenever the land is sold for suburban purposes at a price high enough to cover these outlays.

More often large tracts of land are subdivided in anticipation of demand before the land is ripe for residential purposes. It is estimated that population will have to increase at more than twice the rate estimated by the Chicago Regional Planning Association in order to put all the lots laid out in Cook County in

[1] Erich W. Zimmermann, *World Resources and Industries, op. cit.*, Chap. 21, "Tree Crops and the Time Factor of Production," pp. 391–99. By permission of Harper and Brothers, publishers.

[2] *Ibid.*, p. 790.

1931 into use by 1960. In such cases ripening costs are shifted from the farmers to the owners of the subdivisions, and often taxes, interest, and ripening and developmental costs have proved so burdensome that large blocks of land have reverted to the government for delinquent taxes. The tragedy of premature and unsuccessful subdivisions lies not only in the loss of private investment but also in the fact that good farm land is taken out of use and committed to idleness after public improvements have been made, many of them at public expense. "We speak of land 'ripening' into higher uses; this is putting land into cold storage—and loading the community with the 'frozen assets' that result."[1]

This situation was paralleled in the "cut-overs." Land was bought by speculators and colonization companies with the expectation of selling to settlers. Since more deforested land was being created than could be absorbed into farms even in the best years of land selling, a waiting or ripening period was inevitable. After the World War it became apparent that the market for cut-over land had vanished, and the owners let the land revert to the county or state rather than continue to pay the carrying charges. The ripening costs were thereby shifted to the public.

Land does not always move freely from a lower use to a higher use because of the *costs of supersession.* Grain farmers may be aware of the advantage of changing to dairying, yet hesitate because of the cost of the herd, the equipment, and remodeling the buildings. A site occupied by a hotel may be ripe for an office building, but the cost of tearing down the hotel, plus waiting costs and loss of income, may postpone the change until the site is over-ripe. Costs of supersession tend to restrict the ready expansion of the higher uses of land and to that extent make these uses more scarce than they otherwise would be. On the other hand, in periods of optimism, supersession often takes place long before a site is ready for the new use, and the owner is faced with vacancies, lack of income, and costs similar to those encountered in premature subdivisions. The gap between two uses is

[1] Herbert D. Simpson and John E. Burton, *The Valuation of Vacant Land in Suburban Areas,* (Institute for Economic Research, Monograph 2, 1931), p. 44. See also Philip H. Cornick, *Premature Subdivision and Its Consequences* (Institute of Public Administration, Columbia University, 1938), Chaps. 1–6.

often bridged in unique ways: the porch of a dwelling is replaced by a small store or shop, the house is remodeled for offices or converted into a rooming house or apartment.

Costs of Production and the Value of Land. To the settler who has cleared a piece of land, who has expended money and effort in working, waiting, and risk-taking, the visible and indirect costs are real. If he were asked to name a price for his land or to fix a price for the products of his land, the operator certainly would take these costs into consideration—all of them would enter into his price. However, once these costs have been expended the owner is helpless to command a return. The settler is not in a position to demand a price for potatoes sufficient to repay the efforts of clearing or to give him a return on his investment. Neither can the owner of an apartment or office building demand a rental based upon cost of production and get it. This is called *fixity of the investment* and refers to the fact that after working, waiting, and risk-taking have been expended in creating land as a factor of production, or spent in the annual costs of cultivation and maintenance, the operator cannot force the consumer to pay a price which will cover costs of production. He has to accept the price or rent established by the market, except in those rare cases where the landowner is in a monopoly situation, particularly in the direct sale of land. Fixity of the investment is, of course, not peculiar to land but has particular significance in those forms of land use with long waiting and ripening periods.[1]

Furthermore, for land that has had costs of production, rent becomes a return on the capital represented by the work, waiting, and risk-taking the operator has sunk in the land. Returning to Table 9, on C land $14 is expended in current outlays for labor, fertilizer, machinery, buildings, etc., and the necessary management, and $3.00 is left as rent out of the $17 the operator receives for the total product of 34 bushels. If the farmer has spent $60 per acre in reclaiming this land, the $3.00 rent represents a return of 5 per cent on the investment in land.

However, in the valuation process "costs of production" are ignored or have only an indirect bearing on land values. Buyers

[1] Dorau and Hinman, *Urban Land Economics, op. cit.*, pp. 164–67. "Fixity of the investment" as used here should not be confused with "it is hard to get your money out of real estate once you have invested in it," and other concepts of "illiquidity."

look to future incomes and rents as their criteria of values; even present incomes serve only as guides in their judgments. In a new community they are interested in the $60 "production costs" only as an alternative to paying more than $60 for cleared land, but if the prospect for future income fails to justify a price of $60, costs of reclamation are past history as far as influencing the value of land is concerned.

The 5 per cent return on the investment, resulting from a rent of $3.00 on $60 production costs, is also bound to change. Should farm prices fall and the rent decrease to $1.50, the settler will realize only 2½ per cent on his investment. Buyers will base their offers on the $1.50 rent and the settler may have to sell at $30 per acre and take a loss of $30.

In cities it is primarily the earning power of the renting public that determines the market price of rentable space, whether for offices or apartments, and the selling price of the buildings reflects their earning power. How quickly the price of structures responds to rents is illustrated by an apartment house built in 1924 for $65,000. Cities were prosperous in the next few years and in 1929 the building was sold for $100,000. After the depression set in the apartment reverted to the mortgagee for $59,000, and in 1932 it was listed at $20,000, but no buyers were willing to take it even at that figure. Since 1933 the price has risen consistently, and in 1938 the owner refused an offer of $50,000. Within ten years the price ranged from almost double to less than one-third of the cost of production.[1]

The usual trend of land rents was consistently upward until 1920. Based upon the original reclamation costs, the higher rents soon represented a far greater return on the investment than 5 per cent. The rise in rents quickly became capitalized into land values and the new owner received only the current rate of return on his money; in fact, in the period of high anticipated values, less than the usual rate. By this time the value of the land had little or no relation to its "cost of production." The $16,000,000 paid for the skyscraper site in Table 13 may have been paid for land costing little or nothing as far as production costs were concerned.

When land has been made usable, its physical durability has

[1] W. A. Helwig, "Basic Thoughts and Average Figures," *Journal of Real Estate Management*, February, 1938, p. 343.

an important influence on the economic supply of land. After Grant Park was created by filling in Lake Michigan, or after new islands were pumped out of the ocean sands in Florida and California, no further production costs were necessary. In contrast to durable land, buildings and other capital goods begin to deteriorate as soon as created and disappear in a relatively short time. Land once created remains a part of the total supply, but buildings and other capital goods must be produced periodically or repaired continuously or else fail to remain a part of the supply.[1]

Other forms of land, however, do not have the indefinite life of urban sites. Agricultural land can and does wear out. Fertilization is similar to the maintenance cost of buildings. Prevention of erosion, weed control, upkeep of drainage, irrigation structures and levees may be regarded in the same light. If these costs are not met currently, the soil continues to deteriorate or revert to its former state. Once run down, it has to be rebuilt and rehabilitated precisely as a neglected building has to be rebuilt or replaced. In some cases land may be so depleted or destroyed that it does not pay to restore it; soil is gone but *space* remains. "Producing economic land" is really a continuous process.

Although land is the most indestructible form of durable capital goods, it should be pointed out that "destructibility" is a matter of degree rather than a difference in kind. Some forms of capital goods are short lived, it is true, but machinery and skyscrapers are relatively durable, and some structures such as the Pyramids and ancient temples have stood for thousands of years. Land itself varies in durability, from mineral resources, which, when removed, leave a mere hole in the ground, to the space of urban sites which remains a part of the economic supply of land as long as man has any use for it, present or potential.

The fact that city land yields an income without costs for maintenance or a sinking fund for replacement, both of which are needed for buildings, explains one of the chief differences in the economic behavior of land and buildings in urban land utilization. Note the depreciation item in Table 13. Because the structure will become obsolete before it wears out physically, the valuation of the building is based upon a series of incomes for a

[1] Herbert D. Simpson, "The Incidence of Real Estate Taxes," *American Economic Review*, June, 1932, pp. 220–22.

definite number of years, whereas the valuation of the land is based upon an *indefinite* series of incomes. In fact, it can normally be assumed that the incomes from the building will gradually decline as the end of its economic life approaches.[1]

Finally, it should be observed that land is subject to speculation and unusual booms, many of which coincide with new developments in transportation such as the Erie Canal.[2] Others seem to start spontaneously, as, for example the Florida boom of 1925 during which land values reached fabulous heights. A $40,000 lot in a Florida city soared to $600,000, and an 80-acre farm near a booming city was sold for $240,000 after three deals. In the words of the authors of a book written when speculation was at its height, "Exclamation points lose their emphasis when relating incidents like that." [3] However, the crash came, leaving wreck and ruin in its wake.

It might be said that land booms are no different from other "bubbles," such as the famous tulip craze of Holland. However, the aftermath of a land boom is a misfortune not only for the individuals who lose their money or are left stranded in half-baked subdivisions, but also for the public which has squandered money on roads, schools, and public services that have to be paid for by solvent taxpayers after the bankrupt landowners have let the land revert to the public through tax delinquency.

Residual Nature of Land Income and Value. Throughout our analysis of proportionality, rent, and value, land was made the residual claimant, i.e., labor and capital were assigned the first claims to the income from the application of labor and capital to land. It should be emphasized again that under many circumstances land has almost the first claim. The tenant who has made a contract to pay a certain rent for a farm, office, or apartment finds that rent is not something which can be paid after all other bills are settled. The farmer or home owner soon realizes that interest and stipulated payments on the principal are among the first claimants to income. However, rents and mortgage payments cannot maintain their first claim over long periods of time,

[1] Babcock, *op. cit.*, Chap. 27, "Depreciation, Obsolescence and Building Life."

[2] Cornick, *op. cit.*, Chap. 1, "Early Subdivision Booms and Their Consequences." A. M. Sakolski, *The Great American Land Bubble* (New York, Harper's, 1932).

[3] F. P. Stockbridge and J. H. Perry, *Florida in the Making* (New York, De Bower Pub. Co., 1926), p. 295.

or even over short periods with violent fluctuations in the earning power of tenants or purchasers.

The apartment house mentioned above can serve as an illustration. Assume that a rental of $1.00 per square foot was charged in prosperous times. This not only paid for all costs but left such a handsome profit that the $65,000 building could be sold for $100,000. When the depression came the new owners were in no position to command a return or dictate a rental such as would sustain the price they had paid. Suppose their income was only 25 cents a square foot. Against this income are the following charges, payable in about the order indicated:

1. Operating expenses, wages, fuel, water, and repairs to utilities.
2. Taxes and insurance.
3. Long time capital costs, such as repairs on the building, and the depreciation fund.
4. Interest on the investment in the land and building.

Unless operating expenses, such as the janitor's pay and repairs, are met the apartment will not be habitable. These items therefore have the first claim; even taxes and insurance may have to be postponed. No money is available for major repairs and depreciation. Bondholders or the mortgagee will have to go without dividends or interest; they have the last claim. If the property is foreclosed it will merely mean a change in ownership, as costs and income are the same under new management.

Should this rental situation continue, the building will begin to deteriorate for lack of repairs and in time the owners may have it demolished just to save taxes. In other words, if there is not enough income to maintain the "capital elements" they disappear. The land or space remains unchanged, however, building or no building.

Inasmuch as all the returns went to the labor-capital inputs and nothing to the land, theoretically this apartment site should be no-rent land and consequently practically valueless. But in this case the value of the land will not become zero; it will merely fall to the level of potential values for other purposes.[1] In abandoned mining or lumbering towns land values may approach zero or disappear completely.

[1] This is also in line with Babcock's principle that land is residual only when it is in its highest and best use, which is often hypothetical. In all other cases the building is residual. *Valuation of Real Estate, op. cit.*, Chaps. 2 and 27.

It is also true of agriculture that human beings have the first claim to the products of the land. Unless enough is raised to feed them, they starve or go on relief. Unless farm laborers are remunerated they cease to work. Next come the investments in capital goods such as seed, fertilizer, tools of agriculture. Unless the income is sufficient to buy or replace them from year to year, production is halted. The more durable forms of capital do not have to be repaid immediately. The length of time in which this is necessary varies directly with the durability of the instrument in question. Over the first few years fences and buildings will not need attention but, like the apartment building, they will disappear if the farmer does not have income to replace or repair them. Agricultural land can go longer without being repaired or replaced than the other forms of agricultural capital; as such it becomes the factor to be "rewarded" after the others have been paid. The owner would prefer to receive a small return rather than let the farm lie idle and receive no return whatsoever.

However, inasmuch as farm land is subject to deterioration, the income of the operator must be sufficient to cover the cost of maintaining the productivity of the land, and herein it differs from the space occupied by the apartment. Furthermore, at any time when the existing economic supply of land is not sufficient to fill the needs of consumers, new land will be brought into production only when prospective producers deem it likely that their future income will reward them for investing their money in the "cost of producing" more land considered in *all* its phases. Land may be regarded as a residual claimant only because of the relatively longer time available for the adjustment of income to the supply price of land, and not because land differs in kind from other forms of durable capital goods.

VI

AGRICULTURAL LAND

Agriculture uses more land than any other industry. In 1935 the farms of the United States embraced over 1,000,000,000 acres, or more than 55 per cent of the total land area. Forests cover only 615,000,000 acres, of which 185,000,000 acres are woodlots on farms and really a part of agriculture. However, strictly speaking, agricultural land uses extend beyond the line fences of the farmers; probably another 600,000,000 acres of the remaining public domain, land in federal forests, Indian reservations, state lands, and railroad land, are used for grazing or dry farming. The mere area involved, the diversity of agriculture, its relation to other land and water uses (through erosion and flood control, for instance), the relationship of agriculture to urbanization, migration, and other national policies, tend to make agricultural land problems of paramount importance to the nation.

TYPES OF FARM ORGANIZATION

Self-sufficing and Peasant Agriculture. Primitive agriculture was a self-sufficing enterprise in which food, clothing, shelter, and fuel were produced for home consumption. Under crude methods of cultivation there could be little or no surplus for exchange. However, in certain favored regions as on the Nile, the Tigris, the Euphrates, and the fertile soils of the Mediterranean basin, the art of agriculture soon developed far enough to permit specialization, and the food surplus entered the commerce of the ancient world.

In America the pioneer was part hunter and part self-sufficing farmer. One reason for this was the lack of a market for his surplus. The transportation of farm produce from Ohio, Indiana, and Illinois by flatboat in Lincoln's boyhood gives some idea of the difficulty of finding a market to provide the little cash needed for kitchen utensils, salt, gunpowder, and the other simple necessities of the frontier.

The South developed commercial agriculture very early because it had exportable tobacco, indigo, rice, and, later, cotton; yet the plantation had many self-sufficing features. It was not long, however, before the frontier farm took on commercial aspects, especially after settlement reached the prairies. Here the soil and climate were conducive to specialized crops. Farm machinery, barb-wire, windmills, and other products of the Industrial Revolution helped the transformation, and canals and railways provided market outlets in the rapidly industrializing East. Many of the functions associated with the self-sufficing farm, such as making the implements, the clothing, the butter and cheese, and canning, were rapidly transferred from the farm to the factory. By raising only a few crops and buying the necessities and luxuries, the modern farmer can now have all the luxuries, gadgets, and necessities that his money can buy, but he is also placed at the mercy of the "price system." The financial success of a specialized farm depends upon the difference in the price of what is bought and what is sold, and herein lies the "farm problem."

Many who have been touched by the plight of the farmer in this depression advocate a return to agrarianism even though it reduces the material standard of living. In fact, they consider this a part of the merit of the plan.[1] This means a return to self-sufficing or peasant farming. However, the latter term has unhappy connotations to Americans who associate peasants with serfs and downtrodden individuals, or at least with farmers living on a low economic scale. European writers claim that the peasant is not necessarily a poor man; he often has great abundance, but his entire scheme of farm management is aimed at full corn cribs, bursting barns, and a well-filled cellar. Since he produces for his own needs primarily, the peasant has greater independence and security, but to the degree that he is actually self-sufficing he must forego the products and services of the modern world. On the other hand, it is claimed that peasant farming does not necessarily preclude the sale of products. In Germany even small farms of 12½ to 25 acres send two-thirds of their products to market, while the larger peasant farms sell from 80 to 90 per cent of their output. What, then, distinguishes the peasant farmer from the

[1] Troy J. Cauley, *Agrarianism* (Chapel Hill, University of North Carolina Press, 1935).

self-sufficing or the commercial farmer? It is said to be a definite attitude toward his occupation, the land, and life in general. This is difficult to define but is nevertheless distinguishable from the attitude of the commercial farmer whose behavior is guided by prices and whose outlook is conditioned by his contacts with a commercial and urbanized society. Perhaps the best example in America is the French-Canadian habitant. "The habitant is not worried because he cannot afford a car or a radio. He has his family, his church, his own people round about him, plenty of fuel, plenty of food (of a crude sort), the fresh air, and the freedom of the woods. He does not look forward to the day when his little village will be a metropolis, with all the glare and noise and mechanical contrivance which the Anglo-Saxon seems to think is civilization. Hence he is not disappointed if things go slowly." [1]

However, to some writers peasant farming is more a matter of land tenure and inheritance than of farm organization or self-sufficiency. The outstanding characteristic which distinguishes the German peasant farm from the capitalistic enterprise, according to Dr. Max Sering, is the fact that the former is "family managed" and is a "home and a heritage" with peculiar non-commercial forms of inheritance. In Yugoslavia family ownership is even stronger than in Germany. Under the leadership of the father or older members of the family, several married brothers and sisters and other blood relations live on one farm and in one household; sometimes twenty to eighty people live together in this communal fashion. The estate is in reality the common property of the family, and not the head's to dispose of as he likes.[2]

The self-sufficing and peasant types of agriculture are more prevalent in Europe and Asia than in America and other new countries. Zimmermann says, "Even today the bulk of mankind depend in the main on their own toil and skill to assure their own food supply. Probably the larger part of the world's food is still

[1] A. R. M. Lower and Harold A. Innis, *Settlement and the Forest and Mining Frontiers* (Toronto, Macmillan, 1936), p. 89. See also André Siegfried, *Canada, op. cit.*, Chaps. 5 and 13.

[2] M. Sering, "The Relations of Land Tenure to the Economic and Social Development of Agriculture," *Proceedings of the Fourth International Conference of Agricultural Economists* (London, Oxford University Press, 1937), pp. 73–86.

Table 17

NUMBER, TENURE STATUS, LABOR EXPENDITURES, SIZE OF FARMS, AND VALUE OF LAND AND BUILDINGS PER FARM BY FARM TYPES, 1930 [1]

Type	Number	Percentage of Total	Number Tenant Operated	Percentage of Class Tenant Operated	Percentage of Class Reporting Expenditures for Labor	Average Size of Farm (Acres)	Value of Land and Buildings per Farm
Cotton	1,640,025	26.1	1,192,195	72.7	28.3	72	$2,960
General	1,044,266	16.6	281,213	26.9	47.4	138	7,199
Dairy	604,837	9.6	129,444	21.4	59.9	139	9,865
Self-sufficing	498,019	7.9	132,377	26.6	19.5	70	2,447
Animal Specialty	479,042	7.6	156,777	32.7	65.1	230	16,276
Cash Grain	454,726	7.2	233,068	51.3	65.4	352	17,580
Crop Specialty	431,379	6.9	201,586	46.7	45.4	109	6,162
Part-time	339,207	5.4	*	*	*	47	3,445
Poultry	166,517	2.7	21,126	12.7	40.5	62	5,981
Fruit	141,418	2.3	16,155	11.4	75.5	71	17,997
Truck	84,561	1.3	27,917	33.0	58.6	60	9,734
Stock Ranch	71,000	1.1	10,969	15.4	61.7	2,912	28,044
All Other	333,651	5.3	261,538	38.9	21.0	121	7,043
Total	6,288,648	100.0	2,664,365	42.4	41.8	157	7,614

* Included with "All Other." Data not available for this item.

[1] Adapted from U. S. Census, 1930, "Type of Farm."

produced by thoroughly antiquated methods on small patches of land held individually by peasants and other individual cultivators."[1]

Self-sufficing and General Farms in the United States. In spite of the evolution in agricultural production in America, only a part of the farms have become like factories. Most of them are a mixture of self-sufficing and commercial agriculture. Table 17 shows the principal types of farming in the United States, ranging from self-sufficing to highly specialized single-crop farms. Self-sufficing farms are defined as those where the value of the products used by the operator's family is more than 50 per cent of the total value of the entire production. This is far from the usual concept of the self-contained enterprise pictured by some writers, yet it does imply a farm on which the family living is the primary objective. According to the study of types of farming made by the federal census in 1930, the United States had almost half a million self-sufficing farms, the greatest concentrations being in the Appalachians, the cut-over areas of the Lake states, New England, the Ozarks, the area immediately north of the Ohio, and minor scattered areas. Since 1930 a marked trend toward self-sufficing farming has taken place, especially in the South.

Another type of farm with strong self-sufficing features is the "general farm," of which there were over one million in the United States in 1930 (Table 17). These are defined as those enterprises where the value of any one product is less than 40 per cent of the total. Farms of this type raise a variety of crops and to a large extent produce food, fuel, and other products for the use of the home.

Specialized and Part-time Farms. The other classes or types shown in Table 17 indicate the degree of specialization to which agriculture has been carried in the United States. Among the "crop specialties" are potatoes, peanuts, tobacco, sugar beets, and broom corn. The income from "animal specialty" comes primarily from the sale of sheep, hogs, and cattle, but stock ranches are placed in a separate class. Cotton farmers made up 26 per cent of the total number of farmers in 1930, the largest single group.

[1] *World Resources and Industries, op. cit.*, p. 220. By permission of Harper and Brothers, publishers.

Part-time farmers are defined in the census as those operators who spent 150 days or more at non-agricultural work or who reported an occupation other than farmer, provided the farm products did not exceed $750. Part-time farmers normally have two sources of income, one from some non-farm occupation and the other from a small tract of land which in many cases is cultivated by the other members of the family. The heaviest concentration is in the areas adjacent to cities, where good roads and cheap transportation have induced this form of decentralization. They are also found in mining, oil, and lumber areas, or where outside work can be obtained on the highways, on railroads, or in isolated factories. According to recent figures of the 1935 census, farm operators reporting more than 150 days of work off the farm for pay increased by over 30,000 since 1930. The flight-to-the-land was not only to self-sufficing farms on the frontiers but also to part-time farms in the urban hinterland. Even in Iowa the movement was not without significance. However, this form of decentralization was well under way long before the depression and represents a permanent rural-urban pattern of living. Like agrarianism, the part-time farm makes its appeal by offering a certain security to the laborer; and to the industrialist it offers cheap unemployment insurance with little or no responsibility on his part.

Part-time farms have also appealed to those anxious to decentralize industry, and many look upon this form of back-to-the-land movement as a new mode of life and a means of solving both rural and urban problems. "The proper development of rural industrial communities could be made to absorb all the unemployed workers and all the submarginal farm population," said M. L. Wilson at the fifth International Conference of Agricultural Economists at MacDonald College in August, 1938. The subsistence homestead movement embodied these ideas.[1]

CHARACTERISTICS OF AGRICULTURE AS AN INDUSTRY

Organized on the Individual or Family Basis. Although the United States has many types of farming they are all alike in that

[1] Carter Goodrich, *et al., Migration and Economic Opportunity* (Philadelphia, University of Pennsylvania Press, 1936), pp. 618–60. See also O. E. Baker, Ralph Borsodi, and M. L. Wilson, *Agriculture in Modern Life* (New York, Harpers, 1939).

the farm is largely owned individually and organized around the family. There are very few partnerships or corporations, and relatively few farmers hire laborers. In 1930 only 42 per cent of all the farms reported having spent any money for outside labor. Many hire a man or two only during the peak load seasons. Only 28.3 per cent of the cotton farms reported expenditures for labor, although cotton picking is one of the sources of income of people in the towns and villages of the Cotton Belt. More than three-fourths of the fruit farms hired labor, whereas less than one-fifth of the self-supporting farms did so.

The family farm has been criticized by many writers. Sir Daniel Hall calls it the "peasant" or "yeoman" type of land holding and says that while it may be good politically it has serious defects economically, especially from the standpoint of maximum food production.[1] In but few cases are land, labor, and capital combined in proper proportions; the usual situation is that the farm either is undermanned or has surplus labor. Small farms cannot use machinery effectively. Financing, buying, and selling are likewise inefficient. Socialists have long pointed out the waste on small farms, "each requiring the upkeep of separate live-stock, houses, barns, fences, machinery and other equipment; each demanding separate journeys to markets for purchases or sales; each necessitating separate haggling over crops."[2]

Up to the present time economic forces have favored the independent farm units. This accounts for the six and four-fifths million farms in the United States. These independent farms are largely responsible for the individualism of the American farmer, one of the characteristics of the frontier which is admirable in many respects but a disadvantage in other ways. Both psychological and economic forces have been responsible for the lack of united action among farmers. They have been less successful than any other group in combining to control their numbers or regulating production or controlling the area to be devoted to farming. This is due to the great numbers involved, the scattered territory on which farmers live, and the nature of the industry

[1] He advocates large corporation farms of 2,000 to 10,000 acres under the control of competent managers, thus opening farming to men of large capacities. See his article, "Feeding the World," *Atlantic Monthly*, May, 1925.

[2] H. W. Laidler, *Socialism in Thought and Action* (New York, Macmillan, 1919), p. 15.

itself. The industry is therefore one of cut-throat competition, nationally and internationally.

Contrary to the predictions of socialists and alarmists, large-scale or corporation farming has not superseded the family farm. The economies in buying and selling, in management, in the use of machinery and man-power claimed for the large farm, whether owned by corporations or individuals, are more theoretical than actual. The irregularity of the work on most farms, its seasonal nature, the uncertainties of the weather, and the difficulties of overseeing laborers when scattered over a large area are some of the factors which militate against "bonanza" farms. Being without many of the self-sufficing features, they are fully exposed to the vicissitudes of nature and cycles of the competitive system, hence they lack the security of the diversified farm.

No doubt certain types of agriculture in favored regions lend themselves to "gigantic units," but up to the present time the trend has not been in that direction to any alarming degree. Large-scale farming has been profitable in the wheat sections through the use of the combine and power machinery, but it is still predominantly in the family or individual form of organization, notwithstanding some highly publicized "corporation farms." Whether a successful cotton picker will revolutionize cotton farming by substituting large units for the present small farms remains to be seen.[1]

Throughout the entire world agriculture tends to center around the family as the economic unit. While this has many admirable aspects it also sets a limit to the size of the business enterprise. The acreage operated has to be adjusted to the amount of work the farmer and his family can deliver, with the maximum set by the peak load at harvesting or other critical periods. If additional labor can be hired at this time the size of the unit can be increased materially.

The family-sized farm has been defined as that area which will give full employment at productive labor to the farm family and give the farmer a high standard of living. Other writers speak of that area which will *support* a family, which could be defined as a

[1] Clarence A. Wiley, "The Rust Mechanical Cotton Picker and Probable Land-Use Adjustments," *Journal of Land and Public Utility Economics*, May, 1939, pp. 155–67.

mere subsistence unit since the term "support" is very flexible. All these definitions place an upper limit on the amount the farmer is permitted to earn—a high standard of living, subsistence, or just enough to keep the family employed at productive labor. No such limit is proposed for the entrepreneur in other occupations and industries. The entrepreneur in the steel business is frankly after the largest profits and income. As long as agriculture is organized as it now is, we must not be surprised if farming loses the boy who has the enterprise and capacity to organize a corporation, head a railroad system, or manage a chain of restaurants.

Table 17 gives some idea of the size of the average farm business expressed in acres and in value. In 1935 the average farmer operated about 155 acres, somewhat less than in 1930 because of the increase in the small-sized self-sufficing and part-time farms. There was a tendency for farms to decrease in size from 1850 to 1880, but after that farms increased in size owing to mechanization and the expansion of agriculture in the West, where grain farms average over 350 acres and stock ranches average almost 3,000. Truck, fruit, cotton, self-sufficing and part-time farms have the smallest acreage. Using the value of real estate as a test of size, the ranches, cash grain, animal specialty, and fruit farms head the list in 1930 with an average investment of $16,000 to $28,000, whereas the average cotton farm involves less than $3,000 capital. A special study of large-scale farming by the federal census disclosed less than 8,000 farms which could meet the test of having produced $30,000 worth of products in 1929. About one-fourth of them were stock ranches, characterized by large areas, and another fourth were fruit farms usually associated with small tracts. Over 40 per cent of the large-scale farms are located in the Pacific states, the majority being in California.[1]

While agriculture offers security, a fair living, and a steady income—if not in money, at least in food, fuel, and other things furnished by the farm—it does not offer the same opportunities for rare talent as many other callings. There are few if any

[1] R. D. Jennings, *Large Scale Farming in the United States,* 1929 (Bureau of the Census and Bureau of Agricultural Economics, U. S. Dept. of Agriculture, 1933); O. E. Baker, *A Graphic Summary of the Number, Size, and Type of Farm and Value of Products* (U. S. Dept. of Agriculture, Miscellaneous Publication 266, 1937), Figs. 98–105.

millionaire farmers, although there are some millionaires who are farming. In our early history some of our greatest statesmen, such as Washington, Jefferson, and Madison, were farmers, but their fame rests only slightly upon their occupation. On the other hand, the accumulation of property worth $18,000 to $20,000 within the short period during which the American farmer "climbs the agricultural ladder," (as is the case in normal times in some of our better agricultural states) is a praiseworthy accomplishment in an economic society where so few own productive property.

A serious defect of the family farm is the inflexibility of the labor supply and, in most cases, of the land as well. The farmer cannot easily reduce production; he cannot "fire" his family nor easily adjust his acreage. Interest, taxes, and other fixed charges continue whether half of the farm is worked or all of it. It may be more profitable to use all his labor, horses, machinery, and land to raise all he can at the risk of a lower price than to let them remain idle part of the time and raise a small crop at a higher price. The rigidity of the factors of production makes shifting difficult, and the farmer hesitates to make changes in crop practices even when the conservation of his soil is at stake.

The Farm and Home Are One. Another characteristic of agriculture is that the home and farm are one establishment; in fact, some of the functions of the farm are still carried on in the home. If the farmer loses one he loses both. The home gives the feeling of attachment to the farm, which becomes one of the subtle factors determining the behavior of farmers and their children even though they enter other occupations. Only those who have the most commercial relationship to the farm leave the place abruptly; most farmers "retreat" rather than retire from the land. This helps to explain part of the tenure system of America. Furthermore, the home is a substantial part of the farmer's investment. In 1930 the total value of farm dwellings was over $7,000,000,000, more than half of the total investment in farm buildings.

Lack of Control over Production. Because the farmer is so close to nature his work is different from manufacturing and other industries. The farmer is often advised to "control his production." This is possible only to a limited extent for the industry as a whole as well as for the individual farmer. The farmer may enlarge or reduce his acreage, but the output may not be affected at all. After the crops are planted the harvest is largely in the laps of the gods. It is practically impossible to increase the acreage after the seed-time has passed, and it can be reduced only by destroying the growing plants or the crops. There is no possibility of speeding up or reducing production to any extent. Wheat matures in its due season and not before. After the crops are planted they are subject to insects, diseases, floods, droughts, or hail, many of these factors being only slightly under the control of man. Therefore only a rough correlation exists between acreage and crop yields. One can imagine the demoralization in the Ford plant if the same amount of raw material and labor produced a million cars in one year and the next year two million. Yet this happens on individual farms and, to a degree, in the industry as a whole.

The Investment Is "Fixed" in Land and Permanent Improvements. It has been pointed out that fixity of the investment is one of the outstanding characteristics of land. In 1920 almost 70 per cent of the farmer's total investment was in land. This proportion was reduced to 60 per cent by 1930 owing to the fall in the value of the land and the increase in the value of buildings. It will be observed from Table 18 that land values more than

TABLE 18

VALUE OF VARIOUS CLASSES OF FARM PROPERTY, 1900–1935[1]

(Billions of dollars)

	1900	1910	1920	1925	1930	1935
Land	13.0	28.5	54.8	37.7	34.9	32.8
Buildings	3.6	6.3	11.5	11.7	12.9	
Implements & Machinery	0.8	1.2	3.6	2.7	3.3	—
Livestock	3.0	4.9	8.0	4.9	6.1	—
Total Farm Property	20.4	40.9	77.9	57.0	57.2	

[1] Thirteenth Census of the United States (1910), *Abstract of the Census,* pp. 276–277.

Fifteenth Census of the United States, *Agriculture, General Statistics. Summary for the United States, 1929 and 1930,* pp. 38–39. U. S. Census of Agriculture, 1935, *General Report,* Vol. III, pp. 21, 23. This census reported the value of land and buildings as one item and omitted the other items of farm property.

doubled between 1900 and 1910 and almost doubled during the next decade. In 1920 farm real estate, i.e., land and buildings, was worth $66,000,000,000 but 15 years later it had shrunk to a bare $33,000,000,000. ($33,644,000,000 in 1940.)

Fixity of the investment, therefore, has more than the usual significance for agriculture. Very little farm land exists today that has not been cleared, drained, irrigated, or ameliorated in other ways. The time element is important in many crops. Orchards and livestock require years of waiting before the owner can realize on his investment. Money sunk in buildings and equipment also tends to become fixed; nor can the farmer shift from one type of agriculture to another without costs of supersession. It is not difficult to understand the temper of the farmers of the one-crop areas who try to "command a return" by political means, even though one questions the economic soundness of their proposals.

Agricultural Population Is Widely Distributed. Agriculture needs space, and, as has been pointed out before, agricultural nations can expand only by increasing their area—an important factor when population begins to press upon the food supply. The space element also accounts for the scattered and non-nucleated nature of the rural population of America. The 32,000,000 people living on farms in the United States in 1935 were distributed over a billion acres of land, whereas the 95,000,000 urban dwellers occupied perhaps ten million acres or less than half of the acreage occupied by farmsteads. The density of farm population is in inverse proportion to the size of the farm. A survey township of 23,040 acres can be divided into only 8 ranches of about 3,000 acres per ranch, whereas it can support 320 average cotton farms. The costs of roads per family, of schools per pupil, and of other public services per capita (as, for instance, rural electrification) increase as the distance between dwellings increases. This is an important factor in areas of isolated settlement or scattered farms. Where farmers live in villages or in closer communities such costs are reduced. However, good roads, the automobile, the telephone, and radio are overcoming some of the personal disadvantages of space relationships in rural areas.[1]

[1] Lynn Smith, "The Social Effects of Land Division in Relationship to a Program of Land Utilization," *Journal of Farm Economics*, November, 1935, pp. 702–9.

THE DEVELOPMENT AND RECLAMATION OF AGRICULTURAL LAND

Under the various land acts the settlement of the humid area of the United States reached the Mississippi by 1820–30 and by 1880 settlers crossed the 100th meridian. The chief obstacle to agricultural utilization of humid land was the forest. By 1880 about 150,000,000 acres or 22 per cent of the original eastern forest had been removed merely to get at the soil, and most of the trees were destroyed and burned as an obstruction to agriculture.[1] In some places excessive stoniness added to the cost of creating a farm, and especially on the prairies, drainage was often needed to make the land productive. It is difficult to visualize the original state of much of the splendid land of the Corn Belt. An explorer passing across the Ohio line into Indiana in 1823 reported "the country so wet that we scarcely saw an acre of ground upon which a settlement could be made. We traveled for a couple of miles with our horses wading through water to the girth." Immense swarms of mosquitoes and flies made it difficult to stop and pasture the horses.[2]

Drainage has improved over 650,000 farms and almost 45,000,000 acres in the United States, according to the census of 1930.[3] This seems to be an understatement since the census of 1920 reported over 53,000,000 acres reclaimed through drainage. Much of this drained land is of excellent quality and, because it is level, is least subject to erosion. On the other hand, in the enthusiasm for reclamation of 1905–20 large areas were drained which proved to be worthless, or the cost of drainage was too great for the land to carry. Fine recreational areas were destroyed, many of which are now being restored for wild life and forests.

The earliest drainage was on individual farms, but in many cases reclamation was beyond the means of a single landowner or more than one farm was involved. In other cases drainage had to precede the creation of farms. To permit co-operative and com-

[1] See Chap. IX.

[2] "Long's Expedition to the Source of St. Peter's River," quoted in *Land Available for Agriculture Through Reclamation,* Part IV of the Supplementary Report of the Land Planning Committee to the National Resources Board (1936), p. 35.

[3] *Drainage of Agricultural Lands* (Bureau of the Census, 1930), p. 46. See also O. E. Baker, *A Graphic Summary of Physical Features and Land Utilization in the United States, op. cit.,* Figs. 51–53.

munity action, the legal device of the drainage district was created. Since this method is also used in irrigation, flood control, conservation and, more recently, in wind and water erosion control, it will be described in some detail here.

Drainage Districts. Drainage districts derive their powers from the state and are organized under state statutes. Before 1847 they were authorized by special legislation, but in that year Michigan and Ohio passed general enabling acts and other states soon followed. Naturally many variations occur in the laws, but several essential characteristics are common to all.[1]

Organization starts with a petition from the landowners to some public body, usually the county board or one of the lower courts, asking that a district be organized. The numbers of signatures necessary is expressed as a certain proportion of the landowners of the area to be included, or owners of a certain proportion of the acreage, or a combination of the two. After a public hearing a referendum is held, and if the required number favors the establishment of a district, organization proceeds. The required number is usually a majority of the votes cast, but some states dispense with the referendum entirely, especially where the law requires a large number of signers to the petition.

A common provision in drainage laws is that the cost shall not exceed the benefits. In Virginia, for instance, the court may halt the organization of a district whenever the estimated cost of construction, plus three years of maintenance and the cost of damages, is greater than the expected benefits. In California and Wisconsin the approval of a state officer or body is required. These provisions are designed to guard against uneconomic districts, but in the days of wild enthusiasm for drainage not all unwise enterprises were nipped in the bud.

The control and management of the project is placed in the hands of a small board of "drainage commissioners" elected by the landowners of the district or appointed by the court or some other body. Money needed for the construction of ditches, dams, and other engineering works is usually raised by selling bonds, backed by the land in the district. To retire bonds, pay the interest, and

[1] A synopsis of the drainage laws of the thirty-five states reporting organized drainage enterprises is found in Part III of *Drainage of Agricultural Lands, op. cit.* See also R. P. Teele, *The Economics of Land Reclamation in the United States* (Chicago, A. W. Shaw, 1927), pp. 132–40, 174–80.

provide for annual maintenance, assessments are placed upon the land in proportion to the benefits received. If the landowner has suffered damage he is compensated. One of the most important duties of the drainage commissioners is the determination of benefits and damages. After the assessments have been levied they operate in a manner similar to taxes; collection is enforceable by law with penalties, reversion, and other attributes of the power of taxation. In one respect this power is even more potent than that of taxation; not only farms, but railways, telegraph companies, and other corporations, and even counties and municipalities are subject to drainage assessments. Assessments may be levied on federal lands, however, only with the consent of the federal government.[1]

The significance of the district form of organization, whether for drainage, irrigation, or soil conservation, lies in the fact that the district is an independent unit of government with specified powers delegated to it by the state. Districts may cut across town, country, and municipal boundaries and have the right of eminent domain, the power to levy and collect assessments like taxes and to own property. Any landowner unwilling to "join" is forced by the majority to co-operate in the common enterprise, yet democratic procedure safeguards the rights of the minority. To justify these extraordinary powers the petitions are generally required to state that the object of the project is *public* health, utility, convenience, or welfare.[2]

In some states counties are specified as the bodies to carry on drainage, and county officials are placed in charge of the work, but the cost of reclamation is assessed only against the land benefited. However, in Minnesota and Ohio the bonds issued against drainage projects are "backed by the full faith, credit and resources of the county," which means that the county as a whole assumes the obligations whenever the drained area fails to collect the assessments. Northern Minnesota counties have been plunged into financial difficulties because of the failure of drain-

[1] George R. Boyd and R. A. Hart, *Drainage District Assessments* (U. S. Dept. of Agriculture, Bulletin 1207, 1924), pp. 8–9.

[2] Drainage districts, like other *ad hoc* units of government, sometimes cause difficulties when too many layers of government tax the same land. It is easy to "overload the land" and difficult to unscramble the conflicting claims whenever taxes are delinquent.

age projects.[1] In 1930, 56 per cent of all land in drainage enterprises was in county drains. The almost 68,000 enterprises in all types of districts covered practically 84,500,000 acres, an area equal to Iowa and South Dakota. Almost 40 per cent of the area is in the Corn Belt and one-fourth in the Lake states.[2]

Drainage Costs. Drainage is a form of "cost of production" of farm land, and the outlays for maintenance must be considered as part of the annual inputs of labor and capital. In drainage districts the cost of converting wet land, swamps, and marshes into an efficient farm are both private and public, the public costs being those for the levees, ditches, and pumping plant provided by the district co-operatively. As more difficult projects were undertaken these costs became steadily higher, being three times as high in 1915–20 as before 1870. In 1930 the average investment per acre was $8.06, but in several states it was above $20 and in one case above $30. It is estimated that the United States has about 91,000,000 acres of land suitable for crops and improved pasture after being drained, but only one-third of this area can be reclaimed at a cost of $30 per acre or less.[3] With the present trend in the demand for farm products it is doubtful whether it will pay to drain land at costs approaching $30 an acre.[4]

Drainage districts organized before much of the land is in productive use or, in the case of commercial enterprises, before it is even in farms, incur waiting and ripening costs in addition to the easily discernable "production" costs. The postponement of repaying the bonds or of paying interest, permitted by some states, is a cost to someone. The idle land within a district simply increases the burden on the land that is "working." In 1930 only 75 per cent of the land in drainage enterprises was improved. Almost 8,000,000 acres were for sale and reported available for settlement. Failure to meet public costs manifests itself in delinquency in drainage assessments and arrears in paying principal and interest of the bonded indebtedness. While the agricultural depression helped to put many drainage enterprises into

[1] R. W. Murchie and C. R. Wasson, *Beltrami Island, Minnesota Resettlement Project* (Minnesota Agric. Exp. Station Bulletin 334, 1937), 11–15.
[2] *Drainage of Agricultural Lands, op. cit.*, p. 19 and Table I.
[3] *N. R. B. Report, op. cit.*, p. 131.
[4] The Census of 1920 reported almost 40,000,000 acres *in farms* needing drainage. Much of this can be drained at lower costs by farmers individually.

difficulties, others failed or had to be refinanced because they were economically unsound ventures. In 1930 about one-eighth of the acreage in the districts was delinquent and in arrears, and almost 24 per cent was reported idle. In 1933 Congress authorized the Reconstruction Finance Corporation to assist drainage enterprises.[1]

The Swamp Land Act. Almost the first case of federal assistance in land reclamation was the Swamp Land Act of 1850.

TABLE 19

POPULATION AND FARM LAND SUPPLY OF THE UNITED STATES, 1850–1935 [2]

YEAR	POPULATION (MILLIONS)	ALL LAND IN FARMS			IMPROVED LAND*		VALUE OF REAL ESTATE PER ACRE
		Total Millions of Acres	Acres per Capita	Increase in Millions of Acres	Total Millions of Acres	Per Capita Acres	
1850	23	294	12.7		113	4.9	$11.14
1860	31	407	13.0	113	163	5.2	16.32
1870	39	408	10.6	1	189	4.9	18.26
1880	50	536	10.7	128	285	5.7	19.02
1890	63	623	9.9	87	358	5.7	21.31
1900	76	839	11.0	216	414	5.5	19.81
1910	92	879	9.6	40	478	5.2	39.60
1920	106	956	9.0	77	503	4.8	69.38
1925	114	924	8.1	−32	505	4.4†	53.20
1930	123	987	8.0	63	522	4.3†	48.52
1935	127	1,055	8.2	68	514	4.0†	31.16

* Improved land is all land regularly tilled or mowed, land in pasture which has been cleared or tilled, fallow land, land in orchards, gardens, vineyards, etc., and farmsteads. This classification was discontinued after 1920.

† The 1925 and subsequent censuses reported crop land, pasture, woodland. "Land Available for Crops" is crop land plus plowable pasture. This is the figure used for 1925, 1930, and 1935 for "Improved Land."

In 1849 Congress transferred to Louisiana all the swamp and overflow lands within her border to reimburse her for the expenditures she had made in protecting from floods, not only the

[1] *Drainage of Agricultural Lands, op. cit.*, pp. 15, 45; *Land Available for Agriculture through Reclamation, op. cit.*, pp. 37–39; Teele, *op. cit.*, Chaps. VII and VIII.

[2] Based on U. S. Census.

farm land, but the land still in public domain, by the 1,400 miles of levees built by the people of Louisiana. The next year the act was extended to other public land states. The intent of the act was that the swamp and overflow lands donated by the federal government should be sold and the proceeds used for drainage and flood control. Only in rare cases were the funds used for land reclamation; instead they were used for schools, to subsidize railroad construction, and for other purposes. There was fraud in selecting the land granted to the states and more fraud in disposing of it to individuals. The main accomplishment of the Swamp Land Act was the transfer of about 64,000,000 acres of public domain to fifteen states.[1]

Expansion of the Agricultural Land Area before 1920. Table 19 shows the increase since 1850 in agricultural land, measured in terms of "all land in farms" and "improved land." The expansion of the farm area was retarded by the Civil War but rapidly regained its stride. It reached its greatest proportions during the 1890's when the increase was so rapid that in 1900 the farm land and improved area per capita was actually greater than thirty years before.

However, in the first decade of the twentieth century the rapid expansion of the agricultural area was halted; only 40,000,000 acres of farm land were added between 1900 and 1910 and 77,000,000 acres in the next ten years, most of it in the West. The period from 1900 to the close of the World War was one of agricultural prosperity. Free land was gone; rather, settlement was meeting the resistance of the arid and cut-over frontiers, and a temporary decline in agricultural efficiency, in terms of production per capita, was making for a growing scarcity of farm products in the face of a rapidly increasing population.[2] During the first ten years of the century population increased by 16,000,000, and almost 9,000,000 immigrants had come to our shores. Both the population increase and the number of immigrants were the largest in our history. While cities investigated the "high cost of living," farmers were living in a golden era of rising prices for products and land.

[1] Hibbard, *A History of the Public Land Policies*, *op. cit.*, pp. 269–88; Teele, *op. cit.*, pp. 51–61.

[2] O. E. Baker, "The Outlook for Land Utilization in the United States," *Journal of Farm Economics*, April, 1931, pp. 217–18.

Land Policies of the Conservation Era, 1900–1920. The new ratio of man to land aroused an interest in reclamation of all kinds, in cut-over land, drainage, and irrigation. It was felt that land was being worn out, so the problems of erosion, increasing crop yields, and fertilization caught the attention of the public. Settlement and colonization were given additional impetus. Some states gave financial assistance to irrigation districts, to colonization companies, or directly to settlers by loans or special rural credit acts. Some aided settlers in the selection of land or protected them from buying submarginal land. A few established state-directed colonies, notably California and Washington. Private settlement was assisted by the states, through their agricultural colleges and experiment stations, in land clearing, drainage, irrigation, and in other ways. Agricultural education and extension were expanded, because, as James J. Hill put it, "This country cannot feed the population which it must necessarily have within a comparatively few years if it does not change its agricultural methods." [1] The federal government felt justified in reclaiming desert lands by irrigation to increase the food supply and to make arid land available to home seekers.

Most of the states established immigration departments to advertise the opportunities and advantages of the state to settlers.[2] Where no regular immigration official or commission existed, the department of agriculture or some other body often acted in the capacity of immigration stimulator. Canada and her provinces followed a similar policy and in some respects set the pace. In some states semi-official or private chambers of commerce or similar organizations performed this function with the sanction of the public. The Virginia Chamber of Commerce is an example. After the World War, when the back-to-the-farm movement had slackened, this body petitioned Congress to amend the immigration laws to permit "selected, desirable agricultural immigrants" to be admitted "to people Virginia's millions of man-hungry unoccupied tillable acres with desirable, permanent agricultural settlers." [3] The war had given the final impetus to the intensifica-

[1] Van Hise and Havemeyer, *op. cit.*, p. 349.

[2] B. Henderson, *Farm Land Available for Settlement* (Farmers' Bulletin 1271, 1922) lists twenty-six active immigration departments.

[3] Press release of March 21, 1924.

tion and expansion of agriculture by its appeals to patriotism and the stimulus of war prices.

Readjustment of Land Uses, 1920–1930. Even if there had been no other complicating elements, the readjustment of the abnormally expanded agricultural plant to post-war conditions would have been painful enough. However, other factors made matters worse. European countries instituted a policy of self-sufficiency and built up their own productive capacities. This reduced the demand for cotton, wheat, tobacco, pork, and other products which were sold abroad. In 1920 fully 61,000,000 acres of land, or 17 per cent of the total acreage, were used to grow the crops sent abroad. Production in this area had to be adjusted to demands at home. If the "self-contained nation idea" is carried to its final conclusion, a still more drastic curtailment of certain crops will be necessary.

The home market was reduced not only by the declining rate of population growth due to restrictions on immigration and the fall in the birth rate, but also by changes in the consuming habits of our people. The changing styles in women's dress and the introduction of rayon reduced the demand for cotton. The per capita consumption of cereals and some meats decreased, whereas the demand for sugar, dairy products, fruits, and vegetables increased. The shift has been from land-using to labor-using crops. It is significant that this change came in the period of urban prosperity and great urbanization. The accompanying change to more sedentary occupations—to riding in automobiles instead of walking, for instance—reduced the per capita need for food.

While the demand for farm products was decreasing, the farmers' capacity to produce increased in an unforeseen and incredible manner. Mechanization increased the power to operate land from 12 acres per man in 1850 to 34 acres in 1930. In Montana one man, using horses, with some help at harvest time, can handle 320 acres, but with a modern heavy-duty tractor he can manage 1,600 acres.[1] The shift from animal power to tractors, the change from less productive to more productive crops, the improvements in animal breeding and feeding have added 20 to 25 per cent to the productive capacity of the agricultural plant without any increase in crop acreage. These factors have had the

[1] *Yearbook of the U. S. Dept. of Agriculture*, 1932, p. 419.

same effect as if 60,000,000 acres of crop land had been added to the crop area of 1920.

The shift to mechanical power has made another profound change in the demand for farm products. The first of these replacements came when the railroad took the place of the horse. The number of horses in England was reduced from 1,000,000 to 200,000 after this happened. It was estimated that the land needed to feed one horse would feed eight men; consequently, the 800,000 horses displaced by the railroads made room for 6,400,000 additional people in England. Since the railroad "grew up with the country" no such displacement was necessary in America.[1]

In the days of horse-cars, carriages, and wagons, practically all vehicles in city and country were propelled by animal power. Electric streetcars were the first substitution for animal power, but soon the automobile and the truck made the cities practically horseless and, together with the tractor, invaded the rural areas as well. The change has had a double influence on agriculture. The city was a market for horses and mules and for the feed needed for their nourishment. Now the farmer no longer has this market: the motorcar and tractor are the products of the mine and factory and so is the "gas" and oil. Even the farmer is now partly dependent upon the commercial world for the power he once produced on his own acres. Between 1910 and 1926 a decrease of about 6,000,000 draft animals took place. The census of 1935 reports more than 2,000,000 fewer horses in 1935 than in 1930. The land released to produce food for human consumption by 1930 was estimated at 25,000,000 acres. This change came with full force just at the time when so many other factors were affecting the supply and demand for the farmers' products.[2]

Future Demand for Agricultural Land in the United States. Today the United States is struggling with the problem of adjusting land uses to a probable population of 150,000,000 million people by 1960 instead of 200,000,000 or more. Instead of agriculture's absorbing all the land physically available for this purpose, it now is estimated that only about 27,000,000 more acres

[1] *Wisconsin and Iowa Farmer,* Vol. 3, 1851, p. 21.

[2] O. E. Baker, *A Graphic Summary of Farm Machinery, Facilities, Roads and Expenditures* (U. S. Dept. of Agriculture, Miscellaneous Publication 261, 1937), Figs. 3–16.

of crop land above the 1930 harvested crop figures will be needed to feed and clothe the expected increase in population.[1] If the estimate of 2½ acres of crop land per capita is correct, 375,000,000 acres of crop land will be ample to sustain 150,000,000 people. The harvested crop acreage of 1930 was only 15,000,000 acres short of that figure, and the acreage "available for crops," which includes crop failure, idle, fallow, and plowable pasture, was 147,000,000 acres in excess of the estimated acreage needed for this population of 150,000,000 people.[2]

It might even be argued that this future population can be sustained without adding another acre to the land now in farms. Land clearing is still going on; "wood land in farms" as reported by the census is a miniature frontier gradually being pushed back, automatically adding to crop and pasture lands of the nation without having to bring new land into farm ownership. The census of 1925 reported over 4,000,000 acres cleared and added to crop land between 1920 and 1925. This clearing was done on half a million farms, mostly in the newer sections but also on Corn Belt farms. Since the recent exodus to the land has been largely to the wooded sections, much of the increase in crop land is coming from forest and cut-over regions. Other shifts come from converting pasture into crop land and changing to more intensive crops. During the World War decade American farmers increased their crop acreage by 45,000,000 acres, whereas the normal rate of increase would have been but 20,000,000, and the new crop acres came largely from shifts within the farms themselves. In fact, it is safe to predict that improvements in the technique of agriculture will continue, and with a stationary population the area necessary to sustain this population may actually shrink. If the agro-biologists are correct we will be able to produce the crops now grown on 241,000,000 acres on an area the size of Kansas, or 52,000,000 acres!

The above estimates of needs are based upon a more or less commercial type of agriculture. With still greater commercialization and mechanization, and with the use of the best grades of land, the number of farmers necessary to produce the nation's

[1] *N. R. B. Report*, p. 111.

[2] George S. Wehrwein, "Goals in Land Use Policy," *Journal of Farm Economics*, February, 1938, pp. 237–46.

sustenance could perhaps be cut in half. Even today the third of the farmers representing the lowest income-producing farms are responsible for only 5 per cent or so of the farm products entering into commerce. However, the area of land in commercial farms and the number of farmers are both augmented by the thousands of partially self-sufficing farmers, who provide a livelihood for themselves to a considerable degree outside of the price system.

Whether the nation should adopt a policy of commercial agriculture and a small farm population, or should actively promote self-sufficing agriculture with a large rural population and as much land in farms as possible, is the subject of lively debate. Many nations have an active agrarian policy aimed to increase the farmer class, believing that there is no longer a balance between urban and rural populations. German economists, even before the present regime, suggested policies for "the maintenance of a numerous, truly independent, physically and mentally healthy peasant class." This has become the central theme of the German land tenure policy and inheritance laws, both designed to permit as large a proportion of the people to remain on the farms as possible.[1] In the United States also, some economists and sociologists believe that a large rural population is desirable for its own sake. Those who view the rapidly declining birth rate with alarm and note the disparity in birth rates between the city and country favor a large rural and village population as a means of increasing the birth rate. To others the security of self-sufficient farming, the simple life, and the contact with nature make their appeal. Still others consider the country a recruiting ground for the cities. There is also the tradition, though a dying one, that all great men were born in the country, preferably in log cabins, and that a decline in rural population will dry up the source of genius. It is not possible to discuss the pros and cons of the subject here, but it should be pointed out that these philosophies have a definite influence on the land policies of nations, not only on land tenure and inheritance institutions, but also on policies of land utilization. The contrast may be observed in the colonization policies of Ontario and Quebec, the former more or less capital-

[1] C. von Dietze, "Land Tenure and the Social Control of the Use of Land," *Proceedings of the Fifth International Conference of Agricultural Economists, op. cit.*

istic, the latter based upon the life, ideals, and institutions of the habitant.[1]

The Trend in Farm Population in the United States. The surplus of population on the farms is a normal situation. While the frontier was open many farm people followed Horace Greeley's advice and "went West," but from the very beginning farm people have also moved to cities from the rural areas. On the other hand, there is also a less well-known migration from cities to farms. In 1920, for instance, 896,000 people left farms for the cities, whereas 560,000 *moved to the farms.* The net movement was 336,000 in favor of the cities. Were it not for the high birth rate in the country the rural areas would become depopulated. During the readjustment period of 1920 to 1929 urban industry was prosperous. Cities absorbed not only the normal surplus of rural young folks but attracted others as well. Those who had started farming on the frontiers were pulled by the high wages and pushed by the low prices of farm products to abandon their farms and take jobs in the factory. Farm population had shrunk from about 32,000,000 people in 1920 to about 30,000,000 in 1929, accompanied by a decrease of 160,000 farms.[2] It is estimated that 5,000,000 rural people moved into the cities during this period, and if this exodus had continued long enough it would have done much to solve the farm problem. By and by a balance might have been reached, leaving just enough farmers to feed and clothe the cities at prices which would have given them a high standard of living. Sir Daniel Hall stated a few years ago that with proper organization of agriculture only 10 per cent of a country's population need be on the land.[3] Cities were absorbing all who were released from agriculture to such an extent that Robert Murry Haig could say in 1926, "The question is

[1] A. R. M. Lower, "Settlement and the Forest Frontier in Eastern Canada," in Vol. IX of *Canadian Frontiers of Settlement* (Toronto, Macmillan, 1936), Chaps. 7 and 8; A. W. Ashby, "The Relations of Land Tenure to the Economic and Social Development of Agriculture," *Proceedings of the Fourth International Conference of Agricultural Economists, op. cit.*, pp. 87–103; Stephen S. Vischer, "Where Our Notables Come From," *Scientific Monthly*, August, 1937, pp. 172–77; O. E. Baker's writings, particularly "Rural-urban Migration and the National Welfare," *op. cit.*; Cauley, *Agrarianism, op. cit.*; Heske, *German Forestry, op. cit.*, Chap. 21.

[2] Folsom and Baker, *op. cit.*, Figs. 27–49, especially 41–49.

[3] "Feeding the World," *op. cit.*, pp. 678–88.

changed from 'Why live in a city?' to 'Why *not* live in a city?' "[1]

Since the urban depression of 1929 the rural-urban population movement has been retarded. From 1920 to 1929 the net movement from the farms average 662,000 per year. In 1930 it dropped to 212,000, in 1931 it was only 20,000 and was actually reversed in 1932. In that year 266,000 *more* people moved away from the cities than migrated from the country to the urban centers. After 1932 the net cityward movement was partially restored. The reduced migration and the normal increase by births have "dammed up" people on farms. The increase in farms, especially subsistence and part-time farms, as part of this "flight" has been noted elsewhere. Cities became panic-stricken and many proposals were made to get people out of the city onto the soil. Publishers, industrialists, and public officials suddenly became poetic about "Mother Earth" and proposed placing millions on the land in the name of relief for agriculture. Unfortunately, many who left the cities migrated to the frontiers to reinhabit abandoned shacks where a former settler had starved; they merely added to the cost of schools, roads, and relief in the poorest counties of these states. The theory that if a man and land are put together the product will be a self-supporting citizen, simply did not work.

In conclusion, and before discussing the adjustments called for by the new man-land ratio, it might be well to note how the recent changes have upset the old concepts of the "progress of society," rent, value, and the distribution of wealth. Instead of being in the favored position, owners of natural resources in general are experiencing their full share of depression and lack of control over production. Although agricultural land prices behaved in a Ricardian manner, particularly up to the close of the World War, the reaction following the war has been such that the value of farm real estate in 1935 was about at the 1905 level, despite the spectacular back-to-the-land movement between 1930 and 1935. Probably more interesting and significant is the fact that the proposal to nationalize the agricultural land of Great Britain, both in 1925 and more recently, was provoked, not by the fear of excessive earnings for landlords, but by just the opposite. Their returns have become so low, or in some cases ac-

[1] Haig, "Toward an Understanding of the Metropolis," *Quarterly Journal of Economics,* February, 1926, p. 213.

tually negative, that the government has granted aids for drainage and other improvements. It is felt that this condition must end in public control over the land and ultimately in public ownership. Landlords have failed to perform the functions which are expected of them because rents have not been sufficient to permit them to do so.[1]

PROBLEMS IN THE UTILIZATION OF AGRICULTURAL LAND

Problems in agricultural land utilization fall into two classes: (1) those due to shifts in agriculture, which were with us before the depression, and (2) those due to over-expansion and settlement on submarginal land, due to the changes in the status of agriculture since the World War.

Problems Due to Shifts in Agriculture. Before the West was opened, eastern farms enjoyed a fine market in the cities of the seaboard and in a limited export trade. Many of them had been built up with great care and were equipped with buildings that are a joy architecturally to this day. Their security was ruthlessly destroyed when canals and railroads brought in the bountiful harvests of the West and when the newly invented farm machinery favored the large level farms of the prairies. Grain farming became unprofitable, sheep raising shifted to the frontier, and drastic adjustments had to be made.

The repercussion of the fertile Western lands on the East can be traced in the loss of farm land. New England had 18,000,000 acres of farm land in 1850, which gradually increased to 21,000,000, but by 1930 it had shrunk to 14,000,000 acres. The Middle Atlantic states reached their maximum acreage in 1880 with 46,000,000 acres of land in farms, but in 1930 only 35,000,000 million acres were so reported. Part of the decrease is accounted for by the shift to urban uses, highways, and railways, but most of the acreage passed out of use as "abandoned farms."

[1] *The Land and the Nation,* Rural Report of the Liberal Land Committee, 1923–25 (London, Hodder and Stoughton). See also the paper by Ashby and discussion by George Dallas in *Proceedings of the Fourth International Conference of Agricultural Economists, op. cit.,* pp. 101–3, 122–24.

Charles Abrams in his *Revolution in Land* (New York, Harpers, 1939) says "Land in America has become the heritage of the underprivileged. Wretched farms and shabby homes, mortgage debt and tenancy, overcrowding and unwholesome living conditions—all these have become a part of that gloomy heritage." (p. 7.)

The process of abandonment begins with a decrease in the more intensive uses within the farm itself. In 1880 one-third of New England was classed as improved land; in 1920 only 15 per cent. It is estimated that farm land has reverted to brush and forest land at the rate of a million acres per year during the past few decades. Large areas of farm land in the southeastern pine lands are now covered with forests, and fairly salable timber is to be found in Virginia in former cotton fields, with the ridges made by the cultivators still visible. This also is true of other regions of the South.

Farm abandonment is a long-time process. The farm is not abandoned just because there is no economic rent. Not until the improvements on the land have depreciated so far that they fail to function is the battle lost. The self-sufficing elements make possible the persistence of farmers on land which has become submarginal. Standards of living can be lowered until only a few dollars of cash are needed for outside purchases. Production therefore exists on lands below the margin of profitable utilization, both on the advancing frontier and on the older but now submarginal lands. Both margins tend to react on the good farmer on good land insofar as the "marginal" farms sell their products on the market and are competitors of the commercial farmer.

The loss in farms and crop land, however, is no longer confined to the East. In spite of the extraordinary demands upon agriculture during the World War, the farm area of the nation increased only 8.8 per cent (1910–20), but all except three of the states east of the Mississippi reported a decline in the area of land in farms. The decrease of 7,000,000 acres east of the Mississippi was offset by an increase of 84,000,000 in the West. In the next decade the shift was accelerated. An actual decrease in crop acreage took place in practically every state east of the Mississippi and in the Pacific states as well. However, between 1930 and 1935 an extraordinary increase of almost 68,000,000 acres of land in farms was reported; all states except Nevada and California apparently gained in the acreage of farm land.[1]

[1] O. E. Baker, *A Graphic Summary of Physical Features and Land Utilization in the United States, op. cit.*, Figs. 20–35. Some of this "gain" may be due to differences in methods of enumeration.

The paradox of the situation lies in the fact that while abandoned farms appeared in the East, attributed to worn-out soils, to tenancy, and to poor farming, public and private land policies were directed toward bringing more land into farms and reclaiming swamps, cut-over lands, and deserts. Public funds were being spent in creating competition for the farmers already established in the older sections of the country. State and national policies still proceeded on the theory that there cannot be too many farms and farmers.

Over-expansion and Settlement on Submarginal Land. In the "conservation era" of 1900 to 1920 the conservationist and land boomer operated hand in hand. While the former talked of "wise" use, the latter was sure that agriculture was the only "wise" use. Public and private agencies assisted the land seller in "developing" the unused lands and in placing people who had neither experience nor aptitude for farming on cut-over, drained, and irrigated lands.

In the effort to convert all land into farms, the concept of submarginal land was forgotten or hushed up. The fact that a few good farmers had been able to "make a showing" became the basis for believing that the success of subduing the frontier was all in the man and lay in his skill in managing sandy, swampy, or other recalcitrant soils. It was also observed that foreign groups such as the Finns, Slavs, Germans, and others either showed unusual aptitude in clearing land and creating farms or were willing to accept a low standard of living. Serious consideration was given to the settling of foreigners, especially because "native Americans and even old-time immigrants avoid hard pioneering work in the wilderness since they can find opportunities for lighter work and better returns elsewhere."[1] This tended to set a margin based upon the standard of living the settler was willing to accept. The problems in the cut-over areas may serve as an example.

Land Problems in the Cut-over Regions. The difficulties of the cut-over lands have been varied and even conflicting. For many years it was the lag of settlement which caused the major problems. As long as trees were removed to create farms there were no "cut-overs," nor was there any problem of idle land while

[1] Peter A. Speek, *A Stake in the Land* (New York, Harper's, 1921), p. 8.

logging and settlement went forward simultaneously. However, the sawmill soon outdistanced the plow and the vast areas of cut-over lands came into existence. In the decade 1900 to 1910, improved farm land increased at the rate of 6,400,000 acres annually, but cut-over lands overtopped this by increasing at the rate of 9,400,000 acres each year. In the 1910–20 decade the area of improved farm land increased at the rate of 2,500,000 acres per year, but the lumberman added to the cut-over lands four times as much land in the same period.[1]

One reason for the slow development of agriculture in the present cut-over regions was the high cost of producing farms in forested areas as compared to the treeless prairies. Furthermore, the same lumber production which created cut-over land for the Lake states provided the cheap lumber and fencing that made competing prairie agriculture possible. After the Civil War westward moving settlers "by-passed" the wooded sections, and the prairies even attracted the residents of Lake states. Later the opportunities on irrigated lands, in dry farming, and in Canada increased the competition. The lag in settlement created a gulf of "idle" land—land which was not productive either as forest land or as agricultural land. Lumbering companies, having harvested their crop, had no further use for the soil and simply let it revert to the states or counties for taxes. Had it not been for the retardation of westward expansion, the growth in population, and the rise in land values after 1900 which renewed the wave of settlement in the Lake states, this condition would have been augmented and become permanent. However, after 1900 tax-delinquent or reverted land was restored to the tax rolls by colonization companies, by speculators, and by others who felt that the land would soon be wanted for farms and who hoped to share in the rise in land values.

Yet in spite of the rapid development during the conservation era it would have taken 125 years to convert the cut-over lands of the South into farms at the rate of clearing in that period, and 250 years at the rate of settlement which prevailed from 1920 to

[1] *Yearbook*, 1922, *op. cit.*, p. 88. This refers to the predepression decades. The discrepancy became greater after 1920 when land in farms was actually decreasing for a while.

1925. In the Lake states one to four centuries would have elapsed before the available cut-over land could have been turned into farms at the existing speed of settlement. In fact, it would have taken 800 years to get the Upper Peninsula of Michigan settled, providing all of it were suitable for agriculture. Meanwhile ripening costs were creating a load for speculators which no increase in the value of raw land could hope to offset. Under the assumption that the land would be held for agriculture, another wave of tax delinquency was unavoidable. However, the waiting period might have been bridged had we been forest-minded. Even granting that in the distant future the land was destined for an agricultural use, it could have grown another crop of timber or several crops of pulpwood while waiting.

In the second place, in the optimism of settlement the fact was overlooked, consciously and unconsciously, that much of the cut-over land was definitely submarginal for agriculture. As early as 1898 Filibert Roth reported that only 20 per cent of the soil of northern Wisconsin was of a superior quality, 40 per cent was of fair value for agriculture, and 40 per cent was not suited for farming and should remain in forests.[1] While his estimates were not absolutely correct, it is significant that the submarginal character of the land was made public forty years ago. Similar conditions are characteristic of other cut-over states. Had the land been classified and submarginal farm lands removed from sale, a forest policy could have been started in the early part of this century and the cut-overs would be yielding timber products today. However, the land came on the agricultural market, good and bad alike, innocently and fraudulently. In spite of the efforts of immigration departments to guide and advise prospective settlers, many farmers were placed on land which could not support them on any decent standard of living. Here, as in other parts of the United States, submarginal lands were deliberately sold to "suckers." Farm abandonment, therefore, was inevitable even in prosperous years, and cannot be laid entirely at the door of the depression.

Tax delinquency and farm abandonment, however, were pre-

[1] Filibert Roth, *Forestry Conditions of Northern Wisconsin* (Wisconsin Geological and Natural History Survey, Bulletin 1, 1898), p. 8.

cipitated by the break in prices of 1920. Land above the margin under war prices was distinctly below the margin of profitable use after the depression set in. If the depression played havoc with the good farmer on good land, it was doubly disastrous to the settler who was caught in the critical situation of having sunk his money in land, buildings, and equipment, with only a few acres cleared and years of ripening costs ahead. Practically all settlers had to depend on outside labor to tide them over this "grubstake" period, but with the decline in lumbering such opportunities became scarce. Those on submarginal land and those with the least income migrated first to accept city jobs. In time the region was dotted with abandoned farmhouses. Owners of cut-over land—speculators, land companies, and others—saw no further opportunity to sell land to settlers, soon failed to pay taxes, and the land reverted to the states or counties, thus creating a "new public domain" of millions of acres of idle land. The remaining settlers were even more isolated after their neighbors had gone to the cities.

It is estimated that 52,000,000 acres of land laboriously hewn out of the wilderness for farming have been abandoned and are ready for reforestation, and by 1950 this area may be increased by another 25,000,000 to 30,000,000 acres.[1]

The problem spread in ever-widening circles. Local governments had laid out roads, built schoolhouses and courthouses, and planned other public expenditures in anticipation of increasing population and a larger tax base. The depression dashed their hopes. The sawmills continued to remove the remaining timber. Other mills had to shut down during the depression, thereby reducing the opportunity for outside work to settlers. As forests were removed the tax base also decreased, augmented by the tax delinquency on deserted farms and cut-over land. The isolated settlers demanded their share of public services, which became excessive if considered on a per capita basis. A road nine miles long had to be maintained for the benefit of a single settler in one locality. In this case the entire state shared in the excessive cost, because it paid $40 to $50 a year in state aid to the local town for the maintenance of that road. Schools with only three

[1] *A National Plan for American Forestry,* Senate Document 12, 73d Congress, 1st Session, 2 vols. (1933), pp. 151–69.

or four pupils are being conducted at a cost of $300 to $500 per pupil per year, largely paid for out of state funds.

Rural Zoning. After 1929 the problem was aggravated by the city exodus to the land. Abandoned houses were reoccupied and new shacks erected in out-of-the-way places. This meant additional outlays by towns and counties already overburdened with costs and a depleted tax base. This situation brought about the rural county zoning movement in Wisconsin. By an enabling act of 1923, counties were given the power to zone their lands in general, and in 1929 this power was enlarged to permit zoning for agriculture, forestry, and recreation. Beginning with 1933, twenty-five northern and central Wisconsin counties have closed over 5,000,000 acres of land to further agricultural settlement by setting up forestry and recreational districts in which farming is prohibited. The direct purpose was to prevent future isolated settlement with its attendant high costs for public services and also to prohibit settlement on the poorer and submarginal lands of the county. Instead of inviting "suckers," these counties have actually made it illegal to use certain lands for farming. Even with one-third of the area closed to agriculture, almost a fourth of the area of these counties is still unoccupied and open to further agricultural development.

The zoning of marginal lands is important as one of the first attempts to use the police power to control population and direct land uses outside of incorporated places. California preceded Wisconsin in establishing county zoning by permitting individual counties to zone. Both states now have general enabling acts, and other states have followed their example.[1]

Resettlement of Stranded Populations. The shifts in agriculture and the over-expansion and settlement on submarginal lands have left thousands of stranded farmers, many of whom fail to make a decent living and most of whom create excessive public costs. Some people on submarginal land have been there for more than a century, as, for instance, in the Appalachians, and have adopted a way of life peculiar to themselves. The offhand suggestion to set up a gigantic resettlement scheme and move all these people out of the submarginal areas is unrealistic. It was once suggested that the problem of the agricultural surplus

[1] See Chap. XIII for other phases of county zoning.

could be solved by purchasing the land on the margin and "work upward." The futility of this was first seen when it was pointed out that the removal of the "lower half" of the farmers of the United States would affect only 12 per cent of the products entering into commerce. More important still, unless jobs or other land can be found for resettling the farmers, the plan will not work. Unfortunately a period of urban depression is a poor time to try to move people into cities. To place them on better land, where they would be expected to produce more than on their submarginal farms, could hardly be justified when under other programs farmers would be paid to plow under crops and to reduce production from a national point of view. It is also a serious question whether the frontier or mountaineer farmer or squatter can readily adjust himself to commercial agriculture.

In spite of these difficulties it is sound public policy to retire submarginal land from cultivation. The National Resources Planning Board has recommended the retirement of 75,000,000 acres of such land, representing a little over 20,000,000 acres of crop land. This would involve the purchase of about 450,000 farms.[1] In general these areas are located in the hilly forested regions, the drier portions of the Great Plains, regions with serious erosion, and those with light sandy soils.

In the areas zoned against agriculture an additional reason for resettlement arises. Since zoning is not retroactive, those who established their farms before the ordinance was passed are permitted to stay. They are entitled to the same public services as before, and therefore zoning does not remove the defects which it is designed to cure, it can only prevent future costs. Roughly 2,000 such "non-conforming users" live in the Wisconsin zoned areas, of which perhaps one-half are causing unusual expenses for public services. Progress is being made by trading land and by other measures in resettling the non-conforming users. The next step after resettlement is the reorganization and readjustment of local governments to suit the new conditions of land use and distribution of population. A study of the savings that could be made by reorganizing local governments and relocating the isolated settlers of the fourteen northeastern counties of Minnesota

[1] *N. R. B. Report*, pp. 110–11, 175–84.

indicated that $923,400 could be saved annually by both reorganization and relocation and $443,600 by reorganization alone.[1]

Zoning and resettlement complement each other in a land use program. Zoning closes the land to agriculture; resettlement removes the non-conforming settler, thereby leaving a homogeneous district which can be devoted to forestry and recreation. Zoning without resettlement is a job half done. On the other hand, resettlement without zoning may be a job never done. There is nothing to prevent the private owner from starting a farm or selling submarginal land, thus repeating all the mistakes of the past and incurring public costs, and eventually the victim may call upon the public to resettle him or place him on relief. Naturally, a resettlement program must be a long-time program carried out with a full understanding of local conditions and of the settlers' needs and psychology. One of the achievements of rural zoning is that it has been a democratic local movement by which local people have elected to regulate the uses of the land of their county in the interest of public welfare.

Purchase and Reforestation Program of New York State. New York is typical of the older sections of the United States where problems exist because of shifts in agriculture rather than because of over-expansion onto submarginal land. In the East the present use of land is the result of a century or more of experimentation in endeavoring to find the best use for land under changing economic conditions. New York is attempting to find the proper use for land once suitable for farming but now submarginal under the impact of competition of the commercial farms of the West. The belief that what the land needed was "the right kind of farmer" was a constant bait for Western and Southern "suckers." In spite of such new blood, farm abandonment proceeded at the rate of 100,000 acres per year for forty years and after 1928 at the rate of about 250,000 acres per year. It is estimated that there are some 6,000,000 acres of submarginal and idle farm land in New York, yet by a better utilization of the good farm lands this state maintained its position as fifth or sixth agricultural state in the total value of farm products. However, with farm abandon-

[1] O. B. Jesness and R. I. Nowell, *et al., A Program for Land Use in Northern Minnesota* (Minneapolis, University of Minnesota Press, 1935), p. 266. See also Chaps. X and XI.

ment came the usual harvest of isolation, small schools, and high costs for public services as in the cut-over areas.

The land problem was attacked by a series of studies and surveys beginning with soil surveys in 1899 and culminating in the careful land classification surveys made by Cornell University.[1] These surveys and extension work gave the people of the state the background and desire to foster the legislation which followed. General interest in reforestation, begun in 1927, has resulted in state and county forests and a forest taxation law. In 1931 the people approved a constitutional amendment providing for the acquisition of a million acres of abandoned and submarginal farm land for reforestation over a period of fifteen years at a cost of $20,000,000. Sale is entirely voluntary, so the land is purchased at very low figures. Up to October, 1938, 413,688 acres had been purchased, or were under contract for purchase, at an average of $3.89 per acre. When the program is completed large areas will be in solid blocks of forests in which schools, roads, and other public expenditures will no longer be necessary. Besides this, the state is providing itself with a future timber supply and new recreational opportunities. Forests will replace old tumble-down buildings which are depressing evidences of the failure of agriculture on land unsuited for this purpose. The positive side of this land program consists of developing the compact agricultural areas by giving them hard-surfaced roads, rural electrification, good schools and health facilities.[2]

Although New York also has a rural zoning law under which towns can presumably regulate the use of agricultural land, the law has less application than in the Lake states. The state reforestation program will eventually take over most of the submarginal farm land, yet zoning might prove helpful in preventing settlement in abandoned farm areas still in private ownership.[3]

Resettlement and Land Purchase by the Federal Government. The federal government has been engaged in land-use adjustment

[1] For an excellent summary of the studies and surveys see A. B. Lewis, *Methods Used in an Economic Study of Land Utilization in Tompkins County, New York, and in Other Similar Studies in New York* (Cornell University Memoir 160, April, 1934).

[2] Carl E. Ladd, "Land Planning in the Empire State," *New Republic,* August 3, 1932, pp. 306–8.

[3] Robert Whitten, "Rural Zoning in New York," *Journal of Land and Public Utility Economics,* August, 1936, pp. 313–14.

programs for several years. The Subsistence Homesteads program had as one of its objectives the resettlement of stranded populations, and some projects were begun under this organization. The work was transferred to the Resettlement Administration, which more recently was made a part of the Farm Security Administration, which in turn comes under the jurisdiction of the United States Department of Agriculture. The activities of the administration include: (1) the development of three Greenbelt towns, (2) "rural rehabilitation" under which supervised credit is extended to farm families unable to secure credit through the usual channels, and (3) the purchase of over 9,000,000 acres of submarginal agricultural lands—together with the necessary research and co-ordination with other land-use programs, federal, state, and local. Most of the purchasing during 1937–38 was done on the Great Plains because of the acute land problems of the Dust Bowl. Land so purchased is generally turned over to state conservation departments or other state agencies for administration, or to federal departments such as the Forest Service, the National Park Service, etc. Of special interest are the projects designed to turn over a million acres to the office of Indian Affairs to be used for the Indian rehabilitation program. Another three-fourths of a million acres are to be administered by the Biological Survey for the migratory water fowl.

VII

AGRICULTURAL LAND TENURE AND SOIL CONSERVATION

"Tenantry is unfavorable to freedom. . . . The tenant has, in fact, no country, no hearth, no domestic altar, no household god. The freeholder, on the contrary, is the national supporter of a free government, and it should be the policy of republics to multiply their freeholders as is the policy of monarchies to multiply tenants." These were the sentiments of Senator Thomas Hart Benton when he espoused the policy of granting land "without price" to settlers.[1] The idea of freeholders each "under his *own* vine and fig tree" was one of the dominating factors back of American land policies. No wonder it came as a surprise when the census of 1880 disclosed the unwelcome truth that about one-fourth of our farmers were renters, in spite of the fact that millions of acres of land were still to be had for the homesteading. At that time only 536,000,000 acres were in farms, just about half of the acreage of 1935. Since 1880 the proportion of tenant-operated farms has steadily increased until in 1935 over 42 per cent of our farmers were renters and 10 per cent *part-owners,* i.e., owners renting land in addition to the land they own.[2]

AGRICULTURAL LAND TENURE

Mention should be made of a small group of farms operated by hired labor under the supervision of a manager. Only .7 per cent of the farms of the United States are under the supervision of managers, but since these are generally large farms this type of enterprise is more important from the standpoint of area than of numbers. Manager-operated farms embraced 5.8 per cent of the land in farms in 1935. Managers constitute 3 per cent of the farmers, yet they operate over 10 per cent of all the farm land in the Pacific states. Although less important numerically in the Mountain and Plains states, they supervise about one-tenth of the farm land in these regions also.

[1] Hibbard, *A History of the Public Land Policies, op. cit.,* pp. 142–43.

[2] H. A. Turner, *A Graphic Summary of Farm Tenure* (U. S. Dept. of Agriculture, Miscellaneous Publication 261, 1936).

Tenants who rent all the land they cultivate constitute about 17 per cent of the farmers of the East and operate about the same proportion of the farm land. The same relationship holds in the Pacific states, but in this section about one-fifth of the farmers are tenants. In the Corn Belt and Lake states tenants operate a larger proportion of the acreage than their numbers indicate, whereas the opposite is true of all other sections. It is especially noteworthy that although almost 54 per cent of the farmers of the South are tenants they control less than 40 per cent of the farm land. The 53 per cent of the farmers of the 100th Meridian states who are tenants operate only 37 per cent of the land, which indicates that here, as well as in the South, tenant farms are smaller than owner or part-owner farms whereas the reverse pertains to the Corn Belt.

In number the proportion of part-owners ranges from 6.4 per cent of all the farmers of the South to 16.3 per cent of those in the Mountain states, but the proportion of the farm land operated by them is higher than the percentage by number in every section, particularly in the West. In the Mountain states almost half of the farm land is operated by part-owners.

Combining the land rented by part-owners with that managed by tenants, a total of 44.7 per cent of all the farm land of the United States is rented land. In the Corn Belt and Plains states over half of the farm land is rented, while in the South only 42.5 per cent is under this form of tenure. It is remarkable that almost 45 per cent of the farm land of the Mountain states is rented, although only 16 per cent of the farmers are renters. The Pacific and Lake states also have a much larger proportion of their farm land rented than the percentage of tenancy indicates.

Geographical Distribution of Rented Farms. The first two columns of Table 20 show that the regions vary considerably in the number of farms and land in farms. The 100th Meridian states have more farm land than any other region, but the South exceeds all others in the number of farmers. The West and East are comparatively unimportant compared to the Mississippi Valley and the South. For this reason the percentage of tenancy means more in these intensely utilized agricultural regions. The South has 48 per cent of all the tenants of the United States, the 100th Meridian states 22 per cent, and the Corn Belt 16 per

TABLE 20

PROPORTION OF FARM LAND AND OF FARMS OPERATED BY VARIOUS TENURE CLASSES, AND BY REGIONS, 1935[1]

Region	Land in Farms Millions of Acres	Proportion of Total Land in Farms								Number of Farmers (thousands)	Proportion of Farmers in the Various Tenure Classes			
		Operated by				Part Owner Land		Total Area Owned	Total Area Rented					
		Managers	Full Owners	Tenants	Part Owners	Owned	Rented				Managers	Full Owners	Tenants	Part Owners
Northeast	66.6	3.6%	70.2%	17.1%	9.1%	5.9%	3.2%	76.1%	20.3%	715	1.3	75.3	16.7	6.7
South	188.5	3.1	49.7	39.2	8.0	4.8	3.2	54.5	42.5	2,548	0.4	39.4	53.8	6.4
Corn Belt	144.5	1.5	38.8	42.3	17.4	9.7	7.7	49.5	50.0	1,188	0.6	47.6	38.6	13.2
Lake	74.7	1.4	51.8	28.6	18.2	10.7	7.5	62.5	36.1	600	0.5	62.0	24.5	13.0
100th Meridian	343.8	6.7	27.3	36.9	29.1	14.7	14.4	42.0	51.3	1,190	0.5	32.1	53.2	14.2
Mountain	173.9	11.4	23.1	16.1	49.4	21.0	28.4	44.1	44.5	271	1.1	54.4	26.6	17.9
Pacific	62.5	10.3	34.9	22.3	32.5	15.5	17.0	50.4	39.3	300	2.9	67.0	21.2	8.9
United States	1,054.5	5.8	37.1	31.9	25.2	12.5	12.7	49.6	44.6	6,812	0.7	47.1	42.1	10.1

[1] Based on 1935 U. S. Census of Agriculture, Vol. III, *General Report*, pp. 110–125: 134.

cent.[1] It is also in these sections that crops are raised which lend themselves to tenant farming. Almost three-fourths of the cotton farms are cultivated by renters and croppers. One-crop "specialties" in general lend themselves to tenant farming and are admirably suited to the needs of absentee landlords; the share is easily established, the product is readily divided, and the tenant can be supervised without much trouble. The more complex fruit, poultry, dairy farms and stock ranches are largely operated by owners.

Compared to the United States, the proportion of tenant-operated farms is low in Canada; only 10.2 per cent of the Canadian farmers were renters in 1931, and another 9.3 per cent were reported as "owner-tenants," i.e., owners who rented land in addition to their own holdings. However, there is a remarkable similarity in the proportion of tenant farms on the Canadian side of the line in corresponding geographical regions. The high proportion of owner-operated farms in the older sections is even more striking than it is in the eastern sections of the United States (Table 21). On the other hand, the Prairie provinces

TABLE 21

PROPORTION OF FARMERS IN OWNER, PART OWNER, AND TENANT CLASSES, CANADA, 1931 [2]

	Prince Edward Island	Nova Scotia	New Brunswick	Quebec	Ontario	Manitoba	Saskatchewan	Alberta	British Columbia
Owner	94.0	94.2	93.9	93.1	81.9	70.1	66.5	73.0	82.0
Part-owner	4.2	3.1	3.4	3.2	6.9	11.7	18.1	14.9	7.1
Tenant	1.8	2.7	2.7	3.7	11.2	18.2	15.4	12.1	10.9

follow the trend set by the same conditions which are responsible for the high proportion of tenant-cultivated farms of the Great Plains of the United States. The high percentage of part-owners is noteworthy. Ontario and British Columbia hold an intermediate position.

[1] In the South the word "tenants," as used by the census, includes "croppers," and therefore these percentages are not strictly comparable.

[2] Seventh Census of Canada (1931), Vol. VIII, *Agriculture* (Dominion Bureau of Statistics, Ottawa, 1936), Table 14, p. xiv.

The Agricultural Ladder. Senator Benton's dream of a nation of freeholders was possible only as long as the United States and Canada could present a farm in full ownership to every pioneer. But when the second generation was ready to acquire a farm in the older settled areas the land was in private ownership, was cleared and improved, and had buildings on it. It was now a "produced factor of production," valuable, and not to be had without a price. In 1930 the average Iowa farm was worth about $20,000. The prospective purchaser therefore had to have $20,000 before the owner would part with it. It might be presumed that the purchaser could go in debt for the entire amount and pay for the farm out of its earnings. This is conceivable if the land is valued as close to the productive level as possible so that the economic rent can pay the interest on the investment and the principal can be retired out of labor, capital, and management earnings. Yet this is risky, and few owners dare to sell a farm and accept a mortgage of 100 per cent of the value. Even the Federal Farm Loan Banks lend only 50 per cent of the value of the land and 20 per cent of the value of the buildings. This means that the young Iowa farmer should have had about $10,000 as a "down payment."

Around 1918 a study was made by W. J. Spillman, tracing the tenure history of about 2,000 midwestern and prairie farm owners. (Table 22) He found that a third of these farmers had stepped directly from the status of unpaid laborer on the home farm to full ownership. In some cases this meant direct inheritance of the home farm or inheritance of money which enabled the young man to purchase a farm from relatives or others. Another third had rented land as an intervening step, spending an average of nine years in accumulating capital and experience before purchasing a farm; even in this group one-fifth reported acquiring the farm by inheritance. A smaller group spent about ten years working as hired men, whereas one-fifth used both the "hired man" and the "tenant step" on the agricultural ladder. According to the 1920 census, at least 44 per cent of the owners of the United States had been tenants at some time in their careers. Later studies have given us more refined and more extensive data but all point to the fact that the average American farmer "in his time plays many parts," rising from laborer to landed proprietor.[1] This is unlike many foreign countries with distinct tenure classes—laborers, tenants, and landlords—and little movement from one class to another. The

TABLE 22

STAGES PASSED BY 2,112 MIDWESTERN FARM OWNERS IN ACQUIRING OWNERSHIP [2]

	Number	Percentage of Total	Percentage Acquiring Ownership by						
			Homesteading	Marriage	Inheritance	Purchase			
						From Near Relatives	From Others	Total	Age at Ownership
FHTO..	435	20%	1	9	1	12	77	89	36
FHO...	·268	13	4	28	7	6	55	61	29
FTO...	679	32	1	5	23	30	41	71	33
FO.....	730	34	3	4	47	30	16	46	26.5

F = Labor on home farm H = Rural Laborer T = Tenant O = Owner

amount and percentage of tenancy under normal conditions depend upon the number of farmers who include this step in their climb on the agricultural ladder and the length of time they spend in this stage. If the movement is retarded for some reason the proportion tends to increase; if accelerated—by a credit system, for instance—the proportion is decreased.

However, not all movement is pregressively upward on the ladder. According to the 1920 census 11 per cent of the tenants had once owned land; in some states the proportion was as high as one-third. The heavy increase in tenancy since 1930, together

[1] The above study fails to reveal the number of farmers who were born in the city and came to the farm as adults. A study of the history of 2,263 Wisconsin farmers showed that 12 per cent fell in this group, some of them buying farms directly, others passing through one or more of the usual steps of the agricultural ladder. It also fails to show the number who engaged in non-agricultural occupations as a means of accumulating capital toward the purchase of a farm. Just about one-third of these Wisconsin farmers had spent some time in urban occupations. This shows that not every farm boy who "goes to town" stays there; his city job paradoxically becomes a step on the "agricultural" ladder. Furthermore, it also means a transfer of wealth from city to country. B. H. Hibbard and Guy A. Peterson, *How Wisconsin Farmers Become Farm Owners* (Wisconsin Agric. Exp. Station Bulletin 402, 1928).

[2] Based on W. J. Spillman, "The Agricultural Ladder," *American Economic Review Supplement*, March, 1919, Tables 1, 2, and 3.

with the increase in corporate landownership (all of which is leased), indicates that thousands of owners have lost their hold on the ownership rung of the ladder.[1] In other cases the tenant never gets beyond the tenant stage, either preferring to remain a renter or failing to accumulate the necessary capital to purchase a farm. If accumulation of capital rather than tenure status is made the test of progress, a tenant is often further ahead by renting than by buying, especially if land can be rented on terms less than the interest on the investment. However, the uncertainty of tenure, the difficulty of landlord-tenant relationships, and the exclusion from any share in increasing land values are powerful reasons for wanting to become a landowner. There has always been a strong feeling for the freehold among American farmers, particularly among foreign-born white farmers.

The next stage is that of "mortgaged owner." Some farmers enter this stage too soon; they have a hard time to pay the interest and retire the principal even in normal times and may lose their farms in a depression. After the mortgage is satisfied the farmer enjoys a period of unencumbered ownership. The final stage consists of "retreating" from the responsibility of operating the farm by renting it for a while and finally by selling it.[2] Probably more than two-thirds of the landlords of the United States are thus active or retired farmers, only a small number being bankers, merchants, or "professional landlords" making a business of renting land.

Inheritance in Land Tenure. It has been suggested that tenancy could be practically eliminated if all farms were inherited. This, however, leads to some practical difficulties. The father is not always ready to relinquish the management of the farm as soon as the son is of age. Tenancy provides an intermediate stage, a sort of partnership. The fact that about 20 per cent of the tenants of the United States are related to their landlords suggests this. Furthermore, the son can expect to obtain absolute possession of the farm only if he is an only child.

[1] A recent release of the U. S. Census, based on a very limited number of farms, seems to indicate that one tenant out of every eight included in the survey had been an owner.

[2] Charles J. Galpin describes the "retreat" of farm owners in "Tenancy in an Ideal System of Land Ownership," by Richard T. Ely and C. J. Galpin, *American Economic Review Supplement,* March, 1919.

Brothers and sisters are entitled to a share of the property, and the larger the family the smaller will be the share of the son who remains on the farm, and the more he will have to pay out to the others. As noted before, in countries where the law requires that the land be actually divided and given in equal inheritances to all the children, the result has led either to small uneconomic farms or to deliberate control of the size of the family. The son who inherits a farm subject to payments to his brothers and sisters equal to three-quarters of the value of the property is no better off financially than if he had bought a farm outright and had gone in debt to the same extent.

Because the farm must be purchased or transferred as a unit, the refinancing of farms has to be repeated in every generation. Those members of the family who do not inherit the farm itself take a share of the wealth with them whether they move to another farm or to the city. Since about one-third of the farm-born children move to cities, inheritance transferred a fund of wealth from country to cities estimated at three to four billion dollars in the 1920–30 decade. Migrants from the rural areas to the city not only cause a transfer of inherited wealth but, by migrating at the most productive ages, contribute another $2,000 to $2,500 per migrant in the cost of the upbringing and the education of these young men and women. It is estimated that the 6,300,000 net migrants from the farms in 1920–30 represented a contribution of fourteen billion dollars to the urban centers.[1]

This transfer of wealth to the cities is often deplored, but during the westward movement when the surplus young folks moved to the frontier, inheritance transferred wealth from the East to the West, where it was used to create new farms which shortly became competitors of the eastern farmers. The East likewise educated and equipped its future rivals and competitors. From the farmer's standpoint the movement to the cities is less dangerous than the movement to new farms; it creates consumers and not competitors for those remaining on the land.

Just as there has always been a landward movement of city people, there has been a transfer of wealth to rural areas as well. City people who buy farms, the country youth who uses a city

[1] O. E. Baker, "Rural-urban Migration and the National Welfare," *op. cit.*, pp. 87–89.

job as a step on the agricultural ladder, the earnings of part-time farmers, and the remittances and gifts from children living or working in cities represent a flow of wealth to the farms. Cities also contribute substantial sums for the roads, schools, and public services of rural areas through our system of state aid. How far this movement of wealth tends to offset the transfer of capital to urban centers is not known.

The older countries with feudal legacies of entail, primogeniture, and similar institutions have given more attention to inheritance than the United States and other new countries. Furthermore, control of inheritance is often the central theme of their tenure and land policies. Thus the German *Reichserbhofrecht* of 1933 provides for the transference of farms below 125 hectare (309 acres) to one child only, generally the youngest. The other children or relatives are entitled to support and education but have no claim on the capital value of the farm; however, they have the "home refuge right," i.e., if they are unemployed through no fault of their own they may return to the home farm and work there. Furthermore, the farm may not be sold or mortgaged; in fact, the law goes so far as to permit a special court to take over the administration or even possession of the land if the operator neglects his farm or fails to pay his debts. Approximately half of the arable land of Germany is under the *Reichserbhofrecht*.[1]

This, it is claimed, is really a return to the old Germanic concept of landownership which had been sidetracked by the Roman law with its concept of soil only as "capital," individualism of ownership, and the right to bequeath freely—never fully accepted by the German peasantry.[2]

Land Credit and Tenure. High land values are generally, though not always, associated with a high proportion of rented farms. Inasmuch as high-priced land is also the most productive soil, capable tenants prefer to rent this type of land rather than the less productive farms, and landlords prefer to own them purely as a "renting proposition." In such areas land values are high because the bidding of tenants for the land establishes a prof-

[1] C. von Dietze, "Land Tenure and the Social Control of the Use of Land," *op. cit.*, pp. 118–40.

[2] Heske, *German Forestry, op. cit.*, pp. 231–34.

itable contract rent for the owners. Thus, relatively little land becomes available for purchase to the tenant who wishes to climb the agricultural ladder.

It should be just as easy to pay for high-priced land with excellent earning power as to pay for cheap land with a low income per acre. However, the higher the price the larger will be the down payment and the longer the farmer will have to spend on the pre-ownership stages of the agricultural ladder. If the price paid is out of line with economic rent, the period will be longer before the debt can be retired. Many countries have therefore tried to attack the tenant problem by providing adequate land credit to farmers. Among the oldest of these is the Prussian *Landschaft.* These banks issue bonds secured by all the mortgages which the banks hold as the result of loans to the members, thereby placing the credit of the entire association as security for the bonds. The Federal Land Bank has established banks upon somewhat the same principle. Local loan associations are established through which the bank operates. Loans are made up to 50 per cent of the normal appraised value of the land plus 20 per cent of the value of the permanent improvements, not to exceed $50,000 per individual. The rate of interest is fixed as 1 per cent above the rate of the latest bond issue, with a maximum of 6 per cent. The basic rate in 1938 was 4 per cent. This low rate was uniform all over the United States and had a marked effect on reducing the interest rate in those areas where the usual private mortgage rate was high. It was also in these regions that most of the loans were made.

One of the most important features of this act was the recognition of the slow turnover and the time element in agriculture. The loans are amortized, i.e., the borrower pays a stated sum each year consisting of the interest and part of the principal. As the principal is gradually reduced the interest on the remainder is also reduced, therefore a larger and larger share can go to reduction on the sum owed. The common terms are 20 to 30 years, with 40 set as the maximum.

During the recent emergency, arrangements were made for direct loans by the Federal Land Bank to borrowers who did not have to take stock in local associations. The rates were 5 per cent higher than the rates on loans through associations. The same restrictions as to the amount of loans and amortization prevail in this type of loan. On the other hand, the so-called "commissioner loans" could be made up to 75 per cent of the appraised value of the property, up to $7500. The rate is 5 per cent and the loans do not extend over 40 years. The loans could be made until February 1, 1940. Credit is also supplied to agriculture through short and intermediate production loans, and to co-operative associations for shorter periods.

Credit is not a cure-all for the tenant problem. Too easy credit may load a farmer with a debt during an upward swing of prices which has to be repaid during a period of declining farm prices. Even fairly low rates of interest will not solve his problem. It is not the interest but the principal that creates the chief debt burden. Also, low interest means high land values as soon as it becomes the capitalization rate. While the farmers who bought their land at the beginning of the program are helped by low rates of interest, it is doubtful whether later purchasers have any advantage. However, it is impossible to trace the influence of the lower rates of interest on land values since 1916 because of the violent crosscurrents of the War and post-war periods.[1]

Land Tenure in the South. Economic factors alone do not account for the land tenure pattern. In many sections, particularly those with foreign groups, tenancy is almost nil. Custom, inheritance, and other institutional factors are sometimes stronger than the economic elements. In the South human and historical factors operate in the direction of a high proportion of tenant farms. The South raises rice, tobacco, and cotton, all of them good tenant crops. It also has the Negro and a special type of white tenant. This combination explains why in some of the southern states more than two-thirds of the farmers are renters. The tenure situation in this part of the United States cannot be comprehended without an understanding of how it originated.

Contrary to considerable popular opinion, the southern agricultural landscape is not a vast panorama of cotton plantations. Accepting the census definition of a plantation as being a unified agricultural organization of five or more tenant tracts under one management, composed generally of a continuous tract of land

[1] N. J. Wall and E. J. Engquist, Jr., *A Graphic Summary of Agricultural Credit* (U. S. Dept. of Agriculture Miscellaneous Publication 268, 1938).

operated as a single unit with respect to methods of control of labor and production, a recent survey in Arkansas showed that 40 per cent of the tenants of this state are not plantation tenants.[1] Shading from the plantation with its five or more units under central management located in the rich alluvial lowlands of the Coastal Plains, the deltas and the flood plains of the rivers, to the single rented farm of the uplands, a gradual shift in the nature of the tenancy system takes place.

Southern agricultural history is the story of this parallel development. In the uplands, tenancy emerged in much the same manner as in other regions of the United States. However, the plantation system has influenced to a degree the customs and the operation of upland farms. To the rich alluvial lowlands cotton was well suited. Early colonial land policies encouraged ownership in large tracts and cotton provided a crop which could be grown on a large scale, provided a cheap labor supply could be obtained. Negro slaves were imported and the ante-bellum plantation organization resulted.

With the close of the war between the states came the end of the slave plantation system. The liberation of the slaves destroyed the largest part of the property values. Land was cheap and almost valueless as a basis for credit during reconstruction days. The freedmen, unused to a money economy, illiterate, and made peculiarly conscious of their freedom during the carpetbag days, had to be adjusted to the new situation. The planter also had to adapt his method of farming to the new conditions. At first he tried to hire the Negro at cash wages, but this failed because he was not sure of his labor supply since the Negro was not inclined to work as long as he had any money.

Out of this situation the "cropper" system evolved. Large plantations are divided into proper-sized units and each unit rented to a "cropper." The landlord furnishes all the equipment, work stock, and the land, and the crop is divided half and half between landlord and tenant. The cropper is in reality a laborer paid in kind. Since he has an interest in the success of his venture he will stay on the farm until the crop is harvested; thus security of tenure for at least a year is obtained for the landlord, which he

[1] Arkansas State Policy Committee, *Agricultural Labor Problems in Arkansas*, (Published Paper No. 1, October, 1936), pp. 11–13.

did not have under the wage system. However, the penniless cropper has to live until the "crop is made," therefore he must have credit for a large part of the year. So the "credit merchant," the landlord who guarantees the tenant's credit at the bank, and the banker become important elements in the tenure pattern. Sometimes a commissary is established on the plantation itself. Naturally, croppers are supervised, and their state of dependence upon landlords and credit agencies exposes them to exploitation, especially when they are illiterate. Many of them are in constant debt to their employers or to the merchants.

A more advanced type of tenancy is the "third and fourth," under which the landlord receives one-third of the grain and one-fourth of the cotton but also furnishes less to the tenant.[1] The tenant owns most, if not all, of the tools, equipment, and animals and enjoys a greater freedom of management. Other forms of tenure are the usual cash rents and the "standing rent," under which the renter pays a definite amount of the crop, such as a fourth of a bale per acre, irrespective of yield or prices. Many combinations have evolved, such as the "share-cash" and still others depending on local crops and customs. Often the landlords supervise tenants as well as croppers and take care of their credit needs.

The census did not separate croppers from other tenants until 1920. It then appeared that 47 per cent of the Negro tenants were croppers and over 25 per cent of the white tenants were also in this lowest of tenure classes. The number of croppers increased for both races up to 1930, after which there was an ominous drop. The apparent increase in Southern owners and the decrease in tenants and croppers were sufficient to reverse the trend in tenancy in practically the entire South and affected even the national figures enough to reduce the proportion of tenant-

[1] One of the serious stumbling blocks to shifting from cash cropping to more diversified farming involving livestock and pasture is the traditional "third and fourth," not only because such a change is detrimental to the landlord's interests but also because both landlord and tenant believe that this rent is the "right," "normal," or "natural" rent. Tenants have said "they would not rent from landlords so dishonest as not to use a third-and-fourth contract." Thus an educational program designed to change leasing methods must be aimed at changing attitudes and traditions based upon nearly a century of habit and custom. This is an example of how, even in a new country such as the United States, institutions are created and perpetuated. John A. Baker, "A New Lease for a New South," *Land Policy Review,* July–August, 1938, pp. 7–10.

operated farms of the United States from 42.4 per cent to 42.1 per cent, the first decrease in the percentage of tenancy since 1880.[1]

This change in the tenure relationships is due in part to readjustments made in response to the Agricultural Adjustment Act. It was easy for landlords to reduce their acreage of cotton by dismissing some of their croppers and tenants and re-hiring them as laborers. Other renters were simply thrown on the relief rolls.

It is commonly believed that southern agriculture is largely associated with colored farmers. As a matter of fact, in 1935 only 24 per cent of the farmers of the South were colored. Numerically there were fewer Negro farmers in 1935 than in 1910. The number of colored owners in the South reached its peak in 1910; today fewer Negro owners operate farms than in 1900. Likewise, colored tenants have decreased in numbers whereas the number of croppers consistently increased until the last decade.

The tenant problem of the South is therefore as much, if not more, a white man's problem than it is a colored man's problem. In the first place, white farmers outnumber colored farmers three to one, but only 46 per cent of the former are tenants as compared to 76 per cent of the latter. A surprisingly large number of the white farmers, however, are croppers, again the result of historical factors. It is an error to think of the entire white population of the pre-war South as slave owners. Of the 118,000 families in Georgia in 1860, 77,000 held no slaves and were chiefly farmers. The Piedmont and mountain people hardly ever came in contact with slavery; in fact, their economic interests were so opposed to the slave owner that if the Civil War had not come there might have been serious troubles within the South itself.[2] The war and reconstruction days left their mark upon this numerous class, and the present descendants are the heritage of those chaotic periods.

[1] The legal status of tenants, croppers, and laborers has been discussed in another connection. The fact that croppers are really more like laborers than tenants is obscured whenever they are enumerated as "tenants" by the census. The tracts they cultivate are called *farms* and this causes confusion whenever the South is compared with other sections of the country as to the number, size, and trends of "farms," or when a comparison is made in the number of farmers and the tenure classes. Croppers appear and disappear from the census with a mere change in the method of paying them. Standing renters defy classification either as cash or share tenants, yet are important because their legal status is the same as that of cash tenants in several Southern states.

[2] Paul B. Sears, *Deserts on the March* (University of Oklahoma Press, 1935), pp. 55–56; R. P. Brooks, *The Agrarian Revolution in Georgia* (Bulletin of the University of Wisconsin 639, 1914), p. 85.

Some of those referred to as "poor white trash" represent the most acute problems for readjustment and rehabilitation.

The question is raised, is this deplorable situation due to the land tenure system or vice versa? To a large extent these people are tenants and croppers because they are illiterate, thriftless, and shiftless and lack the qualities needed to climb the agricultural ladder. A mere change in land tenure will not solve the problem. Were many of the croppers and tenants given a farm free of debt, it would be only a few years before they would be back to the renter or laborer stage. They are not prepared for independent management of landed property, which exposes them to the temptation to borrow and mortgage their farms, and eventually perhaps to lose them. The same characteristics of the renters also make good landlordship difficult. Unless constantly supervised, the shiftless tenant neglects the crops and may guiltily sneak away leaving debts and the unpicked crop behind him.

On the other hand, it is also true that the cropper and tenant remain renters because of the system under which they work. The weak and illiterate tenant is no match for the landlord or credit merchant, who take advantage of the renter's unequal bargaining power and unequal position before the law. Wherever the tenant is kept in permanent debt it is idle to expect him to rise above the cropper stage.

Tenants in the upland regions, however, are not so completely enslaved by these conditions. They are more predominantly white. Moreover, from the standpoint of independence of operation the tenant in the upland region is more nearly like the owner-operator. Croppers here make up less than 30 per cent of the tenant class, as compared to more than 50 per cent in the lowland area; in fact, nearly three-fourths of the croppers of Arkansas are plantation tenants.[1] The situation in Arkansas is more or less typical of other southern states where both lowland and highland conditions prevail. The plantation system with its peculiar characteristics rarely penetrated into the hills.

Another feature of the land tenure system of the South is its close connection with cotton culture. Table 17 shows that fully 72 per cent of all cotton farms are cultivated by tenants, a higher percentage than for the southern farms as a whole. Since cotton

[1] *Agricultural Labor Problems in Arkansas, op. cit.*, pp. 11–13.

cannot be used for food or clothing until it is fabricated, the landlord has an absolute check on the crop. Even the absentee owner can check his tenants through the cotton gin and the banks. Since it is to the landlord's advantage to have as much land as possible in cash crops, he discourages gardens, feed and food crops which the tenant might use without his knowledge; but to this general statement notable exceptions must be made. The tenant likewise prefers to raise cash crops so that he can meet his debts. Cotton culture also conflicts with other crops at critical times so the grower has to choose between more or less cotton whenever he grows food and feed or cultivates a garden. This affects the owner-operator as well as the tenant. The result is slavery to the one-crop system, an inadequate and unbalanced diet, and full exposure to the price system. Success and failure depend upon the price of cotton on the one hand and the cost of fertilizer, implements, food, and clothing on the other. For decades "diversification campaigns" have tried to break the iron sway of King Cotton and in only a few places has his hold been loosened. The southern agrarians are deeply conscious of this condition and are trying to reverse the emphasis—grow crops for home consumption first, live within the farm, and grow the cash crops merely as the means of securing the little money needed for cash outlays.

Instability of Land Occupation. One of the worst features associated with American land tenure is the instability of land occupation. In 1935 over one-fourth of all farm operators reported that they had been on the farm they were then occupying one year or less. Naturally, tenants are more unstable than owners. Forty-seven per cent of the tenants and 57 per cent of the croppers had occupied their farms less than two years. Almost two-thirds of the white croppers but only 50 per cent of the colored croppers were in this group. Such instability is disastrous to community life and to institutions such as the church, lodge, and school. Schools are practically emptied at moving time, only to be refilled with a new group of pupils after the moving spasm is over. Children form no attachment for a community or a home; the covered wagon is the actual home of many of these roving tenants. Where generation after generation has lived in this fashion there is no desire to own land or to associate one's self with a given community. Some of this moving is legitimate. Some tenants move because the experience and capital they have accumulated on a small farm have prepared them for the management of a larger or better farm, but other tenants move because of difficulties with the landlord or merely because they are restless and think they can do better in the "next county."

The landlord is caught in the same vicious circle. It is difficult to furnish adequate housing to suit the various sized families. He can hardly expect the tenant to do good farming under insecure tenure or to make any improvements from which the renter cannot gain while on the farm. Improvements *to* the land, such as drainage, tiling, clearing, and erosion control, become permanently associated with the farm and accrue to the landlord. Improvements placed *on* the land become *fixtures* which become the property of the landowner unless otherwise stipulated in the rental contract.

Where land is held in speculative ownership the situation is perhaps at its worst. The owner has no interest in the land except to sell it. Since the farm may be sold at any time the renter has no security of tenure and looks upon land as something to exploit. One of the tragedies of involuntary ownership of land by corporations in our best agricultural states is the necessarily temporary possession.

Land Tenure Policies. It is generally admitted that a certain proportion of tenant-operated farms have a place in a system of land tenure. Farms cannot be transferred from one generation to another or to the next buyer without a landlord or a "lendlord." In general, states with a low proportion of rented farms have a high proportion of mortgaged farms. Since about 20 per cent of the tenants reported being related to the landlords, we can assume that this proportion represents a normal rate due to the transfer of farms from fathers to sons or among other relatives. However, if these were the only farms on the rental market, there would be no farms to rent by tenants not related to their landlords. Hence, the ownership of land by non-farmers and others who lease land temporarily or permanently is not necessarily a bad feature in a system of land tenure. In fact, such landlords offer opportunities for non-related tenants to take this step on the agricultural ladder.

Beyond this point, however, efforts should be made to increase the proportion of owner-operated farms by rural credit programs and purchase projects designed to assist people to become owners. This is not easy where sociological conditions have been adverse to private initiative and to climbing the agricultural ladder to ownership. Furthermore, the history of assisted colonization in the United States, whether public or private, is an almost uniform record of failure. Careful study of these past efforts should be made before new projects, either federal or state, should be undertaken.[1]

The second part of the program should aim at making tenant farming *good farming*. Exploitation of the soil and of human

TABLE 23

ANNUAL GAINS AND LOSSES OF PLANT NUTRIENTS FROM THE SOILS OF THE UNITED STATES[2]

(Millions of tons)

Losses Through	Nitrogen	Phosphorus	Potassium	Calcium	Magnesium	Sulphur	Organic Matter
Crops-harvested Area	4.6	.7	3.2	1.0	.5	.5	92
Grazing and Pastures	3.0	.5	3.7	1.0	.5	.4	60
Erosion and Leaching from Harvested Areas	6.5	.9	21.6	39.6	12.0	8.2	130
Erosion and Leaching from Pastures	2.0	.4	7.7	12.0	3.8	2.2	40
Total Losses	16.1	2.5	36.2	53.6	16.8	11.3	322
Plant Nutrients Added *	11.8	1.1	4.8	13.8	4.6	8.7	100
Net Losses	4.3	1.4	31.4	39.8	12.2	2.6	222

* Through fertilizers, crop residues, manures, rainfall and irrigation waters, nitrogen fixation.

beings is not inherent in a system of "dual occupancy of the soil." Some of the finest agriculture of the world is to be found in England, although British farming has been predominantly tenant farming for almost two centuries. The English farmer has preferred to put his capital in equipment, implements, and stock and let someone else own the land. However, it took a century or more of trial and error and experimentation to perfect a system

[1] See W. A. Hartman, *State Land-settlement Problems and Policies in the United States*, (U. S. Dept. of Agriculture, Technical Bulletin 357, 1933), and *N. R. B. Report, op. cit.*, pp. 196–202.

[2] Compiled from Tables 12 and 13, *N. R. B. Report*, pp. 162–63.

under which the tenant has security of tenure and the land is conserved and even built up in fertility. Landlords and tenants together work out the improvements to be made and the share of the cost to be borne by both, and if the renter is disturbed in his tenure, he is paid for his inexhausted improvements left in or on the land.[1] Except for a few private contracts here and there we have no laws, customs, or institutions comparable to the English system and until we do the conservation of agricultural land rests on an insecure basis.

THE CONSERVATION OF THE SOIL

The conservation of agricultural land consists of maintaining the productive power of the soil and protecting it from erosion. Before man used the land for cultivated crops the components of the soil—plants, animals, and inert matter—had become adjusted to one another. Plants and trees died and added to fertility. When agriculture replaced the natural vegetation, plants were removed whole or in part, thereby depleting both chemical elements and humus. Even grazing exhausts the soil.

Maintaining the Fertility of the Land. Table 23, from the report of the National Resources Board, shows the annual balance between deposits in and withdrawals from the soil capital of the United States. The additions consist of certain elements added by nature in rainfall and irrigation water, and of man-supplied elements such as crop residues, manures, lime, marl, fertilizers, sewage, peat, and industrial by-products. Erosion and leaching are by far the most important causes of the loss of soil elements. If it were not for these two factors the additions would exceed the losses in the cases of nitrogen, potassium, calcium, magnesium, and sulphur.

Under good farm management fertility is returned to the soil by the application of farm manure and the use of commercial fertilizers. The net value of the former depends upon the knowledge farmers have of its use and the extent to which it is properly handled and applied to the land. Commercial fertilizers are being used most extensively on the intensively cultivated crops such

[1] Taylor, *Outlines of Agricultural Economics, op. cit.*, Chap. XXV, "Relations between Landlords and Tenants in England"; Ashby, "The Relations of Land Tenure to the Economic and Social Development of Agriculture," *op. cit.*, pp. 96–103.

as cotton, fruit, and vegetables and predominantly in the eastern and southeastern states where the soil is leached by the heavy rainfall. The amount of commercial fertilizer bought depends upon the relative price of the product and the fertilizer. Fertilizers are in a certain sense a substitute for land or labor.

Insofar as we depend upon the addition of fertilizers containing the essential elements lost through cropping, the problem of maintaining the fertility of the soil becomes one of the conservation of certain minerals. Some years ago great concern was expressed over the supply of nitrogen. It was feared that the Chilean deposits would some day be exhausted, but by the use of legumes and nitrogen fixation, the by-products of certain industries are now able to furnish an unlimited amount of this element at low costs. The world once chiefly depended upon German deposits for potash, but large stocks have been discovered in Texas and New Mexico and industrial by-products now furnish an ample supply. Phosphorous, however, is the most critical element. Although the physical supply in the United States is enormous, it is located primarily in the Far West. The location of the mines with respect to the large consuming centers is unfavorable. Sulphuric acid required for the manufacture of phosphate is also bulky. The costs of manufacture depend upon the costs of sulphuric acid, power and of transportation. Recent developments under the Tennessee Valley Authority, however, indicate that great economies in the manufacture of phosphate are in the offing. Again the problem is not one of the total physical supply but of the economic supply as expressed in price.

Soil Erosion. Cropping takes only certain elements out of the soil which can be replaced, and by good management the humus and organic matter can be kept at par. Erosion, on the other hand, takes the soil body itself, and with it all the soil elements.

The physical factors affecting erosion are complex. Whether or not a given farm will erode depends upon the type of soil, the slope, the condition of the ground, and the manner of land utilization. Some soils erode so easily that the surface is removed even though the eye cannot detect an appreciable slope. Where rain falls gently or in a drizzle water has an opportunity to enter the soil and run-off is reduced to a minimum. Sudden, beating rains and cloudbursts do the most damage. The steepness of the slope determines to a large extent whether a given rain will enter the soil or run over the surface. Rain on a steep slope tends to run off, gaining velocity as it proceeds. The greater the velocity, the greater its cutting power and carrying capacity. Since only 75,000,000 of the 350,000,000 acres of crop land are level, agriculture in the United States must be adjusted to a sloping condition of the land.

The condition of the ground is also important. The porosity and absorbing power of the soil are factors in determining whether the water will percolate into the soil or flow over the surface. Forest soils and heavy grass-covered soils are ideal in absorbing power. On the other hand, frozen soils or those saturated with water send the rainfall into the run-off. However, it is not often that soils become completely saturated.

Most important is the manner in which the land is used. Even on steep slopes and with heavy rainfall erosion is reduced to a minimum in a forest. The trees and shrubs prevent the rain from beating on the ground; the plants, roots, logs, and other obstructions keep the water from running over the surface and give it time to enter the soil. The forest litter and porous humus absorb rainfall and direct it into the ground water. Wild grass in its natural condition gives practically the same protection to the soil as the forest. When cut for hay its protective power is decreased, the run-off increased, and some erosion may take place. The run-off is still more pronounced on pastures, especially if closely cropped and packed hard by the feet of animals. In this case there may be run-off but little erosion. The hard surface sheds the water like a roof and yet little of the soil is washed away.

Cultivated crop land, when friable and open, may absorb water for a while, but as soon as the water becomes muddy the pores are sealed and the soil becomes impervious.[1] Now the water joins the run-off and the earth is in an ideal condition to be carried away. Fallow land or crops such as corn with the stalks far apart have little or no vegetation to bind the soil and protect it from the impact of the water, especially if the rows run up and down the hill instead of along the contour.

[1] W. A. Lowdermilk, "Influence of Forest Litter on Run-off, Percolation and Erosion," *Journal of Forestry,* April, 1930, pp. 474–91.

Erosion takes two main forms: (1) sheet erosion, removing a more or less uniform "sheet" of soil, and (2) gully erosion, in which deep gashes are cut into the hillsides. The second is visible to all, but the first is really more important and more subtle. It has stolen the fertility and soil from millions of farms because the farmer has not been aware of what is going on. One reason why we have become so much more conscious of this menace in recent years is that so long as water was operating on the humus-filled topsoil no appreciable loss of fertility was noticeable, but now this tenacious, water-holding layer is removed and the farmer is forced to farm the relatively poorer "B" horizon. Furthermore, the B layer of the soil erodes much more readily. It is estimated that almost 50,000,000 acres of arable farm land have lost practically all of their topsoil or have been so severely gullied that they are useless for further tillage. Van Hise stated that about 4,000,000 acres were devastated in this fashion by 1910; if these estimates are correct, we have lost 45,000,000 acres in 25 years, or almost 2,000,-000 acres a year.[1]

However, erosion has touched another 87,000,000 acres to the extent of practically removing all the topsoil, thereby reducing the farms to a very low stage of productivity or making them practically submarginal. And almost 468,000,000 acres have lost from one-fourth to three-fourths of the topsoil through water erosion.

The regional distribution of the problem of erosion is shown in Table 24, compiled from the report of the National Resources Board. It will be noted that the Northeast and the Lake states have comparatively little or no erosion, and that more than half of the land in the South, the Corn Belt, and the Pacific states is exposed to the action of wind and water. Most subject to these influences by far are the 100th Meridian and Mountain states. It should be noted that the data for sheet erosion, wind erosion, and gullying are not exclusive, i.e., the same area may have two or even all three of these forms of soil wastage.[2]

When stated in terms of farms or money, the losses from

[1] Charles R. Van Hise, *The Conservation of Natural Resources in the United States* (Macmillan, 1910), p. 310.

[2] See also A. E. Parkins and J. R. Whitaker, eds., *Our Natural Resources and Their Conservation* (New York, Wiley, 1936), p. 77; *Soil Erosion: A Critical Problem in American Agriculture, op. cit.*

Table 24

EXTENT OF EROSION IN THE UNITED STATES BY PERCENTAGE OF THE AREA OF THE ECONOMIC REGION[1]

	Little or No Erosion	Sheet Erosion			Wind Erosion				Gullying				Not Defined
		¼ to ¾ of Topsoil Gone	¾ or More of Topsoil Gone	Total Sheet Erosion	Moderate	Severe	Destroyed	Total	Occasional	Severe	Destroyed	Total	
Northeast	63.4%	30.0%	4.3%	34.3%	*	*	*	1.1%	19.6%	0.1%	*	20.5%	*
South	45.4	31.1	14.5	45.6	*	*	*	*	39.8	5.7	*	46.0	*
Corn Belt	42.5	47.9	7.1	55.0	*	*	*	0.1	34.1	18.8	*	52.9	*
Lake States	63.3	20.9	*	20.9	10.5	4.8	*	15.4	14.8	3.4	*	18.3	*
100th Meridian	16.6	31.9	10.9	42.8	27.9	8.2	*	37.0	23.9	14.1	*	38.5	6.0
Mountain	9.2	36.0	13.2	49.2	17.7	6.4	*	24.5	24.4	37.3	*	61.7	20.4
Pacific	40.1	44.7	5.1	49.8	3.4	2.3	1.6	7.3	38.8	9.3	*	48.6	4.0

* Less than one per cent.

[1] Based on data from *Soil Erosion: A Critical Problem in American Agriculture,* Part V of the Supplementary Report of the Land Planning Committee to the National Resources Board, 1935.

erosion become staggering. Fifty million acres divided into farms of 100 acres each would support a half million families. Bennett estimates the annual monetary loss of productivity at $400,000,000. The tragedy is that so much of this wealth is irreplaceable. These estimates do not include the losses due to the filling of reservoirs and the abandonment of irrigated areas depending on the reservoirs, the losses attributable to interference with navigation, the costs for dredging streams, removing debris from highways, and the destruction of streams for fishing and recreation.[1]

Since erosion can be prevented through proper land utilization, which is under the control of the land occupier, the solution of the problem is fairly simple as far as the techniques are concerned but difficult when these techniques have to be carried out within the framework of privately owned land. Erosion on steep slopes can be prevented by maintaining them in forests or pastures, properly managed to control the run-off. Terraces, contour cultivation instead of cultivating up and down the slopes, and good farm management which will increase the fertility and restore the humus content, are accepted practices. On some farms combinations of two or more of these may be necessary. Where gullies have formed, dams and other engineering works and the planting of grass and trees in the "draws" can stop the progress of a gully but can do little to restore the soil which has gone down the rivers. While these practices are generally known, their application to specific circumstances is still a matter of experiment. Much work is being done at experiment stations and in demonstration areas to perfect our knowledge of the techniques of erosion prevention and control.

Economic Factors of Soil Depletion. It would seem that agricultural land should be one of the natural resources easy to conserve. No waiting or carrying costs are involved; merely such practices as will keep up the fertility of the land as nearly on a par with the original fertility as possible and hold the soil in place. Yet during the short life of the United States an area equal to the size of Minnesota has been completely devastated by erosion, and three times this area or the equivalent of the East

[1] H. H. Bennett, "Soil Erosion and Its Prevention," in Parkins and Whitaker, *op. cit.*, p. 75. See also H. H. Bennett's recent book, *Soil Erosion* (New York, McGraw-Hill, 1939), especially the historical treatment in the first three chapters.

North Central states has been severely injured. In other places soil fertility has been depleted. "Indestructible" agricultural land is a myth, and the reason why it has been depleted and destroyed is that it must have paid the farmer to do so. It is useless to argue that it *should pay* to maintain or build up soil fertility unless the operator has a long-time interest in the soil. Soil has an exhaustion value similar to a forest or a mine. The American farmer has often found it more profitable to exhaust the virgin fertility of one farm and move to a new farm than to try to maintain or restore the fertility on his old one. The farmer who claimed he was a good farmer because he had worn out four farms already was not far from the truth if judged by narrow "economic" standards. Part of the blame must rest on our land policies. The homestead law which gave away land to every home seeker made it more profitable for the pioneer to wear out a farm and ask Uncle Sam for another. Why spend money for repairs and upkeep on an old car when a new one can be had for the asking? The oversupply of farm land which made farm products cheap was not conducive to spending money for maintaining soil fertility. Exploitative agriculture was the profitable agriculture. The farmer might have been told that if he kept his farm in full fertility it would be worth much more in the future, but in balancing an uncertain future against a very real present the present usually won.

After 1900 the time seemed ripe for a stabilized agriculture, with prices rising and the reservoir of free land distinctly limited. But the World War intervened and no doubt was a factor in undoing the progress made in conservation by the Roosevelt crusade. One of the by-products of a stabilized agriculture might well have been a less commercial attitude toward land, similar to the subtle relationship of man to land which is so characteristic of European farming. It is found in isolated cases in America and here an island of well conserved soil may be found in a sea of desolate eroded land.[1]

However, the question is still unanswered: "Why should the farmers permit basic wealth to vanish now that they no longer can get land for the asking and farms are worth thousands of

[1] O. E. Baker, "The Agricultural Prospect," in Parkins and Whitaker, *op. cit.*, pp. 231–36.

dollars?" The reason lies partly in the fact that many of them did not realize what was happening until it was too late, especially in connection with sheet erosion. And now the problem is no longer prevention, but cure. With reforestation, seeding of new pastures, fertilization, reduction in the acreage of soil-depleting crops, terracing, dams, and other works, most of which cost money and labor, the farmer is often not in a financial position to make the necessary outlays. This certainly is the plight of those who bought land during the boom and are now retiring the debt with low-priced farm products. A study of the relationship between the debt per acre and the cropping system in Iowa shows that the debt-ridden farmer had to sell double and triple the amount of cash crops to meet his financial obligations, which meant more land in corn. Erosion prevention and control become closely related to public policies of debt adjustment, refinancing, and readjustments in the credit system, and even of enlarging the size of farms.[1]

Another reason for the American farmer's attitude toward land is to be found in the tenure system. It is to the renown of American agriculture that it has afforded opportunity for landless immigrants, laborers, and tenants to become landowners and eventually to reach the status of landlord, living in security from rent or interest. However, some "climbers" used the tenant stage to make money to buy a farm and then used the farm to make money enough to retire to the village, the city, or to California. The farm, whether rented or owned, was not looked upon as a home but as a factory. This attitude is quite in contrast with the Old World feeling toward the soil. In older nations land has become more than "a mere object of utility or even 'capital.' It became sacred ground . . . part of the national organism, the foundation of the lives of those who were, those who are, and those who are to come. Such land may indeed be cultivated and used by the individual, but it may never become the object of arbitrary action by an individual. . . . The peasant . . . for many generations has cultivated the soil for the race." [2]

[1] R. Schickele, J. P. Himmel, and R. M. Hurd, *Economic Phases of Erosion Control in Southern Iowa and Northern Missouri* (Iowa Agric. Exp. Station, Bulletin 333, 1935), pp. 221–28.

[2] Heske, *op. cit.*, p. 231. The German is even more vigorous: *"Der Bauer baute den Boden fuer das Volk, er bebaute den Boden des Volkes."*

Perhaps as American civilization matures something of the same feeling toward the land will develop; on the other hand, it is by no means to be taken for granted that America should copy this almost mystical attitude toward the soil. On a new soil, under free conditions and without any feudal heritage to hinder, it is reasonable to expect that America will create its own system of land tenure and means of land-use control. History may repeat itself but it does not necessarily have to repeat the same institutions.

If the American farm owner's "conservation relationship" to his farm is weak, it is practically non-existent in the case of the tenants. This is in part due to the insecurity of tenure under which the average renter cultivates his land. He prefers cash crops so that he can "cash in" during his short stay, but the important cash crops such as cotton, corn, tobacco, and the cereals are among the most soil-depleting crops in American agriculture. The Iowa study mentioned above traces relationships between erosion and the proportion and type of tenant-operated farms. Unless the tenant expects to own the farm he is renting, he has little inducement to maintain its fertility, eradicate weeds, control erosion, and keep the buildings in repair. The solution will be found in more owner-operation, and in a system of renting which will encourage the tenant to improve the soil and will reimburse him for his improvements whenever he is not permitted to enjoy the full fruits of his labor.

Soil Conservation Districts. Probably no natural resource offers more difficulties in the formulation of a conservation policy than agricultural land. It is true that farm land is affected by a public interest and that no landowner, including the farmer, has absolute and exclusive rights to land. However, there is considerable reluctance to assert the public's right in farm land. "It should be the aim and policy of any national erosion-control program to avoid the imposition of restrictive legal regulations on the use of the land unless of absolute necessity," says the Report of the National Resources Board.[1] It advises obtaining voluntary co-operation whenever possible, but where voluntary co-operation is not forthcoming the use of state or local land-use controls is advocated. Van Hise in 1910 felt that the erosion problem was

[1] *Op. cit.*, p. 174.

serious enough to justify public regulations of land-use practices.[1] Kansas passed a law designed to control wind erosion as early as 1913, and Texas enacted a law permitting the creation of wind erosion districts.[2] The real impetus, however, to erosion control by collective action was given in 1935 when Congress passed a law authorizing the Secretary of Agriculture to require the enactment of suitable state legislation as a condition to the expenditure of federal funds for erosion control in the states. The Department of Agriculture has worked out a model law which has been modified to suit the legal requirements of the state statutes. Under this act the state permits the setting up of districts under the supervision of a State Soil Conservation Committee. A petition of twenty-five land occupiers (which includes renters as well as owners) starts the organization; a public hearing and referendum complete it. The district is governed by a group of five supervisors, three elected and two appointed by the state committee. The most important power of the supervisors is the formulation of land-use regulations which, upon the approval of the required number of land occupiers, become obligatory upon all living within the boundaries of the district, and violations are punishable by fine as a misdemeanor.[3] Exceptions and variations may be made by a board of adjustment also provided by the statute. Districts are not given the taxing power but may accept grants from state and federal sources. Organization of districts has proceeded rapidly, the first one being the Brown Creek Soil Conservation District in North Carolina (August 4, 1937).[4] By 1940 more than two hundred and twenty districts had been organized in twenty-seven out of the thirty-six states that passed enabling acts. Approximately 120,000,000 acres were included in these districts. Undoubtedly these districts will, and in fact should, operate for some time before enacting land use regulations, to permit ample time to gain experience with voluntary action.

[1] Van Hise, *op. cit.*, p. 314.

[2] Discussed in Chap. VIII.

[3] Regulations may require contour cultivating, lister furrowing, strip cropping, planting of trees and grasses, specifications of cropping programs, and the construction of terraces and dams.

[4] Philip M. Glick, "State Legislation for Erosion Control," *Soil Conservation* (U. S. Dept. of Agriculture, November, 1937), pp. 120–25. Also "The Soil and the Law" by the same author, *Journal of Farm Economics,* May and August, 1938.

Public Control and Assistance. A second form of control may be exercised by public and private lending agencies and through rental contracts.[1] Something of this kind has been done for a decade or more by the Federal Land Bank of Houston, which operates more in an advisory capacity than by coercion. The practice of setting up a farm management program for Rural Rehabilitation clients is proving successful and points to the possibilities of similar plans and contracts by other government agencies and even private banks. The leases for tenants which the Resettlement Administration makes with its clients contained provisions aimed at protecting the land against deterioration. Not only are tenants encouraged to improve their farms, but serious neglect of the soil and erosion constitute a breach of contract under which the tenant or purchaser may lose his right to occupy the land.[2]

Inasmuch as the private owner performs a function which is of public benefit by conserving a resource, it may be argued that there is an obligation on the part of the public to share the costs of conservation. Unless the millions of individual landowners conserve the soil on their individual holdings, the nation will suffer from floods, silting of streams and reservoirs, and all the other disasters which follow in the wake of erosion. But what is the share which the public should bear? Part of this share can legitimately be spent for more education, research, and demonstration. The Soil Conservation Service has been set up for this specific purpose, and the costs of readjusting the farm layout, terracing, fertilization, reforestation, and engineering works are shared by both the government and landowner. The problem remains, however, whether the farmer is financially able and willing to "carry on" after the demonstration ceases.

How far the public should go in giving direct assistance to farmers for conserving the soil is an unsettled question. This assistance may come in the form of exempting woodland and sloping land from taxation, provided they are not grazed and burned and are properly managed to prevent erosion and runoff. This is the substance of a Wisconsin statute and by July 1939 more than

[1] Donald R. Rush, "The Use of Credit in a Land-use Program," *Land Policy Review*, May–June, 1938, pp. 12–16.

[2] L. C. Gray, "Land Policies and National Progress," Address at the meeting of the Association of Land Grant Colleges, November 17, 1936.

29,000 acres had qualified for exemption, of which over 8,000 acres were listed as sloping land.[1] Direct aid is given through the Agricultural Adjustment Administration under which farmers receive federal funds for observing soil conservation practices. The nation seems to be definitely committed to assisting farmers in conserving the soil, but it is the belief of many who are anxious for successful conservation that this activity be divorced from all schemes of production control, and that the payments should be in direct proportion to the results obtained. Unless this is done public money will be spent without commensurate gains in public welfare.

[1] Section 70.11, *Wisconsin Conservation Bulletin,* July, 1939, Vol. IV, pp. 6–8.

VIII

THE UTILIZATION OF THE ARID LANDS

Walter Prescott Webb calls the line of demarcation between the humid and arid sections of America an "institutional *fault*," comparable to a geological fault, roughly following the 98th meridian. At this fault the ways of living, travel, and land utilization, and even the laws and institutions had to be modified. Since the change in humidity is so gradual, the people who first crossed this line did not immediately realize this change. "In the new region—level, timberless, and semi-arid—they were thrown by Mother Necessity into the clutch of new circumstances. Their plight has been stated in this way: east of the Mississippi civilization stood on three legs—land, water, and timber; west of the Mississippi not one but two of these legs were with-drawn,—water and timber,—and civilization was left on one leg—land. It is small wonder that it toppled over in temporary failure." Thus Webb graphically states the problem of conquering arid America, a conquest which is not yet finished.[1]

To the west of this fault lies somewhat less than half of the land area of the United States, yet when the population of the humid lands of the west coast and their cities are subtracted, this half contains approximately only 7 per cent of the people of the United States. Its problems are not those of congested populations but of "manless land," great costly spaces, and arid "pioneer fringes." It is of interest to all Americans because two-thirds of the area of the eleven western states belongs to the federal government and is therefore the common possession of all citizens. Some of it is in parks and forests, the largest areas of recreational land in the country, but a larger portion is merely public domain, a great neglected resource sorely in need of conservation. It is neglected partly because the East has rarely understood the problems of the arid West.

[1] *The Great Plains* (Ginn, 1931), pp. 8–9. Or as carved on a deserted shack, "30 miles to water, 20 miles to wood, 10 miles to hell, and I gone there for good." Mari Sandoz, *Old Jules* (Boston, Little-Brown, 1935), p. 213.

CHARACTERISTICS OF THE ARID REGION

As the pioneers moved westward they first reached what J. W. Powell called the "sub-humid region," in which rainfall gradually decreases from 28 or 30 inches to 20 inches. At the 20-inch rainfall line the "arid region" begins. This line weaves back and forth from the 100th meridian, being to the east of it in the northern part of the Plains and to the west of it in Kansas, Oklahoma, and Texas. Because of the more intense evaporation in the southern areas, the *effective* 20-inch rainfall line tends to become a more or less straight line coinciding rather closely with the 98th meridian. The arid region of Powell, however, should be divided into *semi-arid* and truly *arid,* as suggested by Thornthwaite, because the problems of using the land and of conservation differ, being more crucial in the former.[1]

In Canada the 20-inch rainfall line continues its path northward to Hudson Bay, but the arid region, as indicated by short grass, does not occupy the entire territory to the west of this line; it merely covers an oblong area with Calgary, Saskatoon, and Regina on its northern edge. North and west of this region is the "grove belt," with occasional clumps of trees interspersed with tall grass which in turn merges into the northern coniferous forest.

Climate. The arid region is characterized by great variations in climate, especially in the mountain and plateau region where altitude affects the rainfall and temperature. There are also extreme variations from year to year; drought may come not only in one year but in a series of years, two to four out of ten, as was the case from 1930 to 1936. On the plains the hot winds of summer from the south or southwest sear the crops, while in winter "northers" and blizzards add to the discomfort and hazards of life. Hail is also more prevalent in the arid sections than east of the 100th meridian.

The Inter-mountain region does not have such large areas of

[1] "Subhumid" and "arid" were the designations used by J. W. Powell in his famous *Report on the Lands of the Arid Regions of the United States* (Govt. Prtg. Office, 1879). The eastern boundary of the range territory as delineated in *The Western Range* also falls between the 98th and 100th meridians. Senate Document 199, 74th Congress, 2d Session. See also Webb, *op. cit.*, p. 21, and Thornthwaite, "The Climates of North America According to a New Classification," *Geographical Review*, October, 1931, pp. 633–35.

uniform characteristics as the Great Plains. Temperature decreases not only with latitude but also with altitude. Rainfall varies from 60 inches or more to 10 inches or less within a short distance. The mountains catch the rain-bearing winds and are often forested, while the plateaus and valleys are arid. The distribution of precipitation throughout the season is not uniform; unlike the plains, where the rainfall comes in the early part of the growing season, in the southern part of the Inter-mountain area about 35 per cent of the rain falls in July and August. The northern part has a more uniform distribution of moisture but summer is the driest part of the year.[1]

The second "leg" on which eastern land utilization rested, according to Webb, was water. Because of the lack of effective moisture agriculture became more and more precarious as the settler moved into the sub-humid and finally the arid region. Here nature seems to play tricks with man. During the wet years immigrants swarmed in, and the belief gained ground that "rainfall follows the plow." The burning of the prairie and even the electricity from telegraph wires and railroad tracks were credited with a mysterious influence on precipitation. But within a few years comes the dry cycle, "with the heavens like brass." Drought gradually burns the crops and pastures, and if it continues over a number of years the country becomes severely depopulated.

The West Coast has been the goal of many "Dust Bowlers" during the recent drought. The alternate dry and wet phases of the weather cycle have been responsible for waves of pessimism and optimism in regard to the permanent occupation of the Plains. Maps in the atlases and geographies of the 1850's indicate "The Great American Desert" on the High Plains. In 1860 the Commissioner of Statistics of Minnesota reported that the whole space between the 98th meridian and the Rocky Mountains was a "waterless, timberless, desert-like country" "unfitted for the use of the husbandman," and that the "tide of immigration is even now arrested upon the brink of a sterile waste which covers half of the national domain." [2] But the wet years returned, and in 1883 one railway company alone maintained 124 agencies

[1] See *Atlas of American Agriculture*, Part II, *Climate*, Section A, "Precipitation and Humidity" (U. S. Dept. of Agriculture).

[2] J. A. Wheelock, *First Annual Report of the Commissioner of Statistics* (Hartford, Case, Lockwood, 1860), p. 32.

throughout the Scandinavian countries, Netherlands, Germany, and Switzerland to bring immigrant settlers to the Plains. Some of them homesteaded land as far west as western Nebraska.[1]

However, the deficiency of water goes beyond its inadequacy for farming. The wooded section had abundant streams, springs, and lakes. The old oaken bucket could be lowered into a well of clear water only a few feet deep. On the plains wells had to be drilled from 30 to 300 feet deep and pumped in all but a few favored places where artesian water was to be had. Well-drilling machinery had to be invented before water was available over a large part of the plains.[2] The great depth also called for power to lift the water, which was solved by the windmill. This device was employed by the railroads before the farmers and ranchers of the plains found it useful. Many windmills are homemade, and since there is plenty of wind this type of power is cheap. An adequate water supply is a boon to both ranchman and farmer. During the dry cycles it enabled settlers to maintain themselves with a few acres of irrigated land. Today the windmill makes the home with modern conveniences possible on the plains.[3]

The Soils. When the pioneers crossed the "fault" from the forests to the grasslands they also came into new soil regions. On the transition zone they preferred to clear the forests and shunned the prairies. The farm papers of the fifties and sixties are filled with arguments as to why the latter are unsuited to agriculture and human habitation, but when farmers finally tried the prairies they discovered an unusually fertile soil, level and without stones, which did not have to be cleared. When the obstacles of the shortage of wood and water were surmounted, the so-called Prairie-earths became the famous Corn Belt, and the black prairies of Texas and Oklahoma developed into the most productive cotton lands of the nation. The next soil zone, the Black-earths, lies west of the 20-inch rainfall line and its western boundary roughly marks the western limit of the original tall grass vegetation. In the more arid regions the short grass prevailed; this in

[1] *Possibilities of Shelterbelt Planting in the Plains Region* (Lake States Forest Experiment Station, U. S. Forest Service, 1935), p. 79. *Old Jules, op. cit.*

[2] Senator Peter Norbeck of South Dakota was a professional well driller in his youth and was proud of the fact that he was the "only well digger in the Senate." *New York Times,* editorial, December 22, 1936.

[3] See Webb, *op cit.*, pp. 333–48, 375–82.

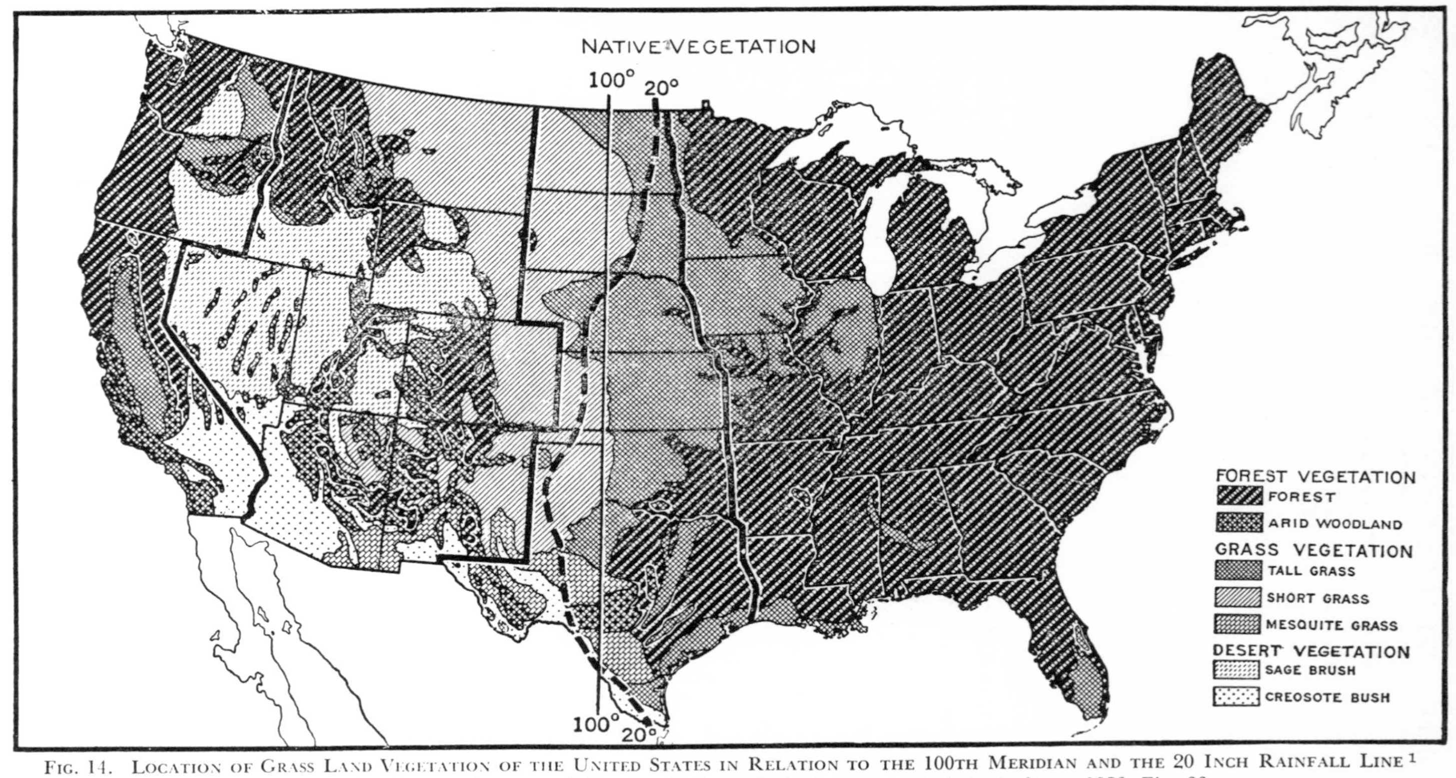

Fig. 14. Location of Grass Land Vegetation of the United States in Relation to the 100th Meridian and the 20 Inch Rainfall Line [1]

[1] Based on C. V. Piper et al., "Our Forage Resources," *Yearbook of the U. S. Department of Agriculture*, 1923, Fig. 33.

turn merged with mesquite grass and other dry land vegetation.[1]

Soils developed under arid conditions, and with a grass cover, differ from forest soils. In general the latter occur where rainfall is greater than evaporation, and the percolating water carries the soluble salts into the lower strata and the ground water. In the more arid regions the water enters only a few inches and in returning brings the salts upward, making the soil alkaline instead of acid. Vegetation is sparse and roots penetrate only 12 to 18 inches. This thin layer of roots and plants is the "thin line of defense" against the action of wind and water. This is essentially the condition in the short-grass region.

In the "tall grass" areas the grass grows to a great height and as it dies forms a layer of rich black soil of great fertility, neither alkaline nor acid. Legumes add nitrogen and the dead prairie animals add the phosphorous. Grazing and fire are a part of the normal experiences of the grasslands. Unless grazed there is a surplus of dry growth which shuts out the sunlight and obstructs the growth. Fires used to be set by the Indians or by lightning or meteorites before the white man came.

The Prairie Landscape. On the plains the pioneer found himself in a new environment, so different from the forest bounded horizon of the humid regions that one of Rolvaag's characters exclaims, "Why, there isn't even a thing that one can hide behind."[2] This was another reason why the early settler avoided the prairies, which came far to the east of the 20-inch rainfall line in parts of Minnesota, Wisconsin, and Illinois, whereas the forest frontier invaded Missouri, Oklahoma, and Texas almost as far west as the 98th meridian (Figure 14). The natural treelessness of the prairies is a mystery to the layman who observes good-sized trees acting as shelter belts on the farms of the plains. The settlers missed the forests and their longing for trees is indicated by the fact that Arbor Day originated, not in a forested country, but in Nebraska under the sponsorship of J. Sterling Morton, one time Secretary of Agriculture, in 1872. Over 700,000 acres of trees have been planted on the plains by private individuals under the stimulus of the Timber Culture Act and other federal acts as well as the various state tree bounty laws. The success of these

[1] Compare Fig. 13 with Figs. 12 and 19 of O. E. Baker, *A Graphic Summary of Physical Features and Land Utilization in the United States*, *op. cit.*

[2] O. E. Rolvaag, *Giants in the Earth* (New York, Harper's, 1929), p. 29.

plantings tends to demonstrate the feasibility of the extensive shelter belts sponsored by the federal government.[1]

However, the absence of wood also had practical implications. In the humid sections the settler found abundant logs for cabins and farm buildings; on the prairies trees grew only along the water courses. Sod houses were often the first habitations, but later the railroads brought in sawed timber. The treeless prairies called for tremendous amounts of lumber, which came largely from the pineries of the Lake states and hardwood forests of the Appalachians. The demand from this source drained the Lake states, and by 1880 helped to make Chicago the greatest lumber port in the world. Fuel and especially fencing were in demand. The forests furnished both. The prairie farmers did not even have stones for fencing. They tried hedges, some of which are still to be seen, but barb wire finally solved the problem.[2]

The animals, as well as the vegetation, had adapted themselves to arid conditions. Many were remarkable for their speed, such as the jack rabbit and antelope, and all were unusual in that they could survive with little or no actual water supply. Some of them vanished with the coming of the white man; others survived and have become pests, notably the ground squirrels, prairie dogs, kangaroo rats, and jack rabbits. The buffalo or bison furnished the Indians with food, clothing, and shelter. No animal did more to dominate the life and institutions of a people than did the buffalo, says Webb. Its extermination not only made room for the cattle of the white man, but helped to destroy the Indians as well.[3]

The Plains Indians also differed from those of the forested areas. Their mode of life was adapted to the treeless expanses of the West. They were nomadic, and with the introduction of the horse they became extremely mobile and formidable. Their skill in riding and in the use of the bow and arrow was almost incredible. It is said that the Indian could carry a hundred arrows and shoot them from his horse so rapidly that one or more arrows was in the air all the time, and each was shot with force enough to drive the shaft through the body of a buffalo. The covered

[1] *Possibilities of Shelterbelt Planting, op. cit.*, Sec. 8. Recent reports indicate a high degree of success in this venture.

[2] Webb, *op. cit.*, pp. 280–318.

[3] *Ibid.*, pp. 33, 42–44.

wagon caravans had to devise a technique of defending themselves against such enemies; in fact, the white man was no match for the Indian until the six-shooter was perfected.

Climate and the Indians kept the Spaniards out of the plains, even though they had settled in Mexico long before the English established colonies on the eastern seaboard. The Americans were repulsed there by the same forces until machinery, barb wire, railroads, and the six-shooter aided their advance. Until then, they crossed the plains only to reach other forested areas in Oregon, gold in California, or trade in New Mexico. The Mormons settled in an arid region, but they also crossed over the plains in their effort to secure isolation. The "fault" marked a limit to the expansion of slavery, cotton, and the plantation because they could not utilize the arid lands. On the other hand, the small farmer was adjusting himself to prairie agriculture by 1850 and was winning the fight for the homestead. Soon new "free" states would be asking for admission to the union and no new "slave" states could be formed to hold the balance of power in Congress. The South chose to "withdraw from a contest whose decision had been written and sealed by the hand that spread the Great Plains across the path of the westward-bound pioneer." [1]

Transportation. The East had navigable rivers, the Great Lakes, and canals; the Plains had rivers that look well on a map but flow in the wrong direction for the westward-moving pioneer. Besides, most of them were of little use even for eastbound freight and passengers since they were not navigable for appreciable distances. The horse became the medium of transportation for the Indian, the cowboy, the pony express, and the settler. The covered wagon caravan technique of travel was evolved to migrate to Oregon or to carry goods over the Sante Fe Trail. The cattle drive was a method of transporting commodities that could provide their own mode of locomotion. Camels were introduced in 1855 for travel from Texas to California but proved to be a failure. Had the experiment succeeded, it might have linked California closer to the South than to the North.[2]

[1] *Ibid.*, pp. 184–202, at 202.

[2] George P. Marsh was an advocate of the use of camels in the Southwest. See *Smithsonian Institute Report*, 1854, pp. 98–122, and his *The Camel, His Organization, Habits and Uses Considered with Reference to His Introduction into the United States* (Boston, Gould and Lincoln, 1856).

Railways finally solved the transportation problem. However, promoters were reluctant to build into the "Great American Desert" ahead of population. Their objective became the Pacific and the plains were merely an obstacle to be crossed in as straight a line as possible. In spite of the immense amount of land granted to them by the federal government, some of them went bankrupt and others were in financial distress for a while. Once established, railways became influential factors in bringing in population. Extensive advertising campaigns in northern Europe brought a multitude of foreign immigrants, especially into the northern portion of the Plains. State immigration agencies assisted the railways in this program. Railways also aided in fighting the Indians and destroying the buffalo, thereby making the country safe for agricultural development.

The story was repeated in Canada. "Railroads and continually improving transportation are as essential as rain and sun to progressive settlement on the Canadian prairie," says W. A. Mackintosh. In the Prairie provinces the wheat had to find an outlet via eastern Canada to reach the overseas markets. The first Canadian railroad reached Winnepeg in 1883, and from this point the railway net has spread in a fan-like fashion to the northwest as far as the Peace River country. Very little of the prairie area is now more than fifteen miles from a railway.[1]

In spite of the efficient transcontinental systems and a favorable rate structure, the West is still at a disadvantage because of its distance from the great consuming centers of the East. On a 1,100-pound steer Illinois has an advantage of $2.85 over Nebraska and $8.50 over Idaho in freight rates.[2] In the Intermountain region there is more than distance to contend with, as the mountains act as a barrier over which all products have to be lifted whether shipped east or to the Pacific. The long hauls and steep grades over which the products of this vast area must be carried to market make transportation costly. Conversely, machinery and manufactured goods must travel the same route, and the added freight increases the cost of production and of living for the western farmer. Besides, the country is not as well served

[1] Mackintosh, *Prairie Settlement, op. cit.*, Chap. III, p. 46.

[2] *The Western Range, op. cit.*, p. 13.

by railroads as the humid area. There are many places more than twenty-five miles from "the civilizing rails." [1]

RANCHING

Historical Development of Ranching. Ranching is almost as old as the settlement of America. In 1519 the Spaniards introduced horses and cattle into Mexico, which finally overspread Texas, California, and even the Great Plains farther north. From 1609 to 1611 cattle were imported into Virginia and turned loose in the open woods. Other herds were introduced at St. Augustine and Biloxi, and in the English colonies in general. By the middle of the seventeenth century cattle were being driven in from the Connecticut Valley to Boston for slaughter. The Shenandoah Valley, Monongahela Valley, and the Piedmont of the Carolinas and Virginia were in these times great cattle regions. A battle of the American Revolution at the "Cowpens" in South Carolina gives evidence of the ranching in early days. Many of Marion's men and Sumter's soldiers were cowboys. In fact much of the technique of ranching—the cowboy riders, the corrals, the branding, and the long drive to the market—was evolved before ranching reached the arid lands. Later on Ohio began to feed cattle on corn and the fattened cattle were sent to the East in competition with eastern feeders. The Mississippi River opened a market at New Orleans. Hogs also were raised on the nuts and acorns in the forests and were driven to market across the mountains. "Travellers were astonished to see on the highways droves of 4,000 or 5,000 hogs going to an eastern market," says Turner. "It was estimated that over 100,000 hogs were driven eastward from Kentucky alone." [2]

After the development of canals and railroads, the nature of the industry changed. Cattle were shipped into the Corn Belt to be fattened for the market, and the meat packing centers shifted to Chicago and other cities still nearer to the source of supplies.

Ranching in the Southwest and West. Ranching was started in Mexico by the descendants of the Spanish settlers who appropriated their herds of cattle and horses from the wild animals on

[1] Mark Jefferson, "The Civilizing Rails," *Economic Geography*, July, 1928. See his map of North America, p. 222.

[2] F. J. Turner, *The Rise of the New West, op. cit.*, p. 101.

the plains. The Mexican ranchers gradually moved northward into Texas, and English pioneers drifted into the same area from the lower Mississippi Valley. At first the markets were too far away and there was little trade except in hides and tallow. The northern plains remained under the control of the Indians until after the Civil War, but even before 1860 ranching began to encroach on this territory from the East. Wild cattle were much less numerous here than in Texas, and domestic animals were brought from eastern farms and turned loose.

After the Civil War the power of the Indians was broken. Texas, with its mild climate, now became the breeding ground from whence immense herds migrated northward. Only the breeding stock was retained at home; the rest were started northward on the historic Chisholm, Montana, Yellowstone, or other trails, as far west as Oregon and north even to British Columbia. Where the trails crossed the railroads "cow towns" arose from which cattle were shipped to the East and where cowboys celebrated after the lonely days on the trail. This northward movement of southern men brought North and South together in a unified West with its own unique social and political characteristics.

In the early eighties ranching began to attract outsiders. Cattle sold for $20 to $25 per head "range delivery" and, as in many other booms, were expected to go higher. Grass was "free" and cattle nearly so. Northerners, easterners, and even Englishmen of wealth and rank were attracted by the profits and romance of ranching. Ranchers and cattle increased till "the land was not able to bear them." By 1885 the country was overstocked and the carrying capacity greatly reduced. In 1886 a great "die" took away thousands of cattle, especially in the northwestern states, and millions of dollars were lost. In 1893 the Southwest had the same experience and even greater losses were experienced. After the reaction the industry was placed upon a more business-like basis.

However, about this time the cattleman also experienced the competition of the arable farmer, who was homesteading the land, and of the range sheepman. Sheep had been introduced into New Mexico and California by the Spaniards as early as 1700, and moved westward with the frontier. After 1870 the cattleman began to fight the "nesters," or homesteaders, and the sheepmen, often in armed conflict, which helped to give the West its reputation of being "wild and woolly."

In Canada the first wild cattle were seen in 1874, having strayed from one of the United States forts. In 1879 the Canadian Government brought in a thousand head of breeding cattle from Montana, and the industry developed rapidly until 1900. After that the encroachment of the farmers reduced the area available for grazing and also forced the ranchman to buy land, which added to his costs. Sheep and horses have also been grazed in the Prairie provinces but there has been a marked decline in the latter.[1]

The Domain of the Ranchman. The retreat of the cattle and sheep ranches before the plow once gave the impression that ranching was destined to become obsolete. But failures in dry farming have proved that there is a permanent place for ranching and that the passing of the cattle kings was merely a change in the organization of the industry. About 587,000,000 acres are today utilized for semi-arid and arid pastures, an area almost equal to all the land used for crops and humid pasture combined. It is true that it is an area of relatively low carrying capacity. Even if crop land were pushed to its extreme physical limits there would still be 468,000,000 acres which would be used for grazing or not used at all.

These arid lands must not be considered a mere residuum. They have qualities of their own which make them excellent grazing lands. Arid regions are less subject to certain animal diseases, and even though cold, the temperature is more endurable because of the dry atmosphere. The grasses are more palatable and nutritious than in humid sections, and the fact that they cure on the ground and serve as winter feed is another advantage. The ideal range is one with nutritious grasses, good water, and natural protection in winter afforded by a rolling and broken topography.

Characteristics of Ranch Management. In comparison with the farmer occupied with general agriculture, the ranchman is to a greater degree at the mercy of nature. He depends almost entirely upon the natural grasses to furnish feed for his herds and

[1] R. W. Murchie, William Allen, and J. F. Booth, *Agricultural Progress on the Prairie Frontier* (Toronto, Macmillan, 1936), Chap. V, "Ranching on the Prairie Provinces."

flocks. The abundance or absence of these grasses determines the carrying capacity of the land. The weather varies from year to year. A period of drought may find him without feed for his stock; he must either sell his animals, often in poor condition and at a time when thousands of others have to do likewise, or else attempt to hold on and take his losses through starvation.[1] Many ranchers now provide supplemental feed which reduces the losses by starvation but adds to the cost of business.

Because he uses natural grasses the ranchman's problem of management consists of so conducting the grazing that the grasses will perpetuate themselves, and if possible increase in quality and quantity.[2] Where land is entirely under private ownership conditions should be ideal for this purpose. The number of animals can be adjusted to the carrying capacity of the range, but this is not an easy task since rainfall is so variable from year to year. Grazing should also be adjusted to the life cycle of the plants so that the range will re-seed itself. Good management includes rotation of pastures; in Texas the ranchmen often include goats and sheep in their system because these animals can utilize the rougher ground and the grasses and shrubs not eaten by cattle. Supplemental feeding and artificial watering places in the form of wells are also part of the ranch management in many places.

The ranges vary greatly with respect to pasturage. Formerly the semi-arid Great Plains were used for grazing on the all-year basis. The rapid settlement of much of this region has so reduced the pasture area that it has generally become necessary to shorten the grazing season and resort to winter feeding. The Intermountain region still has some areas of year-long range, but very often the higher levels are grazed in the summer and the valleys and basins in the winter. This necessitates driving the animals from one range to another, but it helps the range to maintain itself if not otherwise over-grazed.[3]

Compared with ordinary farming, ranching requires large areas of land. In Sutton County, Texas, over 44 per cent of the

[1] A. L. Walker and J. L. Lantow, *A Preliminary Study of 127 New Mexico Ranches in 1925* (New Mexico Bulletin 159, 1927), p. 33.

[2] E. O. Wooton, *Factors Affecting Range Management in New Mexico* (U. S. Dept. of Agriculture, Bulletin 211, 1915), pp. 32–33; Arthur W. Sampson, *Range and Pasture Management* (New York, Wiley, 1923), Chap. 111.

[3] C. V. Piper, *et al.*, "Our Forage Resources," *Yearbook of the U. S. Dept. of Agriculture,* 1923, pp. 392–95.

ranches had at least 20,000 acres of land each, less than 2 per cent being below 2,500 acres. In New Mexico the ranches in the better watered district averaged 34.2 square miles and in the most arid district about 38 sections.[1] A study of Arizona and New Mexico ranches revealed an average of 40,000 acres and 35,000 acres respectively for these two states.[2]

A ranch also involves a larger investment than a farm and this investment is distributed differently, as shown in Table 25. The cattle ranches investigated by Walker and Lantow averaged about $75,000 and ranged from $30,000 to $185,000 in value. Water development is an important item which in some cases ran up to $40,000 per ranch. Cattle represent about one-half of the total investment.

TABLE 25

INVESTMENT PER RANCH ON 112 NEW MEXICO CATTLE RANCHES

Land	$24,531	Cattle	$35,134
Buildings	4,527	Other Livestock	1,470
Water	3,904	Miscellaneous	1,806
Fences	3,265		
		Total	$74,637

Finally, cattle have a long cycle of development which means that the ranch has a slow turnover. The ranch also supplies very little food for the family. Ranching is like one-crop agriculture or a mine in this respect, rather than like the average farm. Its product must all be sold and the provisions for the family must be bought.[3]

Ranching and Property in Land. Early ranching was conducted on "free grass" or, rather, free land. The first herds were to be had for the capture and branding. No one was concerned with land. It was still a part of the public domain, or, in Texas, the property of the state. Even the railroads were as liberal as the government with their lands in those days.

[1] Walker and Lantow, *op. cit.*, p. 37.

[2] Wooton, *The Relation of Land Tenure to the Use of the Arid Grazing Lands* (U. S. Dept. of Agriculture Bulletin 1001), p. 27.

[3] B. Youngblood and A. B. Cox, *An Economic Study of a Typical Ranching Area on the Edwards Plateau of Texas* (Texas Agric. Exp. Station, Bulletin 297, 1922), pp. 23–30, 69–78.

As other ranchmen began to drift into the country with their flocks they fell into the predicament of Abraham and Lot. And, as in the case of these ancient ranchers, "with the whole land before them" it was easy to "separate" and select "well watered" spots and agree that each was to have a sufficient amount of land to maintain his breeding stock and its increase up to the proper marketing stage. Thus developed the "law of the range" which later became the custom and the law, for it must be remembered that ranching often preceded established government. Once such rights were established they were in essence property rights respected by all and subject to purchase and sale as land itself is sold nowadays. No rent was paid for the grazing rights, yet the land was not common property where everybody could pasture cattle. The first comer had the right under the law of the range to secure for himself the right to water and land against all others. Yet the land was not private property in the legal sense.

The cattle were kept within the approximate area by cowboys acting as line riders, who tried to keep the herd together. In spite of the line riders much inter-mingling of cattle took place, especially when the "northers" caused the cattle to drift southward for miles. But each cattleman had his own brand and each year a roundup was held, the strayed cattle returned to the owners, the young stock branded, and the salable cattle sent to the market. Around 1870 the wire fence came into use and took the place of the line riders. This enabled the cattleman to stake out his claim and control his herd, but it also led to serious abuses. Great companies fenced from 20,000 to 50,000 acres of the public lands and kept others out by force of arms. The range became cut up and the free movement of cattle was prevented. Fencing was declared illegal by the Department of the Interior, and by 1890 the public domain was again open.[1]

More serious than the "fence wars" among the stockmen were the fences of the farmers, who were rapidly coming into the more humid parts of the ranch country and were taking up the land under the various homestead acts. These "nesters" or "grangers," as the cattlemen called them, pre-empted especially the land with water. By using the water for irrigation they sometimes depleted the streams to such an extent that the cattle suffered. Very often

[1] Hibbard, *A History of the Public Land Policies, op. cit.*, pp. 476–78.

the nester selected some strategic point in the valleys or near a supply of water and by fencing his quarter section broke up the drives or deprived the ranchman of water. "The fences crept snake-like around the water holes, isolated many sections of grazing lands, and killed the open range by thirst."[1] The old quarrel between Abel, the "keeper of sheep," and Cain, the "tiller of the ground," was re-enacted, but the government favored those citizens to whom it had granted land for farming. In 1892, in the "Rustlers War," the cowboys "surrendered ostensibly to the cavalry, practically to the farmer," says Rollins.[2]

In Texas the second step in the development of property was leasing. In 1883 legislation was passed providing for the leasing of the state-owned grazing lands, although these lands are subject to purchase at all times. Leasing, however, preceded purchase. The ranchman was afraid that if he did not lease the land someone else would and thereby establish stronger rights to the land than the law of the range. At first the leases merely covered the land on which the water was found, or where the headquarters were located, and all the remainder was free grass as before. However, competition among Texas cattlemen forced the last step, namely the complete freehold. At first only the strategic lands were purchased, the water-bearing lands and the headquarters, and the remainder were controlled through a lease or even as "free grass." The leasing period came to an end about 1904 to 1906 in Texas.[3] This gradual shift to the complete freehold is peculiar to Texas and is not yet completed. But in the other parts of the West other conditions obtain to which we shall return later.[4]

Land Policies and Ranching. In Canada provision was made in 1872 for grazing as a form of land use by granting land adjacent to farms for grazing purposes. In 1876 leases were granted to anyone, and, as modified in 1882, the act provided for the leasing of as much as 100,000 acres for twenty-one years at one cent an acre, provided the ranchman met the requirements as to stocking

[1] Philip Ashton Rollins, *The Cowboy* (New York, Scribners, 1922), p. 30.
[2] *Ibid.*, p. 31.
[3] Youngblood and Cox, *op. cit.*, p. 71. Hibbard, *op. cit.*, pp. 479–83.
[4] For a good history of ranching in Montana see Robert S. Fletcher, *Organization of the Ranch Cattle Business in Eastern Montana* (Montana Agric. Exp. Station, Bull. 265, 1932).

of the leasehold. However, such leases were subject to cancellation on two years' notice if the land was needed for settlement. This did not trouble the ranchmen very much in the early days, but when settlers began to come in it added greatly to the insecurity of tenure. The act was amended several times but always to the disadvantage of the ranchman. Although an amendment to the Land Act Regulations in 1925 has given somewhat more stability to the grazing industry, insecurity is still an undesirable feature in many sections. The maximum acreage leasable to one individual has also been reduced.[1]

Not until the Grazing Homestead Act of 1916 was grazing recognized as having a place in the public land policies of the United States. Somehow pasturage was treated as a passing phase of land utilization to be replaced by arable agriculture, especially after dry farming had demonstrated its feasibility. The deterioration of the range was not considered important because the land would come under the plow eventually, just as forest fires were viewed with complacency because the burning only made clearing easier for the settler.

John Wesley Powell's "Pasturage Districts." It is interesting to review J. W. Powell's suggestions for a land system in the arid regions. He recognized three great land uses: (1) irrigable land, which, however, would absorb only a small percentage of the total area (in Utah, for example, only 2.8 per cent was considered capable of irrigation); (2) timbered lands on the highlands, also limited in extent; (3) "pasturage lands," to utilize all the rest of the acreage, with perhaps small irrigated gardens or fields for grain and feed near the ranch headquarters. To this end he advocated the classification of the land so that the first two classes and the mineral lands could be separated from the grazing lands and an adequate program of alienation and use set up for each class.

It is significant that farming as we know it, aside from irrigated agriculture, was not a part of his program. The policies were definitely for grazing, irrigation, and timber. His observations led him to suggest the minimum area for a ranch as four sections or 2,560 acres. He had seen how water could be monopolized by homesteading the strategic quarter sections, so he sug-

[1] Murchie, Allen, and Booth, *op. cit.*, pp. 54–59.

gested a new method of surveying and of land registration. He recommended the organization of pasturage districts (strangely prophetic of the Taylor Grazing districts) with a minimum of nine members, each of whom would be permitted to acquire four square miles of land through the existing homestead laws. The districts were to be more or less self-governing bodies making their own rules and regulations. However, instead of being in the square blocks of the rectangular survey, the district was to be surveyed in such a manner that all members would have frontage on the available water supply for the stock and for irrigation. The tracts, though equal in area, might be irregular in shape to take advantage of the topography and other natural conditions; they were to be surveyed, mapped, numbered, and registered in a manner similar to the platted lots of cities or the government lots on meandered streams. Instead of nine residences scattered over a township, these were to be grouped, to use Powell's own words, so "that the inhabitants of these districts may have the benefits of the local organization of civilization—as schools, churches, etc. and the benefit of cooperation in the construction of roads, bridges and other local improvements." [1]

Later Land Laws and the Pattern of Land Ownership. Instead of adopting a well defined grazing policy, the alienation policy for the benefit of agriculture was continued, with a few tardy modifications to suit Western conditions. By using the Timber Culture Act, the Desert Land Act, the Timber and Stone Acts, as well as the usual homestead acts, the agricultural settlers continued to pick the best lands. The ranchman requiring a much larger acreage for an economic holding had to resort to agricultural acts to acquire what he needed and often used fraudulent methods to obtain the necessary land. Even in Texas, where the ranchman could enter eight sections, cowboys and other ranch hands filed on land and then sold out to their employers.

The first federal act to recognize ranching was the Grazing-Homestead Act of 1916 already mentioned. This law permitted the homesteading of 640 acres on the lands "which are in the opinion of the Secretary of the Interior chiefly valuable for grazing and raising forage crops, which do not contain merchantable timber, are not susceptible of irrigation from any known source

[1] *Report, op. cit.*, pp. 22–23.

of water supply, and are of such character that 640 acres are reasonably required to support a family."

Very few settlers succeeded on the grazing homesteads. Most of them were speculators who made the minimum of improvement, put in their residence, and then sold the land for about $3.00 an acre. A little dry farming was attempted but the land was often so arid that the harvest did not return the seed.[1] If the

PRINCIPAL KINDS OF LAND OWNERSHIP IN THE 11 WESTERN STATES

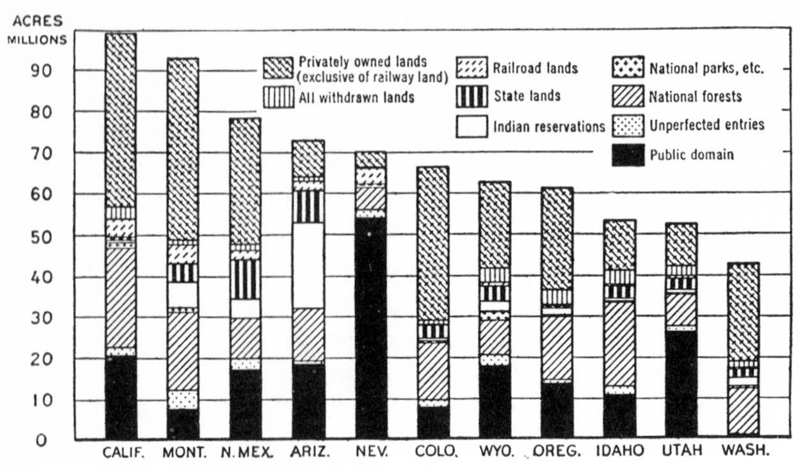

FIG. 15[2]

intention of the law was to add citizens and taxpayers to the state it was a failure. About 99 per cent of the land ultimately went into the hands of stockmen already on the ground.

Most of the land now in public ownership is of a similar character, and in late years counties as well as states have acquired a "new public domain" by taking title to tax-delinquent land. The land tenure of the Pacific and Mountain states is shown in Figure

[1] Will C. Barnes, "The Story of the Range," Hearings before a Subcommittee of the Committee on Public Lands and Surveys, U. S. Senate, 69th Congress, 1st Session (1926). "A large colony of such settlers in the Rio Grande Valley of northern New Mexico, west of the town of Taos, visited in 1922, was composed mostly of veterans and young men from near-by towns, school teachers, clerks in stores (many of them women), almost none of them practical stock raisers. Few of them . . . intended to live permanently upon their tracts. They were for the greater part hauling water for domestic purposes as well as to water the few head of livestock they owned—a cow or two, a few horses for work purposes, chickens, and here and there among the Mexicans small bunches of goats, for meat and milk." (p. 1629.)

[2] From *Land Utilization and the Farm Problem* (U. S. Department of Agriculture Miscellaneous Publication No. 97, 1930).

TABLE 26

LANDOWNERSHIP BY TYPE OF AGENCY IN PETROLEUM COUNTY, MONTANA, 1934 [1]

Type of Agency	Number of Separate Tracts	Average Acres per Tract	Total Number of Acres	Percentage of Total
Public agencies				
Federal	216	1,124.6	242,906	22.7
State	96	675.3	64,828	6.1
County	207	551.7	114,205	10.7
Corporations				
Railroads	53	468.8	24,884	2.3
Investment and mortgage companies	51	294.7	15,032	1.4
Commercial banks	40	218.3	8,731	0.8
Insurance companies	63	374.0	23,560	2.2
Land banks	39	425.7	16,601	1.5
Miscellaneous corporate groups (principally sheep and livestock companies)	77	315.1	24,259	2.3
Individuals				
Residents of Montana	1,035	271.8	281,318	26.2
Non-residents of Montana	961	265.9	255,523	23.8
Total	2,838	377.7	1,071,847	100.0

15. After all the publicly owned land is accounted for, there remain only 255,000,000 acres or 34 per cent as private lands subject to taxation. The almost 8,000,000 acres in Indian allotments are not taxable. Land in farms occupied roughly 218,000,000 acres in 1930 but had increased to 236,000,000 by 1935. In recent years considerable farm land has been transferred to the ownership of banks, insurance companies, and other lending corporations, all of which adds to the complexity of the land-tenure pattern and the problems of the local governments.

The problem of the public administrator and private owner is complicated by the distribution of these various types of land. None of it occurs in solid blocks to any extent, federal, state, and private lands being intermingled, which makes the pattern of ownership extremely complex (Figure 16 and Table 26).[2]

[1] Table 8 of R. R. Renne, *Montana Land Ownership* (Montana Agric. Exp. Station Bulletin 322, 1936).

[2] Renne, *Montana Land Ownership, op. cit.; Tax Delinquency and Mortgage Foreclosures* (Montana Agric. Exp. Station, Bulletin 319, 1936). See also his articles,

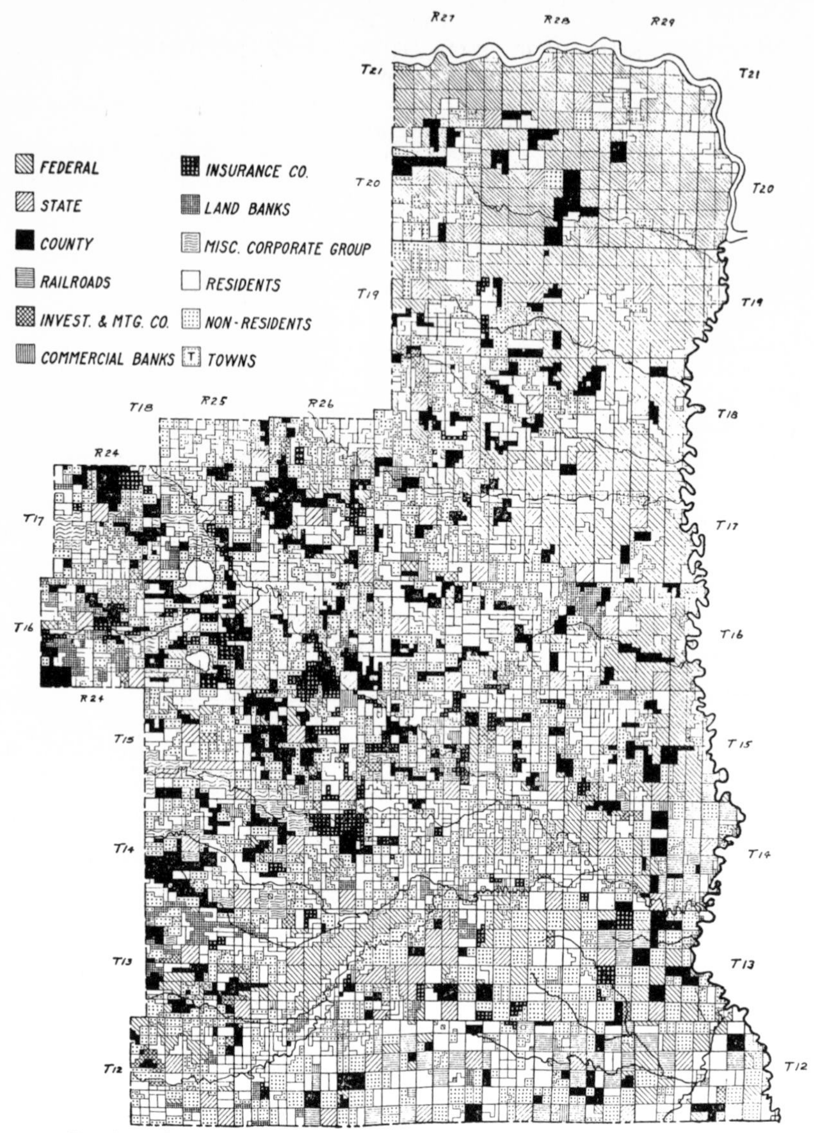

FIG. 16. OWNERSHIP PATTERN OF PETROLEUM COUNTY, MONTANA, 1935 [1]

The Problem of the Ranchman in Securing an Economic Unit. The ranchman had the problem of securing an economic holding from these various and sundry types of land existing in a crazy

"Western Land Policies and Recent Ownership Trends," *Journal of Land and Public Utility Economics*, February, 1936, and "Significance of the Ownership Pattern to Land Use Planning," *Journal of Farm Economics*, August, 1935.

[1] Montana Agricultural Experiment Station Bulletin 322, 1936.

quilt of tenures. Naturally he selected the land with water on it and obtained title to that. This gave him control over all the other land dependent on this water, especially if the land was still public domain. By the law of the range, he was entitled to the use of the land to a point midway between his own water and that of a neighbor. In practice both herds used either supply by the courtesy of the respective owners. But any newcomer had a right to come in, find water or "develop" it, and claim the right to graze halfway to the next water hole. The stockmen on the ground often bought out the interloper or developed another watering place near the newcomer, thereby restricting his range, and then waited for dry years to starve him out.[1]

The worst offenders in this respect were the sheepmen. Sheep crop the grass more closely than cattle, can survive with less water, and often defile the watering places. For these and other reasons there has often been war between cattlemen and sheepherders, which resulted in considerable loss of human life and the destruction of thousands of sheep. In Nevada the ranchmen bought up the water until the ownership of 5 to 10 per cent of the land now controls 90 to 95 per cent of the range. Such water monopoly is responsible for the concentration of holdings in this state. By purchasing the key forties from among the school sections of the state lands, the owners acquired control of the land for miles around. One such ranch is eight miles long and three miles wide, but dominates some seventy square miles of public domain. This control prevents even farm lands from being put to the best use.[2]

In contrast to Texas, where most of the land is privately owned, the stockmen of the other southern range states own very little land, except the strategic area. They lease railroad, state, and Indian lands or depend upon the national forests and the open range. The 125 ranches studied in New Mexico embraced these various lands as indicated in Table 27.

The competition to buy or lease the favored ranch tracts "inflated" the land values just as the values of western forests were inflated. This high capitalization of land has to be borne by the

[1] Wooton, *Factors Affecting Range Management*, *op. cit.*, p. 26.

[2] George Stewart, *This Public Domain of Ours* (Utah Circular 49), pp. 24–26. Romanzo Adams, "Public Range Lands—A New Policy Needed," *American Journal of Sociology*, Vol. XXII, pp. 324–51.

TABLE 27

OWNERSHIP OF THE LAND USED BY 125 NEW MEXICO RANCHES [1]

(Average per ranch)

	ACRES		PERCENTAGE OF TOTAL
1. Owned Land	8,365		21.4
2. Public Domain	10,028		25.6
3. Leased Land	20,811		53.0
State		8,528	21.7
Railroads		1,802	4.6
Private		6,764	17.3
Forest		3,174	8.1
Indian and Other Lands		513	1.3
Total	39,204		

livestock or the "converting" part of the enterprise. The owned land has to pay taxes and these rest heaviest on the poorest soils. If the carrying capacity is 100 acres per cow and the tax only 5 cents per acre, each animal has to sustain a $5.00 annual levy. Naturally delinquency is excessive. Credit is based upon livestock in the range country and the risks involved make the rates high, 9½ to 10 per cent. The most economical way to meet these costs, as well as the handicaps of distance from the market, is the use of the cheap grass supplied by the range. As soon as the ranchman has to depend upon supplemental feed, excessive costs begin to appear. In his efforts to cover these costs the ranchman has steadily increased his herds and overstocked the range. Since there were no regulations on the use of the public domain, the unmerciful competition for grass on this free land caused a rapid deterioration of the grass cover. Indian, state, and county-owned lands are leased and are under somewhat more regulation, the federal forests most of all. Taking all these lands together, the grazing capacity of the entire western range has been depleted by 52 per cent, ranging from 30 per cent on federal forests to 67 per cent on the public domain. The privately owned lands have not escaped; they are said to be depleted by 51 per cent of their normal carrying capacity.[2] The nutritious grasses disappear first

[1] Table 9, New Mexico Agric. Exp. Station Bulletin 159.
[2] *The Western Range, op. cit.*, p. 7.

and the unpalatable plants and foreign species, such as Russian thistle, invade the land. Over-grazing is not fully appreciated as yet because the animals are now using the poorer vegetation, but it is showing its effects in greater death losses, and "calf drops" are only half or two-thirds of what they are under normal conditions. One of the most drastic adjustments the stockmen will have to make in order to conserve and restore the carrying capacity of the range is a reduction of 38 per cent in the herds.[1]

Over-grazing has not only depleted the carrying capacity of the range, but is responsible for wind and water erosion and floods. Several hundred million acres have already lost several inches of their top soil, and their productive capacity has been reduced one-fourth to one-half. Eighty per cent of the entire range is eroding, ranging from almost all of the public domain, 80 per cent of private land, to less than 40 per cent of the federal forests. Floods have increased and the eróded material is being deposited in the streams. This is a serious menace to the great dams upon which irrigation depends so much in the West. "More than 5.8 billion dollars is invested in irrigated land and improvements, as compared to about 4.1 billion dollars in range livestock and related ranch properties. Each of the 475 million acres of range land yielding water or contributing silt to streams supports an investment of $12.27 in irrigation works, lands, and facilities, and this figure would be still higher if the investments for power and municipal water supplies were added." [2] In other words, it would pay to manage the range lands merely to maintain irrigation even if there were no cattle on the "thousand hills" of the West.

The "hoof that broke the sod" has proved to be as dangerous as the "plow that broke the Plains" and the mere transfer of the 50 million acres that should have remained in grass, but are now plowed up, to their original condition without proper management will accomplish little. The history of the public domain also indicates that resources will not be automatically conserved by public ownership *per se*. It has been recognized that to hold the public lands "in trust" for the possible homesteader without

[1] *Ibid.*, pp. 11, 47. See also the special sections of this report on "Excessive Stocking," "Rule-of-Thumb Management," "Financial Handicaps," "Private Ownership—Land and Livestock."

[2] *The Western Range, op. cit.*, p. 25.

regulation or administration was wrong from both public and private points of view. It is a good example of a natural resource going to rack and ruin because of faulty institutional arrangements. Some westerners favored transferring the entire body of land to the states for administration and ownership and this plan was approved by a committee appointed by President Hoover in 1931.[1] While favored in some western states the plan was as violently opposed in others. The controversy was practically closed by the enactment of the Taylor Grazing Act in 1934. This act is based upon the experience gained in regulating grazing on federal forests and by local grazing associations.

Grazing Control on Federal Lands. Because pasturage has always been considered secondary to forest production and watershed protection on federal forests, the regulation of grazing was an accepted policy from the beginning. Grazing can and does interfere with reforestation and forest management so the number of animals permitted admission was regulated by a renewable permit ranging from one to five years. Permits are granted only to actual owners of stock and of land and are not transferable. A sufficient amount of feed to carry the stock through the winter is another stipulation. By carefully holding the number of cattle to the carrying capacity of the forests, depletion has been held down to 30 per cent, as compared with 51 per cent on private land. Judged by trends, over three-fourths of the federal forest land is now on the upgrade, whereas 85 per cent of the land in all other ownerships is on the downgrade.[2] The area of federal forests eroding and contributing to the silting of streams is far below that of the land in other ownerships. Stockmen at first resented this form of control but have gradually been won over as the good results became apparent. In Montana a beginning was made in the setting up of grazing districts which preceded the Taylor Grazing Act of 1934.[3]

The Taylor Grazing Act authorizes the withdrawal from entry

[1] Charles Winter, *Four Hundred Million Acres* (Overland Publishing Co., Casper, Wyoming, 1932). *Report* of the Committee on the Conservation and Administration of the Public Domain, Jan. 1931.

[2] *The Western Range, op. cit.,* pp. 7–8.

[3] R. B. Tootel, *Grazing Districts: Their Nature and Possibilities in Range Land Utilization* (Montana Agric. Exp. Station, Bulletin 127, 1932); H. H. Saunderson and N. W. Monte, *Grazing Districts in Montana: Their Purpose and Organization Procedure* (Montana Agric. Exp. Station Bulletin 326, 1936).

of 142,000,000 acres of the public domain. This includes most of the land of any value; about 15 per cent of the unappropriated land is not affected, although for the present all of the public domain has been withdrawn pending classification, and until executive withdrawal is modified the homestead laws cannot be used for further private entry. The administration of the lands withdrawn is placed with the Department of the Interior, in which a Division of Grazing has been established. Broad powers are given to the Secretary of the Interior to regulate the occupancy and use of the land by regulating the number of livestock that shall be permitted to graze within a district, the season of grazing, and to collect reasonable fees for the use of the public domain. Grazing districts are set up for purposes of administration, and an exchange of lands with other public or with private landowners to "block up" respective ownerships is permitted.

By 1940 over 50 grazing districts had been established embracing about 258,000,000 acres of which 135,000,000 were public domain and the remainder were in other ownerships, private, state and county. Although a notable step in the direction of placing the public domain under administration, it is recognized that the act is not perfect. Advisory boards consisting of local stockmen share in policy making. It is claimed that they have placed too much emphasis on grazing to the neglect of watershed protection, forests, wild life and recreation. It is also feared that, unless great care is exercised in its administration, the privileges of the large land owners will be enlarged and that they may obtain vested rights in the grazing on the public lands.[1]

DRY FARMING

History of Dry Farming. Dry farming is of great antiquity. The great nations of ancient times were in arid and semi-arid regions. China, Mesopotamia, Egypt, Palestine, Mexico, and Peru are outstanding examples. While these countries developed irrigation and were in part pastoral, there are evidences that dry farming was also practiced. In the Bible Jeremiah speaks of the fallow. Ruins in Tunis give testimony of a dense population without irrigation.

Dry farming methods were developed independently in Utah,

[1] *The Western Range, op. cit.*, pp. 32–33, 285–94.

California, Washington, and the Great Plains, from about 1863 to 1880. In Utah the discovery was accidental. Some settlers had tried to irrigate their farms from Malad Creek in the Bear River Valley and found that the water was alkaline. In their despair the starving men plowed up the sagebrush land, sowed some grain, and to their surprise reaped a fair harvest. In Canada the practice began in 1885 when Angus MacKay noted the effect of summer fallow on crop yields. Certain individuals, the experiment stations of the West, and the dry farming congresses have aided materially in developing the technique of this practice.

Because of the aridity of the climate, dry farming must conserve the limited moisture. This is usually accomplished by the summer fallow. The object is to open the soil so that the rains can penetrate it, to work the land to keep out the weeds, and to prevent the evaporation of the water until the crops can appropriate it. Fallowing also rests the land and helps the process of nitrification, an important factor in one-crop agriculture. Fallowing means leaving a portion of the farm idle, i.e., plowed but unsown, while the remaining part is in active production. Dry farming therefore requires double the area of a humid farm for the same acreage in crops. In some regions, however, fallowing is practiced every third or fourth year instead of every other year. As the technique of dry farming has been perfected, the practice of fallowing has been modified and even found unnecessary in some places. On the Great Plains, where rain falls during the growing season, it is not as important as in the Palouse country of Washington, where the rain falls mainly in the winter. In fact, it is impossible to generalize concerning the various practices of soil management.[1]

As might be expected, the technique of dry farming was not learned in a day. The early settlers or "nesters" were careful to select the moist river bottoms, much to the disgust of the ranchmen. Later it was usually the wet period of the weather cycle that brought in a wave of settlers, who succeeded in these favorable years even though they used the methods suitable to humid

[1] William E. Leonard, "The Wheat Farmer of Southeastern Washington," *Journal of Land and Public Utility Economics,* January, 1926, pp. 23–39; Byron Hunter, *Dry Farming Methods and Practices in Wheat Growing in the Columbia and Snake River Basins* (U. S. Dept. of Agriculture, Farmers Bulletin 1545).

farming. One such influx came in the 1880's when covered wagons swarmed into western Kansas and Nebraska "like locusts," encouraged by the railroads, town-site promoters, and speculators. By 1896 the dry years had decimated the area. A more recent boom was enacted in the "Triangle" of Montana and in the corresponding triangle on the Canadian side of the line. This had been a cattle country since 1880. By 1907 homesteaders began to crowd out the cattlemen. A series of years of high rainfall and no troubles with weeds or insects started the boom. The war prices for wheat and low production costs helped the fever. The year 1916 was the climax. Wheat was $2.00 a bushel and this land yielded 30 to 50 bushels to the acre. Just as in the earlier days it was believed that "rainfall follows the plow," and business men and bankers shared the optimism of the farmer. Land values rose rapidly because profits were in direct proportion to the area cultivated. Lands just patented were contracted for at $25 to $50 an acre.

Dry farming practices were not followed; no one believed that the weather might change and even the best technique will not guarantee a crop in some years. The dry farmer must build up not only a reserve of moisture but also a reserve of feed and capital. The Mandan Indians and, later, the early Utah settlers stored up grain for dry years. But the eastern farmers attracted by the boom were not versed in dry farming technique; much less were those coming from eighteen other occupations, including two deep-sea divers who have served as the classic examples of misfits in arid agriculture ever since the boom collapsed.

But after 1916 the tide turned. In 1917 the drought set in. Russian thistles began to appear on the farms. Those who had practiced slipshod farming failed completely. The next year was worse than 1917. Mortgage debts incurred in the days of plenty came due but there were no reserves to draw upon. Everyone had expected the "rainy day" to last forever. Both the United States and the Canadian governments made loans with which to buy seed, but 1919 was so dry that the seed did not germinate in some places and even the native grasses made no growth. The next three years were somewhat better, but grasshoppers and cutworms destroyed crops in many places in 1920. By this time the disaster was complete. Cattle and wheat prices fell. Foreclosure, closed banks, and the abandonment of 80 to 90 per cent of the farms in the Triangle greeted the visitor to Montana in 1923.[1]

There is a tradition in the Northwest, as in all pioneer regions, that it takes three sets of settlers to conquer a new country. It is said that the first two groups are not "good" farmers but that the third set really "knows how to farm." Probably the real explanation is that by the time the third group comes upon the scene the new technique has been mastered. The fact is that in the Triangle those farmers who had followed dry farming practices in spite of the temptation to put the entire tract into wheat were the ones who held on during the drought. These farmers also had shelter belts, gardens, a few cows, and poultry.

Characteristics of Prairie Farming. The farms of the humid section were and still are relatively small. They were settled before the days of large-scale farm machinery, and with hand tools the settler could neither clear nor cultivate a large acreage. Besides, fencing was expensive. It took years to "produce" a full-sized farm. The larger the tract the greater were the ripening costs.

On the prairies "God had cleared the fields," as Herbert Quick put it. Large areas could be used productively the first year, and the ease with which the first harvest was produced encouraged the farmer to get more land at once. With barbed wire fencing and large-scale farm machinery to cultivate, sow, and reap, the area a family could operate became still greater. With horse power at his command the prairie farmer could handle about 320 acres of land without hired help except at seeding and harvest time. While the homestead of 160 acres was sufficient in the humid section of the prairies, it was only half enough for an economic holding in the region of the 100th meridian. The eastern congressmen never seemed able to visualize the need for larger acreages on the plains, and not until 1904 was the homestead act modified to permit the settler to acquire 640 acres under the Kinkaid Act, which, however, was restricted to western Nebraska. Five years later the Enlarged Homestead Act granted 320 acres, thereby recognizing the fact that under a system of fallowing only half of the farm may be producing in a given year. Unfortunately

[1] M. L. Wilson, *Dry Farming in the North Central Montana Triangle* (Montana State College, Extension Bulletin 66, 1923).

these acts were enacted after settlers had passed beyond the 100th meridian. However, by using a combination of the land acts, a settler could get a maximum of three quarter sections, and in later years the farms were gradually enlarged by purchase or by renting additional land. Nevertheless, many of the farms of the wheat-producing areas are still uneconomical in size.[1]

It is not only the need of fallowing that calls for large farms. The low production per acre and the vicissitudes of the area make low-cost extensive farming necessary if dry farming is to succeed. Another handicap is that the plains are adapted to one-crop agriculture, highly commercial in its nature. The security of the diversified or self-sufficient farm is absent. Wheat predominates, with flax, rye, and barley in the northern part and sorghum crops in the southern part as supplementary crops. The latter were imported from the dry lands of Asia and Africa and have been an important factor in the utilization of the southern plains. Among them are kaffir, milo, feterita, sudan grass, and Egyptian wheat. Another unforeseen invasion of the area beyond the 98th meridian has come with the shifting of the Cotton Belt into western Texas and Oklahoma. Between 1919 and 1928 an increase of over 9,000,000 acres of cotton took place in these two states, also the result of mechanization.[2]

The introduction of machinery adapted to the crops grown on the plains reduced the cost of production per man and per acre as soon as the size of the unit could be adjusted to the machine. As the machines increased in size and as mechanical power was introduced, the area which a farmer and his family could handle was increased once more and the cost of production reduced. Lower costs of operation permitted the cultivation of land with less and less rainfall and still lower productivity. Between 1910 and 1920 the acreage in wheat increased 51 per cent and in the next decade 15 per cent, in spite of the agricultural depression. The combine-harvester created another minor revolution. First used in the Pacific states, it was introduced on the plains about 1918 and immediately met with favor. It reduced the necessity for extra labor at harvest time and permitted a still larger acreage per man. It is one of the factors depopulating the

[1] *N. R. B. Report, op. cit.*, p. 159.

[2] P. H. Stephens, "Mechanization of Cotton Farms," *Journal of Farm Economics*, January, 1931, pp. 27–36.

dry farming areas without decreasing the land in cultivation. In place of the 35,000 wheat farmers in Montana in 1915–17, only 14,000 remained in 1929, operating a larger acreage than in 1917.[1] In Kansas at least 2,000 to 3,000 acres are necessary for an efficient unit, especially if a part of the farm is in native pasture. With a proper combination of crops and livestock a farmer can operate 5,000 to 6,000 acres, representing an investment of $50,000 to $200,000 in land and equipment, which raises the question whether a typical farmer can secure capital for such an undertaking. Corporation farming seems a logical solution, yet in 1931 less than one per cent of the wheat grown in Kansas was produced on corporation farms.[2]

Large farms mean long distances to neighbors and isolation from markets, schools, and churches. This problem is being solved by the automobile. It permits the operator to live in a village or small city where the community institutions are provided, yet he can reach his farm in no more time than the old-fashioned eastern farmer took to harness his horses and get to the fields. Mechanical power also does away with the cost and inconvenience of maintaining horses, especially during the winter. Mechanization has ushered in the part-time wheat farmer or the "suitcase farmer" as he is known locally. The suitcase farmer often follows other occupations but works his farm during seeding and harvest. During winter he lives in the larger towns or even in Florida and California. The reduction in population affects not only the farming areas but the rural villages and cities as well.[3]

Over-expansion of Arable Agriculture into the Grazing Domain. The improved techniques, combined with a series of profitable years, especially the war years, have expanded arable agriculture beyond its proper sphere. Dry farming has invaded some of the best range lands, thereby driving the livestock to the already overstocked ranges. It is estimated that over 50,000,000 acres now under the plow should have been left in grass; about half of this land has already been abandaned, much of it even before it could be patented. To reconvert plowed land, nature

[1] "Farm Mechanization," *Yearbook of the U. S. Dept. of Agriculture,* 1932, pp. 417–20.

[2] W. E. Grimes, "Social and Economic Aspects of Large Scale Farming in the Wheat Belt," *Journal of Farm Economics,* January, 1931, pp. 21–26.

[3] Grimes, *op. cit.; Yearbook,* 1932, *op. cit.*

may take 25 to 50 years. At least 15,000,000 acres will have to be re-seeded, and the expense is so great that it must be done by the public. Some of the land now abandoned was fertile, but cropping and erosion have made it sub-marginal. This raises the question of whether dry farming as it is now conducted can ever be maintained as a permanent system of agriculture.[1]

The maladjustment in land use was dramatized by the dust storms of recent years. The plowed plains and overgrazed ranges have always been subject to dust storms, but several years of deficient rainfall had dried the soil and in May, 1934, with little vegetation to hold it, the heavy winds began to lift the fine soil from the wheat lands of Canada, the Dakotas, Minnesota, Nebraska, and adjacent country, and to carry it overland far out into the Atlantic. It was estimated that every square mile in the vicinity of Washington had above it 101 tons of soil in suspension during the storm. In some cases the soil was carried away as far as the plow had loosened the earth. Farm buildings and roads were buried, and distress, sickness, and even death accompanied these storms. The census of 1935 graphically reveals the disaster of 1934 in reporting the large acreage in idle fallow and crop failures. In the 100th Meridian states almost half as much land was "crop failure" as was in harvested crops.

However, this storm and the series of dry years are not an isolated phenomenon. From Table 24 it will be noted that 37 per cent of the area of the 100th Meridian states, almost one-fourth of the Mountain states, and 15 per cent of the land in the Lake states is subject to wind erosion. While much of the western land now under the plow should be restored to grass, a large area can be maintained in arable agriculture by proper methods of tillage. If stubble is not plowed under entirely it helps to protect the soil. Plowing up ridges crosswise to prevailing winds, "strip farming" with alternating strips of seeded and fallowed land, and shelter belts have proved to be effective.[2]

Besides individual attempts to control wind erosion, a beginning has been made in setting up co-operative or community efforts to do so. In 1935 Texas passed an act permitting the creation of Wind Erosion Conservation Districts, which are co-

[1] *The Western Range, op. cit.*, p. 19.

[2] Charles E. Kellogg, *Soil Blowing and Dust Storms* (U. S. Dept. of Agriculture, Miscellaneous Publication 221, 1935).

extensive with the county boundaries and are administered by the regular county officials, but with powers separate from those of the county. These districts are declared to be "agencies of the State of Texas charged with the responsibility of conserving the natural resources of the soil." Upon the petition of fifty tax paying voters an election is held and a majority of the "legally qualified tax paying voters" of the district must vote in favor of forming a district. The officers have the power to enter upon any land in the county, make the necessary improvements, and charge the costs to the landowners, but only after due notification and public hearings. Furthermore, the costs must not be in excess of the benefits received. This assessment constitutes a binding first lien against the property. Because wind erosion affects the public highways, provision was made to transfer a certain proportion of the road and bridge money to wind erosion control purposes. The districts are also empowered to borrow money and receive grants from units of government or outside agencies.

In Kansas the county commissioners may enter private land and charge the expenses of controlling erosion against the land in the same manner as taxes, but costs may not exceed $1.00 per acre. New Mexico, Oregon, and Oklahoma have also passed wind erosion control laws recently.[1]

Finally, land use adjustments are being made by the purchase of land by the federal government, begun under the Resettlement Administration and continued under the Soil Conservation Service. Some of this land will be held in large blocks and restored to grazing, other tracts are being acquired as part of an adjustment program looking toward better land use and better adaptation of the size and type of farms to the region. States and counties are also concerned with the management and administration of land which has reverted through tax delinquency.[2]

With the upward turn in the rainfall cycle the plains are re-

[1] Geo. S. Wehrwein, "Wind Erosion Legislation in Texas and Kansas," *Journal of Land and Public Utility Economics,* August, 1936, pp. 312–13; E. H. Teagarden, "Control of Wind Erosion," *ibid.* November, 1937, pp. 420–21; H. A. Hockley and Herman Walker, Jr., "1937 State Legislation for Control of Soil Erosion," *ibid,* May, 1938, pp. 210–217.

[2] R. J. Penn and C. W. Loomer, *County Land Management in Northwestern South Dakota* (South Dakota Agricultural Experiment Station Bulletin 326, September, 1938).

turning to a more prosperous condition, but the problem of establishing a permanent form of land use in this part of America is still unsolved. One element in the picture is the fact that the arid region appeals to a peculiar type of settler. Some of them are like prospectors, always looking for a lucky strike and roaming about hoping to find it. The "dry lander" is attracted by the large areas, mechanized production, and the gamble with nature. The very necessity of pitting intellect against the fierceness of the drought appeals to many, and this spirit is as important as the economics of the case. There seems to be a natural separation of farmers in the West; some preferring the small areas, close associations, the security and the crops of the irrigated farms, and the others the expansive area of the dry farm. The ranchman is of still another temperament. Many who thought they would like dry farming have found the struggle too much for them. Not more than 15 per cent seem to have stayed with it. As E. V. Willcox wrote in 1920, long before the present droughts, "Have you more of the right stuff in you? If not it's only a question of time when the black stem rust, the grasshoppers, the hot winds, the sand storms, the drought or sheer loneliness will get you. You will long to hear the rain drops on the roof and you will leave the 'never-never' country." [1]

IRRIGATION

Irrigation is an ancient and a spectacular form of land utilization and reclamation. It appeals to the imagination to make the desert "blossom as the rose" and convert a sage-brush tract into a highly cultivated farm. Arid country is unusually healthful and the scenic beauty surrounding many of the irrigation projects adds its appeal. The ability to control the water supply and to apply moisture when and where it is needed is in sharp contrast to the situation of the farmer who must wait for natural precipitation. Railroads and promoters were not slow in capitalizing the advantages of irrigation. The promotion began in the 1880's and by 1890 had reached the stage where books and periodicals were devoted to irrigation.[2] J. W. Powell's article published in 1894, showing that there was a limit to the area which could be irri-

[1] "West of One Hundred," *Country Gentleman*, January 10, 1920, p. 42.

[2] William E. Smythe, author of *The Conquest of Arid America*, (New York, Harper's, 1900), published *The Irrigation Age* during the 1890's.

gated, was resented and caused much debate. He showed that if all the rain falling on the 750,000,000 acres of the arid country were caught and distributed over the land, about 75,000,000 acres could be irrigated; but the practical area he placed at 40,000,000 acres after making allowance for artesian water, pumped wells, and flood plain waters.[1] That he was conservative is shown by the latest estimate of 51,000,000 acres of potential irrigable land, of which 25,000,000 acres are now in enterprises capable of supplying water to land, but of which less than 19,000,000 acres were actually irrigated in 1930.[2]

Whether all of the potential irrigable area of the arid region will be cultivated depends more upon the economic than the physical availability of the water. Irrigation is not the only use for water in the West, and the supply will have to be shared with stockmen, cities, and domestic users; in fact, in some regions there is a fierce conflict for the limited supply. Some states have to choose between more city population and more irrigated land. Furthermore, the area now irrigated represents the less costly projects; the newer enterprises in general are more expensive and can be undertaken only as prices of farm products rise or costs of construction are reduced. The National Resources Board Report estimates that an additional 4,000,000 acres can be irrigated at less than $50 per acre for reclamation, about 3,000,000 acres with an expenditure of $50 to $100 per acre, another 3,000,000 acres at costs ranging between $100 and $200, and somewhat over 1,000,000 acres at more than $200 per acre.[3]

Nature of Irrigation Farming. In the arid area land is not the limiting factor, but water is the "fourth" and scarce factor of production. The scarcity is both physical and economic. As the above figures show, less than 40 per cent of the available area is being watered today. The first irrigators merely diverted water from a stream and irrigated a tract near the river, requiring neither a dam nor a long expensive canal to store and carry the water. Later projects required expensive engineering works, flumes, canals carrying water for miles, and dams. The chief source of

[1] *Irrigation Age,* February, 1894, pp. 54–65; March, 1894, pp. 99–105; and later issues.

[2] *N. R. B. Report,* p. 129, and U. S. Census, 1930, *Irrigation of Agricultural Lands.*

[3] *Op. cit.,* p. 129. The costs on 15,000,000 acres had not been determined at the time the report was published.

water on the earlier enterprises was from streams and could be carried inexpensively to the farms by gravity, but pumping and storage have now increased in importance. In 1910 gravity supplied water to 89 per cent of the irrigated area, in 1930 to only 66 per cent. Then gravity systems required an investment of $26 per acre irrigated, as compared to $110 thirty years later.[1]

In order to irrigate properly the land must be smooth and slope in such a manner that the water can be led to all parts of it. Leveling is often required, the cost of which usually runs from $5 to $10 an acre but often reaches $35 or $40, and even $100, an acre. There have been cases where it has proved more expensive than the cost of the water itself.[2] Finally the settler must provide himself with the usual farm equipment—house, barns, tools, fences, and machinery. There are also many community expenses in a new country, roads, bridges, schools, churches, and other governmental costs. Taxes are usually high. The pioneers often want to do in ten years the equivalent of what their forefathers did in a hundred.[3]

Since some time must elapse before crops can be harvested, the settler must "grubstake" himself and his family for several years. Therefore he should have a considerable sum of money with which to start an irrigated farm, or have the credit with which to meet the production costs and the carrying and ripening costs which accumulate before he can expect any return.[4]

[1] U. S. Census, 1930, *Irrigation of Agricultural Lands,* pp. 30 and 31.

[2] *A Survey of Reclamation* (New York, McGraw-Hill, 1924), reprint of nine articles from the *Engineering News Record* published October to December, 1923, p. 15.

[3] *Ibid.,* pp. 22–23.

[4] The cost of improving an 80-acre farm on the Newlands project of Nevada was reported as follows:

Levelling land, building checks and small ditches	$3,000
House and barn	1,500
Work team and farm implements	1,000
Living expenses, one year	500
Taxes, operation, maintenance, incidentals	300
Initial payment on water right	200
Dairy herd of 20 cows, or other livestock to eat fodder crops	2,000
	$8,500

The cost of development of irrigated land in California in 1922 was found to be $146 an acre, plus land, $7,000 for a 40-acre farm. If the farm was planted to alfalfa the cost was $170 an acre, and if put out in orchards even $200 per acre. This does not include the cost of the land or the construction cost of the water right. *Federal Reclamation by Irrigation,* Senate Document 92, 68th Congress, 1st Session, pp. 126–27.

Irrigation is a special type of agriculture with a technique of its own. Soils must be treated differently under irrigation than under ordinary conditions. Much has been learned about the behavior of soils since we began to irrigate, but much is still to be learned. The quality of soils under irrigation is just as varied as under ordinary agriculture. Some soils are submarginal even though the water supply is adequate. One of the problems of the irrigation farmer is the rise of alkali, brought to the surface by capillary water. If enough water can be applied these salts may be carried downward into the drainage. In other places the soil has become waterlogged and unfruitful. Drainage will usually remedy these conditions, but this adds materially to the cost of developing and maintaining agriculture under irrigation. Where water is stored the life of the storage may be limited by the rate with which silt is accumulating in the reservoirs. Silt deposits filled the Austin (Texas) dam in thirteen years, and the Elephant Butte Dam is being filled at the rate of 20,000 acre-feet per year. The Zuni Reservoir in New Mexico was silted to over 70 per cent of its capacity in twenty-two years. Irrigated land is a good example of a factor of production which can be kept in a productive state only with the constant application of labor and capital. If silting is not prevented, the dams, the flumes, and the thousands of acres "under the ditch" may have to be scrapped like a worn out machine or a depreciated building. Hence the need for a co-ordinated land policy embracing not only the irrigated land, but also the range land, the dry farming areas, and the forests.

The irrigator's ability to apply water to his crops when they need it and in just the right amounts is often more theoretical than real. This can be done only when there is an abundance of water relative to the land, which was true when irrigation first began, but a shortage appeared when the land-water ratio was reversed. By 1913, over 40,000 appropriators had listed their claims for water in Montana by filing on 56,000,000 second feet of water or enough to irrigate an area twice the size of this state.[1] Institutions and laws had to be devised to determine rights to water; this phase of the subject will be elaborated in Chapter XI. But even if all "under a given ditch" have adequate water in a year of plen-

[1] P. L. Slagsvold, *Montana's Irrigation Resources* (Montana Agric. Exp. Station Bulletin 315, 1936).

tiful rainfall, in a drought some or all may not have enough water to mature the crops. In many localities the streams are filled in the spring and early summer while the snows are melting in the mountains, but they dwindle during the late summer and fall when some crops still need water. Such a condition can be remedied by proper storage, but this means outlays for dams and canals. Additional storage is a crying need on many projects, but the high cost of construction relative to prospective returns is the limiting factor in many an irrigation development. Unless the land can be operated intensively, high overhead costs cannot be met and land cannot be used intensively unless climate, soils, and markets are favorable.[1]

The irrigation farmer has the task of meeting the higher costs of production by more efficient techniques and higher yields. However, the usual picture of highly specialized crops and more intensive farming on irrigated land is true of only a portion of the enterprises, and the yields are not always superior to those on humid lands of the same quality. With the exception of rice, the products grown on irrigated land are the same as those raised in the humid sections. Forty-six per cent of the area in irrigated crops was devoted to hay crops in 1929 and almost 27 per cent to cereals, grains, and seeds. Intensive agriculture, such as vegetables, absorbed 5.3 per cent of the area, sugar beets 3.4 per cent, and orchards and fruits 10.2 per cent. Almost half of the acreage devoted to sugar beets in the United States and over 10 per cent of the area in hay crops are on irrigated land.[2]

If the farms are redivided into the usual "type of farming" groups it will be found that fruit farms are the most numerous, representing 21.3 per cent of the total. Crop specialty farms rank second with 17.2 per cent, which includes sugar beets, field peas, beans, hay, or white potatoes. Cotton is the most important product on the irrigated farms in Arizona, New Mexico, and Texas. Dairy and general farms each make up about 10 per cent of the total.[3]

Instead of specializing for the distant market, the irrigation projects began in 1910 to furnish supplemental feed and concentrates for the fattening and feeding of range stock, thus integra-

[1] *Ibid.*, pp. 14–17.
[2] *Irrigation of Agricultural Lands, op. cit.*, p. 326.
[3] *Ibid.*, pp. 285, 131–32.

ting ranching and crop farming. In some cases the ranchman owns only the ranch land and buys his feed; in other cases there is a combination of grazing and growing of feed on the same enterprise. Thus a farm may lie partly in an irrigated tract and partly outside.[1] This accounts for some of the large farms reported as irrigated farms. The usual picture of all irrigation farms as small tracts is contrary to facts. They are as varied in size as the non-irrigated farms, and in many states the preponderant size is the same for both. Although their area ranges from farms of less than 3 acres to over 800 farms containing 10,000 acres or more, the most usual size on the Plains falls between 100 to 174 acres, whereas in the Mountain and Pacific states the prevailing size is 20 to 49 acres.[2]

Land Policies and Irrigation. From the description of irrigation farming and its requirements it is easy to see why the usual land acts failed to meet the needs of the irrigation farmer as completely as they failed to meet those of the ranchman or the dry farmer. The early irrigators wanted small tracts, and none of the land acts permitted the entry of 20 or 30 acres. In Utah 16 to 30 farmers wanted a quarter section and "got by" the land laws by having one of their number enter the land and divide it long before the patent was issued to the entry man.[3] In this connection Major Powell's *Report* is again a pertinent contribution. He proposed irrigation districts to be organized by a minimum of nine settlers, each to have no more than 80 acres. The district was to be platted in a manner similar to his grazing districts, so as to get away from the rectangular survey and take advantage of natural conditions. Water was to inhere in the land and any member of the district who failed to irrigate within five years after entry would lose his right to water.[4]

Instead of a sensible plan such as this Congress passed the Desert Land Act in 1877, believing that it would meet the needs of the irrigator. A large tract was considered necessary to bear the cost of providing a water supply, so the entryman was granted

[1] *The Western Range, op. cit.*, p. 17; Ralph H. Brown in Parkins and Whitaker, *Our Natural Resources and Their Conservation, op. cit.*, pp. 133–35.

[2] *Irrigation of Agricultural Lands, op. cit.*, p. 265.

[3] George Thomas, *The Development of Institutions under Irrigation* (New York, Macmillan, 1920), pp. 39–41.

[4] *Report, op. cit.*, pp. 27–33.

640 acres of non-timbered land "which will not without irrigation, produce some agricultural produce." The area was reduced to 320 acres in 1890. The settler paid $1.25 per acre, but title did not pass until he had expended at least $3.00 an acre for improvements and had reclaimed at least one-eighth of it. Since the title remained with the government until the land was actually irrigated, the settler could not obtain a loan upon his land for the purpose of reclaiming it. The act failed to accomplish its purpose for the cause of reclamation. Thomas sums up the reasons for its failure as follows: "The area was altogether too large for the individual irrigator to reclaim and altogether too small for the capitalist to consider with the view of supplying water and selling it to actual settlers. The act fell far short of accomplishing the purposes of its promoters."[1]

As a matter of fact, because this act did not require residence and permitted the purchase of the land, it became a favorite with speculators and ranchmen who wanted to get large tracts of land. Ditches were made by plowing a furrow that began where there was no water and ended where there was no field to be irrigated, and other clever methods were devised to obtain land under the act.[2] By June 30, 1926, over 32,500,000 acres had been claimed under this law, but the area covered by proofs of compliance was only a little over 8,500,000 acres. The difference represents some lands in the process of reclamation but many more in abandoned schemes.

Irrigation, A Community Enterprise. While the first irrigation was started by individuals, it soon became necessary for a group to band together and arrange co-operatively for taking water from a stream to irrigate a group of farms. It is estimated that fully three-quarters of the irrigation enterprises involve two or more individuals. In some cases there are as many as 5,000 farmers "under one ditch." Human relationships are therefore important, both during the construction period and after. Irrigation farmers usually live close together and are brought into constant association because of their mutual relationship to land and water. They are confronted by the question of the division of work on the ditches, the distribution of costs, and the parceling of

[1] Thomas, *op. cit.*, p. 233. See also pp. 39–41.
[2] Hibbard, *op. cit.*, pp. 424–34.

the water among individual farmers. It is significant that closely knit religious communities, such as the Mormons, or colonies such as Greeley, Colorado, which had their origin in the collapse of Fourierism in the East, have been among the most successful of the irrigation projects. In fact it is claimed that the compulsion to co-operate and live together is producing a unique rural life on the irrigated lands.[1]

Financing the Irrigation Enterprise. The irrigator has two sets of costs, the production and ripening costs on his own farm and those associated with the enterprise as a whole. The latter must be undertaken before water is available for the farm, and this means that money has to be raised and expended long before returns can be realized from the land. The longer the period between the beginning of construction and the time when the first harvest can begin to repay the production and ripening costs, the heavier the burden. Unless the irrigators have the capital, ways and means must be found whereby the project can be financed from the outside. This broadens the human relationships another step; irrigation involves not only the farmers, but also construction companies, stock and bond holders, financing companies, and even local and state governments.

The earliest form of co-operative enterprise in community irrigation was started and financed by the Mormon church. The church furnished the money necessary to support the settlers during the construction period; the co-operators were paid in stock and as the enterprise got on its feet they repaid the money advanced by the church.

Commercial enterprise entered the field by building irrigation dams and flumes with the hope of recovering the costs by selling water to irrigators. In some cases the companies also owned the land and hoped to sell it to future farmers with or without water rights. Usually the money was raised by selling stocks and bonds, and a considerable boom was started in this form of investment. However, practically all such companies have failed and the investors lost heavily. The promoter's hope of success was based upon the belief that it was water which "created the high land values" of the irrigated land, and he felt that settlers *must* have

[1] John A. Widtsoe, *Success on Irrigation Projects* (New York, Wiley, 1928), Chap. 10.

the water which only the company could supply. But the land in its natural state was very cheap; it could even be homesteaded in many cases, and the cost of carrying it was low. There was no compulsion to buy water. Many of the first occupiers were mere speculators who hoped to sell to real farmers after the irrigation works were built. So the land lay idle. Meanwhile the irrigation works deteriorated, sand drifted into the flumes, and interest charges accumulated. After only a few years of watchful waiting the landowners bought the canals and works at a fraction of the real cost.[1]

The experience of the ordinary company led to the *Carey Act* of 1894. One of its purposes was to stimulate irrigation by granting a million acres to such of the arid land states as would provide for the reclamation of the land. The states sold these lands at low prices only to those who made a contract with the construction company to purchase water rights. Thus the land and water were tied together, and when everybody had paid his share of the cost of construction to the company, the dam and engineering works belonged to the water-users, organized as a co-operative enterprise or an irrigation district.

The actual engineering was done by a private company but under regulations prescribed by the state and federal governments. By tying the land and water together, speculation in land and "freezing out" of the company were made impossible. The fact that the federal and state governments were involved in the Carey Act projects gave the impression that bonds of the construction companies were backed by these governments. Millions of dollars of Carey Act bonds were sold and much money was lost since there was no such guarantee. The bonds were merely based upon the settlers' notes for water rights before construction was begun. Delays in construction and in getting settlers on the land strained the finances of many companies and caused their failure. Another contributing factor was that the title to the land remained with the federal government until the lands were "irrigated, reclaimed, and occupied by actual settlers." Settlers could not offer the land as a security for loans, and although vari-

[1] Teele, *Economics of Land Reclamation, op. cit.,* also "The Financing of Non-Governmental Irrigation Enterprises," *Journal of Land and Public Utility Economics,* October, 1926, pp. 427–41; U. S. Dept. of Agriculture Bulletin 1257; Elwood Mead, *Irrigation Institutions* (New York, Macmillan, 1903).

ous ways were devised to get around this difficulty they have not yet been successful in overcoming it.

In 1930 less than one per cent of the irrigated area was served by Carey Act projects, a decrease of almost 84 per cent since 1920. This is due to the fact that as soon as the engineering works are paid for, the project is no longer listed as a Carey Act enterprise but as a co-operative project or as an irrigation district.

Co-operative Associations and Districts. In the co-operative forms of organization, landowners either raise money among themselves or borrow it. Stock is issued and held by the water-users, the stock representing the right to a certain amount of water. In some cases stock may be owned independently of the land and, although this is not considered desirable, it has not developed serious abuses.[1] Almost a third of the irrigated area was under these forms of organization in 1930.

The Wright Act of California (1887) was the first law permitting the formation of *irrigation districts,* which are now common to all the arid land states. Whenever a certain proportion of the landowners of an area vote to form a district, all other landowners are compelled to come into the project. The number of voters necessary to force this action and their qualifications vary with different states and are prescribed by the law. The district becomes a separate unit of government and may levy assessments against all the land in the district; these levies are treated in the same manner as taxes and the taxing machinery is used to enforce and collect them. The assessments may be uniform on all lands or may be apportioned according to the benefits the landowner receives or according to the water allotment. The taxing power is the great element of strength and tends to make the bonds safer investments, yet not all districts have been successful. The principal reasons for delinquent districts have been: the opposition of influential landowners to the organization of districts, the inclusion of unproductive land, inadequacy of the water supply, engineering difficulties, exploitation, and insufficient settlement of the land. As a rule, districts are organized by existing communities which can begin to repay costs within a few years after the improvements have been made. Further stability of the

[1] R. B. Tootel, *An Inventory of Montana Irrigation Projects* (Montana Extension Bulletin 124, 1932), pp. 62–96.

irrigation district's finances is established by certification of bonds by ten of the arid states and the purchase of bonds by others.[1] Although irrigation districts also had their period of boom and reaction, they have increased in importance. In 1920 less than 10 per cent of the irrigated area was in irrigation districts, while in 1930 almost 18 per cent was so governed, the increase being due to a large extent to the shift from other forms of organization to the district form.

RECLAMATION BY THE FEDERAL GOVERNMENT

In 1902 an important step was taken when direct construction of engineering works was launched as a public enterprise. This was partly the result of the enthusiasm for conservation aroused by Theodore Roosevelt, which was aimed especially at the Malthusian specter and supported by the idea that since the remaining public land was of little use to the settler without water it was the duty of the government to furnish the water. The provision of more self-supporting and home-owning farms was part of the same policy. The Reclamation Bureau was set up as the "homemaking branch" of the government, and the ideal of self-supporting farms was often stated in the literature of the times. If this meant owner-operated self-sufficiency, the ideal has not been realized, since most irrigation farms are under commercial and specialized operation, and 23 per cent of them were operated by tenants in 1930.

By this time (1902), the simpler enterprises had been undertaken and the record made by private enterprise had not been entirely successful. It was believed that the government could carry on construction of these more expensive works more economically. The plan was for the federal government to build dams and other engineering structures and for the settlers to pay for them in ten annual installments without interest. The nonpayment of interest was justified on the grounds that the public was benefited by the establishment of homes and settled communities, and this "bonus to the landowners" was to be considered as compensation in part for the hardships and uncertainties of pioneering. Otherwise no subsidy was involved, and, as settlers

[1] Wells A. Hutchins, *Irrigation Districts, Their Organization, Operation, and Financing* (U. S. Dept. of Agriculture Technical Bulletin 254, 1931).

paid for their share of the cost of construction, the works were to be turned over to them as a co-operative or an irrigation district enterprise. The money received was to be used to finance new projects. No money was to be appropriated for reclamation; only the sums received from the sale of public land within the western states were to be used for this purpose.

Within a few years after the work was started it was found that ten years was too short a period for the repayment of the costs of providing the water. In 1914 the time was extended to twenty years, and after the post-war depression set in drastic reorganization was necessary. It should be noted, however, that certain weaknesses became apparent during the period of rising prices before the World War and remained acute in spite of the boom prices of the war years. One weakness lay in the fact that the cost of construction was greater than the income from the land could sustain. Regarding this the National Resources Board Report curtly says: "The placing of settlers on government projects at a cost much greater than might be found elsewhere is not only indefensible economically but it also fails of social justification."[1]

Failure of agriculture on the federal reclamation projects was not the result of faulty construction. The gigantic dams and marvellous tunnels, flumes, and other engineering works are remarkably well constructed and free from the graft at times associated with government construction. It is true that in some cases the estimates of costs were below the actual costs and the settlers were saddled with a larger debt than they expected. Some of the projects were poorly selected, but this was largely the fault of the law which provided that the projects must be located in the states where public lands were being sold. Some states with many highly feasible projects consequently had to be content with few developments, while in others inferior projects had to be undertaken in order to comply with the law. Four projects were abandoned and sold or disposed of in other ways. Furthermore, lands of low fertility were taken into the project, yet it was expected that every acre should carry an equal burden irrespective of its nature.

The main difficulty, however, was with the human equation. Some of the land "under the ditch" was in private hands and be-

[1] *Op. cit.*, p. 194.

came subject to speculation. Many of the settlers had paid too much for the land. This cost, together with that of the water rights, became a heavy load to carry, and the farmer preferred to blame his condition on the government's reclamation plan rather than on private miscalculations. In too many cases the settler was unfamiliar with irrigation agriculture or had too little capital to start farming under irrigated conditions. The law made no provision for examining the settlers as to their experience or capital. In fact, the law did not permit selection. If two men applied for the same tract of land the choice was by lot and not by merit.

Finally, it was difficult for the government to deal with the settlers through its agents on the projects. A voter can always air his grievances and induce his congressman or senator to intercede for him, and this is what happened. Those who could pay held off, waiting for the relief action in behalf of the weaker farmers, and then they applied for the same relief for themselves.

Settlement on government projects was very slow—a characteristic, it seems, of irrigation development in general. Teele observed that not more than 50 per cent of the area of American irrigation enterprises was irrigated twenty years after the project was started, which means that ripening costs are extremely heavy.[1] On the northern plains the irrigation projects were also at a disadvantage after the War when compared to dry farming and ranching. Raising grain on small irrigated farms could not compete with mass production by machines and power on the larger areas. The irrigated farms could not be shifted to more intensive crops because these were not suited to the climate; even to change to sugar beets and dairying was not easy. The irrigators could not meet their obligations to the government. A "fact finders committee" was appointed which reported in 1924 that repayment should be made on the basis of 5 per cent of the settler's gross annual production based on a ten-year average. However, it was found that some farmers would then have a century to pay for their share of construction, so, by an act of Congress, the period was limited to forty years. The committee also recommended that a system of credit be established and that the soils be examined and readjustments in payments be made. Nearly 200,000

[1] Teele, *op. cit.*, p. 191.

acres were found to be temporarily or permanently unproductive and about $27,000,000 of obligations were written off. It was also decided that in the future all projects were to be tested for economic as well as engineering feasibility and prospective settlers were to have two years of actual farm experience and at least $2,000 in money or equipment. But the farmers have been no more successful in meeting their payments than before, and since 1932 the government has granted one moratorium after another.

During the drought period of 1930–35 the irrigation projects were oases in the midst of desolation. In spite of the fact that some of the projects were short of water, irrigators were still in a better condition than their dry-farming neighbors. They had diversified crops for home use and irrigated crops carried the livestock in the country adjacent. The greater security in time of drought has once more raised enthusiasm for irrigation and a demand for federal projects, in spite of the fact that the financial success of public projects is doubtful. Repayments have been so slow that the revolving fund has failed to revolve and a certain amount of subsidy has crept in; yet this can be justified if reclamation is put on the same plane as rivers and harbors and flood control.[1]

This, however, does not meet the criticism that reclamation brings more land into use just at a time when other government agencies are struggling with the "surplus" and crop reduction. The proponents of irrigation try to meet this argument by pointing out that the crops raised on federal projects are negligible or non-competitive.[2]

Our future policy will depend somewhat upon our philosophy in regard to the position of the West in our national scheme. The local benefits of reclamation have been justified because such a large part of the area of the West is in federal ownership for the benefit of the entire nation and is non-taxable for local purposes. The creation of taxable values, new centers of population, and new arable lands is warranted as one way for the federal government to reimburse the West for its contribution to the cause of conservation.[3] Because of its inter-relation with grazing and dry

[1] Sherman Johnson, "Irrigation Policies and Programs in the Northern Great Plains Region," *Journal of Farm Economics,* August, 1936, pp. 543–55.

[2] Elwood Mead, "The Place of Federal Reclamation in a Federal Land Policy," *Proceedings of the National Conference on Land Utilization,* 1931, pp. 17–23.

[3] National Land Use Planning Committee, Publication IV, March, 1933 (mimeographed).

farming further irrigation development is justified to salvage or rehabilitate these other land uses. The reclamation projects are playing an important part in the resettlement program, and readjustments in land use are being made by the Farm Security Administration and the Soil Conservation Service which has taken over the work of the Resettlement Administration.

This is no argument, however, for uncontrolled development of new projects; rather, for conservative additions to old enterprises. The National Resources Board cautions that "economic feasibility" should include national and regional as well as local considerations. Local communities should be required to share in the costs of reclamation, since they also benefit from such projects. Such a requirement would have a sobering effect on local chambers of commerce and other boosters.[1] Furthermore, the settler himself should not be forgotten. Unless the project has soil adapted to irrigation and an adequate water supply, and unless he is asked to pay charges which bear a direct relation to the income his farm is able to deliver, the irrigator will again be the victim of "uneconomic feasibility." [2] Whether Boulder Dam and the Grand Coulee projects can meet these tests remains to be seen.

Land Policies for the Arid Lands. The federal government is now engaged in buying misused land in the arid regions and restoring it to grazing. Farmers are being resettled, many of them on the unoccupied areas of existing irrigation projects. The government also has the gigantic task of giving aid to drought-stricken families.[3] The question, however, is raised of how far state and national governments can go to correct land practices by purchase. It places an enormous financial burden on them to do so, and removes more and more land from the tax rolls. Furthermore, unless the public lands are properly administered the history of misuse of the soil on the public domain may be re-enacted.

Zoning has been suggested to control the use of land, similar to the zoning of submarginal humid areas, but the problem is much more difficult in the arid sections. The division between

[1] *Report,* pp. 193–95.

[2] Sherman Johnson, *op. cit.,* p. 554.

[3] Their plight is vividly described in John Steinbeck's *The Grapes of Wrath* (New York, Viking, 1939).

different land types is not so distinct and their uses are so intermingled. The setting up of clear-cut districts with permitted and prohibited land uses for each is formidable, if not impossible.

Finally, the specter of the weather cycle will not down. Can any zoning ordinance prohibiting arable agriculture and settlement within a given area be enforced when the rains begin to fall and the eternal optimism of the westerner again prevails in the land? "It can safely be said," wrote Isaiah Bowman, "that some of the land that will be purchased under any present national scheme will some day be resold to settlers because of increasing rainfall over a period long enough to hearten the bolder spirits and lead again to a forward push of settlement. It can be predicted with complete assurance that members of Congress will rise 30, 40, or 50 years from now and declaim against the shortsightedness of the legislatures and leaders of 1934–1935 who talked as if the whole West were becoming a desert once more, the grass lands permanently destroyed, the ground water level permanently lowered and the land faced with permanent disaster." [1]

[1] "Our Expanding and Contracting 'Desert'," *Geographical Review,* January, 1935, p. 52.

IX

FOREST LAND

To the settler of the South "as in the North the forest was a hostile thing occupying the ground which he needed for corn and beans, even though it furnished him with game, fuel, and building material. All was fair in the struggle against this handicap, and no weapon, not even his sharp ax, was more powerful than fire. So the use of fire against the forest became a part of the ritual of the poor man. He has literally burned his way west, from the pine lands of the Carolinas to the black jack cross-timbers of Oklahoma and Texas." [1] So universal has been this reaction of the pioneer to the forest that the French habitant burned and slashed with the same abandon in 1725 as the later Ontario farmer of whom it is said he "cordially hates a tree." [2]

This almost vicious attitude toward the wilderness not only is responsible for depleted wealth and for landscapes that are nightmares, but, what is more important, has left us with blunted sensibilities toward the forest and the scenic resources it represents. It is the task of conservation to conserve this great natural resource and also to rehabilitate the attitudes and institutions of a people still enslaved to the settler's psychology of conquest. Nowhere is this more important than in forests, even though the pioneer had the same feelings toward the grasslands, game, and mineral treasures.

THE FOREST AS A MINE

Forest Depletion. Nearly half of the United States, or 822,000,000 acres, was once covered with woodland (Figure 14). Of this area the farmer cleared 150,000,000 acres to make room for crops and did not even convert the wood into boards or fuel. It is estimated that another 50,000,000 acres were cleared by farmers, and the wood was used for some practical purposes.

[1] Sears, *Deserts on the March, op. cit.,* p. 59.

[2] Lower and Innis, *Settlement and the Forest and Mining Frontiers, op. cit.,* pp. 21, 38–39.

Clearing for agriculture was thus responsible for the destruction of about 200,000,000 acres, or 24 per cent of our original forest area.[1]

The original forest area of Canada—1,300,000 square miles—carried about 925,000,000,000 cubic feet of timber; about 27 per cent of this volume remains. It is estimated that only 13 per cent has been cut for use; some of the remainder was removed to clear the land but much more was destroyed by fire.[2]

Of course, there never was a time when some of the cutting was not for fuel, for construction, for shipbuilding, or for export. England depended on the colonies for tall pines for the masts of the royal navy and for naval stores.[3] However, lumbering as a business did not really develop until our own cities furnished a market and until the steam-driven sawmill had been perfected.

While the rapid reduction of our forest resources is to be deplored, especially the depletion due to fires and waste, the fact must not be overlooked that the American people benefited from the bountiful supply of forests placed here by nature and profited by the competition in the lumber industry which gave them cheap lumber. It is difficult to appraise what this has meant to the economic development of the nation. Wood has been used for every conceivable purpose. The Census of 1880 reported the value of saw logs for that year at about $140,000,000 and the wood used for fencing at $100,000,000, but forest-derived fuel was estimated to be worth over $326,000,000. Railways, steamboats, manufacturing plants, and mining establishments were among the heavy users of fuel wood. Railways were also using $10,000,000 worth of ties annually.[4] In spite of the use of natural gas, coal, oil, and electricity, 28 per cent of our total wood consumption to-day is for fuel.

Much has been said about America as a nation of home owners, but few people realize that the abundant and cheap building material furnished by our forests helped materially to make this

[1] Greeley, *et al.*, "Timber, Mine or Crop?" *op. cit.*, pp. 84–88.

[2] Roland D. Craig, "The Forest Resources of Canada," *Economic Geography*, July, 1926, pp. 412–13.

[3] Canada developed a profitable export trade very early, much to the detriment of agriculture since the farmer-lumberer too often preferred the more exciting life of the lumberman. Lower and Innis, *op. cit.*, Chap. III.

[4] Charles S. Sargent, *Report on the Forests of North America* (U. S. Dept. of the Interior, Census Office, 1884).

possible. Ninety-eight per cent of the rural dwellings are built of wood and, in spite of the use of substitutes, urban construction still calls for large quantities of wooden building materials.

The depletion of the forests, spectacular and reckless as it was in America, is not peculiar to the New World. In all parts of the world forests were removed to give place to crops, but before the days of mechanization this was a slow and gradual process. In many parts of Europe forests were depleted to obtain the charcoal used for smelting before mineral coal was used for this purpose. Great Britain has only 5 per cent of her original forests left; France, Spain, Italy, and Greece have from 10 to 20 per cent, but Finland and Sweden have about half of their ancient forests still intact. Thus forests have been pushed more and more to the margins of agricultural production and therefore tend to occupy residual lands. This gives the impression that forests can grow anywhere, but forests also are limited by climatic and soil factors. Only one-fourth of the earth's surface is capable of growing trees of saw timber size. The area capable of growing soft woods is also restricted and is chiefly in the northern hemisphere.

Migration of Lumbering in the United States. Lumbering began in the vicinity of the Atlantic seaboard as a local or neighborhood industry. Mills were established along the rivers which furnished the power to operate the saws, transported the logs to the mill, and carried the finished products to markets. The St. Lawrence and its tributaries were almost ideal for lumbering. Reaching far inland, these rivers tapped the great white pine region of North America, and the lakes, waterfalls, and ample snowfall facilitated the woods operations and the transportation of logs and lumber. In the United States the rivers and Great Lakes were supplemented by canals, but the railways fairly revolutionized the industry. Long-distance transportation permitted production in regions remote from the market and large-scale production soon superseded the small local mills. With all this came the concentration of ownership of the timber lands in the hands of corporations and "lumber kings." When most of the timber was exhausted in the Lake states the center of lumber production shifted to the South and finally to the West. Table 28 shows this shift from 1850 to 1933. After the bulk of the timber had been cut and the large mills had moved on to other

TABLE 28

PERCENTAGE OF TOTAL LUMBER CUT BY SECTIONS; PRICES, PER CAPITA CONSUMPTION, AND LEADING LUMBERING STATES, 1850–1933

YEAR	NEW ENG-LAND	LAKE STATES	SOUTH	PACIFIC	PRICE *		PER CAPITA CON-SUMPTION FT. B.M. †	LEADING LUMBERING STATE ‡
					Hard-woods	Soft-woods		
1850	54.5	6.4	13.8	3.9	—	$24.35	235	New York
1860	36.2	13.6	16.5	6.2	$12.24	24.45	260	Pennsylvania
1870	36.8	24.4	9.4	3.6	24.89	37.70	350	Michigan
1880	24.8	33.4	11.9	3.5	31.62	38.41	370	Michigan
1890	18.4	36.3	15.9	7.3	33.07	34.48	435	Michigan
1900	16.0	27.4	25.2	9.6	39.29	34.06	460	Wisconsin
1914	9.0	10.5	47.7	19.3	54.94	42.76	400	Louisiana
1926	3.8	5.6	42.1	38.4	101.15	66.70§	325	Washington
1933	3.0	2.8	32.3	44.1			116	

* First quality in eastern markets, 1 inch per M. board feet. U. S. Dept. of Agriculture, Statistical Bulletin 21, Table 76, p. 118.

† *Ibid*, Table 60, p. 112, data for year preceding until 1914. The highest per capita consumption was 525 ft. b.m. in 1906.

‡ *Ibid*, Table 55, p. 65. Washington led in 1905–13, and again in 1915–25.

§ This price is for 1925.

areas, the small mills, characteristic of pioneer days, returned. These operate on the odds and ends of virgin stumpage or on the less valuable species and eventually on second growth. In the Northeast and other places where large-scale production never developed, the small mill has always had the advantage.

As the sawmills increased in size, lumbering became a big business, with heavy investments in equipment and land. And as the area of available forests narrowed, competition to secure adequate future reserves became intense in the remaining forests of the West, and the industry became "subject to speculation, capitalization, taxation and carrying charges incident to private ownership." [1] Competition in the industry at all times and the burden of increased carrying charges in later years have resulted in over-production and surplus plant capacity. Lumbermen say that they are forced to cut under these conditions, let the cut-over land revert for taxes immediately, and liquidate the heavy plant and timber investments. The forest "as a mine" has the same

[1] Greeley, "Some Public and Economic Aspects of the Lumber Industry," *op. cit.*, pp. 5–18.

problem of overproduction and depletion as the oil and coal industries.

The consumer felt the consequences of the migration to distant states in higher prices. The sixteen industrial states east of the Mississippi and north of the Ohio and the Potomac consume about half of the lumber produced in the United States and contribute only one-tenth of the supply, yet this region was for many years the banner lumber-producing area of the country. In 1819 Maine led all the states in lumber production; New York had first place from 1830 to 1850, and Michigan from 1870 to the close of the century; but since 1905 some southern or western state has claimed this distinction. This means that the great consuming centers must now "import" much of their lumber from a distance of almost 3,000 miles. In the six years 1914–20 the average haul increased from 350 to 480 miles. In 1920 the lumber traffic engaged 2,000,000 freight cars at an expense of $250,000,000, or $7.30 for every thousand feet of lumber. Only thirty years earlier the average freight was not over $2.00 per thousand.[1] Considerable lumber from the Pacific Coast now reaches Atlantic cities via the Panama Canal. The change in producing areas is reflected in the prices. First quality soft woods sold for $24 per thousand in eastern markets and remained uniformly low as long as 50 to 60 per cent of the lumber cut came from the East or the Lake states. A decided upward trend in prices took place after 1905 (Table 28).

Social Consequences of a Shifting Industry. The lumberman adjusts his operations to the necessities of a shifting industry. The sawmill, the lumbering town, and the immediately dependent industries expect to move and do so as soon as the supply of timber is exhausted. Many of the structures are built for temporary occupancy to begin with. But when the sawmill "pulls out," the community suffers. Many examples can be cited of decaying towns and abandoned railroads, and even pulp mills with their heavy equipment may be forced to move to new regions. All exploited forest regions have felt the effects of depopulation. Farms depending on the local markets created by woodworking industries are left stranded; others become stranded when the railroads are scrapped for lack of freight. Land values decline as

[1] *Yearbook of the U. S. Dept. of Agriculture,* 1922, pp. 114–23; U. S. Forest Service, *American Forests and Forest Products* (U. S. Dept. of Agriculture, Statistical Bulletin 21), p. 118.

the timber is cut and villages and farms are abandoned. Local governments often make public improvements during the days of the thriving industries, but the payment for them and their maintenance later falls upon a dwindling population and a declining tax base. It is only natural for the local residents to be anxious to see "farms follow forests" and to have agriculture and other occupations help them with the burden of government and community support.

The Problem of Idle Land. The results of the lag in settlement and finally of the recession of the agricultural frontier have already been discussed.[1] As idle land, yielding no income, cut-over land is mere space, absorbing public revenues and giving nothing in return. Immediate reforestation could have restored it to an income-producing basis, but nothing was done for reasons to be elaborated later. Reforestation also came into direct conflict with the agriculture expansionists, who conceded that the foresters should have the submarginal land on the "worst first" theory of land utilization.[2] However, no land speculator or colonization company would admit that it had any land unsuitable for agriculture, nor would public officials and immigration departments willingly confess that their county or state was cursed with land so poor as to be fit only for forests! "So as I figured it out," said one forester, "to make headway, forestry must first debunk agriculture." This he did with the vigor of a crusader and was soon ably assisted by the agricultural depression.[3]

Waste, Fire, and Other Losses. A shifting extractive industry engaged purely in mining a resource under severe competition, such as lumbering has been, can afford to take only the choicest trees or parts of trees and neglect or waste the rest. As a rule only about one-third of the annual cut is used for saw timber, and often mature trees are used for fuel, pulpwood, and similar products. Other wastes occur in the utilization of the saw log. Sweden has a large paper industry which uses wood such as is now wasted in the United States. However, some woodworking firms of the United States have done much to salvage the usual wastes

[1] Chap. VI, "Agricultural Land."

[2] P. S. Lovejoy, "The Worst First Theory," *Journal of Forestry,* April, 1926, pp. 351–57.

[3] Lovejoy, "Concepts and Contours in Land Utilization," *op. cit.* See also his articles in *Country Gentleman* during 1920–24.

in sawmills and convert them into useful products. The Forest Products Laboratory at Madison, Wisconsin, is doing notable work in the better utilization and conservation of wood products.

Fire has been a scourge which has destroyed not only timber but human lives as well. In 1871 the Peshtigo fire in Wisconsin burned 1,200,000 acres and took 1,500 lives. In 1881, 138 lives were lost in a Michigan fire and 400 in the Hinckley fire of 1894 in Minnesota. These and other historic fires burned virgin timber, but later fires swept over cut-over and second-growth timber again and again. The cut-over fires were regarded lightly because they were considered a help to the land-clearing settler. However, they destroyed the humus of the soil and the seeds and young trees which might have yielded a second harvest even without the care of man.[1] Although fire fighting has become a part of our forest policy, fire losses represented a drain on our forests of 1,390,000 board feet during 1925–29, as compared to roughly 55,000,000 board feet used for lumber, pulpwood, fuel, etc. Losses from insects, diseases, wind, drought, and other causes took another 3,402,000 board feet from our forest capital (Table 29). In Canada it is estimated that fire destroys one-third as much

TABLE 29

AVERAGE DRAIN ON THE FORESTS OF THE UNITED STATES, 1925–29, COMPARED WITH ESTIMATED NORMAL FUTURE REQUIREMENTS[2]

	Average Annual Drain 1925–29		Tentative Normal "Requirements"	
	Million Bd. Ft.	Million Cu. Ft.	Million Bd. Ft.	Million Cu. Ft.
Lumber	38,000	7,371	32,000	6,207
Pulpwood	1,474	589	4,363	2,623
Fuel Wood	7,047	4,003	7,047	4,003
Other Products	8,121	2,532	8,121	2,532
Total Commodity Use	54,642	14,495	51,531	15,365
Fire Losses	1,390	871	695	436
Losses from Insects, Disease, Wind, Drought, etc.	3,402	985	2,552	739
Total Drain	59,434	16,351	54,778	16,540

[1] Lovejoy, "Cloverland—Watch Its Smoke," *Country Gentleman,* March 27, 1920.
[2] N. R. B. Report p. 138.

timber as is converted into useful products, although other authorities claim that fire is destroying as much timber as is being cut.[1] Under a theory of inexhaustibility the idea of forest protection came late in the forest policy of America.

Present Status of Forests of the United States.[2] When comparing the present status of forests with the original stand, *acres* are a deceptive unit of measurement. Even the virgin forest was not all of saw timber caliber. It ranged from stands which the census of 1880 reported as having 200 cords or more per acre to some with less than one cord.[3] Lovejoy described an area of the Northern Peninsula of Michigan as "so poor that the original forest was hardly worth stealing."[4] Canada's forests consist of 460,000 square miles of merchantable timber, as compared with 748,000 square miles on which the timber is either inaccessible or too small for profitable utilization.[5] The United States has about 615,000,000 acres of "forest land," of which approximately 495,-000,000 acres can be called "commercial forest." The qualitative value of these forests is indicated by the fact that approximately 99,000,000 acres, or 20 per cent, consist of virgin timber of saw timber size, while 90,000,000 acres, or 18 per cent, are second growth also capable of conversion into saw timber. Almost one-fourth of the area has trees which have reached cordwood dimensions, 102,000,000 acres are restocking in a fairly satisfactory manner, but 83,000,000 acres, or 17 per cent, have been so damaged by fires and other causes that they are not restocking or only in a very imperfect manner. The tragic fact is that almost one-fourth of the commercial forest area of the Lake states and the South are "non-stocking," whereas the bulk of the merchantable timber is in the Far West (Table 30).

How does the present stock of timber and the annual growth compare with the drain upon our forests? Table 30 shows that we still have a stock of "old" mature growth of timber on hand. This is not increasing but is in a sort of stationary state. On the other hand, the second growth, cordwood, and the restocking areas are adding to the supply of wood. In the period of 1925–29 growth

[1] Craig, *op. cit.*, p. 413.
[2] See *N. R. B. Report*, *op. cit.*, pp. 140 and 141, for maps.
[3] Sargent, *op. cit.*, has a series of maps showing density of forests in these terms.
[4] "Concepts and Contours in Land Utilization," *op. cit.*, p. 385.
[5] Craig, *op. cit.*, p. 396.

amounted to just about one-half of the total drain in timber in general but supplied only one-fifth of the requirements for saw timber. The present rates of growth are not adequate to meet the requirements as set up (Table 29) by the National Resources Board and based upon what were normal requirements during a period when the "country was conscious neither of depression or unusual prosperity." [1] It is anticipated that there will be a decrease in the demand for lumber, also in the losses and drains caused by fire, insects, and diseases, but that the requirements for wood pulp will increase fourfold over the 1925–29 level. The expected increase in the demand for this form of wood will have a decided influence on our forest land policy. Now more than half of our pulpwood is being imported, mainly from Canada.

Even in Canada the annual drain from cutting plus fires and other losses exceeds the annual growth. Russia is the great source of wood for the importing countries of western Europe. Even though she has two-fifths of the coniferous forests of the world, the exhaustion of her readily accessible supplies is in sight within a decade or two, and within thirty-five years in western Siberia. Alaska and the humid tropics have enormous areas covered with forests, but the cost of getting the timber to the consuming centers is such that only higher prices can make their exploitation profitable. The United States cannot rely on imports to meet its requirements except at markedly increased costs for lumber.

However, "requirements" cannot be divorced from abundance, scarcity, and prices. Countries with abundant supplies of original forests and low prices use more wood products than those in which forests are scarce. The first five countries in order of per capita consumption of wood in the 1920's were Alaska, Finland, the United States, Chile, and Norway. The per capita consumption is much smaller in countries with dense populations who have to depend upon man-grown forests, such as Germany, France, and the United Kingdom.[2] In the United States the maximum per capita consumption was reached in 1906; today it is practically one-fourth of what it was 30 years ago. When prices rose it paid to use substitutes. In spite of the feverish activity in reforestation at the present time, a deficiency of timber, though

[1] *N. R. B. Report*, p. 138.
[2] *Yearbook of the U. S. Dept. of Agriculture*, 1923, p. 483–87.

TABLE 30

DISTRIBUTION OF THE COMMERCIAL FOREST AREA OF THE UNITED STATES BY CHARACTER OF GROWTH BY AREA AND BY PERCENTAGE OF TOTAL AREA OF EACH REGION[1]

(Millions of acres)

	Total Forest Land Acres	Saw Timber Areas				Cordwood Areas		Fair to Satisfactory Restocking Areas		Poor to Non Restocking Areas	
		Old Growth		Second Growth							
		Acres	% of Total	Acres	% of Total	Acres	% of Total	Acres	% of Total	Acres	% of Total
East*	54	8	14.7	13	24.2	15	28.2	12	22.3	6	10.6
Lake	56	3	4.8	2	4.3	9	15.9	28	50.4	14	24.6
Central	64	2	2.6	20	30.4	26	39.8	12	19.1	5	8.1
South	191	14	7.5	43	22.5	53	27.6	37	19.5	44	22.8
Mountain †	63	33	37.0	7	10.3	12	18.5	6	9.8	5	8.5
Pacific	67	39	58.3	5	7.9	7	10.0	6	9.1	10	14.5
Total	495	99	20.0	90	18.2	121	24.5	102	20.6	83	16.7

* Middle Atlantic and New England.

† North and South Rocky Mountain areas.

[1] *A National Plan for American Forestry, op. cit.*, p. 126. These regions do not correspond precisely with those suggested in Chapter II.

not a "timber famine," is in sight between the exhaustion of virgin timber and the full realization of the second-growth forests and present plantings.[1] Prices will tend to rise and demand to fall until a balance of drain and growth is established on a lower level of requirements.

Conservation of Forests. As long as the forest is treated as a mine its conservation involves the same type of costs as the holding of a supply of coal or petroleum. The private owner has to consider the interest on his investment, taxes, protection costs, and the risks of fire, wind, and disease, balanced against possible future incomes. However, even though timber was "treated as a mine," was it not reasonable to assume that the conservation of forests would prove a profitable undertaking as the supply of virgin timber approached exhaustion? Would not constantly rising prices more than offset the holding or carrying costs? As a matter of fact, the anticipation of a "timber famine" impelled the rush to the South and West among lumbermen, anxious to block up their holdings and acquire the remaining timber before the supply was depleted. The establishment of federal forests limited the available area for private ownership still further. Both lumber companies and private speculators entered the competition. Naturally the price was run up and timber resources were capitalized at enormous figures. Money had to be borrowed to finance these purchases and timber bonds, a special form of security, appeared about 1905. These bonds paid 6 to 7 per cent but, in general, interest rates ranged from 5 to 8 per cent.

The private timber owner now had to figure his costs on this extravagant capitalization Local governments were not slow to raise assessments on properties which were being bought and sold at princely prices. It took only twelve years to double the investment in timber with simple interest at 6 per cent, and from six to ten years with compound interest. Table 31 shows the cost of holding a typical West Coast quarter section for eight years after purchase during the boom.

Instead of starting with an investment of only a few dollars per acre in 1907, the timber operator was faced with carrying $4,000 until he was ready to cut. In eight years his investment

[1] *N. R. B. Report,* p. 143.

had become 170 per cent of that of 1907.[1] Even if timber had been exactly like oil, an exhaustible, non-replaceable resource, it is doubtful whether prices of forest products could have kept pace with such rapidly mounting costs.

However, the story of Western timber took another turn. The owners might have recovered more of their costs if the timber

TABLE 31

COST OF HOLDING 160 ACRES OF TIMBER LAND, 1907–15

Purchase price, 1907	$4,000
Simple interest @ 6% on purchase price	1,680
Taxes	940
Simple interest on taxes	158
Fire protection, cruising, etc.	44
Total	$6,822

famine had materialized, but unexpected supplies of second-growth merchantable timber in the East and South appeared on the market, and substitutes for wood kept prices from going up. Today there is as much discussion of overproduction in the lumbering industry as in agriculture. This is an example of the danger facing all resource owners. There is no assurance that substitutes will not be found for any of the resources we are now using and therefore no guarantee that the future installments will pay for the costs of their conservation.

It has been suggested that even under the cut-out-and-get-out method of logging it would have been good conservation to dispose of the slash to prevent fires, to leave sufficient seed trees, to prevent the destruction of small trees and seedlings by careful logging operations, and to cut only the mature trees. Yet all these procedures involve costs or reduce profits. The logger who tried to conserve was forced into line by the lower costs of his competitors who "let the devil take the hindmost."

With the original stock of timber almost exhausted, conservation today no longer means withholding the supply from the market to insure a future supply but replenishing the vanished resource and putting idle acres to work. The crime of treating the forest as a mine was not that trees were used, but that nothing

[1] Greeley, "Some Public and Economic Aspects of the Lumber Industry," *op. cit.*, p. 17.

was done to shift to a "forest as a crop" policy, which might have given us a second or even a third crop of timber by this time. This does not mean that a tree should have been planted for every one removed, but certainly much more of the 495,000,000 acres of commercial forest land could be producing second growth of merchantable size instead of "restocking fairly" or not at all.

Insofar as the people of the United States thought at all of the future timber supply in the post-Civil War period, they had faith that private enterprise would supply the nation with forest products. But we are now forced to the conclusion that private enterprise has failed to conserve and replenish the forest resources. The professional lumberman cannot be blamed entirely, although he is often made the scapegoat. The logger was not in business to grow trees but to harvest them. He bears about the same relation to the forest as the custom thresherman does to farming; both handle the crop after it is grown but do not sow or cultivate it. Furthermore, it is a moot question whether any lumberman who tried to keep large tracts for reforestation or selective logging would have found public support in an era when all our land policies favored the "plow following the ax." But if the lumberman did not feel inclined to invest in the business of growing trees, why did not other investors find it profitable to do so? This leads us to a consideration of the costs and income of forests "as a crop."

THE FOREST AS A CROP

Characteristics of Forest Production. A mere collection of trees or trees growing separately do not make a forest. Farm wood lots are ordinarily not forests even though they may yield occasional saw logs. Trees growing in a real forest crowd one another and kill out the weaker members and the lower branches by their shade; this produces a long straight bole free from knots and almost cylindrical in shape, sometimes a hundred feet or more in length. Logs of this kind are the delight of the lumberman, producing a maximum of lumber with a minimum of waste, boughs, and brushwood. A tree in the open or in a small grove does not grow this way. It has branches close to the ground and the lumber is likely to be gnarled and full of knots. Therefore a real forest must be one of considerable area.

The second outstanding feature of forestry is the length of time required to grow a "crop" of trees to saw log size. Some trees grow very slowly at first, then increase their growth, and finally slow down; as maturity is reached, growth almost ceases. The value of the tree grows with age because of the greater cubic content of usable wood and the improvement in quality as it grows older. Finally decay sets in and the tree dies. This cycle varies with the species. Soft woods start with a rapid growth and reach maturity in 30 or 40 years, whereas conifers and hardwoods grow slowly at first, then accelerate their growth and continue it for a long time. In other words, the "rotation" period for soft woods is much less than for hardwoods, and the forester cuts and replants the former every 30 or 40 years, whereas conifers reach maturity much later. The rotation also varies with soil and climatic conditions as well as with species.

Unlike agricultural crops, forests have really no one period of harvest. Trees may be cut as soon as they are a few years old and used for poles, Christmas trees, firewood, or fence posts. A few years later they may be used for railroad ties or telegraph poles and later still for saw logs of various sizes. The forester can practice "low forest culture" and cut at the age of 75 years or so, or he can practice "high forest culture" and wait 100 or even 150 years. The temptation, however, for the private owner is to convert his resource into cash as soon as he finds difficulty in carrying the costs.

Forestry also differs from agriculture in the relative importance of the factors of production. Since trees can grow on rough land, often submarginal for farms, the cost of the land is relatively low. However, as the forest develops the trees become the valuable capital goods. Nature plays a more important role here than in agriculture. Trees cannot be "bred" in the same sense that new varieties of crops have been evolved, nor can their growth be accelerated appreciably by cultivation. The forester merely guides the growth, thins where it is needed, removes the dead trees, and protects the forest against fire and diseases. The labor per acre is very small and much of it can be done in the winter; this indicates once more that large areas are needed for profitable forestry.

Forestry has an advantage over agriculture in one respect.

Crops with a definite period of harvest must be stored, which means costs for storage space, for holding the product, and depreciation, as well as gambling with price changes. The forester, on the other hand, can store his products "on the stump" without costs and can cut heavily or lightly in any one year to take advantage of the market. While it is presumed that a definite proportion will be harvested each year under sustained yield management, the cutting quotas of several years may be grouped. These advantages are believed to justify a lower rate of return for forest investments than for business investments.[1]

Finally, forestry is like agriculture in being conditioned by the gradations in land. Certain parts of the country have more moisture, more suitable forest soils, and longer growing seasons than others and will grow trees better than less favored sections. Just as land may be submarginal for agriculture, so there are soils unsuited to commercial forest production.

Costs of Reforestation or Afforestation. Reforestation with planting is necessary on about 83,000,000 acres of land classified as "poor or no restocking," provided the land is suitable for this purpose. In addition, the submarginal farm land now being retired will have to be afforested in the humid areas. It is interesting that in an old country like Germany about five million acres are classified as idle, waste, or submarginal agriculturally and recommended for afforestation.[2]

Suppose an entrepreneur were to engage in reforestation, starting with bare land as he will have to do on "non-stocking" land. Assuming that he adopts a 50-year rotation, what will be the cost of growing trees? The costs consist of the original outlay for land, trees and planting. Every year he will have extra expenses for taxes, fire protection, and forest labor. His total costs will consist of all the actual outlays with compound interest up to the time of his harvest. This method is justified since he might have taken the alternative opportunity of placing his money in a bank and reinvesting his annual interest for fifty years. However, he is justified in taking only a low rate of interest according to the opinion of forest economists.

During the time the trees are growing the operator has no

[1] Heske, *German Forestry, op. cit.,* pp. 91–93.
[2] Heske, *op. cit.,* pp. 149–51.

income except from thinnings and some fuel. Since forests are being sought for recreational purposes, the private forest owner may find it possible to lease his land for a game preserve or other recreational purposes and thereby add to his income while waiting for the "crop" to mature. Profit will depend upon the difference between costs and income after fifty years of waiting and risk. However, it should be noted that if income just covers costs, including interest, all outlays have been returned in full plus compound interest. In other words, the interest has become a part of income.

If the forest owner planted and harvested only one plot he would have only one crop and he would be through. But by planting a new area every year he can have a series of consecutive plots which after fifty years will yield a continuous harvest providing each plot is replanted as soon as cut. The timber harvested in any one year is expected to carry the entire costs of the business as a whole for that particular year. This "clear-cut-and-plant" method, employing only a single species, was once used extensively in Germany. Today the *Dauerwald* (continuous forest) is favored because it recognizes the principle that the true forest consists of a variety of species which, with all the innumerable living organisms, constitutes a harmonious biological unit. Clear cutting destroys this harmony. The *Dauerwald* principle postulates the cutting of single trees in such a manner "that the forest hardly notices it."[1] Selective cutting of mature trees may be carried on in such a manner that the annual cut will not exceed the annual growth, and "sustained yield management" results from such a practice. Only the annual increment is removed; the capital remains intact.

In the United States forestry can be started in the majority of cases without resorting to planting on bare land. As Table 30 shows, about 223,000,000 acres of the second-growth forests have reached cordwood dimensions or are restocking naturally in a satisfactory manner. Many cut-over areas have seed trees which will restock the whole region in time if fire is kept out. Some lumber companies have left seed trees as a part of their regular practice and are securing a continuous harvest. These lands do not have to go through the waiting process required when plant-

[1] *Ibid.*, Chap. 2, "Development of Sustained Yield Forestry."

ing has to be done. Fire protection, however, is absolutely essential.

A change in the demand for wood products is going on which also affects the nature of forestry. Relatively the demand for pulp, cellulose for rayon, insulating and fabricated boards, and similar uses is increasing, while the demand for saw timber is decreasing. This means that in the future the aim may be to grow the largest crop of cellulose in the shortest possible time, cut the trees, and repeat the process. Species may be selected with this purpose in mind. This will mean a shorter rotation period, lower total interest charges, and the usual objections of time and interest will no longer hold to the same degree.

Costs under Sustained Yield Management. As an illustration of the costs and income on a forest operating on a sustained yield basis the case of a jack pine tract being managed for pulp wood production may be used.[1] (Table 32.) It is assumed that the tract consists of 40,000 acres of second growth naturally restocking jack pine of which 1,000 acres will be logged each year. The average production is assumed to be 20 cords per acre and the average stumpage value, i.e. the value of the wood of the tree as it stands in the forest, "on the stump," is placed at $1.00 per cord. Consequently the annual gross income derived from the harvested tract will be $20,000 in terms of stumpage value.

The costs involved in producing this gross income year after year consist first of all of fire protection for the entire tract of 40,000 acres. At 10 cents an acre the owner will spend $4,000 annually for this purpose. Slash disposal costs of 17½ cents per acre are charged as part of logging costs which are subtracted from the selling price of the wood as part of the calculations of arriving at stumpage values.

The value of jack pine land is about $1.00 per acre and since this is the permanent part of the investment, 4 per cent annual interest should be charged, or $1,600. The value of the timber can be estimated by assuming that if the stumpage value of the mature tract is $20,000, the other 39 tracts will range from this

[1] Raphael Zon, *Timber Growing and Logging Practice in the Lake States* (U. S. Dept. of Agriculture Bulletin 1496, 1928), pp. 32–35. The method of calculation described in this bulletin is reproduced above and in column 1, Table 32, except for taxes. The author assumed 15 cents per acre, making an annual tax $6000 in place of $6600.

figure to practically nothing on the least mature tract, an average of $10,000 for the 40 tracts or $400,000 for the entire tract. With an assumed tax rate of 15 mills on the full stumpage value the annual taxes will be $6600. Balancing cost and income there is left a net annual return of $7800 or $7.80 per acre and 19.5 cents per acre owned.

TABLE 32

COST AND INCOME ON A TRACT OF JACK PINE FOREST UNDER SUSTAINED YIELD MANAGEMENT

	General Property Tax	Wisconsin Forest Crop Tax
Returns, 20,000 cords @ $1.00 per cord stumpage value	$20,000	$20,000
Fire protection, 10 cents per acre on 40,000 acres	4,000	4,000
Interest on the value of the land $40,000 @ 4%	1,600	1,600
Taxes 15 mills on $440,000 land and timber	6,600	....
Tax on land 10 cents per acre Forest Crop Tax	....	4,000
Severance tax, 10 per cent of stumpage value of tract cut, $20,000	....	2,000
Annual cost of carrying the investment	12,200	11,600
Net return on total acreage	7,800	8,400
Net return on per acre cut	7.80	8.40
Net return per acre owned	.195	.21
Cost of production per cord	.61	.58

The proper use of interest in calculations of this kind is much debated.[1] Yet if money is borrowed, interest is the price paid for the use of money and is an obvious cost similar to the outlays for wages or taxes. Besides, it is difficult to see why interest on the value of the land is justified while interest on the value of the timber is not. If interest were charged at the rate of 4 per cent on the stumpage value of $400,000, the operator would have an addi-

[1] D. M. Matthews, *Management of American Forests* (New York, McGraw-Hill, 1935), Chap. XII, "The Nature of Capital and Income in Forest Business."

tional $16,000 annual costs and the total outlays would exceed the income by $8,200 but with *all* interest charges omitted the net income would be increased by $1,600 over the figures in column 1 of Table 32.

If these figures are typical it would seem as though forestry should attract capital seeking conservative returns. No doubt there is considerable truth in the statement: "The main obstacle to the practice of forestry in this country is the mental attitude which fails to regard the forest as a permanent, crop-producing entity and which takes no cognizance of the possible profits in permanent forestry as compared with the destructive 'mining' of timber from forested land." [1]

In contrast to the United States, Central Europe has invested large sums in sustained yield forestry. The owners regard them as good investments yielding a dependable annual income, though not a high return. The rate of return is not considered as important as the safety of the income and of the business itself. The ease of administration and social prestige add to the desirability of forest ownership, and an expected advance in timber prices with a rise in income and capital value are added inducements. Furthermore, the risks from fire have been reduced both by prevention and suppression and by forest fire insurance. For instance, the largest single fires in Germany since 1800 have burned over only 15,000 to 17,500 acres and many other fires have done little damage. Private and mutual forest fire insurance companies are found in France, the Scandinavian countries, and Finland as well as Germany.[2]

Reasons usually mentioned in America for the reluctance of private enterprise to engage in forestry are taxes, interest, and the uncertainty of prices of timber. The complaint that taxes are a serious obstacle to forestry is universal.

Taxation of Timber Lands. High taxes affect three types of forest land: (1) mature timber and timber under sustained yield, (2) cut-over land, (3) land being reforested. Taxes constitute a large part of the cost of holding timber for future cutting. With certain exceptions, forest taxation has not been burdensome in

[1] *Forest Land Use in Wisconsin,* report of Wisconsin Committee on Land Use and Forestry (Madison, Executive Office, 1932), p. 76.

[2] Heske, *op. cit.,* pp. 98–100 and Chap. 25, "Forest Fires and Forest Fire Insurance"; Matthews, *op. cit.,* Chap. XIX.

the United States as a whole, but the difficulty has been *uneven* taxation due to differences in assessment, or differences in the rate, or both. In 1932 the rate on rural property in the forest counties of Wisconsin ranged from 15 mills to 60 mills. When such inequalities exist forest owners cut the timber in areas where the taxes are unreasonable and hold it where they are moderate.

The effect of high taxes on the owner practicing sustained yield operations is shown in Table 32. Under the assumed 15-mill rate the operator pays $6,600 per year, but if his tract were located in the county with the 60-mill rate he would have an annual tax bill of $26,400 and annual costs would exceed the returns by $12,000.

Taxes tend to be excessive in forested or partly forested areas because of the high cost of local government characteristic of sparsely settled areas. These areas have so little other property to tax that most of the burden falls on forests and this burden tends to increase as the cut-over area increases. The fact that an outside corporation pays the tax often leads to inefficiency and extravagance in local government. Some communities deliberately build schools and roads lavishly at the expense of timber owners, who retaliate by removing the tax base as rapidly as possible. In other cases the timber owners control local politics and manipulate the taxing machinery in their favor. One of the most needed reforms is the reorganization of local government to suit the needs of thinly settled timbered areas. The unorganized territory of Maine seems to be ideal for this purpose.[1]

In cut-over land, whether held for future agricultural development or for possible reforestation, taxes are the main item in the ripening and holding costs. It is not generally recognized how much these speculatively owned lands have contributed to the treasuries of local governments while in the possession of hopeful private owners. Although relatively low in value they form the major portion of the land area of most of the cut-over regions. In proportion to sale value they are usually over-assessed, particularly in the recent period of declining land values. Over-assessment is one of the reasons why the cut-over lands are the

[1] Fred Rogers Fairchild, *et al., Forest Taxation in the United States* (U. S. Dept. of Agriculture, Miscellaneous Publication 218, 1935), especially, Part 8, pp. 281–339.

first to "go delinquent," and delinquency in turn increases the tax burden on the remaining timber, the farm land, and resort and urban property.

While *excessive* taxation is largely responsible for the burden on mature timber or cut-over land, on land in the process of reforestation the fault lies in the form of the tax itself. It is maintained that the general property tax is not suited to forestry because the operator on a 40-year rotation will make 40 tax payments before he receives an income. The burden has been compared to 40 separate taxes on a farmer's crop during one summer. Taxes so paid are really an advance to the public by the owner out of an *expected* income. In Table 32, taxes will be small in the early stages of growth but will increase by $15 per year per 1,000 acres at the rate of forest growth and prices assumed. Before the owner can harvest his crop of jack pine on "plot 39" he will have paid $6,600 in taxes during the 40 years on this one plot. Various states have tried to modify the general property tax by so-called "forest crop laws." [1]

Forest Crop Laws. From the owner's standpoint a reasonable yield or severance tax payable at the time of cutting would be the most desirable tax. However, with a severance tax in an area where most of the land has to go through a waiting period the local community will be without adequate revenue for 40 years or more. Various states have tried a combination of property and yield taxes with payments from the state to the local units of government in lieu of taxes. The Wisconsin forest crop law can serve as an example. The law is optional; the owner may enter land under the law subject to the approval of the state conservation commission. This body is empowered to reject land more suitable for agriculture or recreation on the one hand or land submarginal for commercial forestry on the other. The owner pays only 10 cents an acre on the land and the state matches this payment with another 10 cents per acre.[2] The 20 cents are divided as follows: 40 per cent goes to the town, 40 per cent to the school districts in which the forest crop lands are located, and 20 per cent to the county. At the time of cutting the state receives

[1] Summarized and described in Fairchild, *et al., op. cit.*, pp. 341–404.

[2] Whenever the forest crop appropriation of the state is not sufficient to pay the full 10 cents per acre the available funds are prorated. This does not affect the annual tax of 10 cents contributed by the owner.

10 per cent of the stumpage value as a severance tax.[1] Mature timber may also be entered, but the taxes paid by the owner and the severance taxes differ from the above rates.[2] Although the owner enters into a contract to practice forestry in a manner satisfactory to the conservation department, he may withdraw his land at any time, but he is then required to pay the real estate taxes that would ordinarily have been charged against the land less all the taxes he has paid while under the forest crop law. Interest is charged on the former and allowed on the taxes actually paid by the owner.

The tax burden of the owner of the jack pine holding under the Wisconsin forest crop law is shown in Table 32, column 2. In this case the land tax of $4,000 plus the 10 per cent severance tax of $2,000 are almost the same as the low 15-mill tax under the general property tax. Michigan's forest crop law with the tax on land and severance tax, almost identical with that of Wisconsin, has been nullified by the low rate on general property under the 15-mill tax limitation law.

The laws of other states depart from the Wisconsin law primarily in the amount of the taxes on land and timber, in not requiring contractual relations between the owner and the state, and in not fixing a definite sum for the land tax but leaving the bare land subject to the prevailing general property rate, or by granting exemptions without the yield tax.[3]

Laws of this type have been tried since a Michigan act of 1911, but have failed to promote private forestry to any appreciable extent. This suggested the idea of a non-optional tax, under which all land classified as forest land by a state authority is automatically placed under the forest crop law and becomes subject to the special tax. It was hoped that this would check tax delinquency on cut-over land and keep it on the tax roll. California provided for such a plan by constitutional amendment in 1926, and Oregon copied the plan by statute in 1929 and

[1] In case the severance tax yields more than the state has contributed during the 50 years, plus interest, the surplus goes to the local units of government.

[2] The first year the owner pays 40 cents an acre as land tax, but if he cuts in this year his severance tax is only 2 per cent of the stumpage value. The second year the land tax is 35 cents and the severance tax 3 per cent, etc., until in the tenth year they are 10 cents per acre and 10 per cent of the stumpage value respectively.

[3] Fairchild, *et. al., op. cit.*, pp. 341–404, 281–339.

Washington in 1931. Experience with non-optional laws is too recent to be conclusive.

The Forest Taxation Inquiry criticizes all yield tax laws on the ground that they favor forest owners as compared with other property owners. Other defects are also pointed out and to overcome these objections the Inquiry offers three substitutes. One of these is the "deferred timber tax plan" which is especially significant when the owner has to wait for a period of years before he can harvest any timber products. Under the general property tax he would be subject each year to taxes as shown in column 1 of Table 32 but with no assurance that the tax rate will remain 15 mills and with the taxes increasing annually as the taxable value of the forest increases. But under the deferred timber tax plan he pays only the tax on the land while the state pays to the local units of government the tax on the timber at the assessed values and rates as determined by local officials.

However, the year the owner starts to cut he begins to reimburse the state for deferred, accumulated taxes, not by paying them all at once, but by paying a fixed proportion of the stumpage value of the products harvested that year. The proportion is fixed by law and it has been suggested that 30 per cent would be an acceptable rate where property taxes do not exceed 15 mills. Any deferred taxes in excess of this amount will be carried forward to be paid in succeeding years. The only subsidy lies in the fact that the state does not charge any interest. The element of subsidy in the forest crop law is in the fixed 10 cents per acre tax on the land, irrespective of value, and the fixed 10 per cent of the stumpage value paid when the trees are cut, contrasted with the total reimbursement by the owner under the deferred timber tax plan.[1]

Unless accompanied by a reduction in the cost of government and by honest and efficient assessment, this tax is in itself no solution to the problem. This statement also applies in respect to the two other plans suggested by the Forest Taxation Inquiry, an "adjusted property tax" and a "differential lumber tax." Under the former plan the annual tax is reduced in proportion to the deferring of the income by a rather complicated method of calculation, and under the latter plan timber would be

[1] *Ibid.*, pp. 594–602.

classified and the assessment again reduced to the degree of deferment suggested.[1]

Interest and Credit. The "cost of money" is another factor in the cost of producing trees. In Table 32 only 4 per cent is used, but in a new country rates are usually 6 per cent and may be 8 or 10 per cent. Interest was an important item of cost in financing timber operations in the Far West. Low interest will be a significant factor in favor of timber growing in the East where rates are generally lower. Furthermore, as the country matures all capital investments tend to yield a relatively lower rate of return than when the nation was younger.

The precariousness and peculiar nature of the forest as an investment are reflected not only in the attitude of investors in forest property but also in the reluctance of credit agencies to lend to the investors. Even in Germany, with its long experience in conservative, well-managed forests, the lack of suitable credits is an outstanding problem. The long-time nature and slow turnover of agriculture, given as reasons for government credit, are exaggerated many times in forestry. Forestry needs credits extending over generations, non-callable mortgages and amortization payments which will permit the retirement of the debt out of income from sustained yield management. The proper appraisal of the property so as to give the owner as large a loan as possible is also important. Capitalization of the annual income at a low rate of interest is recommended and the loan should be a generous proportion of the value so obtained.

On the other hand, lenders have been reluctant to lend money on forests because of the risks involved as well as the slow turnover. Fire and insect damage are always present. More serious, however, is the fact that the borrower is in a position to reduce or wipe out the value of the security by removing the timber. For this reason it is necessary for the creditor to exercise a certain amount of supervision and control over the debtor's forest operations. Some German credit institutions even insist on the control of the management by state forestry officials. Many of them have made the loans only on the value of the bare land. Since 1880 the Prussian *Landschaften* have made loans on both forests

[1] Fairchild, *et al., op. cit.,* pp. 521–640. In contrast to our experiments with a simple special form of forest taxation, German forests seem to thrive under a complicated series of income, property, and inheritance taxes. Heske, *op. cit.,* Chap. 24.

and land but have insisted on annual reports, inspection, and insurance. It has been suggested that a quasi-public loan plan similar to the Federal Farm Loan system should be established to assist and stimulate private forestry in the United States.[1]

It has been claimed that private forestry is a safe and certain investment, and therefore a low interest rate is justified in the calculation of costs and the capitalization of income. In conclusion, one cannot help compare this claim with the fact that even in a country such as Germany, where there has been conservative sustained forestry, lenders are unwilling to invest in forest properties.

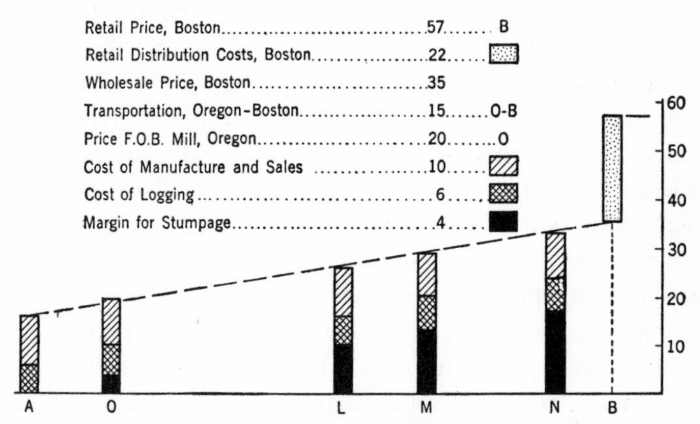

FIG. 17. VALUE OF STUMPAGE AS DETERMINED BY PRICES IN THE MARKET AND COSTS OF TRANSPORTATION

Uncertainty of Prices. The value of stumpage in the United States is determined by the price of the finished product on the eastern markets minus the cost of selling, distribution, transportation, manufacturing at the mill, and logging. Douglas fir selling in Boston at $57 retail is worth about $4.00 on the stump in Oregon (Figure 17). These are the average costs; the more efficient firm can distribute for less and the more competent mill operator can manufacture and log at costs below the outlays of the less efficient operator. Let us assume that $15 transportation charge, plus other costs, allows $4.00 for stumpage at 0. At A, being farther from the market, prices will be such that only logging and sawmill costs are covered, leaving nothing to be assigned

[1] Heske, *op. cit.*, Chap. 26. *A National Plan for American Forestry, op. cit.*, pp. 1125–34.

as the present value of stumpage. Assuming identical distributing, manufacturing, and logging costs, $11 will be left for stumpage at L, $13 at M, and $18 at N.

A higher price for the finished product in Boston transmitted down the line may leave a margin for stumpage at A, but it will also call forth a larger supply by permitting less efficient mills from A to N to operate and all operators will increase output by bringing trees from greater distances to the mills, the use trees of a lower quality, and "closer" lumbering. The higher price may also react on demand, promote the use of substitutes, and a new equilibrium will be established between supply and demand.

The value of stumpage so determined represents the price the average operator can afford to pay for standing timber. The trouble has been that competition for forest land has driven stumpage prices above this level or carrying costs have thrust the investment beyond this point. Furthermore, the private operator who wishes to reforest or to carry on sustained yield management will determine whether or not he should do so by observing the stumpage value or anticipated stumpage value at his location. For instance, if operators feel that A will be permanently "marginal" they certainly will not plant trees and incur all the other costs only to find the stumpage value to be practically nil. On the other hand, costs of transportation act as barriers to competition from distant sources of timber (even though these have been grown without "costs of production") to such an extent that operators at L, M, and N have a real incentive to engage in forest enterprises. However, as long as finished lumber of Douglas fir quality sold for $35 to $40, forest owners had little inducement to grow trees for profit even in the East, except in anticipation of the exhaustion of the virgin timber of the South and West.[1]

Whether prices will rise considerably in the future is a debatable question. The decreasing rate of population growth will have a depressing effect on the demand for forest products. Competition of substitutes for wood is another factor of uncertainty. In fact, research is under way aimed at "holding, recapturing and expanding" the market for forest products.[2]

[1] H. H. Chapman, *Forest Management* (Albany, J. B. Lyons, 1931), Chapter V.
[2] C. P. Winslow, "Enlarging the Consumption of Forest Products," in *A National Plan for American Forestry, op. cit.*, pp. 1355–95.

In spite of the difficulties of private forestry enumerated above and the favorable attitude toward government ownership in Europe, private forests predominate outside of Russia. About half of the forests in Italy, Germany, and Denmark are privately owned. Two-thirds of the forests of France, Finland, Austria, and Belgium are in private ownership, and the proportion is even greater in Norway, Sweden, Great Britain, and Ireland.[1] In fact, in Germany there is even a feeling against "monopolization" of forests by the state.

Institutional Factors in European Forestry. In comparing Europe with America, Europe's many institutional factors and long experience with man-made forests must be taken into consideration. In the first place, the unique social attitude there toward land, and especially toward forests, "as a trust belonging to the nation of which only the usufruct may be claimed" by the occupier is an important element. It explains the acceptance of public restrictions on the management of private forests, which are unknown and would be unworkable in the United States in the present stage of its development. The most important regulation is the requirement to reforest all cut-over land within a specified time, for the violation of which the owner is punished by fines and even imprisonment. Financial inability is not accepted as an excuse, and state officials have the power to reforest private land if the owner fails to do so. Land clearing is permitted only under strict regulations. In some German states even clear cutting as part of forestry is allowed only after official approval. Many states restrict the partition or division of forest properties.[2]

Another institution which stabilizes and promotes private forestry is entail. In Germany about one-eighth of the total forest area is in entailed estates, in which case the forest cannot be sold or divided upon inheritance and the order of inheritance itself is regulated. The forest must be managed to keep the capital unimpaired; the owner has a right to the usufruct but he may not touch the substance or capital or impair it by neglect. Entail has resulted in tracts of adequate size, stability of owner-

[1] Raphael Zon and W. N. Sparhawk, *Forest Resources of the World* (New York, McGraw-Hill, 1923), I, 19–24.

[2] Heske, *op. cit.*, pp. 258–64. Sparhawk, "Public Regulation of Private Forests," in *A National Plan for American Forestry, op. cit.*, pp. 993–1050.

ship and operation, and a "lively initiative which is lacking in state forests." In reality the property belongs to the family, a *perpetual* person, yet the temporary occupant is often motivated to make the forest a model of management.[1]

One American forester has concluded that in the United States no ordinary business concern ever has been or will be attracted to forestry since the returns will be below 4 per cent and the investment cannot be sold easily (i.e., it lacks liquidity). Only certain large mineral and paper concerns are now practicing sustained forestry as a minor adjunct to their regular business. He feels that the United States should permit the formation of similar "legal personalities" with privileges in taxation, protection at public expense, and loans at a 3 per cent rate of interest. Private and public holdings should be "blocked up," since sustained forestry on scattered holdings and wood lots is impracticable, but private forests should be supervised by the Federal Forest Service to insure proper management.[2]

FOREST LAND POLICIES

Non-commercial Uses of Forests. Trees are only a part of the environment with which the forester deals. Tree roots hold the soil in place, but the shrubs, grasses, and other plants making up the forest cover are equally important elements in controlling erosion and furnishing food for animals and birds. Soil, water, plants, and animals form part of the biologic whole which is commonly called the forest.[3] The tree may be worth more in the forest than as lumber and firewood because the forest is so intimately interrelated with other land uses. The forest's relation to climate and its influence on the water table and on stream flow were recognized a century ago and no doubt exaggerated by early scientists, followed by a tendency to swing in the opposite direction and deny the influence of forests on climate. It is admitted that the climate *within* the forest itself is the result of forest influences and is different from the climate of non-forested areas, but the controversy centers on the alleged modifications of the climate of surrounding areas through forests and how far these

[1] Heske, *op. cit.*, pp. 102–10.

[2] C. A. Schenck in *Forestry News Digest*, January, 1937, p. 25.

[3] F. A. Silcox, "Forests and Flood Control," Supplement to *Science*, October, 1936, p. 5.

modifications extend. The shelter belt across the plains was proposed primarily for its influence on the velocity of the wind, its effect on reducing the blowing of soil, for increasing the soil moisture by catching the snow, and for the purpose of protecting the farmsteads against the severe winter winds. How much the "belt" will influence climate is the subject of much debate.[1] Zon and Sparhawk claim that 30 per cent of a nation's land should be maintained in woodland for non-economic reasons, except in such insular countries as England and Holland. Fernow, on the other hand, does not believe that a given percentage can be uniformly applied.[2]

An interesting example of the influence of "forest climates" is found in the wooded areas of the Lake states. In these states the heavy snowfall makes snow removal an important item of cost in highway maintenance. Artificial snow fences are installed at critical places along the roads to keep the snow from drifting onto the right of way. However, trees are now being planted as "living snow fences." In the wooded areas the natural forest performs this function.

The difference in the cost of snow removal on tree lined roads as compared with open roads in Gogebic County, Michigan, illustrates the economic importance of the action of the forest. In the last eight years, with an average of 147 inches of snowfall per year, the cost of removing snow on sheltered roads was $78 a mile, on semi-sheltered highways $111, and on unprotected, windswept roads $350 a mile annually. The cost of maintenance is also higher on the unsheltered stretches in summer. It would be a saving in regions of heavy snowfall to keep the margins of the highways as timbered strips in public ownership or to zone the roads to prevent the cutting of timber within a certain distance from the right-of-way.

Beauty and recreation as related to forests are closely associated with the economic life of such regions as New England, New York, and the Lake states. Their lakes and streams are eagerly sought by summer visitors, but these bodies of water are

[1] *Possibilities of Shelterbelt Planting in the Plains Region, op. cit.,* Secs. 6, 9; L. R. Waldron, "Can Trees Reclaim the Weather?" *Country Gentleman,* November, 1934.

[2] *Forest Resources of the World, op. cit.,* I, 1. See also Zon, "Forests and Water in the Light of Scientific Investigation," *op. cit.,* and Bernhard E. Fernow, *Economics of Forestry* (New York, Crowell, 1902), p. 68.

unattractive without forests. Public money spent for restoration and maintenance of forests is economically justified in these areas merely to maintain the recreation industry, which means resorts, tourists, hunters, fishermen, and nature lovers. The millions of visitors to federal forests show the importance of the woodlands in a scheme of recreation. However, most of the forests to be maintained exclusively for non-economic purposes or for their influence on other land uses must be publicly owned since they yield little or no income for the private owner.

Property in Forest Land. The discussion so far has pointed out some of the difficulties encountered by the private owner engaged in reforestation or in conserving this resource. In many respects the various governments—federal, state, and municipal—can reforest or conserve much more efficiently and at lower costs than the individual. They are less concerned with the time element since the life of a nation is considered unlimited. Instead of paying taxes, they are supported by taxes, and can normally borrow at lower rates of interest than can an individual or a corporation.

It is interesting, therefore, to examine the world situation both historically and otherwise with respect to property in forests. Forests, whether privately or publicly owned, have always been "affected with a public interest." In the pre-feudal days they were the common lands outside of the villages and often served as barriers or boundaries. Their use for hunting, pasturing, or fuel was open to all, but as the feudal lord came into more power he began to assume control over the forests in the interests of the chase. In fact, the word "forest" came to mean "hunting grounds," whether these were forested or not, and might include pastures, crop land, and villages. This fact had special significance in England.

City forests began to appear with the royal encouragement of town building. Gifts of land, including forests, were made to the cities. Other city forests were acquired by purchase and by forfeiture of mortgages among the nobility. Another turn of the wheel came when many of these forests became public property during the revolutionary times of the early nineteenth century. Under the influence of the doctrines of Adam Smith, however, the various governments of Europe began to dispose of their forests to private individuals. In Germany this policy was soon reversed because *laissez faire* was not the proper doctrine for a forest policy. Other countries, however, went much farther in permitting forests to become private property. The result of all these movements is a great variety of ownership, from communal forest, through various kinds of private forests, to public forests owned by nations, states, and cities. Communal forests are still the prevailing form of forest property in some cantons of Switzerland.[1]

As the forests came more and more under the control of the feudal lords, these lords restricted the rights of the peasants in order to preserve the game. This incidentally helped to prevent the undue destruction of the forest, even though the communal freedom was lost. Nevertheless, the peasants did not lose all their rights through this change in ownership. Servitudes or rights akin to property rights grew out of the feudal relations or were granted to conciliate the peasants, which rights consisted primarily of privileges to pasture cattle and hogs in the forest and the liberty to take litter and wood. These rights were strengthened rather than weakened with time, and in order to extinguish these servitudes the peasants were often paid in cash or given parcels of forest land in exchange for them.[2]

The European servitudes or easements offer a striking illustration of the influence or property relationships on production. The owners of these rights have for centuries persisted in using the forests for grazing. Under most circumstances grazing is detrimental to natural regeneration because the animals destroy the young trees. England was deforested not so much by the cutting of timber as by the unregulated grazing by sheep under rights established in the fifteenth and sixteenth centuries. The British Government has millions of acres of public lands which could be reforested, but since these are encumbered by grazing rights, it has to buy land free from such rights. In the same way grazing has been detrimental in France, Germany, and the Mediterranean countries.[3] Repeated attempts have been made to regu-

[1] Fernow, *Economics of Forestry, op. cit.,* and *A Brief History of Forestry* (Tóronto, University Press, 1907); Heske, *op. cit.,* Chaps. 4, 5, 6, 19.

[2] Fernow, *History of Forestry, op. cit.,* pp. 86–90; Heske, *op. cit.,* Chap. 20.

[3] See Arthur E. Morgan, "The Goat Versus the Forest," *American Forests,* June, 1932, pp. 337–39.

late grazing rights in the interests of reforestation, but with varying degrees of success.

Grazing is allowed in our national forests under a "permit system" which gives the Forest Service the power to control the manner, amount, and time of grazing. No one is given an interminable right under this plan, which means that the stockmen are using the public range under somewhat uncertain conditions. A plan was proposed which would have given the stockmen rights to the use of a specific area of land in the forests, which rights would have been perpetual, transferable, and negotiable. Foresters at once pointed out the similarity of this plan to the servitudes of Europe. Since national forests are established primarily for watershed protection and forest production, and since grazing is a secondary use of a purely private nature, it is highly important that subsidiary uses be kept subsidiary, always subject to regulation and repeal whenever they are out of harmony with the primary uses. It is in the interest of sound public policy that servitudes do not develop in the public forests of America.[1]

The experience of the world proves that because of the peculiar nature of forests as a crop, the public is justified in making the growing of timber for commercial purposes a public function. In practically every country of the world public forests are found side by side with private forests. About two-thirds of the world's forests are publicly owned, yet this in itself is not a guarantee that they are managed efficiently. The largest areas of publicly owned forests are to be found in the less developed regions such as the tropics, northern North America, and Asia; in such regions the nations merely own enormous tracts of "unmanaged" virgin forests, quite unlike the managed forests of Central Europe. In many southern European countries the percentage of forests in public ownership is greater than in France and Germany but the management is far inferior. Wherever public control over private forests is effective, or economic conditions are favorable to private forestry, government ownership is less urgent.

[1] See P. L. Butterick, "The Forester and the Shepherd," a series of articles in *American Forests and Forest Life,* February, March, April, and May, 1926; also a similar article by the same author in *Journal of Forestry,* February, 1926, pp. 141–52; Henry S. Graves, "The New Public Lands Controversy," *American Forests and Forest Life,* January, 1926; Sparhawk, *Forest Rights in Foreign Countries with Especial Reference to Grazing Rights* (U. S. Dept. of Agriculture, Circular 456, 1937).

The Forest Policy of Canada. Canada offers an example of a new nation which has retained its forest land in public ownership, in direct contrast with its neighbor to the south. The plan of not alienating forest land grew out of the early policy of taxing timber which had been floated down the Ottawa and St. Lawrence. This developed into a plan of charging for the right to cut timber, with the Crown retaining possession of the land itself. The provinces have inherited this policy and have retained it in principle.

Canada's first attitude toward the forest was the same as that of the United States, i.e., that it was a passing resource, and therefore the government wanted to get all it could out of the sale of timber before alienating the land for settlement. However, it was soon realized that some of the land should remain in forests; this realization called for a classification of the land, separating the part to be retained in public ownership from the part to be alienated for settlement. Quebec and Ontario have classified their lands and set up machinery for forest administration, but in many cases pressure is brought to have certain lands declared agricultural. This is done either by legitimate settlers or by bogus settlers and companies who, after obtaining title to the land, strip it of timber and abandon it. Theoretically, land classification should withhold agricultural settlements from submarginal agricultural land; practically, this is not always effective.

The provinces grant timber "licenses," "berths" or "limits," and other concessions specifying the area and the time within which the company may lumber the tract. The usual time of one year was found to be too short for the pulpwood companies, so the period has been extended to eight or more years, the tracts have been increased in size and a more permanent tenure provided for. The companies usually pay a certain fixed royalty per cord and agree to put up a mill of a given value or one employing a certain labor force. Some grants with renewals run over forty years.[1] Probably 90 per cent of the forest lands of Canada are in public ownership, yet the history of exploitation, fires, and administration is not so very different from that of the United States. In other words, mere public ownership is no guarantee

[1] Lower and Innis, *op. cit.*, Chaps. VI, VII, and IX.

that a nation can withstand pressure groups when trying to safeguard its natural resources against misuse and exploitation.

The Forest Policy of the United States. No positive forest policy existed in this country for more than a century. The agricultural land laws were not suited to the needs of the lumberman, who needed large tracts for an "economic holding." However, the land acts were no particular hardship. The Act of 1820 permitted the purchase of any sized area at $1.25 per acre; besides, timber stealing from the public domain and fraudulent acquisition of land was not unknown. Millions of acres were obtained through the use of agricultural college and military scrip. In 1878 two acts designed to aid settlers and miners were passed—the Timber Cutting Act and the Timber and Stone Act—but both were used by large lumber companies to obtain great tracts of valuable timber at a low price. Over 12,500,000 acres had been acquired by lumber companies under the latter act by 1923, at prices averaging from $2.50 to $3.68 per acre, varying with the years the act was in operation.[1]

However, interest in forestry and conservation of forests was not lacking in America even before the Civil War. Attempts were made by various states as early as 1868 to encourage timber culture by tax exemption acts. Arbor Day was instituted in 1872, and Dr. Franklin Hough was appointed in 1877 by the Commissioner of Agriculture to study the forest situation. The census of 1880 prepared the creditable report on the forests of North America noted before. In 1886 the Division of Forestry was created by statute as a part of the Department of Agriculture and Dr. Bernhard E. Fernow placed in charge. He was a trained forester who comprehended the pioneer psychology of America, and with remarkable tact he knew how to create an interest in forestry and to win the confidence of the lumberman and the general public. He did noteworthy educational work through associations, by lecturing at American universities and establishing forest schools in the United States and Canada. During his leadership in the department two of the most important laws affecting forestry were passed by Congress, "the first of which brought the old King's Forest theory back by definite establishment of national forests"

[1] Hibbard, *A History of the Public Land Policies, op. cit.*, pp. 463–70.

(1891) and the second provided for their protection and administration (1897).[1]

The act of 1891 permitted the reserving of land from the public domain to be retained in federal ownership for forestry purposes. The significance of this act lies in the further reversal of the policy of alienation of the public domain already begun by the withdrawal of Yellowstone National Park in 1872. President Harrison immediately began withholding lands for federal forests and President Cleveland continued this program. For some years violent opposition to this policy arose and great difficulty was experienced in protecting the new form of public property. Mere ownership had to be replaced by vigorous administration. Pinchot succeeded Fernow in 1898, and with Theodore Roosevelt's administration came a lusty policy of enlarging the area of federal forests and enforcing their protection and maintenance. In 1911 the Weeks law was passed permitting the purchase of land needed for the protection of watersheds, and in 1924 another act provided for the purchase of land for timber production. Federal forests are no longer confined to those states with remaining public domain, and their purposes now include every form of forest use from recreation to commercial timber production. Table 33 shows the extent of the federal forests in 1934. Since then about 70,000,000 acres have been added under the present vigorous conservation policy.

State Forests. State forests antedate federal forests. New York established a forest "preserve" in the Adirondacks and Catskills in 1885 from land reverted to the state through tax forfeiture. Other areas were added by purchase. The attempt to maintain a true forest had a checkered career and in 1894 the people of New York, by a constitutional amendment, created the Adirondack Park and prohibited the use of this area for logging or commercial purposes of any type. In 1929 the state inaugurated the reforestation of submarginal agricultural land described earlier.

Pennsylvania is second in the extent and completeness of its

[1] Jenks Cameron, *The Development of Governmental Forest Control in the United States* (Johns Hopkins University Press, 1928), p. 201. For the work of Fernow see pp. 196–201, 210–14.

state forest program. Some of the other eastern states and the Lake states have fair-sized state "forests." However, the statistics on state forests must be used with discretion. Many state forests are the remnants of federal land grants or consist of large tracts of forested, cut-over, or restocking lands obtained through tax

TABLE 33

PRESENT AND RECOMMENDED OWNERSHIP OF FOREST LANDS AND SUGGESTED INTENSITY OF MANAGEMENT BY TYPES OF OWNERSHIP [1]

Millions of Acres

	Area in 1934	Recommended by 1960	Type of Management Recommended		
			Intensive	Extensive	Protective
Private					
Farm Woodlands....	150	124			
Industrial..........	285	133			
Total Private........	435	257	114	87	56
County and Municipal..	5	5	3	1.5	0.5
State	17	77	49	14	14
Federal *	...	...	129	48	80
National Forests.....	113	243			
Public Domain......	24	10			
Other.............	21	23			
Total Federal.......	158	276			
Total Public........	180	358			
Grand Total........	615	615	295	150.5	150.5

* To the 257,000,000 acres listed under "type of management" have been added 19,000,000 acres in "specialized areas" to make the total of 276,000,000 acres of all federal forests.

delinquency, but without adequate administration. In other cases the state has not made a clear-cut distinction between a "park" and a "forest." If *forests* are defined as "areas either specifically set aside by legislative act or established under legislative authority contemplating their permanent retention and administration by the state for forest (as distinguished from essentially park) purposes and organized into definite units of administration," there were in 1932 about 4,000,000 acres in state forests in 405 separate

[1] Adapted from Tables 25 and 26, *N. R. B. Report,* pp. 209–10.

units.[1] State parks of the forest type contained a total of 2,500,000 acres. Using the above distinction, New York had only 74,000 acres in forests in 1932 but over 2,000,000 acres in parks. In the United States as a whole, in 1932, over 6,000,000 acres of state-owned "forest" land were *not* under forest administration.[2] The National Resources Board Report of 1934 estimates about 17,000,-000 acres in state forests of all types (Table 33).

Town and Municipal Forests. As early as 1790 the town of Danville in New Hampshire established two small town forests which are still in existence.[3] Today New York leads both in number and acreage in this type of forest ownership. Many serve chiefly as protective forests for municipal water supplies; others have brought in some revenues through the sale of forest products, but their most important role will be for recreation. Town and municipal forests cover about a half million acres.[4]

County Forests. New York and Wisconsin lead in the area of county forests. In the former the state helps counties to establish forests by contributing a maximum of $5,000 per year per county for the purchase of land, reforestation, and maintenance. Stability of ownership is ensured by the stipulation that the area must forever be kept in forests for watershed protection, recreation, timber production, and other forest uses. The county board of supervisors may sell the products of these forests under the regulation of the state conservation commission.

Wisconsin counties were empowered to establish forests by grant or purchase, but the present county forests are almost without exception the result of the reversion of tax-delinquent land to the county. Under the Wisconsin law counties could take title to land after three years of failure to pay taxes, but the time was extended to five years by the 1935 legislature. Taking title is optional, but counties have found it advantageous to do so because of the peculiar relationship of the school districts, the towns, and the state to the county in the tax system.[5] However,

[1] *A National Plan for American Forestry, op. cit.*, pp. 833–42, 824–30.

[2] *Ibid.*, pp. 825–28.

[3] *Town* refers to the New England town or the subdivision of a county, often called *townships* in other states.

[4] *A National Plan for American Forestry, op. cit.*, pp. 843–47.

[5] Taxes are collected by the town treasurer, not only for his town but for the school districts, the county, and the state as well. If, however, because of tax delinquency the local treasurer fails to collect the total levy of all these units of

mere ownership of forest and cut-over lands did not create *forests.* The impetus toward active forest administration came when the forest crop law was changed to permit counties to enter tax-reverted land under the law, subject to rejection or acceptance by the conservation department. The state pays 10 cents an acre to the towns, to be divided among the school districts, the town, and the county in a manner similar to private forest crop land payments. The state aids the county in its forestry program by contributing 10 cents an acre from another fund for reforestation, administration, and maintenance under the supervision of the state conservation department. When the timber is cut the state receives 50 per cent of the stumpage value. County forests are for all practical purposes "co-operative" forests in which the county furnishes the land while the state stands most of the other costs.

The forest crop law complements and completes the rural zoning program. Zoning by merely prohibiting agriculture in forest and recreational districts is negative. Positive measures are needed to effect the growing of trees in the areas designated as forest zones. The forest crop law offers inducements to both private landowners and counties to practice forestry. The growth of county forests has been very gratifying: on March 15, 1938, 1,746,647 acres of county-owned land were entered under the forest crop law, as compared with 162,476 acres under private entry. Many Wisconsin counties have acceptable reforestation and management programs under way. In 1934 the area in forests belonging to all local units of government of the United States was estimated at about 5,000,000 acres (Table 33).[1]

Public Forests and Local Governments. One of the arguments against any public ownership of land is that as public property it is not a part of the tax base. This is of special signifi-

government, he is required to pay the state's share in full, then the school levy, next the town's share, and the county is paid the remainder. All tax-delinquent lands are sent up to the county treasurer for further collection. The Wisconsin county as the residual claimant becomes the owner of tax-reverted lands. It naturally became the unit for planning, zoning, and reforestation.

[1] Viewed in all its ramifications, the Wisconsin forest crop law is more than a tax measure and a means of assisting counties overwhelmed by tax-delinquent and idle lands. One of its purposes is to promote forestry and complement the zoning and planning movements. See F. B. Trenk, *The County Forests of Wisconsin* (Wisconsin Conservation Department, 1938).

cance in forest landownership because forests require such large areas which must be "blocked up" for efficient administration. However, except for protective and recreational forests, the forest is expected to produce an income which conceivably may bring more revenue to the unit of government that owns it than could be obtained by taxing the land as private forests. Nevertheless the public forest is tax exempt as far as all the *other* taxing units are concerned. In the case of federal and state forests the situation is intensified because these larger units of government can raise money by inheritance, income, and other forms of taxation, whereas the towns, counties, and school districts usually derive from 75 to 90 per cent of their revenues from real estate. The federal forests occupy, on the average, about one-fifth of the areas of the counties in which they lie, varying from 2½ per cent in Maine to almost 47 per cent in Idaho.[1] A study of selected counties in Pennsylvania showed that 19 per cent of the area of these counties was either in national forests, in state forests, or in game land and therefore untaxable by the counties.[2]

As long as forests are created by reserving a part of the nontaxable public domain, by dedicating lands already in state ownership to this purpose, or by using tax-reverted lands, the situation is not serious since these lands were not taxable anyway. However, where school districts, towns, and counties have been set up on the basis of private land ownership and considerable areas of land are later converted into public forests, the financial condition of these governmental units often becomes critical. This is also true whenever forest crop or tax exemption laws reduce the annual revenues. The payment of 10 cents an acre by the state to local governments under the Wisconsin forest crop law is in recognition of this dilemma; so is the "deferred timber tax" recommended by the Forest Taxation Inquiry.

The division of federal forest income among minor units of government was provided by an act of Congress in 1908. Under this act 25 per cent of all the money collected from the sale of forest products or for the use of the forests (as, for instance, for grazing) is paid to the state to be distributed to the counties in

[1] *A National Plan for American Forestry, op. cit.*, p. 1105.

[2] E. A. Ziegler, *Forest Taxation in Pennsylvania* (Pennsylvania Department of Forests and Waters, Bulletin 55, 1936), pp. 9–10.

which these forests lie for the use for schools and roads. By a law of 1913 another 10 per cent of the income is spent for roads and trails within the national forests, and special appropriations have been made for highways on private lands adjacent to or within federal forests. The contributions in lieu of taxes solve the problem where mature timber is being harvested, but today much of the federal forest area consists of recently acquired cut-over land on which harvests are "a long way off," whereas the reduction in the tax base and the need for revenue are immediate. Pennsylvania has met this situation by paying 5 cents an acre to counties in lieu of taxes on national forests until the 25 per cent of the forest income paid by the federal government is equal to or exceeds the state's contribution. It also pays 5 cents an acre (2 cents for schools, 2 cents for roads, and 1 cent for the county) on state forest lands, and 4 cents on "auxiliary forest" lands, which are similar to the Wisconsin forest crop lands.[1]

The question may be raised, however, whether local units of government are entitled to substantial donations in lieu of taxes as a long-term policy. Public purchase and zoning should be followed by the relocation of the isolated settlers as part of a permanent land policy so as to reduce the need for public services. With redistribution of the population, unnecessary roads and schools can be closed and local units of government consolidated or reorganized. In other words, local government should eventually be adjusted to a forest-farm-recreation scheme of land utilization. One danger of the aids in lieu of taxes is that they may tend to preserve types and functions of local government which should be reconstructed.

The Future Forests of the United States. Within a quarter of a century a remarkable shift in the general attitude toward forests has taken place. Since the World War, with a stationary population in sight, we have become reconciled to a restricted area for agriculture, which leaves the remainder of the country for other uses, presumably forestry and recreation. Foresters, in place of begging for land, are now implored to "put idle land to work."

It is not easy to project a single policy for forest land because forests have such multiple uses. For instance, it is estimated that

[1] Ziegler, *op. cit.*, p. 6.

470,000,000 acres of forest land are needed for watershed protection. This purpose may or may not conflict with timber cutting or with other forest uses, least of all with recreation. However, wherever "protection forests" have little or no commercial value or where the protective function requires severe restriction of the commercial use, such woodlands remain or become public property.

Another approach would be to set up purely material standards, starting with the requirements of a given population and stating them in board feet and cubic feet, as is done in Table 29. From this the area of land that will satisfy the annual "drain" with a given intensity of management can be determined. However, "requirements" are not a fixed amount; people will buy more or less timber and wood products depending on the abundance or scarcity of these products as expressed in price. This is the primary reason for the great differences in wood consumption of the various nations.

This raises the question of possible policies which a government could pursue. It might deliberately use as much land as possible with intensive management so as to make timber abundant and prices low; in fact, it could ignore costs of production entirely in order to stimulate home building and help agriculture and industry. There is some fear among private timber owners that this may happen. It is interesting and reassuring that older nations have followed a policy of selling timber on the competitive market, which is also the federal forest policy in the United States. "The state forest administration may not sell its timber below the current market prices, for that would make all the other forest owners suffer for the benefit of the timber merchant, would depress the value of all the forest property in the State, would impair the ability of private owners to pay taxes, and would reduce the incomes of the communes and foundations," says Heske in discussing the principles of state forest management.[1]

"Normal requirements," as employed in Table 29, might be used as a basis for determining the area of land needed to supply the United States with forest products at various intensities of management. However, the competition of other land uses is

[1] *German Forestry, op. cit.*, p. 84.

recognized in the proviso, if the "land can be spared from other uses," and the economic aspects are given due weight in the statement, "if the cost of establishing and maintaining the forest does not outrun the value of the product," due consideration being given to the non-economic and social values of the forests.[1] "Economic feasibility" is therefore one of the tests used by the Forest Service in making these estimates and recommendations.

The land which can be spared from other uses is estimated at 615,000,000 acres and presumably will be the same in 1960 when population has become stationary. To meet requirements for wood products three types of management are recommended. Intensive management is to be adopted on 295,000,000 acres, extensive administration on about 150,000,000 acres, and about 150,000,000 acres are recommended for protective management with mere protection against fire, insects, and disease, the land to be used mainly for wild life, recreation, and watershed protection.

Table 33 also shows the present and recommended ownership. Almost one-fourth of the 615,000,000 acres is now owned by farmers. This form of woodland is expected to decrease to some extent by 1960, but a drastic reduction of all other private forest land is anticipated and a notable increase in state and federal forests is suggested.

Private ownership is considered suitable for "mature and second growth timber favorably located in relation to markets and other factors and not burdened with taxes and interest payments on borrowed capital."[2] This means that privately owned forest land will be confined almost exclusively to the East and South, with a few scattered tracts in the Lake states and the West. The National Resources Board also suggests aiding the private owner by tax reforms and loans but insists on some control over production and on requiring compliance with certain standards of silvicultural methods and sustained yield management.[3]

The Farm Wood Lot. In 1930 the sale of fuel, fence posts, poles, saw and veneer logs, pulpwood, and ties added $242,000,000 to the farmers' income in the United States.[4] These figures are impressive but deceptive. Much of this income is the re-

[1] *N. R. B. Report,* p. 137.

[2] *Ibid.,* p. 209, also maps, pp. 207–11.

[3] *Ibid.,* pp. 211–13.

[4] See Figs. 217–20 of U. S. Dept. of Agriculture Miscellaneous Publication 267.

sult of clean cutting and sale of the "timber capital," and probably only a small proportion came as annual production from sustained yield managed woodlands. Moreover, of the 185,000,000 acres reported as woodland in farms in 1935, 108,000,000 acres were also used for pastures. But if grazing is not carefully regulated it will mean the ultimate extinction of the wood lot. As already pointed out, cattle and sheep trample and eat the seedlings, leaving only the mature trees. As the "grandfather" trees die the wood lot becomes a grove. The leaf litter disappears and grass takes its place. This process is hastened by burning over the woodlands to secure better pastures; almost 8,000,000 acres were reported as burned over in 1924. Eventually even the grove disappears. This is a deliberate part of the clearing process on many farms, but on others farmers are not aware of the damaging effects of grazing or burning on their woodlands. Much has been said about the function of forests in controlling run-off and preventing erosion, but this is true only of *forests,* and not of pastures with a few trees left in them. If wood lots are to contribute to erosion control they must be managed to achieve this purpose. It is significant that the *Bauernbusch* or "farm forests" of Germany are also in poor condition because of unguarded grazing and the removal of forest litter. One of the critical points in the land use program both at home and abroad evidently is the farm wood lot which, because of its ownership, is peculiarly at the mercy of uninformed and unregulated private property. The Cooperative Farm Forestry Act of 1937 is designed to assist farmers in wood lot management through technical advice, cooperative agreements for the establishment and care of farm woodlands, and the furnishing of planting stock.

Management of Private Forest Land. Even though the public ownership recommended in Table 33 becomes a reality, 133,000,000 acres or over 20 per cent of the total forest area will remain in private ownership in addition to the 124,000,000 acres in farm woodlands. Perhaps the goal of 358,000,000 acres of public forests will not be reached because of the strain on federal, state, and local budgets and the resentment of local governments at the reduction of their tax bases by public purchases. However, only a small fraction of the private forests are under adequate management today, and the problem of persuading American forest owners to treat their forests as a crop and not as a mine is still unsolved. The institutions and attitudes toward land which are such important factors abroad are absent in America. In spite of the assertion that sustained yield management as an investment is attracting capital, European countries do not trust "economic" and "institutional" forces alone to conserve and maintain forests, but use public regulations to reinforce them by insisting on proper forest practices. Controls and restrictions must be adapted to the institutions and traditions of our own country before they will be accepted and prove enforceable. These should be supplemented by public aids and inducements as exemplified by the forest crop laws. A plan has been suggested under which private owners would retain ownership but the government would manage the forests, pay a share of the income to the landowner at the time of cutting, and pay the local governments a stated yearly sum in lieu of taxes. This plan meets some of the present objections and difficulties. Private owners would be relieved of all responsibilities of sustained yield management, public treasuries would not be called upon for enormous outlays for land purchase, and local governments would be satisfied by having a definite and dependable income.[1]

[1] Sparhawk, "A Possible Program of Public Regulation," in *A National Plan for American Forestry, op. cit.*, pp. 1343–54; Conrad H. Hammar, *Extending Public Control and Management of Forest Land without Purchase* (Missouri Agricultural Experiment Station, January 12, 1938, mimeographed).

X

THE ENVIRONMENT AND RECREATIONAL LAND

The Environment. "It is upon the surface of the land, its natural beauties or its man-made ugliness, that we are compelled to gaze most of our waking hours," is the observation of a noted British geographer.[1] Undoubtedly our surroundings, whether man-made or natural, have an influence on our lives, consciously or unconsciously. "There is little question that many of the attributes most distinctive of America and Americans are the impress of the wilderness and the life that accompanied it. If we have any such thing as an American culture (and I think we have), its distinguishing marks are a certain vigorous individualism combined with ability to organize, a certain intellectual curiosity bent to practical ends, a lack of subservience to stiff social forms, and an intolerance of drones, all of which are the distinctive characteristics of successful pioneers," says Aldo Leopold in making a plea for the preservation of the wilderness, the environment which produced these qualities.[2]

One step further is the uninhabited wilderness whose highest and best use is no "use" at all. "It's the great spaces that appeal," says Stephen Leacock. "To all of us here, the vast unknown country of the North, reaching away to the polar seas, supplies a peculiar mental background. I like to think that in a few short hours in a train or a car I can be in the primeval wilderness of the North; that if I like, from my summer home, an hour or two of flight will take me over the divide and down the mournful shores of the James Bay, untenanted till yesterday, now haunted with its flock of airplanes hunting gold in the wilderness. I never have gone to the James Bay; I never go to it; I never shall. But somehow I'd feel lonely without it." [3]

Into this natural environment man has introduced his works.

[1] L. Dudley Stamp, "Planning the Land for the Future," *Science*, December 7, 1934, pp. 507–12, at p. 507.

[2] "Wilderness as a Form of Land Use," *Journal of Land and Public Utility Economics*, October, 1925, pp. 398–404, at p. 401.

[3] *Funny Pieces* (New York, Dodd Mead, 1936), p. 291.

In many cases, particularly the cities created by the Industrial Revolution, they are anything but beautiful. H. L. Mencken says that some "titanic and aberrant genius" must have "devoted all the ingenuity of hell to the making" of some of the steel towns. "It seems incredible that mere ignorance should have achieved such masterpieces of horror. There is a voluptuous quality in them. They look deliberate."[1]

The extreme development of man-made urban environment has created the impression that all cities are hideous and must by their very nature be hideous. There is also a philosophy that all great cultures have come from the soil and a deliberate dispersion of the city is necessary. However, the relation of man to his environment is not as simple as all this; the frontier and open country may be a moral and physical slum, whereas some races and nationalities forced off the land and compelled to live in cities have maintaned a vigorous culture and made notable contributions to art, science, music, and scholarship. But it is not necessary to accept specific dogmas to appreciate the influence of environment on our lives. One of the accepted purposes of city and regional planning is the ordering of land uses, not only for their ordinary functioning, but also for harmony and beauty. The "city ugly" is no more inevitable than the "denuded and disorderly landscapes" which are the aftermaths of exploitative lumbering and mining.

While the country and city seem opposites, "neither can exist for human use without some tincture or leaven of the other."[2] Gardens, trees, and parks are a part of cities, and buildings and other man-made structures are a part of the country. The two together form the environment in which the modern mobile man lives, works, commutes, and spends his leisure. The control of the urban environment lies with the city, but that of the countryside rests with a large number of units of government, which adds to the complexities of planning.

We are prone to think of scenery as the unusual, existing at given places, and above the ordinary landscape in scenic quality.

[1] Quoted in Benton Mackaye, *The New Exploration* (New York, Harcourt, 1928), p. 142. See also Mumford, *Culture of Cities, op. cit.*, Chap. III, "The Insensate Industrial Town," and Chap. 4, "Rise and Fall of Megalopolis."

[2] Patrick Abercrombie, *Town and Country Planning* (New York, Holt, 1933), p. 19.

It is interesting to observe the enthusiasm of Patrick Abercrombie for the English countryside, an "amenity" consisting not only of the "wild" but also of the "tame." "Nothing, not even the extremest mechanization of farming can prevent the country from being the town dwellers' chief contrasted recreation and relaxation; its only rival is the sea." The humanized, tame and cultivated country he calls "the most beautiful in the world." [1] This suggests that we have much to learn in appreciating our natural, ordinary environment and preventing its disfigurement.[2]

RECREATIONAL LAND

As a part of the intelligent planning of all land uses in order to constitute a harmonious environment, there is a need for planned recreational land. Recreation means different things to different people and may take different forms at various times. To some it is mere diversion, pleasure, or amusement. The theaters, movies, circuses, Coney Island, dance halls, night clubs, and road houses thrive as commercial enterprises in response to the demand for amusement. To other people recreation means what the word signifies—refreshment of mind and body, a creation anew of the physical and spiritual man. This means primarily the outdoor forms of recreation.

Up to a few years ago it was hardly necessary to set aside land for outdoor recreation for the occupations of many people took them into the open. Modern callings are becoming more and more sedentary. We are becoming a nation of city dwellers surrounded by an artificial and man-made atmosphere, and the time for leisure is increasing. The 84-hour work week of 1840 has practically been cut in half and we may soon have the 30-hour week. It is important that the play instincts of man be developed properly and not permitted to degenerate. Cities have recognized this fact in their plans for parks, playgrounds, and recreational centers.

Recreational land as such is also necessary because other uses have absorbed most of the land once public property. Even private land was once open to all, but with the increase in population and the more intensive use of land the private owner has asserted

[1] *Ibid.*, Part III, pp. 217 and 225.
[2] *Ibid.*, pp. 228–48: "Rural Preservation: Disfigurement."

his rights. The owner of a farm did not object to his neighbors' hunting, fishing, or picnicking on his property, but when hordes of strangers began to use (and abuse) his property he "posted" the farm. The owner also found that he could turn the recreational qualities of his land into money and began to charge for the privilege of using his place. Even Niagara Falls was once so surrounded by private property that no one could get a decent view of the falls without paying for the privilege. In 1880 Canada and New York bought the necessary riparian land and made it into a public park.

Even though we respect the private owners' rights to land for productive purposes, we often experience a feeling of resentment whenever land is "posted" to keep out picnickers, hikers, hunters, and nature lovers whose use of the land does not or need not interfere with its commercial utilization. The solution of the problem takes on a twofold aspect: the reconciliation of private property rights with the "rights" of the public to the reasonable use of such land for recreational purposes, and the provision of public land specifically dedicated to recreation.

The creation of parks, forests, and other forms of recreational land has been slow and has had to overcome much opposition. Instead of being considered the "highest land use," it has had to compete with alternative private land uses which often outbid the public recreational interests. Recreational land is considered "sentimental," while other land uses "make money" and pay taxes instead of costing the taxpayers money for purchase, upkeep, and maintenance! Central Park of New York City was the achievement of William Cullen Bryant and other public-spirited citizens. Heroic efforts were necessary to keep the area free from encroachments and true to the ideals of a park. Yellowstone National Park was about to be seized by private individuals for speculation when, in 1872, President Grant approved an act setting aside the Yellowstone land as "a public park or pleasuring ground." Not until 1890 were other national parks set aside out of the public domain.

Whenever commercial uses have clashed with the use of land for recreation it has been a colossal task to arouse public opinion. The famous big trees of California are an example; entreaties of men like Theodore Roosevelt and John Muir were needed to spur others to action. Many of the recreational areas now set aside for public purposes were made possible by the generosity and activity of individuals interested in the public welfare. In California William Kent purchased the grove of giant trees now known as Muir Woods National Monument for the express purpose of saving these trees from the ax, only to find that the tract was to be condemned by eminent domain for a reservoir site. The day was saved by deeding the property to the federal government. Another example is the Palisades Park. The beauty of the Hudson was being destroyed at this point by quarrying the rocks. About $2,500,000 was raised by private subscription and taken to the New York legislature with the proposal that they match this sum to save the Palisades. The result was what has been called "The Greatest Park in the World." [1]

Since then many public-spirited individuals and societies have championed the cause of public recreational land. The civic organizations represented by the Federated Societies,[2] the conferences on outdoor recreation and on parks, and the various groups interested in conservation and recreation in general indicate the growing public interest in this field.

The Enjoyment of Nature. The recreational motive is so varied with individuals that it defies description and classification, so the general term "enjoyment of nature" will have to cover a multitude of desires. To some this term means hunting and fishing, but to another the companionship of wild creatures is so intimate that he refuses to "shoot" his prey with anything but a camera. The latter form of recreation can be just as exciting as the former. One person is satisfied with walking in a more or less artificial park, whereas another is not happy unless he is in a trackless wilderness. Some enjoy nature by driving in a closed car through a state or national park and are delighted with the guides, crowds, hotels, roads, and dance halls of the usual summer resort, whereas the "nature lover" flees from these as from perdition.

[1] See a book by that name describing the Palisades Interstate Park by Arthur P. Abbott (New York, Historian Publishing Co., 1914).

[2] The Federated Societies on Planning and Parks consist of the American Planning and Civic Association, American Institute of Park Executives, American Park Society, and National Conference on State Parks.

The perplexing problem is to find a land policy of sufficient magnitude and breadth to satisfy all demands for outdoor recreation.[1]

Primeval Areas. Recognition of the desire for isolation is found in the provision of "primeval areas." These are defined as "unmodified tracts of land with accompanying plant and animal life where the normal processes of nature continue undisturbed by man and where all forms of life are given sanctuary," or, more concisely, as "an area where ecological forces are not modified by artificial treatment." [2]

In federal forests such tracts consist primarily of virgin forests which are to remain untouched and are usually from 1,000 to 2,000 acres in extent. It is recommended that from 250,000 to 2,000,000 acres constitute a primeval area. Only land in large tracts and in federal ownership, such as the parks, forests, public domain, and Indian reservations, can furnish the requisite areas. The National Park Service is also setting aside, against encroachment of the general public, areas with unique natural features and "research reserves" to preserve geologic phenomena and biotic communities. Fortunately for the primeval areas "only one motorist in hundreds will venture a mile from his car; the rest are amply content with the road, and the museums, lectures and pleasures of developed centers." [3]

The Wilderness. This form of land use is described as a "wild roadless area where those who are so inclined may enjoy primitive modes of travel and subsistence." Its primary feature is the absence of modern modes of travel, the motorcar or motorboat, and of hotels and resorts. The shrinking of the wilderness is due not so much to the advance of agriculture or even of lumbering, because the wilderness areas are not suited to these land uses, but rather to the extension of roads everywhere in the effort to catch the tourist's dollar. Administratively the wilderness can be a part of the regular park and forest system.[4]

For the nature lover and the scientist, and for those anxious to preserve an area of nature undisturbed by man, a much smaller tract than the primeval area and wilderness as discussed above will

[1] For an analysis of the components of recreation see Aldo Leopold, "Conservation Esthetic," *Bird Lore,* March–April, 1938, pp. 101–9.

[2] *N. R. B. Report, op. cit.*, p. 219.

[3] *Ibid.*

[4] Leopold, "Wilderness as a Form of Land Use," *op. cit.*, p. 398.

often suffice. A few acres in the rougher spots of a forest or park will do, if left undisturbed by the public or by some public-spirited landowner. Many species of plant life are on the way to extinction, as is the case with some birds and animals.[1] Destruction of forests, grazing and drainage, the burning of wood lots, together with the unthinking and selfish picking of flowers and shrubs by vacationists, are responsible for this situation. Much educational work needs to be done with both children and adults to make them appreciate how fast our native plants are disappearing. Legislation has been necessary to prevent some of our species from being destroyed completely by "flower lovers" who pick the flowers and even tear up the roots, then throw away their wilted trophies before they reach home.[2]

The Trail. To provide a means for the enjoyment of nature by those who cannot use the extensive wilderness and who feel more at home and safer in more civilized surroundings, the trail is a solution. This is a path laid out over public and private lands for hikes. "Wandering" has long been a favorite method of recreation in Europe, and hiking over trails following forests, mountains, and other scenic areas is becoming an enjoyable method of spending a vacation in America. Hostels and inns provide moderately priced accommodations. One of the first trails was visioned by Benton Mackaye—the Appalachian Trail which extends from Maine to Georgia. Bridle paths and canoe trails are suggested for those who prefer other methods of travel to hiking.

Riparian Recreational Uses. The use of water for recreation —boating, fishing, bathing, and enjoyment of its beauty—is part of our very nature. Pollution probably affects more people from this standpoint than any other. Waters filled with sewage and trade wastes are usually devoid of fish, a menace to health, and offensive to those who want to use them for bathing or boating. Even the beaches of the Great Lakes and the oceans are not free from pollution and oil wastes.

People in general have not appreciated the place of water as

[1] *The University and Conservation of Wisconsin Wildlife* (Bulletin of the University of Wisconsin, Serial 2211, February, 1937).

[2] For a list of plants in danger of becoming extinct, those in need of protection, those which may be picked in moderation, and those which are plentiful, see *Teaching of Conservation in Wisconsin Schools* (Curriculum Bulletin of the Wisconsin Department of Public Instruction, May, 1937), pp. 67–68.

part of the environment. A lake or marsh, even though useless for fishing or for summer resorts, is nevertheless a part of the landscape. The gently flowing stream is as important as rapids, dells, or waterfalls. It is an attractive part of the rural landscape, but too often it is narrowed, cribbed, and confined whenever it flows through a village or city. Buildings are placed close to the stream and sometimes even encroach on the bed, thereby increasing the flood hazard. Usually the backs of the buildings face the water and the river is used as a dump for tin cans, rubbish, garbage, and sewage unless the law interferes. How much better it would be to treat the stream banks as a parkway and so conserve the natural recreational qualities of the stream. Harrisburg, Pennsylvania, offers an example of the use which can be made of the river front for recreation.

Zoning Riparian Uses. An amendment to the Wisconsin county zoning enabling act in 1935, permitting the regulation of land uses along natural water courses, had as one of its purposes the exclusion of industries from river valleys as well as the preservation of the stream banks for parks and parkways pending the time when they can be purchased and used for these purposes. Recently Jefferson County, in southeastern Wisconsin, passed a zoning ordinance which took advantage of this amendment. "Conservancy districts" were set up in the valleys of the two principal rivers, ranging from half a mile to about two miles in width. The riparian land on several large lakes has also been placed in conservancy districts. The regulations prescribed for these districts are similar to those for urban residential zones, including minimum lot sizes and maximum building height for residences. Their effect will be the exclusion of all business and commercial structures, including stores, taverns, dance halls, tourist cabins, junk yards, and billboards, thereby reserving the riparian land for farms, permanent residences, summer homes, and cottages. This signifies an attempt to preserve the amenities of the river and lake shores and to prevent their disfigurement.[1]

In addition to the problem of preserving riparian land and the waters themselves, the question of public access must also be con-

[1] J. M. Albers, "New Uses for County Zoning: The Jefferson County, Wisconsin, Ordinance," *Journal of Land and Public Utility Economics,* November, 1938, pp. 460–62.

sidered. This may be handled either by providing more public land or by modifying the rights of the riparian owners. Although 45 per cent of our population lives within fifty miles of salt water or the Great Lakes, only one per cent of the shore lands are public property. Cities and other units of government have failed to retain or acquire sufficient shore property for bathing beaches, parks, drives, and parkways. This holds true not only for areas with large metropolitan centers and congested populations but also for rural states. There is the problem of controlling the shore lines of practically every one of the thirty-eight lakes listed in the *Report on the Iowa Twenty-five Year Conservation Plan* in order to insure adequate public access.[1] Few so-called "scenic drives" permit more than an occasional glimpse of the lake, ocean, or stream along which they are laid out.

Areas of Historical and Archeological Interest. Historic places have a universal appeal. Much of the travel to Europe, to the East, and to Quebec is generated by the desire to visit places noted for their history and because here the past has been preserved in castles, churches, forts, and other structures. The federal government, through the National Park Service, is preserving historic places, battlefields, and mementos of the original Indian civilization. States are maintaining their first capitol buildings and other structures of historic interest. However, it would be a fine thing for local communities to honor illustrious acts of peace as well as of war. Mementos of the struggles of the pioneers are vanishing rapidly and, once destroyed, can never be replaced except as replicas or restorations. The early churches, mills, log cabins, covered bridges, village sites, historic trees, rural cemeteries, and Indian mounds are among the structures and areas which should be preserved, or at least marked. Many states, notably Virginia and Montana, are using roadside markers to point out to travellers the historic spots on or near the highway on which they are motoring.

WILD LIFE, HUNTING, AND FISHING

Depletion of Wild Life. Probably no resource has suffered more from the encroachment of civilization than wild life, i.e.,

[1] Iowa Board of Conservation and Iowa Fish and Game Commission (1933), pp. 55–68.

wild birds, fish, and animals. The abundance of buffalo, deer, ducks, geese, fish, and other creatures before the white man came is almost unbelievable. Today many species are extinct or sorely depleted. The destruction began with the removal of the forest. Lumbering destroys the home of game and fish and forest fires complete the ruin. The dredging machine, the ax, and the plow have been highly effective in destroying wild life because the creatures were deprived of food and cover. On the other hand, the new environment has been favorable to some species.

In addition to the destruction of the natural environment, civilization has introduced features to which wild creatures have not become accustomed and perhaps never will. Domestic cats destroy more birds than any other animal except man. Poison intended for other animals is often fatal to birds. They also lose their lives by flying into lighthouses, arc lights, and other illuminated objects which blind them at night. Telephone and telegraph wires also take a heavy toll of bird life because they cannot be seen at times of low visibility. The number of animals killed by railway trains and automobiles is appalling.[1]

In some cases mistaken though sincere efforts at efficient land utilization have resulted in the depletion of game. When the Germans adopted the clear-cut-and-plant method of forestry, using spruce and pine exclusively, natural food for deer became so scarce that artificial feeding became necessary. In fact over-artificial forestry almost extinguished bird life in these "wood factories."[2]

Industries and cities have been injurious to water creatures through pollution. In the industrial sections of the East many streams are without any living organisms whatsoever. Oil from steamers is destroying oyster beds and fish by excluding oxygen from the water, and birds have been seen with feathers so smeared with oil that they were unable to rise from the sea and fell easy victims to hunters.[3]

[1] Junius Henderson, *The Practical Value of Birds* (New York, Macmillan, 1927), pp. 88–108.

[2] Aldo Leopold, "Deer and Dauerwald in Germany," *Journal of Forestry,* April and May, 1936; also "*Naturschutz* in Germany," *Bird Lore,* March–April, 1936, pp. 102–11.

[3] W. C. Adams in *Proceedings of the National Conference on Outdoor Recreation,* 1924, p. 39; Elmer C. Aldrich, "A Recent Oil-pollution and Its Effect on the Water Birds of the San Francisco Area," *Bird Lore,* March–April, 1938, pp. 110–14.

Another cause for the extinction of wild life is modern weapons in the hands of "butchers" and "pot hunters." "If the wild creature population were turned over exclusively to their mercies, there would not be a living thing left in a decade. With dynamite, net and machine gun they would wipe bare the lands and waters of the continent. . . . One of this precious crew boasted that in a single year he had killed 139,000 game birds and animals."[1] In contrast to the butcher is the sportsman who "has no business interest in killing and no sadistic perversion to satisfy. He believes in giving animals a chance, a fair gamble with death."[2] The sportsman has a sincere interest in game conservation, although often the methods his organizations suggest are fantastic and "anti-conservational."

Those who thoughtlessly or maliciously assist in the extermination of wild life fail to realize the economic value of birds and animals. Fur, food, feathers, and other products derived from birds, beasts, and fish are worth millions of dollars annually. Birds, bats, moles, shrews, snakes, skunks, and other creatures hold myriads of insects in check. The damage done to crops and fruit by birds is usually far outweighed by their destruction of insects; the trouble is that the farmer is aware of the former but is often ignorant of the latter. Just as important are the aesthetic and recreational values of wild life as part of the environment—the songs and beauty of birds and the presence of furry creatures. This fact is appreciated by resort owners, who want deer, porcupine, and bear for the enjoyment of their guests. In some places they have protested against open seasons for deer for this reason, and resorts sponsor twilight drives for the purpose of seeing the deer during the summer months.

Wild life requires extensive areas, and to maintain and enhance this resource a land policy will involve: (1) land set aside primarily for this purpose, with no encroachment of other uses, or with the other uses kept strictly secondary; (2) areas managed more intensively for specific species of game, usually public but perhaps also private; (3) forest-game combinations of uses; (4) park-game and (5) farm-game combinations.

Land Used Primarily for Game. The wild and rocky lands of

[1] Stuart Chase, *Rich Land, Poor Land* (New York, McGraw-Hill, 1936), p. 181.
[2] *Ibid.*, p. 183.

Alaska, Canada, the Rockies, the Olympic Peninsula, the Everglades, and the deserts represent the wilderness type of landscape where wild animals are left under the condition of nature, with as little interference with the "law of tooth and claw" as is consistent with keeping all the species alive. It would appear, with 46 per cent of the area of the United States classed as "grade 5" land, "essentially incapable of tillage," that wild life, hunting, and fishing should have ample scope. However, some of the species use the same type of land as grazing animals, and a conflict arises both in the national forests and on the public domain. Bighorn or mountain sheep, formerly widely dispersed over the rugged sections of the West, are now confined to areas too rugged for or otherwise unusable by livestock. Antelope and elk compete with range cattle. It is feared that the Taylor Grazing Act has strengthened the hold of local livestock interests on the public lands of the West, to the detriment of wild life and recreation.

In view of the prospect of a stationary population and a limited demand for forest products, much of the forested land can and should be managed for recreation. This means not only for hunting and fishing but for the broader and more intangible aesthetic uses. As Lovejoy points out, this will mean planting trees for deer food and deer yards instead of for pulp and logs. Later the area may be closed to shooting and reserved entirely for the enjoyment of nature. Any merchantable wood will be a mere by-product.[1] Leopold suggests that only half of our forest area be developed for intensive silviculture and the other half devoted entirely to "floral and faunal conservation." "In other words pull our working plans down out of the cliffs and rocks and let those places grow game and scenery." [2] This concept also fits into that of the wilderness and primeval areas.

However, public administrators have not generally accepted this form of "forest" management, nor are they always in a position to do so. Under the Wisconsin forest crop law no land is acceptable which will not give a reasonable assurance of developing a stand of merchantable timber. This means that individuals or counties cannot be assisted in managing forest land for recrea-

[1] Lovejoy, "Concepts and Contours in Land Utilization," *op. cit.*, pp. 388–91.

[2] Leopold, "Deer and Dauerwald," Part II: "Ecology and Policy," *Journal of Forestry*, May, 1936, p. 464.

tion, wild life, or scenery. Furthermore, the public is given the right to hunt and fish on all forest crop land, but subject to the regulations of the conservation department, which prevents the owner from capitalizing on the hunting or fishing qualities of his property.

Game and Bird Refuges. Other forms of public game land are the bird and game refuges under the jurisdiction of the several states and several federal departments, particularly the Biological Survey and the Forest Service. Human encroachment on nesting and feeding areas of migratory birds make refuges particularly important for ducks, geese, and similar birds. The program for refuges in the Mississippi Valley for feeding, nesting, and resting grounds is under way. The area per refuge should not be less than 10,000 acres, and 50,000 acres is an efficient maximum. "An ideal system of refuges would contemplate a series of major projects approximately 300 miles apart in each of the four major flight lanes and extending from the Canadian border to the southern limits of the United States." Groups of smaller refuges might well be created close to these larger ones.[1]

Refuges for upland game and animals are managed with the idea of a central core of land where game is not disturbed and with various rings of buffer areas offering successively less protection. The land may consist of both public and privately owned land.

Game in Parks and Public Forests. Wild life and game can also be administered as part of other public land uses, particularly parks and forests. The national parks are for the purpose of conserving the scenery, natural and historical objects, and wild life. However, the tendency is to fit wild life into a "park" policy. Game and wild animals of interest to tourists are tolerated and others, especially those which feed on game (predators), are "controlled" or slated for extermination. Coyotes, mountain lions, wolves, and similar species are not wanted, whereas bison, elk, and antelope are protected. This policy is not without its critics.[2]

"A forest is a certain territory of woody grounds and fruitful pastures, privileged for wild beasts and fowls of Forest, Chase and

[1] *N. R. B. Report,* pp. 148–49.

[2] See V. E. Shelford, "Conservation of Wild Life," in Parkins and Whitaker, *Our Natural Resources and Their Conservation, op. cit.,* pp. 492–95.

Warren, to rest and abide in, in safe protection of the king for his princely delight and pleasure. . . ." So reads the definition of a forest in an old book on forest laws.[1] Even this short definition makes it clear that the forest was privileged ground for animals under the "safe protection of the king." Furthermore, it consisted not only of tree covered ground but of "fruitful pastures," and might include other lands. During this period of forest history the forester was actually a game manager concerned with trespass, deliberate preservation of mast trees, predator control, and restraints on the kill. Forest courts administered special forest laws with unusual severity.

Later, with the shift in emphasis in forestry, and especially commercial forestry, game became secondary and often hostile to forest practices because game ate the young trees or stripped their bark. However, the more natural *Dauerwald* is less antagonistic than the older highly commercial forest management to game and wild life. In America, in the first enthusiasm for forestry, it was assumed that reforestation would automatically restore the habitat for game and fish. But it was soon discovered that rabbits, mice, deer, and even birds interfered at times with forest management, and the conflict between the hunter who wanted rabbits and the tree planter who did not was on. Forest experiment stations are now examining the relationships between wild life and forests in order to reconcile the two.[2]

One of the difficulties of forest-game relationships in the national forests lies in the fact that while the federal government owns the forest the states claim jurisdiction over game. The legal status of game on federal forests has never been settled. One result is that some states have centered their game policy on the destruction of predators. This causes an unrestrained increase in deer which, true to the Malthusian law, gives rise to a pressure of population on the food supply and carrying capacity of the forest. In the western states game policies are often determined by those who pasture stock in the federal forests. They can influence the game policies even though forest policies are determined by another level of government.[3]

[1] John Manwood, *A Treatise of the Laws of the Forest* (London, 1665).

[2] Leo C. Couch, "Forest-Wild Life Relationships: What Has Been Accomplished through Research," *Journal of Forestry*, September, 1938, pp. 913–15.

[3] Shelford, *op. cit.*, p. 495.

Game on Farm Land. Even though farming has been responsible for the destruction of the habitat of some wild life it has not exterminated all species; in fact, certain types have actually increased. The robin, the meadow lark, and the cardinal have become more numerous and rabbits, squirrels, and skunks seem to have adjusted themselves to farming conditions. Most of the trappers in the United States are farm boys and about half a million are engaged in this occupation.[1] It is possible through adjustments in farm management to restore breeding, nesting, and feeding grounds on the average northern farm, especially those with marsh, swamp, wood lots, or with trees and shrubs along fences. In many places introduced species, such as pheasants, are really semi-domestic game raised by farmers, which take on the legal status of wild game under certain conditions. While the biological problem of raising game is by no means solved, the real problem is to get farmers and other landowners to permit the game to raise itself (with some intelligent assistance) and to present it when grown to the general public for sport. The issue lies in the property relationships of game and land.

Property in Game. Game is the classic example of qualified property, although it is commonly called the property of the state. "We take it to be correct doctrine in this country that the ownership of wild animals, *so far as they are capable of ownership,* is in the state, *not as proprietor,* but *in its sovereign capacity, as the representative,* and for the benefit of all its people in common," said the Minnesota Supreme Court.[2] The words "not as proprietor" and "as representative of all its people" indicate the qualified nature of the ownership. A Wisconsin court also held that the state "has no proprietary right in the ice nor in the fish that inhabit such waters or in the fowls that resort thereto."[3] This decision was quoted to deny the right of the state to sell carp taken from the lakes. However, the question is more or less academic because the state's power to regulate the manner and time of taking game and other restrictions is ample for purposes of conservation. This power extends even to prohibiting the shipment of game outside the state on the ground that the state has the

[1] Van Hise and Havemeyer, *op. cit.,* p. 420.

[2] *State* v. *Rodman,* 58 Minnesota 393, 59 N. W. 1098 (1894). (Italics in text are ours.)

[3] *State* v. *Rosemiller,* 114 Wisconsin 169R.

right "to confine the use of the game to those who own it, the people of that state." [1] It may for the same reasons pass hunting laws in favor of its own citizens as against the rights of nonresidents.

But if the state has no proprietary right in game, neither has the landowner. Rabbits that consume the crops of a farmer cannot be claimed if they escape to a neighbor's farm, but tame and domestic animals can. Whether a deer raised on a private preserve or animals in a menagerie are "wild" or "tame" has presented knotty questions to the courts. Absolute property in game is acquired by an individual whenever he obtains possession according to the manner prescribed by law. This is in accordance with the Roman rule and holds against the landowner's right who, because of his ownership of the soil, might claim the right to wild animals found upon it or flying over his land.[2] However, the owner can buy a license as well as the outside hunter, and "being on the ground" has the prior right to "reducing game" on his farm "to possession." Nevertheless, the average farmer or wild land owner has little interest in protecting or managing game, especially if he finds sportsmen assuming that a hunting license gives them the right to hunt on anyone's property. The horde of city hunters who, in their ignorance or excitement, shoot farm animals, leave gates open, or break fences have caused legislatures to strengthen private owners' rights against trespass. However, "free hunting" is still a part of our pioneer heritage; perhaps also a revolt against the medieval monopoly of kings and noblemen to the chase. It also accounts for the feeling against private game preserves with their "Private" and "No Hunting" signs. But this sentiment is giving way. In 1934 the Lower Peninsula of Michigan had 220 hunting and fishing clubs, a few of them owning from 10,000 to 18,000 acres.[3]

As far as the individual farmer is concerned, he will be induced to practice game management for the sport of the general public if there is an income either monetary or psychic, or both, sufficient to cover his "costs," which may be more psychic than

[1] *Geer* v. *Connecticut,* 161 U. S. 519 (1896).

[2] Robert H. Connery, *Governmental Problems in Wild Life Conservation* (New York, Columbia University Press, 1935), Chap. IV, "The Sphere of the State Government in Wild-Life Conservation."

[3] Wilber O. Hedrick, *Recreational Uses of Northern Michigan Cut-over Lands* (Mich. Agric. Exp. Station, Special Bulletin 247, 1934), pp. 26–30.

real. Although he does not own the game he may lease the hunting rights to outsiders, which is one form of income and either he or the lessee can exercise control over the kill so that no more than the natural increase is shot each year. In some cases a group of farmers have posted fairly large areas and issued supplementary hunting licenses or permits to hunters. This gives them control over hunting as well as over trespass.

Fish and game are now protected by a multitude of game laws regulating weapons, seasons, and the regions open for sport, under the powers of the federal and state governments and involving even international treaties. The work of the government also includes research, raising fish in hatcheries, raising game, and other practices designed to increase the supply of game and fish. The Biological Survey, the Bureau of Fisheries, the Forest Service, and the various state conservation departments are the chief agencies for these purposes.[1]

TOURISTS AND THE HIGHWAY

The Tourist Flow. The various factors which lure men into the out-of-doors—whether a mere desire for a change of scene, the enjoyment of nature, the love of the water, the desire to visit historical places or "scenery," or to hunt and fish—are responsible for the modern tourist travel. This has reached gigantic proportions since the invention of the automobile and the building of good roads. According to the United States Travel Bureau, 69 per cent of the tourists use their personal automobile, 23 per cent use the railroads, 7 per cent travel on buses, and 1 per cent use the airplane.[2] This has created a new industry, the "tourist business," which has been especially beneficial to states lacking the usual economically valuable resources but which have mountains, rocks, waterfalls, forests, lakes, and seashore to look at and an agreeable climate to enjoy. So lucrative and also so competitive has this business become that $50,000,000 or more was spent in 1930 in advertising their scenery by various states, local communities, and business interests involved in catering to tourists.

Recreational use is estimated to have brought, in 1930, $90,-000,000 to Minnesota and $200,000,000 to Michigan, with Wiscon-

[1] Connery, *op. cit.*
[2] *New York Times,* August 21, 1938.

sin about halfway between. Both Michigan and Wisconsin consider the tourist trade their second most important source of income. According to *Commerce Reports* almost 16,500,000 tourists entered Canada in 1927 and spent $197,000,000. American tourists in Europe spent over a half billion dollars abroad.[1]

Surveys made by various states and the federal Bureau of Public Roads reveal something of the mobility of the American people and their habits en route. It is estimated that 2,500,000 out-of-state cars visit Michigan in a year, almost 2,000,000 come to Wisconsin, and 500,000 visit Florida. However, the distance travelled is far less than is ordinarily supposed. The Pacific states receive only one-eighth of their out-of-state traffic from states east of the Mississippi, and almost 80 per cent of Michigan's tourist flow originates in the East North Central states. More than half of the summer visitors to Wisconsin come from Illinois. Florida attracts 90 per cent of her traffic from the area east of the Mississippi and almost two-thirds of the cars come from the South.[2]

The fact that the mass movements of tourists are local and restricted in distance is important from several standpoints. In the first place, states with recreational attractions located near the centers of wealth and population have a decided advantage over those located at greater distances. Connecticut, for instance, has beautiful hills and woods, more than 1,000 lakes, a river frontage of 7,600 miles, besides a coast line extending along her entire southern boundary. More than 20,000,000 people live within a radius of 150 miles of the central part of the state, which makes Connecticut not only easily accessible for the motoring tourist but also suitable for estates, summer homes, and cottages.[3] Another illustration is afforded by the upper eight states of the Mississippi Valley, which have roughly 30 per cent of the urban population of the United States, 27 per cent of the total population, more than 30 per cent of the taxable wealth, and one-third of the motor vehicle registrations—all important factors in gen-

[1] George S. Wehrwein and K. H. Parsons, *Recreation as a Land Use* (Wisconsin Agric. Exp. Station Bulletin 422, 1932), pp. 7–12.

[2] L. E. Peabody and I. M. Spashoff, "Tourist Travel in the United States," *Public Roads* (pub. by U. S. Dept. of Agriculture), August, 1937, pp. 101–16.

[3] N. L. Whetten and V. A. Rapport, *The Recreational Uses of Land in Connecticut* (Connecticut Agric. Exp. Station—Storrs, Bulletin 194, 1934), pp. 6, 9–10.

erating the tourist flow. The mere accessibility of the recreational regions of the Great Lakes states becomes an assurance that the bulk of the midwestern tourist traffic will be into these states.

In the second place, the restricted travel range of the tourist with average income and leisure time means that recreational facilities should be provided in this range insofar as natural features are available. For example, Iowa's conservation plan sets up a goal of a county park within 10 miles of every person in Iowa and a state park within 25 miles.[1]

The Highway as a Means of Recreation. "The whole world of out-door recreation is at the command of the motorist. One end of the road is at his door step. At the other end is the place of his desires."[2] This applies to the urban dweller who seeks the open country and to the farmer who comes to the city or village for recreation. The mingling of commercial with recreational traffic, however, creates complicated traffic problems; one interferes with the other. Congestion and the danger of accidents have reduced the pleasure of driving. Adjustments must be made for the "Sunday driver" on the regular roads or special highways should be designed for recreational motoring.

While the prophecy made a few years ago was exaggerated, that one-third of our population would soon live in trailers, nevertheless this new form of housing must be given more consideration. Unquestionably it has permitted people to live cheaply while following the climate or visiting scenic places. This has appealed especially to the older age groups in our society. On the other hand, it has placed new demands upon public facilities, the cost of which are not easily recaptured by taxation. Trailers slow up traffic, make new demands upon the margins of the highways, and create problems of housing, sanitation, and public services. Land-use policies, especially in suburban areas and "trailer towns," will have to include provisions for land, light, sewers, and other public utilities and regulations to safeguard health and safety.[3]

[1] Iowa State Planning Board, *Second Report,* April, 1935, p. 129.

[2] F. V. Colville, in *Proceedings of the National Conference on October Recreation,* 1924, p. 27.

[3] The Jefferson County (Wis.) zoning ordinance excludes tourist camps with two or more cottages or space for more than two trailers or house cars from the forest and conservancy districts but permits them in the agricultural districts pro-

To complete the "highway as a means of recreation," its margins should be equipped with various public facilities. Private enterprise has provided filling stations, garages, eating places, "tourist homes," cabins, and spaces for trailers. Cities and villages have public camping grounds and states and counties are providing wayside parks and other areas along highways, equipped with benches, tables, refuse cans, and water. Parking space and "tournouts" should be provided at points of historical interest and scenic views so that the tourist can enjoy the landscape without parking on the right of way. A complete highway system might also include special provisions for horse drawn vehicles, bridle paths, and even a path for the lone pedestrian. Footpaths are a part of the English landscape and the trail movement in this country will magnify their importance here.[1] Special scenic and recreational highways are also being laid out, but the mileage of such roads is still small. Besides offering a smooth dustless pavement, the highway and its margins should be pleasing and beautiful. An outstanding example is the George Washington Parkway from Washington, D. C., to Mount Vernon.

The Roadside Environment. The highway and the automobile constitute the modern means of putting people in touch with environments other than their own. The roadside has been called the "front yard of the nation"; if that is true, then the owners of adjacent land are the architects of the roadside landscape.[2] Whether the landscape is ugly, repellent, or beautiful depends to a considerable extent on the landowners along the highway. In fact, billboards and nuisances of all kinds would be no problem if farmers and other landowners refused permission for them or refrained from using the land for such purposes.

The farmer may argue that he is not in business to furnish scenery for tourists. Even granting this, he should be concerned with his own environment. The farm and home are one, and there is no reason why the farmer himself should gaze "all his

viding 800 square feet of ground are furnished for each cabin or trailer and the sanitary facilities meet with the regulations of the State Board of Health. The grounds must also be enclosed by a fence or hedge 5 feet high.

[1] See Benton Mackaye and Lewis Mumford, "Townless Highways for the Motorist," *Harper's*, August, 1931, pp. 347–56.

[2] J. M. Bennett, *Roadsides: The Front Yard of the Nation* (Boston, Stratford, 1936).

working hours" on ugly landscapes or upon huge signs on his barn or silo and ugly advertising along his fences. The fact is that the farmer is a landscape architect on a larger and higher scale than the planner of an estate or city home site. "It is higher," says Aldo Leopold, "because it is functional. The farm is or can be a beautiful organism, the estate is at best a painted picture." [1]

Looked at from a purely materialistic angle, the landscape has an advertising value of its own. This is especially important for states that attract millions of people who come to see the scenery. Whether he is conscious of it or not, the traveller carries away impressions of dilapidated farmsteads, abandoned shacks, and a butchered wood lot, or of fine farms with monolithic silos and the red barns so much admired by modern artists. The tourist flow automatically brings future buyers to see farms, forests, factories, and industries; it is not necessary to carry advertising to the buyer. Whether this advertising makes a favorable or unfavorable impression depends on what the tourist sees.

The Impact of the Highway on Its Margins. Highways are the unifying bands which tie all land uses together. They are built at enormous expense to the taxpayers, and insofar as the adjoining landowners profit by what Pomeroy calls "the impact of highway traffic on abutting property," the owners enjoy an economic advantage donated gratis by the public. This advantage consists of the greater accessibility to the market or the opportunity to sell goods and services to the stream of passengers. Therefore the public has the right to regulate the benefited land, to protect its investment from intrusions and types of business which endanger safety and health or affect the amenities of the countryside.

Controlling Land Uses on Highways—Zoning. A striking example of uncontrolled development is reported on the road connecting Los Angeles with San Bernardino and Riverside. One and a half million dollars were spent on this road, which today carries 15,000 vehicles every twenty-four hours. Shortly after the highway was finished 50 per cent of the frontage was occupied by business places, an average of 41 per mile. Not only was the appearance of the landscape desecrated, but at each business place cars cut in and out, park on the right of way, and mix slow with

[1] Private memorandum.

fast traffic. More than half of the motor accidents are said to be due to this "marginal" and "interstream" friction.[1]

In sharp contrast with this instance, which can be duplicated a thousand times anywhere in the United States, is another California example.[2] San Mateo County, just south of San Francisco, affords a recreational outlet for some 600,000 people. One of the finest recreational roads is the Skyline Boulevard along the Santa Cruz mountains, with spectacular views of the Pacific Ocean and San Francisco Bay. The forty miles of this boulevard in San Mateo County are protected by zoning, some by ordinances of the local units of government and the remainder by a county ordinance which restricts the land uses in a strip 1,000 feet on each side of the highway. Only seven small business districts are permitted, at properly spaced intervals. In these restricted districts agriculture, hotels, single and multiple dwellings, and a limited number of retail businesses are allowed, but no billboards. The operators of the retail business places must obtain permits from the county board of supervisors, who have the right to control the location of business, the advertising on the structures, and the design of the building itself. Although architectural control might have some difficulty in the courts, it has worked well in practice. On the long stretches between business districts only agriculture and single-family dwellings are the approved uses. Most of the other roads in San Mateo County are also zoned.

The above example illustrates the principles of highway zoning in general. The highway and its margins are linear in character and therefore the restricted district assumes a linear shape. While many authorities insist on "comprehensive zoning," under which the entire county is zoned and the highway included as part of the comprehensive zoning, others claim that the strip from five hundred feet to a fourth of a mile from each side of the road is affected by public interest and might legitimately be restricted by the state directly, primarily on the basis of safety, general welfare, and aesthetic grounds.[3] In fact, it is maintained that whenever the highway strip runs through local business zones the

[1] American Nature Association, *Quarterly Bulletin*, July, 1938, pp. 9–12.

[2] *Ibid.* See also Hugh R. Pomeroy, "Roadside Control in California through County Zoning," *Roadside Bulletin*, June, 1937.

[3] Albert S. Bard, "Highway Zoning or Mere Regulation—Which?" *Roadside Bulletin*, June, 1937.

local provisions should be modified within the strip, because here business is largely "traffic attracted" and not the usual urban type of establishment. Furthermore, if left to local units to zone, the restricted areas often become spotted. Businesses and billboards immediately crowd into the unzoned areas, where they remain as non-conforming uses after the dilatory local units have decided to zone their part of the county.

No doubt the state could use the police power directly in controlling land uses which affect the welfare of the highway. It has also been suggested that the state acquire the right to control the margins by easements or deed restrictions. Scenic easements by the states of Virginia and North Carolina protect the Blue Ridge Parkway. However, the general opinion prevails that zoning should be done by communities even though local pressures are often strong enough to prevent the enactment of the ordinances or to take the "teeth" out of restrictions.

While the zoning of the Skyline Boulevard illustrates primarily the restricting of a recreational highway, the same principles may be applied with modifications to high-speed, heavy-traffic roads and even to rural highways. On the former the objective should be to carry traffic at an uninterrupted high speed, except where business has become sufficiently congested, and here the speed should be reduced to 25 miles an hour. To avoid too much interruption, business establishments should be concentrated in special districts and might well be restricted to those services needed by the traveller, which excludes dance halls, outdoor zoos, junk yards, and similar establishments. Billboards belong exclusively in the congested business districts. Setback lines should be made uniform so that all structures are far enough from the pavement to keep all parking off the right of way. The zoning of highway margins is a good example of the regulation of one land use for the benefit of another.

Outdoor Advertising. This is one of the most difficult and controversial highway problems. Cities have limited, through zoning, the areas within which signs are allowed, and such regulations have been sanctioned by the courts.[1] One place where billboards tend to congregate is in the ribbon developments of

[1] *Cusack Co.* v. *City of Chicago,* 242 U. S. 526 (1916), upheld a city ordinance regulating billboards in residential districts on the grounds of safety, health, and morals.

taverns, "hot dog" stands, and similar forms of business, a part of the out-thrust of cities. This, however, is only one phase of the unregulated land uses in the rural-urban fringe left to the control or lack of control of weak or apathetic rural governments. County zoning of the suburban type is designed to correct this situation.[1]

Other places where billboards are erected are on well-travelled highways because the more passengers the greater is the number of people reached by the advertiser. Here signboards increase the hazards of driving. Even though billboards are not placed on dangerous curves they tend to distract the motorist. To say that the driver does not *have* to look at the signs would be an admission that the posters are not read and therefore of no value to the advertiser. It is the job of the billboard to attract the eye, otherwise it is valueless to the advertiser.

The most frequent criticism, however, is that the presence of outdoor advertising on scenic highways, boulevards, and rural roads is out of harmony with the landscape. This also applies to garish filling stations and other structures. While it has long been possible to regulate billboards wherever they are a menace to health, morals, or safety, restrictions based upon aesthetic grounds are on a less firm legal foundation.[2] Massachusetts, through a constitutional amendment, now has limited power to control outdoor advertising from this standpoint.

States now regulate billboards by permits and licenses and taxation based upon the size of the signs, as well as by zoning. Outdoor advertising can be relegated to business districts through zoning. Billboard companies, however, insist on a status similar to *any other* business, while planners claim that the community has the right to classify business and restrict billboards to *specified* business districts. On this theory outdoor advertising was excluded from the business districts along the Skyline Boulevard. Probably the real difficulty lies in the passive attitude of the public in being willing to tolerate disfigurements of the landscape.

It is believed that zoning will never be fully effective as a means of controlling outdoor advertising until it is made retroactive and empowered to abolish existing billboards. While courts

[1] See Chap. XIII.

[2] However, in a case involving architectural approval a California court upheld the ordinance. American Society of Planning Officials, *News Letter*, December, 1938.

would consider the forcible removal of expensive non-conforming structures unreasonable, the billboard is not an expensive structure. Billboards and junk yards were abated on Long Island through the retroactive action of zoning.

Disadvantages of Landownership on Highways. The impact of the highway on abutting property is not always an advantage to the landowners. The constant stream of cars often interferes with farm operations and endangers the lives of children who have to use the highway to get to school. An improved road running through submarginal land does not necessarily make the region supermarginal. This circumstance is often neglected in the zoning of marginal areas.

The modern highway and automobile have intensified the conflict between the private owner and the recreation-seeking public because many more people are brought into contact with farms, forests, and other non-urban land. The general public has assumed not only the right to hunt but to help themselves to Christmas trees, fruit, and flowers. Even apple trees were held quasi-public property by Pennsylvania courts until the legislature defined the right of the landowner to his trees and fruits.

TYPES OF PUBLIC RECREATIONAL LAND

Broadly speaking, recreational land may be for *intensive* or *extensive* use, though in practice these shade into each other or may be combined on a given area. Among the intensive uses are playgrounds, tennis courts, ball parks, swimming pools, beaches, and "in-town parks," more or less artificial, providing amusements which may be enjoyed by the crowd. "Commons," "squares," and parkways, which serve as pleasure traffic arteries, are also among the intensively used recreational land areas. Most of these are forms of urban recreational land but may also be found in the rural areas.

Urban Parks. In the development of cities the need for a fairly large area, kept in a more or less natural condition, was recognized as soon as population crowded out the open spaces around homes and along the streets. Curiously enough, the large spacious cemeteries served this purpose during the 1830's. Mt. Auburn in Boston, Laurel Hill in Philadelphia, and Greenwood in New York for a decade or so satisfied the dual purpose of burial and pleasure ground. However, the funerals and ever growing number of tombstones soon made the two uses incompatible.[1]

The next step was a park of the Central Park type, the parlor of the city, where people rode in stylish carriages or promenaded to see and be seen, to enjoy the trees, the swans on the lakes, and the flowers arranged in artificial beds. The purpose changed as time went on and now, surrounded by the city and with automobiles seeking the nearest way, many of the stately parks are losing their original restful nature and are in danger of becoming mere thoroughfares. Rock Creek Park in Washington, Golden Gate Park in San Francisco, Druid Hill Park in Baltimore, and Lincoln Park in Chicago are sharing the fate of Central Park in this regard.

So long as people travelled with horse and buggy, parks in the cities or on the outskirts were ample, but since the automobile has "broken the bonds of the city" it has become possible for many people to visit beaches, parks, forest preserves, and reservations of natural scenery at considerable distances from the city. To meet this need larger tracts for more extensive uses have been established, of which the Chicago Forest Preserves are a good example. These forests are managed from a recreational standpoint, and in spite of rather intensive use their forest character has been preserved and enhanced.

The recreational land considered so far has been urban and metropolitan. In 1930 the 1,070 cities with a population of 5,000 or more reported a total recreational area of all types of 308,805 acres, or an acre for every 208 persons. Planners have set the goal at one acre for every 100 persons and a similar ratio for the metropolitan *area,* i.e., roughly 50 miles from the center of the metropolitan "district," which is defined by the United States Census as the central city, satellite cities, and all the intervening and adjacent open territory having a population density of at least 150 people per square mile.[2]

Parks in the Metropolitan Area. People who drive with some objective are often looking for a restful spot for a picnic or where the children can play. Since the range of the average driver of

[1] *The Central Park,* by the Central Park Association (New York, Thomas Seltzer, 1926), pp. 22–23.

[2] *N. R. B. Report,* p. 146.

this type is about 100 miles during a day's vacation, other parks should be available within this range. It has been suggested that within this radius enough open spaces be provided to equal the area of all the cities, a total for the United States of about 9,000,000 acres.[1] Parks and parkways planned for this class of driver will relieve the pressure on the private land for recreational purposes. Iowa's plan of a county and state park within driving distance of every citizen, rural or urban, sets up a commendable standard.

Granting the need for parks and other recreational facilities within the metropolitan area, the question arises as to which units of government shall furnish the land and bear the expense. The central city usually has the finances and power to create parks within its jurisdiction, but its people also use the recreational facilities of the entire region. Smaller cities and villages may have areas of great natural beauty, lakes, or beaches which should be developed as public recreational grounds but may not be financially able to do so. More often they refuse because, while the costs fall on them, the benefit goes to the entire region and especially to the central city. Rural towns and counties usually take the same position.

One way to overcome this is to form a metropolitan park district. This was done in 1893 in Boston, where a metropolitan park commission was created so that in "the important matters of a wise provision for outdoor recreation and the preservation of forest, shore and river front, Boston and its neighbors are in effect a single community." [2]

County Parks. Another way to provide these facilities is to enlist the larger units of government, particularly the state and the county. About 100,000 acres of county parks were reported in 1930. The majority of the counties reporting one or more county parks lie in metropolitan regions. However, many rural counties have established park systems by setting aside scenic areas, picnic grounds, beaches, and other areas designed primarily for the enjoyment of local people.

State Parks. Almost 4,000,000 acres are in state parks which, because of their accessibility to large congested populations, are

[1] *Ibid.*

[2] Harlean James, *Land Planning in the United States for City, State, and Nation* (New York, Macmillan, 1926), p. 250.

visited by more people annually than all the federal parks and forests put together.[1] However, the term "parks" includes a great variety of types of recreational land—small areas surrounding a monument or historic building, and mere picnic and camping grounds, as well as areas which meet the test of having unique or unusual natural features. Some contain historic or prehistoric sites or unique botanic and forest conditions which should not be exposed to intensive recreational uses at all. These should really be made "state monuments." Too often the various uses are hopelessly mixed on a small area. Wherever a park has multiple uses it is recommended that intensive uses be isolated from the others. Administrators, however, often have to compromise to satisfy the different demands made upon the park by the vacationing public.

National Parks. The National Park Service administers areas of superlative scenery or of outstanding historic, prehistoric, or scientific importance. It has under its jurisdiction over 15,000,000 acres. Beginning with the Yellowstone in 1872 the number of parks has grown to 24. The service also administers 67 national monuments and 37 other areas such as military parks, battle sites, and cemeteries.

National parks are "areas inclosing scenery of quality so unusual and impressive or containing natural features so extraordinary as to possess national interest and importance contradistinguished from local interest." This standard differentiates national from state parks and is an ideal to which the Park Service has tried to adhere, in spite of the pressure from localities which realize on the monetary value of having a park in the neighborhood. Strict adherence to this standard means that national parks must be located where nature has placed features of impressive or unusual scenery and not necessarily where the most people live which is not a handicap to the true purpose of *preserving* these natural wonders. The danger lies in the growing intensification of the use of national parks. The attendance has jumped from a few hundred thousands to millions of people, many of whom have no interest in the parks as nature. They visit them because it is a "trophy" of their vacation. Roads are demanded so that they can get around fast "and enter in their little books a schedule of

[1] *N. R. B. Report,* p. 146.

having seen this, that and the other object."[1] Wild life is threatened or becomes semi-domesticated and Coney Island features are introduced to cater to the amusement addict and souvenir hunter. Private residences are found in some of our national parks and there is pressure for more. There is also the constant threat of private interests against the holding of these areas for public use. "Not a Congress has passed for at least 20 years without the introduction of one measure or more providing that water rights in a park be under one condition or another assigned to some particular interest or individual."[2] Other pressures are for private mining and lumbering rights. The state parks are beset with similar dangers.

National Monuments. These are primarily of historical or archaeological interest, usually smaller, and lacking the distinction of parks. The Petrified National Monument is an example. Forty square miles of petrified forest have been set aside for this monument and the taking of specimens, hunting, and shooting are prohibited in this area. Another example is the first farm entered under the Homestead Act of 1862 by Daniel Freeman in Nebraska. Many states have likewise preserved their former capitols, battlefields, Indian mounds, and unusual or historic trees as "parks."

Forests. The forest permeates a great many forms of outdoor recreation. It is an important element in the landscape whether found in city parks, tree-lined streets, country roads, or wilderness and primeval areas. The tourist enjoys trees as they line the highway or appear in wood lots, shelter belts, or private and public forests. Michigan creates a forest environment by leaving a strip of timber on each side of the road or planting these margins with trees. The forest furnishes sport for the hunter and fisherman and that "contact with the eternally young soul of nature, which helps, as nothing else can, to preserve in us the spirit of youth which we so desperately need in the fight against age which we must all make from the hour of our birth."[3] It adds to the qualities of

[1] Henry Baldwin Ward, "What Is Happening to Our National Parks?" *Conservation,* July–August, 1938, p. 21.

[2] *Ibid.* See also Struthers Burt, "Damnable Damming," *Hunting and Fishing,* November, 1938.

[3] Glenn Frank, "Forests and America's Future," *American Forests and Forest Life,* December, 1930, pp. 743–44.

other forms of scenery. A lake or stream without trees on its banks loses most of its charm. Some timber owners now leave belts of timber around the lakes instead of clearing to the water's edge. Even mountains and the seashore become more pleasing and charming when trees are part of the landscape.

Public forests in general are managed so as to include recreation as one of their several purposes. Many municipal and town forests and forest preserves are used almost entirely for outdoor recreation. The Adirondack State Park is the outstanding example.

State and national forests try to co-ordinate the three uses: commercial, protective, and recreational. In the management of federal forests recreation is considered "dominant" in areas of exceptional scenery or of natural and historic interest, or in areas which have or are likely to have intensive use by large numbers of people. No other uses are permitted to interfere with the dominant use. In areas where recreation is less important the uses may be co-ordinated or recreation is subordinated to other forest purposes. One reason for this restriction on recreation is the fire hazard. The wide use of federal forests by the public can be judged by the increase from 3,000,000 to 32,000,000 annual visitors between 1917 and 1931.

The Administration of Recreational Land. The practical management of recreational land is beset with difficulties. It is important that recreational opportunities be made available within the region of population concentration. Here it is necessary to plan for the maximum population, rural and urban, and to select the accessible areas which will be needed before they are used for other purposes and before their natural features are wholly or partially destroyed. Furthermore, land values rise even for submarginal farm land within metropolitan areas, and the longer the purchase is postponed the more expensive the land becomes. It is therefore desirable to acquire recreational areas before they are needed; the ripening costs have to be borne by the governments involved.

The second problem is the question of which unit of government is to provide and maintain the parks, forests, beaches, and other public recreational land. The expenses involved are considerable. The parks and playgrounds of New York City are costing $250,000 a year merely to repair the damage caused by "barbarians" who destroy trees, shrubs, benches, swings, and buildings.[1] To cover some of these costs it has been suggested that a charge be made for the use of the parks, zoos, and playgrounds. This is contrary to the spirit of public recreation. However, a charge for services, such as parking space or the rental of recreational equipment, is not unreasonable.

Whenever the purpose of a park is the preservation of natural historic or prehistoric features the location must be determined by these features, without much regard to their accessibility or the number of people who want to or are able to use them. However, administrators of such areas feel that they get support for their work in proportion to the number of people who visit the park. If 500,000 people visit Yosemite they become evidence that the park is "justified." However, this requires the introduction of facilities for transportation and for the comfort and convenience of the crowd, which in turn impairs the primary objective of the park. On the other hand, the Park Service has made admirable use of its opportunity to educate the numerous visitors by means of guided trips, campfire lectures, publications, museums, and special exhibits at strategic places. Similar programs are being offered in public forests, municipal and state parks.[2]

Another unsettled problem is that of overlapping jurisdiction of the various governmental departments. Seven or eight separate agencies of the federal government are administering recreational land and these are not always co-ordinated with state and local programs.

PRIVATE RECREATIONAL LAND

Mountains, waters, forests, and a favorable climate have attracted men from immemorial times to purchase land for private recreational purposes. "Watering places" were famous early in our history, and Florida, Colorado, and California have long been renowned for their recreational attractions. In 1846, even before all of the Northwest Territory had attained statehood, William Cullen Bryant visited Mackinac Island and wrote that people had

[1] *New York Times*, editorial, October 6, 1938.

[2] See "Educational Recreation," in Part XI of the *Supplementary Report* of the Land Planning Committee to the National Resources Committee (1938), pp. 242–49. F. W. Luening, "Undertones in the Forest Symphony," *Journal of Forestry*, Sept., 1939.

already begun "to repair here for rest and refreshment from the southern borders of Lake Michigan."[1]

Private recreational land and structures may be divided into two broad classes, "commercial" and "non-commercial," but the line of distinction is not always exact. Among the former are hotels—sometimes a single structure, sometimes with cottages for rent. In many places individual cottages may be leased. "Taking in summer boarders" is another phase of the same activity. Private or commercial beaches, summer theaters, dance halls, and picnic grounds also fall in this class. Summer camps for boys and girls operated by the Scouts, religious organizations, or by private individuals for profit are semi-public in their nature.

The non-commercial lands include: (1) estates with large areas of land and elaborate buildings generally in the vicinity of large cities, the typical "play farms" of the wealthy, (2) summer homes which range all the way from $100,000 establishments, similar to estates, to modest homes and cottages, (3) recreational clubs for golf, hunting, fishing, yachting, and (4) beaches and general recreation.

Geography of Recreation. Land selected for private recreation consists primarily of mountainous or hilly forested land commanding elevation and scenery and riparian land on the oceans, the Great Lakes, inland lakes, or streams. In Connecticut estates are found principally in the vicinity of New York City and in the picturesque Berkshire Hills. Summer home buyers are attracted to the Berkshires but the heaviest concentration is along Long Island Sound. In the Southern Peninsula of Michigan about 40 per cent of the recreational lands are on the shores of the Great Lakes and the remainder principally on inland lakes. In Wisconsin private recreational land occupies a thin fringe on inland lakes, along some of the larger streams, as well as on the shores of the Great Lakes.[2]

However, not all lake shore property is capable of "resort development." Well wooded, high shores or sandy beaches suitable for bathing are in the greatest demand. Many beautiful clear-water lakes are almost devoid of fish, whereas lakes with low swampy shores and abundant vegetation provide ideal condi-

[1] E. O. Wood, *Historic Mackinac* (New York, Macmillan, 1918), II, 401.

[2] Whetten and Rapport, *op. cit.*, pp. 9–10; Hedrick, *op. cit.*, pp. 15, 31–36; Wehrwein and Parsons, *op. cit.*, pp. 4–6.

tions and food for fish but are almost useless for summer homes and resorts.

For the northern recreational areas a cool climate, especially cool nights, and dry sunshiny weather are ideal. The fact that frosts can be expected at any time during the summer in some of the northernmost counties of the Lake states curtails agriculture and even slows up forest growth but attracts summer visitors trying to escape the heat and humidity of the Corn Belt. The Lower Peninsula of Michigan has the same level of temperatures in July as Florida has in January. The southern regions attract the northerners during the winter by their mild balmy climate and ocean beaches, while the West has become famous for its dude ranches.

Recreation as a Land Use. Aside from the money brought into geographically favored regions by tourists, the use of land for recreation has other beneficial effects. In the first place, recreational land is absorbing large areas of substandard agricultural land. In New England farm abandonment has taken place primarily on hilly and rough land, exactly the kind of land suitable for reforestation and recreation. This means that these land uses are complementary rather than conflicting; only near cities or on the coast have recreational uses encroached on farm land. In Connecticut roughly 313,000 acres or 10 per cent of the total area of the state is in private recreational land—and 416,000 acres or one-eighth of the state if public lands are also included. Over 10 per cent of Washington County, R. I., is classed as recreational land. These New England figures are naturally exceptionally high and cannot be duplicated in sparsely settled areas.[1]

Recreational property had an unusual boom in the Lake states about 1925. Speculators were buying "anything called a lake lot." This boom created the impression that recreational land would absorb the bulk of the idle and tax-delinquent lands and solve the "land problem" for these states. However, a study of the possible development of this form of land use in the two best Wisconsin resort counties made it clear that only 8.5 per cent of the land area of one and 15.7 per cent of the area of the other could expect to become private recreational land unless game preserves absorbed non-riparian lands. In other words, from 84

[1] Whetten and Rapport, *op. cit.*, pp. 35–36.

to 93 per cent of the land had to find uses other than for private recreation even in the most favored counties.[1]

Although recreational lands occupy limited areas they hold a position in the tax base out of all proportion to their size. Riparian land suitable for resorts and summer homes is scarce and is bought and sold at front foot values like urban property. In Washington County, R. I., recreational land makes up three-eighths of the entire valuation of the county, and is assessed at almost $460 per acre, in contrast to about $44 per acre for the land not in recreational uses.[2] In many localities of the resort areas of Wisconsin and Michigan private recreational lands pay from one-half to more than three-fourths of all the property taxes. So important is this form of real estate in Connecticut that the value of all farm property in 1930 was only about 11 per cent greater than the total recreational real estate values.[3]

Finally, recreation offers employment in combination with agriculture and forestry. The further development of a forest-farm-recreation economy is especially significant in marginal areas where part-time work is important to the farmers on small or partly cleared farms or to those on substandard soils. Summer visitors must be housed and fed and farmers are finding a local market for milk, eggs, chickens, and other farm products at hotels, resorts, and summer homes. Those with lake shore property have sometimes built cottages for lease. Others rent tourist rooms to tourists or take in boarders, although the automobile seems to have destroyed the traditional New England "summer boarder type of business."[4] Farmers and members of their families also find employment in the building trades, in stores, garages, hotels, and resorts, on golf courses, as guides, in renting boats and selling bait.

Problems of Private Recreational Land. One of the problems associated with private recreational land is excessive and premature subdividing of lake shore property. Usually the plat is so planned that all lots face the lake, but sometimes "wildcat" operators lay out hundreds and even thousands of small lots only

[1] Wehrwein and Parsons, *op. cit.*, pp. 20–24.

[2] W. R. Gordon, and B. E. Gilbert, *Recreation and the Use of Land in Washington County* (Rhode Island Agric. Exp. Station Bulletin 258, 1937), pp. 41–51.

[3] Whetten and Rapport, *op. cit.*, p. 36.

[4] Gordon and Gilbert, *op. cit.*, p. 70.

a few of which are riparian. Access is inadequately furnished by reserving a part of the shore for public use.

Over half of the 16,000 registered lots in three northern Wisconsin counties were laid out between 1923 and 1928, all of which had to be carried on the tax rolls as separate descriptions. When the boom collapsed over 9,000 or almost 56 per cent of all these lots remained unsold and became tax delinquent. The cost of advertising and selling them was more than the counties received in taxes on the remainder of the lots.

Because lots are often made too small, problems of health, sanitation, and congestion arise at the very place where people expect to find fresh air, sunshine, and healthful and unpolluted waters. Sometimes the promoter has made ample provisions against such contingencies and enforced them through private deed restrictions. "In other instances, residents already located have organized themselves into informal as well as legal associations and have adopted a set of building restrictions, inaugurated programs of road building, extended light, power and water facilities, erected club and bath houses. Real estate companies have not infrequently made requirements as to minimum cost and type of building that may be erected to insure a desired standard of development. Towns have made similar stipulations and enforced restrictions." [1]

Densely settled areas have available an array of measures to control land uses; the problem is more difficult in sparsely settled areas under rural forms of government and usually without adequate machinery for enforcement. In Wisconsin control over platted subdivisions was made statewide in 1927 for those counties in which plats are not subject to the jurisdiction of cities or county park commissions.[2] This law requires the submission of plats to the State Board of Health, the Real Estate Brokers Board, and the Director of Regional Planning, thereby giving these bodies a chance to check wildcat and unsatisfactory plats. Under a Lake and Stream Shore Platting and Sanitation Code the Board of Health has insisted on riparian lots with at least 60-foot frontages and a minimum area of 8,000 square feet. The width of roads is prescribed and the proportion of the lot which can be

[1] Gordon and Gilbert, *op. cit.*, p. 21.

[2] *Wisconsin Revised Statutes*, 1937, Chap. 236.

covered by the building. Rules in regard to sanitation, water supply, cesspools, garbage and refuse disposal have been laid down which must be entered in the deeds to the property as restrictions and filed with the plat for approval.[1]

A second form of control employed in the farm-forest-recreation region of Wisconsin is zoning. Nine counties have established "recreation districts" involving about 380,000 acres of land. These districts are modified forestry preserves which, in addition to the usual forest and recreational uses, also permit yearlong residence so that owners of resort property or their managers or caretakers can maintain a permanent residence. All other uses are excluded—business, industry, and agriculture. Farms are prohibited because of the fire hazard incident to land clearing and to preserve the amenities of the lake shores as already described. This is still rather rudimentary zoning but indicates the possibilities of regulating land in the interest of recreation. The conservancy districts of Jefferson County are essentially residential-recreational districts excluding many uses ordinarily associated with recreation, such as taverns, hotels, tourist camps, and billboards.

[1] Wisconsin Platting and Sanitation Code (4th ed., revised, 1938).

WATER RESOURCES

Laws, customs, and institutions governing the use of water are as old as civilization and have grown in volume and complexity as more people came to use the same source of water. Springs and wells were among the first forms of property of nomads. In arid regions irrigation laws were evolved to solve the complicated problem of the conflicting claims to a limited supply of water. A different set of laws developed under the humid conditions of England and northern Europe. Therefore, in discussing the utilization of water as a resource or the use of land as affected by water, the legal and institutional framework is basic. The discussion in this book is not intended to serve as a treatise on water rights; rather, it will be directed toward showing how these rights affect the utilization of both land and water.

Man is concerned with water because of its destructive as well as beneficial aspects. On the beneficial side are its functions in plant growth, in irrigation, and in domestic, industrial, and urban uses, all of which diminish the volume or change the nature of the water; and its use for fisheries, navigation, water power, and recreation, which do not consume or modify to any appreciable extent the substance of water. Where water becomes relatively scarce many of these uses conflict. Irrigation may deprive cities of water for domestic and industrial purposes, or it may lower a stream sufficiently to injure navigation. Hence the development of laws and institutions governing irrigation control.[1]

FLOOD CONTROL

The impression prevails that floods are the result of the destruction of forests and the "unbalancing" of land use through human occupation. However, De Soto encountered floods on the Mississippi in 1543, and many other inundations are on

[1] This is indicated by the very titles of two books dealing with irrigation: Mead, *Irrigation Institutions, op. cit.*, and Thomas, *The Development of Institutions under Irrigation, op. cit.*

record before the Mississippi Valley was settled.[1] Nevertheless, destruction of human life and of property could take place only after man had encroached on the flood plains and deltas and after the fertile lands and other commercial advantages had lured him to locate farms and cities in the path of inundations. Moreover, there is ample evidence that the modification of the earth by man has seriously affected the relation of water to land and has exaggerated flood conditions.[2] Many solutions have been suggested, and the first efforts "to keep the river from the door" were by levees.

Levees. As early as 1717 levees were begun at New Orleans; in fact, land grants by the King of France were conditioned on the building of levees by the planters, and in the early history of Louisiana police juries compelled all who lived within seven miles of the river to work on the dikes. Up to 1850 the riparian owners were still building levees privately with little direct aid from counties and parishes but with some supervision by those local units of government. This meant piecemeal building, and the gaps between the levees were invitations for the river to enter upon the land.

The second step was the creation of levee districts in the 1850's, under state statutes. These districts carried the brunt of flood control until about 1927. They were political units, having the power to levy taxes and issue bonds against the property of the district, to use eminent domain to condemn land, and to own the levees and other property needed for flood control. As a rule they were loosely supervised by a state board of engineers.[3] The legal framework was similar to that of drainage or irrigation districts.

Levee building was interrupted by the Civil War and the reconstruction period. During the war both armies demolished levees on the plea of military necessity, and after the war a series of floods continued the process of destruction. By 1870 the levee districts were impoverished. The taxable value of the land in

[1] E. A. Sherman, *The Protection Forests of the Mississippi River Watershed and Their Part in Flood Prevention,* (U. S. Dept. of Agriculture, Circular 37, April, 1928, p. 3); Arthur DeWitt Frank, *Development of the Federal Program of Flood Control on the Mississippi River, op. cit.,* pp. 13–15; Ben Hibbs, "Water to the Sea," *Country Gentleman,* June, 1937.

[2] See Chap. II.

[3] A. D. Frank, *op. cit.,* pp. 15–16, 137–40.

1870 was only 25 per cent of that in 1860, and more than half of the fertile Yazoo Valley had reverted to the state for taxes.

The Swamp Land Act was the first attempt to share the burden of flood control with larger units of government. Had the states lived up to the intent of this law, sold the 64,000,000 acres of land granted to them by the federal government at a substantial figure, and used the proceeds to protect and drain the lands, much soil might have been reclaimed, either by aiding local districts or by direct state flood control and drainage. However, by 1870 the lands had been sold and the money spent for other purposes. The people of the Mississippi Valley now turned directly to the federal government for assistance. The Mississippi River Commission was created in 1879. Money was granted to the levee districts with the requirement that a certain proportion of the costs should be raised locally. All this was done under the guise of assisting navigation; not until 1917 was money appropriated directly for flood control. This was not a serious matter, however, since levee building was necessary for both purposes.

The Mississippi River Commission's plan for flood control was "levees only," the method approved by the United States Army engineers ever since 1822. It is true that floods broke through the crevasses from time to time, but the reason given was that the system was not complete or that the levees had not been brought to standard height and base. For a long period no great floods came and the people in the lower valley felt secure behind their earthen walls. The rude awakening came in 1927 when the water poured through 225 crevasses and inundated 18,000 square miles. The direct and indirect losses in property are placed at about half a billion dollars. Only the heroic work of the Red Cross and other agencies kept the loss of life as low as 250 deaths.

The layman who reads of the success of accepted forms of flood control on other rivers is inclined to agree with a statement made in 1852 that the Mississippi "seems to defy all acknowledged laws of hydrodynamics" and "frequently disappoints calculations based upon recognized principles."[1] Part of the difficulty lies in the nature and extent of the Mississippi drainage. It includes

[1] A. D. Frank, *op. cit.*, p. 99, quoting Senate Executive Document 49, 32d Congress, 1st Session, 1852, p. 30.

41 per cent of the area of the United States and lies in thirty-one states or parts of states. Practically all the run-off of this gigantic area is funneled through the Mississippi below Cairo. Only the Arkansas, the Red, and a few other minor rivers join the "Father of Waters" below this point. Thus the area which suffers most from floods contributes the least. As Charles Ellet pointed out in 1852, "The process by which the country above is relieved is that by which the country below is ruined,"—implying that the control of floods on the Mississippi is of nation-wide concern.[1]

The flood of 1927 brought sharp criticisms upon the "levees only" policy. Gifford Pinchot called it "the most colossal blunder in engineering history."[2] The critics of levees pointed out that to confine a river which normally spreads over fifty miles of flood plain between dikes only a mile or more apart simply "sets the river on edge." After all, water is a "solid fluid." Formerly great natural outlets—the secondary channels—relieved the main stream, but these were closed by levees as early as 1844. The only remedy was "bigger and better levees." Some critics claim that there is a physical limit to the height of dikes because the delta soil cannot support the weight of high earthen structures, especially on the wet ground of old sloughs and lake beds. This, however, is stoutly denied.[3] More sinister, if true, is the contention that, since the Mississippi is an aggrading stream below Cairo, its bed is rising and is becoming higher than the surrounding flood plain. This is scornfully dismissed by the engineers, who claim that the surveys made in 1882, 1894, and 1904 indicate no significant change in the cross section of the river; the bed has neither risen nor "scoured."[4] However, students of sedimentation maintain that the gradual raising of the bed of the river, beginning with the delta, is inevitable.

Forests and Flood Prevention. The question has been raised many times of whether it is not more feasible to *prevent* floods in the vast territory which contributes the water than to *control*

[1] A. D. Frank, *op. cit.*, p. 25.

[2] *Manufacturer's Record*, June 9, 1927, p. 55.

[3] See William H. Haas, "The Mississippi River—Asset or Liability," *Economic Geography*, July, 1931, pp. 257–58; A. D. Frank, *op. cit.*, pp. 127–28; "The Problem of Mississippi River Flood Control," *The Staple Cotton Review*, February, 1937, pp. 8–9.

[4] A. D. Frank, *op. cit.*, pp. 128–29.

floods by levees or other engineering works after the water has reached the lower Mississippi. Following the 1927 flood the role of forests in flood prevention was hotly debated and still is. The Mississippi River Commission recognized the beneficent effect of trees as an aid to flood prevention but it was not willing to build a complete flood control policy on forests. Some of the critics of the "forest-flood" policy claim that measurements on the Merrimac River of New England indicate little or no relation between deforestation and stream flow and assert that cultivated land has as much protective influence as forests. They also point out that floods swept over the Mississippi Valley before the land was settled and that it would take 533,000 square miles of forests to reduce the height of a flood at Memphis by one foot. Furthermore, when the ground is saturated or covered with sleet and ice, forests can do little to hold a heavy rainfall such as fell in January, 1937, or during the Dayton flood of 1913. Foresters, in general, recognize the necessity for levees, reservoirs, and by-passes as flood control measures.[1]

Even granting the function of the forest as a means of preventing floods, it happens that most of the land in the Mississippi Valley is suitable for agriculture. This precludes keeping the Corn Belt and a large part of the Lake states in forests or permanent grasses. However, the areas most likely to produce floods—the steep, rocky, and impervious soils, usually submarginal for agriculture—may easily be placed in forests for both "production" and "protection" purposes. This was recognized in the Weeks law of 1911 which was the first act authorizing the federal purchase of forest lands but was restricted to the buying of areas considered vital for the protection of watersheds of navigable streams.

Reservoirs for Flood Control. The Report of the Inland Waterways Commission of 1908 said that the only "logical way to control a river" was to control the water in the tributaries, and the only way to prevent floods was to build reservoirs to "catch and temporarily hold the flood waters." This idea is also em-

[1] *Ibid.*, pp. 110–12. *Relation of Forestry to the Control of Floods in the Mississippi Valley*, House Document 573, 70th Congress, 2d Session, 1929, pp. 50–51; Hibbs, *op. cit.*, p. 8.

bodied in the plans suggested by *Little Waters,* but not as an exclusive method of erosion and flood prevention.[1]

Probably the best known reservoir system is the Miami Conservancy District in Ohio established after the Dayton flood. Flood waters are held in five reservoirs and gradually released so as not to inundate the lands and cities below. At other times the reservoirs are empty. The district was organized under the Ohio law of 1914 making conservancy districts political subdivisions of the state with the right to tax all lands benefited; in fact, power has been granted to assess even lands outside of the district. The land in the retention basins (which are flooded when the dams are filled) was bought by the district, and the farms were rearranged, the buildings moved to higher ground, and the land resold subject to flood easements. Some of the farms which are flooded only in part were not purchased but flood easements were obtained from the owners. Roads, railways, and even a village were relocated. Easements were obtained on 25,000 acres and 30,000 acres bought outright.[2] The Muskingum and other Ohio river valleys are now building reservoirs under Ohio conservancy district plans.

Although the effectiveness of reservoirs to control floods on the smaller streams has been proved, grave doubts are expressed as to their feasibility on larger rivers or their ability to prevent floods on the main stream, even though the tributaries are under conservancy districts. Engineers claim that all the reservoirs built or under construction in the state of Ohio will have only a minor effect on the volume of the Ohio River. Besides, the cost is considered to be too great. It was estimated that it would cost $1,292,000,000 to build enough reservoirs on the head waters of the tributaries of the Mississippi to reduce the height of floods 5.7 feet at Cairo and 5.4 feet at the mouth of the Red River.[3] However, sentiment is more liberal today than it was 10 years ago

[1] *Inland Waterways Commission Report,* Senate Document 325, 60th Congress, 1st Session, 1908, p. 451; Person, *et al., Little Waters* (Soil Conservation Service, *et al.,* 1935), pp. 57–69.

[2] S. Graham Smith, "The Conservancy Lands," *Miami Conservancy Bulletin,* December, 1923.

The value of the sediment which floods were expected to bring to the farms in the retention basins was exploited when the district advertised "Inexhaustible Farms for Sale." *Bulletin,* April, 1920.

[3] A. D. Frank, *op. cit.,* p. 107.

in favor of reservoirs as an aid to control but not as an exclusive measure to eliminate floods.[1]

A subject much debated is whether it is feasible to combine power development with flood control; if this can be done the current can help pay for the cost of the dam. This idea was rejected in the Miami Conservancy District and generally is not considered advisable by engineers because the two purposes are in conflict. To control floods the reservoirs should be empty when the inundation starts so as to hold back as much water as possible. On the other hand, power dams must be kept filled to provide a continuous "head." [2] The two purposes are nevertheless combined by the Tennessee Valley Authority by providing additional height above the part of the dam used for power. The Norris Dam has 137 feet of water for power purposes but an additional 79 feet can impound over 2,000,000 acre-feet of water before the water flows over the dam.[3]

The "Outlet" Method of Flood Control. The plan of reducing the volume in the river by allowing the water to follow its old secondary channels was generally opposed by engineers before 1927 because they were afraid that the secondary channel might become the new channel and with the decreased velocity sedimentation might take place in the main stream below the "break." However, the relief which New Orleans experienced in 1922 and again in 1927 after the levees were broken demonstrated the feasibility of outlets. The flood control plan finally adopted as a result of the 1927 disaster included floodways in addition to levees. One of these "safety valves" is in southeastern Missouri, another in southern Arkansas and northern Louisiana, two are in the Atchafalaya River in Louisiana, and the last is the Bonnet Carre spillway which takes water out of the Mississippi into Lake Pontchartrain.

"Comprehensive" Flood Control. Senator Newlands, Gifford Pinchot, J. Russell Smith, and others have been ardent supporters of a comprehensive plan which would rely not on any one technique but on all methods of flood prevention and control, coordinated to obtain the maximum results. Even if this principle

[1] Person, *et al., op. cit.,* pp. 38–39.

[2] A. D. Frank, *op. cit.,* p. 108.

[3] Harold L. Ickes, "In Defense of the New Deal Power Program," *New York Times Magazine,* November 7, 1937, p. 23.

is accepted the problem still remains of determining how much the nation can afford to spend for flood control and, with only a given sum available for this purpose, how to allocate the money to reforestation, reservoirs, levees, spillways, etc., so as to get the maximum prevention and regulation. Because of the widely different approaches of foresters, engineers, economists, and others, the complexion of the board or commission entrusted with "comprehensive" flood control would have much to do with determining the technique or combination of methods that are employed.

It should be pointed out that the discussion so far has dealt almost exclusively with the Mississippi. Many other regions in the United States need flood control, and methods considered inadequate for our largest river may be quite suitable for rivers with different characteristics.

Economic and Legal Aspects of Flood Control. Legal and economic questions are raised when flood waters encroach on land uses either temporarily or permanently. The Miami Conservancy District is an example of the adjustment of property rights. The question also appears when land is flooded through outlets or spillways. The Jadwin plan of 1928 had no provision for the payment of damages or flowage rights, on "the theory that floodways were natural outlets that had been appropriated by man, who must suffer the servitude imposed, and, therefore, could not expect damages when the flood waters were turned upon him." [1] This is an interesting attitude toward "natural outlets appropriated by man." Were the same philosophy extended to include the entire area naturally flooded and appropriated by man, governments in general would have no responsibility for flood control. For a while Congress did nothing about floodway damages but finally made the states responsible for acquiring flood rights or easements or for paying damages to landowners.

The assumption of responsibility for flood control by the nation as a whole is an important change in policy which has significant implications. Before 1927 all federal funds had to be matched by local contributions. However, because of the heavy losses to local districts on the Mississippi during the flood of 1927 and the fact that they had already contributed $242,000,000 and

[1] A. D. Frank, *op. cit.*, p. 226; also pp. 224, 242, 250–52.

the federal government only $71,000,000, Congress decided that the latter should bear the entire expense of the new projects. Federal aid has since been extended to other rivers, which means that flood control is practically on the same status as irrigation, navigation, and "rivers and harbors." The arid states watched this trend with some alarm as early as 1904 because they saw in it a rival for appropriations for irrigation.[1]

To frustrate "pork barrel" methods in flood control, the Water Planning Committee of the National Resources Board has recommended that federal appropriations be made: "(a) only where there is reasonable protection against maximum floods; (b) only where the total benefits justify the expense; (c) only where there are responsible and legally constituted authorities with which to deal; (d) to an extent not greater than 30 per cent of the cost of labor and materials where the benefits are chiefly local; (e) to an extent greater than 30 per cent only in proportion to benefits definitely applicable to recognize national interests; (f) to a full 100 per cent only where the benefits are almost wholly of national interest." [2]

The provision that flood control should be undertaken "only where the total benefits justify the expense" is an important one. The cost of building levees is a cost of "producing" the land protected by them and the annual expense of maintaining them is a part of the yearly input of labor and capital. At what point will the reclamation and maintenance costs overtop the value they create? As long as this was the individual responsibility of the riparian owner he made the decision and took his loss if he had miscalculated. Shifting the burden to levee districts did not shift the burden to Santa Claus; it merely came home in taxes. It is estimated that by January 1, 1928, the total indebtedness of the levee districts was $820,000,000, which far exceeded the assessed valuation of the districts. In this they resembled many drainage and irrigation districts.

However, with the burden transferred in whole or in part to

[1] *Ibid.*, p. 82.

[2] *N. R. B. Report, op. cit.*, p. 273. There are as yet few guiding principles in determining the benefits of flood control. See Gilbert F. White, "The Limit of Economic Justification for Flood Protection," *Journal of Land and Public Utility Economics*, May, 1936, pp. 133–48, and H. L. Lutz, "Financing Flood Control Measures in the Mississippi Valley," *ibid.*, May, 1929, pp. 169–75.

the federal government the question of feasibility is easily forgotten. It has been said that "flood control is a matter of money and earth, each in sufficient volume and properly applied." [1] The question raised by the editor of the *Engineering News Record,* December 29, 1927, still awaits an answer: Is it good economy to spend a third of a billion dollars to save land worth a half billion dollars when there is so little need for agricultural land? [2] However, wholesale evacuation and "giving the land back to the river" will hardly be feasible in the Mississippi Valley since so much money has already been spent to reclaim some of the richest land in the South. Besides, not only farm land but railroads, roads, industries, and even cities may be involved. Here protection is justified, yet it may be more feasible to relocate these man-made elements than to try to protect them against inundation. It is proposed to move Shawneetown, Illinois, four miles to a new site twenty-five feet above the record watermark of the Ohio, and a new city is planned for the inhabitants.[3]

Since flood control is now more or less a federal function, it has become a part of the national *land* policy. All new projects may well be examined from the standpoint of whether it would not be cheaper to buy such farms as are subject to floods, and use the land for forests and recreation.

Zoning may be used to correct and direct land uses so that they will fit the natural regimen of streams. In 1937 the Wisconsin county zoning law was amended to permit county boards "to regulate, restrict and determine the areas along natural water courses, channels, streams and creeks in which trades and industries, and the location of buildings for specified uses may be prohibited." Under this law county ordinances may restrict the encroachment of buildings and industries on river areas subject to floods. Existing structures remain as non-conforming uses which, with depreciation and obsolescence, will eventually be eliminated. Since the act permits the regulation of land uses in general, restricted districts can be set up along rivers in which

[1] A. D. Frank, *op. cit.*, p. 220.

[2] Based upon the assessed valuation of $504,000,000 on the 17,000,000 acres in the 31 levee districts, and new flood control appropriations estimated at $300,000,000. The Jones-Reid bill passed in 1928 carried an appropriation of $325,000,000. This does not take into consideration the $363,000,000 spent by local and federal governments before 1927.

[3] *New York Times,* July 18, 1937.

agriculture and residences are prohibited and forests, wild life, recreation, and other land uses not damaged by floods may be encouraged. Non-conforming uses may be purchased, as is suggested for the marginal land areas.[1] Cities may also use the zoning power in a similar manner to direct their growth away from the flooded areas.

But the problem of floods is related not only to land use but to water use. Is the rushing of water to the oceans as smoothly and swiftly as possible making the best use of the water? The question has been raised whether this is good "conservation"; should it not be restrained to add to the percolating water or used for water power en route? The answer to these questions rests upon the findings of physical scientists and engineers before the economic phases can be appraised.

NAVIGATION

The beneficial uses of water are of two types—*usufructuary* and *proprietary*. The former includes navigation, water power, and fisheries, in which people have only rights in the water as it flows by, rights in the *use* of an unstable and transitory property object. In the latter the ownership tends to be in the substance of the water itself. Irrigation water and water for domestic, municipal, and industrial uses are examples.

Of all the uses for water, navigation is usually paramount, and if other uses conflict with it, they must give way. A navigable body of water is a public highway for commerce and pleasure. This gives the public the right to take ice, to fish, and to use the water for navigation subject only to the police regulations of the state. No impassable obstructions such as dams or bridges may be built on a navigable stream unless provision is made for free navigation. Locks have to be constructed to permit boats to pass around a dam and bridges are built so they can be opened to allow the passage of vessels. The city of Chicago maintains almost fifty bridges of the jack-knife or drawbridge type to permit a few sand barges and similar craft to use the river.

[1] The Jefferson County, Wisconsin, ordinance has the provision "that no building or structure shall hereafter be erected or structurally altered adjacent to any lake or stream unless it be so situated that the basement floor shall be above the high water mark." This applies to the entire county insofar as the towns have approved the ordinance. This is an example of "flood zoning" under the enabling act as amended. Albers, "New Uses for County Zoning," *op. cit.*, pp. 460–62.

The Rights of the Public in Navigable Waters. The rights of the public in a navigable stream include public regulation, controlling and directing the flow of streams, the right to impede and accelerate the flow, to deepen the channel, to change it or even make an entirely new channel, and to remove obstructions. If these acts inflict injury upon private property, usually no compensation is paid because navigation is considered to be clearly in the interest of public welfare.

Land Beneath Water, the Property of the State. In a navigable stream, excepting in a few states, river beds are the property of the state. The state has a proprietary interest in the land beneath the water. Florida has sold the phosphate found in stream beds, Arkansas sold sand and gravel, and in 1913 Kansas declared by statute that sand, oil, or minerals in river beds are the property of the state, subject to sale or grant. Similarly, lake beds are the property of the state and the riparian owner's rights cease at the water's edge.

Although the federal government once owned the land comprising the public domain in full proprietorship, courts have held that the United States did not have ownership of lake and stream beds. These had to be held in trust while the state was still unorganized or under territorial government, awaiting the time when it could enter the union on equal footing with other states.[1] Then the submerged lands became the full property of the state subject to use, sale, grant or lease as any other state property.

Wisconsin is among the few states permitting the riparian owner to own the river bed of a navigable stream (but not of a lake), subject only to the rights of navigation. The consequences are worth citing to illustrate the loss of public rights by such a policy. By virtue of the ownership of the bank riparian owners obtained the valuable privilege of erecting buildings on piles up to the middle of the stream. This privilege adds to the value of riparian property. Because the navigability of the Rock River had already been impaired by dams, bridges, and other encroachments it was held by the courts that the buildings were not a

[1] *State* ex rel. *Dawson* v. *Akers et al.*, 92 Kan. 169, 140 Pac. 637, 40 Ann. Cas. 543; *Illinois Steel Co.* v. *Bilot,* 109 Wis. 418; *U. S.* v. *Utah, U. S. Daily,* April 17, 1931.

material impairment of navigation.[1] In 1887 the legislature tried to make these structures nuisances, but the act was declared unconstitutional because it would have taken property without due process of law and without compensation.[2] Wisconsin courts even declared that ice on streams, whether navigable or non-navigable, belongs to the owner of the bed of the stream.[3] Thus one early decision set in motion a train of events which destroyed valuable public rights and gave extraordinary privileges to stream bank owners. However, a recent court decision preventing private owners from building a store over the same river in another city has strengthened public as against private rights to navigable streams in this state.[4]

On the Great Lakes and the oceans both jurisdiction and ownership of land beneath the water are involved. The oceans are without ownership and the control of any particular nation ceases at the three-mile limit. The jurisdiction of the states bordering on the Great Lakes or arms of the sea, such as Chesapeake Bay, extends to established boundary lines, within which each state regulates fishing according to its own laws. About two-thirds of the fresh water fish caught in the United States come from the Great Lakes but this resource is badly depleted principally because, although the states agree through conferences on measures for regulation and rehabilitation, individual states have refused to enact these regulations into laws because of pressure from commercial fishermen. Land under water on the Great Lakes belongs to the state having jurisdiction, but only the land near the shores has any economic significance.

The paramount rights of the public on navigable waters are matched by equally cogent rights of the private individual over the water and the bed whenever a lake or stream is not navigable. Although the *land* beneath the water is strictly private property, the riparian owner does not gain possession of the water itself. He may not use it or obstruct its flow to the damage of other riparian owners living on the same stream, but the rights to fish, to take the ice, and to exclude trespassers belong exclusively to him.

[1] *State* v. *Carpenter,* 68 Wis. 168 (1887).

[2] *Janesville* v. *Carpenter,* 77 Wis. 288 (1890).

[3] *Reyson* v. *Roate,* 42 Wis. 543 (1896).

[4] *S. S. Kresge* v. *Railroad Commission,* 204 Wis. 479; 235 N. W. 4; 236 N. W. 667.

Tests of Navigability. Because of the differences in the rights of public and private owners on navigable and non-navigable waters it is highly important that the two be clearly distinguished. When is a river navigable? As defined in earlier times in England, only waters subject to tidal flow were considered navigable. Later, certain non-tidal streams were also included, and the term "navigable in law" was used. In the United States the presence of large rivers and fresh water lakes made another change in the concept necessary, and "navigability in fact" was made the test. Both federal and state laws define the term "navigability in fact," and naturally the variations are numerous. In lumbering states streams were important as a means of getting saw logs to market, so streams of sufficient capacity to float logs six inches in diameter were declared navigable even if they were capable of doing so only for a part of the year.

"Navigability in fact" is also the test of public rights on lakes and ponds. This is complicated by the impression that lake beds are private property if a lake has not been "meandered" when the original survey was made. (See Chapter IV.)

Various court decisions have made it clear, however, that meandering cannot make navigable a lake which is not so in fact, nor can the failure to meander make non-navigable a lake which is capable of navigation as defined by the statutes. Nevertheless, some landowners claim that, since the legal description of their land, as publicly recorded, includes these lakes, they therefore own the submerged land. Others urge that since they have paid taxes on the entire description they have *title* to the land beneath the water. The courts have held otherwise.[1]

Each state, however, has determined its own test of navigability. Massachusetts, for instance, in 1647 fixed the dividing line between public and private lakes at ten acres. Wherever the statutes define a navigable stream as one that will float a log or a canoe, the rights of the public are extended to tiny bodies of water, a fact of great importance to the fisherman, canoeist, and all riparian recreational uses. The Ordinance of 1787 even declared that "the carrying places" between navigable waters "shall be common highways and forever free . . . without any tax, impost or duty therefore." Even though this article was later

[1] *Mendota* v. *Anderson,* 101 Wis. 479; *Doeme* v. *Jantz,* 180 Wis. 225.

incorporated into the Wisconsin state constitution, the Supreme Court of that state declared that this provision applied only to commercial portages in existence in 1787!

Decline in the Importance of Navigation. Navigation rights were formulated at a time when streams and lakes were the chief means of transportation, in fact so important in national defense that the jurisdiction over navigable waters was vested in the War Department of the federal government, where it still rests.[1] The question might well be raised whether at the present time other uses for streams, as, for instance, for water power or flood control, are not more important or whether navigation should be permitted to interfere with land transportation and with uses of land in conflict with navigation. Why should the state be forced to put "lifts" in bridges with a depth hardly sufficient to float a scow or rowboat? Or why should river craft have the right of way over automobile traffic? An important conflict has arisen over the fur animal law in Wisconsin. The law permits the fencing of land to confine beaver, muskrats, and other animals, but beaver and muskrats require water, and if navigable water is included in the fenced area the public cannot be excluded. However, the Wisconsin courts in 1908 declared that a distinction could well be made between "streams capable of floating logs and timber only at certain periods and the streams capable of more extended and constant navigation." Later decisions hold in effect that the legislature has the right to designate which of the uses of a stream is of the greatest public benefit and to enact laws giving preference to the "highest" uses.[2]

Another reason why other uses for water might well take precedence over navigation is the decline in the relative importance of this form of transportation in the United States. The

[1] Thus both the federal and state governments have jurisdiction over navigable waters. The definition of navigability by federal statutes is simply streams "suitable for use for the transportation of persons or property in interstate or foreign commerce." (Sec. III of Federal Water Power Act.)

[2] It is interesting that Article IV of the Colorado River compact reads: "Inasmuch as the Colorado River has ceased to be navigable for commerce and the reservation of its water for navigation would seriously limit the development of its basin, the use of its waters for purposes of navigation shall be subservient to the uses of such waters for domestic, agricultural and power purposes. If the Congress shall not consent to this paragraph, the other provisions of the compact shall nevertheless remain binding."—National Resources Committee, *Regional Factors in National Planning, op. cit.*, p. 65.

Great Lakes traffic in iron ore, coal, grain, and similar products has maintained its volume, but freight shipments have declined for other products, including flour. River commerce had dwindled to small proportions when the conservation movement kindled new interest in the subject. In fact, it was on a river trip organized by the Mississippi Valley Waterway Association (a group of St. Louis business men whose object was to see that the Mississippi was made navigable) that Theodore Roosevelt, Gifford Pinchot, and others were inspired to call the famous "governors' conference" of 1908.[1] (See plate facing page 271.)

Funds for river and harbor improvements to assist commerce have long been favored as a means of "bringing home" federal money for local interests. Paradoxically, the demand for funds has increased proportionately as transportation shifted from rivers to railways, highways, and airplanes.[2] It is estimated that over $4,000,000,000 have already been spent on our waterways. The Ohio River improvement has cost the federal government $132,000,000, a sum which would "build four parallel two lane $45,000-a-mile roads from Pittsburgh to Cairo." The $228,000,000 spent on the rivers between Pittsburgh and New Orleans "would construct two parallel $100,000-a-mile double track de luxe railways completely equipped" between these two cities.[3] The nine-foot channel on the upper Mississippi is expected to cost $175,000,000, or $5,000,000 more than Boulder Dam, which means an expenditure of about $265,000 per mile for the 660-mile stretch.

It is doubtful if these expenditures will equalize the disadvantage of water traffic as compared with rail and automobile transportation. Speed is important for most freight except for certain raw materials. The handicap of water transportation is indicated by the fact that the round trip between Pittsburgh and New Orleans can be made by train or truck in less than four days, whereas it would take a modern tug and barges thirty days with no

[1] Pinchot, "How Conservation Began in the United States," *op. cit.*, p. 263.

[2] Control over navigable waters is exercised by Congress, based upon the delegated power "to regulate commerce with foreign countries and among the several states" (Art. I, Sec. 8, No. 3). The same clause is the basis for federal aid to commerce. The control over waters for other purposes is left to the states, and its extent varies from complete control in New York to practically no regulation at all in other states. H. D. Padgett, "Legislative Aspects of the Use and Control of Water Resources," in *N. R. B. Report*, p. 377.

[3] A. E. Parkins, "Our Waterways and Their Utilization," in Parkins and Whitaker, *Our Natural Resources and Their Conservation, op. cit.*, pp. 366–67.

delays or stops. Four days at least are needed to pass the hundred locks in the up and down trips on the Ohio.[1]

Even though the taxpayers are bearing the entire cost of making rivers navigable whereas railways have built their own roadbeds, and though rates for water transport are less than railroad rates, no significant revival of river navigation took place after 1908; in fact, in 1918 the federal government undertook the building and operation of a fleet of modern tugboats and barges on the Mississippi and the Warrior-Tombigbee rivers to demonstrate the feasibility of inland water transportation. This venture has been of doubtful value.[2]

Navigation has been a convenient cloak to accomplish worthwhile purposes which are not permitted directly to the federal government. Although Congress had approved the Colorado River compact which stated that the Colorado had ceased to be navigable, the Supreme Court stopped Arizona from enjoining the building of Boulder Dam by declaring that the Colorado *was* navigable and the dam would improve its navigation. Floods were controlled under the same caption until 1917. States also used "navigation" to obtain the use of streams for power. The Tennessee Valley Authority is now permitted to sell electric current as a by-product of its navigation and flood control programs. The danger of such a procedure is that "improving for navigation" has to be undertaken not for its own sake but to accomplish other purposes, in spite of the fact that water transportation is declining in importance.

RIPARIAN RIGHTS

Nature and Extent of Riparian Rights. Although water is public in navigable bodies, the owner of land bordering on a lake or stream acquires certain rights in the water by reason of his ownership of riparian land which non-riparians do not enjoy. Having access to the stream or lake, he can enjoy the scenery, fish, swim, bathe, skate, and build piers and wharves, subject only to the rights of navigation. He has the right to the deposits brought by the river, to new lands added by the action of the stream, but he also suffers the damages of riparian erosion. Rivers tear away

[1] *Ibid.*

[2] *Ibid.*, pp. 361–64, 367–71. Recent reports seem to be more optimistic, however.

the land in one place and build up the shores in another. Farms are destroyed and towns threatened by destruction or left far "inland" by capricious streams. In other places farms are enlarged and property relationships become very complicated under such conditions.[1] Where rivers form boundaries between states or counties, questions of jurisdiction may be raised and the ownership of the river bed becomes involved. The Mississippi and Missouri are notorious for riparian erosion and changes in their channels. Expensive revetments and other engineering works are often necessary to keep a river in its place.

The land area which can claim riparian rights varies with the laws of the respective states. In some states only the tract originally entered when the land was acquired from the government has riparian rights, or only the 40-acre tracts so entered. Sometimes the entire tract in one ownership has these privileges even though assembled from several holdings, but in other states the rights are restricted to the smallest parcel of riparian land making up the consolidation. Usually the portion of the tract sold loses the right unless the right is conveyed in the deed. A road between the land and a body of water dispossesses the rest of the tract if the title to the right of way has been deeded without reservations as to the riparian rights. These facts are of great importance not only in the arid regions but also for recreational lands situated on lakes and streams. Thus an 80- or 160-acre farm on a lake enjoys riparian rights, but the sale of a strip of land along the water's edge, no matter how narrow, deprives the remainder of the farm of these rights, unless protected by deed restrictions. However, riparian lands must lie in the watershed of the stream to which they are riparian, except in Oregon.[2] Finally,

[1] The changing channel and the tearing down and rebuilding of land cause many lawsuits. In one instance a farmer homesteaded on an island in a river. A flood came and washed it away. A few years later the river rebuilt the island, adding many acres to it, and joined it to the mainland. The law holds that the land added to the bank becomes the property of the bank owner, but if an island is not completely washed away, all the land subsequently added to the island becomes the property of its owner. In this case the owner of the island was able to prove that it had not completely vanished. In another case a farmer bought 120 acres of bottom land of which a flood destroyed all but 12 acres. Sixteen years later his farm was not only restored but actually 40 acres larger than before. A. B. Macdonald, "The Treacherous Big Muddy," *Country Gentleman,* November 1, 1924, p. 18.

[2] Donald M. Baker and Harold Conkling, *Water Supply and Utilization* (New York, Wiley, 1930), pp. 221–23.

since the land beneath water is, with few exceptions, the property of the state, the riparian owner's rights cease at the water's edge. He has no right to extend a boundary fence into a navigable lake, nor can he stop people from using the water offshore.

Riparian Rights and Recreation. Riparian rights give unusual values to shore properties. All along the North Shore above Chicago land values reflect the desirability of lake frontage for residential purposes. Industries requiring water or the facilities of water transportation compete for land on rivers, lakes, or oceans. Private recreational land is practically a fringe of riparian land around lakes, often sold by the front foot while the territory not in touch with water sells at farm or cut-over land prices.

To the extent that a lake is completely surrounded by privately owned land and the public is excluded, a monopoly is created and this exclusive right of riparian owners has seriously interfered with the use of waters for public recreation. It is interesting to see how the various states are trying to recover or protect the rights of the people in this respect. The New Jersey Department of Conservation has been given the power to acquire the fresh water ponds and the lands riparian to them. By another law the owner of such ponds may retain title to them, but he is exempt from taxation if he grants free access to the public for boating and fishing. An ordinance of the Massachusetts Bay Colony of 1641 provided that "every inhabitant who is a householder shall have free fishing and fowling in the great ponds, bays, coves, and rivers so far as the sea ebbs and flows within the precincts of the town where they dwell, unless the freemen of the town have otherwise appropriated them; provided that no town shall appropriate to any particular person or any persons, any great pond containing more than ten acres of land. . . . For great ponds lying in common it shall be free for any man to fish or fowl there and may pass and repass on foot through any man's property for that end, so they trespass not upon any man's corn or meadow." The fact that the rights to the ponds were reserved for "householders" gave them the status of common property rather than public property. This is emphasized in the opinion of the Attorney General of the state in 1923 when he said that the title to the waters and the soil beneath the waters was now in the hands of the commonwealth for the benefit of the public, provided such ponds had not been granted to a town or a private person before 1647. He also ruled that while the ancient ordinance specifically mentioned "fishing and fowling," this did not exclude other rights and public uses which the progress of civilization and the increasing wants of the community might demand. The right of access was tested in 1924 and the rights of the public were upheld.[1]

Another plan to provide public access to lakes is to reserve or buy part of the shore for public ownership. The Wisconsin stream platting law requires that whenever riparian land is platted a public road must be run to the water every half mile. Some Canadian and Australian provinces reserve a strip of land along the banks of rivers in public ownership.[2] This was also the practice under the Roman law.

Water Power. The most valuable riparian right is the privilege of developing water power. The riparian owner has the right to use the natural fall in a river occasioned by a difference in the level of the stream where it first touches his land and where it leaves his property, but he cannot alter the level of the water or pollute it. Since every riparian owner from the source to the mouth has the same corresponding right, no one owner has an absolute right and no utilization must interfere with the equal utilization of other riparian owners. On navigable streams power rights are also subordinate to public rights, the most important being navigation.

Were these limitations strictly interpreted, riparian rights would hinder rather than help in the development of water power. The law, however, permits more favorable constructions than the riparian doctrine seems to hold. It allows a *reasonable* interference with the natural flow of a stream; water may be impounded a *reasonable* length of time to accumulate a "head" sufficient to drive a turbine. However, the building of a dam involves changing the level of the stream, and if the operator does

[1] Raymond H. Torrey, *State Parks and Recreational Uses of State Forests,* National Conference on State Parks, Washington (1926), pp. 53–55.

[2] Adams, *Rural Planning and Development, op. cit.,* pp. 51–52. Elwood Mead, *Helping Men Own Farms* (New York, Macmillan, 1920), p. 205.

Minnesota is reserving from sale a strip of land two rods wide on meandered lakes and public waters on state owned land.

not own all the land which will be flooded he encroaches on the rights of other riparian owners. He must obtain the consent of the owners and compensate them for damages. If only one of them refuses to sell, the entire project may be blocked, or at least exorbitant prices may be asked for the land to be submerged.

To help the water power operator to obtain the necessary flowage, the state came to the rescue. Under the "Mill Acts" of colonial Massachusetts and other states the water power owner was empowered to flood his neighbor's land and pay damage for the injury inflicted thereby. The state granted the prerogative of eminent domain to a private individual, who in turn had to devote his mill to a public use and agree to public regulations, including the fixing of a price for his services. The courts of some states refused to uphold the mill acts, however.

Another way to obtain the right to condemn property was evolved in Wisconsin. In the early history of the state, water power owners asked the legislature for a franchise to "improve navigation." This being a public purpose, the right of eminent domain could be used to obtain the submerged lands. This seems like a bit of fiction, but in the lumbering days the building of dams actually did improve navigation; so does a series of dams on a shallow stream, providing locks are built to take boats around the dams. That is the principle employed on the upper Mississippi to provide a 9-foot channel. However, when the state helps a private owner to obtain his power in this way it is no longer strictly speaking *riparian property* but rests on a grant or franchise of the state subject to state regulation and control.[1]

Public Control over Water Power. Since 1915 the Public Service Commission of Wisconsin has had control over the waters of the state. It must approve the construction of dams and is empowered to refuse to grant a permit if scenic beauty would be destroyed thereby. The statute says that "the enjoyment of natural scenic beauty is declared a public right." The commission must approve the plans for the construction of the dam and may take possession of any water power if it should be proved that it had come under the control of a trust. The commission also decides cases involving lake and dam levels, which is a matter of

[1] E. A. Gilmore, "Riparian Rights in Wisconsin," Senate Document 449, 61st Congress, 2d Session (1910).

considerable importance to recreational riparian owners and cranberry growers, as well as to water power operators.

The basis for the power of Congress to control water power lies in the right of this body to regulate navigable waters. It may also control water power developments if the power enters into interstate commerce. Congress assumed positive control in 1899 and 1910 by prohibiting the building of dams on navigable waters except as authorized by Congress. The numerous requests for permits and the large amount of work involved in determining whether or not they should be granted led to the creation of the Federal Power Commission in 1920. This body is now charged with these duties. However, the same act also strengthened the powers of the United States over streams; in fact, federal control has been extended to those non-navigable streams "which affect the navigable capacity of navigable rivers." The Supreme Court has not had an opportunity to pass on the constitutionality of this act but it has been upheld in lower courts on the basis that its chief purpose is the "protection of navigation."[1]

IRRIGATION

Irrigation is a proprietary use of water and concerns the use of land as well as of water. In no other use is the legal and institutional framework so important in securing the best use of both resources and in no other case are property relationships more complicated. When land is irrigated, water is taken bodily from the stream and consumed in the production of plants, although some of it finds its way back into the stream or ground water by seepage. Unlike the riparian owner who is expected to return the full volume of water undiminished and unpolluted, the irrigator depletes the stream and where the water supply is limited only a limited number of farms can be served.

The problem lies in the establishment of rights to water, not merely to a use as it passes, but to a use akin to proprietary possession of the body of the fluid itself. The first arrival is in a position to *claim* all the water in a stream whether he uses it or not, but the one who establishes his farm nearest the source of the stream is physically in a position to deprive all others of water by appropriating it before it can reach them. Even granting that

[1] Padgett, *op. cit.*, p. 378.

a reasonable number of claimants appeared and were willing to take a proportionate share of the water, what is a proportionate share? These are age-old questions.

Irrigation laws are found in the code of Hammurabi, seven hundred years before Moses. In the Mediterranean region the scarcity of water and the demands for irrigation and municipal uses led to a system of water rights which was codified in 550 A.D. in the legal Digests of Justinian and recognized throughout the Roman Empire.[1] The Spaniards practiced irrigation in our arid Southwest before the English came and established codes and laws governing the use of water. The English did not copy any of them, but developed their own laws as the result of hard knocks and experience with their environment, the laws being singularly like those evolved by other peoples under similar conditions.

The Appropriation Doctrine. One form of doctrine was that of *appropriation*. Under this it was held "that he who first turned the stream of water from its course or of a lake from its bed, and applied them to a beneficial and continuing use was first in property right in that stream commensurate to and concurrent with that use."[2] Since the right of appropriation goes to the first claimant it is important that he have some means of proving that he was first. Hence laws have been enacted prescribing how priority is to be established. However, the irrigator is not permitted to claim the entire supply but only the amount necessary to water a reasonable area of land under irrigated conditions. Furthermore, he must actually *use* the water; if he does not begin to do so after a reasonable time, or ceases to use the water, his right to its use is forfeited or abandoned. Since the amount allowed to each irrigator is fixed, this involves the physical measuring of the water. So a voluminous body of law has grown up dealing with the acquisition, defining, and enforcement of rights to irrigation water.[3]

[1] "An irrigation channel was called a *rivus* and all persons participating in its water right were *rivales* or rivals, a term which came to be applied to rivals in love by the old Roman comedies,—with peculiar appropriateness, for competition in water rights was keen, equity in them was jealously guarded, illicit draughts were common, and quarrels were frequent."—Ellen Churchill Semple, *The Geography of the Mediterranean Region* (New York, Holt, 1931), p. 466.

[2] R. H. Hess, "Arid Land Water Rights in the United States," *Columbia Law Review*, June, 1916, pp. 484–85.

[3] See Thomas, *op. cit.;* Teele, *Economics of Land Reclamation, op. cit.*, Chap.

The appropriation doctrine does not necessarily make for the best use of water. As was stated in the resolutions of the "League of the Southwest" in January, 1919, "The history of irrigation throughout the world has shown that the greatest duty of water is had by first using it upon the upper reaches of the stream and continuing the use progressively downward. In other words, the water should first be captured and used while it is young, for it can then be recaptured as it returns from the performance of its duties and thus be used over and over again."[1] The "recapture" has reference to the fact that in mature irrigation projects as much as 30 per cent of the water returns to the streams as seepage or can be used on lower lying land.[2] However, should the first appropriator not have located on the upper reaches of the river, the water must be permitted to flow the entire length of the stream to satisfy his claim. If a shortage occurs, he is entitled to his full quota and all others have to take a reduced portion or even go without water. Where the doctrine of priority is applied between states it forces everybody to scramble for water on the "first come, first served" precept, whether the state is ready for development or not. The best land may not get the water, nor is the most efficient use necessarily made of the water.

On the other hand, the appropriation doctrine has features which help to bring the best land into use. The selection of land for irrigation is very flexible under this principle. The irrigator does not have to live on a stream. His farm may be a mile away from a body of water, yet he may divert the water and carry it wherever it is required for beneficial use, without returning the water or any part of it to the natural stream in any manner. "The appropriator may, under certain circumstances, change the point of diversion as well as the place of application of the water; he has a property right in the water lawfully diverted to beneficial use and may dispose of the same separate and apart from the land in

---

IX; Teele, *The Western Farmers' Water Right* (U. S. Dept. of Agriculture, Bulletin 913); Mead, *Irrigation Institutions, op. cit.;* and especially S. T. Harding, *Water Rights for Irrigation* (Stanford University Press, 1936).

[1] *Regional Factors in National Planning, op. cit.,* p. 59. The "duty" of water is the amount required to produce an annual crop as expressed in terms of acre-feet. The requirement varies with the crop: from 5 acre-feet for rice, for instance, in California, to about 1 acre-foot for other crops.

[2] Harding, *op. cit.,* p. 27.

connection with which the right ripened to any one who will continue such use without injury to the rights of others."[1] The fact that an irrigation ditch passes over the land of another necessitates the exercise of eminent domain, or of some power akin to this, to force the landowner to agree to the building of the ditch.

The doctrine of appropriation grew out of the needs of the 1849 gold miners, who had to establish working rules where no government existed. The person first in time was the first in right in establishing his claim to land and water. This possessory right was recognized by California as a state in 1851, and later by the federal government. Utah accepted it under the leadership of the Mormon church, and Colorado incorporated it in its constitution in 1876. It was well adapted to an unsettled region with ample water to supply the demand, but was not so well suited where population began to press upon water resources. As time went on, many of the exclusive rights were modified and many states began to enact careful water codes with state agencies to regulate the settlers' rights.

The Modified Riparian Doctrine. The appropriation doctrine, however, was not the only one tried in the West. Settlers coming from the humid East were accustomed to the riparian doctrine and tried to apply it in the arid West. Once more modifications had to be made when men crossed the "institutional fault" of the 98th meridian. Since the riparian doctrine prohibits the diminution of the volume of the stream, it is directly contrary to the needs of the irrigator. But this was modified by using the elastic adjective *substantial,* which was interpreted to mean nothing less than a real injury to the riparian owners above or below the irrigator involved.

The fact that the non-riparian owner of land is not entitled to water under the riparian doctrine was overcome by an appropriate definition of "riparian." "Courts have even denominated lands of one watershed as riparian to streams of another, the diversion and return of water at points on the lands of the appropriator has been widely held to be an unessential element of the common law, and the rights of way for irrigation works have been ac-

[1] Justice Elliott of the Colorado Supreme Court in *Oppenander* v. *Left Hand Ditch Co.* (1892), 18 Colorado 142, 148–49; 31 Pac. 854. Quoted in R. H. Hess, "The Colorado Water Right," *Columbia Law Review,* December, 1916, pp. 662–63.

quired by condemnation."[1] The riparian doctrine holding that the right to water is a part of the right to land has been modified so that the ownership of water can be separated from landownership.[2] In fact, this doctrine has been so greatly modified by law and by court decisions in the western states that Dr. Teele declares, "It seems probable, therefore, that within a few years the riparian doctrine, so ill adapted to an arid region, and never intentionally adopted in our own arid region, will cease to be a hindrance to the best use of our water resources."[3]

The question of the appropriation vs. the modified riparian doctrine was also complicated by the fact that some of the Western states are only partly arid, as, for instance, the Pacific states and the 100th Meridian states. Here the use of water for irrigation often conflicts with its use for navigation and power. Although California started with the appropriation doctrine, through the decision of the case of *Lux* v. *Haggin* in 1884 the riparian doctrine was put in its place but adapted to the dual nature of the state. States wholly within the arid region, such as Utah, are not troubled by this problem.[4]

Public Relationships of Water under Irrigation. In the adaptation of old laws and customs to new conditions it was inevitable that water should demand new property relationships and different institutions for public control and regulation. Dr. Teele says: "A water right is a right to the future use of something which past experience indicates will be in existence perennially. The property, therefore, is not a material thing that can be segregated, stored or protected as can a material thing such as money, goods, or land. This immaterial quality renders water rights peculiarly 'social phenomena' since they are not a form of property that an individual can hide away or protect through his own efforts."[5] The "social aspects" of the problem have compelled the arid states

[1] R. H. Hess in *Bailey's Encyclopedia of American Agriculture* (Macmillan, 1909), IV, 161.

[2] The separation of water from land is necessary where irrigation works are constructed by a company which sells water to irrigators. Such a company may own no land and the water "attaches to the ditch" instead of to the land. In other cases farmers sell their excess water to neighbors. See Thomas, *op. cit.*, pp. 54–55, and Mead, *Irrigation Institutions, op. cit.*, pp. 82–87.

[3] *Economics of Land Reclamation, op. cit.*, p. 262.

[4] For a brief summary of irrigation laws see *Irrigation of Agricultural Lands, op. cit.*, pp. 26–29.

[5] *Economics of Land Reclamation, op. cit.*, p. 256.

to take aggressive measures of control and even to establish state ownership of the waters subject to appropriation. Colorado declared in her constitution, "The water of every stream not heretofore appropriated, within the state of Colorado, is hereby declared to be the *property of the public,* subject to appropriation as hereinafter provided." (Art. 16, Sect. 5.) Wyoming went a step further and in 1890 provided in her constitution that, "The water of all natural streams, springs, lakes or other collection of still water, within the boundaries of the state, are hereby declared to be the *property of the state.*" (Art. VIII, Sect. 1.) The latter has been called the Civil Law Doctrine and is based upon the idea that water is the actual property of the Crown and can be disposed of by sale or grant to individuals. Since the state has succeeded to the prerogatives of the Crown the action of Wyoming and Utah in declaring waters the property of the state is quite logical. However, a decision of the Wyoming Supreme Court has held that the state merely controls the water as a sovereign under its police powers and not as a proprietor. It was stated that there was no appreciable distinction between the phrases "property of the public" and "property of the state," the state being "vested with jurisdiction or control in its sovereign capacity."[1] The intention no doubt was to establish actual state proprietorship. The waters were to be disposed of by grant by a Board of Control which would determine the manner of disposal and which was empowered to withhold and refuse permits. The state was then in a position to make a complete plan for the utilization of its water resources. However, it seems that the usual procedure of acquiring rights common to the Western states was in vogue even before the decision of the court referred to.[2]

The doctrine of state ownership of waters offers no particular difficulty wherever the public domain has been completely alienated, but the question of the proprietorship of waters on the federal lands of the Western states is still unsettled. According to one view, the federal government "became not only the owner of the lands but also the owner in a strict and proprietory sense of the right to use the waters of these lands" when it acquired territory

[1] *Farm Investment Co.* v. *Carpenter,* 9 Wyo. 110. See also Teele, *Economics of Land Reclamation, op. cit.,* pp. 260–62.

[2] Teele, *op. cit.,* p. 262. Thomas, *op. cit.,* p. 46.

through purchase or cession. Conferring statehood passed political powers, not property rights, according to this theory advanced in the leading case of *Lux* v. *Haggin*.[1] Nevertheless, under the theory of the Colorado doctrine all rights to water rest upon state sovereignty and state law, which implies that the *state* controls the waters even within national forests, parks, and the remaining public domain—Indian reservations excepted. However, the federal government has repeatedly asserted its claim to the ownership of these waters, although Congress has taken a conciliatory attitude and avoided conflicts with state jurisdiction as, for instance, in the Reclamation Act. Until this matter is definitely decided no comprehensive plan for the utilization of Western waters will be possible.[2]

The Functions of the State in Irrigation Regulation. Two schools of thought have grown up in regard to the function of the state in irrigation; one favors public guidance and control, the other leaves as much as possible to private initiative. Wyoming is the outstanding example of the former, Colorado of the latter. Wyoming and several other states have given public officials the right to refuse permits to appropriate water if such permits are believed to be in conflict with public interest. Colorado merely places filings on water on record and does not investigate whether water is actually available or not. Investors have sometimes been defrauded because they believed that approval of their filings by the state was a guarantee that water was available. Conflicting rights have to be settled in the courts. On the other hand, the freedom to file on all possible water resources has stimulated private initiative. It has been pointed out that the greatest development has taken place in the states with the least public control, such as Colorado and California, whereas Wyoming, the leader in such control, is the most backward in development.[3]

The two points of view are also manifested in the attitudes of Colorado and Wyoming toward the utilization of water. Colorado recognizes the right to a *definite quantity of water* which may be used on any land the irrigator wishes or of which he may sell a part to his neighbor. Water is therefore used on as much land as

[1] 69 Cal. 255 (1886).

[2] N. D. Padgett, "Legislative Aspects of the Use and Control of Water Resources," *op. cit.*, p. 379.

[3] Teele, *Economics of Land Reclamation, op. cit.*, pp. 268–70.

possible, and used economically. Wyoming, on the other hand, grants water for specified areas of land, with the maximum amount fixed by law. The right is said to be appurtenant to the land and may not be transferred. It was feared that the water users might be exploited by the water owners if the two were separated. However, no such evils have appeared, and the economic disadvantage of attaching water to land has become so evident that Wyoming and other states now permit transfers, provided that the rights are attached to some other specific tract. Where land is the fixed factor the tendency is to use water lavishly and uneconomically. This is given as another reason for the more rapid development of irrigation in states following the Colorado system, namely California, Montana, and Utah. The various forms of irrigation projects also differ in regard to attaching water to the land. Mutual stock or co-operative companies tend to divorce land and water, whereas irrigation districts, the Carey Act, and Federal Reclamation projects tend to consider water appurtenant to the land.

Conflicts over Water Rights between States. Conflicts regarding the rights to irrigation water have arisen not only between individuals and projects but also between states. The conflicts involving states are especially interesting because they bring into sharp focus the theories of water ownership and control. One such dispute involved the Arkansas River, which rises in Colorado but flows through Kansas, Oklahoma, and Arkansas. It was contended that the withdrawal of water in Colorado for irrigation had injured the land and the people of Kansas, the people claiming the right to the entire undiminished flow of the river under the riparian doctrine in vogue in that state. Colorado, on the other hand, demanded the right to the use of all the water originating in her borders on the basis of the "sovereign right of ownership to said waters." However, in a case involving the Laramie River, rising in Colorado and flowing into Wyoming, both states had accepted the appropriation doctrine but with certain differences. Again Colorado claimed all the waters of the river, but Wyoming contended that "priority" should apply regardless of state lines and that because she had made appropriations enough to use the entire flow of the Laramie she was therefore entitled to the entire volume of the stream. The United States Supreme

Court, in the *Kansas* v. *Colorado* case, allowed Colorado the use of the water already appropriated but held that any further depletion might be denied. In the *Wyoming* v. *Colorado* case the court upheld the priority doctrine, nevertheless granting Colorado a fixed amount of water in the Laramie. In both cases the court did not decide between doctrines of ownership but rather judged the question of equitable division or apportionment of the waters between the states in controversy.[1]

Instead of waiting for the courts to decide the apportionment of water, state compacts have been made between Colorado and Nebraska and between Colorado and New Mexico, an interesting illustration of the sovereignty of the states. A more ambitious "treaty" has been attempted involving the seven states in the Colorado basin. A compact was made in 1922 dividing the waters between the upper and the lower basins. These two basins divide approximately at the Utah-Arizona line. However, the main controversy is over the apportionment of water between California and Arizona, both of which are in the lower basin, so the principal points at issue remain unsolved. Arizona has refused to ratify the compact.[2]

FOOD RESOURCES IN WATER: DOMESTIC AND MUNICIPAL USES

Fish rank third in the total quantity of meat consumed in the United States; and to them must be added the vast quantities of shellfish, oysters, and other sea foods taken from the shallow waters of the arms of the ocean. These valuable resources are constantly being jeopardized by pollution. Some European countries have a unique system of "water" farming in rotation with "land" farming. Low places are converted into ponds and used for fish and fowl for one or two years, then are drained and sowed to grain for an equal period. Each crop benefits its successor.[3]

The first and most primitive use for water was for drinking

[1] *Kansas* v. *Colorado* (185 U. S. 208; 206 U. S. 46: 1901–1907). *Wyoming* v. *Colorado* (259 U. S. 149, 496; 260 U. S. 1: 1922).

Padgett, *op. cit.*, p. 378, cites James Graffon Rogers as saying that the U. S. Supreme Court did not establish the principle of equitable division, rather "it does say there must be an equitable limit to conflicting sovereignties, a fair adjustment of their otherwise complete and entire right of assertion and an apportionment not of water but of natural benefits."

[2] A complete description of this state compact is found in *Regional Factors in National Planning*, *op. cit.*, pp. 53–70. See also Padgett, *op. cit.*, p. 380.

[3] Person, *et al.*, *op. cit.*, pp. 65–67.

purposes for man and beast. In arid countries water may be so scarce that it is often restricted to this one use and even bathing and domestic uses are regulated. In humid areas water is usually plentiful enough for these purposes so that no serious conflicts arise until large cities begin to emerge. Cities use water for many purposes besides home use—for street sprinkling, parks, fire protection, sewage, and sanitation. Private dwellings, offices, and manufacturing plants use enormous quantities of water, most of which is returned to the stream in volume but polluted by sewage and trade wastes. Water is also important in moving the waste matter of cities; often the same stream which furnishes drinking water for the city also receives the discharge of sewage and polluted wastes. This is also true of the Great Lakes. Lake Erie provides water for some thirty-six cities in the United States and Canada, and Chicago, Milwaukee, and other lake ports are dependent on Lake Michigan for their water. At one time both cities discharged their sewage into the lake and lengthened their intakes to avoid contagion. Chicago now runs some of her city waste into the Chicago River and, by diverting water from Lake Michigan, carries the sewage into the Desplaines, Illinois, and Mississippi rivers. The city is permitted to use only a limited amount of lake water for this purpose, but it was claimed that even this amount had lowered the level of the lakes. Since both Canada and the United States border on the Great Lakes, the controversy became international.

Sewage can be absorbed and purified by running water but many trade wastes cannot. Paper mills, tanneries, and chemical works not only use large quantities of water but also dump into the streams industrial wastes which kill wild life and fish and destroy the recreational value of the streams. In the East waters are also polluted by mine drainage. Contaminated waters are a handicap to industry. Corrosion and scale in the locomotives of the railways running east of Pittsburgh are costing these roads from $12,000,000 to $20,000,000 a year.[1]

Since three-fourths of the population served by water systems use surface water, the seriousness of pollution is obvious. It is claimed that 85 per cent of the rivers of America are somewhat contaminated, but progress is now being made in controlling the

[1] *N. R. B. Report,* p. 315.

situation. Cities are building disposal plants which purify the water before it returns to the streams and also salvage the fertilizing materials contained in the sewage.

Where heavy concentrations of population require a large volume of water, it is often necessary to go hundreds of miles for an adequate supply. San Francisco gets water from the Hetch-Hetchy Valley 155 miles away, and Los Angeles is using water from the Colorado River 300 miles away. Where state lines have to be crossed, problems of jurisdiction arise. Boston and the nearby cities proposed to get a diversion from the Connecticut River basin, but Connecticut claimed that this would impair navigation, increase the danger of pollution, and take away flood rights. New York and New Jersey became involved in a similar controversy and both cases were carried to the United States Supreme Court. In spite of the riparian doctrine, the court held that water could be diverted to a different watershed and divided unequally between states on the basis of the need for the water.[1] If state rights and strict interpretation of the riparian doctrine were to prevail, cities in small states would be severely hampered, if not actually stopped, in their development because of the lack of water.

UNDERGROUND WATER

Percolating water found in the interstices between soil and rock particles constitutes a vast resource of water. It is estimated that if it were brought to the surface it would form a lake from 500 to 1,000 feet deep.[2] Some of this water is found in the soil proper, but artesian water lies in a porous rock layer between two impervious layers of rock. About half of the people of the United States depend upon water from wells, and so do many industrial plants. In 1930 about 12 per cent of the area of irrigated land also obtained its water from wells and springs.

Human occupation has affected underground water as it has influenced other realms of nature. The removal of ground water through wells has lowered the water table in many parts of the United States, and droughts have aggravated the situation. As early as 1927 it was reported that the water level had fallen 48 feet

[1] *Ibid.*, p. 377. *Connecticut* v. *Massachusetts* (282 U. S. 660, 1931); *New Jersey* v. *New York* (283 U. S. 336, 1931).

[2] Parkins and Whitaker, *op. cit.*, pp. 290–92.

in five years in Indiana, and some of the cities had to shift to surface water for their needs.[1] It is also claimed that the drain upon subsurface water in the Great Lakes region was an important element in reducing the seepage into the lakes and streams and consequently an important factor in lowering the level of the Great Lakes.[2]

The rights to underground water are even more complicated than the rights to surface water because the supply is invisible and the volume and direction of flow are usually unknown. Some water occurs in basins; other underground water is moving, very slowly of course, but where a current can be established the legal rights are similar to those in the waters of a surface stream.

Under the common law the owner of the surface has full property rights to the water beneath his land. However, water, petroleum, and natural gas are "fugitive minerals" which flow freely from one place to another, propelled by gravity or in response to pressure.[3] The owner of a well is often in a position to exhaust the water supply underneath an entire community. Artesian water, if allowed to run, or if wasted or used excessively, may be depleted to the detriment of the other users dependent on the same supply. This is especially important in arid regions, and here court decisions and laws have modified the old English common law. In the case of *Katz* v. *Walkinshaw* in California the doctrine of "correlative right" was laid down, and this has been generally followed in other arid states.[4] The owner has the right to use water to the full extent if the supply is sufficient; if not sufficient, each landowner is entitled to a reasonable share.

This doctrine applies to percolating waters and artesian as well as non-artesian basins, but it does not apply if the water is drawn from an underground stream whose channel is known and defined. All underground water is presumed to be percolating until proven otherwise. Arizona courts have also sustained the law declaring underground waters of the state to be public waters, subject to appropriation under the supervision and control of the

[1] Lewis S. Finch, "Water Shortage in Indiana," *Journal of the American Water Works Association,* March, 1927, p. 337.

[2] Herman L. Fairchild, "Changing Levels of the Great Lakes," *Scientific Monthly,* March, 1926, pp. 193–99.

[3] The property relationships of oil and natural gas will be discussed in Chap. XII.

[4] *California Court Reporter,* Vol. 141, p. 116.

state engineer. Water used for stock watering or domestic purposes was exempted.[1]

New Mexico probably has the most comprehensive laws dealing with underground water. The waters of underground streams, channels, artesian basins, reservoirs, or lakes having reasonably ascertainable boundaries are declared to belong to the public and subject to appropriation for beneficial use. Artesian waters which have been declared public are under the control of the state engineer, from whom permits must be obtained before drilling can be begun. Waste below the surface, on the surface, or while the water is being conducted to the "point of beneficial use" is prohibited. Wells abandoned for four years revert to the state for appropriation. Provision is also made for Artesian Conservancy Districts.[2]

CONFLICTS IN CLAIMS TO WATER

In this chapter the importance of the legal framework in the economical uses of water and land has been stressed. Since water is not subject to proprietorship in most of its uses, the value created by water tends to attach itself to the land that it touches. This is especially important in riparian land but is also true of irrigated land.[3] Another peculiarity of water is that it often creates monopolistic control over land. The owner of a spring, well, water hole, or river bank in an arid region literally has control over all the land dependent on that water supply. Water power and wharf properties also tend to become monopolized. It is for these reasons that water has been made subject to considerable social control, as previously noted.

Furthermore the uses and rights in water resources often come in conflict. A river is a unit from its source to its mouth and under natural conditions is so balanced that any disturbance by man sets in motion consequences which bring difficulties or disaster. The Sacramento-San Joaquin system of California affords a striking example. The rainfall is only 10–15 inches in the San

[1] Teele, *Economics of Land Reclamation, op. cit.,* pp. 279–81. D. W. Murphy, "Rights to Underground Water Sustained in Arizona Decision," *Engineering News Record,* December 8, 1927.

[2] New Mexico Laws, 1931, Chap. 131; Session Laws, 1935, Chap. 43.

[3] William Melcher, "The Economics of Federal Reclamation," *Journal of Land and Public Utility Economics,* November, 1933, p. 393.

Joaquin Valley but increases to 30 inches in the northern end of the Sacramento Valley; practically all of this rain falls in the winter and most of it reaches the ocean in less than two months. Flood control and drainage are therefore necessary side by side with irrigation.

One of the first conflicts in water uses came from the hydraulic mining on the head waters of the Sacramento, which brought debris into the rivers, choking the channels and spreading the material over the farms of the valley floor. A federal court in 1884 prohibited further operations, but under congressional action a limited amount of mining has been permitted. The second conflict came when irrigation depleted the waters of the Sacramento. Today the city of Sacramento is the head of navigation about 60 miles from the mouth of the river and the War Department has issued repeated warnings that navigation below Sacramento must be maintained. The diminished flow has also permitted salt water to back up into the rivers and channels of the delta of the two rivers, menacing crops worth $30,000,000 annually and threatening a highly attractive industrial area with a hundred manufacturing plants depending upon the river for fresh water. The seriousness of the conflict is indicated by the following statement: "The year 1920 had proven that the Sacramento River was an exhaustible stream and the same year saw the initiation of a lawsuit between the delta lands and the up-river lands, which cost the litigants some $250,000 in money. Barely had the Supreme Court written its last pronouncement on this suit, when a new one was started. The new suit brought in the water users of both the great valleys and involved every right to the use of the waters, whether flood or summer flow, of the two rivers flowing to the bay, and their tributaries. It, in effect, set every diverter of water against his brother diverter, and it set one great section of the state against another great section. It involved every angle of the water law; riparian rights, the right of appropriation, with all the uncertainties of beneficial application and due diligence, rights on tidal and navigable streams, and many other details, that must be fought over to establish finally what is called a water right. . . . The diverters of water might readily be called upon to put up more in cold cash in the defense of their water rights than the construction of their irrigation works originally cost them. And in the end no more water would be flowing in the Sacramento River than now flows."[1]

California has had in mind for some time a "co-ordinated plan" to correct the situation. The strategy lies in storing the heavy winter rains for release during the dry months; this will also hold back the waters that produce the floods in the lowlands and the delta region. Water released from the dams in summer is expected to create electricity, to provide ample supplies for irrigation and for municipal and industrial uses, and also maintain the volume of the river necessary for navigation and hold back the salt water from the delta. More ambitious still is the plan to take water from the Sacramento and lower San Joaquin rivers and by a series of conduits and pumping plants to alleviate the deficiency in ground and stream water on the upper San Joaquin basin.[2]

Co-ordinated development of water resources is also contemplated in certain state laws setting up districts with powers similar to drainage or irrigation districts but much more comprehensive. The Brazos Conservation and Reclamation District of Texas is set up to provide erosion and flood control, promotion of irrigation and drainage, conservation of water for domestic, municipal, commercial, and industrial enterprises and water power where it may be co-ordinated with other and superior uses and "subordinate to the uses declared by law to be superior."[3] The preservation of equitable rights over the watershed in the beneficial use of storm, flood, and unappropriated waters and the "prevention of the escape of any such waters without maximum public service" are also important purposes. Perhaps it is significant that navigation is not included and that the state proposes to accomplish a comprehensive plan of conserving the water resources without using navigation as a subterfuge.

[1] William Durbrow in Bulletin 4, Department of Public Works, Division of Water Rights, *Proceedings of the Second Sacramento-San Joaquin River Problems Conference and Water Supervisor's Report* (1924). Also see Bulletin 12, Department of Public Works, Division of Engineering and Irrigation, *Summary Report on the Water Resources of California;* National Resources Committee, *Drainage Basin Problems and Programs* (December, 1936), and National Resources Board, *Inventory of the Water Resources of the South Pacific* and *Great Basin Drainage Areas* (1935).

[2] For comprehensive water use planning in Russia see M. Ilin, "How We Reconstruct Nature," *Harper's,* January, 1935, pp. 163–74.

[3] Texas Statutes, Art. 8194.

XII

MINERAL AND POWER RESOURCES

Energy in the Modern World. Mineral and power resources are important not only for their own sake but because of their influence on other land uses. Primitive man started his conquest of nature with the use of animate power—his own muscle and that of animals. Slaves were the chief source of energy at first, since man only gradually domesticated the beasts. The earliest efforts to use wind and water were feeble, largely because the use of metals was still in its infancy. As long as this condition lasted man was not the "earth conditioning" creature pictured by Marsh.

The invention of the steam engine was literally a revolution in the use of energy and the metallurgical arts. Iron and coal gave birth to railways, mining, modern shipping, factories, and steel skeletons for buildings. The source of energy was shifted from the farm and forest to the mine.

A second shift came with the invention of the internal-combustion engine. This displaced steam to some extent, but its chief influence came in the substitution of individual transportation for mass transportation. Furthermore, pipe lines proved to be a more mobile and flexible method of transferring energy from where it is mined to where it is used than the older forms of transportation.

Electricity is not a new form of energy but a new form of transmitting the energy created by fuels and water power. The factory no longer has to be a power plant but it can buy a clean, highly divisible, easily controlled and transported power, which may also be used for light, for heating, and in chemical and metallurgical processes. Electricity has given new impetus to water power development.

Agriculture today, with its modern machinery and energy, is a far cry from the farming which depended on animate power. Mineral fertilizers, power, and machinery have changed the productive power of the soil, and steam- and gas-propelled transportation has literally doubled the area of commercial agriculture.

The machinery used in lumbering, earth-moving, irrigation, and drainage has helped to make man a "geographical factor." Its chief impact, however, may be seen in the concentration of population and in urbanized ways of living. The modern city dates from the beginning of the iron and coal "age." [1]

Rapid Utilization of Mineral Resources. While minerals and metals were used by mankind from the earliest days, the present enormous development in their utilization has taken place within the memory of men now living. Since 1815 the white population of the world has trebled but the output of tin has increased 26-fold, of copper 63-fold, of the mineral fuels 75-fold, and of pig iron 100-fold. In 1815 the ferrous alloys and aluminum were little more than curiosities. Even the fertilizer minerals were developed as late as the nineteenth century. The growth of mineral production in the United States is remarkable. More coal and iron have been mined since 1905 than in all the preceding years. The value of our mineral production per capita increased from $7.00 in 1880 to $52 in 1921.[2]

The rapid depletion of mineral deposits became of great concern in the "conservation era." Dire prophecies of the exhaustion of iron, coal, and petroleum reserves filled the popular magazines. However, the demand has flattened out. Up to 1910 everything had to be created—the railroad net and rolling stock, ships, bridges, pipe lines, machinery, and automobiles. The saturation point has been reached for many of these items, especially in view of the impending stationary population. Even though obsolete and in need of replacement, the old bridge or car returns second-hand metal to the furnace as "scrap" and reduces the drain on the mines. In the period 1910–14 scrap copper and lead were each equal to 14 per cent of mine production; by 1924–28 the proportions were 38 and 40 per cent respectively; but in 1933 the tonnage of "secondary" copper was one and one-third times the mine output and scrap lead equalled 82 per cent of the virgin mined metal.[3] About 33 per cent of the total annual demand for steel making comes from sources other than pig iron.[4] This is one of

[1] Zimmermann, *World Resources and Industries, op. cit.,* Chaps. 4, 5, 23.

[2] C. K. Leith, *World Minerals and World Politics* (New York, McGraw-Hill, 1931), pp. 3–6.

[3] *N. R. B. Report, op. cit.,* pp. 429–30.

[4] Zimmermann, *op. cit.,* p. 601.

the reasons for the "surplus" and "excess plant capacity" in the mineral industry.

Classification of Mineral Resources. In this chapter it is necessary to discuss mineral and power resources as a unit, yet they are highly diverse in their characteristics and economic behavior. Broadly considered, "minerals" include not only those resources generally recognized as minerals such as iron, copper, lead, and the precious metals, but also coal, petroleum, natural gas, water, and the rock materials such as marble, granite, limestone, and slate. These may be grouped on the basis of uses, as follows:

1. Rocks—largely used in construction (granite, marble, sand, clay, cement).
2. Fertilizer minerals (nitrates, phosphates, potash).
3. Energy resources (coal, petroleum, natural gas, water).
4. Ferroalloys (manganese, chrome, nickel, vanadium).
5. Copper, lead, zinc.
6. Gold, silver, platinum.
7. Miscellaneous metallic minerals (aluminum, arsenic, tin, mercury).
8. Miscellaneous non-metallic minerals (asbestos, borax, graphite, gypsum, salt).

Other classifications are "metallic" vs. "non-metallic" and "expendable" vs. "non-expendable." The expendable minerals are those which disappear in use, largely the energy and fertilizer minerals, whereas the non-expendable minerals are those which tend to accumulate—gold, silver, iron, or copper. The problem of conservation is naturally much more serious with the former than with the latter. Another grouping is that of "basic" vs. "contributory." The three basic minerals are: coal, "the reducer and energizer"; iron, "the harnesser and magnetizer"; and copper, "the conductor of electrical energy." These three "lay the foundations of human control of the forces of nature." [1] All others are contributory.

CHARACTERISTICS OF MINERAL LANDS

Minerals Provided by Nature. The *land* aspect of mineral resources is the one of greatest importance for our discussion. In the first place, minerals are an outstanding example of the wealth

[1] Walter H. Voskuil, *Minerals in Modern Industry* (New York, Wiley, 1930), pp. 22–23. Zimmermann, *op. cit.*, pp. 433–35.

provided by nature without the aid of man. Man has not produced them, neither can he add to the supply as made by nature. Minerals cannot be grown. This fact greatly affects the public's attitude toward mineral resources. The feeling that these resources are a heritage of the people justifies heavy taxation and stringent public control or public ownership in the minds of many people.

Exhaustibility of Mineral Resources. Another characteristic of mineral lands is the exhaustibility or non-permanence of the resource. The mine has only one crop; as the minerals are removed the value of the land, insofar as it depends on the minerals, decreases. The income from mines is therefore limited and is not like the rent of land, a constantly recurring return. This has an important bearing on mine valuation and taxation.[1]

Because of the exhaustibility of mines, the mineral industry is a shifting one. As older supplies are exhausted or costs of extraction rise, a move is made to newer districts. Changes in technology or the substitution of one mineral for another also cause readjustments in the industry and shifting from one region to another. Even more significant is the fact that industries dependent on these resources must shift also. The exhaustion of the ore supplies of the Great Lakes region will mean a movement of iron and steel production to the ore regions of the Southeast and to the Atlantic. Exhaustion means depopulation and a declining tax base similar to the decline noted in connection with forests, only more acute. Forest land has possibilities of restoration or of changing to agricultural or recreational uses; the mine has no alternative or abandonment value.

Small Spatial Requirements. Mineral lands require very little space and therefore do not conflict with other land uses except in rare cases.[2] It has been estimated that mining occupies about 24,-

[1] Destructibility of minerals as "land" does not hold for the non-expendable minerals as goods. Gold and silver have existed as coins and jewelry for thousands of years. Objects made of iron, copper, stone, and cement last for decades and even centuries, not necessarily in their original form but after being rebuilt or recast. Metal objects are the most durable of all goods.

[2] One exception is the strip mining of coal in Illinois. More than 15,000 acres of farm land were stripped and destroyed during the past 20 years. It is estimated that more than 184,000 acres of Illinois land are underlain with coal. See H. W. Hannah and Bert Vandervliet, "Effects of Strip Mining on Agricultural Areas in Illinois and Suggested Remedial Measures." *Journal of Land and Public Utility Economics,* August 1939, pp. 296–317.

000,000 acres or approximately the same area as the land in farmsteads of the United States. Since so much mining is done underground and yet the surface property has to be bought and sold on a spatial basis, many conflicts arise. If a vein slants the owner's right ceases as soon as the vein leaves his property, the power to tax likewise stops, as well as the jurisdiction of municipalities. The federal mining laws have modified the ancient doctrine by permitting the owner of the "apex" or top of a mineral vein to follow the vein wherever it may lead. Since veins do not have any regular form this practice leads to serious complications.[1]

Mineral Deposits Are Highly Localized. A corollary to the small spatial requirements is the highly localized character of most mineral deposits. Anthracite coal, for instance, is found principally in one small section of Pennsylvania. Ninety per cent of the radium produced in the past few years came from one deposit, and until 1924 about 60 per cent of the world's supply of vanadium came from one mine. A single mine produces 75 per cent of all the molybdenum. Sometimes the mineral may be widely distributed yet a few rich deposits control the market. Thus 80 per cent of the world's sulphur comes from five deposits controlled by two companies. In other cases concentrated ownership may arise out of exclusive control of patents or of fabrication or reduction plants, control of marketing facilities, or exceptional entrepreneurship. Aluminum, steel, and copper are examples.

The setting here seems perfect for monopoly control, yet competition is never absent or else is just around the corner. All metals are subject to the competition of substitutes, of scrap, new deposits, and the discoveries of chemical science. High prices tend to stimulate activity in all these phases. However, this does not mean that the monopolistic elements that remain may not be detrimental to public welfare and should not be subject to public control. On the other hand, coal, petroleum, and natural gas are so widely distributed and the ownership of the land so diffused that fierce competition takes place and results in overproduction and overexpansion of the industry.[2]

The spatial concentration and uneven distribution of minerals are international as well as intranational. For instance, 40 per

[1] C. K. Leith, *Economic Aspects of Geology* (New York, Holt, 1921), p. 350.
[2] *N. R. B. Report,* pp. 417–18.

cent of the world's gold comes from the Transvaal and 90 per cent of the platinum is mined in the Ural Mountains. This means that certain countries have a monopoly of strategic metals, important in peace-time industry or absolutely essential in modern warfare. Alloys are particularly important. Only fourteen pounds of manganese are needed to manufacture a ton of steel, yet without the alloy it is not steel. The ferroalloys are found in only a few places, often in backward countries.[1]

Another element that tends to concentrate mineral industries is the fact that modern mining calls for expensive machinery, deep tunnels, efficient methods of transportation, and large reserves of land for future exploitation. This naturally tends to concentrate the industry in the hands of powerful companies and in those places where the quality and quantity of ore deposits make large-scale operations profitable. Even the mining of precious metals, once a "free for all" source of wealth in the days of the gold rushes, has largely given place to commonplace machine production.

CHARACTERISTICS OF MINING

Speculation and Risk. One of the differences between surface land use and underground mining is that, by and large, mineral treasures are hidden. They can be found only by arduous prospecting, by digging or drilling in many places until ore or oil are found—although geological knowledge and modern techniques have taken much of the luck and chance elements out of prospecting. Nevertheless, in 1930 over 21,000 wells were drilled in the United States, of which 32 per cent were dry and a total loss to the investors. The annual expenditure for drilling averages about $500,000,000.[2]

The rewards in mining are therefore very uneven. The returns to a few lucky individuals are excessive, but these are balanced by the losses of those who venture time and money but receive nothing. It is a question whether the total return to successful investors is equal to the total outlay of those who are unsuccessful. Even in some of the most successful districts there is no large surplus over expenditures.[3] Mining investments re-

[1] *Ibid.*, pp. 442–43. Leith, *World Minerals, op. cit.*, pp. 48–52.
[2] Zimmermann, *op. cit.*, pp. 502–4.
[3] Leith, *Economic Aspects, op. cit.*, pp. 330, 334.

flect the risk of the industry and the investor is never sure whether he has put his money into a wildcat scheme or a legitimate enterprise.

However, the gambling instinct is the one that helps to keep private capital risking another throw of the dice. There seems to be no limit to the amount of capital which can be enticed into the oil drilling game, for instance. "The failure of nine does not deter the tenth from risking his last penny on the speculative venture." [1] This is one of the most important factors in the overproduction of oil and the failure to conserve it.

Locational Disadvantages. Because mineral deposits are strictly localized they are a good illustration of the principles noted in Chapter V. If too far removed from the centers of consumption they remain unused until the price of the mineral or the cost of transportation becomes such that the mine can be exploited profitably. The mobility of petroleum and natural gas, through railways, steamships, and pipe lines, frees these resources to a considerable extent from this limitation. Furthermore, the price of the mineral tends to become the cost of mining plus the cost of transportation insofar as it is widely used by a dispersed population. Coal is a good example. Anyone living some distance from the coal fields is surprised at the cheapness of this fuel in the coal mining regions.

Depth of the Deposit Increases Costs. Mining, however, is subject to a unique distance factor, namely, the depth from which the deposit has to be lifted. Oil and gas are exceptions in that they often lift themselves in the form of spectacular gushers, but for regular oil production pumping has to be used with surprisingly low yields. In 1930 the wells of the United States as a whole produced an average of only 7½ barrels a day, ranging from an average of 1 barrel a day in Eastern fields to about 16 barrels in the West.[2]

In the solid minerals the economic depth is a question of the cost of bringing the minerals to the surface compared with their value when they get there. The economic supply will always be far less than the physical supply. "It is almost needless to say," said William Stanley Jevons in 1860, "that our [English] mines

[1] Zimmermann, *op. cit.*, p. 529. By permission of Harper & Brothers, publishers.
[2] Bureau of Mines, *Petroleum in 1930*, p. 860.

are literally inexhaustible. We cannot get to the bottom of them; and though we may some day have to pay dear for fuel, it will never be positively wanting."[1] The cost of taking coal from a deep pit may be so great that for all practical purposes the coal seams have been emptied to the bottom and swept clean like a cellar. Borrowing from von Thünen once more, one might say that if a ton of coal has to be expended in mining and bringing that ton to the surface the economic limit of the coal supply has been reached.

Careful estimates of British geologists indicate that only 7 per cent of the physical supply of coal in the United Kingdom has been mined, yet miners have been forced to descend 3,700 feet below the surface and, at shallower depths, to use seams as thin as 14 inches. The average depth of coal workings in Great Britain is 1,023 feet, as compared to 262 feet in the bituminous coal mines of the United States. Copper mines in Michigan have gone a mile below ground.[2]

Costs of Extraction and Exploitation as Limiting Factors. Many mineral resources are outside of the sphere of economic utilization because of the cost of exploiting thin seams, and the expense of smelting or fabrication. Many low-grade ores are not mined because it does not pay to smelt them. In some cases present methods of mining are leaving these in such condition that they may never be recovered; in other instances only a higher price or an improvement in the technique of extraction is needed to make them available. In still other cases the application of more power will bring the desired result. For petroleum the economic supply depends in part on the depth to which wells can be sunk. Its economic availability was increased enormously when engineering technology made a depth of 12,000 to 15,000 feet possible.

Statistics of the reserves of minerals are very deceptive unless the difference between the physical and the economic supply is kept in mind. Nickel, which is produced in small quantities in only a few places, is twice as abundant as copper, five times as abundant as zinc, ten times as abundant as lead, and fifty to one hundred times as abundant as tin.[3] The figures for coal, iron,

[1] Quoted in Wright, *Population, op. cit.*, p. 83.

[2] Zimmermann, *op. cit.*, p. 467. *N. R. B. Report*, pp. 396–97.

[3] Zimmermann, *op. cit.*, p. 437.

and oil reserves hide the fact that the supplies of the future can be obtained only by a greater expenditure of energy and costs.

The Law of Diminishing Returns in Mining. This "supreme law of extractive industries" means that speeding up production reduces efficiency and involves going to greater depths, thus rapidly increasing the costs of production. To escape the law, operators tend to shift to new territory, especially in such widespread resources as coal. A rise in prices also induces thousands of wagon mines and "snow birds" (i.e., operators who mine only in winter) to start working. Surplus plant capacity is thereby established without regard to the effect on the industry. Moreover, it does not necessarily follow that mines cease operation because prices fall, a condition similar to that in agriculture and forestry. Since the mine has no alternative use, the owners have the choice of continuing work or complete idleness. To maintain the plant in idleness means overhead costs greater than in the average industrial establishment. Many mines will be made unfit for work by the escape of gas or will become filled with water. Besides, the usual carrying costs, taxes, interest, and maintenance continue as before.

Unusual Labor Conditions in Mining. Mines are usually in places where little or no alternative opportunities exist for the miners. The operator often feels a responsibility to the workman to keep the mine going, and yet labor is a large part of the cost of operation in many cases. In Great Britain, for instance, about 70 per cent of the expense of mining coal is labor cost. This item is also important in the United States and is reflected in the labor situation. The competitive advantage of operators in the non-unionized areas of West Virginia and Kentucky, plus some physical advantages, has caused a decided shift in the industry from the unionized areas to these two non-unionized states.[1]

As a result of these factors many mines are now submarginal. Unwisely opened mines produce much the same conditions as premature agricultural developments or "unripe" suburban subdivisions. Taxes become burdensome and stranded communities bear the brunt of the disaster. It is said that the condition of stranded metal and coal miners is "perhaps the most tragic of any group of American workers. . . . This is now recognized to be

[1] *Ibid.*, pp. 472–78.

a social responsibility and where necessary a government responsibility."[1] The mine worker not only has the economic hazards of a shifting, seasonal, or erratic industry, but his work is also injurious to his health and more dangerous to life and limb than any other major occupation. Falling rocks, explosives, gases, flooding, high temperatures, excessive humidity, and harmful waters and dusts are among the perils of mining. Dust is especially harmful. It is not to our credit that, with the exception of Chile, the United States is the most backward nation in the world in mine accident prevention.[2]

THE POWER RESOURCES AND THEIR STRATEGIC POSITION

Because they are expendable resources (with the exception of water power), and because so much of our modern civilization

TABLE 34

SOURCES OF ENERGY IN THE UNITED STATES

	Percentage of Total	
	1923 *	1933 †
1. Coal	65%	58.4%
Bituminous	—	50.3
Anthracite	—	8.1
2. Oil	18.	21.4
3. Firewood	6.	5.5
4. Water power	4.	6.3
5. Natural gas	4.	5.8
6. Work animals	3.	2.5
7. Wind	.1	.1

* F. G. Tyron and Lida Mann, "Mineral Resources for Future Populations" in *Population Problems*, ed. L. I. Dublin, Boston, Houghton, Mifflin, (1926), p. 123.

† S. S. Wyer, "Man's Shift from Muscle to Mechanical Power," cited in Zimmermann, *op. cit.*, p. 543.

depends upon them, the power minerals are of special significance. Our dependence on stored-up energy is almost appalling. One-half of the energy used in the United States comes from bituminous coal, a little over one-fifth from oil, 8 per cent from anthracite, and almost 6 per cent from natural gas—a total of almost 86

[1] *N. R. B. Report,* pp. 423–25, at 425.

[2] *Ibid.,* pp. 435–37.

per cent. Water power furnishes 6.3 per cent, followed closely by firewood with 5.5 per cent, while animate energy, "animal muscle," is only 2½ per cent and wind only 0.1 per cent of the total. The small proportion contributed by water power is surprising, but it has become relatively more important since 1923, and so has natural gas.

Coal. The problems of the coal mining industry have been noted; they present the paradox of overproduction in a resource that after all is exhaustible. Under the present adjustments in society food and water alone outrank coal as necessaries of life and over a billion tons per year are mined to furnish fuel, electricity, gas, heat for metallurgical processes, and transportation, particularly through the railways. In spite of this demand it is said that coal mining was overdeveloped twenty, forty, and even fifty years ago. In 1929 the bituminous coal industry was burdened with a huge surplus of plant capacity due to many causes and not simply to the World War. The excess capacity has been a prime factor in the cut-throat competition, the resource waste, the financial losses, the low wages, and the turbulent labor relations of this industry. The problem of capacity is twofold—first, to reduce the present surplus and, second, to control unwise expansion in the future so as to prevent a repetition of past overdevelopment.[1]

In view of the situation in bituminous coal it is a grave question whether the rapid expansion of water power under the sponsorship of the government is altogether sound. The National Coal Association has pointed out that the development of 6,500,000 horsepower on the St. Lawrence would destroy the market for 58,000,000 tons of bituminous coal annually, do away with 19,000 freight trains per year, and affect 100,000 coal mine employees.[2] The Planning Committee for Mineral Policy cautiously said, "The fundamental relationship among the three great sources of power—coal, oil and hydro plants—should be understood and articulated in any broad power program, and the protests of the coal miners and mine workers against alleged too rapid development of hydo-electric projects at public expense warrants careful study to determine their merit."[3]

[1] *N. R. B. Report,* pp. 403–4.

[2] E. A. Holbrook, *The Coal Industry and the Government's Hydro-electric Plants* (National Coal Association, Washington, D. C.), p. 12.

[3] *N. R. B. Report,* p. 424.

In support of hydro plants it is often argued that they conserve coal by leaving it in the ground. It would be more logical to mine the coal as long as it can furnish cheaper power than water, and later switch to the permanent type of power. This can be produced at any time and will be produced as soon as coal becomes expensive enough.[1] Besides, the need for conservation is understood better today than in 1910. Then it was feared that there "would be no more coal" in a hundred years. The known physical reserves are said to be 3,182,000,000,000 net tons, enough to last over 2,000 years at the 1929 level of consumption. However, the public will become aware of a growing scarcity as we resort to thinner or less accessible seams and beds of poorer quality; therefore, elimination of waste, careful mining, and the proper utilization of coal is still important.[2]

Petroleum and Natural Gas. Second in importance as a source of energy in the United States is petroleum, but this does not indicate its importance for high-speed locomotion and for lubrication. "Lubricating oil is perhaps the most important key commodity of modern machine civilization. Even if petroleum furnished no other product but lubricating oil, it would have to be considered one of the most important natural resources." [3] This point is emphasized here because the public is conscious primarily of gasoline, only one of the many products of petroleum. It is estimated that $15,000,000,000 is invested in automobiles in the United States, and during the past 75 years this country produced and consumed two-thirds of the world's production of oil, although its share of the total world reserves did not exceed one-fifth.[4] Kerosene, once the chief product of petroleum, is now of small importance. Gas and fuel oil, asphalt, paraffin, and petroleum coke are other products.

Just as in the case of coal, a "surplus" exists in the production

[1] Cf. "Had our government followed the policy of carefully restricting the alienation of mineral resources so that the value of the coal might be higher, the water powers of America would probably have been fully utilized a generation ago."—L. C. Gray, "Economic Possibilities of Conservation," *Quarterly Journal of Economics,* May, 1913.

[2] G. S. Rice, A. C. Fieldner, and F. G. Tyron, "Conservation of Coal Resources," in *Transactions of Third World Power Conference,* Vol. VI (Washington, Government Printing Office, 1936).

[3] Zimmermann, *op. cit.,* p. 486. By permission of Harper and Brothers, publishers.

[4] *N. R. B. Report,* p. 405.

of petroleum, largely due to the land relationships under which oil is exploited. The right to drill for oil goes with the ownership of the surface, but petroleum is a migratory mineral and moves in the direction of decreased pressure propelled by the pressure of gas. The owner of a 10-acre lot can drain the petroleum from a whole geological field. Adjacent property owners must drill at once or lose the oil beneath their own property. Operators put their wells close to the boundaries of their tracts, or even in the corners, so as to drain, not only beneath the surface they own but that of their neighbors. The neighbors follow by planting wells opposite those already started. Then a mad race begins to bring in the first "gusher" and to drain the pool before the next well also taps the same resource. As more wells "come in," less pressure is available for each one and production goes down. Inefficient methods of drilling and of controlling the escape of gas, and loss when the oil flows too fast are some of the reasons why the waste of this resource is indescribable.

"The United States, through the Geological Survey, has spent millions of dollars in learning and proving that oil does not occur in 160 acre tracts, yet tries to do so by fiat, or, at least ignores legally the fact that oil is migratory." [1] This paradox results from the fact that jurists applied the same reasoning to oil that had been applied to game—*ferae bestiae naturae,* i.e., the landowner does not have title to the wild game on his land until he has reduced it to possession.

Van Hise predicted in 1910 that if the consumption of petroleum continued to increase as it had in the past, oil supplies might be exhausted by 1935.[2] Since then the amazing fields in Texas, California, and Oklahoma have come into production, and technological advances in drilling, rejuvenation, and refining have added substantially to the economic supply of oil. Cracking alone has doubled our potential gasoline resources.[3] Nevertheless, the National Resources Board Report points out that the United States is depleting its resources faster than any other country with oil reserves of major importance, and predicts a shortage within

[1] C. G. Gilbert and J. E. Pogue, *Petroleum, A Resource Interpretation* (U. S. National Museum, Bulletin 102, Part 6), p. 61.

[2] *The Conservation of Natural Resources in the United States* (New York, Macmillan, 1910), p. 48.

[3] Voskuil, *op. cit.,* p. 149.

the next fifteen years which can only be prevented by the discovery of new fields.[1]

Almost 6 per cent of our total supply of energy comes from natural gas. Natural gas is a by-product of oil production and is often wasted. In 1931–32 the wastage in the Oklahoma City field averaged 300,000,000 cubic feet per day, and 1,000,000,000 cubic feet were blown into the air daily in the Texas Panhandle in 1934. The latter amount is equal to 40,000 tons of coal.[2] Natural gas conservation is dependent upon a revamping of the same fundamental property relationships as apply to petroleum. Unit development and the operation of entire pools should be substituted for the "law of capture." This is being applied on federal lands and should be extended to private lands.

Water Power. During the "conservation era" the fear of a shortage of energy minerals was somewhat allayed by the belief that water power would become an adequate substitute. Van Hise quoted W J McGee as saying that water power "exceeds our entire mechanical power in use, would operate every mill, drive every spindle, propel every train and boat and light every city, town and village in the country." [3] However, water power has certain limitations even though electricity has freed it of its former earth-bound character. It cannot take the place of coal in certain metallurgical processes nor can it furnish power for ships or take the place of gasoline in automobiles, trucks, and tractors. The electric automobile has now passed into memory, along with the "steamer." Furthermore, the localization of water power is still a stubborn fact. At the present time electric current cannot be sent profitably for longer distances than 300 miles. The per-mile cost of lines rises rapidly with the distance, and the loss in power transmitted becomes progressively greater. This is likewise a limiting factor in the proposal to burn coal at the mines, convert the energy into electricity, and transmit the current. Unless large quantities of water are available at the mine for condensing purposes, this plan also is impracticable. About 400 to 500 tons of water are necessary for every ton of coal burned. It is estimated that the Hudson Avenue Generating Station in

[1] *Op. cit.*, p. 405.
[2] *Ibid.*, p. 406.
[3] Van Hise, *Conservation*, *op. cit.*, p. 120.

New York uses twice as much water as do the inhabitants of Greater New York for domestic purposes.[1]

The region around Niagara, which comprises about one-fourth of the water power resources of the United States and Canada, lies in the very heart of manufacturing and population concentration and is able to market its power readily. On the other hand, the Puget Sound region, which has one-third of the potential water power, is far from the power-consuming centers. A third concentration lies in the Boulder Dam area and a smaller one in the southern Appalachians.[2] Insofar as industries depend more on cheap power and relatively less on the market and raw materials, they can be attracted to areas with abundant hydro-electric power. Nitrate fixation, aluminum reduction, and paper making seek power sites. The cheap, steady power of Niagara has drawn industries using current for electric furnaces that operate twenty-four hours a day. The city of Niagara has grown from a village of 8,000 to an industrial city of 80,000.[3]

The impression is general that water power is *cheap* power because nature carries rainfall to the top of elevations and all man has to do is to put a turbine in the path of the water as it rushes back to the sea; steam, on the other hand, requires fuel which has to be mined, transported, and laboriously fed into furnaces. If fuel and labor were the only costs, the advantage would be with water power. However, other factors must be considered.

Only a few water power sites have a uniform flow like Niagara. Most of the streams have high water in the spring or fall and low water at other times, especially in winter when the supply is locked up by freezing. On such streams the operator has the choice of building a plant suited to the minimum flow or one suited to the maximum, using steam stand-by plants to keep the supply of current at the maximum. Another alternative is to build storage dams, but then the capital investment becomes higher for the hydroelectric plant than for the corresponding cost of the powerhouse and equipment of a steam plant. Unlike steam plants, which can be built in units as the demand for cur-

[1] Zimmermann, *op. cit.*, p. 568.

[2] E. Huntington and F. E. Williams, *Business Geography* (New York, Wiley, 1926), pp. 139–47.

[3] Zimmermann, *op. cit.*, p. 577.

rent grows, the dam generally must be built for ultimate capacity. Surveys, the cost of acquiring flowage rights, the dam with its fishways and locks, not forgetting the invisible carrying costs of interest and taxes during construction, tend to make the investment considerably above that of a fuel power plant. Operating costs, on the other hand, are higher for the latter—for labor and especially for fuel. However, improvements in the use of fuel have been so remarkable that this difference is becoming less marked, whereas the cost of putting up the dams at less and less economical sites is becoming greater. As a consequence, the superior advantages of water power in many places are lessened and in some places have disappeared.

The most effective way to use both steam and hydro plants is through a co-ordination of the two in a so-called "Grid system" wherever this can be done. Surplus power in one plant may be utilized at places where low water has created a deficiency and steam and water can supplement each other.[1]

Other Substitutes for Mineral Fuels. Many suggestions have been made in the way of substitutes for mineral fuels. For instance, alcohol could be substituted for gasoline, but it would take our entire corn crop to replace the gasoline now being used per year. The energy in a whole year's production of human food is equal to only 3 per cent of our annual production of fuel.[2] Wind power has been used for centuries but it has not proved as efficient as might have been expected. The tides, direct energy from the sun, and even the atom have been considered as power sources, but these forces are either very uncertain and variable or else their utilization awaits new discoveries in physics and chemistry. Until then, conservation of mineral resources, especially the energy minerals, is of paramount importance.

THE CONSERVATION OF MINERAL RESOURCES

Costs of Conservation to the Producer. Since mineral resources are definitely limited and exhaustible, their conservation may be thought of as a rationing or husbanding over a period of years, just as a group of shipwrecked sailors might ration a limited

[1] *Ibid.*, pp. 568–83. Voskuil, *The Economics of Water Power Development* (Chicago, A. W. Shaw, 1928), Chap. III.

[2] Dublin, *Population Problems, op. cit.*, pp. 135–36.

supply of food in order to make it last as long as possible. In the case of minerals, the theoretical ideal might be that future generations should have an equal share with present generations. Assuming the nation's life to be a million years (although every nation presumes it has infinite life), the present generation would therefore be entitled to use one millionth of the coal reserves in one year. However, the present generation refuses to accept this point of view. It is not interested in people living a million years from now, in fact its interest rarely goes beyond two generations. While it might be agreed that something should be left for unborn future generations, most people want a much larger fraction than the equal share "right now."

The example may be made more reasonable, however. According to the National Resources Board Report, "The proved reserves of oil recoverable by the usual methods of production are estimated to be about 13 billion barrels which would last approximately 15 years at the 1933 rate of consumption."[1] In other words, the present rate of consumption may be assumed to be about 1,000,000,000 barrels a year. To complete the illustration, assume also that no more reserves are in sight and that the public is aware of this fact. It is desired to conserve the 13,000,000,000 barrels by restricting output so as to extend the period of use from 15 to 60 years. Clearly the rate of consumption must be cut to 25 per cent of the present volume, less than 250,000,000 barrels per year, or the supply will not last. Managing an exhaustible supply in this way conforms to Zimmermann's definition: "Conservation involves a reduction in the rate of disappearance or consumption, and a corresponding increase in the unused surplus at the end of a given period."[2]

This way of rationing the supplies placed on the market should meet the test of "orderly and efficient" use and "wise use"—words sometimes used in defining conservation—since it avoids hoarding on the one hand and dumping the supply on the market on the other.

Assuming the oil to be on privately owned land this plan permits the owner to market his resource in sixty annual installments. Whether he leaves the oil in the ground or drills it and

[1] *Op. cit.*, p. 405.
[2] Zimmermann, *op. cit.*, p. 790.

stores it above ground, the principle is the same, except that his costs will be higher in the second case.

Immediately the owner is faced with ripening or carrying costs. As in the case of forests, he has to consider his original investment, annual costs for protection, insurance, legal charges, and taxes, with interest on all these outlays compounded until the time when the resource is placed on the market. In the illustration used above these costs may be set up for each of the sixty annual installments. The last quantity sold will have charged against it its share of the original investment, and sixty payments of taxes with interest on all outlays. If his receipts cover all the costs the owner will have all his money back plus compound interest. If the income fails to cover the costs so set up, he has simply earned a lower rate of interest than was anticipated or no interest at all. Perhaps the investment may fail to return even the actual outlays.

However, this assumes that the price of oil will remain the same for sixty years. Given an exhaustible and irreplaceable resource, would it not be more reasonable to expect the price to rise as the point of exhaustion is approached? If this were true each succeeding installment would sell for more than its predecessor, and the later returns should more than cover the accumulating costs and leave a larger profit for the owner. This would perhaps meet the definition that conservation seeks to secure as great or even greater *income* from the exploitation of natural resources as is enjoyed by present generations.[1] It is not even necessary that the owner should place *equal* installments on the market. Let the earlier ones be greater and the others less and the same general conditions would obtain, but they would not result in the same total income and costs.

Why should not conservation pay if rising prices tend to cover the costs of conserving the resource for future generations? Unfortunately, there is no guarantee that prices will rise sufficiently to cover the costs; in fact, they may not rise at all. It is not realistic to assume that "no substitute is in sight." Many minerals are interchangeable. Oil, bituminous coal, and natural gas have been substituted for anthracite to such an extent that the anthra-

[1] Conrad H. Hammar, "Economic Aspects of Conservation," *Journal of Land and Public Utility Economics,* August, 1931, p. 290.

cite industry remained stationary between 1916 and 1926 and has been declining ever since. Perhaps the best "conservation" would be to get anthracite out of the earth as fast as possible because in another fifty years hard coal may be as useless as the rock in which it is embedded.

Furthermore, the owner cannot be certain that new fields will not be discovered or that new processes will not double the economic supply of oil. The experience of lumber operators who banked on a timber famine, described in Chapter IX is a case in point. The operator also cannot predict the extent of the importation of oil from foreign countries.

Another assumption is that individual owners will co-operate and control the drilling, storage, and marketing of oil or that they will consent to government control of the industry. This could be accomplished by agreements, trusts, or cartels. The history of the oil industry, however, shows the futility of voluntary agreements.[1] Under highly competitive conditions, with unequal financial power to withhold, concerted action becomes impossible. Goaded by high carrying charges or by the desire to take advantage of the withholding policy of others, agreements are broken and the other producers are forced to fall in line.

It might be argued that those who adopt the policy of conservation should welcome the failure of competitors to conserve; let the violators exhaust their supply now, and in the future the lion's share will fall to those who have withheld. Practically, there are few investors or even corporations in such a favored financial position that they can accept losses in the present in the hope of future gains, even if these could be guaranteed, to say nothing of the fact that there is no assurance of adequate future prices.

Conservation is impossible for the individual under cut-throat competition. Various industries faced with this fact are vainly casting about for a means of stabilizing conditions and for some way to get united action to prevent the enormous physical losses of such resources as coal, oil, and gas. Yet unrestricted competition, made mandatory by the anti-trust laws, still prevails. It was an interesting paradox of the Roosevelt conservation era that an

[1] John Ise, *The United States Oil Policy* (New Haven, Yale University Press, 1926), Chap. III.

anti-trust campaign and crusade for conservation were on the stage at the same time. As Zimmermann says, "The trust buster and the conservationist were strange bed fellows," and he adds, "the great weakness of the Rooseveltian conservation campaign lay in the unwillingness or inability to draw logical conclusions from their own proposals." [1]

Costs of Conservation to the Consumer. So far the discussion has centered on the reaction of the producer to holding his oil reserves for sixty years instead of allowing them to be consumed in fifteen years. However, the consumer is also concerned. At the present rate of production or "overproduction," a billion barrels of oil are placed on the market every year, and the automobile driver gets his gasoline at a price of about 15 cents plus taxes. If the supply were deliberately cut to one-fourth of the present amount, it is reasonable to suppose that the consumer would have to pay 40 to 50 cents a gallon and that a large number of cars would stay in the garage. There is no escape from the results of a policy of restricting the present supply in order to leave a surplus for future generations, namely, higher prices for the present generations. Whether the withholding is done by private owners or by the government is immaterial. The test of the sincerity of a conservation crusader should be his willingness to pay more for exhaustible resources today in order that shadowy future generations may also have oil, coal, game, forest products, or natural gas. Perhaps the majority of our people, when confronted with this test, will applaud Senator Howe of Wisconsin who said in a speech in 1871: "I am . . . ready to labor by the side of the senator from Massachusetts for the welfare of the government today . . . but when he calls upon us to embark very heavily in the protection of generations yet unborn, I am very much inclined to reply that they have never done anything for me and I do not want to sacrifice too much." [2]

Perhaps the method described above goes beyond the popular concept of conservation. Some writers emphasize "elimination of waste" and point to the progress made in engineering, in mining, and in efficient utilization of the resource after it is mined.

[1] *Op. cit.*, p. 785. By permission of Harper & Brothers, publishers.

[2] Quoted in John Ise, *The United States Forest Policy* (New Haven, Yale University Press, 1920), p. 53.

Much progress has been made in this respect, it is true, and much accomplished without increasing costs. Many conservational measures can be carried out without governmental control, direction, or ownership. C. K. Leith says that the mineral industry desires conservation as much as the public and has done much to eliminate wastes and to project their operations over a long period. The larger and stronger a corporation is financially, the easier it is to do this. The anti-trust laws, whatever their other merits, may be anti-conservational in their application to mining.[1]

Finally, the policy of conservation must conform to the characteristics of each specific mineral. This means one thing for an exhaustible resource and another for iron and copper, which accumulate above the earth's surface after being mined. It is conceivable that with a stationary population only a small amount of new iron will be needed to keep up the accumulated stock and to replace losses by rust, corrosion, wear, and casualties such as shipwrecks. The question might even be raised whether society would not benefit by getting minerals like copper out of the earth and using them freely, shifting them from one use to another as the demand shifted.

MINERAL LAND POLICIES OF THE UNITED STATES

Policies before the Conservation Era. In view of the need for conservation and the public interest in minerals, especially since they are vital to national defense and survival, the question of adequate public control and public ownership is more important in this form of land than in any other. The United States started with a policy of alienating the surface of the public domain but reserving the minerals and leasing mining rights. This was before much was known about minerals, so the laws specifically reserved only gold, silver, copper, lead, and salines. However in 1829 lead mines and lands in Missouri were opened to sale, and in 1846 Congress authorized the sale of the reserved lead mines and lands in Arkansas, Iowa, Illinois, and Wisconsin. This policy was extended to other areas soon afterward and to coal in 1864.

Gold was discovered in California before the state had any governmental organization, and miners obtained mineral lands under local customs. By 1866 a billion dollars in gold and silver

[1] *World Minerals, op. cit.*, Chap. VI, "Conservation."

had been taken from the public domain without the soil's becoming property in the manner prescribed for agricultural lands. In 1866 Congress recognized and validated the rights so acquired and "provided that the mineral lands of the public domain should be free and open to exploitation and occupation and to acquisition by conforming in general to local customs," i.e., "the general mining law became one of possessory occupation."[1] This means, in short, that the miner neither leased the land from the government nor acquired it under one of the land acts used by farmers and lumbermen. Coal lands, however, were alienated under a policy of sale in 1864, and in 1870 to 1872 the "principle of sale and purchase" was extended to mineral lands, in general at $2.50 to $5.00 per acre.

Withdrawals and Leasing after 1906. One of the definite results of the "conservation era" was the change in our mineral land policy. Beginning with the coal and oil classifications and withdrawals of 1906, and the act of Congress of 1914 setting up the leasing of coal lands in Alaska, this policy was extended to include the leasing of potash lands in 1917 and by subsequent acts to other minerals within the public domain. Private individuals may obtain the right in fee to metalliferous minerals and through *leases* the right to mine coal, oil, gas, or phosphate on all federally owned land, except national parks and monuments and Indian reservations. About 35,000,000 additional acres have also been sold on which the government has reserved the mineral rights. Royalties received from the leases up to July 1, 1934, amounted to

[1] *N. R. B. Report,* p. 421.

In view of the present interest in districts for conservation it is noteworthy that the same device was used by miners before state or territorial governments could provide rules and laws. Before Colorado became a territory in 1861 the country was divided into "mining districts," some less than a mile square, others more extensive, which became permanent geographical units in place of towns, townships, and sections for the purpose of describing the location of real estate of all kinds. By-laws were adopted at a meeting of miners and provided for officers, including a recorder who kept a record of claims and transfers, and a judge who carried out the rules. The regulations defined the name and boundaries of the district designated by natural objects and described the manner of making a claim, the number of feet which should constitute a claim, and the amount of surface allowed. As in water rights, non-use forfeited the right to hold the land, so the amount and kind of work required to hold a claim were prescribed. The Colorado customs were based upon those established in California and these in turn can be traced to Mexican and Spanish codes. When the territory was organized the district regulations were recognized to have all the force of laws. R. S. Morrison, *Mining Rights in Colorado* (Denver, Chain & Hardy, 1879), pp. 3–18.

about $108,000,000, of which only 10 per cent is retained by the federal government, 37½ per cent going to the states and the remainder to the reclamation fund. This system has proved advantageous to the industry and to the government although some administrative features need adjustment. Government ownership proved to be especially advantageous in holding back oil production, whereas the opposite condition in private fields demoralized the markets.[1]

Public Ownership of Mineral Lands. In view of the difficulties of conservation by the individual, much can be said for public ownership of mineral lands. This does not imply government operation any more than public ownership of forests necessarily means government lumbering. By merely retaining ownership of the public domain the government makes no outlays for land, and even if it should purchase mines it has the advantage of obtaining money at low rates of interest. The government does not have to pay taxes or secure the usual profits of the private investor. Furthermore, mineral resources are publicly owned in Canada, France, Germany, Spain, Russia, Italy, Mexico, and nearly all of the South American countries, partly as a conservation measure and partly as a factor in their defense programs. Most of the countries of western Europe have also reserved the undiscovered mineral resources on private property to their governments, except when previously conveyed to private owners or, in some cases, where the minerals occur at the surface. The same policy is followed with some variations in the British colonies and in Latin American countries. Such mineral properties are "open for development either by the owner of the surface or others on a rental, lease, specific tax, labor, or concession bases." The government holds the title, exacts tribute, and more or less directs and controls the operation.[2]

In spite of the arguments which can be marshalled in favor of public ownership of mineral lands, the National Resources Board Committee for Mineral Policy did not recommend the general extension of public ownership of minerals now in private ownership, with the exception of the purchase and retirement of a por-

[1] *N. R. B. Report,* pp. 419–22. Special acts have opened leasing on Indian Reservations from time to time in which case the royalties go to the tribe or allottee.

[2] Leith, *Economic Aspects, op. cit.,* p. 344.

tion of the coal reserves and of some submarginal coal mines, and the holding in public ownership of tax-delinquent mineral deposits until the minerals are needed, when they are to be leased with royalties paid to the state. Said the committee: "Whatever the abstract merits of public ownership may be, private ownership is so inherently a part of the American genius and tradition, and is so firmly entrenched, by law and custom, as a national policy, that the practical difficulties alone of any general reversal of the status quo at this late date appear insuperable. However, future conditions cannot be foreseen and the committee recognizes the possibility that restoration to public ownership of minerals now privately owned may sometime become a desirable feature of national policy."[1] It was felt that the problems could best be solved under private ownership, with government control and supervision.

Regulations in the Interest of Conservation. Because so much of the difficulty arises out of the unrestrained competition in coal, oil, copper, and other minerals, it is proposed that the industry be permitted to control competition under federal supervision, and in the case of coal to fix maximum and minimum prices with adequate safeguards for the workers and consumers.[2] Furthermore, the police power seems strong enough to enforce laws against unnecessary loss, destruction, or waste. This is supported by a decision of the United States Supreme Court.[3] However, even though the power exists, the real test lies in the willingness of the people to use the instrument at their command.

Taxation. Heavy taxation of minerals is based upon the feeling that the public has more interest in these resources than in the others and is entitled to a larger share of the income. Mines being immobile, the local governments are prone to take advantage of this characteristic of land, especially if the reserves are in absentee ownership. However, the tax on mineral land operates much as the general property tax on forest land. Mine owners build up reserves in order to assure a future supply of raw ma-

[1] *N. R. B. Report,* p. 423.

[2] *Ibid.,* pp. 400–415, 417–18.

[3] *Champlin Refining Co.* v. *Corporation Commission of Oklahoma,* 286 U. S. 230, 233. "Land owners do not have absolute title to the gas and oil that may permeate below the surface. . . . The right to take and thus acquire ownership is subject to the reasonable exertion of the power of the State to prevent unnecessary loss, destruction, or waste."

terials for their plants. Much of the ore will not be needed for some time to come, which means that the carrying charges soon make "holding" unbearable. Operators must open their mines to provide an income to meet taxes and other outlays, thus forcing selective mining, hasty methods of extraction, and waste. The severance tax would induce better conservation but might encourage concentration of ownership, speculation, and monopoly. It has been suggested that owners be relieved of ad valorem taxes on reserves representing "a reasonable ratio to their production." On reserves held beyond the ratio the ad valorem taxes should be maintained or increased. Should this result in tax delinquency and reversion of the land so taxed, the state could lease the reverted land to the companies. In addition the state should also lay a reasonable output tax on all mines.[1]

INTERNATIONAL ASPECTS OF MINERALS

The localization of minerals makes practically every nation dependent on others for certain minerals. For instance, the United States, the outstanding mineral country of the world, has to depend on foreign countries for antimony, chromite, nickel, tin, manganese, asbestos, bauxite, and platinum and is largely dependent on foreign sources for still other minerals.

However, the generous supply of fuels—coal, oil, and natural gas—and of iron, copper, and other vital resources places us at the head of the list of manufacturing and industrial nations. The United States is part of the region centering around the North Atlantic which has the highest concentration of minerals on the globe. The North Atlantic countries have in their possession the major resources of coal, iron, copper, lead, zinc, oil, and gas. Their power resources enable them to do five times the mechanical work of Russia, China, and India combined, although they have only one-third as much population as these three countries. "With a fifth of the world's population, this group of countries is doing about 2/3 of the world's work. The United States alone is doing about 40% of the world's work, and its next competitor, Great Britain, about a quarter as much as the United States. . . . From this belt originates the commercial and in some cases the political, control of a preponderant part of the mineral produc-

[1] *N. R. B. Report*, pp. 426–28, at p. 427.

tion of the rest of the world."[1] These nations have experienced the greatest urbanization and commercialization, and also have the "sinews of war."

"Any nation can start a war, but capacity to sustain it effectively under modern conditions is about commensurate with its industrial power based on minerals, particularly the mineral fuels, iron, copper, lead and zinc. The time is gone by when military strength can be measured mainly by the number of men available."[2] The military rank of a nation therefore tends to correspond with its rank in available mineral resources. This places at a disadvantage the Mediterranean, South America, Asia, and, for the present, Germany. Great Britain's mineral resources are widely scattered over the entire empire, which makes her position somewhat precarious. Naturally there has been a desire to develop all resources within the nation and to build up reserves in foreign countries.

One way of building up reserves is to buy scrap metals. Italy and Japan began buying American scrap iron even before 1935, and later Great Britain, Poland, China, and Germany were added to the list of our customers. A second method is to annex actual territory, as happened with Alsace and Silesia, or to establish controls or possession in backward countries. However, the world was pretty well staked out by the time the minerals became of major importance and part of the world's history has been the reshuffling of ownership, of which Manchuria is an example. A third way of gaining control of minerals is through "peaceful penetration." American, French, and English nationals or corporations seek minerals and obtain concessions in so-called "backward nations." Through the property control exercised by their nationals, nations obtain control over mineral resources. For instance, Great Britain and France control the chrome supplies of the world through their concessions in Rhodesia and New Caledonia. Great Britain controls the tin supply of the Malay States.

Ideally, the world would be better off if absolutely free ex-

[1] C. K. Leith, "Exploration and World Progress," *Foreign Affairs,* October, 1927, p. 133. In his later work, *World Minerals and World Politics* (*op. cit.,* 1931), he says that the United States does one-half of the world's work.

[2] Leith, *World Minerals, op. cit.,* p. 142.

change of minerals gave them the benefit of comparative advantage to the fullest extent. But unfortunately the policy of nations has been to take advantage of their monopolistic positions, a policy which has become intensified by "wars and rumors of wars." To secure a supply of its own, to become independent of foreign supplies, tariffs are used to stimulate mining and fabrication at home. Others use export tariffs to secure revenue, control markets, or conserve the minerals. Chile has placed an export tariff on nitrates and Peru on copper and vanadium. Bounties, embargoes, and taxes are other political measures used.[1] In some cases the governments participate in the exploration, production, and marketing of mineral products or give special rates on the railroads. Other nations have nationalized their mineral resources; some have aided their nationals to get concessions in foreign countries. Probably in no field of production is there so much public interference, subsidy, and control as in the mineral industry.[2]

Exploitation in Undeveloped Nations. The problems of the exploitation of mineral resources in a country not sufficiently developed to do its own exploitation are certainly perplexing. The experience of the United States in Mexico is an example. Here nationals used to one set of laws came in contact with a people who held a very different conception of property in mineral land. When a conflict of this kind arises, the home country is called upon to protect the "legitimate interests" of its nationals and usually does so under one pretext or another. It generally deplores or ignores "exploitation."

Surely a sovereign nation has the right to do as it pleases with its own resources. It may argue that it prefers to conserve them for its own people, to be exploited in the future when they are ready for it. Practically, its policy in this respect will be dictated by the North Atlantic nations, the great exploiters of mineral wealth in the past, who will furnish the great political and commercial thrust against the rest of the world in the future. Among these North Atlantic nations, the United States is the chief

[1] B. B. Wallace and L. R. Edminister, *International Control of Raw Materials* (Brookings Institution, 1930).

[2] Leith, *World Minerals, op. cit.,* Chaps. IV and V.

mineral exploiter and will continue so even though we, or any other nation for that matter, refuse to call a spade a spade and admit we are exploiting.

"Our thesis, if you please," says Leith, "is acceptance of the principle that might makes right, but only to the extent and in the sense that nature's environment creates might. Human volition plays little part, and it seems futile to argue this as a moral or ethical question. This concentration of power, with its consequences, is no more right or wrong than nature's original distribution of resources."[1] However, he makes a plea for intelligent, open exploitation with due regard for the rights of the peoples whose resources are being developed. He favors international agreements to secure freedom of exchange of minerals and agreements on methods of exploitation.

[1] "Exploration and World Progress," *op. cit.*, p. 137. See also John Donaldson, *International Economic Relations,* Chap. XII: "Public, Foreign and International Control of Raw Materials; the Question of World Monopoly of Essential Supplies."

XIII

URBANIZATION AND URBAN LAND

"History and archeology teach us that since time immemorial the city has been the center of civilization by which the surrounding region has been raised from barbarism to culture. Science and art, philosophy and higher religion may indeed be regarded as the natural products of city life. The city existed before the state, which was created by it." [1] The persistence of certain cities, even though political states have come and gone, is remarkable. Damascus, Jerusalem, Rome, and the Hanseatic cities are examples. City life is really as old as civilization. Even in primitive times people congregated in villages for more effective co-operation and for defense. Defense has been a factor in the location of cities even in modern times—Boston situated on a peninsula, New York, Paris, and Venice on islands are examples, and Fort Pitt became Pittsburgh.

Religion and politics have also been important elements in urbanization. The ancient oriental city developed around a god and a king, who formed the center from which religious and political power radiated. The court and the temple, the army and the priests were the nucleus of population, which in turn attracted merchants and gave impetus to manufacturing. Babylon became a city of a million people. Rome, Athens, and Jerusalem owed their origins to religion and political power. Some of these ancient cities are still religious capitals. In America, Salt Lake City is perhaps the best example of a "religious city." Many of our state capitals and county seats, and the capitals of many nations were located by some legislative body or by the decision of a ruler. Sometimes these sites were advantageously located for other purposes and "political cities" have become large and prosperous, but not in every case. Recreational areas also attract concentrations of people.

Although large populations lived in cities in ancient times,

[1] Karl Kekoni, "The Problem of the City," *Scientific Monthly*, December, 1937, pp. 547–54, at 547.

the medieval period was not conducive to urbanization on a large scale. London probably had no more than 25,000 people in the thirteenth century and not over 40,000 at the beginning of the fifteenth. According to Ashley, only ten cities in all England contained more than 5,000 people in the year 1400. Famous cities like Nuremburg and Strasbourg had fewer than 20,000 people and their area was small in proportion; the former covered about 340 acres, the latter only 193.[1]

One reason for the deficiency of urbanization was the lack of sanitation and of modern techniques. Sewage was thrown into the streets where hogs acted as scavengers until the next rain washed it into the streams. Water was drawn from these streams, from springs, or the town pump. Sanitary conditions were indescribable. It is said that a city could be detected by its odor miles away. Contagious diseases struck terror among the people, who "fled from the plague" into the open country. Even the cities of the American colonies were decimated by deaths or by the enforced removal of residents because of the want of sanitation and medical attendance.[2] It is an interesting fact that Malthus included "great towns" among the positive checks to population as late as the early part of the nineteenth century. Only the constant migration from rural districts kept cities alive.[3]

Modern Techniques and Urbanization. Many of the modern techniques which make urbanization possible are less than a hundred years old. One hundred and fifty years ago London still used wooden water pipes. Iron pipes did not come into general use until 1810–20. In 1700, New York householders were ordered to burn lights in their front windows "in ye Darke of ye moon," and every seventh householder was required to hang out a lantern or candle on a pole.[4] Gas for street lighting came into use in 1824 and electricity in 1885. Modern transportation has permitted the separation of the residential part of the city from the industrial and commercial sections, and now people commute

[1] W. J. Ashley, *An Introduction to English Economic History and Theory,* 2 vols. (New York, 1894), II, 11.

[2] *A Century of Population Growth* (Bureau of the Census, 1909), pp. 11–12.

[3] Mumford, however, insists that the medieval town was more sanitary than is generally supposed. It had ample open spaces and was planned better than the more modern cities. *Culture of Cities, op. cit.,* Chap. I.

[4] L. H. Robbins, "A Panorama of Eventful 'Firsts,'" *New York Times Magazine,* November 26, 1933, p. 13.

fifty miles or more to their work. Health departments, hospitals, and strict rules of quarantine have practically eliminated such dread diseases as smallpox and leprosy, and other contagious diseases are under control. Millions of human beings now live in close contact yet are practically as free from contagious diseases as those living in the open country.

Cities have gained great material and cultural advantages. The theater, the opera, symphony orchestras, art galleries, museums, and cathedrals are urban institutions some of which are to be found only in the metropolitan centers. People are attracted to the urban centers because there they can market their special talents. In the city their dollar will buy more of the material comforts, luxuries, and entertainment than anywhere else. All this has tended to widen the gulf between the standards of living of rural and urban areas. Civilization has done more for the city than the country, not as the conscious effort on the part of any group, but merely as the result of economic forces and technical improvements. Added to the economic opportunities offered by cities are the cultural and other advantages which draw people into the cities.[1]

MANUFACTURING AS AN URBANIZING FACTOR

None of the factors enumerated so far has had the power to create numerous large cities; it remained for manufacturing and commerce to bring into being the modern metropolis.

Manufacturing was once a household industry and as such was not necessarily an urbanizing factor. Shoe manufacturing in colonial New England was of this type. However, power, machinery, and the factory building, by centralizing all processes under one roof, also centralized labor and management. Laborers now went to the factory and naturally wanted to live close by. This concentration of workers attracted the second layer of occupations—the stores, tailors, banks, and the professions—and soon a complete urban center was established. Since industry is such an important "city builder," one key to the location of cities is the force or forces that locate industries.

Some industries are located by the natural resources them-

[1] *Our Cities: Their Role in the National Economy,* Report of the Urbanism Committee to the National Resources Committee (Government Printing Office, Washington, 1937), pp. 1–25.

selves. Extractive industries must be carried on where nature has placed the ore, soil, forests, fish, or recreational advantages. However, extractive industries are not great city builders. Fishing hamlets, lumbering towns, and agricultural villages rarely become large enough to be called cities. Only 9 per cent of the mine workers live in cities of more than 25,000 people. Almost 67 per cent live on farms or in villages of 2,500 or less. Paradoxically, the automobile has proved to be a centralizing instead of a decentralizing force in the mining regions. It has permitted miners to move into the city to take advantage of its cultural and social opportunities and still work in the outlying mines.[1]

Power has always been an important element in fabrication. Water power was important before the age of steam but was "earth-bound," which meant that raw materials had to be brought to the source of power and finished products retransported to the market. Falls and cascades along the famous "Fall line" from New England to the Carolinas became important factory sites. It is an interesting fact that in the first decade of the nineteenth century the ratio of manufactures to population was higher in the South than in New England.[2] Water power also influenced city sites in other parts of the United States, as, for instance, Minneapolis.

Weber's Law of the Location of Industries. The Location of Raw Materials. While natural resources and water power tend to localize certain industries, others are free to locate where they please. Coal, oil, and natural gas, especially when their energy is distributed through electricity, may also be sent wherever they are needed, i.e., they are not earth-bound like the water wheel. When all these factors are mobile, where is the most economical place to build a factory? To answer this question Alfred Weber formulated a theory of the location of industries.[3] He reduced all the factors to weight and distance, hence his principles should operate in a communistic as well as a capitalistic society.

Wheat and flour may be used to illustrate Weber's law, and

[1] Goodrich *et al.*, *Migration and Economic Opportunity*, *op. cit.*, pp. 303–10.

[2] Katharine Coman, *The Industrial History of the United States* (New York, Macmillan, 1907), pp. 249–54, at 249.

[3] *Theory of the Location of Industries,* ed. Carl Joachim Friedrich (Chicago, University of Chicago Press, 1929).

transportation may be expressed in ton-miles for either product. Flour milling is a "weight losing industry" and characteristic of a large number of fabricating plants: 270 pounds of wheat will make a barrel of flour weighing 196 pounds. Disregarding by-products, if wheat is turned into flour at the wheat fields only 196 pounds of product will have to be transported, whereas if the wheat is moved to the point of consumption and milled there, 270 pounds of freight will have to be transported for every barrel of flour manufactured. Other things being equal, it is evident that the aggregate costs of transportation will be least with the mills located near the wheat fields, which is where the majority of them were first established.

However, it costs about 25 per cent more to transport flour than wheat. Reduced to equivalent pounds, the cost would be equal to transporting 245 pounds of wheat. This reduces the locational advantage of the mill near the wheat fields (w), but not enough to move it to the point of consumption (c).

Again, the mill needs fuel to grind the wheat. Suppose that it takes 25 pounds of coal to manufacture a barrel of flour, and that the coal has to be shipped from the point of flour consumption (*c*). The cost of transporting the coal added to the cost of transporting 245 pounds of flour would bring the "flour costs" up to the "wheat transportation costs" and the location of the mill would be a matter of indifference; should it take more than 25 pounds of coal the mill would operate more economically at *c*. A water power site reducing the cost of power to the equivalent of 15 pounds of coal could shift the location to *y*, assuming the same form of transportation from *y* to *c* as from *w* to *c*.

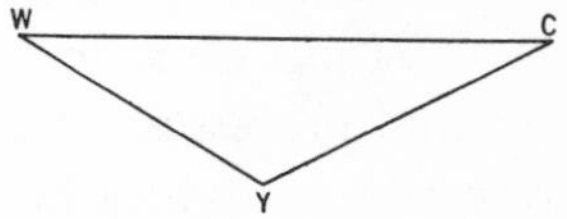

W C
Y

The problem becomes more complex where several weight losing raw materials are combined and by-products have to be considered. Here Weber uses a "parallelogram of forces," each of the materials pulling in its direction with a force proportionate to its respective weight or "equivalent weight," the point of location being the resultant of the various "pulls." The general tendency is for the place of fabrication to be located near the raw materials rather than near the market, and entirely at one deposit if the weight of this deposit is equal to the weight of all the rest plus the weight of the resulting product.[1] Fuel is an extreme case of a weight-losing material; it disappears entirely during the fabrication process and does not enter into the weight of the finished product. Coal, being so heavy and bulky, therefore tends to attract factories of all kinds to the coal mines.

The iron and steel industry furnishes an illustration of the importance of fuel as a locational factor. Coke is an important ingredient in smelting. Since one ton of coal reduces to 1,200 pounds of coke, this weight losing element attracted coke manufacture to the coal mines. And since it takes several tons of coke to smelt a ton of ore, this became another reason for the ore to go to the coal. Moreover, as steel and rolling mills are great consumers of heat and energy, they also found a situation near the coal mines advantageous. In the final analysis 4 to 4½ tons of coal are consumed in making one ton of finished steel products.[2]

Pittsburgh and the neighboring sections of Pennsylvania were ideal for the location of the iron and steel industry. This region got an early start by the discovery of ore in 1790. Ore, coal, and limestone could be concentrated by floating them down the Allegheny and Monongahela rivers to their junction. From here the nails, knives, pots, skillets, builders' tools, and agricultural implements needed on the frontier were floated down the Ohio and Mississippi rivers or carried northward to St. Louis and the upper river ports. The discovery of petroleum and natural gas in the same general region merely intensified its advantage for iron and steel manufacturing.

As time went on it was found economical to integrate the various processes. Economies in the entire range of processes rather than savings in individual processes became locational factors. As Zimmermann puts it, "The question no longer is where is the logical place to build a blast furnace or a Bessemer converter or an open hearth or a rolling mill; it becomes one of finding the most suitable location for such a giant manufacturing complex as the Gary works of the United States Steel Corporation, or the Sparrow's Point plant of the Bethlehem Steel Corporation, or the

[1] *Ibid.*, pp. 48–67 (at 64), 227–52.
[2] Zimmermann, *World Resources and Industries, op. cit.*, pp. 621–22.

combination iron, steel, and automobile works of the Ford Motor Company at Fort Dearborn." [1]

However, the iron and steel industry has spread to other regions. One reason is that ore has to be brought from Minnesota to Pittsburgh via the Great Lakes and overland by railway. Lake freighters and railways bringing ore from the Superior region do not want to go back empty and can afford to haul coal cheaply. Economically this has placed coal nearer the source of ore, and Erie, Buffalo, Cleveland, Toledo, Detroit, and other cities have become centers of iron and steel manufacturing.

Birmingham, Alabama, has also become a center of iron and steel fabrication. Here coal, iron, and limestone are found almost within sight of each other, and the cost of assembling is low. However, the cost of mining the ore is greater than on the Mesabi range, and the much discussed labor advantage in the South is considered debatable. Birmingham's chief disadvantage is its isolation from the centers of consumption, in spite of the cheap water transportation via the Black Warrior barges to Mobile.[2] Another interesting shift is toward the Atlantic. Sparrow's Point, near Baltimore, depends primarily on foreign ores and has the advantage of the markets along the Atlantic coast and in foreign countries. The location on the sea also permits shipbuilding by the steel corporation.

The Influence of the Market on the Location of Industries. Raw materials are not the only element in plant location; markets are also important. The heavy concentration of population in and around the eastern iron and coal region furnished a market close to the raw materials.[3] But the extension of the railways shifted population westward, and now the upper Mississippi Valley is one of the greatest iron and steel markets of the world and may become the most important.[4] In response to the "pull of the market," Gary, Indiana, was born. Duluth, St. Louis, Milwaukee, Joliet, and other mid-western cities have also become

[1] *Ibid.*, p. 623. By permission of Harper & Brothers, publishers.

[2] *Ibid.*, p. 630. Langdon White, "Geography's Part in the Plant Cost of Iron and Steel Production at Pittsburgh, Chicago and Birmingham," *Economic Geography*, October, 1929, pp. 327–35.

[3] Scrap iron also accumulates in greatest quantities in areas of dense population, which strengthens the locational advantage of the East.

[4] Zimmermann, *op. cit.*, p. 628.

iron and steel fabrication cities. Plants using iron in the later stages of manufacturing can economically be located at some distance from the source of fuel, and machinery manufacturing concerns are still more widely dispersed.[1]

In contrast to the weight losing industries are those whose products are heavier, more bulky, or more perishable than the raw materials from which they were made. These tend to locate near the market. Manufacturing of farm machinery followed the agricultural frontier because it cost more to ship the machines than the iron and steel used in their fabrication. Concerns making paper boxes, barrels, furniture, and similar bulky articles locate near the point of consumption. Bread and other perishable foods which have to be sold fresh are made within city delivery distance of the consumer. The cost of transportation acts as a tariff wall and hastens the development of local industries in areas isolated from the usual manufacturing centers. On the other hand, the urbanization induced by the heavy industries of the East furnished such an extensive market that this region has also attracted the "weight gaining" industries, thereby giving employment to still more labor.

The weight, size, or bulk of the package and the distance in miles are physical factors, but freight rates and time are economic factors. In establishing rates, the value of the product, as well as its weight and bulk, is taken into consideration, and the higher rate on the finished product may offset the weight lost in manufacture. The controversy between eastern and western millers has resulted in the same rate for wheat as for flour, which has tended to shift the flour milling industry to Buffalo and intermediate points. Many examples can be cited to show that the freight rate structure is often the determining element in factory location. "The power to make freight rates has been called the power to turn a wilderness into a city or a city into a wilderness." [2] Much of the work of rate regulation is concerned with alleged discriminations between places, commodities, and persons.[3]

However, not all factors are "agglomerating," to use Weber's term. While steam was centripetal in its influence, electricity and

[1] Huntington and Williams, *Business Geography, op. cit.,* Chaps. 25, 26.

[2] D. Philip Locklin, *Economics of Transportation* (Chicago, Business Publications, Inc., 1935), p. 504.

[3] *Ibid.,* Chaps. 22–25.

the automobile are centrifugal in their action on the location of industry to the extent of shifting factories into the outlying regions of the cities.[1] Other "deglomerating" elements are high rents, high land values, traffic congestion, and high transportation costs within congested areas. It is interesting also to find that almost 60 per cent of the manufacturing establishments which left New York City in recent years and which gave reasons for their departure mentioned the vague but significant reason of "racketeering in business and labor."[2]

Labor as a Factor in the Location of Industries. Last, but not least, in plant location is the cost of labor. Variations in wage scales, efficiency, skill, unionization, and labor laws are all taken into consideration by the factory operator whenever he seeks a location. In the shoe industry the questions of raw materials, of machinery, and the market are not determining factors in themselves. The industry has in a large measure followed the labor supply. It is said that a plant would theoretically be justified in locating 1,000 miles from the point of cheapest access to materials, fuel, and markets in order to take advantage of a 10 per cent saving in labor costs.[3] Shoe manufacturing is one of the most widely dispersed industries of the United States and a favorite one for chambers of commerce, real estate agencies, and other promoters to sponsor and attract.[4] The much discussed migration of cotton mills to the South is not so much a movement to the raw materials as to take advantage of lower wages and of the more effective control over labor by employers in this region. This is very important in cotton fabrication, where 55 per cent of the value is added by manufacture.[5]

The type and supply of labor are also important. The women's clothing industry caters to style and seasonal demand. It must be close to the "high-class trade" and prefers a reservoir of labor which can be hired on a moment's notice and laid off when the demand ceases. Even shoes which follow the styles

[1] *Our Cities, op. cit.,* pp. 29–30.

[2] *New York Times* editorial, April 2, 1937.

[3] Edgar M. Hoover, Jr., "The Location of the Shoe Industry in the United States," *Quarterly Journal of Economics,* February, 1933, p. 256.

[4] Hoover, *Location Theory and the Shoe and Leather Industries, op. cit.* The entire book deals with the location of a typically foot-loose industry. Labor is treated in Chaps. XIII and XIV.

[5] Goodrich *et al., op. cit.,* pp. 377–78.

must be manufactured close to the market. Only the largest cities can meet these requirements, and only a central location in the city will do.[1] Sometimes a major industry supplies a secondary source of labor. Silk and rayon mills have located in Pennsylvania where the men work in the mines and heavy industries and the textile mills can take advantage of the supply of women workers.

While the above factors are the main elements in plant location, they do not explain why every factory "is where it is."[2] Some factories are located accidentally or through the efforts of a superior entrepreneur as, for instance, rubber manufacturing at Akron, Ohio, and automobile manufacturing in Michigan.[3] Once located, the "early start," inertia, heavy investment in the structures and land, local attachments and connections are retarding factors in relocation. The shift comes less through migration of existing plants and more through the establishment of new factories and branches at a new location. Flour milling has spread in this fashion from Minneapolis and steel from Pittsburgh. Such trends create new centers of population, and retard the growth or even cause a decrease of population in the older centers.

While manufacturing has been an agglomerating force, it has also created the "insensate industrial" town with all its ugliness, slum areas, and barbarism. It is claimed that the cities of Germany, with their inheritance of craftsmanship and strong cultural traditions, have never become typical "factory towns" as have the cities of England. The extremely rapid development of industry in Great Britain is responsible for its unattractive industrial cities,

[1] *Ibid.*, pp. 346–48.

[2] In the selection of a site for a refinery and rolling mill for monel-metal, the points in plant location were ranked as follows: (1) fuels, 33%, (2) labor, 25%, (3) living conditions, 10%, (4) power, 10%, (5) supplies, 6%, (6) climate and transportation, each 5%, (7) building costs, taxes, and laws, cost and quality of site and water supply, altogether, 6%. *Industrial Survey of Upper San Francisco Bay Area* (Bulletin 28A, Dept. of Public Works, California, 1930).

[3] "Manufacturers tell us that the original location of manufacturing plants is, in the majority of cases, not a matter of deliberate choice. It is generally determined by the accident of the residence of factory owners rather than by a comparison of the advantages of various cities. . . . [but] There is a kind of 'natural selection,' resulting from the competitive struggle for existence, that produces a greater mortality among thóse firms that are not advantageously located."—Edwin M. Fitch and Ruth L. Curtiss, *Industrial Trends in Wisconsin* (Bulletin of the University of Wisconsin, General Series 1674, 1933).

and the same is true of America.[1] But manufacturing is less of an urbanizing force today than it was forty or fifty years ago. In 1890 wage earners comprised almost 20 per cent of our urban population; in 1930 only 12.8 per cent. In spite of a notable increase in factory output, a decrease in actual numbers of factory workers took place between 1920 and 1930.

TRANSPORTATION AND COMMERCE IN CITY LOCATION AND URBANIZATION

Considered historically, manufacturing was not the first cause of urbanization. Many of the early cities prospered primarily because they facilitated the exchange of commodities. By caravan and by ships the ancient peoples of the Orient exchanged food, clothing, and luxuries. Tyrus, "situate at the entry of the sea," became "a merchant of the people for many isles." In the Christian era the monasteries, churches, and castles were convenient places to hold fairs, and finally the merchant came on the scene and established a fixed place of business.[2] Venice, Genoa, London, Paris, and the Hanse cities prospered with the decline of the feudal regime and the development of the mercantile system.

The first American cities were of commercial origin. Cities were located on such harbors as had water connection with the interior. Montreal, New York, Philadelphia, and Baltimore had excellent river systems penetrating the hinterland; Boston less so. With the mountains as a barrier and only poor land transportation available, the rivers and the oceans were the chief highways. A ton of freight could be brought from Europe for $9.00; it could not be moved over thirty miles of wagon road for that price. Even coal was imported from Liverpool.[3]

Harbors on Lakes and Oceans. However, a physically fine harbor does not necessarily create a city. Labrador has many good harbors but no cities. What is needed is a hinterland with goods seeking a market outlet and demanding goods in exchange. In some cases artificial harbors are built if necessary, or poor ones are improved at enormous expense. Los Angeles is one example,

[1] Kekoni, *op. cit.*, pp. 550–51; Mumford, *op. cit.*, Chap. III.

[2] N. S. B. Gras, *An Introduction to Economic History* (New York, Harper, 1922), p. 104.

[3] B. H. Meyer, *History of Transportation in the United States Before 1890* (Carnegie Institution of Washington, 1917).

and most of the harbors of the Great Lakes are man-made. While ships were small they could use the rivers, arms of the oceans, and other shallow waters, but as ocean vessels became larger, the really important harbors narrowed down to those with deep water and adequate dock facilities, such as New York, Seattle, San Francisco, and Montreal.

The Influence of Rivers and Canals on the Location of Cities. The era of water transportation practically laid the foundation for the pattern of city distribution in the United States as it exists today. At least 69 of the 93 cities with a population of 100,000 in 1930 were in existence by 1850, and among those cities not yet founded at that time, the locations of Seattle, Tacoma, Portland, and Duluth were also determined by convenient water facilities.

The head of navigation where land routes met water routes, the junction of two rivers (Pittsburgh), a break in navigation where goods had to be reloaded (Louisville), these were typical points of origin of cities. Fords, bridges, and ferries have also been determining factors, as the names of many cities will testify today.

St. Louis is perhaps the most outstanding river town of the great Ohio-Mississippi-Missouri system. This system gave access to 35 rivers and 12,000 miles of navigable water for steamboats designed to navigate "on a heavy dew." New Orleans, however, was at the apex of the system and a great ocean port as well. In 1851, in spite of canal connections with the East, 95 per cent of the beef, lard, pork, flour, and corn from Cincinnati went down the river to New Orleans. By 1840 the "Crescent City" lacked only a few hundred inhabitants of being the second city in the United States; New York was first and Baltimore was second. It had 102,000 people at that time and St. Louis about 16,500 inhabitants.

The natural waterways were soon supplemented by canals, the most important being the Erie Canal, which "fixed the destiny" of New York, energized Buffalo and Albany, and stimulated city growth all along its route—especially where water power was also available, at Rome, Syracuse, and Rochester. Urbanization was likewise stimulated on the Great Lakes, and the success of the

Erie Canal led to a wild orgy of canal building, particularly by the rival cities of New York.

River and canal transportation, however, has serious disadvantages. Traffic has to follow directions laid down by nature to fixed points, irrespective of the final destination of freight. For instance, river transportation sent products to New Orleans for export where they had to be trans-shipped for a long sea voyage to Europe. Only riparian lands, or lands within a short distance of water, could be served by the rivers and canals, and large areas of the country were left to primitive wagon transportation or none at all. Water traffic is slow, and was suited only to the cheap and bulky farm products of pioneer days, with their leisurely methods of travel. In the nineteenth century the steamboat became a social institution as well as a freight carrier.[1] Another disadvantage was that many of the rivers and all of the canals were of shallow draft, and reloading to larger craft was necessary at certain points. Traffic was often interrupted by low water in summer and always by the ice in winter in the northern states. Even on the Great Lakes and on the St. Lawrence navigation closes for several months.

Railways as Urbanizing Factors. Railways started as feeders for water transportation, to connect seaboard cities with the immediate hinterland, or one city with another to avoid water detours.[2] Thirty years after the first railway was built the rails had reached the Pacific, and in another thirty years the main pattern of the railway network had been fixed. The initial urbanizing influence was practically exhausted in sixty years.

Being man-made, railroads should be free to build anywhere and to avoid the earth-bound limitations of waterways; yet the eastern terrain is such that the roads had to follow the same lines of least resistance used by the hunter, the wagon-borne pioneer, and the canals. This can be observed by noting the routes of the railways connecting the eastern cities with Chicago and St. Louis. South of the Potomac the barrier was so formidable that it was not crossed by a railway until 1882. Following the same route

[1] Garnett Laidlaw Eskew, *The Pageant of the Packets* (New York, Holt, 1929), pp. 87–137.

[2] For instance, the short cut from Lake Erie to Chicago via railway avoided the long lake voyage through Lakes Huron and Michigan.

as the waterways and heading for the same terminals, the railways did not at first create new cities but immensely strengthened the locational advantage of those which could profit by the new mode of transportation. Everywhere the railways came into direct competition with water transportation, and by their greater regularity and greater speed, by not requiring reloading, and also by "unfair" rates, they soon shifted the axis of freight movement in the United States to the east-west direction.

West of the Mississippi, however, railways preceded settlement to a considerable extent, raced across the plains, and sought the easy passes through the Rockies to connect with the seaports of the Pacific. It is remarkable how many of the same lines serve Los Angeles, San Francisco, Portland, Seattle, and Tacoma. On the eastern edge of the plains these "transcontinental" lines started from river-located "gateway" cities, especially from points where the Mississippi and Missouri had to be bridged. In spite of their origins on the edge of the plains, all these lines except the Southern Pacific have access to Chicago, which has become the railway center of the country. St. Louis is also a radiating point, principally for the southwestern railways, as Winnipeg is for the Canadian railways.

In 1840, when New Orleans was almost the second largest city in the United States, Chicago was a struggling village. But in 1870 Chicago had surpassed New Orleans, and in 1880 was ahead of St. Louis. It owed its origin to lake and river and, later, canal transportation, but it leaped forward when the railways had to skirt the lower point of Lake Michigan to reach the West and Northwest. A series of advertisements published around 1930 recited the fact that the "Windy City" was served by 37 railroads, that a passenger train entered and left every minute of the day and a freight train every 2½ minutes. The urbanizing influence of a railroad center of such magnitude was shown by the fact that over 80,000 men were employed merely to handle freight.[1]

Although railways were first built to connect existing cities, they soon became forces for locating new urban sites. New cities and villages sprang up at every depot, and those at junctions and intersections were usually doubly favored. On the plains, villages were moved bodily to the railway. One of the striking features

[1] Advertisements of the Public Service Company of Northern Illinois, 1929.

of the railway map is the radiating pattern around such cities as Indianapolis, Des Moines, Wichita, Fort Worth, and Dallas. Beyond the 100th meridian there are practically no north and south lines, an interesting indication of the east-west axis of travel and freight movement on the plains.

Railroad corporations soon appreciated the benefit they were conferring on a community and learned how to extract bonuses and donations. In the region beyond the Mississippi, especially, they became powerful economic and political factors.[1] At all times they have influenced the welfare of particular cities through the rate structure. Usually the larger cities have the advantage over smaller cities, and those with competing lines or competing water transportation have a decided bargaining advantage over those on single lines. Furthermore, the necessity for speed and promptness in both passenger and freight traffic has given the larger cities another advantage. The express trains and "streamliners" thunder by the small town, which must be content with local freight and passenger service.

The Panama Canal. Before the Panama Canal was built, practically all the freight originating in the Mountain and Pacific states was oriented to the East. However, the canal has so reduced the expense of freight shipments between the two coasts that it costs less to ship from Philadelphia to San Francisco by ocean than from Denver to San Francisco by rail. The ocean rim has felt this influence in the growth of population. It is estimated that, in 1910, 38 per cent of our people lived within 50 miles of salt water or the Great Lakes, but in 1930 the figure had grown to 45 per cent. Between 1920 and 1930, 67 per cent of the population growth took place in this 50-mile belt.[2] Large sections of the West have become more isolated and inland cities such as Spokane and Pendleton have felt this influence on their welfare.[3]

The Influence of Motor Transportation and Highways on City Location. The automobile and the hard surfaced road are so recent that it is almost forgotten that roads, turnpikes, plank roads, and the famous Cumberland road preceded canals and

[1] Glenn Chesney Quiett, *They Built the West: An Epic of Rails and Cities* (New York, Appleton-Century, 1934).

[2] Statement of Representative S. B. Pettengil before the Traffic Club of Chicago, *New York Times,* March 24, 1937.

[3] McKenzie, *op. cit.,* pp. 154–57.

railways. In 1828 more than a thousand wagons operated by organized freight companies brought the products of the West over the Cumberland road to Baltimore, and the "stone rivers" of Pennsylvania helped to build the cities of the middle states.[1]

During the time when canals and railways overshadowed highways, roads were purely of local concern and served as lines of communication between farm and city, farm and railroad, or farm and water. Cities naturally were interested in this form of transportation which connected them with their immediate hinterlands, but intra-city traffic was monopolized by water and rail transportation and to a limited extent by electric interurban lines.

The first effect of the automobile and truck was to enlarge the trade area of cities, thereby making it possible for the central city to serve a larger area. The relation of the central city to its satellite cities was also changed, the suburban residential trend was accelerated, and the movement of industries from the main city to the periphery encouraged. This phase of highway transportation did not change the general pattern of city distribution but it has tended to intensify the position of large cities by giving them closer connections with their "metropolitan regions."

The motorcar is less earth-bound than the railway or waterway. With roads on practically every section line, the automobile can cut across from one city to another. This has been of special advantage to cities which formerly could be reached only by roundabout rail connections, notably on the plains where so many of the lines run only east and west.

However, the bulk of freight and passenger traffic is between large centers of population. To meet the needs of this traffic, straight, wide, and well constructed roads between big cities have had the first rights on the public treasury. Once these superhighways are laid down, automobile, bus, and truck traffic becomes almost as channelled as that of the railways. Some of these fine highways parallel the railways and merely reinforce the former location of some cities; in other cases old railroad towns

[1] "Men quickly built stone rivers (roads) to meet Nature's lack . . . inland Pennsylvania developed systems of transportation beyond anything known in other colonies, bred in her wheat fields horses of nation wide fame, built wagons to match her crops and very early set to work on canals."—Archer Butler Hulbert, *Soil: Its Influence on the History of the United States* (New Haven, Yale University Press, 1930), pp. 39–40. See also Locklin, *op. cit.*, pp. 31–36.

have become stranded because the new highway is some distance away.

Air Transportation in Relation to City Growth. Airplanes are entirely free from the limitations of tracks, roads, and other factors which limit surface transportation to earth-bound routes. The great speed of the airplane has shrunk the earth to a fraction of its former size. To reach Valparaiso, Chile, by steamer from New York is a seventeen days' trip; by plane it takes only three and a half days. Dinner in New York and breakfast in Los Angeles are a commonplace today, and the Manhattanite can leave his desk on Friday afternoon and reach Bermuda the same evening. Speed is invaluable for mail, express, high-priced freight, and passenger traffic, and because of the intense competition for trade all the great commercial nations are rapidly expanding their air service for international trade.[1]

The effect of the airplane on the distribution of population and on urbanization remains to be seen. No doubt cities of some importance will spring up around the fuel depots, hangars, hotels, and other facilities associated with landing fields and junction points as, for instance, Bermuda.

On the other hand, air transportation seems to strengthen the position of already existing large cities. Large commercial planes must carry passengers, mail, and freight on scheduled trips in sufficient quantities to be profitable ventures. Only metropolitan centers can supply the necessary traffic; all other cities are "overpassed." Furthermore, only cities with adequate airports and landing fields can hope to utilize this form of transportation; this factor again favors the larger cities unless smaller cities are assisted by the state or other units of government.

Functions of the Commercial City. One of the functions of the commercial city is to trade with its own hinterland, to exchange manufactured goods for the fuel, food, fibers, and raw materials of its trade territory. However, the fully developed commercial city also acts as a collecting and distributing agency for its hinterland. "The commercial city is like a giant sitting at the gateway of his estate. With one hand he sweeps up the products which the people of his hinterland prepare; with the other he reaches far out to other people, strangers perhaps, and

[1] McConnell, "The Race for Aerial Trade Routes," *op. cit.*, pp. 348–65.

offers his people's products in exchange for something which he can hand back to his own subjects."[1] The power of this giant depends upon the wealth of his empire and the efficiency of the means of transportation at his disposal, for the purposes of both concentration and distribution. Such cities developed even in ancient times. Ancient Tyre "trafficked" in the wares of Tarshish, Syria, Judea, Arabia, and fifteen other places enumerated by Ezekiel. London has become the great entrepôt dealing in goods brought from the ends of the earth for sale and resale to the entire world.

Commerce also includes exchanges, banks, and other financial and credit institutions, and these became effective influences in the upbuilding of London, Paris, Amsterdam, and New York. The entrepreneurship functions, of managing, advising, and risk bearing, also tend to center in the larger cities. The metropolitan center may be compared to the captain's bridge connected with all parts of the ship by devices for communication. The railway, the telephone, the telegraph, and air mail carry the directions of the "captain of industry" to all parts of his enterprise.

The Distribution of Trade Centers. So far the discussion has dealt with industrial cities and commercial centers all more or less located by distinct natural or economic advantages. However, if all physical factors are uniform as in von Thünen's Isolated State, nevertheless a definite pattern of village and city distribution will take place according to the unique principles of Walter Christaller.[2] In an Isolated State minus the central city, with population more or less evenly distributed, the inhabitants will need to buy certain articles, sell their surplus, and use the services of physicians, bankers, and other professional persons. Christaller holds that these services and functions will establish themselves at trade centers, evenly distributed over the surface at the vertices of equilateral triangles. The area served by each village is a small hexagon, the size of which is fixed by the distance the furthermost residents find it convenient to trade at the center. However, the small "market" villages cannot furnish all the

[1] Huntington and Williams, *op. cit.*, p. 316.

[2] *Die Zentralen Orte in Süddeutschland, Eine ökonomisch-geographische untersuchung über die Gesetzmässigkeit der Verbreitung und Entwicklung der Siedlungen mit Städtischen Functionen* (Jena, Gustav Fischer, 1933). See also Hoover, *Location Theory and the Shoe and Leather Industries, op. cit.*, p. 19.

services the people need. Certain of the centers therefore become the place where these more specialized functions are rendered—for example, most of the professions—with the result that these particular villages expand to small city dimensions. These larger centers will also be evenly spaced, each "serving" six trading villages. A third and even fifth segregation will eventually emerge, still larger cities and fewer in number, which furnish those specialized services which are uneconomical for cities lower in the hierarchy.

Christaller applied his principles to South Germany with striking results. Naturally, the pattern becomes distorted as soon as variations in services, in density of population, in natural resources, and in costs of transportation are introduced. For instance, if in Figure 12 of Chapter V the three centers of extraction are considered to be centers of distribution, the size of the region each will serve will depend on the cost of delivering the goods to the hinterland and on the speed and efficiency of service. If A, B, and C are wholesale centers selling identical goods, these goods will sell at retail in the surrounding territory at the cost at the center plus transportation and retailing costs. A certain territory will be reserved for A, B, and C respectively, but at the edges B can outsell A at *x* if the goods can be delivered at less cost, more quickly, or in better condition.

CITIES IN AMERICAN NATIONAL ECONOMY

The city building factors discussed so far have transformed a rural frontier into a full-fledged urban industrial society in 150 years. When the first census was taken in 1790, over 96 per cent of the people of the United States were living in the open country or in cities with less than 8,000 inhabitants. Only six cities had more than 8,000 people at this time. In 1930 the urban population of this country was 56.2 per cent of the total population, *urban* being broadly defined as those people living in incorporated places with more than 2,500 people. Two-thirds of our people live in incorporated places. The majority of Americans live in 3,165 cities, five of which have a population of over a million and 93 of which have over 100,000 inhabitants. Nearly 30 per cent of the people live in "large" cities, meaning cities of 100,000 or more, but if those living on the peripheries are included it may

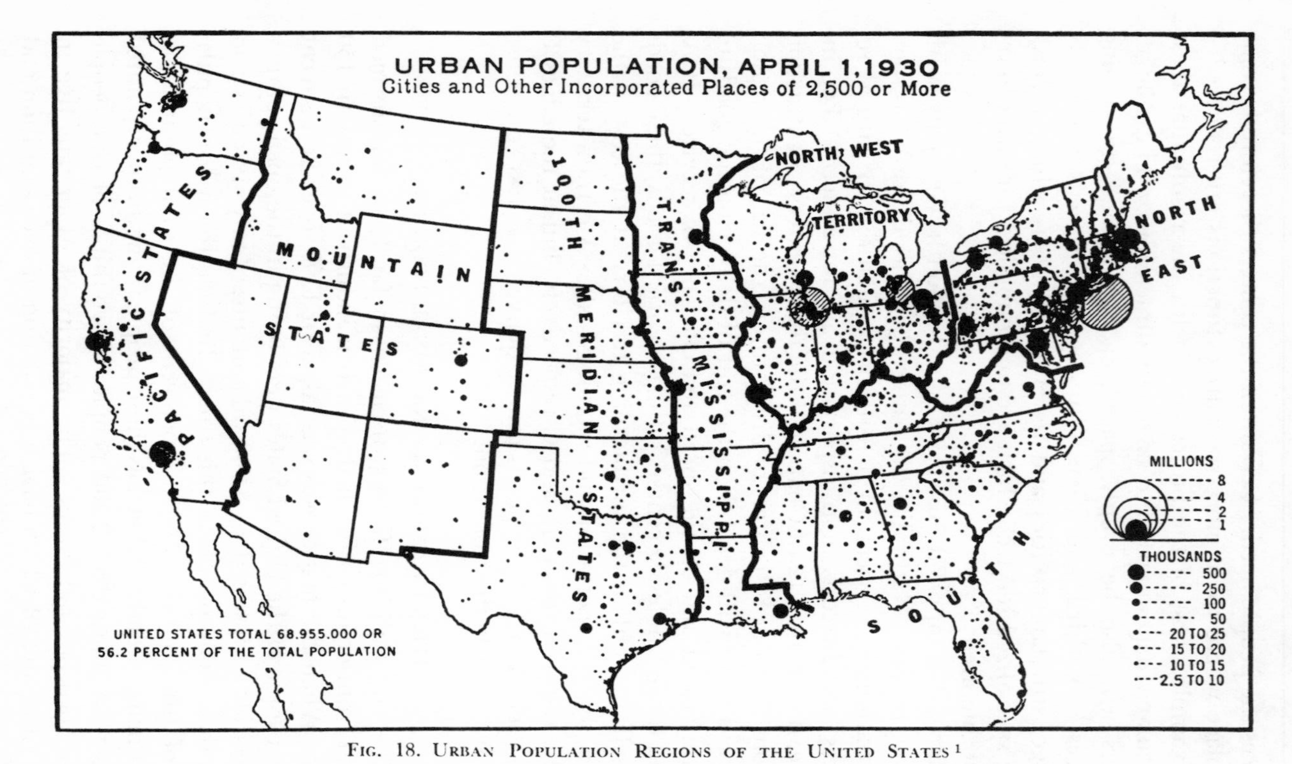

Fig. 18. Urban Population Regions of the United States[1]

[1] Base map from United States Department of Agriculture Miscellaneous Bulletin 265. J. C. Folsom and O. E. Baker, *A Graphic Summary of Farm Labor and Population* (1937), p. 21.

be said for all practical purposes that half of the people of the United States live in large cities.[1]

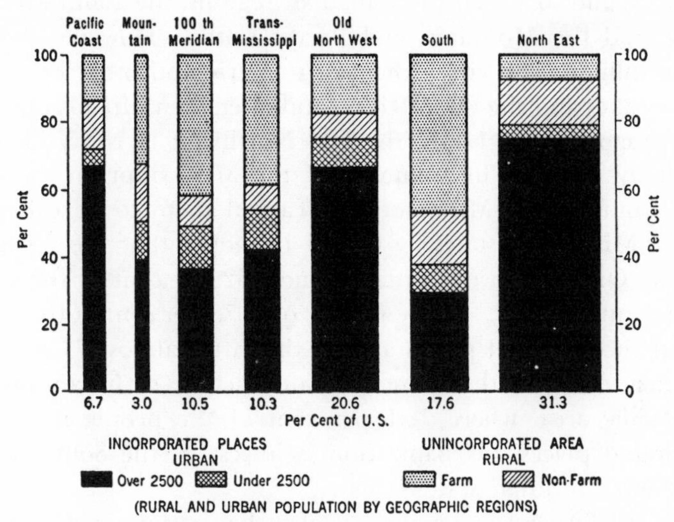

FIG. 19. DEGREE OF URBANIZATION OF THE UNITED STATES BY THE REGIONS SHOWN IN FIGURE 18 [2]

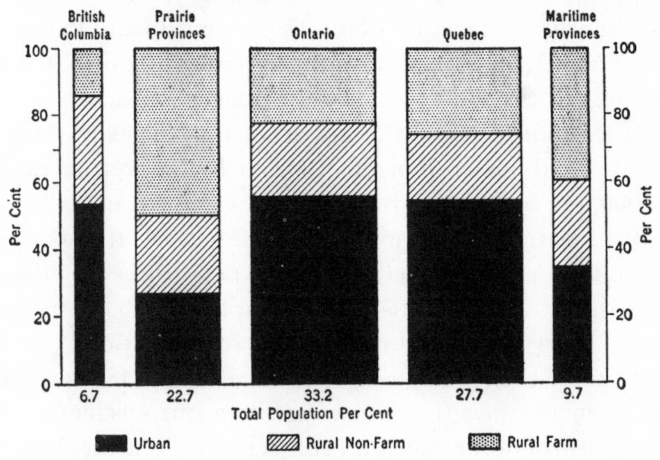

FIG. 20. DEGREE OF URBANIZATION OF CANADA BY REGIONS [3]

The figures for the nation as a whole do not give an adequate picture of city growth in the various sections. To show this more graphically, a somewhat different grouping of states has been

[1] *Our Cities, op. cit.*, pp. 1–3.

[2] Based on the United States Census, 1930, *Population*, Vol. II, Tables 6–8.

[3] Based upon data from *Canada Yearbook*, 1936, pp. 122–131. See Fig. 3, p. 47.

made to correspond with the historical progress of urbanization. The northeastern region is identical with the same region in Figure 3, and so are all the Canadian regions, the 100th Meridian states, and the Mountain and Pacific states. However, because of the influence on city growth of the Erie and other canals, the Great Lakes and the Ohio River, and later the railroads centering in Chicago and St. Louis, the Old Northwest territory has been set off by itself. The influence of the Mississippi on the states from Louisiana to Minnesota has caused them to be called the "Trans-Mississippi states." It will be noted that the Northeast and the Old Northwest contain almost 52 per cent of the people of the United States. In the former over 78 per cent of the people live in incorporated places and in the latter almost 74 per cent. Another section with almost the same degree of urbanization is the Pacific area, where 72.1 per cent of the people live in incorporated places. Urbanization is lowest in the South and in the 100th Meridian states.

Figure 20 shows the degree of urbanization in Canada by regions, calling places of 2,500 or more "urban." Over 46 per cent of the people of Canada are thus classed as urban, ranging from 55.2 per cent in Ontario to about 27 per cent in the Prairie provinces. The high degree of urbanization in British Columbia corresponds to the same situation in our Pacific states.

Another indication of the importance of cities in America is indicated by the fact that in 1932 urban governments spent $4,250,000,000 or one-third of the entire governmental expenditures of the nation, a sum exceeding the federal, the state, or the total non-urban local governmental expenditures for that year. Municipalities of the United States employ 1,250,000 persons or one out of every three public employees of the nation.[1]

In spite of their tremendous responsibilities, cities are handicapped in many ways from carrying them out efficiently. Cities are the creatures of the state and subject to the statutes enacted by state legislatures, whose members are often unacquainted with urban problems. "Home rule" is still fragmentary and unsatisfactory. Unfortunately, many states pre-empt important sources of revenue for themselves, leaving the cities to supply the enormous revenues necessary for urban governments chiefly from the

[1] *Ibid.*, p. 3.

general property tax. Recent tax-limitation legislation has often played havoc with city finances until readjustments could be made and other sources of revenue discovered.[1]

The cities also have a direct relation to the remainder of the country through the migration of rural people to urban centers. This migration probably accounts for 6,500,000 of the 14,600,000 increase in urban population between 1920 and 1930.[2] What it means in the transfer of people, inheritance, and wealth has already been pointed out (Chapter VI). This migration is also responsible for the peculiar population structure of cities, there being more middle-aged people in the cities than in the rural areas, where the younger and older age groups predominate.

Net immigration from foreign countries added about 3,000,-000 to the urban population in the decade 1920–30. Probably not more than 5,000,000 of the 14,600,000 increase, or 35 per cent, can therefore be attributed to births over deaths in the urban centers themselves. The foreign-born and their children make up nearly two-thirds of the population of the cities of 100,000 or more. This proportion becomes progressively smaller as the size of the city decreases, until in the rural areas only one-sixth of the population is foreign-born or of foreign parentage.

In addition to the foreign immigrants and their children, American cities have also attracted Negroes from the southern rural areas and smaller cities.[3] The city has traditionally been the melting pot. "It has not only tolerated but rewarded individual differences. It has brought together people from the ends of the earth *because* they are different and thus useful to one another, rather than because they are homogeneous and like-minded."[4]

The rapidity and degree of urbanization have made many people apprehensive. Some writers echo the age-old fear of cities and claim that the city is altogether sterile and evil. Others fear the effect of urbanization on the birth rate. Frank Lloyd Wright speaks of the "disappearing city" and hopes for its dispersion and

[1] A. M. Hillhouse and Ronald B. Welch, *Tax Limits Appraised*, Public Administration Service, Chicago, 1937, pp. 28–31.

[2] National Resources Committee, *Population Statistics*, Part 3: "Urban Data" (Washington, 1937), p. 11.

[3] *Our Cities, op. cit.*, pp. 9–12. *Population Statistics*, Part 3, *op. cit.*

[4] Louis Wirth, "Urbanism as a Way of Life," *American Journal of Sociology*, July, 1938, p. 10.

elimination, whereas Mumford would create a "new urban order."[1]

Unfortunately also, the concentration of economic power has gone so far that only a few cities have the qualifications of a "metropolis."[2] These are located largely north of the Potomac and Ohio and east of the 100th Meridian states, a concentration within a concentration. The metropolis has become the dominant center for the dissemination of ideas and culture through the newspapers, the magazines, and, more recently and more potently, the movies and the radio. The large city sets the style in the theater, art, dress, and fashions. Its literature interprets the hinterland according to urban standards. Europe, for instance, gets its idea of America from New York because this city is in the main line of communication between the two continents. In many respects New York is spiritually and psychologically closer to Europe than it is to America. A healthy reaction against the metropolitan monopolization of intellectual life, art, and literature is now under way, led by the militant regionalists.[3]

THE CITY IN ITS REGIONAL SETTING

The Legal City. What is a city? Where does the city end and rural territory begin? The medieval city with its walls, gates, and moat was easily distinguished from the open country, but what about the sprawling, star-shaped modern city? The legal city, i.e., the territory over which the city has jurisdiction, is not an adequate test of urbanized territory. Some cities, notably Los Angeles, have enlarged their boundaries to include considerable areas of farm land, whereas everybody recognizes that many "city people" live outside of the city limits.

Density of population or numbers are sometimes used to distinguish a city from rural districts. "For sociological purposes a city may be defined as a relatively large, dense, and permanent settlement of socially heterogeneous individuals."[4] The city thus defined cuts across all political jurisdictions, and this definition is

[1] Wright, *The Disappearing City* (New York, Wm. Farquhar Payson, 1932). Mumford, *op. cit.*, Chap. VII.

[2] Gras, *Introduction to Economic History, op. cit.*, Chaps. 5 and 6, at p. 186.

[3] Donald Davidson, "Lands That Were Golden," Part I, New York and the Hinterland, *American Review*, October, 1934, pp. 545–61.

[4] Wirth, *op. cit.*, p. 8.

inadequate for statistical purposes. Many states differentiate unincorporated territory, villages, and cities on the basis of numbers. In Wisconsin, for instance, a group of people numbering 150 living on a half square mile of land may incorporate as a *village,* and when population reaches 1,000 may incorporate as a *city.* However, units of government are not obliged to incorporate whenever a certain density of population has been reached, so the same state may have rural townships with 3,000 to 10,000 inhabitants, villages with 10,000, and cities with less than 1,000. In New Hampshire, Rhode Island, and Massachusetts the densely populated portions of towns are not separately incorporated or politically distinct from the rural territory, and it is not the usual practice to incorporate cities until population has reached 10,000.

Urban, Rural, and Farm Population. The United States Census classifies all incorporated places with more than 2,500 people and all unincorporated towns and places with a population of 10,000 or more and with a population density of more than 1000 per square mile as *urban.* On this basis 56.2 per cent of our people were urban in 1930. The census also distinguishes *farm* population from all others and reported in 1930 that 24.6 per cent of our people fell in this class, leaving about one-fifth of the population neither "farm" nor "urban." It is possible to segregate another 7.5 per cent as living in incorporated places with less than 2,500 people, but this classification gives little clue to their rural or urban character. Some of these villages are sophisticated satellite "bedroom towns" on the edge of a metropolis; others are mere crossroads hamlets as rural as the farms about them.

About one-eighth of the population is called *rural-non-farm* in the census. This is also a heterogeneous group consisting of rural residents not on farms, of storekeepers, rural ministers, crossroads garage men, night club operators, and the rural village folks, plus unincorporated mining, lumbering, and fishing hamlets and the residents of unincorporated and often densely settled areas on the outskirts of cities. Figure 21 shows the distribution of our population by these categories but unfortunately fails to present an adequate definition of a city.

Metropolitan Districts. To get a more realistic picture of the truly "economic" and "sociological" city in measurable terms, the federal census officials have set up "metropolitan districts."

These consist of the central city, the adjoining municipalities, and all other civil divisions with a population density of not less than 150 per square mile. A civil division with a smaller density was included, as a rule, if surrounded by other divisions having the proper density, or if contiguous to the central city. The territory

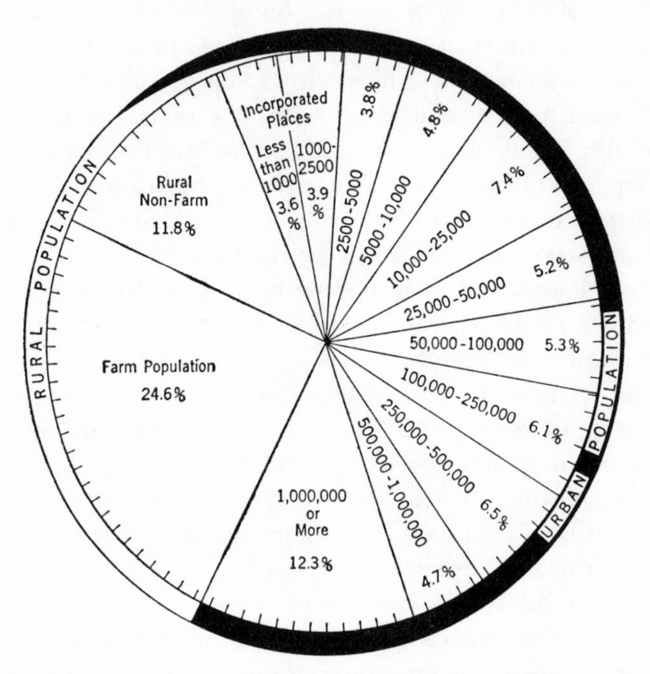

Fig. 21. Distribution of the Population of the United States by Rural and Urban, and by Cities of Various Sizes, 1930 [1]

included must have a minimum population of 100,000 to be called a "metropolitan district." [2] Many metropolitan districts lie in more than one county and several straddle state lines, notably New York, Chicago, Cincinnati, and Kansas City. The United States has 96 metropolitan districts. How urbanization "grows on what it feeds" is shown by the fact that while the total population of the United States increased by 16.1 per cent between 1920 and 1930, the 85 districts for which comparable data were available increased 24.9 per cent. However, there were striking differences in the rates of growth in the various components of the district.

[1] Based on U. S. Census, 1930, *Population,* Vol. II, p. 9.

[2] *Metropolitan Districts,* Bureau of the Census (1932), pp. 5–6.

Central cities increased 22.3 per cent, satellite cities 36.2 per cent, and the remaining areas 54.8 per cent during this decade.

Urban vs. Rural Land. If it is difficult to define a city, it is just as difficult to distinguish urban from rural *land*. Are the house and two acres occupied by a factory worker living a mile from the city a "farm" or a part of the city? The census authorities have not solved this question satisfactorily. One definition, however, distinguishes urban from rural land by the size of the parcels and the complement of public utilities or facilities such as streets, sidewalks, sewers, and water mains.[1] Nevertheless, this classification would omit all land in the process of subdividing and it would not include much of the land of the metropolitan district as defined by the census.

The Metropolitan Region. Beyond the metropolitan district and "urban land," as defined above, there is still other territory over which the city casts its influence. This metropolitan region also lacks exact definition but is characterized by the close association many of its people have with the central city. Roughly, it is the commuting area from which people come to work in the city. Physically they live in the country; economically, socially, and culturally they are a part of the city. They keep up this close connection through the telephone, the daily paper, and the automobile. It is therefore a region of heavy traffic which rapidly thins out as the outer edge of the region is reached. The daily commuting passenger traffic to the business section of Philadelphia was distributed as follows in 1932: coming less than 5 miles, 195,000 people; 5 to 20 miles, 175,000; 20 to 40 miles, 13,000; and over 40 miles only 7,000 people.[2] Of those coming from beyond the five mile radius, 37 per cent came in cars, 21 per cent by railroads, and 42 per cent by trolley, ferry, bus, subway and elevated.

The metropolitan region is important from the standpoint of planning because it is an economic and social unit within which all the inhabitants are interested in the same objectives—adequate transportation facilities, parks, water supply, sewerage, and control over the private utilization of land. Unfortunately for planning and the administration of planning, both the "metropolitan

[1] E. M. Fisher in McKenzie, *The Metropolitan Community, op. cit.*, Chap. 15.

[2] *The Regional Plan of the Philadelphia Tri-State District,* (Regional Planning Federation, 1932), p. 136. See also National Resources Committee, *Regional Planning,* Part II: "St. Louis Region," (Washington, 1936).

district" and the "metropolitan region" consist of many units of government, ranging from the metropolis to the rural town.

The *trade area* is another form of city hinterland. It represents the area from which people come for retail buying, banking, and in smaller places to attend the church and school or to use the library. Most of these services are impersonal, and the purchaser does not necessarily consider himself a "citizen" of the city, but of his own rural territory. On the other hand, he may also be a part of the region defined above.[1]

The *hinterland* may be used as a general term embracing all the land of the suburban area, the metropolitan region, and the trade area. Strictly speaking, it is the domain of the "giant" described by Huntington and Williams and includes the entire region served and "dominated" by a given city.[2]

Economically and sociologically the city no longer has a medieval wall with gates and moats. Urban land extends as far as its economic potency can be felt. Sociologically the city affects all "who have come under the spell of the influences which the city exerts by virtue of the power of its institutions and personalities operating through the means of communication and transportation."[3]

THE STRUCTURE OF CITIES

The Land-Use Pattern of Cities. An airplane view reveals the typical American city as a sprawling mass of structures of varying size, shape, and construction, crisscrossed by a checkerboard street pattern which here and there assumes irregularities. The city is most densely built up at the core. Here one or more tall structures will loom up grotesquely, marking the location of the central business district. If the city is large the number of skyscrapers will be correspondingly multiplied and they will reappear irregularly at places somewhat distant from the city center, indicating the location of subcenters. The central business district flattens out abruptly toward the edges, where the city's light manufacturing and warehouse areas may be recognized, and along the

[1] J. H. Kolb, *Service Relations of Town and Country* (Wisconsin Research Bulletin 58, 1923). J. H. Kolb and R. A. Polson, *Trends in Town-Country Relations* (Wisconsin Research Bulletin 117, 1933).

[2] Gras, *op. cit.*, pp. 194–96, 209 *f.*; 295–314.

[3] Wirth, *op. cit.*, p. 5.

water fronts or railway tracks appear the smoking chimneys of the "heavy industrial" district. The light manufacturing and warehouse area is interspersed by ramshackle structures which constitute the blighted areas and slums; adjacent to this belt are to be found the tenements and workingmen's homes. The remainder of the city consists primarily of the residential sections, which also contain stores, parks, schools, churches, and similar structures.

The general shape of these belts is circular, with the commercial section and its "100 per cent location" at the center, but the symmetry of the total configuration is usually warped by water fronts, rivers, elevations and depressions in the topography, and by the proximity of other cities.

Beyond the built up parts of the city the urban out-thrust into the metropolitan region follows along the main transportation lines, especially railways and the radiating highways. This tends to make the city star-shaped. At intervals along the railway lines and the through highways, often as uninterrupted extensions of the city proper, are the suburbs and satellite towns, some industrial and others residential. Between the settled areas are the open farm lands, country clubs, subdivisions, country estates, and perhaps parks and forest preserves, all of which are a part of the metropolitan region.

Since American cities did not start with a blueprint or plan, these districts and their relationship to one another are the result of economic forces which, in the main, have placed the various land uses "where they belong."[1] The city is a living organism in which these elements have arranged themselves according to the economic demands of the public. The arrangement is by no means perfect and much needs to be done by wise planning and zoning to make the city a livable community and an effective place to work. The fact that some industries have left the city because of traffic congestion indicates the failure of economic forces alone to secure for us an efficient city structure.

Natural Elements Affecting City Structure. Certain natural factors have a definite influence on city structure and often become the point of origin from which the city develops. The water front of a river city determines the location of wharves, warehouses, lumber yards, coal docks, and factories. These uses

[1] See "Competition of Land Uses in Cities," Chap. V of this volume.

have the "first choice" of this site. Railroads seek low, level ground, and since this is often along the river or water front, the same area attracts both forms of transportation. Railroads likewise attract heavy industries and warehouses, so railway stations and freight yards become important points of origin. Inland towns often originate along highways, or at the junction of two or more roads, but the structure of many seaport and railway cities is also influenced by highways. Broadway in New York City is part of the Albany Turnpike, and airplane views of Chicago, Baltimore, and Boston will show how radiating country roads have become important factors in their structure.

Natural features also influence the location of residential areas. The first choice goes to those who are financially able to outbid all others for the finest views, wooded tracts, lake frontage, and moderate elevations, with freedom from noise, smoke, and traffic. Such residential districts are usually located at considerable distances from the industrial and commercial areas, often in suburban and satellite cities. The recreational features of the city and metropolitan region are also usually located with respect to natural features, but most of the other urban land uses are practically "foot-loose" and follow the principle of "situs."

Economic Location or Situs. Situs is often considered the chief characteristic of urban land. It is, however, not a fixed quality of land, as fertility or the presence of minerals may be. Because of human preferences, a given corner may be an excellent place for a grocery. The services of the land at this place are high and valuable. But a new street is opened and people find another corner more convenient. The old location loses its situs quality. The owner cannot take his site to the new corner; all he can do is sell out and move to the new place. Land is immobile and situs must be used where it is.

As was noted in Chapter V, each city has a "100 per cent location." Why a certain retail area should reach the peak of land values is not easily explained, but once it is established it becomes the center from which all other land uses radiate and values decline. "If we investigate the reasons why site rent increases steadily toward the center of the city, we will find it in the labor saving, the greater convenience and the reductions of the loss of time in connection with the pursuit of business."[1] In a word, accessibility means ease of contact. It is at the heart of the city that contact is secured with the least recourse to transportation. Transportation is costly in time and in the expense of overcoming friction. Costless transportation would do away with situs; there would be no "centers" and no advantage of location manifesting itself in high values. In fact, the "peak" of land values would disappear. This, however, would not apply where space did not permit all to enjoy equal advantages. For instance, only a certain number of people can own land on a given lake or river. Even though the rest could get costless transportation to such a lake or river, private riparian ownership would keep them from it.

Because the best sites are limited, the price paid for space is such that the owner finds it profitable to utilize the land intensively so as to create as much economic space as possible. Hence the high buildings providing easy contacts within a very limited area. "The financial district is in effect one big structure; the streets practically cleared of all except pedestrian traffic are little more than corridors and air shafts."[2]

Various utilizers bid for the better sites, thereby establishing a scale of rents or values which only those utilizations performing the most valuable services per unit of area can afford to pay. As was pointed out before, in this way utilizations are sorted and assigned by economic competition to various sites which, taken together, make up the structure of the city.[3] Examples of this competition are familiar to all observers. In New York manufacturing establishments are being crowded out of Manhattan; in fact, there is a tendency to split up an industry into its various economic functions and to move each function to that part of the metropolitan region where it can be performed most economically. In a business consisting of manufacturing, storage, and office management, it became uneconomical to use high-priced land for manufacturing and storage, and one by one these functions were moved to New Jersey or Long Island. Finally only the

[1] J. H. von Thünen, *Der Isolierte Staat, op. cit.*, pp. 212–13.

[2] R. M. Haig, "Toward an Understanding of the Metropolis; The Assignment of Activities to Areas in Urban Regions," *Quarterly Journal of Economics*, May, 1926, p. 427.

[3] Chap. V.

managerial offices were left at the old location. Some offices have even moved their files to low rental areas rather than keep them in expensive offices. A counteracting force to dispersion is the increased strain upon the managers' power to conduct a business so scattered.[1]

The area with the "100%" business locations and the financial district also attracts theaters, motion-picture houses, and hotels. In the largest cities distinct sub-districts can be noted—for theaters, hotels, furniture stores, department stores, etc. Even buildings become specialized, such as the "medical arts buildings," "merchandise marts," and others catering to those in one business or profession. On the other hand, some shopping districts are located away from the main lines of traffic because they appeal to the more fashionable trade or offer parking space. Even small cities now have outlying shopping centers. Some of the large department stores establish branches in these centers, whereas other stores find these locations so profitable that they do not care to enter the central district at all. The outlying business districts become advantageous locations for the smaller cinemas, for doctors, dentists, lawyers, and other professional men. "Light" wholesale houses prefer to locate their establishments near the retail centers.

The residential structure of cities has become just as specialized as the commercial and industrial. The central business section provides housing through hotels and apartments akin to hotels. In the transition area beyond the business district are the dilapidated residences, rooming houses, and tenements which furnish housing for transients, single persons, "bohemians," and childless families. Much of this land is ripening into another use, or is expected to do so, and is held by absentee speculators with the hope that hotels, stores, and skyscrapers will be erected on these lots. Land values are inflated but rents may be low. Buildings are crowded and in disrepair and sanitary facilities are inadequate or completely lacking. It is in this belt that the newest immigrants, including the Negroes, find their first homes.

At its periphery this area merges with the district of workingmen's homes, often multiple dwellings which command relatively low rent but are in a better state of repair than the slums. This

[1] Haig, *op. cit.*, pp. 416–17.

area, in turn, shades into the middle-class apartment house area with its own local business center. The residents of this section of the city have a higher level of income, pay higher rent, and command better facilities than those nearer the center. The outer zone of the city proper is the single-family residence area where land is considerably cheaper and where, consequently, more spacious dwellings with garages, yards, and larger open spaces may be bought or rented. Beyond this area is the suburban zone with its scattered estates, golf courses, residential communities, and industrial area, interspersed with truck gardens, farm lands, and embryonic residential subdivisions.

However, psychological and sociological factors account for other forms of residential districts. Fashion and the exclusiveness of old residential areas become reasons for living in certain sections; they add prestige and "tone." Spatial segregation also takes place by reason of color, nationality, economic status, and personal preferences. These have produced the German sections, the "Little Italies," the Lower East Side, Harlem, Greenwich Village, and other well-known localities. They bring in another element of difficulty in housing and in providing for education and recreation.

In a growing city none of the elements of city structure is fixed. The commercial and industrial areas enlarge and crowd in upon the residential areas. Apartments and hotels move into single-family districts. The city expands on its outer edges into the rural areas. One of the hopeful features of city planning and zoning is that plans can be made and control measures used to anticipate and direct the movement of land uses in socially desirable directions.

Classification of Urban Land. As noted before, *urban land* exists both in cities and in the rural-urban fringe and is not easy to classify. It may be classed as land and water areas and as developed and undeveloped areas. The proportion of non-utilized land varies widely in American cities, depending upon how closely the city is built up and how much rural territory has been annexed.

Table 35 shows the average percentage of the land in various uses in sixteen typical "self-contained" cities. It will be noted that 40 per cent of the land is vacant. Omitting this part of the city's area, column 2 shows the percentages in terms of the developed area only. The many sub-classes are shown in the "New Building Classifications" for New York City.

NEW BUILDING CLASSIFICATIONS (1937) [1]

A. ONE-FAMILY DWELLINGS:

1. Two Stories and Attic (Detached, Small or moderate size)
2. One Story (permanent living quarters)
3. Large Suburban Residence (Two story—high class)
4. City Residence
5. Attached or Semi-Detached (Two story)
6. Summer Cottages
7. Mansion Type
8. With Store
9. Miscellaneous (Old buildings, attached frame houses, etc.)

B. TWO-FAMILY DWELLINGS:

1. Two Story Brick
2. Two Story Frame
3. Converted (From One Family)
8. With Stores
9. Miscellaneous (City Type, old, etc.)

C. WALK-UP APARTMENTS:

1. Semi-Fireproof (Over 6 families, built after 1920)
2. Three to Six Families
3. New Law (Built prior to 1920)
4. Old Law Tenements (With or without stores)
5. Converted Dwelling
7. New Law With Stores (Built prior to 1920)
8. Semi-Fireproof With Stores (Built after 1920)
9. Miscellaneous

D. ELEVATOR APARTMENTS:

1. Semi-Fireproof (Over 6 families, built after 1920)
2. Semi-Fireproof (Built prior to 1920)
3. Fireproof (Standard Construction)
4. Cooperative and High-Class Type
5. Apartment Hotels (With or without stores)
6. Fireproof—With Stores
7. Semi-Fireproof With Stores (Built prior to 1920)
8. Semi-Fireproof With Stores (Built after 1920)
9. Miscellaneous

E. WAREHOUSES:

1. Fireproof—One Story
2. Fireproof—Two Stories or over
3. Semi-Fireproof
4. Frame
9. Miscellaneous

F. FACTORY AND INDUSTRIAL BUILDINGS:

1. Heavy Manufacturing (Fireproof)
2. Special Construction (Printing Plant, etc., Fireproof)
3. One Story—Fireproof
4. Semi-Fireproof
9. Miscellaneous

G. PUBLIC GARAGES AND GASOLINE STATIONS:

1. Public Garage—Two or more stories

[1] From Report of the Dept. of Taxes & Assessments of the City of New York.

2. Public Garage—One Story (Semi-Fireproof or Fireproof)
3. Garage and Gas Station Combined
4. Gas Station—With Enclosed Lubrication Plant
5. Gas Station—Without Enclosed Lubrication Plant or Workshop
8. Garage with Showroom
9. Miscellaneous—Gas Stations and Public Garages

H. HOTELS:

1. Highest Type (Savoy Plaza, Waldorf, etc.)
2. Over 15 stories (Roosevelt, Taft, etc.)
3. Commercial—Over nine stories
4. Fireproof—Under nine stories
9. Miscellaneous

J. THEATRES:

1. Small Moving Picture—No Vaudeville Stage (With or without stores)
2. Moving Picture and Vaudeville Type (Designed for Vaudeville—whether or not so used)
3. Large Moving Picture Houses (Paramount, Capitol, of Manhattan, etc.)
4. Legitimate Theatres (Theatre sole use of building)
5. Theatre as part of building of other use
9. Miscellaneous

K. STORE BUILDINGS (TAXPAYERS INCLUDED).

1. One Story Store Building
2. Two Story Store, or Store and Office
3. Department Stores
9. Miscellaneous

L. LOFT BUILDINGS:

1. Over Eight Stories (Mid-Manhattan Type)
2. Fireproof—Loft and Storage Type
3. Semi-Fireproof
8. With Retail Stores
9. Miscellaneous

O. OFFICE BUILDINGS:

1. Fireproof—Up to Nine Stories
2. Ten Stories and Over (Side street type)
3. Ten Stories and Over (Main street type)
4. Tower Type
5. Semi-Fireproof
6. Bank Building (Designed Exclusively for Banking)
9. Miscellaneous

S. MISCELLANEOUS BUILDINGS:

1. Places of Public Assembly (Concert Halls, Lodge Rooms, etc.)
2. Private Schools, Libraries, Museums, Hospitals, Sanitaria
3. Resort Hotels, Country Clubs, Road Houses, Yacht Clubs
4. Stadia, Race Tracks, Base Ball Fields, Outdoor Swimming Pools
5. Grain Elevators, Coal Pockets, and Similar Industrial Properties
6. Piers
7. Amusement Places—Resort Bath Houses, Boat Houses
8. Riding Academies, Stables and Sheds
9. Unclassified

U. UTILITY STRUCTURES

X. EXEMPT PROPERTY

V. VACANT LAND

TABLE 35

AVERAGE PERCENTAGE OF LAND USED FOR VARIOUS PURPOSES IN SIXTEEN CITIES OF THE UNITED STATES[1]

Total City Area		Total Developed Area	
Use	Percentage	Use	Percentage
1. Single family	21.8	1. Single family	36.1
2. Two family	1.3	2. Two family	2.1
3. Multiple dwelling	0.7	3. Multiple dwelling	1.1
4. Commerce	1.4	4. Commerce	2.4
5. Light industry	2.0	5. Light industry	3.2
6. Heavy industry	1.7	6. Heavy industry	2.7
7. Railroad property	3.2	7. Railroad property	5.5
8. Streets	20.2	8. Streets	33.6
9. Parks	4.0	9. Parks	6.3
10. Public and semi-public	4.5	10. Public and semi-public	7.6
11. Vacant land	40.0		

One-fifth of the entire area of these sixteen representative cities, or one-third of the developed area, is utilized by streets. This area not only is non-taxpaying land but it has to be covered with concrete or other surfacing material and then maintained and kept free from snow and dirt. Parks and other public property, plus the area of the streets, remove almost half of the land of these cities from the tax roll.

The area devoted to "commerce," which contains the sky-scrapers and other business structures and which epitomizes the city to the average citizen, occupies less than 2 per cent of the total area of these cities. Less than 10 per cent of the total area is in commercial uses and almost one-fourth devoted to residential uses. While these figures hold for the sixteen cities, they cannot be considered representative of any given city. City structure depends too much upon the nature of the individual city—whether it is a central city or a satellite, a capital, industrial or commercial city—to have any degree of uniformity.

CITY PLANNING AND HOUSING

The youthful city directed all its efforts toward physical growth and material gain; it was surging ahead too rapidly for

[1] Harland Bartholomew, *Urban Land Uses* (Cambridge, Harvard University Press, 1932), p. 146.

any reflections on the ultimate results of its activities. The cries of the few farsighted ones were drowned by the hammering of the riveting machine. The day has come, however, when serious thought is being given to a more orderly and planned procedure. Crime, bad housing, health problems, tangled traffic, deflated land values, corrupt government, economic insecurity, rapid obsolescence and blight, lack of articulation between communities and industries, and many other serious problems are dead weights on continued progress.[1] Planning is necessary to redirect city structure.

Nowhere are people thrown into closer relationship than in cities. This in itself calls for greater control over the activities of individuals, as can be seen in the regulations governing health, sanitation, traffic, and land utilization. Urban life is made possible only by warning signs and by regulation for the benefit of all at the expense of the freedom of the individual. The public has more direct interest in the land in cities than in rural land; not only is much land in public ownership, but the restrictions on private land use have to be more rigid.

City planning in the United States grew out of a number of streams of thought and activities. One of the most important was the need for regulation and direction in housing. As early as 1857 a commission was appointed in New York to examine the tenement situation, and from then on the terrible conditions in our major cities challenged the idea of *laissez faire* in land use. Municipal engineers saw the need for the proper ordering of the public utilities. Other groups became important factors through their interest in "civic improvement." Still others approached city planning from the field of landscape design and were especially helpful in park development before people became conscious of the concept of planning the city as a whole. The work of Frederick Law Olmsted is outstanding in this respect.[2]

Two examples of planning have influenced the movement in the United States. The first was the plan by L'Enfant of the city of Washington, a plan made before the city was built. The streets were laid out in irregular rectangles and a system of diago-

[1] For a further discussion see *Our Cities, op. cit.*, pp. 9–28, 55–70, 73–78.

[2] Harlean James, *Land Planning in the United States for City, State, and Nation, op. cit.*, Chaps. 3 and 4.

nal avenues imposed upon the "gridiron" layout. Sites were designated for the capitol and the "white house," and a mall a sixth of a mile wide was laid out along which public buildings were to be placed. The plan was neglected for many years, but was revived in 1900.[1]

The other example was the World's Fair in Chicago in 1893, which occurred after a long period of mediocre taste in architecture. The most eminent architects, engineers, sculptors, painters, and landscape architects "cooperated to produce a marvellous spectacle which touched the dormant emotions of many Americans and so left a profound effect upon the building of cities." [2] Unfortunately, the impression was so strong and vivid that the classical style was copied slavishly in the "City Beautiful" idea of planning. It took years before Louis Sullivan's ideas broke through the old architectural traditions and became the "cause triumphant." [3]

Elements of the City Plan. Before any plan for a city can be made, a thorough survey of its physical features, its structures, its transportation and traffic systems, and its public recreation lands should be made.[4] The planner is then ready to make a blueprint outlining the streets, parks, playgrounds, and other public areas, and to designate the private uses of land, generally grouped as commercial, industrial, and residential areas. In making his blueprint he will be guided by a few general rules; a fixed set of principles has not yet been formulated. Some of these will be given here just to present a more vivid picture of plan-making.

In the *street design* the main arteries of traffic should connect with the trunk lines coming into the city and other arteries bringing traffic from outlying districts. If possible, traffic should be classified and streets set aside for each class. Arterial highways should be able to carry fast-moving traffic at high speed with the fewest stops practicable. The planner will, so far as possible, avoid having heavy, slow-moving traffic cross a main arterial road. Minor streets can be narrower and follow irregular lines instead

[1] *Ibid.*, pp. 35–39, 52–54.

[2] *Ibid.*, p. 47.

[3] Thomas E. Tallmadge, *The Story of Architecture in America* (New York, Norton, 1936), Chaps. 6, 8, and 9.

[4] See *Suggestion for Use in Making a City Survey (Industrial and Commercial)* (U. S. Department of Commerce, Bureau of Foreign and Domestic Commerce, 1938).

of being direct. Pleasure drives and boulevards are generally laid out to follow routes of natural beauty and are not designed for commercial traffic. Adequate traffic connection between freight terminals and the water front, or between these two and the business section, should be kept in mind.

The width and arrangement of the streets is also important. It must be remembered that streets are covered with expensive pavements, and some cities have from 20 to 30 per cent of their total area covered in this way. There must be a balance between the desire for wide beautiful streets, traffic needs, and the costs involved in wider streets. The arrangement of street-car tracks, curbs, sidewalks, grass strips, and trees all become important factors in planning and should conform to the type of street and its use for business, residential, or industrial purposes.

The rapidly increasing number of motorcars is the despair of the city planner. City plans made thirty years ago contemplated horse-drawn vehicles. The streets are now inadequate. Many cities are taking the position that public streets are for *moving* traffic and are regulating and even prohibiting parking wherever congestion is especially troublesome.

Rail and water transportation and, more recently, airports are important features of a city plan. Water fronts and railway stations were often the first points of origin and were located before the city ever thought of a plan. Once located, it is extremely difficult and costly to move them. In Chicago the various railways located their stations as close to the "Loop" as possible, and now this area is hemmed in by a "Chinese wall" of rail property. Only a few of the streets in the Loop extend beyond it. Only four of the north and south streets of this part of the city extend two miles between Chicago Avenue and Roosevelt Road, and all traffic leaving the Loop is forced upon these four streets.[1] Just now air transportation is engaging public attention and an increasing number of cities are considering airports. The proper location of airports, especially in relation to the city and to other transportation agencies, is a nice problem in planning.

The growing demand for recreational land in cities has been discussed above.[2] Professor Henry V. Hubbard suggests eight

[1] James, *op. cit.*, p. 199.
[2] Chap. X.

different classes of recreational areas, five of which are playgrounds and three are parks. The playgrounds comprise: (1) fields for adults for baseball, football, tennis, etc.; (2) playgrounds for boys above twelve with apparatus such as parallel bars, etc.; (3) similar playgrounds for girls above twelve; (4) playgrounds for children below twelve equipped with sand boxes; (5) special facilities such as bathing beaches, skating ponds, etc. The parks are: (1) the "reservation," a tract of forest land in the country in connection with city forests or urban water supplies, such as the Chicago Forest Preserves; (2) the large park or "country park," to be subjected to rather intensive use but keeping some of the aspects of a country park; (3) the town park, which is more accessible and is used intensively. Parks should be located so as to take advantage of natural features yet should be in relation to population density and the transport system.[1]

Some cities combine parks and playgrounds, but city planners generally hold that the two uses should be separated. Neither should parks be used for public buildings. Playgrounds should be located as near to the congested populations as possible.

Other features of city planning include the location of public buildings, schools, fire stations, city hall, police stations, and county, state, and federal buildings. Some years ago planners strove to locate these buildings in "civic centers," but this is no longer being done. The planner must also keep in mind sewerage, water supply, and the other elements of "city housekeeping."

It should be realized that the above is a catalogue of the elements of a plan for a large city. Smaller cities will not need all the park spaces suggested by Hubbard nor will the street layout include everything enumerated.[2] Furthermore, how these elements will be arranged to secure harmony, convenience, efficiency, and beauty depends on the skill and vision of the planner. The designers of Radburn, New Jersey (the "City for the Motor Age"), of the Greenbelt Towns sponsored by the federal government, and the garden cities of Letchworth and Welwyn used the same elements as the speculative promoter who lays out a stereotyped, gridiron subdivision, but the results are as different as

[1] Hubbard, "Park and Playgrounds," in *Proceedings of the Fourteenth National Conference on City Planning*, Springfield, Mass., June 5–7, 1922, pp. 2–29.

[2] See Russell Van Nest Black, *Planning for the Small American City* (Chicago, Public Administration Service, 1933).

Frank Lloyd Wright's Taliesen is from a house constructed by a jerry-builder.

The public features of the city plan involve primarily the right of eminent domain. The right to purchase land for streets, parks, water fronts, and playgrounds is well established because their public purpose is evident. However, it is often desirable for the city to condemn more than is actually needed for public purposes. In the case of widening a street, this is at times desirable so that the city can protect the usefulness and beauty of the public improvement by controlling the land adjoining. Sometimes remnants of lots will be left which, after such *excess condemnation,* can be reblocked or sold to adjoining property holders. Since the widening of the street often enhances property values, the city could frequently receive enough income from the sale of this property to pay for the entire improvement, but the practice has not always had the sanction of the courts.

The Regulation of Private Land Uses—Zoning. All the elements of planning discussed above dealt with publicly owned land or land under the full control of the municipality. But the planner also has on his blueprint his ideal of how the private land should be used. In this he will be guided by the principles of city structure and will assign certain sections for commercial uses, others for industrial purposes, and last, but not least, certain areas will be set aside for residential purposes. Within these areas it is highly important that incompatible land uses be prohibited. It is not desirable that factories or warehouses be located in a residential area, bringing noises, odors, and heavy traffic into a quiet neighborhood and thereby endangering health and safety and depreciating property values.

Zoning recognizes first of all certain general *use areas.* Usually these are subdivided into several classes, such as "Class A, B, and C Residential Districts." Within the districts for each use, zoning ordinances customarily prescribe the height to which the building may be carried, the area of the lot that may be covered, and the restrictions as to rear yards, side yards, and courts.

In the early history of zoning the theory was that the "higher" uses should be protected against "lower" uses. Some authorities of zoning are urging that since each district for a specific use has its own characteristics—its own type of streets, for instance—

therefore *any* other use not in conformity with the district is out of place.

Much of the success of land use regulations depends upon the efficiency of zoning. Some cities merely set up a few restrictions in certain areas and call this zoning. Modern zoning is not merely restrictive but looks to the future to guide city development. For instance, as the commercial section grows and becomes ready to expand into the residential erea, a prescribed time, place, and manner of opening new areas for the stores and offices will direct this expansion. An adequate city plan will try to foresee this expansion and be ready for it.

Building Height Limitations and Traffic Congestion. One of the most controversial subjects is the control of the height of the skyscrapers. It is contended that skyscrapers are dangerous to health, that they cut off sunlight so that artificial light has to be used in the lower offices, that they are fire-traps and elements of great danger in case of earthquakes and storms. These objections have been met fairly successfully, but the main reason for height limitation is the claim that high buildings tend to aggravate traffic congestion, both vehicular and pedestrian. However, traffic congestion is much more of a factor with stores than with office buildings. Table 36 shows the result of a one-day count of people going in and out of office buildings, stores, and a hotel in Milwaukee. The number of people entering the four office buildings was only a little more than the number shopping at one of the "ten cent" stores, yet the office buildings ranged from 16 to 23 stories in height. Most astonishing, perhaps, was the small amount of traffic furnished by the 25-story hotel and the 10,000 people who shopped at the two-story chain store. Facts such as these assist the planner when working with street width, traffic control, and parking problems.

Housing and Home Ownership. The problem of housing is not exclusively an urban problem. The stranded settler in the "cut-overs," the miner, the share cropper generally live in substandard dwellings. If brought together as a city they would constitute the worst slums on earth because rural houses lack the conveniences usually, though not always, found in urban houses. Nevertheless, congested housing brings with it peculiar problems of its own. Crowding, insanitary conditions, disease, crime, and

TABLE 36

DAILY PEDESTRIAN TRAFFIC IN AND OUT OF VARIOUS TYPES OF BUILDINGS IN MILWAUKEE, 1937 [1]

	STORIES *	HOURS	NUMBER ENTERING	NUMBER LEAVING	PEAK HOURS	
					Entering	Leaving
1. Office Building A	23	7 A.M.—7 P.M.	3,817	3,549	12–1 P.M.	11–12 A.M.
2. Office Building B	20	" "	2,534	1,981	7–8 A.M.	5–6 P.M.
3. Office Building C	16	" "	1,883	1,638	1–2 P.M.	4–5 P.M.
4. Office & Bank Bldg.	18	" "	8,116	8,061	1–2 P.M.	12–1 P.M.
5. Hotel	25	8 A.M.—8 P.M.	2,978	2,740	5–6 P.M.	5–6 P.M.
6. Department Store	7	9 A.M.—6 P.M.	48,293	43,530	2–3 P.M.	2–3 P.M.
7. Chain Store	2	" "	10,339	10,323	3–4 P.M.	3–4 P.M.
8. "Ten Cent" Store	2	" "	15,759	12,661	12–1 P.M.	12–1 P.M.
9. Department Store in Outlying Business District	4	" "	6,649	6,895	12–1 P.M.	3–4 P.M.

* Estimated. Not comparable exactly because of set backs and the composite use of some of the buildings.

[1] *Milwaukee on the Go: A Pedestrian and Vehicular Traffic Survey*, compiled and mapped by Charles B. Bennett, City Planner, Board of Public Land Commissioners (published by the *Milwaukee Journal*, 1939).

delinquency are associated with poor housing though not necessarily caused by substandard housing.

Much has been said about the growing proportion of rented farms in the United States, which automatically means "rural homes." In 1930, however, 53.2 per cent of *non-farm* homes were rented, as compared to 42 per cent of farm homes. The proportion of rented dwellings varies widely with cities and is not necessarily correlated with large cities. About 80 per cent of the dwellings in Manhattan are rented, but the figure for the Bronx is higher and for Brooklyn lower. Birmingham, Alabama, is very near to New York in its percentage of tenant occupied houses, whereas Portland, Oregon, Salt Lake City, and St. Paul have less than 50 per cent of their families living in rented dwellings.

Since the majority of city people are tenants, this means that one group must invest in land and structures while another group buys housing as a commodity from landlords. The interests of these two groups are not identical and often antagonistic. The respective bargaining power becomes the rent-determining factor. The public acts as umpire to see that the landlord furnishes sanitary and decent dwellings, and during emergencies courts have upheld the public regulation of house rents to protect the tenant. However, the public may not always be an unbiased umpire.

The reasons for the high proportion of rented dwellings and the poor housing of cities are manifold. Urban housing is difficult because there are so many kinds of persons and families to be housed. The traditional farm or village family and home have been metamorphosed. Many single persons and childless couples want extreme mobility and do not care to be tied to a given spot. Their wants have to be satisfied by the hotel, boarding house, and kitchenette type of apartment. Many of the activities of the old household, such as baking, laundering, sewing, and dressmaking, are now largely done outside of the home. Education, recreation, and the care of dependents are more or less public functions or are furnished by private enterprise. The members of the family have become more individualistic. Less space is needed and more conveniences are demanded. The house began to shrink to the flat as early as the 1880's in response to these forces. Land values also forced the economy of space afforded by the multi-family type of dwelling. These institutional factors affect the living of all groups in urban society. Many well-to-do have forsaken the single-family house for luxurious apartments, accessible to theaters, stores, and offices. All of these factors have tended toward less home ownership and more rented dwellings.

Housing and home ownership may also be approached from another angle. Who can afford a modern home in the average city? It is a rule-of-thumb principle that no more than two, or at the outset three times the gross annual income should be spent for a home. With this in mind, the relation of income to home ownership is striking. The average annual family income of the American people in 1929, at the very peak of prosperity, was $2,800.[1] The median income was $1,700 per family per year, which means that half of the families were earning less than this figure. The distribution was as follows:

Annual Income		Number of Families	Percentage
Below	$1,000	6,000,000	21%
Less than	1,500	12,000,000	42
Less than	2,500	20,000,000	71
Above	5,000	2,000,000	8
Above	10,000	600,000	2.3

The realtor's slogan "Own your own home" is meaningless to probably half the families of the United States because $3,000 is inadequate to buy a lot and erect a modern house, except in villages, on farms, in the warmer sections of the country, or where materials and labor are inexpensive.[2] Stuart Chase feels that only those with *assured* incomes of $3,000 per year or more can afford the luxury of the "owned" home. The security of the income is highly important. During the depression the foreclosure of homes in cities was quite as tragic as on the farms. Philadelphia, the "city of homes," had 170,000 foreclosures between 1920 and

[1] Maurice Leven, Harold G. Moulton, and Clark Warburton, *America's Capacity to Consume* (Brookings Institution, 1934), p. 55. The above includes farmers as well as non-farmers.

[2] This statement should be modified in the light of recent experiments in low-cost housing by both public and private enterprises. However, the above income figures are too optimistic for the present time. For figures based upon depression conditions see "Family Income and the Urban Housing Market in the United States," *Federal Home Loan Bank Review*, December, 1938, pp. 70–73.

1938, or 40 per cent of the owned dwellings. The nation as a whole had 1,600,000 foreclosures between 1926 and 1936. It is estimated that a million homes were saved by the Home Owners Loan Corporation. The significance of this condition is that those in the lower income brackets will tend to be inadequately housed whether they own or rent, and if they rent they are at the mercy of the rental market.

The incentive to home ownership is also weakened by the fact that with a stationary population in sight only a few cities can expect to expand very much. With the tendency of cities to flatten out into the peripheries and of old residential areas to decrease in value, the home owner must expect, in addition to the physical depreciation of his house, stationary, if not declining, land values. It is doubtful speculation to expect "unearned increment" to pay for a home.[1]

Furthermore, the burden of taxation on property has become excessive in many cities and is felt to be another deterrent to home ownership. This feeling has gained such momentum that laws have been passed and even constitutions amended in nine states, definitely limiting the tax on real estate for all purposes. The overall limits range from 1½ to 5 per cent of the value of the property, and it is generally held by the proponents of tax limitation that the lower limit, 15 mills per dollar, is the preferable rate. By July, 1937, thirteen states had also passed laws providing for the exemption of "homesteads" of a certain value from taxation, generally restricted to owner-occupied properties.[2]

An important factor in promoting home ownership is sufficient and reasonable credit. Home buying is by its very nature installment buying and for many people the largest investment they ever make. In this field the building and loan associations have played an important part, but in the present stringency the federal government has assisted in refinancing existing homes and furnishing credit for new dwellings. The question is pertinent whether private enterprise can furnish adequate housing at prices low enough to fit the incomes of the lower income groups. Pub-

[1] Stuart Chase, "The Case against Home Ownership," *Survey Graphic,* May, 1938; Babcock, *The Valuation of Real Estate, op. cit.,* pp. 69–78; and Chap. 7.

[2] See Abrams, *Revolution in Land, op. cit.,* Chapters 5, "Decline of the Home"; 6, "Drift into Tenancy"; 8, "The Mortgage"; 9, "The Land Tax"; 10, "Construction," and 15, "New Deal in Land."

lic housing has been undertaken because it is believed that the time has come to put housing for the lower income groups in the same category as public education and recreation, to be furnished at public expense and subsidized to the extent that the income level of the client is inadequate to pay for reasonably decent shelter. In this connection the programs of the federal government should be studied. Much more has been done in foreign countries than in America in furnishing public housing.

METROPOLITAN REGIONAL PLANNING

The close relationship of the city with the metropolitan region calls for planning the entire region as a unit, instead of piecemeal and often inharmonious planning by the individual units of government which comprise the region.

The Elements of the Regional Plan. These are surprisingly similar to those of the city plan—highways, railroads, airports, and water transportation; a full complement of recreational land to serve the entire region; sewerage, water supply, control of pollution; and the assignment of industrial, commercial, residential, and agricultural uses to various districts. It is on the periphery of the urban areas that planning and zoning are in the full sense of the word *directional,* because the planner can project the future uses of the land before the pattern is set and the land forms solidified. Zoning and other controls may be employed to regulate the uses he has assigned to each tract.

Sometimes it is necessary to have some type of land use regulation in the metropolitan region in unincorporated areas where zoning restrictions do not exist or are inadequate. In such cases *private deed restrictions* may be used. Subdividers sometimes designate a given lot line, specifying a given type of improvement, and stipulate other restrictions on the utilization of land in deeds, mortgages, and leases. Civic organizations, real estate boards, and property owners' protective associations sometimes use similar extra-legal methods to induce the utilizers of property to conform to the standard desired by the community.

If the problem of blueprinting a metropolitan region is more difficult than planning a city, the problem of transferring the plan to the land is much more so; because not one but many municipalities must accept the "master plan" and adopt the land use districts and regulations contemplated in the plan. This is sometimes accomplished by metropolitan districts and boards which, like other "districts," are units of government that can and do cross the boundaries of the regularly constituted units. Boston began in 1889 with a Metropolitan Sewerage Commission embracing eighteen towns. Water supply, parks, and, finally in 1923, planning for the whole region (now consisting of forty cities and towns) have come under the control of metropolitan boards.

County Zoning in Regional Planning. County zoning usually does not affect an entire metropolitan region, but it is effective within the jurisdiction of a county in controlling land uses. Early in the 1920's the zoning power was granted to individual counties in California and Georgia and in some other states to towns. In 1923 Wisconsin passed the first general enabling act under which any county may regulate land uses and out of which the "rural type" of zoning evolved. By 1937 Michigan, Indiana, California, and Washington had also passed general enabling acts permitting rural zoning, while the Virginia, Tennessee, and Illinois acts were confined to suburban zoning. Township zoning acts of the urban type had already been passed in the New England and three Middle Atlantic states. Since 1937 Pennsylvania has passed a comprehensive act under which both rural and suburban zoning are possible. Tennessee, Georgia, Virginia, Florida, Michigan, Colorado and Minnesota have broadened their laws or added new statutes during 1937–39. Florida has tried some direct state zoning by using a legislative decree to set up an exclusive residential area adjacent to the city of Tampa.[1]

An example of county zoning designed to regulate metropolitan regional land uses is that of Orange County, California. This county is south of Los Angeles and has a highly attractive orchard section, fine riparian land along the ocean, and the outthrust of urban land uses from Los Angeles and its own cities. From the latter arose the usual problem of the metropolitan area and a districting ordinance was passed setting up, in addition to three residence districts, two business districts, one district for light

[1] Herman Walker, Jr., "Recent Progress in the Enactment of Rural Zoning Enabling Legislation," *Journal of Land and Public Utility Economics,* August 1938, pp. 333–39. See *ibid,* August 1937 for the Pennsylvania Act, November 1937 and 1939, Tennessee, August 1939, Colorado, and February 1940 for Minnesota.

industries, and four interesting non-urban types of districts, as follows:

> *Roadside Agricultural Districts,* designed for use along primary and scenic highways to restrict outdoor advertising and scattered commercial uses and to preserve the fundamental non-urban character of the highway frontage;
>
> *Estates Districts,* establishing high-quality open types of residential use, the minimum land unit being one acre;
>
> *Small Farms Districts,* permitting one- and two-family dwellings and incidental uses common in suburban areas, the minimum land unit being 20,000 square feet;
>
> *Mountain Estates District,* set up primarily to regulate the spacing of dwellings in summer resort subdivisions in forest areas, minimum land unit 10,000 square feet.

In each of these districts the maximum height of the buildings, the minimum building site area, the space for front, rear, and side yards are prescribed. The ordinance also provides for an "unrestricted district," from which only dwellings are excluded, and an "unclassified district" for the extensive undeveloped areas and grazing and farming lands.[1]

Control of Subdivisions. It is important to recognize that much of the future development of American cities is under the control of private individuals. A realty concern obtains a tract of land outside of the city limits where city ordinances have no jurisdiction. When it lays out the streets it fixes the pattern for all time to come, yet the width may not be adequate, they may not connect with existing arteries, and no provision may have been made for future increase in traffic. The subdivider may or may not provide for parks. These matters are of great public concern, yet the subdivider is tempted to put as much land as possible into the lots which he can sell, and as little as possible into the streets and parks which he must donate to the public.

Considerable progress has been made in securing this much needed control over the region outside the city. In some cities unofficial planning associations are at work gathering data and making plans for the *region* as well as the city. Subdividers and others responsible for the future of the region are persuaded to

[1] L. Deming Tilton, "The Districting Plan of Orange County, California," *Journal of Land and Public Utility Economics,* November, 1936, pp. 375–91, at p. 382.

make their land utilization conform to the general plan, usually with some success. In some cities metropolitan commissions have obtained legal and effective control through legislation, as in Boston. Other cities have the power to control planning within a certain distance beyond the city limits.

While satisfactory progress has been made along some of these lines, little has been accomplished by zoning or any other land use regulations to restrain the premature subdividing of non-urban land for residential purposes. Undue optimism, speculation, and even fraud were behind the laying out of residential sites around Chicago, Detroit, New York, and other cities. The consequences of wildcat subdividing are remarkably similar to the events on the agricultural forest fringe. Land is taken out of agricultural use and frozen as residential plats which cannot be restored to the former use except in unusual cases. When the boom collapses thousands of lots remain unsold, and the ripening and waiting costs drive the realty companies into bankruptcy and force them to let the land revert for taxes. The tax-reverted lands, a "new public domain," bring the same headaches to local units of government as they do to the counties or the state in the cut-over areas. The lands remaining on the tax roll now have to carry the burden of government expenses, which have been driven to excessive heights by the cost of the new streets, sewers, schools, and other public services demanded by the subdivider and the clients. "If the whole of the surplus plotted acreage is fully improved as now laid out, excessive costs of street improvements alone will amount to from 125 to 150 million dollars" in New Jersey, according to the New Jersey State Planning Board.[1] The few owners who built homes in these speculative subdivisions have their counterpart in the isolated stranded settlers in the marginal areas of the forest-farm frontier.

However, it is not only platted property that furnishes problems in unplanned suburban areas. The hit-and-miss home seeker who buys land on the "shoe string" developments along radiating highways is also setting a pattern of land use which becomes fixed before the city can reach him with some form of land use control. Meanwhile billboards, junk yards, hot dog

[1] *Land Subdivision in New Jersey,* New Jersey State Planning Board (Trenton 1938), pp. 10–11.

stands, and similar commercial uses crowd into the same sections, the out-thrust of the city which Mackaye so much dreads.[1] And this conglomeration of hideousness is the entrance and front yard to American cities and will remain so until regulations are set up to control the situation. Unfortunately these regulations must now be supplied by weak and sometimes apathetic units of government under township and county zoning enabling acts available in only a score of the states.

Even in those states in which suburban zoning is permitted, little attempt has been made to control wildcat subdividing. It is presumed that residential property is welcome in the rural areas around cities and not detrimental or out of harmony with farming, wood lands, estates, or recreation. Local officials are happy to have new properties to tax, and farmers are glad to sell farm land at "residential values." However, there are times and places where small lot subdivisions are incompatible with the rural landscape consisting of farms and estates. It is really a matter not of "higher" or "lower" land uses but of *incompatible* uses. If this concept of incompatibility is accepted it should be entirely feasible to exclude, not only business and industrial uses, but also small-lot subdivisions from rural areas. Zoning can once more become a directional instrument to guide the use of land for residential purposes by opening only enough rural land to supply the demand for new homes. Zoning, however, must be supplemented by more stringent platting laws and other forms of restriction.[2] Among the latter is the suggestion that a "certificate of convenience and necessity" be required before permission is granted for a new subdivision.

The Planning of Other "Regions." Regional planning began with the metropolitan region in which the city was naturally the center. However, the concept of planning land uses and the man-made structures associated with land has been extended to counties, states, and regions other than urbanized areas. One of these is the Tennessee Valley Authority, which embraces a river valley and is aimed at co-ordinating the use of all natural resources, water and land. A still wider use of the "region" is

[1] Mackaye, *The New Exploration, op. cit.*

[2] Cornick, *Premature Subdivision and Its Consequences, op. cit.,* pp. 324–25 and Chaps. 7–9.

proposed by Mumford, who defines regional planning as "the conscious direction and collective integration of all those activities which rest upon the use of the earth as site, as resource, as structure, as theater. To the extent that such activities are focussed within definite regions, consciously delimited and utilized, the opportunities for effective co-ordination are increased. Hence regional planning is a further stage in the more specialized or isolated processes of agriculture planning, industry planning or city planning." [1]

THE FUTURE OF URBANIZATION

The urban way of life is established and mere movement of industry into the metropolitan region or a wider dispersion of the residential areas will not change its fundamental characteristics. The economies of a certain degree of concentration of work and people will remain so long as transportation is a factor of cost in money, time, or inconvenience. Electricity and modern transportation are acting as centrifugal forces, but no widespread diffusion of industries to smaller cities or the open country is taking place.[2]

Urbanization itself will stop at the balance between rural and urban economies. With a surplus of both food and population on the farms, many more people could be moved to the cities and the remainder, probably half, could raise all the food and fiber needed to support the nation. In other words, the farm population could be reduced from 24.6 per cent to 15 per cent without serious lack of the means of subsistence. Even with a stationary population, city growth can continue as long as urban industries and occupations offer jobs. Rural fecundity is still great enough to maintain and even augment urban population by migration.

Increased urbanization, however, does not mean that all cities will grow, nor that an upper limit may not be reached beyond which a given city can grow. From the engineering standpoint there is no limit to the size of a city; water can be brought from greater distances, sewers made large enough to carry the wastes, streets double decked, tunnels and bridges designed to transport more goods and people. However, the law of diminishing returns

[1] *Culture of Cities, op. cit.*, p. 374.
[2] See the conclusions in Goodrich *et al., op. cit.*, pp. 618–27.

begins to operate and the per capita cost of these services rises at a more rapid rate than population growth. Land values and the cost of living rise; in fact, one of the reasons for the suburban movement is to escape these consequences and yet make a living in the central city. The long distances to work, with the resultant congestion and loss of time, likewise militate against the gigantic city.

We may also expect certain cities to grow and others to decline as economic advantages shift. These shifts are already under way and more changes will occur as the resource base shifts.[1] New sources of power, changes in transportation, a growing nationalism with a consequent decrease in foreign trade may create new conditions for city growth in some sections and drastic declines in others.

[1] See maps, pp. 30–31, of *Our Cities, op. cit.;* also F. G. Tyron, "The Changing Distribution of Resources," in Goodrich *et al., op. cit.,* pp. 251–99.

XIV

CONSERVATION AND SOCIAL CONTROL OVER LAND: A SUMMARY

Reference has repeatedly been made to the "conservation era," the first fifteen or twenty years of the present century. This should not leave the impression that no thought had been given to this subject before 1900; evidences of interest in forest conservation may be found before 1800, and the efforts of individuals, societies, and Congress during the entire nineteenth century are on record.[1] However, the vital attack on the problems of conserving all natural resources was made in 1908 when Theodore Roosevelt called a conference in Washington of the governors of all the states, and in his opening address declared that conservation was the "chief material question that confronts us, second only . . . to the great fundamental question of morality." [2]

Unfortunately, conservation then became a slogan, and many weird proposals were made by popular writers on how and what to conserve. Suggestions for saving wood took such trivial forms as preventing waste in matches, lead pencils, and kindling wood. Reclamation of farm land was undertaken in the name of conservation because of the supposed shortage of agricultural soil. Its meaning was expanded to include health, home beautification, parks, playgrounds, and many other things far afield from land or natural resources.

In reviewing the practical results of this exciting era, Zimmermann concludes, "It is difficult to discover any tangible and far reaching effects of the enthusiasm for conservation which Roosevelt managed to arouse." [3] While this is an overstatement, it must be admitted that the crusade for conservation accomplished less

[1] See Pinchot, "How Conservation Began in the United States," *op. cit.*, pp. 255–65; Ise, *The United States Forest Policy, op. cit.*, Chaps. 1 and 2; Parkins and Whitaker, *Our Natural Resources and Their Conservation, op. cit.*, Chap. 1; R. T. Ely, R. H. Hess, C. K. Leith, and T. N. Carver, *The Foundations of National Prosperity* (New York, Macmillan, 1917), Part I, Chaps. 2, 3, and 4.

[2] *Proceedings of a Conference of Governors*, May 13–15, 1908, ed. W J McGee (Washington, 1909), p. 3.

[3] *World Resources and Industries, op. cit.*, p. 782. By permission of Harper & Brothers, publishers.

than it should have, and largely because the fundamentals of economics and of social philosophy, the problems of property, and the legal aspects of conservation were neglected or ignored.

Conservation Involves the Balance between the Present and Future. The economist cannot solve the problem of conservation. He can only state the conditions under which conservation will or will not take place. The economic factors involved are the costs of conserving as balanced against probable incomes accruing some time in the future. For the purpose of this discussion, Zimmermann's definition will be accepted: "Conservation is any act of reducing the rate of consumption or exhaustion for the avowed purpose of benefiting posterity." [1] It involves more than merely "combining the factors of production" and "elimination of waste"; it involves the deliberate restraint on the use of the resource in the present in order to leave a supply for future generations. This can be applied to the entire gamut of natural resources, from flowers to minerals. The flower picker must realize that to pull up *every* lady's-slipper means no more lady's-slippers next year and every year thereafter. Conservation-minded nature lovers deliberately restrain their desire to pick every flower in order that others living and yet unborn may also enjoy lady's-slippers.

Hunters may either butcher everything in sight or discipline their propensity to slaughter to the extent of shooting only the annual increase, thus leaving enough breeding stock to provide sport for later years and for future generations of Nimrods. In general, the sportsman is willing and ready to do this voluntarily, but he also supports game laws to keep those in line who are not conservation-minded.

Although the supply of fish in the Great Lakes has been sorely depleted by over-fishing, by taking fish from the spawning grounds, and by the destruction of immature fish, political pressure by commercial fishermen has been powerful enough to prevent uniform regulations and proper administration. "The point of view of the average commercial fisherman has been short sighted: he has not been willing to forego a dollar today to save the resource for tomorrow." [2]

[1] *Ibid.*, p. 792.

[2] *Regional Planning, Part VIII, Northern Lake States,* National Resources Committee (1939), p. 47.

Conservation takes a somewhat different form in the case of non-replaceable resources. Here a deliberate reduction in the rate of disappearance in the present is necessary in order to guarantee a supply for the future. Nevertheless, every one of the replaceable resources may be "treated as a mine." This is notoriously true in forest land, and agricultural soil has an exhaustion value similar to minerals. The total destruction of fish, game, and wild life, so that nothing will be left for the future, is also an act of "mining," whether careless or deliberate.

Stated in another way, conservation involves a conflict between the present and the future. Insofar as conservation involves the postponement of income, or the choice of future as against present incomes, the resource owner is confronted with the same psychological elements that are involved in the impatience theory of interest.[1] Five thousand dollars two years from today or 40 years hence are not the same to him as $5,000 this year. In other words, the resource owner discounts the *future* incomes. With a time preference rate of 5 per cent, the $5,000 available in 40 years would have a present worth of only $710 and $5,000 per year over a period of 40 years is worth about $85,000 today. The higher the interest rate the less future incomes are valued in terms of "present worth," and the lower the rate the more nearly will present and future incomes be equal. The best conservationist would be a person whose time preference is *nil.* To him the value of prospective incomes, no matter how far in the future, would be the same as a present income. Such a person does not exist; there is always a conflict between the present and the future, which L. C. Gray says is "the heart of the conservation problem." "The primary problem of conservation," he says, "expressed in economic language is the determination of the proper rate of discount on the future with respect to the utilization of our natural resources."[2]

However, this should not leave the impression that all individuals, communities, and nations always prefer present to future returns. Individuals and corporations invest heavily in long-time enterprises even though their returns are postponed to a distant

[1] Ely, Hess, Leith, and Carver, *op. cit.,* pp. 126–39.

[2] "Economic Possibilities of Conservation," *Quarterly Journal of Economics,* May, 1913, p. 515.

future. All savings for old age and life insurance are of this character; in life insurance the income becomes available only after the death of the investor. In any mature society with ample capital accumulation and low interest rates, the "conflict between the present and future" is not serious enough to prevent investment in conservation enterprises merely because incomes become available in the distant future. The reason for not investing lies rather in the nature of the resource, the uncertainty of the prospective income, and the lack of assurance of favorable public policies toward the investor. Even in Germany, where it is reported that a landowner spent $100 an acre for reforesting stripped coal land because he "considered it his duty to leave the property to his successors in at least as good condition as when he took it over," the private owner is not entrusted with the conservation of forests free from entail, government aid, and public regulation.[1]

In contrast to a mature society which takes thought for tomorrow are some primitive races which have no regard for the future and have a fatalistic outlook on life. It is claimed that a thousand years ago Sinai was reasonably well wooded, and the ruins of dams, cisterns, and terraces indicate a high state of cultivation and a relatively large population. However, the Bedouins who inherited the land have failed to keep up the improvements and have "wantonly and wickedly" wrecked conduits and cisterns "which they were too lazy to use." In this destructive policy they were aided by the camels and goats, which have practically depleted the land of trees and shrubs. It has been aptly said that the Arab is not the "Son of the Desert" but in most cases the "Father of the Desert." "The future worries them [the Arabs] not a jot and with them time is not a dimension, it is merely a state of mind." They created the arid waste in which they live today.[2]

Conservation is therefore primarily a matter of social philosophy differing with individuals, nations, and even sections within the same nation. The lavish use of natural resources in a new country is part of the period of exploitation, capital accumulation, and "digging in." No other policy could have given America such quantities of cheap food, oil, lumber, and minerals, which

[1] "Soils and Men," *Yearbook of the U. S. Dept. of Agriculture,* 1938, p. 133.
[2] C. S. Jarvis, *Three Deserts* (New York, Dutton, 1937), pp. 143, 159–60.

became the exportable surplus and the basis for rapid urbanization. The East reached maturity first and became a champion of conservation before the West was ready to adopt the same philosophy. The West was still in the frontier stage of its development, anxious to exploit the forests, open the mines, and reclaim the deserts, and thus to attract population and create taxable wealth. Westerners were willing to admit that conservation was a splendid ideal of great national importance, but they felt that the burden was falling upon their states. The eastern part of the country had had a free hand in exploiting its resources and building up the industries now denied to the West. Hence the early opposition to national forests, to restrictions on grazing, and to mineral reservations. However, with the development of federal forests, parks, reclamation, and the later grazing and mining policies, much of the opposition to conservation involving public ownership and regulation has disappeared.

To every nation as it approaches maturity comes the necessity of husbanding its resources. "In France," said Ambassador J. J. Jusserand at the American Forest Congress in 1905, "we think much about tomorrows, because we have known so many yesterdays. . . . We have not your boundless resources; we must husband what we possess."[1] If a philosophy of conservation develops it will be expressed in a willingness of the people to restrain themselves, as producers and as consumers, and to set up social controls to accomplish this purpose.

The Costs of Conservation. Much has been said about the *costs* of conservation, the cost of holding land and resources for the future. However, no particular costs are involved in refraining from "mining" natural resources, whether wild flowers or timber, except the psychic or pseudo-economic costs of income foregone through refraining from exploiting the resource. If these resources had been left as part of the public domain, there need have been no waiting or carrying costs for agricultural, forest, or mineral lands or land held for speculation as far as private owners were concerned. The real cost would have come in the fact that state and local governments would have been wholly or partly without a tax base. There were both a public push and a

[1] *Proceedings of the American Forest Congress,* Washington, January 2–6, 1905, p. 24.

private pull to get land into individual ownership. Once in private ownership, however, conservation costs were inevitable. In the case of many resources, notably forests and minerals, carrying costs are important forces in driving the owners to exploit the land to "get out from under."

Finally, the costs of conservation to the consumer must not be omitted. To conserve oil by reducing the annual supply must necessarily mean higher priced gasoline; probably the real test of a conservation policy would be the consumer's willingness to pay 40 cents a gallon in order that his grandchildren also might run a car.[1] The consumer, moreover, is baffled by the revolutionary changes in the use and extraction of non-renewable resources. The "reserves" of coal in tons and oil in barrels are almost meaningless. No one can tell when a technological invention will not double the economic supply or provide a more acceptable substitute. Substitutes have already appeared for anthracite coal, which was once considered a natural monopoly. It may be that in another twenty-five years hard coal will be practically valueless. Could the trend of events be foreseen, the best conservation might have been to use this kind of coal as fast as possible, substituting it for other fuels wherever practicable and finding new methods for its utilization. Science has done such wonderful things that the layman believes everything possible. For this reason, and not always because he is callous toward future generations and their welfare, the average citizen refuses to deny himself the luxury of using natural resources without reservation.

Conservation Policies. If conservation of our natural resources were automatically the product of rational land utilization, or if all individuals were willing "to reduce their rate of consumption for the avowed purpose of benefiting posterity," it would not be necessary to speak of a conservation policy. With greater national maturity also come qualities of foresight, a broader outlook, and a willingness to look into the future. Nevertheless, the experience of older nations should help America consciously to speed up the process; in other words, to inaugurate a policy of education. However, leaving it to education is too easy a solution of the problem and one proposed for too many things. Moreover, a mere knowledge of the facts will not provide

[1] See Chapter XII.

a "social philosophy." The desire to conserve must become a part of the institutions, customs, and thinking of a people who will then gladly make sacrifices without even considering them sacrifices. Even the United States has individual landowners and communities whose ambition is to pass the soil to the next generation unimpaired or perhaps a little more fertile than they received it from the past generation.[1]

Education should also make people, urban as well as rural, aware of the importance of conservation for their community. "The loss of soil or forests" becomes translated into a local loss of income, delinquent taxes, bankruptcy of local governments, and loss of population. Soil conservation districts may serve their greatest purpose by getting an entire watershed to think in terms of a common conservation problem. People meeting together to discuss the pros and cons of rural zoning are becoming self-educated in land use control. Furthermore, as people become sensitive to their environment, they become willing to do many things which have no economic reward whatsoever. They will spend money either privately or by paying taxes to rehabilitate disorderly and devastated landscapes, just as they are willing to spend their money for education or other instruments of public welfare.

Once a social philosophy favorable to conservation has been established, conservation may be fostered by "changing the rules of the game." If anti-trust laws, tariffs, public land policies, and taxation have acted as inducements to exploit natural resources, the repeal of these acts or positive legislation on the other side may also act as incentives to conserve them. For instance, a change in property relationships in the oil fields will work wonders in conserving this resource without costs to the owners or the government. The fact that the application of this principle to the conservation of a given resource may raise the price to consumers or reduce the profits of the resource owner is no argument against it. It is being done by all nations today. Tariffs to protect infant industries or to build up manufactures at home withhold a supply from abroad, create a scarcity at home, and raise the price high enough to permit the domestic manufacturer to carry

[1] Robert B. Goodman, "Our Attitude toward Land—A Contrast between American and European Land Policy," *American Forests*, February, 1935.

on his business. This is neither a condemnation nor a justification of the tariff; it merely indicates that we have a precedent for adopting a positive conservation policy even though it places burdens upon both producers and consumers.

Policies of Public Control over Land. Insofar as land and resources are affected by public interest, no landowner holds title to land to the exclusion of the rights of the public, including future as well as present generations. Our political philosophy must give meaning and content to the vague idea of "public vs. private rights" to land. The right to control land uses exists and lies in the sovereign power of the state and may be exercised through the police power, eminent domain, and taxation. The real question is whether the people are willing to make use of these powers within the rule of reasonableness, as decided by the courts and American traditions.

The American attitude toward land goes back to the Revolution, which swept aside not only political traditions but also the remnants of the feudal system. The Ordinance of 1787 abolished entail and primogeniture, and the frontier Jacksonian democracy emphasized the Jeffersonian concept of land tenure. Allodial tenure, free transfer of title, and grants by the federal government to settlers without reservations or qualifications became a part of American land institutions.[1] This emancipation from feudal land tenure should not be abandoned lightly. Even though entail and other restrictions on land tenure have been favorable to the conservation of forests in Germany, this is not an adequate reason for copying European institutions. While freedom of tenure has brought speculation, over-mortgaging, soil depletion, and erosion, it is hoped that we may create a better attitude toward land and establish direct controls over land without changing the framework of land tenure.[2]

The police power, used directly by the state or by delegation

[1] Note how these elements of land tenure are embedded in Section 14 of Article 1 of the Wisconsin Constitution. "All lands within the State are declared to be allodial, and feudal tenures are prohibited:—Leases and grants of agricultural land, for a longer term than 15 years, in which rent, or service of any kind shall be reserved, and all fines and like restraints upon alienation, reserved in any grant of land, hereafter made, are declared void."

[2] George S. Wehrwein, "Public Control of Land Use in the United States," *Journal of Farm Economics,* February, 1939, pp. 74–85. See also F. F. Elliott's "Discussion," *ibid.,* pp. 85–88.

to local units of government, has permitted the control of land uses, principally through zoning. The various applications have been discussed in the preceding chapters, but it will be noted that zoning can become a directional measure principally on the forest-farm and forest-grazing frontiers, or in the fringe between urban and rural territory. Here shifting land uses may be anticipated and directed according to a plan or blueprint. Sometimes the zoning of one type of land may be used to secure the proper utilization of another type, as, for instance, the control of the margins of the highway in the interests of the safety, convenience, and pleasure of those who use the roads and streets.

While progress in this direction is laudable, it must be realized that many forms of zoning are still in the experimental stage and await the action of courts and the test of administration by the local units of government to which this form of land use control has been entrusted. Part of the problem lies in getting adequate administrative machinery in the "fringe" counties and townships, but perhaps the major difficulty is in getting enforcement by decentralized, democratic, and sometimes indifferent and inefficient local governments.

Zoning, however, is inadequate as a land-use control measure under certain conditions. It can best be used to set up broad classes of land use in areas sufficiently uniform and large enough to meet the test of "equal treatment" of all land within a district. It is of doubtful value, but perhaps not impossible, when used to regulate land practices within the line fence of a given farm or to prescribe forestry regulations within a "forest district." Also, some enabling acts prohibit the retroactive action of zoning, although courts have supported it and certain states now have acts which permit the termination of non-conforming uses by the ordinances.

Conservation districts, however, are prepared to do what zoning cannot do. It will be recalled that these districts are specially created units of government which can cut across the boundaries of local units so as to embrace natural land use areas or regions. They have been used to promote flood control, mining, irrigation, drainage, and, more recently, the control of wind and water erosion and the development of water power.[1] Depending on the

[1] William F. Kennedy, "The Nebraska Public Power Districts," *Journal of Land and Public Utility Economics*, February, 1939, pp. 29–48.

enabling act, districts have the taxing power or the power to assess conservation costs against the land, the costs to be recaptured through taxes. They may borrow money, use eminent domain, and, in the Soil Conservation districts, may place regulations upon land uses within the district—which is truly land use control.

Taxation has been mentioned in connection with various types of land. Its power to influence land utilization is very important. The general property tax is supposed to treat all property alike, but each resource reacts differently to this tax, with the result that in some cases proper land utilization and conservation become impossible. The forest crop laws and special forms of taxes for minerals recognize this point. Exemption from taxation, in whole or in part, is also employed to relieve the burden on homes and farms, to stimulate home ownership, to preserve wood lots, and to attract industries. These are indirect negative methods. Little has been done in America to use taxation as a positive form of land use control. For example, the graduated land taxes of Tasmania and New Zealand have been used to break up large land holdings. These taxes have been suggested in the United States. Taxation might also be used to discourage excessive subdividing and in other ways to direct land uses.[1] However, it is felt by many students of public finance that taxation should be kept strictly a fiscal measure and that other methods should be used directly to control or direct the use of land.

Taxation as a land use control measure should not be confused with the Single Tax. While aimed at land, the Single Tax has a much broader purpose; to its proponents it is a complete social reform similar to socialism. The Single Tax really is neither "single" nor a "tax"; its philosophy does not preclude other taxes, and is essentially a proposal to take economic rent or the "annual value" of land from private rent receivers for public purposes. While the idea of a tax on economic rent did not originate with Henry George, he gave it definite form in his *Progress and Poverty,* published in 1879. He lived during the post-Civil War period when speculation, "land grabbing," cor-

[1] J. V. Van Sickle, "Classification of Land for Taxation," *Quarterly Journal of Economics,* Vol. XLII, pp. 94–116; Yetta, Scheftel, *The Taxation of Land Value* (Boston, Houghton, Mifflin, 1916).

ruption, and fraud were rife, but he over-simplified the remedy for the ills of society by attacking the "unearned increment" in land only. It is aptly said by an admirer of Henry George that if George were living today he would be a "triple-taxer," i.e., he would favor income and inheritance taxes in addition to a tax on land values.[1] "But George's awareness of the political importance of the land," says Mumford, "his clear perception in 1870 of dangers that were to be fully demonstrated by 1890, and the stir that he made in the torpid political and economic thought of his day by introducing into it a vital idea—all this cannot be discounted. Henry George challenged the complacencies of bourgeois economics in terms that the bourgeois economist could partly understand. Less than fifteen years after George's *Progress and Poverty* (1879) was published, Professor Frederick Turner pointed out some of the social and economic implications of the passing of the frontier. From this point on, anyone who ignored the role of the land either in American history or in our current institutional life was guilty of convenient forgetfulness: the fact was established."[2]

Public Assistance in Conservation. Inasmuch as the private owner performs a function which is of public as well as private benefit in conserving the natural resource in his possession, there is ground for, if not an obligation upon the public, the sharing of the costs of conservation with the owner. This precept varies with the resource, and before it is applied the public benefit must be clearly established. The forest crop laws, under which concessions are made to private individuals who agree to practice forestry on lands entered under the law, are an example. The payments to farmers for shifting from soil depleting to soil conserving crops can also be justified under this principle. This has been called another form of "land use control," adapted especially for inducing farming practices within the line fence. Certainly it is only right and proper that whenever the government assists the individual landowner it should lay down the rules under which the grant, subsidy, or donation is made. The legal aspects

[1] Harold S. Buttenheim, "If Henry George Were Writing Today," *Journal of Land and Public Utility Economics,* February, 1935, pp. 1–12.

[2] Lewis Mumford, *The Brown Decades, 1865–1895* (New York, Harcourt, 1931), pp. 46–47. See also Charles A. Beard, "The Frontier in American History," *New Republic,* February 1, 1939, pp. 359–62.

of this form of governmental co-operation in land use control are discussed elsewhere.[1]

Public co-operation with private landowners should not be postponed until the resource is almost depleted. If a policy of co-operation is adopted it would be far better if aid were extended to farmers to *prevent* erosion and control it in its earlier stages rather than to wait until the topsoil is practically gone or deep gullies have ruined the land. Eventually the public will step in to save whatever can be saved, but at enormous costs. When the problem is stated in this way it becomes clear that, besides conservation of the resources, it is also important to consider the cost of doing the job. This means either a small sum spent to prevent soil deterioration or a large bill to control gullies and rehabilitate land almost beyond "cure." As Aldo Leopold has put it, "Whenever a private landowner so uses his land as to injure the public interest, the public will eventually pay the bill, either by buying him out or by donating repairs or both. . . . Abuse is no longer a question of depleting a capital asset, but of actually creating a cash liability against the taxpayer."[2]

This raises the further question of the relation of the public to conservation in general. The argument can be made that conservation is not a private but a public function analogous to public defense. Since the loss of land by physical destruction has the same effect as the loss by military defeat, why not place both on the same basis and make both public activities? How this can be carried out with land remaining private property is not so easily established.

However, assuming a co-operative arrangement between the private landowner and the public, this will mean both social and private costs. How these should be apportioned is an unanswered question. How far the public is willing to go depends once more on social philosophy, custom, and other institutions prevailing at any given time. However, Ciriacy-Wantrup warns: "Thus a society might very well be justified in investing efforts for the conservation of land under conditions where interest rate and expected future returns would make it impossible for individuals to do so.

[1] See "The Remedies: Direct Aids to Farmers," in *Yearbook of the U. S. Dept. of Agriculture,* 1938, pp. 279–88; and Glick, "The Soil and the Law," *Journal of Farm Economics,* August, 1938, pp. 616–40.

[2] "Conservation Economics," *Journal of Forestry,* May, 1934, p. 542.

But society should be perfectly clear and honest about the costs to the community. The true interest rate should be used always in computing these costs. In other words, social costs—for example interest charges—cannot and should not always determine social actions in the field of land conservation. But they should always be thoroughly explored and taken into account by those who make or approve government decisions. The gravest mistake would be the creation ad hoc of some sort of "cost free" land economics in order to make proposed actions appear economically desirable when they are not; although these actions may be of great social value from other aspects and may deserve consideration for that reason."[1]

Conservation of Natural Resources through Public Ownership. The alternative to private conservation of natural resources is attained through public ownership. Since the government has practically no time preference, has a long time point of view, far beyond that of any individual, and can plan for a century where the individual plans for a decade, the people as a whole as represented by the state, can conserve land resources without the psychological and monetary costs to the individual. Carrying and holding costs are also less with no taxes to be paid, and because governments can borrow at very low rates of interest. The public also absorbs all responsibility for the preservation of the resources and can spread the cost over the entire population, present and future, making the per capita burden almost nil. Furthermore, whenever these resources are utilized an income emerges which flows in whole or in part into the public treasury. Timber is sold from public forests, royalties are obtained from the minerals on the public lands, and grazing fees are paid for the privilege of pasturing on federal lands. These revenues are shared with local units of government and cover the costs of conservation in whole or in part.

Public vs. private ownership cannot be decided without considering the nature of the resource. Lands charged with public interest, such as parks, national monuments, and forests necessary for watershed protection and erosion control, are accepted as public land without question. The case is not so clear for other types

[1] Siegfried von Ciriacy-Wantrup, "Economic Aspects of Land Conservation," *Journal of Farm Economics,* May, 1938, p. 472.

of land uses, for reasons discussed in earlier chapters. One significant argument against public ownership is that land is thus removed from the tax roll. This is of special importance to local units of government which have to depend upon the property tax for their chief source of revenue.

Finally, public ownership, as such, is negative and is in itself no guarantee that resources will be conserved. Some of the worst wind and water erosion has taken place on the public domain. Tax-reverted lands are often without any management whatsoever. It is important that resources be placed under the administration of efficient units of government or responsible branches of the government service. Public ownership has been called a form of "land use control" in that proprietorship presumably gives the public owner complete control over the use of land. In practice this is often impossible. Various pressure groups and interested persons are constantly interfering. For instance, the Forest Service is helpless in controlling the game and waters on federal forests since these are under the jurisdiction of the states. Local interests have hindered the regulation of grazing in these forests and the weakest control over resources seems to be on public waters. Even publicly owned European forests are not free from the interference of servitudes and easements.

INDEX